TABLE DES MATIÈRES

PREFACE

Can I learn a language?

Everybody is born with a natural ability to learn languages. You know you can learn a language, because you already learned one - English!

How do I learn a language?

How individuals approach learning a language depends a great deal on their personality. As with any other process, people can approach a task differently, but still obtain similar results. Some language learners like to jump in as soon as they know enough to get started, and continue from there using a deductive method. Others want to understand in detail how a language works before they try to use it.

Both methods have advantages and disadvantages. The most important part of the language-learning process is to constantly try to use the language to express yourself. Always alternate study of vocabulary and structures with attempts to communicate. And above all, practice, practice, practice!

How can the *Horizons* print and online MindTap® combination help me learn?

Horizons is designed to work for you, whatever type of learner you may be. Each section of *Horizons* opens with useful phrases and a conversation allowing you to use new words and sentences to begin to communicate right away and to make deductions about how French works. These openers are followed by rules that explain in detail the structure of French. *Horizons* will also give you "tips" – strategies and practice - on how to understand, read, write, and speak French more easily. You will also find out about interesting aspects of francophone culture and how some of these affect spoken and nonverbal communication.

There are three P's involved in learning a language: patience, practice, and persistence. When you take a language class, you should anticipate spending a lot of time practicing what you are learning. Like developing any other skill, such as playing a sport, drawing, or playing a musical instrument, success in learning a foreign language depends on how much time you spend studying and practicing it. In the *Horizons* program, you will have multiple opportunities to practice reading, writing, speaking, and listening to French in a variety of ways. Online MindTap® adds a new dimension to your practice. In MindTap®, the opening sections, structural explanations, and listening, reading, and writing strategies are accompanied by **Try it!** activities that allow you to check for yourself that you understand the new vocabulary, structures, and strategies. In MindTap®, every section of *Horizons* provides multiple opportunities to practice what you are learning. These activities progress from basic exercises that you can use to check your comprehension and to practice the new vocabulary and structures to tasks that allow you to apply what you learn to communicate with your classmates via partner-chat activities.

Will all this practice make perfect?

Your goal in learning French should not be to say everything perfectly. If you set this goal for yourself, you will probably be afraid to speak. Your goal should be to communicate clearly, but you should expect to make mistakes when speaking. Listen carefully to how French speakers express themselves, and make adjustments the next time you need to convey a similar message.

Although perfection is not the goal of language learners, practice is vital to success. You can learn every vocabulary word and rule in the book, but unless you practice regularly, listening to French and attempting to speak it, you will not learn the language. Use the multiple opportunities to practice and to hear French as it is spoken in the *Horizons* text and MindTap® online to progress to clear communication. Enjoy talking to your classmates in class or in the online chats to develop your speaking skills.

How can I be successful?

1. Avoid thinking that you can just substitute a French word for the equivalent word in English. Most of the time, you cannot translate word for word from one language to another. For example, substituting the equivalent English word for each French word in the following sentence would create a very unusual sentence.

   Nous ne l'avons pas encore fait.
   We not it have not still done.

   You might be able to figure out that this sentence means, "We haven't done it yet," but sometimes translating word for word can give a completely wrong meaning. For example, if you translate the following sentence word for word, you would think that it has the first meaning that follows it, whereas it really has the second.

   Je voudrais vous parler demain, s'il vous plaît.
   I would like you to speak tomorrow, if it you pleases.
   I would like to speak to you tomorrow, please.

   You probably noticed in this last example that one word in English may be translated by several words in French and vice versa (**voudrais** = *would like*, **vous** = *to you*, **parler** = *to speak*, **s'il vous plaît** = *please*).

2. Accept cultural differences since they affect how we communicate. For example, in French, a cultural difference that affects the spoken language is that French society is not as informal as ours. Adults generally do not call each other by their first names, and the words for *sir* and *madam* are used much more frequently than in English. For example, it is normal to say **Bonjour, monsieur** *(Hello, sir),* whereas English speakers just say *Hello.*

3. Spend time with the language, stay focused on your task, and be willing to try to communicate using it.

4. Get help if language learning makes you anxious, or if you need help with how to learn or with a particular concept. Don't wait! Get help when you need it!

5. Have realistic expectations. Learning a language takes time. If you set a goal for yourself to have everyday conversation skills after your second year of study, and if you work hard toward this goal, you will be able to function in most everyday conversation settings; however, you will still frequently have to look for words, you will probably still speak in short simple sentences, and you will often have to use circumlocution to get your meaning across. In **Horizons**, you will learn how to function in the most common situations in which you are likely to find yourself in a francophone region. You will be able to meet someone and have a short conversation with this person after only a few weeks.

6. Keep yourself motivated by thinking about what language can do for you. Remember that in today's international economy, individuals who speak another language have better opportunities. Create a personal goal, such as being able to one day speak fluently, travel and enjoy the cultural diversity in the francophone world, get a job with an international company, or do volunteer work abroad. Most people want to make a difference in the world, and learning another language is a good way to begin!

How can I learn to enjoy studying?

As with any accomplishment, learning a foreign language requires a lot of work. You will enjoy it more if you think of it as a hobby or a pastime and as an opportunity to develop a skill, similar to learning to play a sport or a musical instrument. Here are some training techniques that can help you learn a new language.

- Get into a routine. Devote a particular time of day to studying French. It is best to find a time when you are fresh and free of distractions, so you can concentrate on what you are doing. If you study at the same time every day, getting started will become habitual. Once you are settled working and learning, it becomes fun.
- Make sure that the place where you study is inviting and that you enjoy being there.
- Study frequently for short periods of time, rather than having marathon sessions. After about two hours of study, the ability of the brain to retain information is greatly reduced. You tend to remember what you learn at the beginning of each study session and at the end. What you study in the middle tends to become blurred. To illustrate this, read the following words one time, then turn the page and see how many you remember.

  dog, house, sofa, cat, rooster, room, telephone, mouse, book, pencil, television

  Most people can remember the first word and the last. The longer the list, the harder it is to remember the words in the middle. The same is true with studying. Study smaller "chunks" of material more frequently, and set reasonable goals for yourself. Don't try to learn it all at once.
- Study with a classmate or a friend. It is much easier to practice talking with someone else, and it is easier to spend more time working with the language if you are interacting with another person. Also, by studying with classmates, you will feel more comfortable speaking in front of them, which eliminates some of the embarrassment some adults feel when trying to pronounce foreign words in front of the whole class.
- Play games with the language. It is fun to learn how to say things in a new language. For instance, ask yourself how you would say things you hear on the radio or television in French. If you do know how to say something in French that you hear, your knowledge will become more certain. If you don't know how to say something in French, that's normal if you are a beginner. When you finally learn the word or expression you were wondering about, you will remember it more easily, because you have already thought about it.
- Surround yourself by French. Watch French movies or watch DVDs of American movies in the French-language track, listen to French music, and search the Web for French websites with recent news or topics that interest you. Websites with a lot of pictures are the best, because the pictures give you clues to the meaning of unfamiliar words. You probably will not understand very much at first in movies and songs, but they will motivate you to learn more. They teach you about cultural differences, and they help give you a sense of good pronunciation.
- Don't let yourself get frustrated. If you are frustrated each time you sit down to study, ask yourself why. First of all, make sure that you are not studying when you are too tired or hungry. Also, make sure that you clearly understand your assignment and its purpose. Learn to distinguish a language-learning problem from a problem understanding instructions. If you are confused about what you are to do or why, see your instructor during office hours or contact another student. (This is another reason to study with a classmate!)

LEARNING TECHNIQUES

How can I spend my study time most efficiently?

Individuals organize material differently as they learn it. Some people learn better by seeing something; others learn better by hearing it. The following are some study tips for how to go about learning French. You may find that some of these methods work for you and others do not. Be creative in practicing your French, using a variety of study techniques.

General study tips

- Establish a routine. Schedule a time and a comfortable place to study French and gather what you will need. Once you start working and learning, it becomes fun.
- Study frequently for short periods of time. Remember to avoid marathon sessions. Your brain can't learn everything all at once!
- Learn not to translate word for word. Learn to read and listen to whole sentences at a time.

- Keep a log of your study time. Each time you sit down to study new material, write down the time you begin, when you finish, and two or three sentences summarizing what you studied. By keeping a log, you will know exactly how much time you spend on French. Writing one or two sentences summarizing what you studied helps you check your retention.
- Alternate speaking, listening, reading, and writing activities. By changing tasks frequently, you will be able to study longer without losing your concentration.

Vocabulary-learning techniques

- Use your senses. Pronounce words aloud as you study them. Picture things and activities represented by the new words. Learn useful common phrases such as "What time is it?" or "How are you?" as a whole.
- As you begin to learn a group of new words or phrases from the end-of-chapter vocabulary list, first practice repeating each word after the recording online. Your brain will not retain new words as well if you are unsure how to pronounce them.
- Use flashcards. In MindTap®, you will find a vocabulary list for each section of *Horizons* as well as audio flashcards. You can download those on your phone. Pull up your vocabulary list to study when you do routine tasks, or when you are waiting for an appointment, working out, or in the car.
- Study vocabulary in manageable "chunks." Each morning, write out a list of 20 new words and carry it in your pocket. A few times during the day, spend two minutes trying to remember the words on the list. Take out the list and review the words you forgot for two minutes. By the end of the day, you will have spent just a few minutes and you will have learned the 20 words.
- Test yourself. At the end of a study session, write the English words or phrases on a sheet of paper. Put the sheet of paper away for a few hours. Later, take it out and see how many of the French equivalents of these words or phrases you remember.
- Group words in logical categories. For example, learn words for fruits together, words for animals together, sports-related vocabulary together, etc. Also learn pairs of antonyms together: hot/cold, near/far, to go to sleep/to wake up, etc.
- Use related English words to help you remember the French. For example, the French word for *to begin* is **commencer.** Associate it with *to commence.*
- Remember that we cannot say everything even in our own language. If you do not know a word, try to think of another way to say what you want. Use circumlocution. For example, if you do not know how to say "to drive," say "to take the car" instead.

Grammar-learning techniques

- Play teacher. Try to guess what your instructor would ask you to do if he or she were giving a quiz the next day.
- Do the *Pour vérifier* self-checks in the margins of the text and the **Try it!** activities in Mindtap® to make sure you understand new explanations.

- Use color coding to help you remember grammatical information. For example, all nouns in French are categorized either as masculine or feminine, and you must memorize in which category each noun belongs. When you make flashcards, write feminine nouns on pink cards or with pink ink and use blue for masculine nouns. Use an eye-catching color on flashcards to indicate points you want to remember, such as irregular plurals or verbs that take **être** in th**e passé composé.**
- If you like to use lists to study, organize them so that they help you remember information about words. For example, to remember noun gender, write masculine words in a column on the left and feminine words in a column on the right. If you can visualize where the word is on the list, you can remember its gender.
- Learn to accept ambiguity. Sometimes, as soon as you learn a new rule, you find out that it doesn't always work the way you expect it to.

Pronunciation-learning techniques

- Repeat everything you hear in French under your breath or in your head, even if you have no idea what it means. This will not only help your pronunciation, it will help your listening comprehension and your ability to learn vocabulary. For instance, if you keep repeating an unfamiliar word you hear in your head, when you finally find out what it means, you will remember it very easily.
- Read French words aloud as you study.
- Listen to the audio in the book and MindTap® several times. It is impossible to concentrate both on meaning and pronunciation the first time you listen. Listen at least once focusing on pronunciation only. To get maximum benefit from the listening activities, approach them with the right attitude. It takes time, patience, and practice to understand French spoken at a normal conversational speed. Do not be surprised if you find it difficult at first. Relax and listen to passages more than once. You will understand a little more each time. Remember that you will not understand everything and that, for some exercises, you are only expected to understand enough to answer specific questions. Read through exercises prior to playing the audio, so that you know what to listen for. If you find you do not have enough time to process what is being said, pause the audio to give yourself more time. Most importantly, be patient and remember that you can always listen again.
- Make recordings of yourself and compare them to those of native speakers.
- Exaggerate as you practice at home. Any pronunciation that is not English will seem like exaggeration. Psychologically, it is very difficult to listen to yourself speaking another language. Pretend you are a French actor playing a role as you practice pronunciation.
- Listen to French songs on the Internet. Search for the lyrics and sing along.

THE *HORIZONS* VIDEO PROGRAM, *LES STAGIAIRES*

The *Stagiaires* video revolves around the interactions of the employees at a French company. The episode at the end of each chapter, except the *Chapitre préliminaire* and the *Chapitre de révision,* will allow you to review what you have learned and see it used in everyday conversations.

In this video, we meet two interns, Amélie Prévot and Rachid Bennani. They are just starting their internships at Technovert, a small green-technology company.

Amélie Prévot

Rachid Bennani

Henri Vieilledent is the founder, owner, and leader of this dynamic and fast-growing company. Coffee and croissants are his daily motivators.

Henri Vieilledent

Camille Dupont

His faithful assistant, Camille Dupont, helps him run the business . . . and keeps his coffee-and-croissant supply abundant.

Céline Diop

One of Vieilledent's weapons in his efforts to make the company flourish and remain competitive is Céline Diop. The confident and driven sales manager also becomes an effective and appreciated mentor to the two young interns.

You might not be able to tell right away, but Matthieu Sauvage is a wiz. His area of expertise? Computers. However, interactions with the staff can sometimes be challenging for him. He can be extremely shy and awkward. When the attractive intern, Amélie, joins the Technovert staff, will Matthieu finally take a risk and overcome his painful timidity?

Matthieu Sauvage

Christophe Vieilledent

Finally, Christophe Vieilledent is the company's gofer—though he doesn't go for a lot! The mail delivery and other odd jobs he does around the building do not keep him from indulging in his favorite pastime: reading manga. With a father in high places he can keep a low profile.

ACKNOWLEDGMENTS

We are grateful to a great many people for helping us transform our collective classroom experience into this text. Principal among these are Heather Bradley-Cole and Lara Semones, for the opportunity to work with Cengage Learning and for their support; Esther Marshall, Isabelle Alouane, Denise St. Jean, Beth Kramer, Zenya Molnar, Brenda Carmichael and Lisa Trager; Michelle Mckenna and Betsy Hathaway; Elyssa Healy, Peter Schott, Carolyn Nichols, Miranda Marshall; Jason Baldwin, Jason Clark, Sarah Seymour, Bethany Martin, Nathan Carpenter, Dana Edmunds, Sean Hagerty, Nicole Naudé, Ralph Zerbonia; Severine Champeny, native reader and proofreader, and Katy Gabel, Lumina Datamatics project manager. Our thanks also go to: James Browning for his contribution to the Integrated Performance Assessments and Lori Mele Hawke who contributed to the Visual Preface, Transition guide and sample syllabi. We appreciate Miranda Marshall for her keen attention to detail in the creation of PowerPoint presentations. With special thanks to Yamilé Dewailly, Annick Penant, and Debra Latimer for their invaluable contributions to the quality of this work.

A special thanks to both Jims, Laura, Andrew, Annick, Daniel, and Joel for their patient and loving support. Last, but obviously not least, we thank each other for the tolerance, mutual encouragement, and strengthened bonds of friendship such an endeavor requires.
Merci mille fois!

The Authors and the World Languages team would like to thank the following reviewers of *Horizons* for their comments and advice.

Daniele Arnaud, *MiraCosta College—Oceanside*

James Aubry, *University of Tampa*

Mariana Bahtchevanova, *Arizona State University*

Phillip Bailey, *University of Central Arkansas*

Ahmed Bouguarche, *California State University—Northridge*

Jimia Boutouba, *Santa Clara University*

Karen Breen-Davis, *Atlantic Cape Community College*

Suzanne Buck, *Central New Mexico Community College*

Krista Chambless, *University of Alabama-Birmingham*

Sophie Champigny-Hotel, *Saint Petersburg College*

Mary Clarkson, *Houston Community College*

Nathalie Cornelius, *Bloomsburg University*

Sabine Davis, *Washington State University*

Joan Debrah, *University of Hawaii at Manoa*

Bryan Donaldson, *UC Santa Cruz*

Isabelle Drewelow, *University of Alabama Tuscaloosa*

Mary Anne Eddy, *Purdue University*

Lisa Erceg, *Loyola University Chicago—Lake Shore*

Sonia Ghattas-Soliman, *Grossmont College*

Frederique Grim, *Colorado State University*

Kirsten Halling, *Wright State University—Main Campus*

Julie Hatton, *Sinclair Community College*

Peggy Herr, *York College of Pennsylvania*

Claire Holman, *University of Southern Maine*

Martine Howard, *Camden County College*

Juliet Hubbell, *Arapahoe Community College*

Hannalore Jarausch, *University of North Carolina*

Christine Knapp, *Wayne State University*

Laetitia Knight, *University of North Texas*

Tamara Lindner, *University of Louisiana at Lafayette*

Abbes Maazaoui, *Lincoln University*

Monique Manopoulos, *California State University East Bay*

Florence Mathieu-Conner, *Ivy Tech Community College—Online*

John Moran, *New York University*

Michel Pactat, *Miami University*

Melanie Parham, *Asheville Buncombe Tech College*

Michel Pichot, *Aquinas College*

Fleur Prade, *Central Oregon Community College*

Aaron Prevots, *Southwestern University*

Carol Reitan, *City College of San Francisco—Ocean*

Louis Rochette, *St. Joseph's College*

Mercedes Rooney, *SUNY New Paltz*

Michael Rulon, *Northern Arizona University*

Therese Saint Paul, *Murray State University*

Martine Sauret, *Macalester College*

Alan Savage, *Wheaton College*

Michelle Scatton-Tessier, *University of North Carolina at Wilmington*

Pierre Schmitz, *San Antonio College*

Philippe Seminet, *St. Edward's University*

Karen Sorenson, *Austin Peay State University*

Eric Tessier, *University of North Carolina at Wilmington*

Bryon Warner, *Brenau University—Gainesville*

Robin White, *Nicholls State University*

We would like to recognize those who reviewed the MindTap® for World Languages platform:

Whitney Bevill, *University of Virginia*
Katherine Bevins, *University of Tennessee—Knoxville*
Anne-Sophie Blank, *University of Missouri-St. Louis*
Goedele Gulikers, *Prince George's Community College*

Solene Halabi, *Mt San Antonio College*
Katherine Morel, *North Carolina State University*
Steven Spalding, *US Naval Academy*
Valerie Wust, *North Carolina State University*

World Languages Faculty Development Partners:

Claudia Acosta, *College of the Canyons*
Daniel Anderson, *The University of Oklahoma*
Stephanie Blankenship, *Liberty University*
Amy Bomke, *Indiana University—Purdue University Indianapolis*
Julia Bussade, *The University of Mississippi*
Mónica García, *California State University Sacramento & American River College*
Marilyn Harper, *Pellissippi State Community College*
Bryan Koronkiewicz, *The University of Alabama*
Kajsa Larson, *Northern Kentucky University*

Cristina Moon, *Chabot College*
Marilyn Palatinus, *Pellissippi State Community College*
Tina Peña, *Tulsa Community College*
Joseph Price, *University of Arizona*
Goretti Prieto Botana, *University of Southern California*
Michelle Ramos, *California State University San Marcos*
Eva Rodriguez Gonzalez, *University of New Mexico*
Borja Ruiz de Arbulo Alonso, *Boston University*
Laura Sanchez, *Longwood University*
Steven Sheppard, *University of North Texas*
Sandy Trapani, University of Missouri—St. Louis

World Languages Technology Advisory Board:

Douglas W. Canfield, *The University of Tennessee, Knoxville*
Michael B. Dettinger, *Louisiana State University*
Senta Goertler, *Michigan State University*
Michael Hughes, *California State University San Marcos*

Jeff Longwell, *New Mexico State University*
Theresa Minick, *Kent State University*
Jennifer Rogers, *Metropolitan Community College*
Steven Sheppard, *University of North Texas*

In loving memory of Marc A. Prévost, who contributed so much not only to this work, but to each of our lives. He was a wonderful person who loved teaching the language and culture of his homeland, and he will be missed by his colleagues and students.

Bienvenue dans le monde francophone!

On commence!

Pair work	Video	
Group work	Audio	
Class work		

P

© dvoevnore/Shutterstock.com

LE MONDE FRANCOPHONE
Géoculture: Bienvenue dans le monde francophone!

COMPÉTENCE

GÉOCULTURE: **BIENVENUE DANS LE MONDE FRANCOPHONE!**

Bold-faced words are glossed at the bottom of the page. Try to guess their meanings from the context before looking at the glosses.

On parle français au Québec...

Did you know that French is spoken throughout the world? It is estimated that more than 220 million people speak French world-wide. Two-thirds of these francophones (French speakers) live outside of France in around 40 countries across the world.

In the Americas, French is spoken in several states of the US, in several provinces in Canada, in French Guiana in South America, and on several Caribbean islands.

en Louisiane...

et en Haïti.

Bienvenue dans le monde francophone! *Welcome to the French-speaking world!* **On parle français au** *French is spoken in* **en** *in* **et** *and*

Africa has more francophones than any other continent. In fact, Kinshasa, the capital of the Democratic Republic of the Congo, has more French speakers than any other city besides Paris.

On parle français en République démocratique du Congo...

et au Maroc.

You will also hear French spoken in the South Pacific; for example, on the 121 islands that make up French Polynesia.

On parle français à Tahiti!

Le savez-vous?

Use the map in the back of the book and what you just read to answer these questions.

1. French is spoken in about how many countries?

2. Does French have a linguistic or cultural influence on five continents (Europe, Africa, North America, South America, Asia) and on several islands of Oceania, or on only four continents (Asia, Europe, North America, and Africa)?

3. Kinshasa, the city with the second largest number of francophones in the world after Paris, is the capital of what African country?

4. The term **Maghreb** refers to the area of Northern Africa that includes Morocco, Algeria, and Tunisia. Although French is also spoken in this region, what language would you expect to be the official one?

5. In what four places in South America or the Caribbean where French is spoken?

6. In which ocean is French Polynesia located?

---

au Maroc *in Morocco*   **à** *in*

Greeting people

LES SALUTATIONS FORMELLES

Note *culturelle*

People in France generally shake hands when they meet, and they often do not just say **bonjour.** Instead, they include the word **monsieur** or **madame,** or the person's name. Traditionally, **madame** was used to address married women and **mademoiselle** for unmarried women. The use of **mademoiselle** was banned in official government documents in 2012 to make the treatment of women and men parallel. However, it is not uncommon to hear it used to address very young women. In English, do you prefer to use *Ms.* or *Mrs.* and *Miss*?

Notes

1. Boldfaced words are glossed at the bottom of the page. Try to guess their meaning from the context before looking at the glosses.

2. Audio for items accompanied by this symbol is accessed online. 0-3

To greet adults with whom you do not have a close relationship and those to whom you show respect, say:

0-1
— Bonjour, madame.
— Bonjour, monsieur. Je suis Hélène Cauvin. Et vous, comment vous appelez-vous?
— Je m'appelle Jean-Luc Bertin.
— **Vous êtes d'ici?**
— **Non,** je suis **de** Montréal. Et vous, vous êtes d'ici?
— **Oui,** je suis d'ici.

0-2
— Bonsoir, monsieur. **Comment allez-vous?**
— Bonsoir, madame. **Je vais très bien, merci.** Et vous?
— **Assez** bien.

Et vous? Comment allez-vous?

Je vais très bien.	Assez bien. / **Pas mal. /**	Pas très bien.
	Comme ci comme ça.	

PRONONCIATION

Les consonnes muettes et la liaison 0-4

In French, consonants at the end of words are often silent and **h** is always silent, as it is in some English words such as *hour* and *honest.* The consonants **c, r, f,** and **l** (CaReFuL) are the only consonants that are generally pronounced at the end of a word. However, do not pronounce the final **r** of **monsieur.**

   Mar**c**   bonjou**r**   acti**f**   Chanta**l**

— Bonjou**r**, monsieur. Je m'appelle Pau**l** Richar**d**. Et vous, comment vous appelez-vous?

— Je m'appelle Henri Dula**c**. Comment allez-vous?

— Je vais très bien, merci.

If a consonant at the end of a word is followed by a word beginning with a vowel sound (**a, e, i, o, u, y**) or a mute **h,** the final consonant sound is often pronounced and is linked to the beginning of the next word. This linking is called **liaison.** In liaison, a single **s** is pronounced like a **z.**

   Comment vous‿appelez-vous? Comment‿allez-vous?

Les salutations formelles *Formal greetings*   **Vous êtes d'ici?** *Are you from here?*   **Non** *No*   **de** *from*   **Oui** *Yes*   **Comment allez-vous?** *How are you?*
Je vais très bien, merci. *I'm doing very well, thank you.*   **Assez** *Fairly, Rather*   **Pas mal.** *Not bad(ly).*   **Comme ci comme ça.** *So-so.*

A Prononcez bien!
Two new acquaintances are meeting. Copy these sentences from their conversation, crossing out the consonants that should not be pronounced and marking where liaison would occur.

EXEMPLE Comment‿alle~~z~~-vou~~s~~, monsieu~~r~~?

1. Je suis Chantal Hubert.
2. Bonjour, madame. Comment allez-vous?
3. Très bien, monsieur. Comment vous appelez-vous?
4. Je m'appelle Henri Dufour. Et vous?
5. Vous êtes d'ici?
6. Non, je suis de Paris.

🔊 0-5 Now go back and reorder the six sentences to create a logical conversation. When you are done, listen to the conversation, then practice reading it aloud with a partner.

B Bonjour, monsieur/madame.
Imagine that you are meeting a new French business associate. Read the following conversation with another student, changing the words in italics as needed so that they describe you and your partner.

— Bonjour, *madame.* Comment allez-vous?

— Bonjour, *monsieur. Je vais très bien,* merci. Et vous?

— *Assez bien,* merci. Je suis *Jules Alami.* Et vous, comment vous appelez-vous?

— Je m'appelle *Emma Delors.* Vous êtes d'ici?

— *Oui, je suis d'ici.* Et vous?

— Je suis de *Lyon.*

© Konstantin Chagin/Shutterstock.com

À VOUS!

Imagine that you are just beginning an internship with a French company and are meeting your new colleagues. Review the conversations at the top of page 6. Then, go around the room and greet as many colleagues as possible. Exchange names and ask how the others are doing and if they are from here. *Use formal greetings.*

Note *de vocabulaire*

1. Use **bonjour** to say *hello* at any time of day. Use **bonsoir** only to say *good evening.*
2. Note the abbreviations for **monsieur (M.)**, **madame (Mme)**, and **mademoiselle (Mlle)**.
3. Use **je vais** to say how you are doing. Use **je suis** to say who you are, where you are from, or to describe yourself.
4. **De** *(From)* changes to **d'** before a vowel sound or a silent **h.**

LES SALUTATIONS FAMILIÈRES

Note *culturelle*

When people greet one another in France, they usually shake hands or exchange a brief kiss on each cheek called a **bise**. What do people do when they greet each other in your region?

Note *de vocabulaire*

1. To say *you*, use **tu** with friends, family, etc., and **vous** in more formal relationships. Note that different verb forms are used with each one: **tu es / vous êtes...** *(you are . . .)*. After **et**, use **toi** rather than **tu**.
2. **Salut!** is used to say both *Hi!* and *Bye!*
3. The final **-s** of **plus** is pronounced in **À plus!**, but not in **À plus̸ tard!**

Vocabulaire supplémentaire

Comment t'appelles-tu? /
  Comment tu t'appelles? *What's your name?* (familiar)
Comment vas-tu? *How are you?* (familiar)
À bientôt! *See you soon!*
À tout à l'heure! *See you later (the same day)!*
Ciao! *Bye!* (familiar)
Bon week-end! *Have a good weekend!*
Bonne journée! *Have a good day!*

To greet classmates, friends, family members, or children, say:

 0-6

— **Salut**, Pierre. **Ça va?**
— Salut, Juliette. **Ça va.** Et toi, **comment ça va?**
— Pas mal.

0-7

— Bonjour, je m'appelle Pauline. Et toi, tu t'appelles comment?
— Moi, je m'appelle Lucas. Je suis de Lyon. Et toi? **Tu es d'où?**
— Moi, je suis d'ici.

0-8

Here are several ways to say good-bye. Use **À plus!** and **Salut!** only in familiar relationships. The others may be used in either formal or familiar relationships.

Au revoir! *Good-bye!*   À plus tard! / À plus! *See you later!*
À demain! *See you tomorrow!*   Salut! *Bye!*

PRONONCIATION

*Les voyelles **a, e, é, i, o** et **u***   0-9

When you pronounce vowels in English, your tongue or lips move as you say them, so that the position of your mouth is not the same at the end of a vowel as at the beginning. In French, you hold your tongue and mouth firmly in one place while pronouncing vowels. This gives vowels a tenser sound. Practice saying these sounds.

a [a]:	à	ça	va	madame	mal	assez
e [ə]:	je	ne	que	de	demain	devoirs
é [e]:	café	pâté	bébé	été	préféré	répété
i [i]:	quiche	idéal	Paris	machine	six	merci
o [o]:	bientôt	vélo	hôtel	kilo	mots	trop
u [y]:	tu	salut	Luc	super	du	université

To pronounce the **u** sound, position your mouth to pronounce a French **i** with your tongue held high in your mouth. Then, purse your lips. Compare the vowel sounds in **vous** and **vu.**

The vowel **o** has two pronunciations, [o] or [ɔ], and the vowel **e** has three pronunciations, [ə], [e], or [ɛ]. You will learn more about this in ***Chapitre 3.*** Final unaccented **e** is not generally pronounced, unless it is the only vowel in a word, as in **je:** Franc̸, madam̸, appell̸, un̸, Ann̸.

Compare these words: Mari**e** / mari**é**, divorc**e** / divorc**é**, fatigu**e** / fatigu**é**.

Les salutations familières *Familiar greetings*   Salut *Hi*   Ça va? *How's it going?*   Ça va. *It's going fine.*   comment ça va? *how's it going?*
Tu es d'où? *You are from where?*

A **Prononcez bien!** Listen as different people give their name and indicate whether it is the first or second name shown.

0-10

1. Alisa	Élisa	**5.** Élona	Ilona	**9.** Abdel	Abdul
2. Amélie	Émelie	**6.** Albert	Hubert	**10.** Éric	Ulrick
3. Ali	Éli	**7.** Mariel	Muriel	**11.** Nicolas	Nicolo
4. Éliana	Iliana	**8.** Arielle	Urielle	**12.** Mano	Manu

B **Qui parle?** Read each of these phrases aloud and say whether you would be more likely to hear it in conversation **A** or **B**.

A.

© moodboard/Cultura/ Getty Images

B.

© iStock.com/kali9

1. Bonjour, madame.

2. Salut, Thomas.

3. Très bien, merci. Et vous?

4. Tu t'appelles comment?

5. Vous êtes d'où?

6. À plus!

7. Comment allez-vous?

8. Ça va. Et toi?

9. Comment vous appelez-vous?

10. Tu es d'ici?

Now give a logical response to each of the items above.

C **On dit...** It is your first day in a French class for foreign students in France. What would you say in French . . .

1. to greet your professor during the day? in the evening?

2. to ask your professor's name? to tell him/her your name?

3. to ask your professor how he/she is doing? to ask if he/she is from here?

4. to say that you are doing very well? fairly well? not badly? not very well?

5. to greet a classmate? to ask a classmate's name? to ask where he/she is from? to say what city you are from?

6. to ask a friend how it's going? to tell him/her that it's going well?

7. to say good-bye to someone? to say that you will see him/her tomorrow? later?

 À VOUS!

Review the conversations on page 8. Then, go around the room and meet as many new people as you can in the time set by your professor. Have a short conversation with each person in which you greet one another, exchange names, ask and say how it is going, exchange information on where you are from, and say good-bye. Shake hands or exchange *bises*. Use *familiar* French, rather than formal.

You can access the audio of the active vocabulary of this *Compétence* online.

Counting and describing your week

LES NOMBRES DE ZÉRO À CINQUANTE-NEUF

Note *culturelle*

The French manner of indicating numbers with fingers is with palms facing in and starting with the thumb rather than the index finger, then proceeding to the index finger and on to the little finger. Ask your classmates how they indicate numbers with their hands. Are there any variations by nationality or regional origin?

Comptez de zéro **à** cinquante-neuf, **s'il vous plaît**!

0 zéro

1 un	**11** onze	**21** vingt et un	**31** trente et un
2 deux	**12** douze	**22** vingt-deux	**32** trente-deux
3 trois	**13** treize	**23** vingt-trois	**33** trente-trois…
4 quatre	**14** quatorze	**24** vingt-quatre	**40** quarante
5 cinq	**15** quinze	**25** vingt-cinq	**41** quarante et un
6 six	**16** seize	**26** vingt-six	**42** quarante-deux
7 sept	**17** dix-sept	**27** vingt-sept	**43** quarante-trois…
8 huit	**18** dix-huit	**28** vingt-huit	**50** cinquante
9 neuf	**19** dix-neuf	**29** vingt-neuf	**51** cinquante et un
10 dix	**20** vingt	**30** trente	**52** cinquante-deux…

$2 + 2 = 4$ **Combien** font deux et deux?
Deux et deux font quatre.

$5 - 2 = 3$ Combien font cinq moins deux?
Cinq moins deux font trois.

PRONONCIATION

Les nombres et les voyelles nasales 0-11

Although final consonants are generally silent in French, they are pronounced in the following numbers when counting. In **sept,** the **p** is silent, but the final **t** is pronounced. The final **x** in **six** and **dix** is pronounced like the *s* in *so*.

     cinq   six   sep̸t   huit   neuf   dix

Many numbers also contain nasal vowels. In French, when a vowel is followed by the letter **m** or **n** in the same syllable, the **m** or **n** is silent and the vowel is nasal.

Use the words below as models of how to pronounce each of the nasal sounds. The letter combinations that are grouped together are all pronounced alike.

on / om	[ɔ̃]	onze	bonjour	non	nom
an / am	[ɑ̃]	quarante	anglais	dimanche	chambre
en / em		trente	comment	ensemble	embêtant
in / im	[ɛ̃]	cinq	quinze	vingt	important
ain / aim		demain	américain	mexicain	faim
un / um		un	lundi	brun	parfum
ien	[jɛ̃]	bien	combien	canadien	rien
oin	[wɛ̃]	moins	loin	coin	soin

Although most speakers in France, especially Parisians and young people, pronounce the combinations **un / um** as [ɛ̃], as shown above, you will also hear it pronounced [œ̃]: **un, lundi, brun, parfum.**

Comptez *Count*   **de** *from*   **à** *to*   **s'il vous plaît** *please*   **Combien** *How much, How many*

◀)) **A** **Prononcez bien!** How are the italicized letters in the following French-English
0-12 cognates pronounced? Sort the words under the appropriate columns. Then listen and
repeat, comparing the pronunciation of these words with their English cognates.

*im*bécile *em*blème *ju*ngle *im*pact *am*bition *bu*ngalow *com*plice
*in*stitut *en*semble refr*ain* *an*thologie s*ain*t *am*phibien *bom*be
*an*droïde *con*cert *com*bat bar*on* *em*ployé *en*cyclopédie acti*on*

[ɛ̃] as in **cinq:**	[ɑ̃] as in **trente:**	[ɔ̃] as in **onze:**

B **C'est logique!** How logical are you? Complete each list with the logical
numbers and practice reading them aloud with a partner.

1. ⬚1⬚⬚3⬚⬚5⬚⬚⬚⬚⬚9⬚⬚11⬚⬚⬚⬚15⬚⬚17⬚⬚⬚⬚ **4.** ⬚50⬚⬚49⬚⬚48⬚⬚⬚⬚46⬚⬚45⬚⬚⬚⬚⬚⬚
2. ⬚2⬚⬚4⬚⬚⬚⬚8⬚⬚10⬚⬚⬚⬚14⬚⬚⬚⬚18⬚⬚20⬚ **5.** ⬚55⬚⬚50⬚⬚45⬚⬚40⬚⬚⬚⬚⬚⬚⬚⬚⬚⬚
3. ⬚0⬚⬚5⬚⬚10⬚⬚⬚⬚20⬚⬚⬚⬚30⬚⬚⬚⬚40⬚⬚ **6.** ⬚11⬚⬚13⬚⬚15⬚⬚⬚⬚19⬚⬚21⬚⬚23⬚⬚25⬚⬚

◀)) **C** **Comparaisons culturelles.** Here are the ten countries with the largest
0-13 number of French speakers after France. You will hear the number of speakers.
Fill in the missing numbers.

1. la République démocratique
   du Congo: ___ millions
2. l'Algérie: ___ millions
3. le Maroc: ___ millions
4. le Canada: ___ millions
5. le Cameroun: ___ millions
6. la Belgique: ___ millions
7. la Côte d'Ivoire: ___ millions
8. la Tunisie: ___ millions
9. la Suisse: ___ millions
10. Madagascar: ___ millions

D **En taxi.** You've taken a taxi in a francophone country. Tell the driver the address
of your destination.

EXEMPLE 28, avenue des Champs-Élysées
**Vingt-huit avenue des Champs-Élysées, s'il
vous plaît.**

1. 27, boulevard Diderot
2. 11, rue Petit
3. 19, place Saint-Denis
4. 55, rue Bonaparte
5. 15, rue Sébastopol
6. 12, rue Garibaldi
7. 30, boulevard Gabriel
8. 47, rue du Temple

E **Combien font...?** Read each math problem and give the answer.

1. 2 + 3 =   **4.** 18 + 12 =   **7.** 17 − 11 =
2. 21 + 6 =   **5.** 15 + 11 =   **8.** 50 − 13 =
3. 14 + 16 =   **6.** 54 − 4 =   **9.** 45 − 4 =

LES JOURS DE LA SEMAINE

Note *culturelle*

The first day of the week on French calendars is **lundi** *(Monday)*, not **dimanche** *(Sunday)*. Do you think this would make it more convenient for planning your weekend?

To ask and tell the day of the week, say:

— **C'est quel jour aujourd'hui?**
— **C'est lundi.**

lundi	mardi	mercredi	jeudi	vendredi	samedi	dimanche
⑰	18	19	20	21	22	23
24	25	26	27	28	29	30

Vocabulaire supplémentaire

pendant la semaine *during the week*
sauf *except*

Do not translate the word *on* to say that you do something *on* a certain day. To say that you do something *every* Monday (or another day), use **le** with the day of the week.

| Je travaille **lundi.** | *I work **on Monday**.* (this Monday) |
| Je travaille **le lundi et le jeudi.** | *I work **on Mondays and Thursdays**.* (every week) |

Use **du... au...** to say *from* what day *to* what day you do something every week. Use **tous les jours** to say *every day*.

| Je travaille **du** lundi **au** vendredi. | *I work **from** Mondays **to** Fridays.* |
| Je travaille **tous les jours.** | *I work **every day**.* |

Also notice these words.

le matin	*in the morning(s), mornings*
l'après-midi	*in the afternoon(s), afternoons*
le soir	*in the evening(s), evenings*
le week-end	*on (the) weekend(s), weekends*
avant	*before*
après	*after, afterwards*

Note *de vocabulaire*

1. Days of the week are not capitalized in French.

2. Use **du... au...** to say *from ... to ...* with days of the week when talking about what one does in general every week, but use **de... à...** instead to talk about what one is doing one particular week. **En général, je travaille du lundi au vendredi. Cette** *(This)* **semaine, je travaille de lundi à mercredi.**

3. Notice that you use two words, **ne... pas**, to say what someone does *not* do. **Ne** is placed before the verb and **pas** after it. You will learn more about this in *Chapitre 1.*

Le matin, je suis **à la maison** avant **les cours.**

L'après-midi, **je ne suis pas** à la maison. Je suis **en cours de français** et après le cours de français, je suis **dans un autre cours.**

Le soir, après le cours de français, **je travaille.**

Le week-end, **je ne travaille pas.**

Les jours de la semaine *The days of the week*   **C'est quel jour aujourd'hui?** *What day is it today?*   **C'est lundi.** *It's Monday.*
à la maison *at home*   **les cours** *classes*   **je ne suis pas** *I am not*   **en cours de français** *in French class*   **dans un autre cours** *in another class*   **je travaille** *I work*   **je ne travaille pas** *I don't work*

◀))) 0-14 *Two friends are talking about their schedule this semester.*
— Tu es en cours quels jours **ce semestre**?
— Je suis en cours le lundi, le mercredi et le vendredi.
— Tu travailles **aussi**?
— Oui, je travaille le mardi matin, le jeudi matin et le week-end.

A **Au revoir!** Say good-bye to a friend and say that you'll see him/her on the indicated day.

EXEMPLE   Monday   **Au revoir! À lundi!**

1. Sunday   **3.** Thursday   **5.** Saturday
2. Friday   **4.** Tuesday   **6.** Wednesday

B **C'est quel jour?** Complete these statements.

1. Aujourd'hui, c'est...   **6.** Après le week-end, c'est...
2. Demain, c'est...   **7.** Ce semestre / trimestre, je suis en cours...
3. Après-demain, c'est...   **8.** Je suis en cours de français...
4. Les jours du week-end sont...   **9.** Je travaille... (Je ne travaille pas.)
5. Avant le week-end, c'est...   **10.** Je suis souvent *(often)* à la maison...

C **Emploi du temps.** A student is talking about her week. Select the option in parentheses that is logical in each sentence.

1. Aujourd'hui, c'est (jeudi, le jeudi) et demain, c'est (vendredi, le vendredi).
2. Ce semestre, je suis en cours tous les jours (du, au) lundi (du, au) jeudi. Je ne suis pas en cours (vendredi, le vendredi).
3. Je suis en cours de français (après-midi, l'après-midi).
4. Ce semestre, je suis à la maison le matin (avant, après) le cours de français et je travaille l'après-midi (avant, après) le cours de français.
5. Ce semestre, je travaille (samedi, le samedi).
6. Ce week-end, je travaille (lundi, dimanche) aussi.

Now go back and change the statements so that each one is true for you. If a statement is already true, read it as it is.

D **Et toi?** Complete these statements with the appropriate days of the week to describe yourself. Then, circulate through the classroom to try to find two people who completed at least three of the statements the same way you did. Write down their names.

EXEMPLE   Je suis en cours...
— Je suis en cours du lundi au vendredi. Et toi?
**— Moi aussi, je suis en cours du lundi au vendredi. /
Moi, je suis en cours le mardi et le jeudi.**

1. Ce semestre / trimestre, je suis en cours...   **3.** Je travaille... (Je ne travaille pas.)
2. Je ne suis pas en cours...   **4.** Je suis souvent *(often)* à la maison...

ᴐ **À VOUS!**

With a partner, read aloud the conversation at the top of the page, paying particular attention to pronunciation. Then, redo the conversation to make it true for you. Switch roles and do it again.

You can access the audio of the active vocabulary of this *Compétence* online.

ce semestre *this semester*   **aussi** *also, too*

Talking about yourself and your schedule

MOI, JE...

Use these phrases to talk about yourself. Include the ending in parentheses if you are a female.

Je suis...	étudiant(e).
Je ne suis pas...	professeur.
	américain(e).
	canadien(ne).
	de Chicago.
	d'ici.
J'habite...	**à** Toronto.
Je n'habite pas...	**seul(e).**
	avec **un ami / une amie.**
	avec ma famille.
	avec **un camarade de chambre / une camarade de chambre.**
Je travaille...	**beaucoup.**
Je ne travaille pas...	**à** l'université.
	pour Apple.
Je parle...	anglais.
Je ne parle pas...	français.
	espagnol.
Pour moi, le français est...	intéressant.
	assez **facile.**
	un peu difficile.
	super!
	assez cool!

Je suis canadienne, de Montréal, mais j'habite à Paris avec une amie. Je suis étudiante à l'université.

In the following conversation, two young people meet at a party in Montreal.

— Tu es canadien?
— Oui, je suis d'ici. Et toi, tu es canadienne aussi?
— Non, je suis de Cleveland.
— **Mais** tu parles très bien français! Tu habites ici **maintenant**?
— Oui, **parce que** je suis étudiante à l'université. Et toi, tu travailles ici?
— Non, je suis aussi étudiant.

J'habite *I live*   **à** *in (to, at)*   **seul(e)** *alone*   **un ami** *a friend* (male)   **une amie** *a friend* (female)   **un camarade de chambre** *a roommate* (male)   **une camarade de chambre** *a roommate* (female)   **beaucoup** *a lot*   **pour** *for* **Je parle** *I speak, I talk*   **facile** *easy*   **un peu** *a little*   **Mais** *But*   **maintenant** *now*   **parce que** *because*

A **Moi, je...** Talk about yourself by choosing the words in parentheses that best describe you.

1. (Je suis / Je ne suis pas) étudiant(e).
2. (Je suis / Je ne suis pas) de Los Angeles.
3. (J'habite / Je n'habite pas) à Minneapolis.
4. (Je suis / Je ne suis pas) canadien(ne).
5. J'habite (seul[e] / avec ma famille / avec un[e] ami[e] / avec des ami[e]s).
6. (Je parle / Je ne parle pas) très bien français.
7. Pour moi, le français est (cool / assez facile / un peu difficile / intéressant / super).

B **Descriptions.** A Canadian student is talking about himself. Change the words in italics as needed to make the paragraph true for you.

Je m'appelle *Chris Jones*. Je suis de *Toronto*. Maintenant, j'habite *avec un ami* à *Chapel Hill* parce que je suis *étudiant* à *l'université de Caroline du Nord*. Je parle un peu français. Je parle *anglais et espagnol* aussi. Pour moi, le français est *très facile*.

C **En rond.** Find out more about your classmates. Work in groups of three. For each item, say what is true for you and ask the student on your right about himself/herself, using **Et toi?** He/She will complete the item and ask the person to his/her right the same question, who will answer and then begin the next question.

1. Je m'appelle... Et toi?
2. Je suis... Et toi?
3. Je suis de... Et toi?
4. J'habite à... Et toi?
5. J'habite avec... (J'habite seul[e].) Et toi?
6. Je travaille... (Je ne travaille pas.) Et toi?
7. Je parle... Et toi?
8. Pour moi, le français est... Et pour toi?

D **Et toi?** Imagine that you and your partner meet at an event for international students in Paris. Take turns asking and answering these questions.

1. Comment tu t'appelles?
2. Comment ça va?
3. Tu es étudiant(e)?
4. Tu travailles aussi?
5. Tu es américain(e)?
6. Tu es d'où?
7. Tu habites à Paris maintenant?
8. Tu parles espagnol?

À VOUS!

With a partner, read aloud the conversation on the preceding page, paying particular attention to the pronunciation. Then act it out, adapting it to make it true for you. Afterward, switch roles and do it again.

Vocabulaire sans peine!

Vocabulaire sans peine! notes help you learn vocabulary quickly by pointing out cognate patterns between English and French. Cognates are words that look similar and have the same meaning in two languages.

Note these patterns of adjectives indicating where people are from:
-ain = *-an*
américain(e) = *American*
africain(e) = *African*
-ien(ne) = *-ian*
canadien(ne) = *Canadian*
australien(ne) = *Australian*
How would you say these in French?
Mexican
Colombian

L'HEURE

Quelle heure est-il? *What time is it?*

To tell time *on the hour,* use:

Il est + *number* + **heure(s).**   **Il est trois heures.**   *It's 3:00.*

When telling the time, use **une** for *one.* The word **heures** has an **s** except in **une heure.** Don't use **heure** after **midi** *(noon)* or **minuit** *(midnight).*

Il est une heure.   Il est deux heures.   Il est midi.   Il est minuit.

To tell time *after the hour up to the half hour,* use:

Il est + *number of hour*   **Il est trois heures**   *It's 3:05.*
+ heure(s) + *minutes.*   **cinq.**

For *a quarter after,* use **et quart** and for *half after,* use **et demie.** The word **et** is only used in telling time in these two expressions. With **midi** and **minuit,** use **et demi** without the final **e.**

Il est une   Il est trois   Il est neuf   Il est midi   Il est minuit
heure dix.   heures   heures   et demi.   et demi.
                et quart.   et demie.

After the half hour, you can tell the time *until the next hour.* Use:

Il est + *number of next hour* + **heure(s)**   **Il est six heures**   *It's 5:55.*
moins + *minutes until the hour.*   **moins cinq.**

For *a quarter until the hour,* use **moins le quart.** This is the only time **le** is used in telling time.

Il est deux heures   Il est deux heures   Il est deux heures
moins vingt-cinq.   moins vingt.   moins le quart.

The following clock is useful in visualizing how time is expressed. With **moins...,** remember to use the number of the upcoming hour.

Il est une heure /
deux heures...

moins cinq — cinq

moins dix — dix

moins le quart — et quart

moins vingt — vingt

moins vingt-cinq — vingt-cinq

et demie

Instead of using *A.M.* and *P.M.,* use the following, except with **midi** or **minuit.**

du matin *(after midnight until noon)*   Il est huit heures **du matin.**
de l'après-midi *(after noon until 6 p.m.)*   Il est une heure **de l'après-midi.**
du soir *(6 p.m. until midnight)*   Il est neuf heures **du soir.**

Use **à** to ask or tell *at* what time something takes place.

Le cours de français est **à quelle heure**?

Le cours de français
commence *à* une heure.

Le cours de français **finit**
à deux heures et quart.

To say that you do something *from* a certain time *to* another, use **de... à.**

Le lundi, je suis en cours **de** neuf heures **à** une heure.

commence *starts, begins*   **finit** *finishes, ends*

PRONONCIATION

L'heure et la liaison 0-16

Notice that there is liaison before the word **heure(s)** and that the pronunciation of some numbers changes in this liaison. Practice pronouncing these times.

Quelle heure est _t_il?

Il est deux _z_heures.   Il est sept _t_heures.
Il est trois _z_heures.   Il est huit _t_heures.
Il est cinq _k_heures.   Il est neuf _v_heures.
Il est six _z_heures.   Il est dix _z_heures.

Il est dix heures moins le quart.

A **Prononcez bien!** For each time shown, ask your partner what time it is, using the two times given. Pay particular attention to pronunciation. Your partner will respond with the correct time. Change roles after each item.

EXEMPLE 2:00 Il est deux heures. / Il est deux heures et demie.
— **Il est deux heures ou (or) il est deux heures et demie?**
— **Il est deux heures.**

1. *2:10* Il est deux heures dix. / Il est deux heures et quart.
2. *3:15* Il est trois heures vingt. / Il est trois heures et quart.
3. *4:20* Il est quatre heures vingt-cinq. / Il est quatre heures vingt.
4. *5:30* Il est cinq heures et demie. / Il est cinq heures et quart.
5. *6:45* Il est six heures moins le quart. / Il est sept heures moins le quart.
6. *8:35* Il est neuf heures moins vingt-cinq. / Il est huit heures moins vingt-cinq.
7. *9:50* Il est neuf heures moins dix. / Il est dix heures moins dix.
8. *12:00 A.M.* Il est midi. / Il est minuit.

B **Quelle heure est-il?** Can you tell the time if someone asks you? Take turns asking and telling the time with a partner.

EXEMPLE — **Quelle heure est-il?**
— **Il est une heure de l'après-midi.**

1.  2.  3.  4.

5.  6.  7.  8.

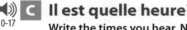 **C** **Il est quelle heure?** Can you understand if someone tells you the time?
0-17 Write the times you hear. Notice how the word **heure(s)** is abbreviated in French.

EXEMPLES VOUS ENTENDEZ (*YOU HEAR*): Il est dix heures et quart.
VOUS ÉCRIVEZ (*YOU WRITE*): **10h15**

VOUS ENTENDEZ: Il est neuf heures cinq.
VOUS ÉCRIVEZ: **9h05**

D **Où êtes-vous?** Say whether or not you are usually at the indicated place or with the indicated people at the time given.

EXEMPLE Le lundi à 9h15 du matin, *je suis / je ne suis pas* en cours.
Le lundi à neuf heures et quart du matin, je suis en cours.
Le lundi à neuf heures et quart du matin, je ne suis pas en cours.

1. Le lundi à 7h00 du matin, *je suis / je ne suis pas* à la maison.
2. Le mercredi à 2h30 de l'après-midi, *je suis / je ne suis pas* en cours de français.
3. Le jeudi à 5h20 de l'après-midi, *je suis / je ne suis pas* dans un autre cours.
4. Le vendredi à 10h45 du soir, *je suis / je ne suis pas* avec des amis.
5. Le samedi à minuit, *je suis / je ne suis pas* seul(e).
6. Le dimanche à 7h30 du soir, *je suis / je ne suis pas* avec ma famille.

E **Quand?** Complete these sentences so that they are true for you the first day of the week you have your French class.

EXEMPLE Je suis à la maison **avant sept heures et demie.**
                                  before   *[time]*

1. Je suis à la maison _____ _____.
                      before   *[time]*
2. Je suis à l'université _____ _____. (J'habite sur *[on]* le campus.)
                      after   *[time]*
3. Le cours de français commence _____ _____.
                                    at   *[time]*
4. Le cours de français finit _____ _____.
                          at   *[time]*
5. Je suis en cours _____ _____ _____ _____.
                     from   *[time]*   *to*   *[time]*
6. Je travaille _____ _____ _____ _____. (Je ne travaille pas.)
              from   *[time]*   *to*   *[time]*
7. Je suis à la maison _____ _____.
                        after   *[time]*

F **Mon emploi du temps.** On a sheet of paper, make two copies of this daily planner, changing it to describe your schedule on one copy and leaving the other one blank. With a partner, take turns describing your schedules. On the blank daily planner, fill in your partner's schedule as he/she describes it to you.

EXEMPLE **Le lundi, je suis en cours de dix heures à une heure. Je travaille de deux heures à quatre heures. Je suis à la maison après cinq heures.**

lundi	
6:00	
7:00	
8:00	
9:00	
10:00	*en cours*
11:00	
12:00	
1:00	
2:00	*travail*
3:00	
4:00	
5:00	*à la maison*
6:00	
7:00	
8:00	
9:00	
10:00	
11:00	
12:00	

You can access the audio of the active vocabulary of this *Compétence* online.

Communicating in class

DES EXPRESSIONS UTILES

Le prof(esseur) **dit aux** étudiants:

Ouvrez votre livre à la page 23.
Lisez l'exercice A.
Fermez votre livre.

Écoutez la question et répondez avec une phrase complète.
Écrivez la réponse au tableau.

Prenez votre cahier, du papier et **un crayon ou un stylo.**

Faites l'exercice A avec **un(e) autre** étudiant(e).

Étudiez les mots de vocabulaire.
Faites **les devoirs en ligne.**

You may also wish to use these phrases.

Comment? Répétez, s'il vous plaît. — *What? Please repeat.*

— Vous comprenez? — *Do you understand?*
— Oui, je comprends. — *Yes, I understand.*
Non, je ne comprends pas. — *No, I don't understand.*

— Comment dit-on *the homework* en français? — *How does one say **the homework** in French?*
— On dit **les devoirs.** — *One says **les devoirs.***

— Que veut dire **votre**? — *What does **votre** mean?*
— Je ne sais pas. — *I don't know.*
— Ça veut dire *your.* — *It means **your.***

— Merci. / Merci bien. — *Thank you. / Thanks.*
— De rien. — *You're welcome.*

Pardon. / Excusez-moi. — *Excuse me.*

---

dit aux *says to the* **Lisez** *Read* **Écoutez** *Listen to* **Prenez** *Take* **votre cahier** *your notebook, your workbook* **un crayon ou un stylo** *a pencil or a pen* **Faites** *Do* **un(e) autre** *another* (**autre** *other*) **Étudiez** *Study* **les mots** *the words* **les devoirs** *the homework* **en ligne** *online*

PRONONCIATION

Les voyelles groupées 0-18

Practice the pronunciation of the following vowel combinations. Notice that the combination **eu** has two different sounds, depending on whether it is followed by a pronounced consonant in the same syllable.

- a + u / e + u / o + u

au, eau [o]:	au	aussi	beaucoup	tableau
eu [ø]:	deux	un peu	jeudi	monsieur
eu [œ]:	heure	neuf	professeur	seul(e)
ou [u]:	vous	douze	jour	pour

- a + i / e + i / o + i / u + i

ai [ɛ]	français	je vais	je sais	vrai
ei [ɛ]	treize	seize	beige	neige
oi [wa]:	moi	toi	trois	au revoir
ui [ɥi]	huit	minuit	aujourd'hui	je suis

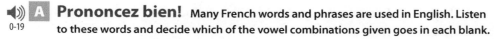

🔊 0-19 **A** **Prononcez bien!** Many French words and phrases are used in English. Listen to these words and decide which of the vowel combinations given goes in each blank.

EXEMPLE Vous voyez *(YOU SEE):* **ai/au** vin___grette
Vous entendez *(YOU HEAR):* vinaigrette/
vi-nai-gret-te / vinaigrette
Vous complétez: **ai/au** vin**ai**grette

1. **ou/oi** c___p d'état
2. **eu/ei** p___gnoir
3. **eu/au** mili___
4. **eu/au** chauff___r
5. **oi/ui** film n___r
6. **oi/ui** haute c___sine
7. **eu/eau** nouv___ riche
8. **eu/au** f___x pas
9. **ai/au** au contr___re

government overthrow
on the contrary
social climber
hired driver
robe
setting
mistake
dark cinema
fine food
vinegar and oil dressing

Now say what each one of the above terms means, using one of the choices given. If you do not know, in French, ask what it means. Pay attention to the pronunciation.

EXEMPLE *Vinaigrette,* ça veut dire *vinegar and oil dressing.* en anglais. / Que veut dire *vinaigrette* en anglais?

⚙ **B** **En cours.** In groups, make up commands your instructor might give you.

> Lisez… / Prenez… / Faites… / Étudiez… / Écoutez… / Écrivez… / Répondez à…

> votre cahier / la phrase / les devoirs / l'exercice / les mots de vocabulaire
> la question / la réponse / un stylo et du papier / votre livre

C **Réponses.** You are visiting Quebec. What do you say… ?

> to thank someone / when someone thanks you /
> to pass through a group / if you don't know / to have something repeated /
> if you don't understand / to ask what **autre** means / to ask how to say *close* in
> French / if you step on someone's foot

L'ALPHABET

When you hear new words, it may be helpful to see how they are spelled. You can ask:

Ça s'écrit comment?	*How is that written?*
Ça s'écrit avec ou sans accent?	*Is that written with or without an accent?*
Ça s'écrit avec un ou deux **s** en français / en anglais?	*Is that written with one or two **s**'s in French / in English?*

A a	**A**nne		**Q** ku	**Q**uentin	
B bé	**B**runo		**R** erre	**R**omane	
C cé	**C**aroline		**S** esse	**S**téphane	
D dé	**D**idier		**T** té	**T**ristan	
E e	**E**mma		**U** u	**U**rsula	
F effe	**F**rançoise		**V** vé	**V**alérie	
G gé	**G**érard		**W** double vé	**W**illiam	
H hache	**H**ugo		**X** iks	**X**avier	
I i	**I**sabelle		**Y** i grec	**Y**ves	
J ji	**J**ules		**Z** zède	**Z**oé	
K ka	**K**arima				
L elle	**L**ola		**é** = **e** accent aigu	**ç** = **c** cédille	
M emme	**M**argot		**è** = **e** accent grave	**'** = apostrophe	
N enne	**N**athan		**â** = **a** accent circonflexe	**-** = trait d'union	
O o	**O**livier		**ï** = **i** tréma	**ll** = deux **l**	
P pé	**P**ascal				

A **Des animaux.** Listen as the names of some animals are spelled out and write them down.

🔊 0-20

EXEMPLE VOUS ENTENDEZ *(YOU HEAR):* A-N-I-M-A-L
VOUS ÉCRIVEZ *(YOU WRITE):* **animal**

B **Les SMS.** Here are some common abbreviations used in French text messages (**les SMS** or **les textos**). First, spell them out, using the French alphabet and numbers. Then, match each one to its equivalent. In some cases, attempting to read the symbols aloud may help you determine the meaning.

> | s'il vous plaît | excellent | mort de rire (*laughing out loud*) | | Tu es OK? |
> |---|---|---|---|---|
> | ciné (*cinema*) | Bonjour. | De rien. | À demain. | À plus! Je sais. |

1. XLnt
2. TOK?
3. SVP
4. Bjr.

5. A+
6. Je c
7. MDR

8. 2ri1
9. a2m1
10. 6né

C **Que veut dire…? Comment dit-on…?** With a partner, take turns asking and telling what each of the following means.

EXEMPLE lisez — **Que veut dire *lisez*?**
— **Ça veut dire *read*!**

> lisez   ouvrez   comptez   faites   autre   tableau

Now, ask your partner how to say each of the following. When he/she tells you, ask how it is spelled in French.

EXEMPLE *read* — **Comment dit-on *read* en français?**
— **On dit *lisez*.**
— **Ça s'écrit comment?**
— **Ça s'écrit L-I-S-E-Z.**

> read   please   You're welcome.
> notebook   How is that written?

D **Préférences.** Share your preferences. Spell out the following things for your classmates to write down and identify. If the name is composed of more than one word, use **espace** to say *space*.

EXEMPLE votre café préféré *(your favorite café)*
VOUS DITES *(YOU SAY):* **C-H-E-Z-espace-M-O-Z-A-R-T**
LES AUTRES RÉPONDENT *(THE OTHERS RESPOND):* **Chez Mozart**

1. votre restaurant préféré
2. votre acteur préféré / votre actrice préférée
3. votre film préféré
4. votre ville *(city)* préférée
5. votre musicien préféré / votre musicienne préférée

Paris, c'est ma ville préférée.

You can access the audio of the active vocabulary of this *Compétence* online.

COMPARAISONS CULTURELLES

L'HEURE OFFICIELLE

It is important to understand **l'heure officielle,** the 24-hour clock, as it is used in all schedules and sometimes in conversations in most countries. Is the 24-hour clock used in your country? In what circumstances? Does using the 24-hour clock make things clearer or less clear to you?

With the 24-hour clock:

- Continue counting from 13 on, instead of beginning with 1 to 12 o'clock again during the P.M. hours. For example, 2:00 A.M. is **deux heures** and 2:00 P.M. is **quatorze heures.**
- Do not use **et, moins, midi, minuit, du matin, de l'après-midi,** and **du soir.** Instead, simply state the minutes after the hour. For example, **deux heures et quart** is **deux heures quinze** and **dix heures moins dix** is **neuf heures cinquante.**

To convert conversational time after noon to official time, add 12 (**une heure de l'après-midi = treize heures**). To convert official time after noon to conversational time, subtract 12 (**vingt heures = huit heures du soir**).

L'HEURE FAMILIÈRE	L'HEURE OFFICIELLE
12h05 minuit cinq	0h05 zéro heure cinq
1h15 une heure et quart (du matin)	1h15 une heure quinze
12h20 midi vingt	12h20 douze heures vingt
1h30 une heure et demie (de l'après-midi)	13h30 treize heures trente
10h40 onze heures moins vingt (du soir)	22h40 vingt-deux heures quarante
11h50 minuit moins dix	23h50 vingt-trois heures cinquante

How would you express each of these times in conversational time? In official time?

12:30 A.M.	3:45 A.M.	1:20 P.M.
10:40 A.M.	12:15 P.M.	11:55 P.M.

Il est quatorze heures cinq.

A **Horaire de train.** You are flying into Paris to study for a month at a French language institute in the town of Le Creusot. The institute's website lists some of the TGV trains you can take daily from the **Gare de Lyon** station in Paris to Le Creusot. Say what time each train arrives, using official time. The first one has been done as an example.

Paris-Le Creusot TGV	
Départ Paris Gare de Lyon	**Arrivée Le Creusot TGV**
5h50	7h09
7h52	9h10
11h51	13h07
13h53	15h11
17h53	19h10
19h58	21h16
20h30	22h46

EXEMPLE 5h50

Le train de cinq heures cinquante arrive à sept heures neuf.

B **À la télé.** You want to watch these shows on TV5Monde, the international French TV station. Take turns asking a partner what time they are on. Answer first using official time, then convert it to conversational time.

EXEMPLE le journal de la RTBF
— **Le journal de la RTBF est à quelle heure?**
— **À six heures trente; c'est-à-dire, à six heures et demie du matin.**

Grille des programmes

Lun 09

Matin		Après-midi		Soir	
04:05	300 MILLIONS DE CRITIQUES	12:00	64' LE MONDE EN FRANÇAIS - 1RE PARTIE	→ 21:16	FABRIQUES CULTURELLES
05:00	FLASH INFO			21:30	TV5MONDE LE JOURNAL
05:02	LE JOURNAL DE RADIO-CANADA	12:23	LE JOURNAL DE L'ÉCONOMIE	21:50	MÉTÉO
		12:27	64' LE MONDE EN FRANÇAIS - 2E PARTIE	21:53	TENDANCE XXI EXPRESS
05:27	TV5MONDE LE JOURNAL AFRIQUE			22:00	DEVOIR D'ENQUÊTE
		12:47	L'INVITÉ	23:37	ITINERIS
05:46	TÉLÉMATIN	12:55	64' L'ESSENTIEL	→ 23:51	MATIÈRE GRISE EXPRESS
→ 06:30	LE JOURNAL DE LA RTBF	13:00	LE JOURNAL DE LA RTS	00:00	TV5MONDE LE JOURNAL
07:00	TV5MONDE LE JOURNAL	13:26	LE COURT DU JOUR - INVENTER DEMAIN	00:10	MÉTÉO
07:20	QUOI DE NEUF DOC?			00:14	L'INVITÉ
07:30	TV5MONDE LE JOURNAL	13:30	FLASH INFO	00:22	LES EXPERTS DU PASSÉ
07:58	TÉLÉMATIN	13:33	ÉPICERIE FINE - TERROIRS GOURMANDS	00:30	MEURTRES À AVIGNON
→ 08:40	UN OBJET, UNE HISTOIRE			01:57	ELLES ONT TOUTES UNE HISTOIRE
08:44	L'INVITÉ	13:59	D'ART D'ART	01:59	VERSION FRANÇAISE
08:53	RÊVES D'HÔTEL	14:02	LE SABRE ET LA KALACHNIKOV	02:26	LE COURT DU JOUR - LES TRAVAILLEURS DE L'OMBRE
09:00	LE JOURNAL DE FRANCE 2	14:54	VISITES PRIVÉES		
09:29	ZAP IN.CH	15:49	NOTRE HISTOIRE	02:30	FLASH INFO
09:55	COURTS SÉJOURS	15:53	VIC LE VIKING	02:32	GOÛT DE / GOOD FRANCE
09:59	INSPIRATION DESIGN	→ 16:05	LE PETIT PRINCE	02:34	CE MONDE EST FOU
10:21	SENTINELLES DE LA NATURE	16:30	PLUS BELLE LA VIE		
10:29	PIQUE-ASSIETTE INVITE LES CHEFS	17:02	VENDÉE GLOBE		
		17:04	LE JOURNAL DE FRANCE 2		
10:55	LES PEUPLES DES MONTAGNES	17:31	TOUT COMPTE FAIT		
		18:10	GÉOPOLITIS		
10:59	SUISSE FOCUS	→ 18:26	QUESTIONS POUR UN CHAMPION		
11:26	MERCI PROFESSEUR!				
→ 11:29	DES CHIFFRES ET DES LETTRES	18:56	OBJECTIF NATURE		
		19:00	TV5MONDE LE JOURNAL		
		19:20	MÉTÉO		
		19:22	LE JOURNAL DU DAKAR		
		19:30	69 MINUTES SANS CHICHIS		

Source: http://www.tv5monde.com/cms/chaine-francophone/programmes/p-86-s5-z302-lg0-La-semaine-d-un-seul-coup-d-oeil.htm

1. Un objet, une histoire
2. Des chiffres et des lettres
3. Le Petit Prince
4. Questions pour un champion
5. Fabriques culturelles
6. Matière grise express

VOCABULAIRE

COMPÉTENCE 1

Greeting people

GREETING PEOPLE

les salutations formelles / familières	*formal / familiar greetings*
Bonjour.	*Hello., Good morning.*
Bonsoir.	*Good evening.*
monsieur (M.)	*Mr., sir*
madame (Mme)	*Mrs., madam*
mademoiselle (Mlle)	*Miss*
Comment allez-vous?	*How are you?* (formal)
Je vais très bien.	*I'm doing very well.*
Assez bien.	*Fairly well.*
Comme ci comme ça.	*So-so.*
Pas mal.	*Not bad(ly).*
Pas très bien.	*Not very well.*
Salut!	*Hi!, Bye!* (familiar)
Comment ça va? / Ça va?	*How's it going?* (familiar)
Ça va (bien).	*It's going fine.*
et	*and*
Et vous?	*And you?* (formal)
Et toi?	*And you?* (familiar)
moi	*me*
merci	*thank you, thanks*

EXCHANGING NAMES

Comment vous appelez-vous?	*What's your name?* (formal)
Tu t'appelles comment?	*What's your name?* (familiar)
Je m'appelle...	*My name is . . .*
Je suis...	*I am, I'm . . .*

SAYING WHERE YOU ARE FROM

Vous êtes d'ici?	*Are you from here?* (formal)
Tu es d'où?	*You are from where?* (familiar)
Je suis...	*I am . . .*
d'ici	*from here*
de (+ city)	*from (+ city)*
oui	*yes*
non	*no*

SAYING GOOD-BYE

À demain.	*See you tomorrow.*
À plus.	*See you later.* (familiar)
À plus tard.	*See you later.*
Au revoir.	*Good-bye.*
Salut!	*Hi!, Bye!* (familiar)

COMPÉTENCE 2

Counting and describing your week

COUNTING TO 59

les nombres	*numbers*
Comptez de... à...	*Count from . . . to . . .*
s'il vous plaît	*please* (formal)
zéro, un, deux, trois, quatre,	*zero, one, two, three, four,*
cinq, six, sept, huit, neuf,	*five, six, seven, eight, nine,*
dix, onze, douze, treize,	*ten, eleven, twelve, thirteen,*
quatorze, quinze, seize,	*fourteen, fifteen, sixteen,*
dix-sept, dix-huit,	*seventeen, eighteen,*
dix-neuf,	*nineteen,*
vingt, vingt et un,	*twenty, twenty-one,*
vingt-deux, vingt-trois,	*twenty-two, twenty-three,*
vingt-quatre, vingt-cinq,	*twenty-four, twenty-five,*
vingt-six, vingt-sept,	*twenty-six, twenty-seven,*
vingt-huit, vingt-neuf,	*twenty-eight, twenty-nine,*
trente, trente et un,	*thirty, thirty-one,*
trente-deux, trente-trois...	*thirty-two, thirty-three . . .*
quarante, quarante et un,	*forty, forty-one,*
quarante-deux...	*forty-two . . .*
cinquante, cinquante et un,	*fifty, fifty-one,*
cinquante-deux...	*fifty-two . . .*
Combien font deux et deux?	*How much is two and two?*
Deux et deux font quatre.	*Two and two equals four.*
Combien font cinq moins deux?	*How much is five minus two?*
Cinq moins deux font trois.	*Five minus two equals three.*

TELLING THE DAY OF THE WEEK

les jours de la semaine	*the days of the week*
aujourd'hui	*today*
C'est quel jour aujourd'hui?	*What day is today?*
C'est...	*It's . . .*
lundi	*Monday*
mardi	*Tuesday*
mercredi	*Wednesday*
jeudi	*Thursday*
vendredi	*Friday*
samedi	*Saturday*
dimanche	*Sunday*

DESCRIBING YOUR SCHEDULE

Tu es...?	*Are you . . . ?*
Je suis / Je ne suis pas...	*I'm / I'm not . . .*
en cours (de français)	*in (French) class*
à la maison	*at home*
dans un autre cours	*in another class*
Tu travailles?	*Do you work?*
Je travaille...	*I work . . .*
Je ne travaille pas...	*I don't work . . .*
Quels jours...?	*What days . . . ?*
le lundi	*(on) Mondays*
le lundi matin	*(on) Monday mornings*
du lundi au vendredi	*from Mondays to Fridays*
le matin	*mornings, in the morning(s)*
l'après-midi	*afternoons, in the afternoon(s)*
le soir	*evenings, in the evening(s)*
tous les jours	*every day*
le week-end	*(on) weekends / on the weekend(s)*
les cours	*classes*
le cours de français	*French class*
ce semestre	*this semester*
avant	*before*
après	*after, afterwards*
aussi	*also, too*

COMPÉTENCE 3

Talking about yourself and your schedule

TALKING ABOUT YOURSELF

Tu es...?	Are you . . . ?
Je suis / Je ne suis pas...	I am / I am not . . .
américain(e)	American
canadien(ne)	Canadian
étudiant(e)	a student
professeur	a professor
Tu habites...?	Do you live . . . ?
J'habite / Je n'habite pas...	I live / I do not live . . .
à... (+ city)	in . . . (+ city)
avec ma famille	with my family
avec un(e) ami(e)	with a friend
avec un(e) camarade	with a roommate
de chambre	
seul(e)	alone
Tu parles...?	Do you speak . . . ?
Je parle / Je ne parle pas...	I speak / I do not speak . . .
anglais	English
espagnol	Spanish
français	French
Pour moi, le français est...	For me, French is . . .
assez cool	pretty cool
assez facile	fairly easy
intéressant	interesting
super	great
un peu difficile	a little difficult / hard
Tu travailles...?	Do you work . . . ?
Je travaille / Je ne travaille pas...	I work / I do not work . . .
à l'université	at the university
beaucoup	a lot
pour...	for . . .
à	in, to, at
maintenant	now
mais	but
parce que	because

TELLING TIME

l'heure	the time
une heure	an hour / one o'clock
Quelle heure est-il?	What time is it?
Il est une heure cinq.	It's 1:05.
Il est deux heures dix.	It's 2:10.
Il est trois heures et quart.	It's 3:15.
Il est quatre heures et demie.	It's 4:30.
Il est dix heures moins le quart.	It's 9:45.
Il est une heure moins dix.	It's 12:50.
Il est midi.	It's noon.
Il est minuit.	It's midnight.
À quelle heure?	At what time?
à... heure(s)	at . . . o'clock
du matin	A.M., in the morning [when telling time]
de l'après-midi	P.M., in the afternoon [when telling time]
du soir	P.M., in the evening [when telling time]
Le cours de français est à quelle heure?	French class is at what time?
Le cours de français commence à...	French class starts / begins at . . .
finit à...	finishes / ends at . . .
de... heures à... heures	from . . . o'clock to . . . o'clock
Je suis en cours de... à...	I am in class from . . . to . . .

COMPÉTENCE 4

Communicating in class

CLASSROOM INSTRUCTIONS

des expressions utiles	useful expressions
Le prof(esseur) dit aux étudiants...	The prof(essor) says to the students . . .
Ouvrez votre livre à la page 23.	Open your book to page 23.
Lisez l'exercice A.	Read exercise A.
Fermez votre livre.	Close your book.
Écoutez la question et répondez avec une phrase complète.	Listen to the question and answer with a complete sentence.
Écrivez la réponse au tableau.	Write the answer on the board.
Prenez votre cahier, du papier et un crayon ou un stylo.	Take (out) your notebook / workbook, paper and a pencil or a pen.
Faites l'exercice avec un(e) autre étudiant(e).	Do the exercice with another student.
Étudiez les mots de vocabulaire.	Study the vocabulary words.
Faites les devoirs en ligne.	Do the homework online.

OTHER USEFUL EXPRESSIONS

Comment? Répétez, s'il vous plaît.	What? Please repeat.
— Vous comprenez?	— Do you understand?
— Oui, je comprends. Non, je ne comprends pas.	— Yes, I understand. No, I don't understand.
— Comment dit-on the homework en français?	— How does one say **the homework** in French?
— On dit **les devoirs.**	— One says **les devoirs.**
— Que veut dire **votre**?	— What does **votre** mean?
— Je ne sais pas.	— I don't know.
— Ça veut dire your.	— It means **your.**
— Merci (bien).	— Thank you., Thanks.
— De rien.	— You're welcome.
Pardon. / Excusez-moi.	Excuse me.

THE ALPHABET

l'alphabet	the alphabet
Ça s'écrit comment?	How is that written?
Ça s'écrit...	Is that written . . .
avec ou sans accent?	with or without an accent?
avec un ou deux **s** en français / en anglais ?	with one or two s's in French / in English?
Ça s'écrit...	That's written . . .

*Pour **l'alphabet** et **les noms des accents,** voir la page 22.*
*Pour **l'heure officielle**, voir la page 24.*

Sur la Côte d'Azur
À l'université

 Pair work

 Group work

 Class work

 Video

 Audio

© Art Kowalsky/Alamy Stock Photo

LE MONDE FRANCOPHONE

Géoculture et Vidéo-voyage: La Côte d'Azur

GÉOCULTURE ET VIDÉO-VOYAGE:
LA CÔTE D'AZUR

France

LA FRANCE
(la République française)

NOMBRE D'HABITANTS: **65 350 000 (Les Français)**

CAPITALE: **Paris**

°Paris

nord
ouest · est
sud

les gorges de Daluis
Côte d'Azur
Grasse
Nice
Antibes
Vallauris
Cannes

La Côte d'Azur est **une des plus belles** parties de la France – et aussi une des plus **fascinantes!**

La Promenade des Anglais à Nice

Nice est **la plus grande ville** de la Côte d'Azur. Nice est **connue pour ses plages** et pour **sa célèbre promenade tout le long de la mer,** la Promenade des Anglais, **l'endroit parfait pour faire une course matinale.**

Une parfumerie à Grasse

La ville de Grasse est connue pour la fabrication de **parfums.**

Les gorges de Daluis **sont** fantastiques et excellentes pour faire du rafting!

Les gorges de Daluis

une des plus belles *one of the most beautiful*   **fascinantes** *fascinating*   **la plus grande ville** *the biggest city*   **connue pour ses plages** *known for its beaches*
sa célèbre promenade *its famous walkway*   **tout le long de la mer** *all along the sea*   **l'endroit parfait pour faire une course matinale** *the perfect place to take a morning run*   **parfums** *perfumes*   **sont** *are*

Le musée Picasso à Vallauris

La plage à Antibes

Voulez-vous voir les œuvres de Picasso?

Les Plages électroniques de Cannes

La plage à Antibes est très belle!

Cannes est connue pour son fameux festival du film et aussi pour le festival des Plages électroniques de Cannes, un festival de musique électro.

Sur la Côte d'Azur, **ça bouge!**

Le savez-vous?

Quelle chose *(What thing)* de la liste correspond à chaque endroit *(each place)*?

le rafting	**le musée Picasso**
une course matinale	**la fabrication de parfums**
les Plages électroniques	

1. Vallauris
2. Grasse
3. la Promenade des Anglais à Nice
4. Cannes
5. les gorges de Daluis

Le musée *The museum*　　**Voulez-vous voir les œuvres de** *Do you want to see the works of*　　**Sur** *On*　　**ça bouge** *it rocks*

AVANT LA VIDÉO

In this video, you are going to visit the **Côte d'Azur,** called the French Riviera in English. Would you like to visit the **Côte d'Azur**?

Recognizing an associated word, either in French or English, can help you guess the meaning of a new word. Using the related word given in parentheses, guess which French word from the list is used in each of these sentences from the video to express the boldfaced English word. Afterwards, read each sentence in its entirety to help you better understand the video.

Respirez	**la journée**
matinale	**initiez**
électroniques	**soirée**
Parfumerie	

1. *Today, we are spending **the day** on the Côte d'Azur.*

   (le jour) Aujourd'hui, on passe _____ sur la Côte d'Azur.

2. *In the morning, **morning** run on the Promenade des Anglais in Nice!*

   (le matin) Le matin, course _____ sur la Promenade des Anglais à Nice!

3. *Later, **evening** on the terrace, cours Saleya in Nice.*

   (le soir) Plus tard, _____ terrasse, cours Saleya à Nice.

4. *And for music fans: the Nice Jazz Festival or the **Electronic** Beaches of Cannes.*

   (électrique) Et pour les amateurs de musique: le Nice Jazz Festival ou les Plages _____ de Cannes.

5. *At the end of the day, **initiate** yourself to rafting for a crazed descent of the Daluis gorge.*

(une initiation) En fin de journée, _____ -vous au rafting pour une folle descente des gorges de Daluis.

6. *In Grasse, visit of the International Museum of **Perfumery. Breathe** deeply!*

(le parfum) À Grasse, visite au Musée international de la _____.

(la respiration) _____ à fond!

▶ EN REGARDANT LA VIDÉO

As you watch the video, determine in what order the activities from *Avant la vidéo* appear.

Bear in mind that you will not understand all you hear. Use what you know and the images to help understand the main ideas.

▶ APRÈS LA VIDÉO

After viewing the video a second time, complete these statements with the correct option from the list. Remember that you will not understand all you hear. Use what you know and the images to help you understand the main ideas.

> **d'orques *(orcas)* et de dauphins *(dolphins)***
> **une promenade le long de la mer à Nice**
> **la fabrication de parfums**
> **à Nice et à Cannes**

1. La Promenade des Anglais est _____.

2. La ville de Grasse est célèbre pour _____.

3. À Marineland, il y a *(there are)* des spectacles _____.

4. Il y a des festivals de musique _____.

Identifying and describing people

LES GENS À L'UNIVERSITÉ

Ce sont mes amis David, Jean, Léa et Lisa.

C'est David, **un jeune homme** français.

Il est étudiant.

C'est Jean, **le frère de** David.

Il n'est pas étudiant.

Il travaille.

David et Jean sont français. Ils ne sont pas de Paris. Ils sont de Nice.

C'est Léa, **une jeune femme** américaine.

Elle est étudiante.

C'est Lisa, **la sœur jumelle de** Léa.

Elle n'est pas étudiante.

Elle travaille.

Lisa et Léa ne sont pas françaises. Elles sont américaines. Léa est à Nice **pour étudier.** Lisa est en France **pour voir sa** sœur et pour visiter la France.

Comment est David?

gros?   mince?   timide? extraverti? intelligent?   bête?   **gentil? méchant?**

David est **petit,** mince et très gentil.

Comment est Léa?

grosse?   mince?   timide? extravertie? intelligente? bête? gentille? méchante?

Léa est **grande,** mince et très gentille!

David et Léa sont **célibataires.** Et vous? Êtes-vous célibataire, **comme** David et Léa, ou **alors** êtes-vous fiancé(e), marié(e) ou divorcé(e)?

Les gens *People*   **Ce sont...** *They are / These are / Those are...*   **mes amis** *my friends*   **C'est...** *He is / She is / It is / This is / That is...*   **un jeune homme** *a young man*   **le frère de** *the brother of*   **une jeune femme** *a young woman*   **la sœur de** *the sister of*   **jumeau (jumelle)** *twin*   **pour étudier** *in order to study*   **pour voir** *in order to see*   **sa (son, ses)** *his/her/its*   **Comment est...?** *What is... like?*   **gentil(le)** *nice*   **méchant(e)** *mean*   **petit(e)** *short, small*   **grand(e)** *tall, big*   **célibataire** *single*   **comme** *like, as*   **alors** *so, then, therefore*

🔊 1-1

David **rencontre** Léa.

DAVID: Salut! Je suis David Cauvin. **Nous sommes** dans le **même** cours de littérature, non?

LÉA: Oui, c'est ça. Bonjour! Je m'appelle Léa Clark. Tu es d'ici?

DAVID: Oui, je suis de Nice. Et toi, tu es d'où?

LÉA: Moi, je suis de Los Angeles, mais j'habite ici maintenant parce que je suis étudiante à l'université.

A **Mes amis.** C'est une description de David, de Léa, de Jean ou de Lisa? Indiquez toutes les possibilités.

	DAVID	JEAN	LÉA	LISA
EXEMPLE				
C'est un jeune homme.	X	X		
1. C'est une jeune femme.				
2. Elle travaille.				
3. Elle n'est pas étudiante.				
4. Il est étudiant.				
5. C'est le frère de Jean.				
6. Il est un peu gros.				
7. Il n'est pas étudiant.				
8. Il est petit et mince.				

B **Et votre ami(e)?** Décrivez votre meilleur(e) ami(e) *(your best friend)*. Utilisez **mon meilleur ami** pour décrire un homme et **ma meilleure amie** pour une femme. Dites au moins cinq choses. *(Say at least five things.)*

EXEMPLES

Mon meilleur ami, c'est Felipe.
Il est de Memphis. Il n'est pas grand.
Il est timide et…

Ma meilleure amie, c'est Sophie.
Elle est de Bangor. Elle n'est pas grande.
Elle est timide et…

> timide/extraverti(e)   gentil(le)/méchant(e)   intelligent(e)/bête
> gros(se)/mince   grand(e)/petit(e)
> marié(e)/célibataire/divorcé(e)/veuf (veuve) *(widowed)*

Maintenant, dites cinq choses pour parler de vous.

EXEMPLE Je m'appelle… Je suis de… Je suis… Je ne suis pas…

🔁 **À VOUS!**

Avec un(e) partenaire, relisez à haute voix *(aloud)* la conversation entre David et Léa. Ensuite, adaptez la conversation pour décrire *(to describe)* votre situation.

You can access the audio of the active vocabulary of this *Compétence* online.

rencontre (rencontrer *to meet* [for the first time or by chance], *to run into* [someone])   **Nous sommes** *We are*   **même** *same*

1. What is an infinitive? How do you say *to be* in French?

2. How do you say *I* in French? *he? she? they* for a group of all females? *they* for a group of all males? *they* for a mixed group?

3. Would you use **tu** or **vous** to address a child? two children? a salesclerk? an adult you've just met?

4. What form of **être** do you use with each subject pronoun?

5. What do you place before a conjugated verb to negate it? What do you place after it? When do words like **ne, je,** and **que** replace the final **e** with an apostrophe (**n', j', qu'**)? What is this called?

6. What is the base form of an adjective? What do you usually do to make it feminine if it ends in a consonant? in **e**? in **é**? in another vowel?

7. What is the feminine form of **gros**? of **canadien**? of **gentil**?

8. What do you usually do to make an adjective plural? What if it ends in **x** or **s**?

9. Is there a difference in pronunciation between **espagnol** and **espagnole**? between **petit** and **petite**? Is the final **s** of the plural form of an adjective pronounced?

Note *de grammaire*

With noun subjects or compound subjects, use the verb form that goes with the corresponding subject pronoun.

David is = he is (**il est**) = **David est**

David and I are = we are (**nous sommes**) = **David et moi sommes**

your friends and you = you (plural) *are* (**vous êtes**) = **tes ami(e)s et toi êtes**

my friends are = they are (**ils/elles sont**) = **mes ami(e)s sont**

DESCRIBING PEOPLE

*Les pronoms sujets, le verbe **être**, la négation et quelques adjectifs*

1. Here are the subject pronouns *(I, you, he . . .)* and the forms of the verb **être** *(to be)*. The word **être** is the *infinitive,* which is the unconjugated form of the verb found in the dictionary. When you conjugate a verb, you change its forms to correspond with the subject. Here is the conjugation of **être.**

ÊTRE *(to be)*					
je	suis	*I am*	nous	sommes	*we are*
tu	es	*you are*	vous	êtes	*you are*
il	est	*he is, it is*	ils	sont	*they are*
elle	est	*she is, it is*	elles	sont	*they are*

- To say *you,* use **tu** when speaking to a friend, family member, classmate, child, or animal. Use **vous** when speaking to an adult with whom you don't have a close relationship or to someone to whom you should show respect, or when referring to more than one person.
- To say *they,* use **ils** for a group of males or a mixed group and **elles** for a group of all females.
- **Je** and other one-syllable words ending in **e** (**ne, le...**) replace the **e** with an apostrophe before another word beginning with a vowel or a mute **h.** This is called *elision.*

2. To negate a conjugated verb, place **ne... pas** around it. Use **n'** before a vowel sound.

NE (N') + *VERB* + PAS		
je **ne** suis **pas**	tu **n'**es **pas**	il/elle **n'**est **pas**
nous **ne** sommes **pas**	vous **n'**êtes **pas**	ils/elles **ne** sont **pas**

3. Adjective forms vary depending on whether they describe a male or a female and whether they describe one person or more than one. The masculine singular form of the adjective is the base form. Add an **e** to change this form to feminine, unless it already ends in *unaccented* **e.** If it ends in *accented* **é** (or any other vowel), add another **e** to form the feminine. Add an **s** to make an adjective plural, unless it ends in **s** or **x.**

MASCULINE		FEMININE	
SINGULAR	*PLURAL*	*SINGULAR*	*PLURAL*
petit	petits	petite	petites
extraverti	extravertis	extravertie	extraverties
jeune	jeunes	jeune	jeunes
marié	mariés	mariée	mariées
français	français	française	françaises

Gros and **gentil** double the final consonant before adding the **e** for the feminine form, as do adjectives ending in **-en,** like canadi**en.**

MASCULINE		FEMININE	
SINGULAR	*PLURAL*	*SINGULAR*	*PLURAL*
gros	gros	grosse	grosses
gentil	gentils	gentille	gentilles
canadien	canadiens	canadienne	canadiennes

PRONONCIATION

Il est + *adjectif* / *Elle est* + *adjectif*
1-2

Since most final consonants are silent in French, you will not hear or say the final consonant of masculine adjective forms, unless they end in **c, r, f,** or **l.** When the **e** is added to make the feminine form, the consonant is no longer final and is pronounced.

petit / petite   français / française

When a masculine adjective form ends in a pronounced final consonant or vowel, or in silent **e**, however, you will hear no difference between the masculine and feminine forms.

espagnol / espagnole   jeune / jeune   marié / mariée   extraverti / extravertie

The final **s** of plurals is not pronounced, nor is a consonant that immediately precedes it, unless it is **c, r, f,** or **l.** The masculine plural forms sound like the masculine singular forms and the feminine plural forms sound like the feminine singular forms. You must pick up the plurality from the context.

Il est petit. / Ils sont petits.   Elle est petite. / Elles sont petites.

1-3

A Prononcez bien! Écoutez chaque *(each)* phrase. C'est une description de **a.** Gabriel Bellon ou de **b.** Gabrielle Lacoste?

EXEMPLE   **VOUS VOYEZ:**   **a.** Gabriel est étudiant.
                                      b. Gabrielle est étudiante.
              VOUS ENTENDEZ: Gabrielle est étudiante.
              VOUS INDIQUEZ: **b. Gabrielle est étudiante.**

a. Gabriel Bellon

1. **a.** Gabriel est grand.
   b. Gabrielle est grande.
2. **a.** Gabriel n'est pas petit.
   b. Gabrielle n'est pas petite.
3. **a.** Gabriel est français.
   b. Gabrielle est française.
4. **a.** Gabriel n'est pas canadien.
   b. Gabrielle n'est pas canadienne.
5. **a.** Gabriel n'est pas gros.
   b. Gabrielle n'est pas grosse.

b. Gabrielle Lacoste

Maintenant, lisez une seule *(a single)* phrase de chaque paire. Votre partenaire va dire si *(is going to say if)* vous dites la phrase **a** ou la phrase **b.**

B Tu ou vous? Demandez à ces personnes d'où elles sont *(where they are from)* avec **Tu es d'où?** ou **Vous êtes d'où?**

> a classmate   a salesclerk   your professor   your professor's young son
> a new elderly neighbor   your parents   a taxi driver
> a couple of friends

C **Quel pronom?** Complétez les phrases avec le bon pronom sujet *(correct subject pronoun)*: **je, tu, il, elle, nous, vous, ils, elles.**

1. David ne travaille pas. _____ est étudiant. Léa ne travaille pas non plus *(either)*. _____ est étudiante aussi.

2. Léa et Lisa ne sont pas françaises. _____ sont américaines. David et Jean sont français. _____ sont de Nice. Ma famille et moi, _____ sommes de Vancouver. Et tes amis et toi, _____ êtes d'où?

3. David et Léa ne sont pas mariés. _____ sont célibataires. Moi, _____ suis célibataire aussi. Et toi, _____ es célibataire ou marié(e)?

D **C'est qui?** Est-ce que ces adjectifs décrivent *(describe)* **David, Léa, David et Léa** ou **Léa et Lisa?** Faites attention à la forme de l'adjectif!

| David | Léa | David et Léa | Léa et Lisa |

EXEMPLE   petit
David est petit.

1. grandes   3. gentils   5. intelligente
2. français   4. extravertie   6. gentilles

E **Gens célèbres.** Travaillez en groupes. Utilisez chacun des adjectifs donnés pour décrire quelqu'un de célèbre (réel ou fictif). Faites attention à la forme de l'adjectif. Après, comparez vos phrases à celles des autres groupes.

grand	grande	petit	petite
LeBron James est grand.			
intelligents	intelligentes	bêtes	jeunes
extraverti	extravertie	timide	mince
méchants	méchantes	gentils	gentilles

F **Descriptions** Formez deux phrases, une à l'affirmatif et une au négatif, pour décrire chacune de ces *(each one of these)* personnes. Changez la forme de l'adjectif comme nécessaire.

grand	petit	extraverti	timide
marié	célibataire	gros	mince
intelligent	bête	gentil	méchant
américain	canadien	jeune	intéressant

EXEMPLE
Moi, je **suis intelligent(e). Je ne suis pas bête.**

1. Moi, je…
2. Mon meilleur ami (Ma meilleure amie)…
3. Mes amis…
4. Le prof (La prof) de français…
5. Les autres étudiants du cours de français…

G Entre amis. Posez ces questions à votre partenaire.

> **EXEMPLE** — **Tu es célibataire ou marié(e)?**
> — **Je suis célibataire / marié(e).**

1. Tu es extraverti(e) ou un peu timide?
2. Tu es célibataire ou marié(e)?
3. Ton meilleur ami (Ta meilleure amie) est intelligent(e) ou un peu bête?
4. Il/Elle est gentil(le) ou un peu méchant(e)?
5. Il/Elle est grand(e) ou petit(e)?
6. Il/Elle est mince ou un peu gros(se)?

H Au contraire! Dites le contraire comme dans l'exemple.

> **EXEMPLE** Les profs à l'université de Nice sont méchants?
> **Mais non! Ils ne sont pas méchants. Ils sont gentils.**

1. Les étudiants à l'université de Nice sont bêtes?
2. Jean et David sont mariés?
3. Ils sont américains?
4. Léa et Lisa sont grosses?
5. Lisa est extravertie?
6. Léa et Lisa sont méchantes?
7. Elles sont petites?
8. Elles sont françaises?

I Comment sont-ils? David parle avec Léa. Complétez ses phrases. Faites attention à la forme de l'adjectif.

> **EXEMPLE** Moi, je… (assez petit / très grand) (gros / mince)
> **Moi, je suis assez petit. Je ne suis pas très grand.**
> **Je suis mince, je ne suis pas gros.**

David et Jean

Léa et Lisa

1. Moi, je… (célibataire / marié) (méchant / gentil)
2. Toi, Léa tu… (extraverti / timide) (mince / gros)
3. Mon frère Jean… (mince / un peu gros) (américain / français)
4. Mon frère Jean et moi, nous… (canadien / français) (bête / assez intelligent)
5. Ta sœur Lisa et toi, vous… ? (français / américain) (célibataire / marié)

STRATÉGIES ET LECTURE

It may seem overwhelming to read a lengthier text in French at first. However, there are strategies you can use to learn to read more easily. This section is designed to help you learn to apply these strategies.

POUR MIEUX LIRE: *Using cognates and familiar words to read for the gist*

1. Cognates are words that look the same or similar in two languages and have the same meaning. Take advantage of cognates to help you read French more easily. There are some patterns in cognates. What three patterns do you see here? What do the last two words in each column mean?

   soudainement *suddenly* obligé *obliged* hôpital *hospital*

   décidément *decidedly* sauvé *saved* île *isle, island*

   complètement? compliqué? honnête?

   généralement? décidé? forêt?

2. Some words may not be cognates, but are related to a recognizable word. Use the hint below to decipher the meaning of the word **pense.**

   Hint: *pensive = deep in thought*   Lisa **pense:** «Il ne comprend pas!»

3. Recognizing words you have already learned in different forms will also help you read. Use the two familiar phrases on the left to guess the meanings of those on the right.

   Comment dit-on *pen* en français?   →   Que dis-tu?

   Je ne sais pas la réponse.   →   Lisa ne sait pas quoi répondre.

A **Avant de lire.** Can you state the general idea of the following sentences? Do not try to read them word by word; rather, focus on the words that you can understand.

Lisa hésite un moment avant de répondre.

C'est juste à ce moment que Léa arrive.

Léa sauve la pauvre Lisa.

David voit Léa et Lisa et s'exclame: «Je vois double!»

David pense que Lisa, c'est Léa.

B **Mots apparentés.** Before reading the following text, *Qui est-ce?*, skim through it and list the cognates you see. You should find about twenty.

Lecture: *Qui est-ce?*

🔊 Lisa Clark is visiting her twin sister, Léa, a student at the University
1-4 of Nice. As she waits for her sister in front of the **musée des Beaux-Arts,** a young man approaches. Since she does not speak French very well, Lisa is unsure what to say when he speaks to her.

— Salut, Léa! Ça va?

Lisa hésite un moment avant de répondre.

— Non, non... euh, ça va, mais... euh... je regrette... je ne suis pas Léa. Je suis Lisa.

— Comment?

Lisa pense: «*He thinks I'm Léa. How do I tell him . . . ?*»

— Non, non, répond Lisa. Vous ne comprenez pas. Je ne suis pas Léa.

— Comment ça, tu n'es pas Léa?

Décidément, ce jeune homme ne comprend rien! Lisa insiste:

— Je ne suis pas Léa. Vous ne comprenez pas! Écoutez! Je ne suis pas Léa! Je ne suis pas étudiante.

— Mais que dis-tu, Léa? demande David. Tu es malade? C'est moi, David. Nous sommes dans le même cours de littérature.

Lisa pense: «*I'm never going to get this guy to understand. He's so sure I'm Léa.*»

C'est juste à ce moment que Léa arrive. La pauvre Lisa est sauvée.

— Salut, Lisa! Bonjour, David!

David, très surpris de voir les sœurs jumelles, s'exclame:

— Mais, ce n'est pas possible! Je vois double! Maintenant, je comprends. C'est ta sœur jumelle, Léa.

— Mon pauvre David! Voilà, je te présente ma sœur, Lisa.

— Bonjour, Lisa. Désolé pour la confusion, mais quelle ressemblance!

A Avez-vous compris? Qui parle: David, Lisa ou Léa?

1. Vous ne comprenez pas. Je ne suis pas Léa.

2. Mais nous sommes dans le même cours de littérature.

3. Je ne suis pas étudiante à l'université de Nice.

4. Je ne parle pas très bien français.

5. Je te présente ma sœur.

B D'abord... Which happens first, a or b?

1. a. David dit bonjour à Lisa.
   b. Lisa arrive au musée des Beaux-Arts.

2. a. David dit: «Bonjour, Léa.»
   b. Lisa pense: «Il ne comprend pas.»

3. a. Lisa hésite à répondre parce qu'elle ne parle pas très bien français.
   b. Lisa répond: «Non, non, vous ne comprenez pas.»

4. a. David comprend que Léa et Lisa sont sœurs jumelles.
   b. Léa arrive.

5. a. David dit: «Désolé *(Sorry)* pour la confusion.»
   b. David comprend la situation.

Describing people

Note *culturelle*

Où habitent la majorité des étudiants en France?

35 % chez leurs parents *(with their parents)*

33 % seuls ou en couple

12 % en résidence collective *(group housing [such as dorms])*

10 % en colocation *(in a shared rental [with a housemate or an apartment mate])*

Remarquez que les résidences universitaires *(university dormitories)* ne sont pas souvent *(often)* sur le «campus» de l'université. Elles sont groupées dans un endroit à part *(grouped in a separate place)* appelé la «cité universitaire». Où *(Where)* habitent les étudiants de votre université?

Note *de vocabulaire*

1. Sympathique is a false cognate; it looks like an English word but has a different meaning. With the abbreviated form **sympa,** do not add **e** to make it feminine, but do add **s** in the plural.

2. Use **le foot(ball)** for *soccer* and **le foot(ball) américain** for *football*.

3. There are three ways to say *my* **(mon, ma, mes)** and *your* [singular familiar] **(ton, ta, tes),** depending on whether the following noun is masculine, feminine, singular, or plural.

1-5

Vocabulaire supplémentaire

optimiste / pessimiste
idéaliste / réaliste

Vocabulaire sans peine!

Noticing cognate patterns can help you learn new words more quickly.

-if(-ive) = *-ive*
agressif = *aggressive*
-ique = *-ic, -ical*
dramatique = *dramatic*
magique = *magical*
statistique = *statistical*
mystique = *mystical*

How would you say these words in French?
impulsive   imaginative
romantic   fantastic

LES DESCRIPTIONS DES GENS

Je suis très...   Je suis **plutôt /** assez...   Je suis un peu...   Je **ne** suis **pas (du tout)...**

jeune / vieux (vieille)

beau (belle) / laid(e)

intelligent(e) / bête
intellectuel(le)

**dynamique /
paresseux
(paresseuse)**
sportif (sportive)

**intéressant(e) /
ennuyeux
(ennuyeuse)**
amusant(e)
marrant(e)

bon (bonne) / mauvais(e)
agréable / désagréable
gentil (gentille) / méchant(e)
**sympathique, sympa /
antipathique**

What are you like, compared to your best friend?

Je suis **plus** dynamique **que mon meilleur ami (ma meilleure amie).**
Je suis **aussi** sportif (sportive) **que** mon meilleur ami (ma meilleure amie).
Je suis **moins** intellectuel(le) **que** mon meilleur ami (ma meilleure amie).

Une **nouvelle** amie, Nadia, parle avec David.

NADIA: **Tes amis** et toi, vous êtes étudiants, non?

DAVID: Oui, nous sommes étudiants à l'université de Nice. Et toi? Tu es étudiante aussi?

NADIA: Non, je ne suis pas très intellectuelle. **Les études** *(f),* **ce n'est pas mon truc.**

DAVID: Et le sport? **Tu aimes** le sport?

NADIA: Oui, je suis assez sportive. J'aime bien le tennis, mais je n'aime pas beaucoup **le football.**

---

plutôt *rather*   **ne... pas du tout** *not at all*   **dynamique** *active, energetic, dynamic*   **paresseux (paresseuse)** *lazy*
ennuyeux (ennuyeuse) *boring*   **marrant(e)** *funny*   **bon(ne)** *good*   **mauvais(e)** *bad*   **sympathique / sympa** *nice*
antipathique *disagreeable, unpleasant*   **plus... que** *more . . . than*   **mon meilleur ami (ma meilleure amie)** *my best friend*
aussi... que *as . . . as*   **moins... que** *less . . . than*   **nouveau (nouvelle)** *new*   **Tes amis** *Your friends*   **Les études** *Studies,
Going to school*   **ce n'est pas mon truc** *that's not my thing*   **Tu aimes** *You like*   **le foot(ball)** *soccer*

A **Ils sont comment?** Complétez les phrases.

EXEMPLE Danny DeVito est (plus, moins, aussi) grand que Tom Cruise.
Danny DeVito est moins grand que Tom Cruise.

1. Johnny Depp est (plus, moins, aussi) beau que Jack Black.
2. Jim Carrey est (plus, moins, aussi) marrant qu'Adam Sandler.
3. Serena Williams est (plus, moins, aussi) sportive que Venus Williams.
4. Scarlett Johansson est (plus, moins, aussi) belle que Jennifer Aniston.
5. Ellen DeGeneres est (plus, moins, aussi) intéressante qu'Oprah Winfrey.
6. Justin Bieber est (plus, moins, aussi) désagréable que Kim Kardashian.

B **Comment sont-ils?** Formez des phrases avec le verbe **être** à l'affirmatif ou au négatif pour parler de vous, de vos amis et de vos professeurs.

EXEMPLE je / timide
Je suis timide. / Je ne suis pas timide.

MOI

1. je / sportif (sportive)
2. je / intellectuel(le)
3. je / paresseux (paresseuse)

MON MEILLEUR AMI / MA MEILLEURE AMIE

6. il/elle / amusant(e)
7. il/elle / bête
8. il/elle / gentil(le)

MES AMIS ET MOI

4. nous / dynamiques
5. nous / sympas

MES PROFS

9. ils / ennuyeux
10. ils / très bons

C **Et vous?** Comment êtes-vous? Comment est votre partenaire?

| très | plutôt | assez | un peu | ne... pas du tout |

EXEMPLE *outgoing*
— **Moi, je suis très / plutôt / assez / un peu extraverti(e). /**
Je ne suis pas (du tout) extraverti(e). Et toi?
— **Moi, je suis très / plutôt... extraverti(e) (aussi). /**
Moi, je ne suis pas (du tout) extraverti(e) (non plus *[either]*).

1. *active*
2. *mean*
3. *lazy*
4. *intellectual*
5. *shy*
6. *boring*
7. *athletic*
8. *married*

À VOUS!

Avec un(e) partenaire, relisez à haute voix *(aloud)* la conversation entre Nadia et David. Ensuite, adaptez la conversation pour décrire *(to describe)* votre situation.

You can access the audio of the active vocabulary of this *Compétence* online.

DESCRIBING AND COMPARING PEOPLE

✔ **Pour vérifier**

1. What are four irregular patterns of adjective agreement?

2. What are the four forms of **beau**? of **vieux**? of **jumeau**? of **nouveau**?

3. How would you say *bigger than? as big as? less big than?*

4. How do you say *better than?*

Sélection musicale. Search for the song "**Exactement**" by **Vive la fête** online to enjoy a musical selection containing these structures.

D'autres adjectifs et le comparatif

1. Remember that adjectives agree in gender and number with the nouns they describe. Note the patterns of these common adjective endings.

MASCULINE	FEMININE	MASCULINE		FEMININE	
		SINGULAR	PLURAL	SINGULAR	PLURAL
-eux	-euse(s)	paress**eux**	paress**eux**	paress**euse**	paress**euses**
-en(s)	-enne(s)	canadi**en**	canadi**ens**	canadi**enne**	canadi**ennes**
-if(s)	-ive(s)	sport**if**	sport**ifs**	sport**ive**	sport**ives**
-el(s)	-elle(s)	intellectu**el**	intellectu**els**	intellectu**elle**	intellectu**elles**

2. **Bon,** like **gros** and **gentil,** doubles the final consonant before adding the **e** for the feminine form (**bon → bonne, gros → grosse, gentil → gentille**).

3. **Beau, jumeau, nouveau,** and **vieux** are irregular, but have a similar pattern.

MASCULINE		FEMININE	
SINGULAR	PLURAL	SINGULAR	PLURAL
beau	beaux	belle	belles
jumeau	jumeaux	jumelle	jumelles
nouveau	nouveaux	nouvelle	nouvelles
vieux	vieux	vieille	vieilles

4. To compare people using adjectives, use:

+ **plus** + *adjective* + **que (qu')**	Je suis **plus grand(e) que** Lisa.
= **aussi** + *adjective* + **que (qu')**	Je suis **aussi mince que** Lisa.
− **moins** + *adjective* + **que (qu')**	Je suis **moins sportif (sportive) que** Lisa.

Instead of using **plus... que** with **bon,** use **meilleur... que** to say *better... than.* You will see both **plus mauvais(e)... que** or **pire... que** to say *worse... than.* Use **en** to say what someone is good or bad *in/at.*

Léa est **meilleure** en français **que** Léa.   *Léa is **better** in French **than** Lisa.*

A **Sœurs jumelles.** Les jumelles Lola et Christine se ressemblent physiquement *(are physically the same)* mais elles ont des personnalités très différentes l'une de l'autre *(from each other)*. Comparez les deux. Faites attention à la forme de l'adjectif.

Lola   Christine

EXEMPLE   dynamique: Lola est **plus dynamique que** Christine.

1. **sportif:** Lola est _____ Christine.

2. **paresseux:** Lola est _____ Christine.

3. **grand:** Lola est _____ Christine.

4. **beau:** Lola est _____ Christine.

B Comment sont-ils? Dites si ces adjectifs décrivent *(describe)* bien ces personnes. Changez la forme de l'adjectif si nécessaire.

EXEMPLE Steve Mandanda (beau, petit) **Il est beau. Il n'est pas petit.**

Steve Mandanda,
footballeur français

Patrick Modiano,
écrivain *(writer)*
français

Claire Denis,
réalisatrice *(film director)* française

Corine Franco,
footballeuse
française

1. Steve Mandanda: gros, sportif, paresseux, dynamique
2. Patrick Modiano: jeune, intellectuel, bête, intelligent
3. Steve Mandanda et Corine Franco: gros, français, paresseux, dynamique, beau
4. Claire Denis: intellectuel, gros, paresseux, américain
5. Corine Franco: sportif, vieux, beau, laid
6. Corine Franco et Claire Denis: français, paresseux, dynamique, laid

C Descriptions. Décrivez ces personnes avec une phrase à l'affirmatif et une autre phrase au négatif.

EXEMPLE Moi, je suis (très) gentil(le). Je ne suis pas (du tout) méchant(e).

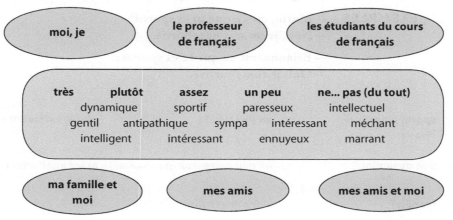

Maintenant utilisez **plus... que, aussi... que et moins... que** et les mots donnés pour faire des comparaisons entre vous et votre meilleur(e) ami(e).

EXEMPLE Je suis plus/aussi/moins dynamique que mon meilleur ami / ma meilleure amie.

ASKING WHAT SOMEONE IS LIKE

✔ *Pour vérifier*

1. When asking a *yes/no* question, what happens to the pitch of your voice?

2. Where is **est-ce que** placed in forming a question?

3. What happens to **est-ce que** before a vowel sound?

4. How can you form a question if you anticipate that the answer is *yes*?

5. How do you normally begin a response to a *yes/no* question in French?

Les questions

There are several ways to ask a question.

1. You can ask a question that is answered *yes* or *no* by just using rising intonation.

Elle est mariée?   Tu es d'ici?

2. You can also ask a *yes/no* or *either/or* question by placing **est-ce que** before the subject and the verb. Note that **est-ce que** becomes **est-ce qu'** before vowel sounds.

Est-ce que tes amis sont étudiants?   Est-ce qu'ils sont intellectuels?

Est-ce que Léa est mariée ou célibataire?   Est-ce qu'elle est étudiante?

3. If you are presuming that someone will probably answer *yes,* you can use either **n'est-ce pas?** *(right?)* or **non?** at the end of a question with rising intonation.

Il est marié, n'est-ce pas?   Il est marié, non?

4. You normally begin a response to a *yes/no* question with **Oui,…** or **Non,…**
— Est-ce que tu es marié?
— **Oui,** je suis marié.
— **Non,** je ne suis pas marié.

A **Personnalités.** Posez des questions à d'autres étudiants pour trouver une personne qui correspond à chaque *(each)* adjectif.

EXEMPLES — Mario, est-ce que tu es sportif?
— Non, je ne suis pas sportif.

— Brianna, est-ce que tu es sportive?
— Oui, je suis sportive.

sportif (sportive) *Brianna*	un peu timide	plutôt extraverti(e)
très dynamique	un peu paresseux (paresseuse)	assez intellectuel(le)
marié(e)	assez marrant(e)	d'ici

Maintenant, présentez un(e) des étudiant(e)s à la classe.

EXEMPLE C'est Brianna. Elle est sportive.

B **Encore des questions!** Formez des questions logiques avec le verbe **être** et posez-les à votre partenaire.

EXEMPLE — **Est-ce que tu es marié(e)?**
— **Oui, je suis marié(e). / Non, je ne suis pas marié(e).**

Est-ce que	tu... nous... tes amis... ton meilleur ami (a meilleure amie)...	marié(e)(s) dans le même cours aussi amusant(e)(s) que toi en cours à dix heures plus dynamique(s) que toi très sportif(s) (sportive[s]) aussi intelligent(e)(s) que toi

C **Et Léa?** Léa répond aux questions d'une nouvelle amie. Utilisez ses réponses pour déterminer quelles questions son amie lui a posées *(her friend asked her)*.

EXEMPLES — **Est-ce que tes amis sont canadiens?**
— Non, mes amis ne sont pas canadiens.

— Lisa et toi, **est-ce que vous êtes d'ici?**
— Non, nous ne sommes pas d'ici.

1. — _____?
— Oui, je suis étudiante.

2. — _____?
— Oui, je suis intellectuelle.

3. — _____?
— Non, les cours ne sont pas difficiles.

4. — _____?
— Oui, les professeurs sont gentils.

5. — _____?
— Non, Lisa n'est pas étudiante.

6. — _____?
— Oui, elle est sportive.

7. — Et ta sœur et toi? _____ _____?
— Non, nous ne sommes pas canadiennes.

8. — _____?
— Oui, nous sommes américaines.

D **Entretien.** Interviewez votre partenaire.

1. Ta famille et toi, vous êtes d'ici? Est-ce que tu es américain(e)?

2. Est-ce que tu es étudiant(e)? Est-ce que les études sont faciles ou difficiles pour toi?

3. Tes amis et toi, est-ce que vous êtes intellectuels? Est-ce que ton meilleur ami (ta meilleure amie) est plus intellectuel(le) ou moins intellectuel(le) que toi?

4. Est-ce que tu aimes le sport? Tu es plutôt sportif (sportive)? Est-ce que tu es aussi sportif (sportive) que ton meilleur ami (ta meilleure amie)? Est-ce que tu es très dynamique ou plutôt paresseux (paresseuse)?

Describing the university area

Note *culturelle*

La vie *(The life)* d'un étudiant universitaire en France est différente comparée à celle *(to that)* d'un étudiant universitaire aux USA. En France, les activités extrascolaires (culturelles ou sportives) sont moins bien développées et font partie de *(are part of)* la vie privée *(private life)* plutôt que *(rather than)* de la vie universitaire. Est-ce que la vie sur le campus est importante pour vous?

Note *de vocabulaire*

1. All nouns in French have a gender (masculine or feminine). Other than those for people, the gender of a noun does not depend on its meaning.

2. To say *a, an,* use **un** before a masculine singular noun and **une** before a feminine singular noun. Use **des** *(some)* before plural nouns. You will learn about this later. For now, learn new nouns with **un** or **une** in front of them to remember the gender.

3. The word **universitaire** is an adjective and must be paired with a noun that it is describing; for example, *university dorms* (**des résidences universitaires**). The word **université** is the noun *the university:* **J'habite près de l'université.**

4. In French, unlike in English, most descriptive adjectives are placed *after* the noun they describe: **un homme** *intelligent.* However, some very common ones (**beau, jeune, bon, grand...**) are placed *before:* **un** *jeune* **homme.** You will learn more about this in *Chapitre 3*.

LE CAMPUS ET LE QUARTIER

Qu'est-ce qu'il y a sur votre campus?

Sur le campus *(m)*, **il y a...**

des salles *(f)* de cours

des bureaux *(m)*

une bibli(othèque) avec wi-fi

une librairie

des résidences *(f)* **universitaires**

un restaurant

un stade des matchs *(m)* de foot(ball) américain

une salle de gym

Dans le quartier *(m)* **universitaire, près de** l'université *(f)*, il y a...

des maisons *(f)*

un **joli** parc des arbres *(m)*

une boîte (de nuit)

un cinéma des films *(m)*

Qu'est-ce qu'il y a...? *What is there...?* **sur** *on* **il y a** *there is, there are* **un bureau** *an office*
une résidence universitaire *a dormitory* **Dans le quartier** *In the neighborhood* **universitaire** *university (as an adjective)*
près de *near* **joli(e)** *pretty*

🔊 1-6 Léa parle avec un ami.

RÉMI:	Comment est **ton** université? Tu aimes le campus?
LÉA:	Oui, il est très agréable.
RÉMI:	Qu'est-ce qu'il y a sur le campus?
LÉA:	Il y a une grande bibliothèque et beaucoup d'arbres, mais **il n'y a pas assez de parkings.**
RÉMI:	Qu'est-ce qu'il y a dans le quartier?
LÉA:	Il y a des cafés, deux ou trois bons restaurants et beaucoup de mauvais fast-foods.

Vocabulaire supplémentaire

un amphithéâtre *a lecture hall*
un arrêt de bus *a bus stop*
une association d'étudiants *a student association*
un bâtiment *a building*
un centre médical *a health center*
un court de tennis *a tennis court*
une fontaine *a fountain*
un gymnase *a gym*
un labo(ratoire) *a lab*
une piscine *a pool*
un service administratif *an administrative office*
une statue
un terrain de sport *a sports field*
un théâtre *a theater* (for live performances)

A **Analogies.** Faites des analogies.

> professeurs   salle de cours   cinéma
> résidence universitaire   parc   fast-food   salle de gym

EXEMPLE des salles de cours: des étudiants
des bureaux: des **professeurs**

1. des matchs de foot: un stade / des films: _____
2. des voitures *(cars):* un parking / des arbres: _____
3. un expresso: un café / des hamburgers: _____
4. des crayons: un bureau / des poids *(dumbbells):* _____
5. une famille: une maison / une camarade de chambre: _____
6. un cours de biologie: un laboratoire *(lab)* / un cours de français:
_____

B **Chez nous.** Décrivez votre université.

1. Le quartier universitaire est (très / assez) *agréable / désagréable.*
2. Le campus est (très / assez) *joli / laid.*
3. Sur le campus, *il y a / il n'y a pas* beaucoup d'arbres.
4. La bibliothèque est (très / assez) *grande / petite* et *nouvelle / plutôt vieille.*
5. *Il y a / Il n'y a pas de* wi-fi dans les salles de cours.
6. *Il y a / Il n'y a pas* beaucoup de résidences universitaires sur le campus.
7. Le restaurant universitaire est *bon / mauvais. (Il n'y a pas de restaurant sur le campus.)*
8. *Il y a / Il n'y a pas* assez de parkings.
9. Près de l'université, il y a *des cafés / un joli parc / une boîte de nuit / une salle de gym / un cinéma…*
10. *Book People / Monster Books / ???* est une bonne librairie près d'ici.

🔁 **À VOUS!**

Avec un(e) partenaire, relisez à haute voix la conversation entre Rémi et Léa. Ensuite, adaptez la conversation pour décrire votre université.

You can access the audio of the active vocabulary of this *Compétence* online.

ton (ta, tes) *your*   **il n'y a pas** *there isn't, there aren't*   **assez de** *enough*   **un parking** *a parking lot*

SAYING WHAT THERE IS

✔ Pour vérifier

1. How do you say *there is? there are? there isn't? there aren't?*

2. What are the two forms of the word for *a*? When do you use each one? How do you say *some*?

3. What do you generally put at the end of a noun to make it plural? When do you not add it? What do you put at the end of a noun to make it plural if it ends in **eau**?

4. In what circumstances do you use **de (d')** instead of **un, une,** or **des**? What is an exception to replacing **un, une,** or **des** with **de (d')** after a negated verb?

5. What is the difference in pronunciation between **un** and **une**? between **des** and **de**? When do you pronounce the final consonants of **un** and **des**?

Note *de vocabulaire*

1. Use **un** before masculine nouns and **une** before feminine nouns to say *one*, as well as to say *a, an*. **J'ai** *(I have)* **deux frères et une sœur**.

2. Use **il y a** to say *there is, there are*. **C'est** and **ce sont** and **il/elle est** and **ils/elles sont** mean *he/she/it/this is* and *they/these are* when identifying or describing someone. You will learn more about this later in this chapter.

Vocabulaire sans peine!

Nouns ending in **-tion** and **-té** are usually feminine. Notice these cognate patterns.

-tion = *-tion*
une nation = *a nation*
-té = *-ty*
une activité = *an activity*
How would you say these nouns in French?
a conversation   an administration
a minority   a majority

*Le genre, l'article indéfini et l'expression **il y a***

1. To say *there is* or *there are* in French, use the expression **il y a (un, une, des...).** To say *there isn't* or *there aren't,* use **il n'y a pas (de...).**

2. All nouns in French have a gender (masculine or feminine). The categorization of most nouns (other than those for people) as masculine or feminine does not depend on their meaning and cannot be guessed. *Always learn a new noun with the article **(un, une)** to remember its gender!*

3. The short word **un** *(a, an),* **une** *(a, an),* or **des** *(some)* before a noun is called the indefinite article. Use **un** with masculine singular nouns, **une** with feminine singular nouns, and **des** with all plural nouns. The word **des** cannot be dropped in French, unlike the word *some,* which can be omitted in English.

	MASCULINE	FEMININE
SINGULAR	un film	une bibliothèque
PLURAL	des films	des bibliothèques

4. To make a noun plural, add **s** to the end of it, unless it ends in **s, x,** or **z.** Nouns that end in **-eau (bureau)** form their plural with an **x (bureaux).**

5. **Un, une,** and **des** change to **de (d')** in the following cases.
- when they follow a negated verb

Il y a **un** stade.	→	Il **n'**y a **pas de** stade.
Il y a **une** bibliothèque.	→	Il **n'**y a **pas de** bibliothèque.
Prenez **des** notes.	→	**Ne** prenez **pas de** notes.
Il y a **des** étudiants dans la classe.	→	Il **n'**y a **pas d'**étudiants dans la classe.

but not if the verb is a form of **être:**

C'est **un** bon restaurant.	→	Ce **n'**est **pas un** bon restaurant.

- after expressions of quantity, such as **assez, beaucoup,** and **combien**

Il y a **combien de** cinémas?   Il y a **assez de** parkings.   Il y a **beaucoup d'**arbres.

PRONONCIATION

L'article indéfini
1-7

Use the very tight sound **u,** as in **tu,** to say **une.** The vowel sound of **un** is nasal. Pronounce the **n** in **un** only in **liaison. Des** rhymes with the **é** of **café,** and **de** rhymes with **je.** Pronounce the **s** in **des** only in **liaison.**

   une résidence   **une** amie   **un** stade   **un** ami   **des** profs   **des** arbres   assez **de** profs

Since final consonants are usually silent, you cannot hear the final **s** of a plural noun and must determine whether a noun is singular or plural from the article. Plurality is often indicated by the sound [e] as in **café (des, les...).**

   un film   **des** films   **un** prof   **des** profs

1-8

A Prononcez bien! Écoutez des descriptions de cette *(this)* salle de cours et indiquez si vous entendez **un**, **une**, **des**, or **de**. Après, regardez la photo et écoutez les phrases encore une fois *(again)*. Indiquez si chaque phrase est vraie **(oui)** ou fausse **(non)**.

	UN	UNE	DES	DE (D')	OUI	NON
1.						
2.						
3.						
4.						
5.						
6.						

B Comparaisons culturelles. Lisez la **Note** *culturelle* dans la marge. Dans une vieille université française, est-ce qu'il y a probablement ces choses?

EXEMPLES   un restaurant universitaire   des matchs de football américain

Oui, il y a un restaurant universitaire.

Non, il n'y a pas de matchs de football américain.

> **un restaurant universitaire**   **un stade**   **des bureaux de profs**
> **une bibliothèque**   **des résidences universitaires**   **des salles de cours**
> **une boîte de nuit**   **des matchs de football américain**

Maintenant, dites s'il y a ces choses *(these things)* sur votre campus.

Note *culturelle*

En France, les vieilles universités n'ont pas de campus dans le sens américain / canadien. Chaque faculté *(Each division)* a *(has)* des salles de cours, souvent dans de vieux bâtiments *(buildings)*, chacune *(each one)* dans une partie différente de la ville *(city)*. Il n'y a pas de bâtiments sociaux, sportifs ou résidentiels. Il y a juste ce qu'il faut pour les études *(just what is needed for studies)*: des amphithéâtres *(lecture halls)*, des salles de cours, une bibliothèque et des bureaux, mais il y a souvent *(often)* un restaurant aussi.

C Chez nous. Complétez chaque phrase avec **un**, **une**, **des** ou **de (d')**. Ensuite *(Then)*, dites si les deux dernières phrases *(the last two sentences)* de chaque groupe sont vraies ou fausses.

1. C'est _____ restaurant.

Il y a _____ bon restaurant sur notre *(our)* campus.   vrai / faux

Il y a beaucoup _____ restaurants dans le quartier.   vrai / faux

2. C'est _____ bibliothèque.

Il n'y a pas _____ bibliothèque sur notre campus.   vrai / faux

Il y a _____ bibliothèque municipale près d'ici.   vrai / faux

3. C'est _____ parking.

Il y a assez _____ parkings sur notre campus.   vrai / faux

Il y a _____ parkings payants *(pay)* près de l'université.   vrai / faux

4. Ce sont _____ arbres.

Il y a beaucoup _____ arbres sur notre campus.   vrai / faux

Il y a _____ parc avec beaucoup _____ arbres dans le quartier près de l'université.   vrai / faux

IDENTIFYING PEOPLE AND THINGS

✔ *Pour vérifier*

Do you use **c'est** and **ce sont** or **il est / elle est** and **ils sont / elles sont** with a noun to identify or describe someone or something? with an adjective to describe? with a prepositional phrase to say such things as where someone or something is or is from? with nationalities, professions, and religions without the indefinite article?

Note *de grammaire*

Don't confuse **il y a** *(there is / there are)* with **c'est / ce sont** and **il est / elle est / ils sont / elles sont,** which are used to say *this/that/he/she/it is* and *these/those/they are*. Remember to use **elles sont** for groups of all feminine nouns and **ils sont** for groups of all masculine nouns or for mixed groups.

C'est un campus. **Il est** beau.
It's a campus. It's beautiful.

Sur le campus, **il y a** beaucoup d'arbres. **Ils sont** beaux!
On the campus, there are a lot of trees. They are beautiful!

Sélection musicale. Search for the song **"Je suis un homme"** by Zazie online to enjoy a musical selection containing these structures.

C'est ou Il est / Elle est

1. All nouns in French are masculine or feminine. Generally, use **il** or **elle** to say *it* and **ils** or **elles** to say *they* when talking about things, depending on the gender of the noun being referred to.

Le campus? **Il** est beau.   Les parkings? **Ils** sont très petits.
La bibliothèque? **Elle** est jolie.   Les salles de cours? **Elles** sont vieilles.

2. Note that **c'est (ce n'est pas)**, as well as **il est / elle est (il n'est pas / elle n'est pas)**, can mean *he is / she is / it is (not),* and **ce sont (ce ne sont pas)**, as well as **ils sont / elles sont (ils ne sont pas / elles ne sont pas)** can mean *they are (not)*. These are not interchangeable.

Use **c'est** and **ce sont**:

- with *nouns* to identify or describe.
  C'est *David.*
  Ce n'est pas *Jean.*
  C'est *un* jeune *homme* sympa.
  Ce sont *Léa* et *Lisa.*
  Ce sont *des amies* sympas.
  Ce ne sont pas *Alice* et *Anne.*

Use **il est / elle est** and **ils sont / elles sont**:

- with *adjectives* to describe.
  Il est *petit* et *sympa.*
- with *prepositional phrases* to say such things as where someone or something is or is from.
  Elles sont *de* Los Angeles.
  Elles sont *en* France.
- with *nationalities, professions* (including **étudiant[e]**), and *religions* without the indefinite article.
  Il est *français.*
  Il est *étudiant.*
  Il est *catholique.*

Nice, c'est une ville de France que j'aime beaucoup.

A **Léa.** Léa parle de ses études. Complétez chaque phrase par **c'est, ce sont, il est, elle est, ils sont** ou **elles sont.**

1. Le cours *(m)* de littérature, _____ mon cours préféré. _____ plutôt facile. _____ à huit heures et _____ dans une grande salle de cours.

2. Mes profs? _____ intéressants. _____ des gens intelligents. _____ à l'université tous les jours. _____ très intellectuels et _____ aussi très sympas.

3. Mon meilleur ami, _____ David. _____ d'ici. _____ un bon ami. _____ très marrant. _____ français. _____ le frère de Jean.

B **Qu'est-ce que c'est?** Identifiez ces personnes et ces choses. Après, décrivez-les *(describe them)* avec l'adjectif le plus logique de chaque paire entre parenthèses. Dans les descriptions, utilisez le pronom *(pronoun)* et la forme de l'adjectif convenables *(fitting)*.

EXEMPLES

café
(grand / petit)
(agréable / désagréable)

C'est un café.
Il est petit.
Il est agréable.

amies
(sympa / antipathique)
(intéressant / ennuyeux)

Ce sont des amies.
Elles sont sympas.
Elles sont intéressantes.

1.
homme
(paresseux /
  dynamique)
(intéressant /
  ennuyeux)
(beau / laid)
(grand / petit)

2.
amis
(gros / mince)
(beau / laid)
(intellectuel /
  paresseux)
(jeune / vieux)

3.
femme
(paresseux /
  sportif)
(gros / mince)
(jeune / vieux)
(grand / petit)

4.
maisons
(nouveau /vieux)
(joli / laid)
(grand / petit)

Talking about your studies

L'UNIVERSITÉ ET LES COURS

Est-ce que vous aimez l'université?

J'aime beaucoup...	J'aime assez...	Je n'aime pas (du tout)...	Je préfère...
les prof(esseur)s	la bibli(othèque)	les devoirs *(m)*	**les fêtes** *(f)*
les étudiants	le labo(ratoire)	les examens *(m)*	le sport
le campus	de biologie	**la salle**	les matchs *(m)*
le livre de français	les cours *(m)*	**d'informatique**	de basket
	en ligne		

Qu'est-ce que vous étudiez?

J'étudie la philo(sophie).   Je n'étudie pas la littérature.

LES LANGUES *(f)*
l'anglais *(m)*
l'espagnol *(m)*
le français

LES SCIENCES HUMAINES *(f)*
l'histoire *(f)*
la psycho(logie)
les sciences po(litiques) *(f)*

LES ARTS *(m)*
le théâtre
la musique
la peinture

LE COMMERCE
le commerce international

LES TECHNOLOGIES *(f)*
l'informatique *(f)*
les mathématiques (les maths) *(f)*

LES SCIENCES *(f)*
la bio(logie)
la chimie

J'aime beaucoup le cours de... Il est facile / difficile / intéressant.

David et Léa parlent de **leurs** études.

DAVID: Qu'est-ce que tu étudies ce semestre?

LÉA: J'étudie le français et la littérature classique. Et toi?

DAVID: J'étudie la philosophie et la littérature classique, comme toi.

LÉA: Comment sont tes cours?

DAVID: J'aime beaucoup le cours de philosophie. Il est très intéressant. Je n'aime pas du tout le cours de littérature, parce que le prof est ennuyeux.

---

la salle d'informatique *the computer lab*   **une fête** *a party*   **Qu'est-ce que...?** *What...?*   **les sciences po(litiques)** *government, political science*   **la peinture** *painting*   **l'informatique** *computer science*   **la chimie** *chemistry*   **leur(s)** *their*

A **Préférences.** Interviewez votre partenaire sur ses préférences.

EXEMPLE le français / les mathématiques
— **Est-ce que tu préfères le français ou les mathématiques?**
— **Je préfère le français.**

1. les langues / les arts
2. le français / l'espagnol
3. la musique / le théâtre / la peinture
4. les sciences / les sciences humaines
5. la chimie / la biologie
6. l'histoire / les sciences politiques / la psychologie
7. le commerce international / les technologies
8. l'informatique / les mathématiques
9. les cours dans les grandes salles / les cours dans les petites salles / les cours dans la salle d'informatique / les cours en ligne
10. les examens / les devoirs / les fêtes

La cour de la Sorbonne

© JOEL SAGET/AFP Creative/Getty Images

B **Opinions.** Faites des comparaisons.

EXEMPLES **Les maths sont plus / moins / aussi faciles que la psychologie.**
La chimie est plus / moins / aussi difficile que la biologie.

les maths	facile	la psychologie
la chimie	difficile	la biologie
la philosophie	intéressant	la littérature
les étudiants	sympa	les profs
les matchs de basket	amusant	les matchs de foot

Vocabulaire supplémentaire

l'allemand *(m) German*
l'anthropologie *(f)*
l'arabe *(m)*
le chinois *Chinese*
la communication
la comptabilité *accounting*
le discours *speech*
le japonais
le marketing
la physique *physics*
la sociologie

C **Entretien.** Interviewez votre partenaire.

1. Qu'est-ce que tu étudies ce semestre / trimestre? Comment sont tes cours ce semestre / trimestre? Comment sont tes profs? Quels cours est-ce que tu préfères? Pourquoi *(Why)*? Est-ce que tu es meilleur(e) en maths, en sciences ou en sciences humaines?

2. Tu préfères être en cours le matin, l'après-midi ou le soir? Tu aimes les cours en ligne?

3. Qu'est-ce que tu aimes à l'université? Qu'est-ce que tu n'aimes pas?

À VOUS!

Avec un(e) partenaire, relisez à haute voix la conversation entre David et Léa. Ensuite, adaptez la conversation pour décrire vos cours ce semestre / trimestre.

You can access the audio of the active vocabulary of this ***Compétence*** online.

IDENTIFYING PEOPLE AND THINGS

✔ *Pour vérifier*

1. What are the four forms of the word for *the* in French? When do you use each one?

2. Besides meaning *the,* what are two other uses of the definite article in French where there is no article in English?

3. When is the **s** of the plural form **les** pronounced?

4. How can you hear the difference between a singular and plural noun?

Sélection musicale. Search for the song **"Salut à toi"** by Kiemsa online to enjoy a musical selection containing these structures.

L'article défini

1. The words **le, la, l', les** *(the)* before nouns are called the *definite article.* The form you use depends on the noun's gender and number and whether it starts with a consonant or vowel sound.

	SINGULAR BEFORE CONSONANT SOUND	SINGULAR BEFORE VOWEL SOUND	PLURAL
MASCULINE	**le** livre	**l'**homme	**les** livres, **les** hommes
FEMININE	**la** librairie	**l'**étudiante	**les** librairies, **les** étudiantes

2. Use the definite article before nouns:

   • To specify items, as when using *the* in English.
   Étudiez **le** vocabulaire à la page 23.   *Study **the** vocabulary on page 23.*

   • To say what you like, dislike, or prefer.
   Je n'aime pas **les** devoirs.   *I don't like homework.*

   • To talk about something as a general category or an abstract noun, as when naming subjects and courses.
   Les langues sont faciles pour moi.   *Languages are easy for me.*
   Les fêtes sont plus amusantes   *Parties are more fun than*
   que **les** devoirs.   *homework.*

   In the last two cases, note that there is no article in English.

PRONONCIATION

La voyelle **e** et l'article défini
1-10

As you know, a *final* unaccented **e** is usually not pronounced, unless it is the only vowel, as in **le.**

   grand**e**   histoir**e**   langu**e**   bibliothèqu**e**   j'aim**e**

Otherwise, an unaccented **e** has three different pronunciations, depending on what follows it.

   • In short words like **le** or **je,** or when **e** is followed by a single consonant within a word, pronounce it as in:
   j**e**   n**e**   l**e**   r**e**garde   d**e**voirs

   • When, as in **les, e** is followed by an unpronounced consonant at the end of a word, pronounce it as in:
   l**e**s   m**e**s   parl**e**z   aim**e**z   étudi**e**z

   • In words like **elle,** where **e** is followed by two consonants within a word, or by a single pronounced consonant at the end of a word, pronounce it as in:
   int**e**ll**e**ctu**e**l   b**e**lle   qu**e**l   **e**spagnol   bask**e**t

Since the final **s** of plural nouns is not pronounced, you must pronounce the article correctly to differentiate singular and plural nouns. Listen carefully as you repeat each of the following nouns. Notice the **z** sound of final **s** in liaison.

le livre	la science	l'étudiant	l'étudiante
les livres	les sciences	les ᶻétudiants	les ᶻétudiantes

🔊 **A Prononcez bien!** Listen as David talks about university life. In each sentence, you will hear the singular or plural form of one of the following nouns. Indicate which form you hear.

1-11

1. ___ le professeur ___ les professeurs
2. ___ le cours ___ les cours
3. ___ l'étudiant ___ les étudiants
4. ___ le devoir ___ les devoirs
5. ___ le livre ___ les livres
6. ___ l'exercice ___ les exercices
7. ___ le campus ___ les campus
8. ___ la bibliothèque ___ les bibliothèques

B Quels cours? Posez des questions à d'autres étudiants pour trouver une personne qui étudie chacune de ces matières.

EXEMPLE — Felipe, est-ce que tu étudies la chimie?
— Non, je n'étudie pas la chimie.

— Élise, est-ce que tu étudies la chimie?
— Oui, j'étudie la chimie.

EXEMPLE 1. 2. 3.

4. 5. 6. 7.

Après, utilisez… **étudie**… pour donner *(to give)* vos résultats.

EXEMPLE Élise étudie la chimie.

C Entretien. Complétez les questions suivantes avec l'article défini (**le, la, l', les**), l'article indéfini (**un, une, des**) ou **de (d')**. Après, posez ces questions à votre partenaire.

1. Tu aimes _____ sport? Est-ce qu'il y a _____ stade sur _____ campus de cette *(this)* université? Est-ce qu'il y a souvent *(often)* _____ matchs de football américain le week-end? Tu préfères _____ foot, _____ football américain ou _____ basket?

2. _____ campus ici est agréable? Il y a assez _____ parkings? Est-ce qu'il y a beaucoup _____ arbres? Est-ce qu'il y a _____ grande bibliothèque? Est-ce que _____ bibliothèque est agréable?

3. Tu comprends bien _____ français? _____ langues sont faciles ou difficiles pour toi? Tu aimes _____ cours de français? Est-ce qu'il y a beaucoup _____ étudiants dans _____ cours? Combien _____ étudiants est-ce qu'il y a? _____ cours est difficile? Est-ce qu'il y a _____ examen aujourd'hui?

D Et vous? Complétez les phrases pour parler de vos cours et de votre université.

1. J'étudie…
2. J'aime beaucoup…
3. Je n'aime pas beaucoup…
4. Je comprends bien…
5. Je ne comprends pas bien…
6. Pour moi, le cours de… est…

VIDÉO-REPRISE

Les Stagiaires *(The Interns)*

The fourth *Compétence* of each chapter of *Horizons* ends with a *Vidéo-reprise* section that reviews the grammar presented in the chapter through activities that revolve around an episode of the *Horizons* video, *Les Stagiaires (The Interns)*. In the video, two students, Rachid Bennani and Amélie Prévot, have just begun an internship at the company Technovert.

Before you watch each episode, you will do a series of exercises that review what you have learned in the chapter and that help you learn more about the characters that you will see in the video.

See the *Résumé de grammaire* section at the end of each chapter for a review of all the grammar in the chapter.

A Qui est-ce? Voici les descriptions des deux stagiaires de la vidéo, Rachid et Amélie. Complétez chaque phrase avec **c'est, il est** ou **elle est.**

____1____ Rachid Bennani.

Sur cette photo, ____2____ au *(at the)* bureau de Technovert.

____3____ un jeune homme sympa.

____4____ intéressant.

____5____ étudiant à l'École de Commerce Extérieur.

____6____ du Maroc *(from Morocco)*.

____7____ Amélie Prévot.

____8____ une femme intelligente.

____9____ française.

____10____ très belle.

____11____ stagiaire *(intern)* à Technovert.

____12____ aussi étudiante.

Maintenant, identifiez un(e) des étudiant(e)s de votre classe et parlez un peu de lui *(him)* ou d'elle. Utilisez les descriptions de Rachid et d'Amélie comme exemples.

B Rachid. Rachid parle de ses *(this)* études. Complétez les phrases avec la forme correcte du verbe **être.**

EXEMPLE Je **suis** étudiant à l'École de Commerce Extérieur.

1. Je _____ en cours tous les jours.
2. Les cours _____ faciles pour moi.
3. Mes profs _____ gentils.
4. Mon meilleur ami _____ étudiant.
5. Mes amis et moi, nous _____ assez intellectuels.

Maintenant, changez les phrases précédentes pour décrire votre situation et posez des questions à votre partenaire basées sur ces phrases.

EXEMPLE — Je suis étudiant(e) à... Et toi? Est-ce que tu es aussi étudiant(e) à...?
— Oui, je suis aussi étudiant(e) à...

C Descriptions. Amélie parle de ses nouveaux collègues à Technovert. Traduisez les adjectifs pour compléter les phrases. Faites attention à la forme de l'adjectif.

EXEMPLE Rachid est un **bon** *(good)* ami.

1.

M. Vieilledent, mon _____ *(new)* chef *(boss)*, est _____ *(smart)*.

Il n'est pas _____ *(young)*, mais il est très _____ *(active)*.

2.

Son fils *(His son)*, Christophe, est _____ *(tall)*, _____ *(thin)* et _____ *(funny)*, mais il est très _____ *(lazy)*.

3.

Matthieu, l'informaticien *(computer specialist)*, est très _____ *(intelligent)*.

Il est _____ *(handsome)* et _____ *(interesting)*, mais il est très _____ *(shy)*.

Matthieu et Rachid sont très _____ *(nice)*.

4.

Céline, la directrice de marketing, est _____ *(intellectual)* et _____ *(athletic)*.

Elle est très _____ *(pretty)* et elle est très _____ *(extroverted)*.

Camille, l'assistante de M. Vieilledent, est très _____ *(smart)*.

Ce sont mes _____ *(good)* amies.

D Mes études. Amélie parle de ses études. Complétez ce qu'elle dit avec un, une, des, le, la, l', les ou de (d'). Ensuite, adaptez le paragraphe pour décrire vos cours, votre université et le quartier près de l'université.

Ce semestre, j'étudie __1__ commerce international et __2__ informatique. J'aime __3__ université parce qu'il y a __4__ salle d'informatique moderne et il y a aussi __5__ nouveau laboratoire de langues. __6__ quartier est beau et il y a beaucoup __7__ arbres. Dans le quartier, il y a __8__ cinéma où on passe *(they show)* __9__ films classiques. J'aime beaucoup __10__ films classiques.

Access the Video *Les Stagiaires* online.

▶ **Épisode 1: Comment sont-ils?**

AVANT LA VIDÉO

Dans ce clip, Amélie, Rachid et Camille parlent de leurs *(about their)* collègues. Avant de regarder le clip, choisissez *(choose)* les adjectifs à connotation positive: **intelligent, paresseux, nerveux, timide, dynamique**.

APRÈS LA VIDÉO

Regardez le clip et dites *(say)* comment Camille décrit *(describes)*:

• Céline   • Christophe   • Matthieu

LECTURE ET COMPOSITION

LECTURE

You are going to read a work from the collection *Paroles* (1949) by Jacques Prévert (1900–1977), one of France's most popular writers of the last century. You have learned to use cognates to make reading easier. You can also usually understand a text more easily if you scan it beforehand to anticipate its content.

On peut deviner! Look at the photo and scan the reading *L'accent grave* and answer these questions to prepare yourself for understanding the text.

1. Where does the conversation take place?

2. What is the student's name? Where have you heard this name before? What was that character famous for saying?

L'accent grave

Le professeur **Élève** Hamlet!

L'élève Hamlet (*sursautant*) ... Hein... **Quoi...** Pardon... **Qu'est-ce qui se passe...** Qu'est-ce qu'il y a... Qu'est-ce que c'est?...

Le professeur (*mécontent*) **Vous ne pouvez pas répondre** «présent» **comme tout le monde?** Pas possible, vous êtes **encore dans les nuages.**

L'élève Hamlet Être ou ne pas être dans les nuages!

Le professeur **Suffit. Pas tant de manières.** Et conjuguez-moi le verbe être, comme tout le monde, **c'est tout ce que je vous demande.**

L'élève Hamlet To be. . .

Le professeur En français, s'il vous plaît, comme tout le monde.

L'élève Hamlet Bien, monsieur. *(Il conjugue:)*
Je suis ou je ne suis pas
Tu es ou tu n'es pas
Il est ou il n'est pas
Nous sommes ou nous ne sommes pas...

Le professeur (*excessivement mécontent*)
Mais **c'est vous qui n'y êtes pas,** mon pauvre ami!

L'élève Hamlet C'est exact, monsieur le professeur,
Je suis «où» je ne suis pas.
Et, **dans le fond,** hein, à la réflexion,
Être «où» ne pas être
C'est **peut-être** aussi la question.

---

un élève *a student, a pupil*   **sursautant** *looking up startled*   **Hein** *Huh*
Quoi *What*   **Qu'est-ce qui se passe?** *What's going on?*   **mécontent** *displeased*
Vous ne pouvez pas répondre...? *Can't you answer...?*   **comme tout le monde** *like everyone*   **encore dans les nuages** *still in the clouds*
Suffit. *Enough.*   **Pas tant de manières.** *Don't make such a fuss.*
c'est tout ce que je vous demande *that's all I'm asking of you*
c'est vous qui n'y êtes pas *you're the one that's not all there*
dans le fond *when you get down to it*   **peut-être** *perhaps*

© Generistock/E+ Getty Images

POUR MIEUX ÉCRIRE:
Using and combining what you know

Certain strategies can help you learn to write better in a foreign language. When you write, avoid translating. It is very difficult to translate correctly. Use and combine what you already know in French instead. Link sentences with words like **et, mais, alors,** or **parce que** to make your writing flow better.

Organisez-vous. You will be writing a short description of yourself and your studies. First, organize your thoughts by completing these sentences in French.

1. Je m'appelle…
2. Je suis de (d')… et/mais j'habite à…
3. Du point de vue *(view)* physique, je suis…
4. Du point de vue personnalité, je suis…
5. Je suis étudiant(e) à… où j'étudie…
6. Sur le campus, il y a…, mais il n'y a pas…
7. En général, j'aime / je n'aime pas l'université parce que…

Compréhension

1. Comment est l'élève Hamlet? attentif ou inattentif? conformiste ou rebelle? intelligent ou bête? marrant ou désagréable ? bon élève ou mauvais élève?
2. Comment est le professeur? patient ou impatient? très sympathique ou un peu antipathique?
3. Qu'est-ce que ça veut dire, **ou**? et **où**? Qu'est-ce que ça veut dire **être ou ne pas être**? et **être où ne pas être**?

Un autoportrait

Write a short paragraph introducing yourself. Use the sentences you completed in ***Organisez-vous*** above to guide you. Remember to use words like **et, mais,** or **parce que** to make your paragraph flow better.

EXEMPLE **Je m'appelle Daniel Reyna. Je suis de San Antonio, mais maintenant j'habite à Austin…**

LES ÉTUDES

How similar (**semblable**) is the French education system to the education system in your area? Read these descriptions of secondary schools and universities in France and compare them to schools in your region, by saying one of the following:

C'est très semblable ici. / C'est assez semblable ici. / C'est très différent ici.

1. The French equivalent of the secondary school diploma is called **le baccalauréat** or **le bac.** There are three types of **baccalauréat** degrees. The **baccalauréat technologique (bac techno)** mixes general and vocational education and prepares students to continue their professional education at the post-secondary level. The **baccalauréat professionnel (bac pro)** is designed to

© LOIC VENANCE/AFP/Getty Images

prepare students to enter directly into the workplace. The **baccalauréat général (bac général)** prepares students to continue on to higher education. Students who pursue the **baccalauréat général** do so in a chosen category (called **série**), **la série littéraire (L), la série scientifique (S),** or **la série économique et sociale (ES).**

2. At the end of their secondary studies, French students must pass a series of difficult national exams, also called **le baccalauréat** or **le bac,** covering all the material they have studied, in order to receive the **baccalauréat (bac)** degree. Students are graded on a scale of 20 and must receive at least 10/20 to pass. Those who score between 8 and 10 may retest, but those who make less than 8 must retake their final year of high school before retesting.

3. Every student who has received the **bac** is eligible for a very low cost university education. Students only pay the equivalent of a few hundred dollars per year to attend French universities, because the government finances higher education.

4. Students have a large range of choices for continuing their education after the **bac,** as listed in the chart on the next page. However, students are only accepted into certain specialized schools or fields by competitive exams. Students often

© Trevor Payne/Alamy Stock Photo

take two years of preparatory courses for the entrance exams to the most prestigious French universities, the **grandes écoles,** which prepare students for high-level positions in the public and private sectors.

Dans une université:	Dans un lycée:
THREE-YEAR DEGREE: une licence	**TWO-YEAR CERTIFICATE:** un BTS (brevet de technicien supérieur)
FIVE-YEAR DEGREE: un master	**TWO YEARS OF PREPARATORY SCHOOL:** les classes préparatoires aux grandes écoles (CPGE)
EIGHT-YEAR DEGREE: un doctorat	
FIVE- TO ELEVEN-YEAR DEGREES: un diplôme de médecine, de chirurgie dentaire ou de pharmacie	**Dans une grande école (GE):**
	THREE- TO FIVE-YEAR DEGREES: un diplôme d'ingénieur, de sciences, d'économie, de commerce, de lettres...

Dans un institut universitaire de technologie (IUT):	Dans une école spécialisée:
TWO-YEAR DEGREE: un DUT (diplôme universitaire de technologie)	**TWO- TO FIVE-YEAR DEGREE:** un diplôme d'art
TWO-YEAR DEGREE: un DEUST (diplôme d'études universitaires scientifiques et techniques)	**THREE- TO FIVE-YEAR DEGREES:** un diplôme de travail social ou de commerce
	SIX-YEAR DEGREE: un diplôme d'architecte

5. In France, most older universities do not have campuses. Each **faculté** *(division or school)* has buildings, often older ones, where classes meet, and often each **faculté** is centered in a different area of town. Many of the more modern universities, however, do have a campus that is more similar to universities in the United States and Canada.

© Nico Tondini / robertharding/Getty Images

Compréhension

1. What is the name of the diploma French students receive when they graduate from secondary school? What do students have to do to earn it? What do you think are the advantages and disadvantages of a system in which students must pass a rigorous cumulative exam in order to receive a secondary education diploma?

2. What are the three types of **baccalauréats**? For students preparing the **baccalauréat général,** in what general fields can they earn their diploma? Would you have liked to pick a major while still in secondary school? What might be the advantages and disadvantages?

3. What options do French students have for continuing their studies after the **lycée**? How do these compare to the options in your area?

4. Who is entitled to a college education? Is it expensive? What are the advantages and disadvantages of making higher education almost free?

5. What are the older French universities like? What is a division, or school, called within a French university?

6. Reread the ***Notes culturelles*** from earlier in this chapter. How much of a role do extracurricular activities and sports play in university life? Can students enter directly into courses of their field of study? Where do most students live? How does this compare to your university?

RÉSUMÉ DE GRAMMAIRE

Je **suis** étudiant(e).

Tu **es** à quelle université?

David **est** à l'université de Nice avec moi.

Nous **sommes** amis.

Vous **êtes** en cours ensemble?

Les cours **sont** difficiles?

Je **ne** suis **pas** grand.

Tu **n'es pas** d'ici!

Il est sympathique.

Il est en cours.

Il est catholique.

Elle est française.

Ils sont étudiants.

C'est un bon ami.

Ce sont mes amis.

— **Il y a** un examen demain?

— Non, **il n'y a pas** d'examen.

C'est **un** nouveau campus.

C'est **une** grande université?

C'est un bon restaurant?

Non, ce **n'est pas un** bon restaurant.

Il **n'y a pas de** restaurants dans le quartier.

Il y a **beaucoup de** fast-foods.

Le campus est beau.

La bibliothèque est grande?

Tu aimes **les** étudiants?

Le prof de maths est sympa.

Je préfère **les** langues.

Les maths sont difficiles.

SUBJECT PRONOUNS, THE VERB *ÊTRE* AND *IL Y A*

Conjugate verbs by changing their forms to correspond to each of the subject pronouns. Here is the conjugation of **être.**

ÊTRE *(to be)*					
je	**suis**	*I am*	nous	**sommes**	*we are*
tu	**es**	*you are*	vous	**êtes**	*you are*
il/elle	**est**	*he/she/it is*	ils/elles	**sont**	*they are*

To negate a verb, place **ne** before it and **pas** after. **Ne** becomes **n'** before vowels or a silent **h.**

Use **il est / elle est** and **ils sont / elles sont** with *adjectives,* to describe people or things, or with *prepositional phrases* to say such things as where someone or something is or is from. Also use them, without the indefinite article, to state professions, nationalities, or religions.

Use **c'est** and **ce sont** instead of **il est / elle est** and **ils sont / elles sont** to say *he/she/it/this/that is* or *they/these/those are* when identifying or describing someone with *a noun.*

Use **il y a** instead of **être** to say *there is* or *there are.* Its negated form is **il n'y a pas.**

NOUNS AND ARTICLES

Nouns in French are classified as either masculine or feminine. The form of the definite and indefinite articles depends on a noun's gender and whether it is singular or plural.

INDEFINITE ARTICLE *(a, an, some)*		
	SINGULAR	PLURAL
MASCULINE	**un** cours, **un** examen	**des** cours, **des** examens
FEMININE	**une** salle, **une** étudiante	**des** salles, **des** étudiantes

The indefinite article changes to **de** (**d'** before vowel sounds) . . .

- after negated verbs (except after **être**).
- after expressions of quantity like **beaucoup, assez,** or **combien.**

The definite article (**le, la, l', les**) never changes to **de**!

DEFINITE ARTICLE *(the)*		
	SINGULAR	PLURAL
MASCULINE	**le** cours, **l'**examen	**les** cours, **les** examens
FEMININE	**la** salle, **l'**étudiante	**les** salles, **les** étudiantes

Le and **la** elide to **l'** before vowel sounds.

Use the definite article . . .

- to say *the.*
- to say what you like, dislike, or prefer.
- to make generalized statements.

ADJECTIVES

Adjectives have masculine and feminine, singular and plural forms, which correspond to the nouns they describe. Add **e** to the masculine form of most adjectives to form the feminine, unless it already ends in an *unaccented* **e.** Add **s** to make an adjective plural, unless it already ends in **s** or **x,** or **z.**

MASCULINE		FEMININE	
SINGULAR	PLURAL	SINGULAR	PLURAL
joli	jolis	jolie	jolies
divorcé	divorcés	divorcée	divorcées
français	français	française	françaises
jeune	jeunes	jeune	jeunes

The following adjective endings have other changes before adding the **e** for the feminine form.

	MASCULINE		FEMININE	
	SINGULAR	PLURAL	SINGULAR	PLURAL
-eux / -euse:	ennuyeux	ennuyeux	ennuyeuse	ennuyeuses
-en / -enne:	canadien	canadiens	canadienne	canadiennes
-if / -ive:	sportif	sportifs	sportive	sportives
-el / -elle:	intellectuel	intellectuels	intellectuelle	intellectuelles

The adjectives **bon (bonne), gros (grosse),** and **gentil (gentille)** double their final consonants in the feminine form.

COMPARISONS

To make comparisons using adjectives, use:

> **+ plus +** *adjective* **+ que (qu')**
>
> **= aussi +** *adjective* **+ que (qu')**
>
> **– moins +** *adjective* **+ que (qu')**

Instead of putting **plus** before **bon(ne)** *(good),* use **meilleur(e)** *(better).*

QUESTIONS

Questions that are answered with **oui** or **non** have rising intonation. You may just use rising intonation or you may begin the question with **est-ce que,** which elides to **est-ce qu'** before vowel sounds.

If you expect the answer to a question to be **oui,** use **n'est-ce pas?** or **non?** to translate tag questions like *right?, isn't he?, can't you?,* or *won't they?* in English.

David n'est pas **grand.** / Léa est assez **grande.**

Il n'est pas **marié.** / Elle n'est pas **mariée.**

Il est **jeune.** / Elle est **jeune.**

David et Jean sont **français.** / Lisa et Léa ne sont pas **françaises.**

David n'est pas **ennuyeux.** / Léa n'est pas **ennuyeuse.**

Il n'est pas **canadien.** / Elle n'est pas **canadienne.**

Jean est **sportif.** / Lisa est **sportive.**

David est **intellectuel.** / Léa est **intellectuelle.**

C'est un **bon** ami. / C'est une **bonne** amie.

Il n'est pas **gros.** / Elle n'est pas **grosse.**

Il est **gentil.** / Elle est **gentille.**

Léa est **plus** intellectuelle **que** Lisa.

Elle est **aussi** grande **que** Lisa.

Elle est **moins** sportive **que** Lisa.

Léa est **meilleure** en français que Lisa.

Le professeur est bon? **Est-ce qu'**il est sympa?

Tu étudies le français, **n'est-ce pas?**

Nous sommes dans le même cours, **non?**

VOCABULAIRE

Identifying and describing people

NOMS MASCULINS

mes amis	*my friends*
un cours (de littérature)	*a (literature) class*
un frère	*a brother*
les gens	*people*
un (jeune) homme	*a (young) man*

NOMS FÉMININS

mes amies	*my friends*
une (jeune) femme	*a (young) woman*
la France	*France*
une sœur	*a sister*
l'université	*the university*

ADJECTIFS

américain(e)	*American*
bête	*stupid, dumb*
célibataire	*single*
divorcé(e)	*divorced*
extraverti(e)	*extroverted, outgoing*
fiancé(e)	*engaged*
français(e)	*French*
gentil(le)	*nice*
grand(e)	*tall, big*
gros(se)	*fat*
intelligent(e)	*smart, intelligent*
jeune	*young*
jumeau (jumelle)	*twin*
marié(e)	*married*
méchant(e)	*mean*
même	*same*
mince	*thin*
petit(e)	*short, small*
timide	*shy, timid*

EXPRESSIONS VERBALES

C'est...	*He is / She is / It is / This is / That is …*
Ce sont...	*They are / These are / Those are …*
Comment est...?	*What is … like?*
Il est / Elle est...	*He is / She is / It is …*
être	*to be*
je suis...	*I am …*
tu es...	*you are …*
il est...	*he is / it is …*
elle est...	*she is / it is …*
nous sommes...	*we are …*
vous êtes...	*you are …*
ils sont...	*they are …*
elles sont...	*they are …*
(pour) étudier	*(in order) to study*
(pour) visiter	*(in order) to visit*
(pour) voir	*(in order) to see*
rencontrer	*to meet (for the first time or by chance), to run into*

DIVERS

alors	*so, then, therefore*
c'est ça	*that's right*
comme	*like, as, for*
de	*of, from, about*
ne... pas	*not*
non?	*right?*
son / sa / ses	*his, her, its*

Describing people

NOMS MASCULINS

tes amis	*your friends*
le foot(ball)	*soccer*
mon meilleur ami	*my best friend*
le sport	*sports*
le tennis	*tennis*

NOMS FÉMININS

tes amies	*your friends*
les études	*studies, going to school*
ma meilleure amie	*my best friend*

ADJECTIFS

agréable	*pleasant*
amusant(e)	*fun, amusing*
antipathique	*disagreeable, unpleasant*
beau (belle)	*handsome, beautiful*
bon(ne)	*good*
désagréable	*disagreeable, unpleasant*
dynamique	*active, energetic, dynamic*
ennuyeux (ennuyeuse)	*boring*
intellectuel(le)	*intellectual*
intéressant(e)	*interesting*
jeune	*young*
laid(e)	*ugly*
marrant(e)	*funny*
mauvais(e)	*bad*
meilleur(e)	*better*
nouveau (nouvelle)	*new*
paresseux (paresseuse)	*lazy*
pire (que)	*worse (than)*
sportif (sportive)	*athletic*
sympathique, sympa	*nice*
vieux (vieille)	*old*

EXPRESSIONS VERBALES

Ce n'est pas...	*He / She / It / This / That isn't …*
j'aime (bien)... / je n'aime pas...	*I like … / I don't like …*
tu aimes...	*you like …*

DIVERS

assez	*rather*
aussi... que	*as … as*
Ce n'est pas mon truc.	*That's not my thing.*
est-ce que...	*(particle used in questions)*
moins... que	*less … than*
ne... pas du tout	*not at all*
n'est-ce pas?	*right?*
plus... que	*…-er than, more … than*
plutôt	*rather*
un peu	*a little*

Describing the university area

NOMS MASCULINS

un arbre	*a tree*
un bureau (*pl* des bureaux)	*an office*
un café	*a café*
un campus	*a campus*
un cinéma	*a movie theater*
un fast-food	*a fast-food restaurant*
un film	*a movie, a film*
un match de foot(ball) américain	*a football game*
un parc	*a park*
un parking	*a parking lot*
un quartier (universitaire)	*a (university) neighborhood*
un restaurant	*a restaurant*
un stade	*a stadium*
le wi-fi	*wi-fi*

NOMS FÉMININS

une bibli(othèque)	*a library*
une boîte (de nuit)	*a nightclub*
une librairie	*a bookstore*
une maison	*a house*
une résidence universitaire	*a university dormitory*
une salle de cours	*a classroom*
une salle de gym	*a gym, a fitness club*

ADJECTIFS

catholique	*Catholic*
joli(e)	*pretty*

EXPRESSIONS VERBALES

Comment est...?	*What is … like?*
Il est / Elle est...	* He is / She is …*
C'est...; Ce n'est pas...	*He / She / It / This / That is …; He / She / It / This / That is not …*
Ce sont...; Ce ne sont pas...	*They / These / Those are …; They / These / Those are not …*
Il y a...	*There is, There are …*
Il n'y a pas (de)...	*There isn't, There aren't (any) …*
Qu'est-ce qu'il y a...?	*What is there … ?*

DIVERS

assez (de)	*enough (of)*
avec wi-fi	*with wi-fi*
beaucoup (de)	*a lot (of)*
combien (de)	*how much (of), how many (of)*
dans	*in*
des	*some*
près de	*near*
sur	*on*
ton / ta / tes	*your*
un(e)	*a, an*

Talking about your studies

NOMS MASCULINS

l'anglais	*English*
les arts	*the arts*
le basket	*basketball*
le commerce (international)	*(international) business*
un cours en ligne	*an online course*
les devoirs	*homework*
l'espagnol	*Spanish*
un examen	*an exam*
le français	*French*
un labo(ratoire) de biologie	*a biology lab*
un livre	*a book*
le théâtre	*theater, drama*

NOMS FÉMININS

la bio(logie)	*biology*
la chimie	*chemistry*
une fête	*a party*
l'histoire	*history*
l'informatique	*computer science*
une langue	*a language*
la littérature (classique)	*(classical) literature*
les mathématiques (les maths)	*mathematics (math)*
la musique	*music*
la peinture	*painting*
la philo(sophie)	*philosophy*
la psycho(logie)	*psychology*
une salle d'informatique	*a computer lab*
les sciences (humaines)	*the (social) sciences*
les sciences po(litiques)	*political science, government*
les technologies	*technical courses, technologies*

EXPRESSIONS VERBALES

Comment sont...?	*What are … like?*
Est-ce que vous aimez...?	*Do you like … ?*
J'aime beaucoup / assez...	* I like a lot / somewhat …*
Je n'aime pas (du tout)...	* I don't like … (at all).*
Je préfère...	* I prefer …*
Qu'est-ce que vous étudiez / tu étudies?	*What are you studying?, What do you study?*
J'étudie...	* I'm studying, I study …*
Je n'étudie pas...	* I'm not studying, I don't study …*

DIVERS

en ligne	*online*
le, la, l', les	*the*
leur(s)	*their*
Qu'est-ce que...? (Qu'est-ce qu'...?)	*What … ?*

Sur la Côte d'Azur
Après les cours

 Pair work   Video

 Group work   Audio

 Class work

© Ulligraphie/Shutterstock.com

LE MONDE FRANCOPHONE
Géoculture et Vidéo-voyage: À Nice

COMPÉTENCE

GÉOCULTURE ET VIDÉO-VOYAGE: À NICE

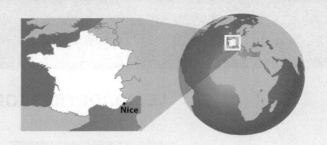

Nice

 NICE

NOMBRE D'HABITANTS: **346 000 (avec son agglomération [*metropolitan region*]: 1 005 000) (les Niçois)**

Nice, **une ville célèbre pour** ses belles **plages** et ses activités culturelles, est **au cœur de** la Côte d'Azur (*the French Riviera* en anglais).

Le Parc de la Colline du Château

C'est sur **la Colline** du château que **les Phéniciens fondent** la ville de Nice. **Plus tard,** un château médiéval **protège la région du sommet** de la colline. Aujourd'hui, **il n'y a plus** de château, mais le Parc de la Colline du Château offre une vue magnifique sur le port, la plage et la ville de Nice.

La Promenade des Anglais et la Baie des Anges

Le Vieux Nice

Ici, les touristes et **les Niçois** aiment **faire une course matinale** ou **faire du roller** et admirer la Baie des Anges et ses belles plages.

Il y a **toujours** beaucoup de gens dans les restaurants et les boîtes de nuit des **rues étroites** de ce vieux quartier médiéval.

---

une ville célèbre pour *a city famous for*　　**plages** *beaches*　　**au cœur de** *in the heart of*　　**la Colline** *the Hill*　　**les Phéniciens fondent** *the Phoenicians found*　　**Plus tard** *Later*　　**protège la région du sommet** *protects the region from the summit*　　**il n'y a plus** *there is no longer*　　**les Niçois** *the Niçois, the people of Nice*　　**faire une course matinale** *to take a morning run*　　**faire du roller** *to go rollerblading*　　**toujours** *always*　　**rues étroites** *narrow streets*

Le vignoble Bellet

Le Château de Crémat

Le vignoble Bellet remonte au temps des Phéniciens. Aujourd'hui, à son Château de Crémat, **vous pouvez déguster du vin** et admirer son «château» **construit** en 1906.

© Fraser Hall/robertharding/Superstock

Le marché Saleya

La beauté et le parfum des fleurs et des fruits et légumes de ce marché enchantent les touristes et les Niçois. Un des légumes les plus appréciés? **La courgette de Nice.** C'est **un endroit parfait** pour **goûter** les spécialités niçoises comme la socca, à base de **farine de pois chiche,** ou **les beignets de fleurs de courgettes.**

Le savez-vous?

Indiquez quel site ou quelle chose va avec chaque *(each)* définition.

> **la Promenade des Anglais**
> **la courgette de Nice**
> **la socca**
> **le marché Saleya**
> **le Parc de la Colline du Château**
> **le Vieux Nice**
> **le Château de Crémat**

1. un vignoble qui date des Phéniciens

2. un endroit qui marque le site de la fondation de la ville de Nice

3. un marché en plein air *(open air)* avec des fleurs et des fruits et légumes de la région

4. le quartier médiéval de Nice
5. une belle promenade le long de la Baie des Anges

6. un plat *(dish)* régional à base de farine de pois chiche

7. un légume dont *(of which)* on utilise la fleur pour faire des beignets

---

Le vignoble Bellet *The Bellet vineyard*   **remonte au temps des** *goes back to the time of the*   **vous pouvez** *you can*   **déguster du vin** *taste wine*   **construit** *built, constructed*   **marché Saleya** *Saleya market*   **La courgette** *The zucchini squash*   **un endroit parfait** *a perfect place*   **goûter** *to taste*   **farine de pois chiche** *chickpea flour*   **les beignets de fleurs de courgettes** *the squash blossom fritters*

AVANT LA VIDÉO

Vous allez visiter Nice à travers la vidéo. Pour vous aider à mieux comprendre, regardez ces photos et complétez les descriptions.

préparation   partie ancienne
huile d'olive   vue panoramique
caves à vin   creusées par les Romains
dégustation   de pop art

1. Une ___ *(panoramic view)* sur la ville de Nice et la mer Méditerranée depuis *(from)* le Parc de la Colline du Château.

2. Le Vieux Nice, la ___ *(ancient part)* de la ville.

3. Le célèbre marché Saleya et une ___ *(tasting)* de socca, plat *(dish)* niçois à base de farine de pois chiche et d'___ *(olive oil)*.

4. La ___ *(preparation)* des beignets de fleurs de courgettes de Nice dans un restaurant régional.

5. Le Château de Crémat, un vignoble qui date des Phéniciens, et ses ___ *(wine cellars)* ___ *(dug by the Romans)*.

6. Dans le musée d'Art moderne et d'Art contemporain, il y a des expositions d'art moderne, ___ et d'art contemporain du bassin méditerranéen.

▶ EN REGARDANT LA VIDÉO

Regardez la vidéo et indiquez dans quel ordre on voit ces scènes.

a. Le Vieux Nice et une dégustation de socca au marché Saleya

b. Un restaurant et la préparation des beignets de fleurs de courgettes

c. La vue sur la ville du Parc de la Colline du Château

d. La Promenade des Anglais

e. Le vignoble du Château de Crémat

f. Le musée d'Art moderne et d'Art contemporain de Nice

▶ APRÈS LA VIDÉO

Regardez la vidéo une deuxième fois et complétez ces phrases.

1. La visite de Nice commence _____.

    a. dans le Vieux Nice

    b. au Parc de la Colline du Château

2. La narratrice *(narrator)* profite d'une visite au Château de Crémat pour _____.

    a. visiter un vignoble

    b. déguster du vin

3. Au marché Saleya, elle voit des fruits et des légumes y compris *(including)* _____.

    a. des courgettes de Nice

    b. des bananes

4. Les beignets de fleurs de courgettes de Nice sont _____.

    a. frits *(fried)* dans l'huile d'olive

    b. cuits au four *(baked)* avec de l'huile d'olive

Saying what you like to do

LE TEMPS LIBRE ET LES LOISIRS (m)

Note *culturelle*

Quels sont les loisirs préférés des Français? Ils aiment, par ordre de préférence: aller au cinéma (25 %), écouter de la musique (21 %), faire de la photographie (19 %), regarder des séries télévisées (15 %). Et vous? Comment est-ce que vous aimez passer votre temps libre?

Note *de vocabulaire*

To say what you *like* in general, use **j'aime**. To say what you *would like* on a specific occasion, use **je voudrais**.

— Qu'est-ce que vous aimez **faire** après les cours en général?
— J'aime...   — Je n'aime pas...   — Je préfère...

— Qu'est-ce que **vous voudriez** faire aujourd'hui après les cours?
— **Je voudrais**...

Le week-end, j'aime **sortir** avec des amis. J'aime...

aller au cinéma
(aller) voir un film

aller au café
(aller) **prendre un verre /
un café**

dîner au restaurant

aller en boîte (de nuit)
(aller) danser
écouter de la musique

faire du sport
jouer au tennis / au basket /
au football / au volley

**courir
faire du vélo**
faire de l'exercice

Après les cours, je suis **fatigué(e)** et je préfère **rester** à la maison. J'aime...

lire

dormir

parler au téléphone
envoyer des textos (m)

jouer de la guitare /
de la batterie / du
piano

regarder la télé(vision)
jouer à des jeux (m)
vidéo

travailler sur
ordinateur (m)
surfer sur Internet (m)

Le temps libre *Free time*   **les loisirs** *leisure activities, pastimes*   **faire** *to do*   **vous voudriez** *would you like*
Je voudrais *I would like*   **sortir** *to go out*   **aller** *to go*   **prendre un verre** *to have a drink*   **prendre un café** *to have a*
cup of coffee   **courir** *to run*   **faire du vélo** *to go biking, to bike*   **fatigué(e)** *tired, fatigued*   **rester** *to stay, to remain*
envoyer des textos *to send text messages, to text*   **de la batterie** *drums*

Vocabulaire supplémentaire

bricoler *to do handiwork*
cuisiner *to cook*
dessiner *to draw*
écrire *to write*
faire de l'aérobic / de la gym(nastique)
  to do aerobics / gymnastics
faire de la muscu(lation) *to do*
  bodybuilding
faire du jogging *to go jogging*
jardiner *to garden*
marcher *to walk*
nager *to swim*
peindre *to paint*
promener le chien *to walk the dog*
voyager *to travel*

David invite Léa à sortir.

2-1

DAVID:	Tu es **libre ce soir**? Tu voudrais **faire quelque chose**?
LÉA:	**D'accord.** Qu'est-ce que tu voudrais faire?
DAVID:	Je ne sais pas. **Ça te dit d'**aller en boîte?
LÉA:	Non, **pas vraiment.** Je préfère aller au cinéma.
DAVID:	Bon, d'accord. **Pourquoi pas.**
LÉA:	**Vers** quelle heure, alors?
DAVID:	Vers sept heures?
LÉA:	D'accord. Alors, à plus tard.
DAVID:	Salut, Léa. À ce soir!

A **J'aime… Je voudrais…** Complétez les phrases pour parler de vos préférences.

1. Après les cours, j'aime… Aujourd'hui, après les cours, je voudrais…
2. Le soir, j'aime… Ce soir, je voudrais…
3. Le vendredi soir, j'aime… Ce vendredi soir, je voudrais…
4. Le samedi, j'aime… Ce samedi, je voudrais…
5. Le dimanche matin, j'aime… Ce dimanche matin, je voudrais…

Note *de grammaire*

Remember that many French verbs that end in **-e** when talking about yourself (**j'aime**) end in **-es** when the subject of the verb is **tu** (**tu aimes**). There is no difference in the pronunciation of the verb. You will learn more about this in **Compétence 2**.

Maintenant, interviewez plusieurs *(several)* étudiant(e)s pour savoir ce qu'ils/ce qu'elles aiment faire et ce qu'ils/ce qu'elles voudraient faire aux moments indiqués ci-dessus *(above)*.

EXEMPLE

> — **Qu'est-ce que tu aimes faire après les cours?**
> — **J'aime rester à la maison.**
> — **Qu'est-ce que tu voudrais faire aujourd'hui après les cours?**
> — **Je voudrais aller au café.**

B **Invitations.** Invitez votre partenaire à faire une des choses suivantes. Ensuite, changez de rôles et faites des projets pour un autre jour.

EXEMPLE demain: jouer au tennis

> — **Tu es libre demain? Tu voudrais jouer au tennis avec moi?**
> — **Oui, d'accord. / Pas vraiment. Je préfère aller au cinéma.**
> — **À quelle heure?**
> — **Vers deux heures.**
> — **À deux heures? Alors, à demain.**
> — **Salut, à demain.**

cet *(this)* après-midi	jouer au tennis / au basket…
ce soir	dîner au restaurant
demain après-midi	aller voir un film
demain soir	faire du vélo
vendredi soir	aller prendre un verre / un café

À VOUS!

Avec un(e) partenaire, relisez à haute voix la conversation entre David et Léa. Ensuite, choisissez une activité et invitez votre partenaire à la faire *(to do it)*.

You can access the audio of the active vocabulary of this *Compétence* online.

libre *free* **ce soir** *tonight, this evening* **faire quelque chose** *to do something* **D'accord.** *Okay.* **Ça te dit de… ?** *(familiar) /*
Ça vous dit de…? *(formal) Do you feel like …?* **pas vraiment** *not really* **Pourquoi pas.** *Why not.* **Vers** *About, Around, Toward*

SAYING WHAT YOU LIKE TO DO

✔ *Pour vérifier*

1. What do you call the base form of the verb that you find listed in the dictionary?

2. What are the four possible endings for infinitives in French? How do you recognize an infinitive in English?

3. When you have more than one verb in a clause, which one is conjugated? Which ones are in the infinitive?

4. Do you use **jouer au** or **jouer du** to talk about playing a sport? When do you use **jouer du (de la, de l', des)**?

L'infinitif

1. To name an activity in French, use the verb in the infinitive. The infinitive is the base form of the verb that you find listed in the dictionary. English infinitives begin with *to*. French infinitives are single words ending in **-er, -ir, -oir,** or **-re,** like **jouer** *(to play),* **dormir** *(to sleep),* **voir** *(to see),* or **être** *(to be).* In French, whenever there are two or more verbs together in a clause, the first verb is conjugated, but verbs that immediately follow are in the infinitive and are translated as *to . . .* in English.

   — Qu'est-ce que tu **aimes faire**? — Est-ce que tu **voudrais sortir**?
   — J'**aime jouer** au golf. — Non, je **préfère dormir**.

2. Use **jouer** *à / au* to talk about playing video or board games and most sports using balls or pucks.

   jouer **à** des jeux vidéo jouer **au** baseball

   Many other sports and activities use **faire** *du / de la / de l' / des.*

   faire **du** vélo faire **de l'**exercice

3. Use **jouer** *du / de la / de l' / des* to talk about playing most musical instruments.

   jouer **du** piano jouer **de la** guitare

4. As with **un, une,** and **des; du, de la,** and **de l'** change to **de (d')** when they directly follow a negated verb or an expression of quantity. **Au** does not change to **de (d')**.

   — Tu joues **de la** guitare? — Tu fais **du** sport le week-end?
   — Non, je **ne** joue **pas de** guitare. — Non, je **ne** fais **pas de** sport.

   — Tu joues **au** football américain le week-end?
   — Non, je **ne** joue **pas au** football américain, mais je fais **beaucoup d'**exercice.

PRONONCIATION

La consonne **r** *et l'infinitif*
2-2

The consonant **r** is one of the few (CaReFuL) consonants that are often pronounced at the end of words. The final **r** of infinitives ending in **-er,** however, is not pronounced. The **-er** ending is pronounced [e], like the **é** in **café.**

| parler | rester | danser | aller |
| regarder | jouer | écouter | dîner |

The **r** in infinitives ending in **-ir, -oir,** or **-re** is pronounced. To pronounce a French **r,** hold the back of your tongue firmly arched upward in the back of your mouth and pronounce a vocalized English *h* sound in your throat.

Pronounce the **-ir** verb ending as [iR], unless the verb ends in **-oir** [waR].

| sortir | dormir | voir |

The **e** in the infinitive ending of **-re** verbs is slightly pronounced when this ending is preceded by a consonant, but not when it is preceded by a vowel.

| faire | lire | être | prendre |

A **Prononcez bien!** Demandez à votre partenaire quelle activité il/elle préfère. Faites attention à la prononciation de l'infinitif.

EXEMPLE lire / regarder la télé

— **Tu préfères lire ou regarder la télé?**
— **Je préfère lire.**

1. faire de l'exercice / dormir
2. sortir avec des amis / inviter des amis à la maison
3. prendre un verre au café / dîner au restaurant
4. regarder la télé / jouer à des jeux vidéo
5. être à la maison / être en cours
6. faire du vélo / courir
7. parler au téléphone / envoyer des textos

Note *de vocabulaire*

To say you don't like either activity, use **ne... ni... ni...** *(neither . . . nor . . .)*: **Je n'aime** *ni* **lire** *ni* **regarder la télé.** To say that you like *both* activities, use **J'aime les deux.**

B **Entretien.** Interviewez votre partenaire.

1. Qu'est-ce que tu aimes faire après les cours? Qu'est-ce que tu voudrais faire aujourd'hui après les cours?
2. Est-ce que tu aimes rester à la maison le week-end? Qu'est-ce que tu aimes faire le week-end? Qu'est-ce que tu voudrais faire ce week-end?
3. Est-ce que tu préfères parler au téléphone ou envoyer des textos?
4. Est-ce que tu aimes aller au cinéma? Tu préfères voir un film au cinéma ou à la maison? Quel film est-ce que tu voudrais voir?
5. Tu aimes jouer à des jeux vidéo? Tu préfères jouer à des jeux vidéo ou lire?

C **Chacun ses goûts.** Circulez dans la classe pour trouver au moins deux personnes qui aiment chacune des *(each of the)* activités illustrées.

EXEMPLE **Daniel, tu aimes surfer sur Internet?**

1.

2.

3.

4.

5.

6.

7.

STRATÉGIES ET COMPRÉHENSION AUDITIVE

POUR MIEUX COMPRENDRE: *Listening for specific information*

It takes time and practice to understand a foreign language when you hear it. However, using listening strategies can help you learn to understand spoken French more quickly.

Often, you do not need to comprehend everything you hear. Practice listening for specific details, such as times, places, or prices. Do not worry about understanding every word.

🔊 **Quand?** Écoutez ces trois scènes. Indiquez le jour et l'heure choisis *(chosen)*.
2-3

SCÈNE A: LE JOUR _____
                   L'HEURE _____

SCÈNE B: LE JOUR _____
                   L'HEURE _____

SCÈNE C: LE JOUR _____
                   L'HEURE _____

© Stockbyte/Getty Images

🔊 Compréhension auditive: *On sort ensemble?*

2-4

You are going to listen to a conversation in which David, Lisa, and Léa run into two of David's friends. Do not try to understand every word of their conversation. Focus on listening for the key information you will need to do the activity. The first time, listen only for how many leisure activities they mention.

A **Vous comprenez?** Écoutez la conversation entre David et ses amis et répondez à ces questions.

1. Est-ce que Thomas et Elsa sont des amis de Léa?
2. Qu'est-ce que Thomas invite David, Léa et Lisa à faire?
3. Qu'est-ce que les cinq jeunes décident de faire ensemble *(together)*?
4. Qu'est-ce que David, Léa et Lisa voudraient faire après?

B **Tu voudrais sortir?** Invitez trois étudiant(e)s de la classe à faire chacun(e) une des activités suivantes *(to each do one of the following activities)*. Utilisez *B. Invitations* à la page 75 comme modèle.

voir un film

jouer au foot

faire du vélo

Saying how you spend your free time

LE WEEK-END

Qu'est-ce que **vous faites d'habitude** le samedi? Vous **passez la matinée** à la maison?

(presque) toujours	souvent	quelquefois	rarement	ne... jamais
(almost) always	*often*	*sometimes*	*rarely*	*never*

En général le samedi matin, je suis fatigué(e) et je **reste** souvent **au lit jusqu'à** 10 heures.

Je **mange** quelque chose.

Quelquefois l'après-midi, j'étudie.

Le soir, je ne reste presque jamais **chez moi. Je vais** souvent au cinéma.

Vous aimez faire du sport? Vous jouez bien au foot? **Quand** vous jouez au foot, est-ce que vous **gagnez** souvent?

Vous aimez jouer de la musique? Est-ce que vous jouez bien du piano?

très bien	assez bien	assez mal	très mal
very well	*fairly well*	*fairly badly*	*very badly*

Je **nage** assez mal.

Je joue très bien au hockey. Je gagne souvent.

Je joue assez bien du piano.

Je **chante** très bien.

---

vous faites (faire *to do, to make*) **d'habitude** *usually, generally* **passer** *to pass, to spend* (time) **la matinée** *the morning* **rester au lit** *to stay in bed* **jusqu'à** *until* **manger** *to eat* **chez moi** *at home, at my house* (**chez...** = *to / at / in / by the house of . . .*) **Je vais (aller** *to go*) **Quand** *When* **gagner** *to win* **nager** *to swim* **chanter** *to sing*

2-5

Léa et David parlent de leurs activités *(f)* du week-end.

LÉA: Qu'est-ce que **tu fais** d'habitude le week-end?

DAVID: Le samedi matin, je reste au lit, le samedi après-midi, je joue au tennis et le soir, j'aime sortir. Et toi?

LÉA: Le matin, j'étudie. L'après-midi, Lisa et moi aimons **faire du shopping ensemble.** Le soir, moi aussi, j'aime sortir.

DAVID :   Alors, tu es libre samedi soir? Tu voudrais sortir? Il y a un bon film au ciné-club **à la fac.** C'est un classique de Truffaut.

LÉA: Oui, oui, j'aime bien les vieux films de Truffaut.

DAVID :   Le film commence à huit heures. Je **passe chez** toi vers sept heures?

LÉA: D'accord! À samedi, alors.

Le temps libre. Complétez ces phrases pour parler de vous.

1. Le samedi, je passe *presque toujours / souvent / rarement* la matinée à la maison. *(Je ne passe jamais la matinée à la maison.)*

2. Le samedi matin, je reste au lit jusqu'à *sept heures / dix heures / ???.*

3. D'habitude, le samedi matin, je mange quelque chose *à la maison / dans un fast-food / au café / ???. (Je ne mange pas le samedi matin.)*

4. Je préfère *faire du sport / courir / nager / ???. (Je n'aime pas faire de l'exercice.)*

5. Quand je fais du sport, je gagne *souvent / quelquefois / rarement. (Je ne gagne jamais.)*

6. Je vais plus souvent au cinéma *seul(e) / avec des amis / avec mon meilleur ami / avec ma meilleure amie / avec ma famille / ???.*

7. Je chante *très bien / assez bien / ???.*

8. Je joue *du piano / de la guitare / de la batterie / ???. (Je ne joue pas d'instrument de musique.)*

Vous dansez bien?

À VOUS!

Avec un(e) partenaire, relisez à haute voix la conversation entre David et Léa. Ensuite, adaptez la conversation pour parler de vos activités du week-end et pour inviter votre partenaire à faire quelque chose.

---

tu fais (faire *to do, to make)*   **faire du shopping** *to go shopping*   **ensemble** *together*   **à la fac** *at the university*
passer (chez) *to pass (by someone's house)*

You can access the audio of the active vocabulary of this *Compétence* online.

TELLING WHAT ONE DOES, HOW OFTEN, AND HOW WELL

✔ *Pour vérifier*

1. How do you determine the stem of an **-er** verb? What endings do you add to it?

2. When do you drop the final **e** of words like **je, ne,** and **le**?

3. What are the three possible English translations of **Il parle français**?

4. When do you use **on** to say *they*? What else can **on** mean? What form of the verb do you use with **on**, whatever the meaning?

5. Where do you generally place adverbs such as **bien** and **souvent**?

6. Which **-er** verb endings are silent? Which ones are pronounced?

Note *de grammaire*

Verbs with infinitives that do not end in **-er**, and a few irregular verbs with infinitives that do, such as **aller,** do not follow the pattern of conjugation shown here. You will learn to conjugate these verbs later. For now, you may want to use these forms to talk about yourself.

I go	**je vais**
I sleep	**je dors**
I do, I make	**je fais**
I run	**je cours**
I read	**je lis**
I take	**je prends**
I go out	**je sors**

Vocabulaire sans peine!

Most English verbs ending with *-ate* were French **-er** verbs that were borrowed into English.

imiter *to imitate*
décorer *to decorate*

Also notice these cognate patterns among **-er** verbs.

-iser = *-ize*
utiliser *to utilize*
économiser *to economize*
-fier = *-fy*
défier *to defy*
identifier *to identify*

How would you say the following verbs in French?

to manipulate, to calculate
to symbolize, to hypnotize
to notify, to justify

Sélection musicale. Search for the song **"Elle chante pour moi"** by Faudel online to enjoy a musical selection using this vocabulary.

Les verbes en *-er,* le pronom **on** et les adverbes

1. Regular verbs are groups of verbs that follow a predictable pattern of conjugation. In French, the infinitives of the largest group of regular verbs end in **-er.** Most verbs ending in **-er** that you have learned, *except* **aller,** are conjugated in the present tense by dropping the **-er** to form the stem and adding the following endings, which correspond to the subject.

PARLER *(to speak, to talk)*	
je parl**e**	nous parl**ons**
tu parl**es**	vous parl**ez**
il/elle/on parl**e**	ils/elles parl**ent**

2. The present tense can be expressed in three ways in English. Express all three of the following English structures by a single verb in French.

I work.
I am working. } Je travaille.
I do work.

We study.
We are studying. } Nous étudions.
We do study.

3. Here are the regular **-er** verbs that you have seen so far.

aimer	dîner	inviter	parler	rencontrer
chanter	écouter	habiter	passer	rester
commencer	envoyer	jouer	préférer	surfer
compter	étudier	manger	regarder	travailler
danser	fermer	nager	répéter	visiter

4. Remember that there is elision of the **e** in words such as **je** and **ne** before a vowel or silent **h.**

j'aime / je **n'**aime pas   j'habite / je **n'**habite pas

5. Use the pronoun **on** to say *they, one, people* when you are referring to people in general. Consider the difference between these sentences.

À Paris, **on** parle français.   *In Paris, **they** speak French. (general group)*
Mes amis? **Ils** parlent français.   *My friends? **They** speak French. (specific people)*

With **on**, use the same form of a verb as that for **il/elle.**

on parle *one speaks / they speak / people speak*

On is also used, instead of **nous,** to say *we*. The verb form is still the same as that used for **il/elle.**

Mes amis et moi, **on aime** sortir. = Mes amis et moi, **nous aimons** sortir. *My friends and I, **we like** to go out.*

6. Adverbs such as **bien, souvent, rarement,** and **beaucoup** tell how well, how often, or how much you do something. In French, these adverbs are generally placed *directly after the conjugated verb,* but usually before an infinitive. **D'habitude** and **quelquefois** may also be placed at the beginning or end of the clause.

Thomas regarde **souvent** la télé.   *Thomas **often** watches TV.*
Quelquefois, je joue **bien** au tennis.   ***Sometimes,** I play tennis **well.***

Notice that **ne... jamais** follows the same placement rule as **ne... pas.**

Je **ne** joue **jamais** au golf.   *I **never** play golf.*

🔊 PRONONCIATION

Les verbes en -er

All the present tense endings of **-er** verbs, except for the **nous (-ons)** and **vous (-ez)** forms, are silent.

je rest~~e~~	il rest~~e~~	ils rest~~ent~~
tu rest~~es~~	elle rest~~e~~	elles rest~~ent~~

Rely on context to distinguish between **il** and **ils,** or **elle** and **elles.** You will hear a difference only with verbs beginning with a vowel sound.

il travaill~~e~~ — il~~s~~ travaill~~ent~~   il aim~~e~~ — ils‿aim~~ent~~

The **-ons** ending of the **nous** form rhymes with **maison** and the **-ez** of the **vous** form rhymes with **café** and sounds like the **-er** ending of the infinitive. There is liaison between the **s** of **nous** and **vous** and verbs beginning with vowel sounds.

nou~~s~~ parlons	nous‿étudions
vou~~s~~ parlez	vous‿étudiez

A **Prononcez bien!** Complétez chacun des verbes avec la terminaison correcte et indiquez si la terminaison est prononcée.

TERMINAISON PRONONCÉE?

EXEMPLE Le samedi soir, j'aim**e** rester à la maison. _____ OUI __X__ NON

1. Moi, je rest___ souvent à la maison le samedi soir. _____ OUI _____ NON
2. Mes amis et moi, nous dîn___ souvent au restaurant. _____ OUI _____ NON
3. Ma famille et moi, on dîn___ rarement à la maison. _____ OUI _____ NON
4. Nous préfér___ dîner au restaurant. _____ OUI _____ NON
5. Mon meilleur ami (Ma meilleure amie) préfèr___ rester à la maison. _____ OUI _____ NON
6. Mes amis aim___ beaucoup sortir. _____ OUI _____ NON

Maintenant, lisez chaque *(each)* phrase à haute voix *(aloud)* et dites si c'est vrai en disant **c'est vrai** ou **ce n'est pas vrai.**

EXEMPLE Le samedi soir, j'aime rester à la maison.
C'est vrai. / Ce n'est pas vrai.

B **Le samedi.** Est-ce que vous faites toujours, souvent ou rarement ces choses le samedi? N'oubliez pas *(Don't forget)* de conjuguer le verbe!

| (presque) toujours | souvent | quelquefois | rarement | ne... jamais |

EXEMPLE dîner au restaurant
Le samedi, je dîne souvent au restaurant.
Le samedi, je ne dîne jamais au restaurant.

1. rester au lit jusqu'à 10h
2. manger à la maison le matin
3. passer l'après-midi chez moi
4. regarder la télé
5. danser en boîte
6. chanter dans un karaoké

Maintenant, demandez à votre professeur s'il/si elle fait souvent les choses indiquées.

EXEMPLE dîner au restaurant
Le samedi, est-ce que vous dînez souvent au restaurant?

Nous aimons dîner dans le Vieux Nice.

C **En cours de français.** Formez des phrases pour décrire *(to describe)* votre cours.

EXEMPLE nous / parler / beaucoup / en cours
Nous parlons beaucoup en cours.
Nous ne parlons pas beaucoup en cours.

1. le prof / parler / souvent / très rapidement
2. les étudiants / parler / très bien / français
3. nous / travailler / beaucoup / en cours
4. nous / aimer / souvent / dormir en cours
5. les étudiants / travailler / bien / ensemble
6. on / regarder / souvent / des vidéoclips en cours
7. je / écouter / toujours / le prof (la prof) en cours
8. les étudiants / manger / en cours

D **Comparaisons culturelles.** Relisez la *Note culturelle* à la page 80. Répondez à ces questions sur la journée typique des Français.

EXEMPLE En France, on écoute plus souvent la radio ou on fait plus souvent une promenade?
En France, on écoute plus souvent la radio.

1. En France, on regarde plus souvent la télé ou on écoute plus souvent la radio?
2. On surfe plus souvent sur Internet ou on écoute plus souvent la radio?
3. En France, on surfe plus souvent sur Internet ou on joue plus souvent au foot?
4. On passe plus de temps *(more time)* devant *(in front of)* la télé ou avec un bon livre?

Maintenant, complétez les réponses à ces questions pour parler de vos amis et vous.

EXEMPLE Tes amis et toi, vous regardez plus souvent la télé ou vous écoutez plus souvent la radio?
Mes amis et moi, on **regarde plus souvent la télé / écoute plus souvent la radio.**

1. Vous regardez plus souvent un film à la télé ou au cinéma?
Mes amis et moi, on…
2. Vous jouez plus souvent à des jeux vidéo ou au foot?
On…
3. Vous aimez ou vous n'aimez pas faire du sport ensemble?
On…
4. Vous dînez plus souvent ensemble au restaurant ou chez un ami?
On…

E **Talents.** Dites comment ces personnes font ces choses.

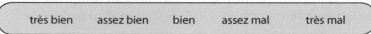

| très bien | assez bien | bien | assez mal | très mal |

EXEMPLE
Ma sœur **joue très bien / assez mal de la guitare.**
Ma sœur **ne joue pas de guitare.**

1. Mon meilleur ami
(Ma meilleur amie)…
Mes amis et moi, on…

2. Mes parents…
Moi, je…

3. Moi, je…
Mon ami(e) *[name a friend]*…

4. Mes amis ___ et ___
[name two friends]…
Mes amis et moi, nous…

F Qu'est-ce qui se passe? Travaillez en groupes pour décrire la scène chez la famille Li ce week-end. Donnez au moins cinq détails.

Étienne   Monsieur Li

Madame Li

Audrey   Louise   Dominique   Georges   Antoine et le chien

G Entretien. Interviewez votre partenaire.

1. Tu es musicien(ne)? Est-ce que tu danses bien ou mal? Est-ce que tu chantes bien? Tu préfères écouter de la musique ou regarder la télé? Est-ce que tu regardes souvent la télé quand tu manges? Tu écoutes de la musique quand tu étudies?
2. Est-ce que tu es sportif (sportive)? Est-ce que tu aimes le sport? Quel sport est-ce que tu préfères, le football américain, le basket, le golf ou le baseball? Est-ce que tu joues au tennis? au golf? au volley? (Est-ce que tu gagnes souvent?)
3. Tes amis et toi, vous passez beaucoup de temps ensemble? Qu'est-ce que vous aimez faire ensemble? Vous dînez souvent ensemble? Vous préférez manger ensemble à la maison, au restaurant, au café ou dans un fast-food?

H Colocataires. Imaginez que vous cherchez un(e) colocataire *(are looking for a housemate)*. Demandez à un(e) autre étudiant(e) s'il / si elle fait les choses suivantes.

EXEMPLE travailler / beaucoup
— **Est-ce que tu travailles beaucoup?**
— **Oui, je travaille beaucoup.**
Non, je ne travaille pas beaucoup.

1. aimer / beaucoup / aller en boîte
2. parler / souvent / au téléphone
3. étudier / beaucoup
4. passer / toujours / le week-end à la maison
5. inviter / souvent / des amis à la maison
6. regarder / toujours / la télé le week-end
7. écouter / souvent / du hip-hop

Après, décrivez *(describe)* votre partenaire à la classe. Dites au moins cinq choses.

EXEMPLE **Il/Elle travaille beaucoup et…**

SAYING WHAT ONE DOES

✔ *Pour vérifier*

1. In verbs like **préférer,** which forms have a spelling change in the stem in the present tense? What is the change? Which forms have stems like the infinitive?

2. In verbs that end in **-yer,** like **envoyer,** which forms have a spelling change in the stem in the present tense? What is the change? Which forms have stems like the infinitive?

3. What is special about the **nous** form of a verb with an infinitive ending in **-ger**? in **-cer**?

4. What is the difference in pronunciation between **é** and **è**?

Vocabulaire sans peine!

Note the following cognate patterns with these verbs with spelling changes.

-nounce = **-noncer**
to pronounce **prononcer**
to denounce **dénoncer**

-erate = **-érer**
to accelerate **accélérer**
to cooperate **coopérer**

How would you say:
to announce, to renounce
to tolerate, to exasperate

Quelques verbes à changements orthographiques

A few **-er** verbs have spelling changes in their stems in the present tense.

1. When the next-to-last syllable of an infinitive has an **e** or **é**, this letter often changes to **è** in all forms except **nous** and **vous.**

PRÉFÉRER *(to prefer)*	
je préfère	nous préférons
tu préfères	vous préférez
il/elle/on préfère	ils/elles préfèrent

RÉPÉTER *(to repeat)*	
je répète	nous répétons
tu répètes	vous répétez
il/elle/on répète	ils/elles répètent

2. In verbs with infinitives ending in **-yer,** the **y** changes to **i** in all forms except **nous** and **vous.**

ENVOYER *(to send)*	
j'envoie	nous envoyons
tu envoies	vous envoyez
il/elle/on envoie	ils/elles envoient

3. With verbs ending in **-ger,** like **manger, nager,** and **voyager** *(to travel),* insert an **e** before the **-ons** ending in the **nous** form. With verbs ending in **-cer,** like **commencer,** the **c** changes to a **ç** before the **-ons** ending in the **nous** form.

VOYAGER *(to travel)*	
je voyage	nous voyageons
tu voyages	vous voyagez
il/elle/on voyage	ils/elles voyagent

COMMENCER *(to start, to begin)*	
je commence	nous commençons
tu commences	vous commencez
il/elle/on commence	ils/elles commencent

The verb **commencer** is followed by **à** before an infinitive.

Je commence à jouer du piano. *I'm starting to play the piano.*

PRONONCIATION

*Les lettres **é, è, c** et **g*** 2-7

Spelling changes occur in verbs to reflect pronunciation. The letter **é (e accent aigu)** sounds like the vowel of **les.**

— Vous préférez passer la matinée à la maison?

— Non, nous préférons passer la matinée au café.

The letter **è (e accent grave)** often occurs in the final syllable of words ending in a silent **e (Michèle),** and sounds similar to the *e* in the English word *let.*

Je préfère aller à la bibliothèque avec Michèle.

In French, **c** and **g** are pronounced soft (the **c** like an **s** and the **g** like a French **j**) before an **e, i,** or **y.** They are pronounced hard (the **c** like **k** and the **g** similar to the *g* in the English word *go*) before an **a, o, u,** or a consonant.

Soft **g:** **Ge**orges, **Gé**rard, **Gi**lbert   Hard **g:** **Ga**brielle, Hu**go,** **Gui**llaume

Soft **c:** **Cé**cile, Mauri**ce**   Hard **c:** **Ca**therine, **Co**lette

The letter **ç** is used to indicate that a **c** is soft before **a, o,** or **u.** In verb endings, use **ç** to keep **c** soft before **o,** and introduce an **e** to keep **g** soft before **o.**

commençons   mangeons   voyageons   nageons

A Prononcez bien! Dans les mots suivants *(following words)*, la lettre **c** est prononcée [s]. Lesquels de ces mots requièrent *(require)* une cédille?

1. menace / menacant
2. facade / facile
3. Nice / nicois

4. France / francais
5. provencal / Provence
6. prononciation / prononcons

Maintenant, dites si vous aimez les gens avec les traits de caractère suivants. Faites attention à la prononciation des lettres **c** et **g**.

J'aime bien les gens... / Je n'aime pas les gens...

> créatifs   cultivés   arrogants   vulgaires
> menaçants   superficiels   imaginatifs   généreux
> calmes   courageux   égoïstes   gentils

B Préférences. Complétez ces questions avec le verbe indiqué et interviewez votre partenaire.

1. Est-ce que tu _____ (préférer) parler au téléphone ou envoyer des textos à tes amis?
2. À qui *(To whom)* est-ce que tu _____ (envoyer) souvent des textos?
3. Avec qui *(With whom)* est-ce que tu _____ (préférer) sortir?
4. Quel jour est-ce que tes amis _____ (préférer) sortir?
5. Vous _____ (manger) souvent ensemble?
6. Est-ce que vous _____ (préférer) dîner ensemble à la maison ou au restaurant?
7. Qu'est-ce que tes amis _____ (préférer) faire le week-end?
8. Tes amis et toi, vous _____ (voyager) souvent ensemble pendant les vacances *(during vacation)*?

Vous aimez aller au café?

C Formez des phrases! Par équipes *(In teams)*, utilisez des verbes en **-er** pour compléter les phrases suivantes. Écrivez autant de *(as many)* phrases que possible. Chaque groupe gagnera *(will earn)* un point pour chaque phrase correcte et logique.

EXEMPLE En cours de français, le professeur...
> **En cours de français, le professeur préfère parler français.**
> **Il écoute les étudiants. Il répète souvent en cours. Il...**

1. En cours de français, les autres *(other)* étudiants et moi, on...
2. À l'université, beaucoup d'étudiants...
3. Quelquefois, je (j')... sur ordinateur.
4. Est-ce que tu... en cours?
5. Le week-end, mes amis et moi, nous...
6. Tes amis et toi, vous... au café?

Asking about someone's day

LA JOURNÉE

Note *culturelle*

D'après une étude récente (*According to a recent study*), chaque (*each*) jour le Français typique consacre (*dedicates*): 11 heures 45 aux besoins (*needs*) physiologiques (dormir, manger, faire sa toilette [*to get cleaned up*]); 3 heures 15 au travail, aux études et au transport; 3 heures 10 aux tâches domestiques (*domestic tasks*) et 4 heures 58 aux loisirs ou aux amis. Combien de temps consacrez-vous à ces activités tous les jours?

Note *de vocabulaire*

1. The adjective **tout** is placed before a noun's article. It means *the whole* or *all* before singular nouns (**toute la journée** *all day*) and *all* or *every* before plural nouns (**tous les jours** *every day*). It has four forms: **tout** (*masc. sing.*), **toute** (*fem. sing.*), **tous** (*masc. plur.*), and **toutes** (*fem. plur.*).

2. Use the following pronouns after prepositions such as **sans, avec,** or **chez.**

avec moi *with me*
avec toi *with you*
avec lui *with him*
avec elle *with her*
avec nous *with us*
avec vous *with you*
avec eux *with them* (m or mixed group)
avec elles *with them* (f)

3. One hears **au gym** as well as **à la gym.**

— Quand est-ce que vous êtes à l'université?
— Je suis à l'université…   tous les jours **sauf** le week-end.
                                du lundi au jeudi / le lundi, le mardi…
                                le matin / l'après-midi / le soir.
                                de dix heures à quatre heures.
                                toute la journée.

— À quelle heure est-ce que vous arrivez à l'université?
— J'arrive à l'université…   à neuf heures quinze.

— Où est-ce que vous **déjeunez** en général?
— Je déjeune…   chez moi / chez des amis / chez…
                                au restaurant (universitaire).
                                au café Trianon / dans un fast-food.

— Qu'est-ce que vous aimez faire après les cours?
— J'aime…   **rentrer** chez moi.
                                aller au parc / à la gym / chez un(e) ami(e)…
                                sortir avec des amis / dormir / manger…

— **Avec qui** est-ce que vous **aimez mieux** sortir?
— J'aime mieux sortir…   avec **mon copain / ma copine.**
                                avec **mon mari / ma femme.**
                                avec **des copains / des copines.**

— Pourquoi est-ce que vous préférez sortir **avec lui / avec elle / avec eux / avec elles**?
— Parce qu'il/elle est…   riche, beau (belle), intelligent(e)…
  Parce qu'ils/elles sont…   amusant(e)s, marrant(e)s, intellectuel(le)s…

— Quand est-ce que vous préférez sortir ensemble?
— Nous préférons sortir…   le vendredi soir / le week-end…

🔊 2-8

Jean **demande** à Léa comment elle passe une journée typique.

JEAN: Quand est-ce que tu es en cours ce semestre?

LÉA: Je suis en cours tous les jours, sauf le week-end. D'habitude, j'arrive à l'université vers dix heures et je rentre vers trois heures et demie.

JEAN: Et après les cours, qu'est-ce que tu aimes faire en général?

LÉA: Après, j'aime rentrer à la maison et dormir un peu.

JEAN: Et qu'est-ce que tu aimes faire le soir?

LÉA: Le soir, j'aime faire quelque chose avec des copains. On aime dîner, aller au cinéma ou prendre un verre au café ensemble.

---

sauf *except*   **toute la journée** *all day*   **déjeuner** *to eat lunch*   **rentrer** *to return, to go back (home)*   **Avec qui** *With whom*
aimer mieux *to like better, to prefer*   **mon copain** *my boyfriend*   **ma copine** *my girlfriend*   **mon mari** *my husband*
ma femme *my wife*   **un copain (une copine)** *a buddy, a friend*   **avec lui (avec elle)** *with him (with her)*   **avec eux** *with them (masc. or mixed group)*   **avec elles** *with them (fem.)*   **demander** *to ask (for)*

A Précisions.

A **Précisions.** Demain, David déjeune avec des amis au café Chez Marie. Quelle est la réponse logique pour chaque question?

1. Quel jour est-ce que nous déjeunons ensemble?
2. À quelle heure?
3. Qui déjeune avec nous?
4. Pourquoi est-ce que tu n'invites pas Thomas?
5. Où est-ce que nous déjeunons?
6. Qu'est-ce que tu voudrais faire après?

a. Au café Chez Marie.
b. Elsa et Cyril.
c. Vendredi.
d. Aller au cinéma.
e. Parce qu'il travaille.
f. À midi et demi.

> ### Chez Marie
> **Pizzas – Snack – Bar**
> **27, rue de Rennes**
>
> euros
>
> **Calzone:** **6,00**
> Tomate, champignons, œuf, crème fraîche
>
> **Marguerite:** **5,00**
> Tomate, fromage
>
> **Poivrons:** **5,80**
> Tomate, fromage, champignons, poivrons
>
> **Reine:** **5,80**
> Tomate, fromage, olives, champignons, jambon
>
> *Service continu de midi à 2h du matin.*

B **C'est vrai?** Lisez chaque phrase et dites si c'est vrai ou si ce n'est pas vrai.

1. Je suis à l'université toute la journée du lundi au vendredi.
2. Nous sommes en cours de français le matin, tous les jours sauf le vendredi.
3. Les jours du cours de français, j'arrive à l'université à neuf heures vingt et je rentre vers cinq heures.
4. Le cours de français est de dix heures à onze heures.
5. Les autres étudiants et moi, on déjeune souvent ensemble.
6. Après les cours, j'aime mieux rester à la maison que sortir avec des amis.
7. J'aime mieux sortir avec mon copain (ma copine).

Maintenant, corrigez les phrases qui ne sont pas vraies.

C **Entretien.** Interviewez votre partenaire.

1. Quels jours est-ce que tu es à l'université? Est-ce que tu restes à l'université toute la journée? À quelle heure est-ce que tu arrives à l'université? À quelle heure est-ce que tu rentres chez toi?
2. Quand est-ce que tu étudies? Où est-ce que tu aimes mieux étudier: chez toi ou à la bibliothèque? Avec qui est-ce que tu préfères étudier?
3. Où est-ce que tu aimes mieux déjeuner? À quelle heure? Est-ce que tu déjeunes souvent chez toi? Où est-ce que tu préfères manger le soir? Est-ce que tu dînes plus souvent chez toi ou au restaurant? Est-ce que tu manges souvent dans un fast-food? Qu'est-ce que tu préfères: les hamburgers, la pizza ou les tacos?
4. Qu'est-ce que tu aimes faire le week-end? Où est-ce que tu aimes mieux sortir avec des copains: au cinéma, au café ou en boîte? Avec qui est-ce que tu préfères sortir? Pourquoi est-ce que tu aimes sortir avec lui (elle/eux/elles)? Quand est-ce que vous aimez mieux sortir ensemble?

À VOUS!

Avec un(e) partenaire, relisez à haute voix la conversation entre Jean et Léa. Ensuite, adaptez la conversation pour décrire votre situation. Changez de rôles.

You can access the audio of the active vocabulary of this *Compétence* online.

ASKING FOR INFORMATION

✔ Pour vérifier

1. How do you form an information question?

2. Does **qui** or **que** become **qu'** before a vowel sound?

3. When are three times you do not use **est-ce que**?

4. How do you say *Who is this? What is this?*

Les mots interrogatifs

1. You have learned to ask questions with **est-ce que**. To ask for information such as *who, what, when, where,* or *why,* add the appropriate question word before **est-ce que**.

où *where*	**Où est-ce que** vous étudiez?
que (qu') *what*	**Qu'est-ce que** vous étudiez?
pourquoi *why*	**Pourquoi est-ce que** vous étudiez le français?
quand *when*	**Quand est-ce que** vous étudiez?
qui / avec qui *who(m) / with whom*	**Avec qui est-ce que** vous étudiez?
comment *how*	**Comment est-ce que** vous passez la journée?
quel(s) jour(s) *(on) what / which day(s)*	**Quels jours est-ce que** vous êtes en cours?
à quelle heure *at what time*	**À quelle heure est-ce que** vous êtes en cours?

Note *de grammaire*

In informal conversation, it is common to ask an information question by placing the question word at the end, without using **est-ce que**. In this case, use **quoi** rather than **que** to ask *what*.

Tu dînes où? = Où est-ce que tu dînes?

Tu manges quoi? = Qu'est-ce que tu manges?

2. Note that **que** becomes **qu'** before a vowel sound, but there is no elision with **qui**. Remember that **parce que** also becomes **parce qu'** before vowels and silent **h**.

— **Qu'**est-ce que tu aimes faire le soir?
— J'aime sortir.
— Avec **qui** est-ce que tu aimes sortir?
— J'aime sortir avec Paul **parce qu'**il est amusant.

3. Do not use **est-ce que** with **qui** when it is the subject of the verb, or with **où** or **comment** when they are followed directly by a form of the verb **être (est, sont...)**.

qui *who*	**Qui travaille** avec toi?
où *where*	**Où est** la bibliothèque?
comment *how*	**Comment est** l'université?

4. Use **Qui est-ce?** to ask *who* someone is. Use **Qu'est-ce que c'est?** to ask *what* something is.

— Qui est-ce? — Qu'est-ce que c'est?
— C'est Jean. — C'est un livre.

PRONONCIATION

Les lettres **qu** et la prononciation du mot **quand** en liaison
2-9

In French, **qu** is usually pronounced [k] as in the word **quiche**. However, you do hear a [w] after the **qu** in words such as **pourquoi**, due to the **oi** that follows it.

qui que quand quelle heure pourquoi

Note that **d** in liaison is pronounced as a **t**.

Quand‿*t*est-ce que tu travailles?

A **Prononcez bien!** Formez des questions en utilisant l'équivalent français des mots interrogatifs donnés. Ensuite, posez-les à votre partenaire. Faites attention à la prononciation de la combinaison **qu** et du mot **quand** en liaison.

1. _____ est-ce que tu étudies? *(What? Where? With whom? When?)*

2. _____ est-ce que tu aimes mieux déjeuner? *(At what time? With whom? Where?)*

3. _____ est-ce que tu dînes le samedi soir en général? *(Where? With whom? At what time?)*

B **Posez des questions!** Travaillez en équipes *(in teams)*. Pensez à *(Think of)* une question appropriée pour obtenir chaque réponse en utilisant un mot interrogatif (**qui, que...**) basé sur les mots en caractères gras *(boldfaced)*. Les équipes sélectionnent tour à tour *(by turns)* un élément. Les équipes gagnent les points indiqués pour chaque bonne réponse.

	A	**B**	**C**	**D**
5 points	Ça va **bien,** merci.	Je m'appelle **Léa Clark.**	Il est **9 heures.**	Aujourd'hui, c'est **lundi.**
10 points	C'est **Lisa.**	C'est **un parc.**	David est **sympa.**	Léa est **à la maison.**
15 points	Lisa aime **la musique.**	Thomas travaille **toute la journée.**	David aime sortir avec **Léa.**	Je rentre **à une heure.**
20 points	**Léa et David** étudient les maths.	Nous aimons mieux **aller au cinéma.**	**Parce que le prof est très intéressant.**	Léa parle **bien** français.

C **Le samedi.** Voici un samedi typique pour Adrien, l'ami de David. Travaillez en groupes pour créer cinq questions sur ce qu'Adrien fait *(on what Adrien does)* le samedi. Utilisez un mot interrogatif dans chaque question. Dites il **fait** pour *he does*, si nécessaire. Ensuite, posez vos questions aux autres groupes.

EXEMPLE Qu'est-ce qu'Adrien fait le samedi matin?

| qui | que (qu') | où | quand | pourquoi | comment |

Étienne   Adrien   Dominique

ses *(his)* copains

ASKING QUESTIONS

✔ Pour vérifier

1. How would you invert the question: **Il est ici?**

2. Do you ever use **est-ce que** and inversion in the same question?

3. When do you insert a **-t-** between a verb and an inverted subject pronoun?

4. Generally, can you invert nouns, or only pronouns? What do you do if the subject of the question is a noun? How would you invert the question: **Marie déjeune à onze heures?**

5. What is the inverted form of **il y a**? of **c'est**?

6. How would you invert: **Où est-ce que vous déjeunez?**

Les questions par inversion

1. You can ask a question using rising intonation or **est-ce que**. You can also use inversion; that is, you can invert (change the order of) the subject pronoun and the verb. Attach inverted subject pronouns to the end of the verb with a hyphen.

   Est-ce que tu travailles le lundi? = **Travailles-tu** le lundi?

2. Invert the *conjugated* verb and the *subject pronoun*. Do not invert a following infinitive.

   Aimes-tu aller au cinéma?   **Voudriez-vous** aller danser?

3. Never use both **est-ce que** and inversion in the same question.

   Joues-tu de la guitare?   *OR*   **Est-ce que tu joues** de la guitare?

4. Inversion is not normally used with **je**.

5. When the subject is **il, elle,** or **on** and *the verb ends in a vowel*, place a **-t-** between the verb and the pronoun. Do not add **-t-** if the verb ends in a consonant, but pronounce the consonant in liaison.

   Parle-**t**-il anglais?   Est _t_ il d'ici?
   Travaille-**t**-elle ici?   Est _t_ elle d'ici?
   Parle-**t**-on français ici?   Est _t_ on près de chez toi?

6. Generally, only subject *pronouns* are inverted, not *nouns*. If the subject of the question is a noun, rather than a pronoun, state the noun first, then supply a matching pronoun for inversion.

   Le prof est-**il** français?   **Marie** parle-t-**elle** français?
   Les cours sont-**ils** difficiles?   **Ophélie et Juliette** étudient-**elles** ici?

   However, remember how to ask questions with **où** or **comment** when they are followed directly by a form of the verb **être (est, sont).**

   Où est le stade?   **Comment sont les matchs?**

7. The inverted form of **il y a** is **y a-t-il**. **C'est** becomes **est-ce**.

   Y a-t-il un café dans le quartier?   **Est-ce** un bon café?

8. To ask information questions, place the question word before the inverted verb. **Qu'est-ce que** becomes **que (qu')** when using inversion.

   Où voudrais-tu aller? **Que** voudrais-tu faire? **Qu'**aimes-tu faire?

PRONONCIATION

L'inversion et la liaison 2-10

When the subject is **il, elle, on, ils,** or **elles,** there is liaison between the verb and its pronoun in inversion.

   Lisa est _t_ elle américaine?   David et Thomas parlent _t_ ils anglais?   Est _t_ on près de chez David?

Thomas   Gisèle

🔁 **A** **Prononcez bien!** D'abord *(First)*, écoutez et répétez ces questions. Ensuite, posez-les à un(e) autre étudiant(e). Faites attention à la prononciation!

🔊 2-11

Gisèle, où est-elle ce soir? Est-elle seule? Étudie-t-elle? Thomas et Gisèle aiment-ils la musique? Dansent-ils bien? Et toi? Aimes-tu danser? Dansons-nous en cours quelquefois? Tes amis et toi, aimez-vous aller en boîte ensemble? Aimez-vous mieux aller au cinéma? Y a-t-il un bon cinéma dans le quartier universitaire?

B **Jouons au tennis!** David parle avec Lisa. Recréez ses questions en utilisant l'inversion.

> **EXEMPLE** Est-ce que tu aimes faire du sport?
> **Aimes-tu faire du sport?**

1. Tu aimes jouer au tennis?
2. Tu joues bien?
3. Tu gagnes souvent?
4. Ton meilleur ami est sportif?
5. Est-ce qu'il joue bien au tennis?
6. Quand est-ce que vous aimez jouer ensemble?
7. Est-ce que tu es libre demain soir?
8. Tu voudrais jouer au tennis avec moi?

C **Et toi?** Posez des questions à votre partenaire pour avoir les renseignements suivants *(following information)*. Utilisez l'inversion.

> **EXEMPLE** *when he/she works*
> **— Quand travailles-tu?**
> **— Je travaille du lundi au vendredi.**

1. *what days he/she is in class*
2. *what time he/she arrives at the university*
3. *what he/she likes to do after class*
4. *with whom he/she prefers to go out*
5. *why he/she likes to go out with him/her*

D **Reprise des questions.** Interviewez un(e) partenaire et complétez les phrases suivantes pour décrire sa *(to describe his/her)* journée le premier *(first)* jour de la semaine où vous êtes en cours de français. Avant de commencer, préparez les questions avec **tu** à poser pour obtenir ces renseignements *(to get this information)*. Après l'interview, décrivez la journée de votre partenaire à la classe.

> **EXEMPLE** Le *[first day of your French class]*, il/elle arrive à l'université *[about what time]*.
> **— Le lundi (Le mardi...), vers quelle heure est-ce que tu arrives à l'université?**
> **— J'arrive à l'université vers dix heures.**
>
> Après, à la classe:
> **Chris arrive à l'université vers dix heures.**
> **Il/Elle...**
>
> Il/Elle arrive arrive à l'université *[about what time]*.
> Il/Elle déjeune *[with whom]*.
> Il/Elle mange *[where]*.
> Il/Elle rentre *[when]*.
> Il/Elle étudie *[with whom]*.
> Il/Elle préfère étudier *[where]*.

Going to the café

AU CAFÉ

Note *culturelle*

En France, dans les cafés et les restaurants, le service *(gratuity)* est toujours compris *(included)* dans le prix. Pourtant *(However)*, certains laissent *(some leave)* un petit pourboire *(tip)* supplémentaire, entre 1 et 3 euros par personne, même un peu plus *(even a little more)* dans un restaurant de luxe. Est-ce que le service est compris dans les cafés et les restaurants de votre région? Laissez-vous toujours *(Do you always leave)* un pourboire ou uniquement si *(if)* c'est mérité?

Vous êtes au café. Qu'est-ce que **vous allez** prendre?

Je voudrais…

un expresso

Donnez-moi…

un café au lait

Je vais prendre…

un thé au citron

une eau minérale

un jus de fruit ou un jus d'orange

un coca (light)

un Orangina

un verre de vin rouge ou un verre de vin blanc

un demi

une bière

un sandwich au jambon

un sandwich au fromage

des frites *(f)*

🔊 2-12

David et Léa **commandent une boisson** au café.

DAVID:	Je vais prendre un demi. Et toi?
LÉA:	Moi, je voudrais bien un chocolat **chaud.**
DAVID:	Monsieur, s'il vous plaît.
LE SERVEUR:	Bonjour. Vous désirez?
DAVID:	Pour moi, un demi. Et pour mon amie, un chocolat chaud.
LE SERVEUR:	Très bien.

Sélection musicale. Search for the song **"L'eau et le vin"** by Vanessa Paradis to enjoy a musical selection containing this vocabulary.

vous allez *you are going* **Donnez-moi**… *Give me* … **(donner** *to give)* **un coca (light)** *a (diet) Coke, a (diet) cola* **un demi** *a draft beer* **commander** *to order* **une boisson** *a drink, a beverage* **chaud(e)** *hot* **le serveur (la serveuse)** *the server*

Après, David et Léa **paient.**

DAVID: Ça fait combien, monsieur?

LE SERVEUR: Ça fait sept euros cinquante.

DAVID: **Voilà** dix euros.

LE SERVEUR: Et **voici** votre **monnaie** (*f*). Merci bien.

A **Tu voudrais?** Proposez les choses suivantes à un(e) autre étudiant(e).

EXEMPLE

— **Tu voudrais une eau minérale ou un coca?**
— **Je voudrais une eau minérale / un coca.**

1.

2.   3.

4.    5.

B **Je préfère...** Pour chaque paire ou groupe de choses indiquées dans l'exercice précédent, indiquez votre préférence. Utilisez **le, la, l'** ou **les** pour indiquer ce que (*what*) vous préférez. Pour dire *neither... nor...*, utilisez **ne... ni... ni...** Utilisez **les deux** ou **les trois** pour dire *both* ou *all three*.

EXEMPLE Je préfère l'eau minérale / le coca.
Je n'aime ni l'eau minérale ni le coca.
J'aime les deux.

À VOUS!

Avec deux autres étudiants, relisez à haute voix la conversation au café. Ensuite, adaptez la conversation pour commander ce que (*what*) vous voudriez. La troisième personne joue le rôle du serveur/de la serveuse. N'oubliez pas (*Don't forget*) de payer.

You can access the audio of the active vocabulary of this *Compétence* online.

---

paient (payer *to pay*) **Voilà** *There is, There are* **voici** *here is, here are* **la monnaie** *the change*

PAYING THE BILL

✔ *Pour vérifier*

1. How do you say **60**? **70**? **80**? **90**?

2. When do you use **et** with numbers? Do you use **et** with 81 and 91?

3. How do you say *one hundred*? Do you translate the word *one*?

Les nombres de soixante à cent et l'argent (m)

— Un thé au citron, c'est combien? / Ça fait combien?

— 3,50 € / 3€50 (trois euros cinquante).

60	soixante	80	quatre-vingts
61	soixante et un	81	quatre-vingt-un
62	soixante-deux	82	quatre-vingt-deux
63	soixante-trois	83	quatre-vingt-trois
64	soixante-quatre	84	quatre-vingt-quatre
65	soixante-cinq	85	quatre-vingt-cinq
66	soixante-six	86	quatre-vingt-six
67	soixante-sept	87	quatre-vingt-sept
68	soixante-huit	88	quatre-vingt-huit
69	soixante-neuf	89	quatre-vingt-neuf
70	soixante-dix	90	quatre-vingt-dix
71	soixante et onze	91	quatre-vingt-onze
72	soixante-douze	92	quatre-vingt-douze
73	soixante-treize	93	quatre-vingt-treize
74	soixante-quatorze	94	quatre-vingt-quatorze
75	soixante-quinze	95	quatre-vingt-quinze
76	soixante-seize	96	quatre-vingt-seize
77	soixante-dix-sept	97	quatre-vingt-dix-sept
78	soixante-dix-huit	98	quatre-vingt-dix-huit
79	soixante-dix-neuf	99	quatre-vingt-dix-neuf
		100	cent

© Oliver Hoffmann/Shutterstock.com

PRONONCIATION

Les nombres 2-13

Some French numbers are pronounced differently, depending on what follows them.

deux	deux cafés	deux ^{z} euros
trois	trois cafés	trois ^{z} euros
six^s	six cafés	six ^{z} euros
huit^t	huit cafés	huit ^{t} euros
dix^s	dix cafés	dix ^{z} euros

A. Prononcez bien! Commandez ces boissons. Faites attention à la prononciation des nombres.

EXEMPLES trois demis   **Trois demis, s'il vous plaît.**
                trois expressos **Trois expressos, s'il vous plaît.**

deux demis	trois demis	six demis	huit demis	dix demis
deux expressos	trois expressos	six expressos	huit expressos	dix expressos

Maintenant, lisez ces prix *(prices)*. N'oubliez pas *(Don't forget)* de faire la liaison avec le mot **euro** si *(if)* nécessaire.

1 €   11 €   2 €   12 €   3 €   13 €   6 €   16 €   10 €   20 €
61 €   71 €   82 €   92 €   63 €   73 €   86 €   96 €   100 €   80 €

B. Votre monnaie. Vous êtes au café et vous payez pour vos amis et vous. Suivez l'exemple.

EXEMPLE 6,85 € (10 €)
                — **C'est combien, monsieur?**
                — **Six euros quatre-vingt-cinq, madame.**
                — **Voilà dix euros.**
                — **Et voici votre monnaie.**

1. 12,98 € (15 €)	**4.** 14,88 € (15 €)	**7.** 2,50 € (5 €)
2. 32,45 € (40 €)	**5.** 36,75 € (40 €)	**8.** 16,80 € (20 €)
3. 23,68 € (30 €)	**6.** 7,95 € (10 €)	**9.** 13,25 € (20 €)

C. C'est combien? Écrivez les prix *(prices)* que vous entendez.

2-14

EXEMPLE Vous entendez: Une baguette, c'est 87 centimes.
                Vous écrivez: **0,87 €**

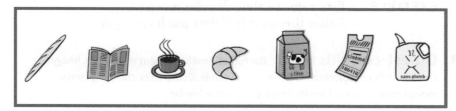

1. un journal	**3.** un croissant	**5.** un billet de cinéma
2. un expresso	**4.** un litre de lait	**6.** un litre d'essence *(gas)*

D. Ça coûte combien? Donnez des prix logiques pour chacune des choses suivantes là où vous habitez. Lisez vos prix à votre partenaire qui va les écrire *(is going to write them)*. Ensuite, changez de rôle.

EXEMPLE Vous voyez: le journal du dimanche
                Vous dites: **Le journal du dimanche, c'est**
                                un dollar soixante-quinze.
                Votre partenaire écrit: 1,75$

1. un billet de cinéma	**4.** un café
2. un hamburger dans un fast-food	**5.** un beau tee-shirt
3. des frites	**6.** un gallon d'essence *(gas)*

VIDÉO-REPRISE

Les Stagiaires

Rappel!
So far in the video, Amélie and Rachid, two new interns at the Technovert company, have met and found out a little about their new colleagues, M. Vieilledent (the boss), Camille (M. Vieilledent's assistant), Céline (the sales manager), Matthieu (the company's shy techie), and Christophe (M. Vieilledent's son and the company's gofer).

See the ***Résumé de grammaire*** section at the end of each chapter for a review of all the grammar presented in the chapter.

In *Épisode 2*, Camille realizes that Matthieu, the company's computer specialist, is interested in Amélie, as he tries to find out from her what kinds of things Amélie likes to do. Before you watch the episode, do these exercises to review what you have learned in *Chapitre 2*.

A **Loisirs préférés.** Camille parle des loisirs préférés des employés de Technovert. Complétez chaque phrase avec le verbe indiqué.

EXEMPLE Christophe aime **lire** *(to read)* des mangas.

1. Matthieu aime _____ *(to play)* à des jeux vidéo et _____ *(to work)* sur ordinateur.

2. M. Vieilledent aime _____ *(to go)* au café où il aime prendre un café et _____ *(to eat)* des croissants.

3. Rachid aime _____ *(to see)* un film ou _____ *(to dance)* avec ses *(his)* amis.

4. J'aime _____ *(to exercise)*. J'aime surtout *(most of all)* _____ *(to swim)*.

5. Amélie aime _____ *(to go out)* avec des amis. Elle aime _____ *(to have lunch)* au restaurant.

6. Céline aime _____ *(to talk)* au téléphone et _____ *(to text)* à ses *(her)* copines.

Maintenant, demandez à votre partenaire s'il/si elle aime faire les choses mentionnées par Camille.

EXEMPLE — **Est-ce que tu aimes lire des mangas?**
— **J'aime lire, mais je n'aime pas les mangas.**

B **Qu'est-ce qu'ils font?** Rachid et Amélie parlent ensemble. Imaginez comment ils complètent les phrases suivantes. Complétez chaque phrase logiquement avec un verbe conjugué et un adverbe.

EXEMPLE mon meilleur ami / jouer au tennis
Mon meilleur ami joue assez bien au tennis.
Mon meilleur ami ne joue jamais au tennis.

> toujours   souvent   quelquefois   rarement   ne... jamais
> beaucoup   assez   (un) peu   ne... pas du tout
> très bien   assez bien   assez mal   très mal

1. moi, je / nager
2. ma meilleure amie / aimer le sport
3. mes amis / jouer au golf
4. je / manger à la maison
5. ma famille et moi, nous / dîner ensemble
6. nous / manger au restaurant
7. ma famille et moi, on / aimer voyager
8. on / voyager ensemble en été *(in summer)*

C C'est combien? Voilà le menu du café en face de *(across from)* Technovert. Demandez à votre partenaire le prix de cinq ou six choses.

EXEMPLE — Un expresso, c'est combien?
— C'est deux euros quarante-cinq.

L'heure du thé

Prix Service Compris (15 %)

Expresso	2,45	Thé (avec lait ou citron)	3,50
Double expresso	4,10	Thé à la menthe	3,50
Café au lait	3,40	Thé au fruit de la passion	3,50
Infusion	3,50	Thé à la framboise	3,50
(Tilleul, verveine, menthe, tilleul-		Cappuccino	4,30
menthe, verveine-menthe, camomille)		Croissants	1,60
Lait chaud	2,90	Confiture pot	1,40
Café décaféiné	2,60	Tartines beurrées	2,80
Double expresso avec pot de lait.	3,60	Grog au rhum	6,10
Chocolat	3,50	Vin chaud	3,75
Café ou chocolat viennois	4,30	Irish Coffee	7,80

Source: L'heure du thé

Maintenant, dites ce que vous aimez prendre.

1. Le matin, j'aime prendre...
2. Le soir, j'aime bien prendre...
3. Avec un hamburger, j'aime prendre...
4. Maintenant, je voudrais...

D Questions. Céline et Amélie décident de sortir ensemble. Complétez leur conversation comme indiqué ci-dessous. Utilisez **est-ce que** pour poser les questions.

— _____ ce soir?
   What would you like to do

— Je voudrais aller voir le film *Star Time.*

— _____?
   Why would you like to see Star Time?

— Parce que c'est un film d'action. Et toi? _____?
   Are you free this evening?

_____?
   Would you like to go to the movies with me?

— D'accord. _____?
   What time does the movie start?

— À 8h30.

Maintenant, recommencez la conversation. Utilisez l'inversion pour poser les mêmes questions.

Access the Video *Les Stagiaires* online.

 Épisode 2: Elle est belle, non?

AVANT LA VIDÉO

Dans ce clip, Matthieu pose beaucoup de questions à Camille au sujet d'Amélie. Quand Céline et Camille se rendent compte *(realize)* qu'il s'intéresse à Amélie, elles parient *(bet)* dix euros: Aura-t-il *(Will he have)* le courage d'inviter Amélie à sortir ou non?

Avant de regarder le clip, imaginez une des questions que Matthieu pose à Camille au sujet d'Amélie.

APRÈS LA VIDÉO

Regardez le clip et notez les questions posées par *(asked by)* Matthieu.

LECTURE ET COMPOSITION

LECTURE

By using cognates and what you already know about cafés, you should be able to make intelligent guesses about what is offered on this café menu. The following exercise will guide you.

Vous savez déjà...
Scan the menu and use what you already know about cafés and restaurants to determine the three main categories of food served at this café.

AU VIEUX PORT DE NICE

NOS SALADES

Salade César _____ 10,50 €
cœur de romaine, fromage gruyère, poulet, croûtons

Salade niçoise _____ 12,95 €
salade, thon, poivron, œufs durs, olives, anchois

Salade mixte _____ 4,75 €
salade, tomates

NOS PLATS

Omelette _____ 7,50 €
jambon, fromage ou mixte

Steak ou poulet frites _____ 16,00 €
frites maison

Pizza à la niçoise _____ 13,00 €
sauce tomate, fromage, olives, thon

NOS SANDWICHS

Jambon _____ 7,50 €
jambon sec ou de Paris

Fromage _____ 7,00 €
gruyère ou camembert

Club _____ 10,00 €
poulet, jambon, fromage, tomate, laitue

© Aaron Black/Aurora/Getty Images

POUR MIEUX ÉCRIRE:
Using logical order and standard phrases

When writing about an activity that you have done often, such as ordering at a café or restaurant, it is useful to start by jotting down the usual sequence of events and typical phrases that are used at each step. This will provide you with a basic framework that you can flesh out with details.

Organisez-vous. You are going to prepare a scene in which two friends meet, talk, and order at a café. Before you begin, make sure you remember how to do these things in French.

- How do you greet a friend?
- How do you call the server over and order a drink?
- How do you talk about what you do on the weekend?
- How do you ask what your companion likes to do and say what you like or do not like to do?
- How do you invite a friend to do something?
- How do you pay the bill?
- How do you say good-bye?

Compréhension

A Mots apparentés. Read the menu and use cognates to identify:

1. Two kinds of sandwiches.
2. Three or four items used in the salads.
3. Two or three items you could order from the *Nos plats* section.

B C'est combien? With a partner, take turns asking each other the price of various items on the menu.

EXEMPLE — C'est combien, le sandwich au jambon?
— Le sandwich au jambon, c'est sept euros cinquante.

Au café

Using your answers from the preceding activity, write a conversation in which you meet another student at a café. You greet each other, order a drink, and start to chat about what you have in common. Remember to add details, such as when you like to do some things or why you do not like to do other things. You finally make plans to do something later, you get the bill, and you pay.

COMPARAISONS CULTURELLES

LES CAFÉS EN FRANCE

En France, le café est une institution sociale. **On ne va pas** au café juste pour prendre un verre, mais aussi pour passer du temps entre amis, pour parler et pour regarder les gens qui passent.

Il y a des cafés **partout** et les cafés reflètent le quartier où **ils se trouvent.**

Il y a des cafés élégants, des cafés de quartier et, **bien sûr**, beaucoup de cafés près des sites touristiques.

Le Procope, datant de 1686 et fréquenté dans le passé par des gens célèbres comme Victor Hugo, Benjamin Franklin et Napoléon, est le café **le plus ancien** de Paris.

Le café du coin est un lieu de rencontre pour les gens du quartier.

Au café, les touristes ont l'impression de voir la France de l'intérieur et de **faire partie de la vie quotidienne** française.

On ne va pas One doesn't go   **partout** everywhere   **ils se trouvent** they are located   **bien sûr** of course
le plus ancien the oldest   **faire partie**   **de la vie quotidienne** to be part of daily life   **Le café du coin** The corner café
lieu de rencontre meeting place

Voilà des **renseignements utiles.**

Dans les cafés, **les prix** sont généralement **moins élevés** au bar et plus élevés sur la terrasse.

Les chaises font face à la rue, parce qu'**un des plaisirs** du café est de regarder les gens qui passent.

Compréhension

1. En France, qu'est-ce qu'on aime faire au café?
2. Quel est le café le plus ancien de Paris?
3. Dans les cafés, où est-ce que les prix sont moins élevés? plus élevés?
4. À votre avis *(In your opinion)*, le café est-il plus populaire en France qu'ici? Qu'est-ce que vous aimez faire au café?

des renseignements utiles *useful information*   **les prix** *prices*   **moins élevés** *lower*   **Les chaises font face à la rue** *The chairs face the street*   **un des plaisirs** *one of the pleasures*

RÉSUMÉ DE GRAMMAIRE

THE INFINITIVE, -*ER* VERBS, THE PRONOUN *ON* AND ADVERBS

Qu'est-ce que tu aimes **faire** le soir?

J'aime **rester** à la maison et **lire** ou **sortir** pour **aller voir** un film.

The base form of a verb is called the infinitive. In English, the infinitive starts with *to (to be, to go, to do . . .)*. French infinitives end in **-er, -ir, -oir,** or **-re.**

parler	**sortir**	**voir**	**faire**
to speak	*to go out*	*to see*	*to make, to do*

The verb following a subject is conjugated. Here is the pattern of conjugation for verbs ending in **-er,** except **aller.**

PARLER *(to speak)*	
je parl**e**	nous parl**ons**
tu parl**es**	vous parl**ez**
il/elle/on parl**e**	ils/elles parl**ent**

Mes amis **aiment** sortir, mais moi j'**aime** rester à la maison.

Nous voyag**e**ons souvent ensemble en été *(in summer).*

Nous commen**ç**ons notre cours à 9h.

With verbs ending in **-ger,** like **nager, manger,** and **voyager,** insert an **e** before the **-ons** ending in the **nous** form.

With verbs ending in **-cer,** such as **commencer,** the **c** changes to a **ç** before the **-ons** ending in the **nous** form.

If the next-to-last syllable of an **-er** infinitive has an **e** or an **é,** like **préférer** and **répéter,** this letter often changes to an **è** in all forms except **nous** and **vous.**

Après les cours, je **préfère** rentrer à la maison. Mais le vendredi après-midi, mes amis et moi **préférons** aller prendre un verre.

PRÉFÉRER *(to prefer)*	
je préf**è**re	nous préférons
tu préf**è**res	vous préférez
il/elle/on préf**è**re	ils/elles préf**è**rent

With verbs ending in **-yer,** such as **envoyer** and **payer,** the **y** changes to an **i** in all forms except **nous** and **vous.**

J'**envoie** souvent des textos.

Vous **envoyez** rarement des textos.

ENVOYER *(to send)*	
j'envo**i**e	nous envoyons
tu envo**i**es	vous envoyez
il/elle/on envo**i**e	ils/elles envo**i**ent

The present tense in French is the equivalent of three present tenses in English.

Je parle français. $\begin{cases} \textit{I speak French.} \\ \textit{I am speaking French.} \\ \textit{I do speak French.} \end{cases}$

À Paris, **on aime** beaucoup aller au cinéma.

Mes amis et moi, **on aime** beaucoup le cinéma.

Use **on** to say *they, one, people* when you are referring to people in general. **On** is also used, instead of **nous,** to say *we.* With **on,** use the same form of a verb as that for **il/elle.**

Je danse **souvent** le week-end.

Je joue **bien** au tennis.

Quelquefois, j'étudie.

Je **ne** travaille **jamais** le samedi.

Adverbs that tell how much, how often, or how well you do something are generally placed immediately after the conjugated verb, but before an infinitive. **Quelquefois** and **d'habitude** can also be placed at the beginning or end of the clause and **ne... jamais** surrounds the conjugated verb.

INFORMATION QUESTIONS

To ask information questions, place the appropriate question word (**où, qui,** etc.) before **est-ce que.**

Où est-ce que tu travailles?	*(Where . . . ?)*
Qui est-ce que tu voudrais inviter?	*(Who . . . ?)*
Avec qui est-ce que tu déjeunes?	*(With whom . . . ?)*
Pourquoi est-ce que tu es ici?	*(Why . . . ?)*
Qu'est-ce que tu voudrais?	*(What . . . ?)*
Quand est-ce que tu déjeunes?	*(When . . . ?)*
À quelle heure est-ce que tu dînes?	*(At what time . . . ?)*
Quel(s) jour(s) est-ce que tu es en cours?	*(What / Which day(s) . . . ?)*
Comment est-ce que tu aimes passer la matinée?	*(How . . . ?)*

Do not use **est-ce que** with **qui** when it is the subject of the verb, or with **où** or **comment** when they are followed by **être.**

You can also form questions by inverting the verb and its subject pronoun. Remember that:

- You do not normally use inversion with **je.**
- If the subject of the verb is a noun, state the noun, then insert the corresponding pronoun to invert with the verb.
- When the inverted subject is **il, elle,** or **on** and the verb *ends in a vowel,* place a **-t-** between the verb and the pronoun.
- The inverted forms of **il y a** and **c'est** are **y a-t-il** and **est-ce.**

THE NUMBERS FROM 60 TO 100 AND MONEY

The **euro** is the official currency of France. A euro is composed of 100 **centimes.** Read prices as:

10,10 € = dix euros dix

84,35 € = quatre-vingt-quatre euros trente-cinq

65,75 € = soixante-cinq euros soixante-quinze

100,50 € = cent euros cinquante

The numbers from 60 to 100 are based on:

60 soixante

70 soixante-dix

80 quatre-vingts

90 quatre-vingt-dix

100 cent

Quand est-ce que tu es en cours?

Quels cours est-ce que tu préfères?

Pourquoi est-ce que tu préfères ces cours?

Où est-ce que tu étudies en général?

Avec qui est-ce que tu aimes étudier?

Qui travaille ici?
Où est la salle de gym?
Comment sont tes cours?

Avec qui aimes-tu mieux sortir?
Qu'aimes-tu faire avec lui?
Comment est-il?
Ton copain **aime-t-il** sortir le week-end?

Aime-t-il aller au cinéma?
Y a-t-il un cinéma près d'ici?
Est-ce un bon cinéma?

— C'est combien, un expresso?
— C'est **deux euros soixante-quinze**

VOCABULAIRE

Saying what you like to do

EXPRESSIONS VERBALES

Qu'est-ce que vous aimez faire?	What do you like to do?
J'aime...	I like . . .
Je préfère...	I prefer . . .
Qu'est-ce que vous voudriez faire?	What would you like to do?
Tu voudrais...?	Would you like . . . ?
Je voudrais...	I would like . . .
aller en boîte (de nuit) / au café / au cinéma	to go to a (night)club / to the café / to the movies
courir	to run
danser	to dance
dîner au restaurant	to have dinner at a restaurant
dormir	to sleep
écouter de la musique	to listen to music
envoyer un texto	to send a text message, to text
faire	to do, to make
faire de l'exercice	to exercise
faire du sport	to play sports
faire du vélo	to go bike-riding
faire quelque chose	to do something
inviter	to invite
jouer à des jeux vidéo	to play video games
jouer au baseball / au basket / au football / au football américain / au golf / au tennis / au volley	to play baseball / basketball / soccer / football / golf / tennis / volleyball
jouer du piano / de la batterie / de la guitare	to play piano / drums / guitar
lire	to read
parler au téléphone	to talk on the phone
prendre un verre / un café	to have a drink / a coffee
regarder la télé(vision)	to watch TV
rester à la maison	to stay home
sortir avec des ami(e)s	to go out with friends
surfer sur Internet	to surf the Net
travailler sur ordinateur	to work on the computer
voir un film	to see a movie

DIVERS

À ce soir!	See you tonight!, See you this evening!
après les cours	after class
Ça te dit de...? / Ça vous dit de...?	Do you feel like . . . ?
un café	a café, a cup of coffee
D'accord!	Okay!
en général	in general
fatigué(e)	tired, fatigued
un loisir	a leisure activity, a pastime
Pourquoi pas.	Why not.
quelque chose	something
le temps libre	free time
un texto	a text (message)
Tu es libre ce soir?	Are you free this evening / tonight?
vers	about, around, toward
(pas) vraiment	(not) really, truly

Saying how you spend your free time

NOMS MASCULINS

le ciné-club	the cinema club
un classique	a classic

NOMS FÉMININS

une activité	an activity
la fac	the university, the campus
la matinée	the morning

EXPRESSIONS VERBALES

Qu'est-ce que vous faites?	What are you doing?, What do you do?
Qu'est-ce que tu fais?	What are you doing?, What do you do?
chanter	to sing
commencer	to begin, to start
faire du shopping	to go shopping
gagner	to win
jouer au hockey	to play hockey
jouer de la musique	to play music
manger	to eat
nager	to swim
passer chez...	to go by . . . 's house
passer	to spend (time)
passer la matinée	to spend the morning
préférer	to prefer
répéter	to repeat
rester au lit	to stay in bed
je vais	I am going, I go
voyager	to travel

ADVERBES

(très / assez) bien	(very / fairly) well
d'habitude	usually, as a rule
ensemble	together
jusqu'à	until
(très / assez) mal	(very / fairly) badly
ne... jamais	never
presque	almost
quelquefois	sometimes
rarement	rarely
souvent	often
toujours	always

DIVERS

chez...	to / at / in / by . . . 's house
on	one, people, they, we
quand	when

COMPÉTENCE 3

Asking about someone's day

NOMS MASCULINS

un copain	a buddy, a friend
mon copain	my boyfriend, my friend
mon mari	my husband

NOMS FÉMININS

une copine	a buddy, a friend
ma copine	my girlfriend, my friend
ma femme	my wife
la journée	the day

EXPRESSIONS VERBALES

aimer mieux	to like better, to prefer
aller au parc / à la gym	to go to the park / to the gym
arriver	to arrive
déjeuner	to have lunch, to eat lunch
demander	to ask (for)
manger dans un fast-food	to eat at a fast food restaurant
rentrer	to return, to go back (home)

EXPRESSIONS INTERROGATIVES

à quelle heure	at what time
avec qui	with whom
comment	how
où	where
pourquoi (parce que)	why (because)
quand	when
quel(s) jour(s)	(on) what / which day(s)
que (qu'est-ce que)	what
Qu'est-ce que c'est?	What is this/that/it?, What are these/those/they?
qui	who(m)
Qui est-ce?	Who is he/she/it/this/that?, Who are they?

DIVERS

avec moi/toi/nous/vous	with me/you/us/you
avec elle/elles	with her/them (f)
avec lui/eux	with him/them (m or mixed)
riche	rich
sauf	except
tout/toute/tous/toutes	all, whole, every
toute la journée	all day
typique	typical

COMPÉTENCE 4

Going to the café

NOMS MASCULINS

l'argent	money, silver
un café (au lait)	a coffee (with milk)
un centime	a cent
un chocolat (chaud)	a (hot) chocolate
un coca (light)	a (diet) Coke, a (diet) cola
un demi	a draft beer
un euro	a euro
un expresso	an espresso
un jus de fruit / d'orange	a fruit / an orange juice
un Orangina	an Orangina
un sandwich au fromage / au jambon	a cheese / ham sandwich
un serveur	a server
un thé (au citron)	a tea (with lemon)
un verre de vin blanc / rouge	a glass of white / red wine

NOMS FÉMININS

une bière	a beer
une boisson	a drink, a beverage
une eau minérale	a mineral water
des frites	(some) fries
la monnaie	the change
une serveuse	a server

NOMBRES

soixante, soixante et un...	sixty, sixty-one . . .
soixante-dix, soixante et onze...	seventy, seventy-one . . .
quatre-vingts, quatre-vingt-un...	eighty, eighty-one . . .
quatre-vingt-dix, quatre-vingt-onze...	ninety, ninety-one . . .
cent	one hundred

DIVERS

Ça fait combien?	How much is it?
Ça fait... euros.	That makes . . . euros.
C'est combien?	How much is it?
chaud(e)	hot
commander	to order (food and drink)
donner	to give
payer	to pay
Qu'est-ce que vous allez prendre?	What are you going to have?
Vous désirez?	What would you like?
Donnez-moi...	Give me . . .
Je vais prendre...	I'm going to have . . .
Je voudrais...	I would like . . .
Pour moi... s'il vous plaît.	For me . . . please.
voici	here is, here are
voilà	there is, there are
votre (vos)	your

Un nouvel appartement

Pair work	Video
Group work	Audio
Class work	

© Pete Ryan/National Geographic/Getty Images

LE MONDE FRANCOPHONE
Géoculture et Vidéo-voyage: En Amérique: Au Québec

COMPÉTENCE

GÉOCULTURE ET VIDÉO-VOYAGE:
EN AMÉRIQUE: AU QUÉBEC

LE QUÉBEC

NOMBRE D'HABITANTS: **8 215 000**

CAPITALE: **Québec**

The word **Québec** (without an article) refers to the city of Quebec and **le Québec** refers to the province.

Le français est la langue maternelle de 21 % (pour cent) de la population canadienne. Les francophones sont **surtout** concentrés dans la province du Québec, où le français est la langue maternelle de 78 % des habitants, mais il y a une présence francophone importante dans d'autres provinces, comme le Nouveau Brunswick, où 32 % de la population parle français. On parle aussi français **aux États-Unis** dans **plusieurs** communautés près de **la frontière** canadienne dans le Maine, le Vermont et le New Hampshire, **ainsi qu'**en Louisiane.

© Becky States/Shutterstock.com

© Alexandra Kobalenko/All Canada Photos/Getty Images

Plus vaste que l'Alaska, le Québec est **la plus grande** des provinces canadiennes et plus de 25 % de la population canadienne habite dans cette province. **Grâce aux grands espaces** de la province, les activités **de plein air y** sont très populaires, surtout les sports d'**hiver** comme le ski, le hockey et **le patinage.**

---

surtout *above all, especially*   **aux États-Unis** *in the United States*   **plusieurs** *several*   **la frontière** *the border*   **ainsi que** *as well as*   **la plus grande** *the largest*
Grâce aux grands espaces *Thanks to the wide open spaces*   **de plein air** *outdoor*   **y** *there*   **hiver** *winter*   **le patinage** *ice-skating*

Fondée en 1608, Québec est la plus vieille ville du Canada.

La ville de Québec est la capitale de la province **du même nom.** Il y a beaucoup de **choses** intéressantes à voir et à faire dans **cette** ville historique. Voudriez-vous dîner dans un restaurant ou aller danser dans une boîte de la Grande Allée?

La Grande Allée est une des rues les plus célèbres de Québec.

Montréal, grand centre culturel et commercial, est la plus grande ville de la province du Québec. À Montréal, il y a une ville **souterraine appelée** le RÉSO. Dans le RÉSO, il y a 30 kilomètres de tunnels et de galeries où **on trouve** des bureaux, des résidences de luxe, des centres commerciaux, des boutiques, des restaurants et des hôtels. Plus de 500 000 personnes utilisent le RÉSO tous les jours. C'est super en hiver!

Il y a de tout dans le RÉSO!

Le savez-vous?

Complétez les descriptions suivantes du Québec.

1. Le _____ est la plus grande province du Canada et plus de _____ % de la population canadienne y habite *(lives there)*. C'est la province francophone la plus importante du Canada!
2. _____ est la plus grande ville de la province du Québec.
3. _____ est la capitale de la province.
4. La _____ est une rue célèbre à Québec avec beaucoup de restaurants et de boîtes.
5. Le _____ est une ville souterraine à Montréal où on trouve de tout!

La ville *The city*   **du même nom** *of the same name*   **choses** *things*   **cette** *this*   **rues** *streets*   **célèbres** *famous*   **Fondée** *Founded*   **souterraine** *underground*
appelée *called*   **on trouve** *one finds*   **de tout** *all sorts of things*

AVANT LA VIDÉO

Vous allez visiter la ville de Québec à travers la vidéo. Pour vous aider à mieux comprendre, indiquez quelle image de la vidéo va avec chaque description.

1. Une vraie ville de hockey, ça c'est Québec.

2. L'art de recevoir *(hosting, receiving)*, ça c'est Québec.

3. Un musée à ciel ouvert *(An outdoor museum)*, ça c'est Québec.

4. Le goût des bonnes choses *(The taste of good things)*, ça c'est Québec.

5. Les grands événements *(events)* sportifs et les grands espaces *(wide open spaces)*, ça c'est Québec.

6. La Grande Allée, c'est juste à Québec.

a

b

c

d

e

f

Qu'est-ce qu'on voit *(see)* dans la vidéo quand on entend *(hears)* les choses suivantes?

1. Aujourd'hui, on va parler de *(we are going to talk about)* spectacles, on va parler de sport, on va parler de notre ville, de ce qui bouge *(what's going on)* ici.
   ☐ la télé ☐ la radio

2. L'art de recevoir, ça c'est Québec.
   ☐ un hôtel ☐ un restaurant

3. Le goût des bonnes choses, ça c'est Québec.
   ☐ un chef ☐ un musicien

4. Les grands événements sportifs et les grands espaces, ça c'est Québec.
   ☐ un match de foot ☐ une femme qui fait du vélo

5. Des projets plein la tête *(A head full of plans)*, ça c'est Québec.
   ☐ un musée ☐ un centre commercial

6. Foncer *(Going full force)*, ça c'est Québec.
   ☐ le hockey ☐ le football canadien

7. La Grande Allée, c'est juste à Québec.
   ☐ des musées ☐ des restaurants

8. La fierté *(pride)*, ça c'est Québec.
   ☐ une fontaine ☐ un monument

▶ APRÈS LA VIDÉO

Est-ce que les phrases suivantes sont vraies ou fausses?

1. La vidéo met l'accent sur *(stresses)* l'histoire de Québec.

2. La vidéo parle de Québec aujourd'hui.

3. La Grande Allée est une avenue avec beaucoup de restaurants.

4. Le sport est important à Québec.

5. À Québec, les gens n'aiment pas l'innovation parce que les traditions sont très importantes.

6. Les gens de Québec aiment beaucoup leur ville.

Talking about where you live

LE LOGEMENT

J'habite...	avec **un(e) colocataire** dans une maison
	avec un(e) camarade de chambre dans
	une résidence universitaire
	seul(e) dans un appartement
	dans un grand **immeuble**
	chez mes parents

Ma maison est...	grand(e) / petit(e)
Mon appartement est...	moderne / vieux (vieille)
Ma chambre est...	joli(e) et confortable
	(trop) cher (chère)

J'habite...	sur le campus	**dans le centre-ville**
	tout près de l'université	**en ville**
	(très / assez) **loin de** l'université	**en banlieue**
		à la campagne

| **Le loyer** est de... | 550 $ (cinq cent cinquante dollars) **par mois** |
| | 1 200 $ (mille deux cents dollars) |

Je n'ai pas de loyer!

Chez moi, il y a six **pièces** (*f*).

Vocabulaire supplémentaire

une buanderie / une lingerie *a laundry room*
une caravane *a travel trailer*
une cave *a cellar*
un duplex *a split-level apartment*
un garage *a garage*
un grenier *an attic*
un jardin *a yard, a garden*
un loft *a loft*
un mobile-home *a mobile home*
un prêt immobilier *a home loan*
une salle de jeux *a game room*
une salle de séjour *a family room, a den*
un studio *a studio apartment, an efficiency*
des W.-C. *(m) a restroom*

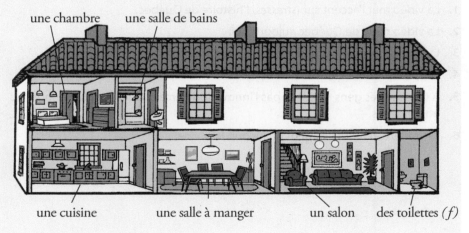

une chambre   une salle de bains

une cuisine   une salle à manger   un salon   des toilettes (*f*)

Sélection musicale. Search for the song **"Le temps de partir"** by Brigitte Boisjoli online to enjoy a musical selection related to this vocabulary.

Le logement *Lodging, Housing*   **un(e) colocataire** *a housemate, an apartment mate*   **un immeuble** *an apartment building*
trop *too*   **cher (chère)** *expensive*   **(tout) près (de)** *(very) near*   **loin (de)** *far (from)*   **dans le centre-ville** *downtown*
en ville *in town* (**une ville** *a city / town*)   **en banlieue** *in the suburbs*   **à la campagne** *in the country(side)*   **Le loyer** *The rent*
par mois *per month*   **Je n'ai pas** *I don't have*   **une pièce** *a room*

🔊 3-1 Adam, un jeune Français, **va** étudier à l'Université Laval, au Québec. Il **pense** habiter avec un ami américain, Robert, qui est aussi étudiant à l'Université Laval.

une fenêtre   l'ascenseur (m)   l'appartement de Robert
au troisième étage (3ᵉ)
au deuxième étage (2ᵉ)
au premier étage (1ᵉʳ) *on the second floor*
au rez-de-chaussée (R.d.C.) *on the first/ground floor*
au sous-sol *in the basement*
l'escalier (m)
la porte

ADAM: Où est-ce que tu habites?
ROBERT: J'habite dans un immeuble dans le centre-ville.
ADAM: **À quel étage?**
ROBERT: Mon appartement est au deuxième étage.
ADAM: Tu habites seul?
ROBERT: Non, j'habite avec mon ami Gabriel.
ADAM: L'université est loin de chez toi?
ROBERT: Non, pas très loin. Et il y a **un arrêt de bus** tout près. C'est très **pratique.**
ADAM: Et l'appartement est agréable?
ROBERT: Oui, j'aime beaucoup mon appartement. Il est assez grand et pas trop cher.

A **Et chez vous?** Complétez les phrases avec les mots en italique.

1. J'habite *dans un appartement / dans une maison / dans une chambre dans une résidence universitaire.*
2. *Mon appartement / Ma chambre / Ma maison* est *sur le campus / près de l'université / loin de l'université.*
3. *Il/Elle* est assez *grand(e) / petit(e)* et *agréable / désagréable.*
4. *Il/Elle* est *dans le centre-ville / en ville / en banlieue / à la campagne.*
5. *Il y a un arrêt de bus / Il n'y a pas d'arrêt de bus* tout près de chez moi.
6. Le loyer *est / n'est pas* trop cher.
7. Ma chambre est *au rez-de-chaussée / au premier étage / au deuxième étage / à un autre étage.*

B **Entretien.** Interviewez votre partenaire.

1. Est-ce que tu habites dans une maison, dans un appartement ou dans une résidence universitaire? Avec qui est-ce que tu habites?
2. Tu habites près de l'université, loin de l'université ou sur le campus? Est-ce que c'est pratique? Est-ce qu'il y a un arrêt de bus tout près de chez toi?
3. Préfères-tu habiter dans le centre-ville, en ville, en banlieue ou à la campagne?
4. Est-ce qu'il y a un escalier chez toi? Il y a un ascenseur?
5. Quelles pièces est-ce qu'il y a chez toi? Dans quelle pièce préfères-tu faire tes devoirs? regarder la télé? manger?

À VOUS!

Avec un(e) partenaire, relisez à haute voix la conversation entre Adam et Robert. Ensuite, adaptez la conversation pour décrire votre propre situation.

Note *culturelle*

Dans les immeubles en France et dans la plupart des pays francophones *(most French-speaking countries)*, faites attention: le premier étage est l'étage au-dessus du *(above the)* rez-de-chaussée. C'est-à-dire *(That is to say)* que le rez-de-chaussée correspond au *first floor / ground floor* aux USA et le premier étage correspond au *second floor.* Au Québec, on trouve *(one finds)* les deux manières d'indiquer les étages.

À quel étage est votre chambre / appartement?

---

va (aller *to go)*   **penser** *to think*   **À quel étage?** *On what floor?* **(un étage** *a floor* [of a building])   **un arrêt de bus** *a bus stop*   **pratique** *practical, convenient*

You can access the audio of the active vocabulary of this *Compétence* online.

GIVING PRICES AND OTHER NUMERICAL INFORMATION

✔ *Pour vérifier*

1. How do you say 100? 1,000? 1,000,000? Before which two of these numbers do you never put **un**?

2. How do you say 1,503? 12,612?

3. In the numbers 200, 2,000, and 2,000,000, which two words would have an **s**, **cent**, **mille**, or **million**? Which one of those words would drop the **s** if another number followed it?

4. Do you use a period or a comma to express decimals in French?

5. How do you say *first*? *fifth*? How do you say *on the* with a floor?

Vocabulaire supplémentaire

un milliard *one billion*
deux milliards *two billion*

Les nombres au-dessus de 100 et les nombres ordinaux

1. Here is how to say numbers over 100.

100 cent	**1 000** mille
101 cent un	**1 001** mille un
102 cent deux	**1 352** mille trois cent cinquante-deux
199 cent quatre-vingt-dix-neuf	**2 000** deux mille
200 deux cents	**602 511** six cent deux mille cinq cent onze
201 deux cent un	**1 000 000** un million

2. Do not use **un** with either **cent** or **mille**. **Cent** means *one hundred and* **mille** means *one thousand*. On the other hand, do say *un* **million**. Use **de (d')** after the word **million** whenever a noun follows it directly.

   cent habitants   **mille habitants**   **un million d'habitants**

3. **Cent** generally only takes an **s** when plural if not followed by another number. Never add an **s** to **mille**. **Million** takes an **s** in all numbers **deux millions** and higher.

   deux **cents** dollars   cinq **mille** habitants
   deux **cent** cinquante dollars   cinq **mille** cinquante habitants

   un **million** d'habitants
   cinq **millions** d'habitants

4. Traditionally, there is no hyphen between **cent, mille,** or **un million** and another number. This traditional spelling is the spelling used in the online activities in ***Horizons.***

   un million trois mille cinq cent quarante-cinq habitants

5. In France and in Quebec, a comma is used to denote decimals, and a space (or a period) is used after thousands or millions.

USA	FRANCE / QUÉBEC
1.5	1,5 (un virgule cinq)
1,000	1 000 *or* 1.000

6. Use **À quel étage?** to ask *On what floor?* To say *on the* with a floor, use **au.** When counting floors, use the ordinal numbers and remember that in many French-speaking countries, the first floor (**le premier étage**) is the floor above the ground floor (**le rez-de-chaussée**).

   —**À quel étage habitez-vous?**   —*What floor do you live on?*
   —**J'habite au troisième étage.**   —*I live on the third (fourth) floor.*

7. In French, to convert cardinal numbers *(two, three, four . . .)* to ordinal numbers *(second, third, fourth . . .),* add the suffix **-ième.** Drop a final **e** from cardinal numbers before adding **-ième.**

   deux → deuxième   **quatre → quatrième**   **mille → millième**

   These ordinal numbers are irregular: **premier (première), cinq*i*ème, neu*v*ième.**

Note *de grammaire*

Adjectives ending in **-er** like **premier** or **cher** take a grave accent mark in the feminine forms: **première, chère.**

A C'est combien? De combien est le loyer ou le prix de ces maisons?

EXEMPLE 900 $ neuf cents dollars

1. 865 $	**3.** 1 545 $	**5.** 999 599 $	**7.** 885 700 $
2. 490 $	**4.** 3 110 $	**6.** 248 525 $	**8.** 1 000 000 $

B Ça coûte combien? Choisissez un prix pour chaque article sur ce prospectus publicitaire *(flyer)*. Ensuite, comparez vos choix à ceux de votre partenaire.

EXEMPLE — Moi, je crois que *(think that)* le téléviseur de 40 pouces coûte… Et toi?
— Moi…

331,88$	349,50$	650,65$
999,99$	1 799,00$	2 499,99$

TÉLÉ À GRAND ÉCRAN — 40ᵖᵒ / 55ᵖᵒ / 60ᵖᵒ

ORDINATEUR PORTABLE ÉCRAN TACTILE — 15,6ᵖᵒ/2 Go / 17,3ᵖᵒ/8 Go

APPAREIL PHOTO NUMÉRIQUE + VIDÉO — écran 3ᵖᵒ

Photos Télé © K. Miri Photography/Shutterstock.com; Ordinateur portable © ifong/Shutterstock.com; Appareil photo © Masalski Maksim/Shutterstock.com; Graphic; © Cengage Learning

Note *de vocabulaire*

1. **Un téléviseur** is used when talking about a *TV set*.
2. In Quebec, the size of such things as TV screens is indicated in **pouces** *(inches)*, shown as **po.**
3. **Go** is short for **gigaoctet** *(gigabyte)*. You can find the words for the latest electronic devices at http://www.fnac.com.

C Chez Robert. Posez les questions suivantes à un(e) partenaire, qui répondra d'après *(will respond according to)* l'illustration.

1. À quel étage habitent Robert et son colocataire? Qu'est-ce qu'ils font *(What are they doing)*?
2. À quel étage habite la jeune femme qui écoute de la musique?
3. Où habitent les enfants? Qu'est-ce qu'ils font?
4. À quel étage est le vieux monsieur? Qu'est-ce qu'il fait *(What is he doing)*?
5. Il y a un ascenseur dans l'immeuble? Il y a un escalier?

l'appartement de Robert

D Le compte est bon. *Des chiffres* (Numerals) *et des lettres est* le plus ancien jeu télévisé *(the oldest game show)* en France. Les participants au jeu utilisent l'addition, la soustraction, la multiplication et la division de six nombres de 1 à 10, 25, 50, 75 ou 100 pour obtenir un nombre entre 100 et 999 en 45 secondes. Lisez les solutions des problèmes suivants.

+ (plus)   – (moins)   × (fois)   ÷ (divisé par)   = (font)

a. 3, 7, 8, 25, 50, 100 = 560
$3 \times 100 = 300$
$300 - 50 = 250$
$250 \times 8 = 2\ 000$
$2\ 000 \div 25 = 80$
$80 \times 7 = 560$

b. 1, 4, 5, 10, 25, 100 = 149
$5 \times 25 = 125$
$125 \times 4 = 500$
$500 \div 10 = 50$
$50 - 1 = 49$
$100 + 49 = 149$

POUR MIEUX LIRE: *Guessing meaning from context*

1. You can often guess the meaning of unknown words from context. Read this passage in its entirety, then guess the meaning of the boldfaced words.

   L'immeuble de Robert **se trouve** dans le centre-ville. Arrivé **devant** l'immeuble, Adam **entre,** il **monte** l'escalier et il **sonne** à la porte de l'appartement de son ami. Une jeune femme **ouvre** la porte. Après un instant, elle **ferme** la porte.

2. Some words may have different meanings in different contexts. For example, the word **bien** can mean *well* or it can be used for emphasis, meaning *indeed.* It may also be used in place of **très,** to mean *very.* Read the following sentences and use the context to decide if **bien** means *well, indeed,* or *very.*

   — Tu comprends **bien**?
   — Oui, mais c'est **bien** compliqué!

   — C'est **bien** ici que Robert habite?
   — Oui, c'est **bien** ça.

3. The word **même** can mean *self, same,* or *even.* Use the context to determine its meaning in the following sentences.

   Les prénoms Gabriel et Gabrielle se prononcent de la **même** manière.
   En France, le premier étage est au-dessus du *(above)* rez-de-chaussée, mais aux USA et au Québec, le rez-de-chaussée et le premier étage sont le **même** étage.
   Je travaille pour moi-**même.**
   C'est **même** plus compliqué que ça.

A **Selon le contexte.** The boldfaced word in each of the following sentences can have a different meaning, depending on the context. Can you guess the different meanings?

Bravo! **Encore! Encore!**
Ça, c'est **encore** plus compliqué.
Je suis au troisième étage, alors je descends **encore** d'un étage pour aller au deuxième?

B **Vous savez déjà...** You already know the boldfaced words in the first group of sentences. Guess the meaning of the boldfaced words in the last sentence, using the context.

Prenez du papier et un stylo.
Lisez le paragraphe.
Le cours de français **commence** à une heure.

La jeune femme **prend** le téléphone d'Adam, **lit** le texto de Robert et **commence** à comprendre la situation.

Lecture: *Un nouvel appartement*

3-2

Adam, un jeune Français, arrive devant l'immeuble où habitent Robert et son colocataire, Gabriel.

Adam regarde un texto de Robert et vérifie l'adresse. Il lit: «Mon appartement se trouve au 38, rue Dauphine. C'est un grand immeuble avec une porte bleue. J'habite au deuxième étage.» «Oui, c'est bien ça», pense-t-il. Il descend du taxi, entre dans l'immeuble et monte l'escalier.

Il sonne à la porte de l'appartement. Quelques instants après, une jolie jeune femme lui ouvre la porte.

— Euh... Bonjour, je suis Adam. C'est bien ici que Gabriel et Robert habitent?

— Gabrielle, c'est moi. Mais...

Adam, très surpris, l'interrompt:

— Gabriel, c'est vous? Euh... Mais vous êtes une femme.

— Eh oui, monsieur, comme vous le voyez, je suis une femme!

— Euh, je veux dire... Euh, excusez-moi. Maintenant, je comprends! C'est que je pensais rencontrer Gabriel, un homme et non pas Gabrielle, une femme. Excusez-moi. Alors, vous êtes Gabrielle. Et moi, je suis Adam, Adam Bertrand. Robert est là?

— Robert?, dit-elle d'un air surpris.

— Eh oui, Robert, mon ami. Il habite ici avec vous, non?

— Mais certainement pas! dit-elle d'un ton un peu énervé.

Quand elle essaie de fermer la porte, Adam s'exclame:

— Un instant, s'il vous plaît. Regardez! Voici l'adresse que mon ami m'a donnée. Elle prend le téléphone d'Adam, lit le texto et commence à comprendre.

— En fait oui, c'est bien ici le 38, rue Dauphine, mais vous êtes au *troisième* étage et votre ami habite au *deuxième* étage.

— Au deuxième étage? Ah! Oui, je comprends maintenant. En France, le premier étage est au-dessus du rez-de-chaussée, mais ici le rez-de-chaussée et le premier étage, c'est la même chose. Alors, je descends d'un étage pour trouver l'appartement de mon ami?

— Oui, c'est bien ça. Au revoir, et bienvenue au Québec, Adam!

— Au revoir, Gabrielle, et merci.

A Vrai ou faux?

1. Adam arrive au 38, rue Dauphine, l'adresse de son ami Robert.
2. Il monte directement à l'appartement de son ami.
3. Il sonne et Gabrielle, la jeune femme qui habite avec Robert, ouvre la porte.
4. Gabriel est un prénom masculin et Gabrielle est son *(its)* équivalent féminin en français.
5. Dans l'immeuble de Robert, on compte les étages comme en France.

B Compéhension. Répondez aux questions suivantes d'après la lecture.

1. Quelle est l'adresse de Robert?
2. Avec qui est-ce que Robert habite?
3. Robert et son colocataire habitent à quel étage?
4. Le deuxième étage aux USA et quelquefois au Québec correspond à quel étage en France?
5. Qui habite au troisième étage de l'immeuble de Robert?
6. Est-ce que Robert habite avec un homme qui s'appelle Gabriel ou une femme qui s'appelle Gabrielle?

Talking about your possessions

DANS LE SALON

Vocabulaire supplémentaire

une cuisinière *a stove*
un lave-linge *a washer*
un lave-vaisselle *a dishwasher*
un lecteur MP3 *an MP3 player*
un (four à) micro-ondes *a microwave (oven)*
une moto *a motorcycle*
un réfrigérateur (un frigo)
un sèche-linge *a dryer*
une table basse *a coffee table*

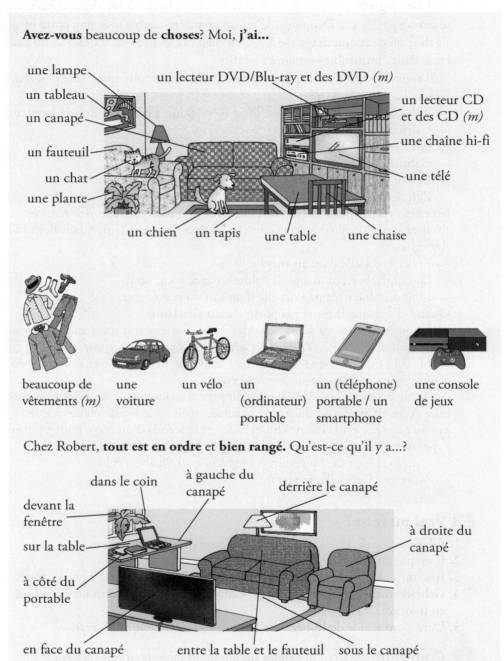

Avez-vous beaucoup de **choses**? Moi, **j'ai...**

une lampe
un tableau
un canapé
un fauteuil
un chat
une plante

un lecteur DVD/Blu-ray et des DVD *(m)*
un lecteur CD et des CD *(m)*
une chaîne hi-fi
une télé

un chien   un tapis   une table   une chaise

beaucoup de vêtements *(m)*   une voiture   un vélo   un (ordinateur) portable   un (téléphone) portable / un smartphone   une console de jeux

Chez Robert, **tout est en ordre** et **bien rangé.** Qu'est-ce qu'il y a...?

dans le coin
à gauche du canapé
derrière le canapé
devant la fenêtre
sur la table
à côté du portable
à droite du canapé
en face du canapé   entre la table et le fauteuil   sous le canapé

Avez-vous (avoir *to have*)   **une chose** *a thing*   **j'ai (avoir** *to have*)   **tout est en ordre** *everything is in order*
bien rangé(e) *neat, put away, straightened up*

🔊 Avant d'arriver au Québec, Adam **cherche** un appartement. Il téléphone à Robert.

ROBERT: Tu cherches un appartement ici à Québec? Écoute, tu sais, moi, je **partage** un appartement avec mon ami Gabriel. **Nous avons** trois chambres; tu voudrais habiter avec nous?

ADAM: **Peut-être.** Comment est **ton** appartement?

ROBERT: Il est assez grand et confortable, mais pas trop cher. Tu aimes les animaux?

ADAM: Oui, pourquoi? **Tu as** des animaux?

ROBERT: Gabriel **a** un chien et un chat. Ils sont quelquefois **embêtants** et ils aiment dormir **partout.**

ADAM: Pas de problème. J'aime bien les animaux. Vous **fumez**?

ROBERT: Non, je ne fume pas et Gabriel **non plus.**

ADAM: Bon, moi non plus. Alors, ça va.

A Cherchez l'intrus! Quel objet de chaque liste ne va pas logiquement à l'endroit *(place)* indiqué?

EXEMPLE sur la table: un portable / une console de jeux / un vélo / des livres

Sur la table, il y a un portable, une console de jeux et des livres, mais il n'y a pas de vélo!

1. sur la table: un lecteur DVD / un portable / un fauteuil / une lampe
2. devant la fenêtre: une table / un tableau / une chaise / une plante
3. dans le salon: un canapé / un lit / un lecteur CD / un chat / une lampe
4. dans la chambre: des vêtements / un chien / un lecteur DVD / une voiture / une télé

B Qu'est-ce qu'il y a? Regardez l'illustration du salon de Robert en bas de *(at the bottom of)* la page précédente. Qu'est-ce qu'il y a à chaque endroit *(place)*?

EXEMPLE sur la table

Il y a des livres et un portable sur la table.

1. devant la fenêtre
2. en face du canapé
3. derrière le canapé
4. à droite du canapé
5. dans le coin
6. sous la plante
7. à côté des livres
8. entre le fauteuil et la table
9. sous le canapé

C Entretien. Interviewez votre partenaire.

1. Tu as beaucoup de choses chez toi? Qu'est-ce qu'il y a dans le salon?
2. En général, est-ce que tout est en ordre et bien rangé dans ta chambre?
3. Est-ce que tu aimes les animaux? Tu as des animaux? Tu préfères les chiens ou les chats?
4. Est-ce que tu fumes?

À VOUS!

Avec un(e) partenaire, relisez à haute voix la conversation entre Robert et Adam. Ensuite, imaginez que votre partenaire veuille *(wants)* habiter chez vous. Adaptez la conversation pour décrire votre situation.

---

chercher *to look for*   **partager** *to share*   **Nous avons (avoir** *to have*)   **Peut-être** *Maybe, Perhaps*
ton/ta/tes *your* (familiar)   **Tu as (avoir** *to have*)   **a (avoir** *to have*)   **embêtant(e)** *annoying*
partout *everywhere*   **fumer** *to smoke*   **non plus** *neither*

You can access the audio of the active vocabulary of this ***Compétence*** online.

SAYING WHAT YOU HAVE

Le verbe *avoir*

✔ **Pour vérifier**

1. What does **avoir** mean? What are its forms? Why might one confuse the **tu, il/elle/on,** and **ils/elles** forms of **avoir** *(to have)* with those of **être** *(to be)*?

2. What does the indefinite article **(un, une, des)** change to after expressions of quantity such as **combien** or **beaucoup**? When else does this change occur?

3. Which of these nouns would have a plural ending with **-x** instead of **-s: un hôpital, un animal, un tableau, un bureau, une table, un canapé**?

1. To say what someone has, use the verb **avoir.** Its conjugation is irregular.

AVOIR *(to have)*	
j'**ai**	nous <u>z</u> **avons**
tu **as**	vous <u>z</u> **avez**
il/elle/on **a**	ils/elles <u>z</u> **ont**

2. Remember to use **de (d')** rather than **des** after **combien** *(how much, how many)*, as you do after other quantity expressions like **beaucoup** and **assez.** Also remember to use **de (d')** instead of **un, une,** or **des** after most negated verbs other than **être.**

AFFIRMATIVE	NEGATIVE	AFTER A QUANTITY EXPRESSION
J'ai **des** chats.	Je n'ai pas **de** chats.	Combien **de** chats as-tu?
After **être:**		
C'est **un** chat.	Ce n'est pas **un** chat.	C'est beaucoup **de** chats.

3. Although the plural of most nouns and adjectives is formed by adding **-s,** words ending in **-eau, -au,** or **-eu** usually form their plural with **-x.** Words ending in **-al** often change this ending to **-aux** in the plural. Acronyms like **DVD** and **CD** do not add **-s** in the plural.

un tableau	un bureau	un animal	un CD	un DVD
des tableau**x**	des bureau**x**	des anim**aux**	des CD	des DVD

Vocabulaire sans peine!

Many adjectives ending in *-al* in English have French cognates with masculine plural forms ending in **-aux.**

régional → **régionaux**

How would you say these words in French? What would their masculine plural forms be?

normal
horizontal
vertical

PRONONCIATION

Avoir et Être
3-4

Be careful to pronounce the forms of the verbs **avoir** and **être** distinctly. Open your mouth wide to pronounce the **a** in **tu as** and **il/elle a.** Contrast this with the vowel sound in **es** and **est.** Pronounce **ils sont** with an **s** sound, and the liaison in **ils ont** with a **z** sound.

ÊTRE: Tu es professeur.
     Elle est professeur.
     Ils sont professeurs.

AVOIR: Tu as beaucoup de cours.
      Elle a beaucoup de cours.
      Ils <u>z</u> ont beaucoup de cours.

3-5
A Prononcez bien! Une amie pose les questions suivantes à Adam.
Vous entendrez *(will hear)* le sujet et un verbe. Si c'est une forme d'**avoir**, complétez la première phrase. Si c'est une forme d'**être**, complétez la deuxième phrase.

EXEMPLE VOUS ENTENDEZ: Tu as
          VOUS COMPLÉTEZ: AVOIR: Tu __as__ combien de colocataires?
                    ÊTRE: Tu ____ le colocataire de Robert et Gabriel?

1. AVOIR: Tu _____ un appartement ou une chambre dans une résidence à l'université?
    ÊTRE: Tu _____ étudiant à l'Université Laval?

2. AVOIR: Ton appartement _____ combien de chambres?

ÊTRE: Ton appartement _____ près de l'université?

3. AVOIR: Il _____ beaucoup de fenêtres?

ÊTRE: Il _____ à quel étage?

4. AVOIR: Tes colocataires _____ beaucoup de choses?

ÊTRE: Tes colocataires _____ étudiants aussi?

5. AVOIR: Ils _____ des animaux?

ÊTRE: Ils _____ canadiens ou américains?

B **Oui ou non?** Vous cherchez un nouveau logement. Complétez ces textos d'autres étudiants qui cherchent un(e) colocataire avec la forme correcte du verbe **avoir**. Ensuite, dites si vous désirez habiter avec ces personnes. Répondez **oui**, **non** ou **peut-être**.

> Nous _____ un très bel appartement et le loyer n'est pas trop élévé (*high*). Les chambres _____ beaucoup de fenêtres et une belle vue.

> Tu aimes les animaux? J'_____ trois colocataires et ils _____ neuf chats.

> Mon colocataire _____ beaucoup d'amis qui fument dans l'appartement.

> Tu _____ une voiture? Mon immeuble n'_____ pas de parking.

> J'_____ un appartement. Il est au cinquième étage, mais nous _____ deux nouveaux ascenseurs.

> L'immeuble n'_____ pas assez d'eau chaude (*hot water*), mais le loyer est de seulement (*only*) deux cents dollars par mois et j'_____ un très joli appartement.

Photo: © Leszek Kobusinski/Shutterstock.com

C **Combien?** Demandez à votre partenaire **combien de** ces choses les personnes indiquées ont.

EXEMPLE ton meilleur ami (ta meilleure amie): cours ce semestre / trimestre

— **Ton meilleur ami (Ta meilleure amie) a combien de cours ce semestre / trimestre?**

— **Il/Elle a quatre cours.**
Je ne sais pas combien de cours il/elle a.
Il/Elle n'a pas de cours.

1. tu: ordinateurs chez toi

2. tu: amis sur Facebook

3. tes amis: photos de toi sur Facebook

4. tes amis: temps libre le week-end

5. ton meilleur ami (ta meilleure amie) cours avec toi

6. ton meilleur ami et toi (ta meilleure amie et toi), vous: amis en commun (*in common, mutual*)

D **Être ou avoir?** Complétez les questions suivantes avec le verbe **être** dans l'espace logique et la forme correcte d'**avoir** dans l'autre espace. Ensuite, interviewez un(e) partenaire en faisant attention à la prononciation.

EXEMPLE Tu **es** souvent sur le campus quand tu n'**as** pas cours?

1. Où est-ce que tu habites? Tu _____ chez tes parents ou tu _____ un appartement, une maison ou une chambre dans une résidence universitaire?

2. Tu _____ beaucoup de place dans ta chambre ou ta chambre _____ petite?

3. Le quartier _____ beaucoup de restaurants et de cafés ou il _____ loin de tout?

4. Et tes amis, ils _____ souvent chez toi quand ils _____ du temps libre?

5. Et toi, tu _____ libre en général quand tu n' _____ pas cours?

SAYING WHERE SOMETHING IS

✔ *Pour vérifier*

1. How do you say *on? under? facing? next to?*

2. What does the preposition **de** mean? With which two forms of the definite article does it combine to form **du** and **des?**

Quelques prépositions

1. You can use the following prepositions to tell where something or someone is. Note that the prepositions in the right column end with **de** when they are followed by a noun, but those in the left column do not.

J'habite **derrière** la bibliothèque.　　J'habite **à côté de** la bibliothèque.
I live behind the library.　　　　　　*I live next to the library.*

De is not used when there is not a noun after the preposition.

J'habite à côté.　　*I live next door.*

sur *on*	**près (de)** *near*
sous *under*	**loin (de)** *far (from)*
entre *between*	**à côté (de)** *next to, beside*
dans *in*	**à droite (de)** *to the right (of)*
devant *in front of*	**à gauche (de)** *to the left (of)*
derrière *behind*	**en face (de)** *across (from), facing*
	dans le coin (de) *in the corner (of)*

2. The preposition **de** *(of, from, about),* which is used as part of some of the prepositions above, contracts with the forms of the definite article **le** and **les,** to become **du** and **des.** It does not change when followed by **la** or **l'.**

CONTRACTIONS WITH *DE*			
de + le	→	du	J'habite près **du** centre-ville.
de + la	→	de la	La salle de cours est près **de la** bibliothèque.
de + l'	→	de l'	Mon appartement est près **de l'**université.
de + les	→	des	Il n'y a pas de parking près **des** résidences.

PRONONCIATION

De, du, des 3-6

Be careful to pronounce **de, du,** and **des** distinctly.

- As you know, the **e** in words like **de, le,** and **ne** is pronounced with the lips slightly puckered. The tongue is held firm in the lower part of the mouth.
- The **u** in **du,** as in **tu,** is pronounced with the tongue arched firmly near the roof of the mouth, like the French vowel **i** in **il,** but with the lips puckered.
- The vowel in **des** is a sharp sound like the **é** in **café,** pronounced with the corners of the lips spread.

A **Prononcez bien!** D'abord, complétez ces phrases avec la forme correcte de la préposition **de (de, d', du, de la, de l', des).** Ensuite, lisez les phrases à haute voix *(aloud)* en faisant attention à la prononciation et dites si chaque phrase est vraie ou fausse.

1. La salle de cours est près _____ ascenseur.

2. Je suis assis(e) *(am seated)* à gauche _____ porte.

3. La porte est près _____ moi.

4. Le professeur est en face _____ un ordinateur.

5. Il y a un tableau en face _____ étudiants.

6. Le professeur est près _____ tableau.

7. Il y a des fenêtres à droite _____ étudiants.

B **Descriptions.** Faites des phrases pour décrire ce salon.

     EXEMPLE les livres / la table
               Les livres sont sur la table.

1. le chat / la table
2. la télé / le fauteuil
3. les plantes / la télé
4. le chien / le fauteuil et la télé
5. le chien / le fauteuil
6. la porte / le fauteuil
7. les livres / l'ordinateur
8. l'ordinateur / la table
9. l'escalier / les tableaux

 C **Qui est-ce?** Utilisez trois prépositions pour indiquer où un(e) des étudiant(e)s de votre classe est assis(e) *(is seated)* et les autres étudiants devineront *(will guess)* qui est la personne décrite.

     EXEMPLE — **Elle est assise près de la fenêtre. Elle est à droite de Brent et elle est derrière Catherine.**
                  — **C'est Julie?**
                  — **Oui.**

D **À vendre.** Avec un(e) partenaire, préparez au moins huit phrases décrivant cette maison.

     EXEMPLE **Quand vous entrez** *(enter)* **dans la maison, les toilettes sont à gauche de la porte et le bureau est à droite. Derrière les toilettes, il y a...**

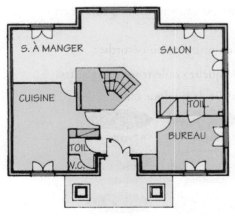
au rez-de-chaussée

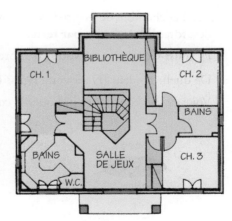
au premier étage

Maintenant, dessinez *(draw)* votre maison idéale. Décrivez cette maison à votre partenaire, qui va la dessiner selon votre description *(who will draw it from your description)*.

Describing your room

LES MEUBLES ET LES COULEURS

Robert **montre** les chambres à Adam.

un poster · un placard · une commode · des rideaux *(m)* · un bureau · un lit · un tapis · une étagère

Voici **ma** chambre. **Les murs** *(m)* sont beiges et le tapis et les rideaux sont bleus. **La couverture** est bleue, rouge et verte.

Ma chambre est toujours **propre** et en ordre. Tout est **à sa place.**

Voici la chambre de Gabriel. **Sa** chambre est souvent un peu **sale** et en désordre. Il **laisse** tout **par terre.**

Et vous? Comment est votre chambre, en ordre ou en désordre?

De quelle couleur *(f)* est votre tapis? De quelle couleur sont vos murs?

Voici des adjectifs pour indiquer la couleur de quelque chose.

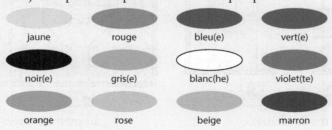

jaune · rouge · bleu(e) · vert(e)
noir(e) · gris(e) · blanc(he) · violet(te)
orange · rose · beige · marron

Les meubles *Furniture, Furnishings* **montrer** *to show* **mon/ma/mes** *my* **un mur** *a wall* **une couverture** *a (bed)cover, a blanket* **propre** *clean* **à sa place** *in its place* **son/sa/ses** *his, her, its* **sale** *dirty* **laisser** *to leave* **par terre** *on the floor, on the ground*

3-7

Robert montre les chambres à Adam.

ROBERT: Voici la chambre de Gabriel, à côté de la cuisine. Sa chambre est toujours en désordre. Il laisse ses vêtements partout.

ADAM: C'est ta chambre en face de la chambre de Gabriel?

ROBERT: Oui, **comme tu vois,** je préfère avoir tout bien rangé et **chaque chose** à sa place.

ADAM: Et ça, c'est ma chambre **au bout du couloir**?

ROBERT: Oui, **viens voir...** Tu as un lit, un bureau et une grande fenêtre avec **une** belle **vue.** J'**espère** que **ça te plaît.**

ADAM: Oui, merci, **ça a l'air bien**!

ROBERT: Les murs sont blancs. Tu préfères une autre couleur?

ADAM: Non, **justement,** le blanc, c'est ma couleur **préférée.**

ROBERT: Moi, je préfère le vert.

A **Chez vous?** **Décrivez votre chambre en choisissant l'adverbe qui convient.**

(presque) toujours   souvent   quelquefois
rarement   ne... (presque) jamais

EXEMPLE Ma chambre est en ordre.
Ma chambre est presque toujours en ordre.
Ma chambre n'est presque jamais en ordre.

1. Ma chambre est propre.
2. Ma chambre est en désordre.
3. Mes livres sont sur l'étagère.
4. Mes vêtements sont par terre.
5. Mes livres sont sur le lit.
6. Je laisse mes vêtements partout.
7. Mes vêtements sont dans le placard ou dans la commode.

B **Les couleurs des choses.** **Complétez les phases suivantes avec le nom d'une couleur.**

1. Ma couleur préférée, c'est le...
2. J'ai beaucoup de vêtements...
3. Les murs de ma chambre sont...
4. La couverture de mon lit est...
5. Les rideaux de ma chambre sont...
6. Ma voiture est...
7. Chez moi, le canapé est...
8. Le tapis de la salle de bains est...

À VOUS!

Avec un(e) partenaire, relisez à haute voix la conversation entre Robert et Adam. Ensuite, imaginez que votre partenaire va habiter *(is going to live)* chez vous et adaptez la conversation pour décrire votre propre maison / appartement.

---

comme tu vois *as you see*   **chaque chose** *each thing*   **au bout de** *at the end of*   **le couloir** *the hall, the corridor*   **viens voir** *come see*   **une vue** *a view*   **espérer** *to hope*   **ça te plaît** *you like it*   **ça a l'air bien** *it seems nice*   **justement** *as a matter of fact, precisely, exactly*   **préféré(e)** *favorite*

You can access the audio of the active vocabulary of this *Compétence* online.

DESCRIBING THINGS

✔ *Pour vérifier*

1. Are most adjectives placed before or after the noun they describe?

2. What are 15 adjectives that are placed before the noun they describe?

3. Where do you place ordinal numbers like **premier (première)** or **deuxième**?

4. What does **seul(e)** mean when it is placed before the noun? after the noun?

5. What are the alternate masculine singular forms of **beau, nouveau,** and **vieux**? When are they used?

La place de l'adjectif

1. In French, most descriptive adjectives, including colors, are placed *after* the noun they describe.

un quartier moderne   une chambre agréable   des murs blancs

2. However, these 15 very common adjectives are placed *before* the noun.

beau (belle)	jeune	bon(ne)	grand(e)	autre
joli(e)	vieux (vieille)	mauvais(e)	petit(e)	même
	nouveau (nouvelle)	meilleur(e) gentil(le)	gros(se)	seul(e) *(only)*

un joli quartier   une grande chambre   de beaux murs

3. All cardinal and ordinal numbers are also placed before nouns.

la première porte   la quatrième maison   les trois chambres

4. The adjective **gentil(le)** may be placed before or after the noun, and **seul(e)** changes meaning depending on its placement. It means *only* or *sole* when placed before the noun, but *alone* when placed after the noun.

un **gentil** colocataire *a nice housemate*   un **seul** homme *only one man*
un colocataire **gentil** *a nice housemate*   un homme **seul** *a man alone*

5. The adjectives **beau, nouveau,** and **vieux** have alternate masculine singular forms, **bel, nouvel,** and **vieil,** which are used before nouns beginning with a vowel sound.

MASCULINE SINGULAR *(plus consonant sound)*	MASCULINE SINGULAR *(plus vowel sound)*	FEMININE SINGULAR
un beau canapé	un **bel** appartement	une belle maison
un nouveau canapé	un **nouvel** appartement	une nouvelle maison
un vieux canapé	un **vieil** appartement	une vieille maison

6. The plural indefinite article **des** changes to **de (d')** when a plural adjective is placed between it and the following noun. **Un** and **une** do not change before singular adjectives.

Tu as **un beau** salon avec **de grandes** fenêtres.
Je voudrais avoir **d'autres** rideaux et **un autre** canapé.

Note *de grammaire*

Remember to use the definite article **(le, la, l', les)** when making generalizations about a whole category of things, as when talking about what type of things you like or prefer. The articles **le, la, l',** and **les** do not change to **de.**

Je préfère **les** vieilles maisons. Je n'aime pas beaucoup **les** maisons modernes.

A **Chez Adam.** Complétez chaque question avec un adjectif *antonyme* de l'adjectif en italique. Notez que ces adjectifs sont placés *après* le nom *(noun)*.

EXEMPLE Tu habites dans une rue *(street) agréable* ou c'est un quartier **désagréable**?

1. Il y a beaucoup de choses *intéressantes* à faire dans le quartier ou c'est un quartier _____?

2. Tu as des colocataires *célibataires* ou c'est un couple _____?

3. Ce sont des gens *extravertis* qui aiment faire des choses avec toi ou ce sont des gens _____ qui restent dans leur *(their)* chambre?

4. Tu as une chambre *propre* ou une chambre _____ et en désordre?

Maintenant, complétez ces questions avec un adjectif *antonyme* de l'adjectif en italique. Notez que ces adjectifs sont placés *avant* le nom.

EXEMPLE Tu as une *grande* chambre ou c'est une **petite** chambre?

5. Tu as de *bons* ou de _____ colocataires?

6. Tes colocataires sont de *vieux* amis ou ce sont de _____ amis?

7. Robert est un *jeune* homme ou c'est un _____ homme?

8. Les parents de tes colocataires habitent dans le *même* quartier ou ils sont dans un _____ quartier?

B **Adam et ses amis.** Complétez les descriptions en mettant la forme correcte de l'un des adjectifs entre parenthèses avant le nom en italique et la forme correcte de l'autre après le nom.

EXEMPLE J'ai une *voiture*. (rouge, petit)
J'ai une **petite voiture rouge**.

1. Mon appartement est dans un *immeuble* dans le centre-ville. (beige, vieux)

2. J'ai un *appartement*. (confortable, nouveau)

3. J'ai deux *colocataires*. (nouveau, sportif)

4. Ils ont beaucoup d'*amis*. (bon, sympa)

5. Les parents de Gabriel ont une *maison* en banlieue. (confortable, petit)

6. Dans le salon, ils ont beaucoup de *meubles*. (cher, vieux)

7. Ils ont un *canapé* dans la salle de jeux *(game room)*. (nouveau, rouge et blanc)

8. Gabriel a un *frère*. (désagréable, petit)

C **Chez toi.** Mettez l'équivalent français de l'adjectif indiqué avant ou après le nom en italique et posez la question à votre partenaire. N'oubliez pas *(Don't forget to)* d'utiliser **de** au lieu de *(instead of)* **des** s'il y a un adjectif pluriel avant le nom.

EXEMPLE Tu as des *profs* avec beaucoup d'expérience ce semestre / trimestre? *(old)*
— **Tu as de vieux profs avec beaucoup d'expérience ce semestre / trimestre?**
— **J'ai de vieux profs mais j'ai aussi de jeunes profs.**
J'ai un vieux prof mais mes autres profs sont jeunes.
Non, je n'ai pas de vieux profs ce semestre / trimestre.

1. Tu as des *profs* ce semestre / trimestre? *(good)*

2. Tu as beaucoup de *cours* ce semestre / trimestre? *(interesting)*

3. Dans quels cours est-ce que tu as beaucoup d'*examens*? *(difficult)*

4. Tu as beaucoup d'amis qui étudient à l'*université*? *(same)*

5. Il y a des *restaurants* dans le quartier universitaire où tu aimes manger? *(good)*

6. C'est un *quartier* où tu aimes passer ton temps? *(pleasant)*

7. Tu as un *logement* près du campus? *(comfortable)*

8. Tu as une *voiture*? *(new)*

IDENTIFYING YOUR BELONGINGS

✔ Pour vérifier

1. How do you say *Gabriel's dog* and *Emma's car* in French?

2. With which two forms of the definite article does **de** combine to form the contractions **du** and **des**?

3. How would you say *the living room's rug* and *the students' rent* in French?

4. Which of the following possessive adjectives have different singular forms for masculine and feminine nouns when translated into French: *my, your* (singular, familiar), *his/her/its, our, your* (singular, formal or plural), *their*?

5. When do you use **mon, ton,** and **son**, instead of **ma, ta,** and **sa** before a feminine noun?

6. Does French have different words for *his, her,* and *its*? How do you say *his house* and *her house* in French? How do you say *his desk* and *her desk*?

La possession et les adjectifs possessifs

1. In French, use a phrase with **de,** rather than *'s* to indicate possession or relationship. Remember that **de** contracts with the articles **le** and **les** to form **du** and **des.** It does not change when followed by **la** or **l'.**

That's my housemate**'s** dog.	C'est le chien **de** mon colocataire.
That's the closet**'s** door.	C'est la porte **du** placard.
They are Gabriel**'s** friends**'** DVDs.	Ce sont les DVD **des** amis **de** Gabriel.

2. Use the following possessive adjectives to indicate to whom something belongs. The possessive adjectives **mon/ma/mes** *(my)*, **ton/ta/tes** *(your* [singular familiar]), and **son/sa/ses** *(his, her, its)* agree in gender and number with the noun that follows them. The forms **mon, ton,** and **son** are used both before singular masculine nouns and before singular feminine nouns beginning with vowels. The possessive adjectives **notre/nos** *(our)*, **votre/vos** *(your* [formal or plural]), and **leur/leurs** *(their)* have only two forms, singular and plural.

	MASCULINE SINGULAR	FEMININE SINGULAR *(plus consonant sound)*	FEMININE SINGULAR *(plus vowel sound)*	PLURAL
my	**mon** lit	**ma** chambre	**mon** amie	**mes** livres
your (sing. fam.)	**ton** lit	**ta** chambre	**ton** amie	**tes** livres
his, her, its	**son** lit	**sa** chambre	**son** amie	**ses** livres
our	**notre** lit	**notre** chambre	**notre** amie	**nos** livres
your (pl./form.)	**votre** lit	**votre** chambre	**votre** amie	**vos** livres
their	**leur** lit	**leur** chambre	**leur** amie	**leurs** livres

— J'aime bien **votre** salon. **Vos** amis passent beaucoup de temps ici?
— Non, en général, nous sommes dans **nos** chambres.
— C'est **la télé de Robert**?
— Non, ce n'est pas **sa** télé. C'est **ma** télé et ce sont **mes** DVD aussi.

3. **Son/sa/ses** can all mean *his, her,* or *its.* Their use depends on the gender and number of the object possessed, not the person who owns it.

C'est **son** fauteuil. C'est **son** fauteuil. Et c'est aussi **son** fauteuil.

PRONONCIATION

La voyelle **o** de **notre / votre** et de **nos / vos**   3-8

Compare the **o** sounds in **notre / votre** and **nos / vos.** The lips are puckered to make both of these sounds and the tongue is held firm, but the **o** in **nos / vos** is pronounced with the back of the tongue arched higher in the mouth than for the **o** in **notre** and **votre.** The letter **o** is pronounced with the sound of **nos** when it is the last sound in a word, when it is followed by an **s,** or when it is written **ô.** Otherwise, it is pronounced with the more open sound of **notre.**

notre chien / nos chiens   votre chat / vos chats

A **Prononcez bien!** Vous visitez la nouvelle maison de vos amis. Formez la phrase la plus logique avec **votre** ou **vos** pour faire des *compliments*. Faites attention à la prononciation de la voyelle **o**.

EXEMPLE meubles (j**o**lis, laids)
Vos meubles sont jolis.

1. loyer (écon**o**mique / tr**o**p cher)
2. salon (conf**o**rtable / désagréable)
3. plantes (j**o**lies / laides)
4. tapis (de b**o**nne qualité / de mauvaise qualité)
5. fenêtres (tr**o**p sales / très pr**o**pres)
6. chien (ad**o**rable / embêtant)

B **C'est à moi!** Un locataire change d'appartement et il voudrait tout prendre avec lui *(him)*, mais l'autre locataire n'est pas d'accord. Jouez les rôles avec un(e) partenaire.

EXEMPLE la plante
— **Bon, je prends** *(I'm taking)* **ma plante.**
— **Ah non, ce n'est pas ta plante. C'est ma plante!**

1. le bureau
2. les rideaux
3. le poster
4. la commode
5. l'étagère
6. les chiens

C **Préférences.** Demandez à un(e) partenaire s'il / si elle aime ces choses. Utilisez **son/sa/ses** ou **leur/leurs** dans les réponses.

EXEMPLES la musique d'Adèle
— **Est-ce que tu aimes la musique d'Adèle?**
— **Oui, J'aime bien sa musique.**
   Non, je n'aime pas sa musique.
   Je ne connais pas *(I am not familiar with)* **sa musique.**

la musique du groupe Coldplay
— **Est-ce que tu aimes la musique du groupe Coldplay?**
— **Oui, j'aime bien leur musique.**
   Non, je n'aime pas leur musique.
   Je ne connais pas leur musique.

1 la musique du groupe Maroon 5
2. les vidéos de Taylor Swift
3. la musique de Carrie Underwood
4. les vieilles chansons *(songs)* des Beatles
5. les livres de J. K. Rowling
6. les films avec Will Ferrell

D **Quelle université?** Comparez votre université avec une autre université dans votre région ou avec une université connue *(well-known)*. Formez des phrases avec **notre/nos** et **leur/leurs**.

EXEMPLE campus / beau
Leur campus est plus beau que notre campus.
Notre campus est plus beau que leur campus.
Leur campus est aussi beau que notre campus.

1. campus / grand
2. cours / chers
3. étudiants / sympas
4. professeurs / intéressants
5. campus / moderne

© Dave G. Houser/Alamy Stock Photo

Giving your address and phone number

DES RENSEIGNEMENTS

Pour **s'inscrire** à l'université, Robert **doit** donner **les renseignements** *(m)* **suivants.**

Quel est votre nom de famille?	Martin.
Quel est votre prénom?	Robert.
Quelle est votre adresse?	C'est le 215, Ursuline St.
Quelle est votre (adresse) mail?	RobMart@airmail.net.
Quel est votre numéro de téléphone?	C'est le (337) 988–1284.
Dans quel pays habitez-vous?	Les États-Unis.
Quel État? (Quelle province?)	La Louisiane.
Quelle ville?	Lafayette.
Quelle est votre nationalité?	Américaine.

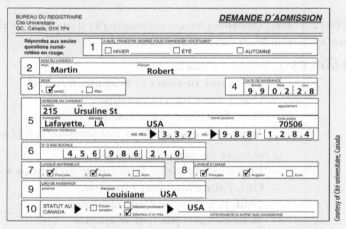

Robert parle de son appartement et son ami Alex lui **pose des questions.**

ALEX: Quelle est ton adresse?

ROBERT: C'est le 38, **rue** *(f)* Dauphine.

ALEX: Et c'est quel appartement?

ROBERT: C'est le numéro 231.

ALEX: Et le code postal?

ROBERT: G1K 7X2.

ALEX: Quel est ton numéro de téléphone?

ROBERT: C'est le 692-2691.

ALEX: Et il est comment, le quartier?

ROBERT: Il est agréable et près de tout.

ALEX: L'appartement n'est pas trop cher? C'est combien, le loyer?

ROBERT: Je partage mon appartement avec deux amis. C'est 825 dollars par mois, partagés entre nous trois. Alors pour moi, ça fait 275 dollars.

---

s'inscrire *to register*   **doit (devoir** *must, to have to)*   **les renseignements** *information*   **suivant(e)** *following*
poser une question *to ask a question*   **une rue** *a street*

A **Quelques statistiques.** Trouvez la réponse à chaque question dans la liste.

> 01   Jean   la Louisiane, le Maine, le New Hampshire et le Vermont
> Marie   Martin, Bernard et Dubois   *Orange, Outlook* et *Google Gmail*
> le Québec   rue de l'Église

1. Quel est le prénom féminin le plus courant *(the most common)* en France?

2. Quel est le prénom masculin le plus courant en France?

3. Quels sont les trois noms de famille les plus courants en France?

4. Quel est le nom de rue le plus courant dans les adresses en France et au Québec?

5. Quelle est la plus grande province canadienne en superficie *(area)*?

6. Quels sont les quatre États aux États-Unis avec le plus grand nombre de francophones?

7. Quels noms de services mail trouve-t-on le plus souvent dans les adresses mail en France?

8. Les numéros de téléphone portable en France commencent par 06 ou 07. Les numéros de téléphone de ligne fixe à Paris commencent par quels numéros?

🔊 3-10   **B**   **Un abonnement.** Un garçon vend des abonnements *(A boy is selling subscriptions)* pour des magazines. Écoutez la conversation et notez les renseignements nécessaires pour complétez ce formulaire d'abonnement.

```
                  SERVICE ABONNEMENTS

MAGAZINE .........................................................................

NOM ................................................................................

PRÉNOM ..........................................................................

ADRESSE MAIL ................................................................

ADRESSE ..........................................................................

CODE POSTAL ................................................................

VILLE ............................... PAYS ..............................

NUMÉRO DE TÉLÉPHONE ...........................................

NUMÉRO DE PORTABLE ...............................................
```

♻ Maintenant, demandez les renseignements nécessaires pour compléter le formulaire d'abonnement à deux étudiants de votre classe.

> **EXEMPLE** — **Quel est ton nom de famille?**
> — **C'est Sodji.**

🔁 **À VOUS!**

Avec un(e) partenaire, relisez à haute voix la conversation entre Alex et Robert. Ensuite, adaptez la conversation pour décrire votre propre situation.

You can access the audio of the active vocabulary of this ***Compétence*** online.

TELLING WHICH ONE

✔ **Pour vérifier**

1. How do you say *this, that, these,* and *those*? When do you use the alternate masculine form **cet**?

2. When do you use **quel** to say *what*? When do you use **qu'est-ce que**? What are the four forms of **quel**?

Les adjectifs *ce* et *quel*

1. To say *this/that* and *these/those*, use **ce (cet, cette, ces).** Notice that the masculine singular **ce** changes to **cet** before a vowel sound.

	MASCULINE		FEMININE
	(plus consonant sound)	*(plus vowel sound)*	*(plus consonant or vowel sound)*
SINGULAR	**ce** canapé	**cet** appartement	**cette** rue
PLURAL	**ces** canapés	**ces** appartements	**ces** rues

Note that this adjective is used to say both *this/these* and *that/those*.

J'aime bien **ces** maisons dans **cette** rue.
*I like **these** houses on **this** street. / I like **those** houses on **that** street.*

2. To say *which* and *what*, use **quel (quels, quelle, quelles).** The form you use depends on the gender and number of the noun it modifies.

	MASCULINE	FEMININE
SINGULAR	**quel** appartement	**quelle** rue
PLURAL	**quels** appartements	**quelles** rues
	Quelle est ton **adresse**?	**Quels meubles** as-tu?

Quel and **qu'est-ce que** both mean *what*, but they are not interchangeable. **Quel** is an adjective and is always followed by a noun. Use:

QUEL	QU'EST-CE QUE (QU')

• directly before a noun
  Tu es de **quel pays**?
	• before a subject and verb
	  Qu'est-ce que tu as chez toi?
	  Qu'est-ce qu'il y a dans ton quartier?

• before **est** or **sont** followed by a noun
  Quel est ton nom?
  Quels sont tes loisirs préférés?	

Note *de vocabulaire*

1. If you need to distinguish *this* from *that*, you can add the suffixes **-ci** and **-là** to the noun.
Ce livre-ci ou ce livre-là? *This book or that book?*
Ces maisons-ci ou ces maisons-là? *These houses or those houses?*
2. **Quel** followed by a noun is also used as an exclamation. It is most often the equivalent of *What . . . !* or *What a . . . !* in English.
Quels chiens embêtants! *What annoying dogs!*
Quelle chance! *What luck!*
Quelle belle maison! *What a beautiful house!*

Sélection musicale. Search for the song "**Je suis**" by Florent Pagny online to enjoy a musical selection illustrating the use and pronunciation of the demonstrative adjective.

PRONONCIATION

La voyelle *e* de *ce/cet/cette/ces*
3-11

You already know that a final **e** is usually not pronounced in French, except in short words like **je.** As you notice in **ce/cet/cette/ces,** unaccented **e** has three different pronunciations, depending on what follows it.
In short words like **ce** and **que,** or when **e** is followed by a single consonant within a word, pronounce it as in:

   je   ne   le   regarde   vendredi

When, as in **ces,** **e** is followed by an unpronounced consonant at the end of a word, pronounce it as in:

   les   mes   parlez   manger   premier

In words like **cette** and **cet,** where **e** is followed by two consonants within a word, or a single pronounced consonant at the end of a word, pronounce it as in:

   quel   cher   belle   elle   cherche

A Prononcez bien! Demandez à votre partenaire s'il/si elle aime les choses suivantes. Faites attention à la prononciation de **ce (cet)/cette/ces**.

EXEMPLE — Tu aimes ce tableau?
— Oui, j'aime bien ce tableau. / Non, je n'aime pas ce tableau.

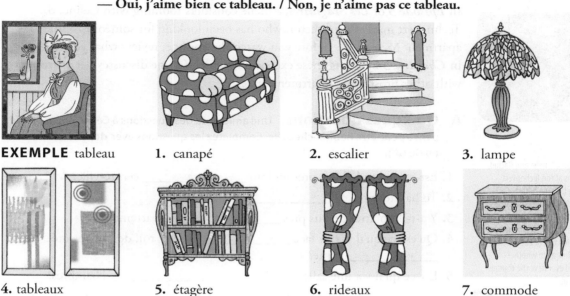

EXEMPLE tableau **1.** canapé **2.** escalier **3.** lampe

4. tableaux **5.** étagère **6.** rideaux **7.** commode

B Entretien. Complétez les questions suivantes avec la forme correcte de **quel** ou avec **qu'est-ce que (qu'est-ce qu')**. Ensuite, posez les questions à votre partenaire.

1. _____ il y a dans ta chambre?
2. Ta chambre est à _____ étage?
3. De _____ couleur sont les murs de ta chambre?
4. ___ meubles as-tu dans le salon?
5. Dans _____ pièce est-ce que tu passes le plus de temps?
6. _____ tu aimes faire chez toi quand tu as du temps libre?
7. _____ tu voudrais changer chez toi?

C Au Canada. Travaillez en équipes *(teams)*. Complétez les questions suivantes avec la forme correcte de **quel/quelle/quels/quelles** et **ce (cet)/cette/ces** comme dans l'exemple. Ensuite, répondez aux questions. La première équipe qui complète tout correctement et qui répond correctement aux questions gagne.

EXEMPLE **Quelle** est la province canadienne avec le plus de francophones?
Cette province est plus grande que l'Alaska.
C'est le Québec.

1. _____ est la plus grande ville du Québec?
_____ ville n'est pas la capitale de la province.
2. _____ est la plus vieille ville du Canada?
Fondée en 1608, _____ ville est la capitale de la province du Québec.
3. _____ pourcentage *(m)* de la population canadienne habite au Québec?
_____ pourcentage est entre 20 et 30 % (pour cent).
4. _____ explorateur est le premier Français à explorer le Canada?
_____ explorateur arrive au Canada en 1534.
5. De _____ couleurs est le drapeau *(flag)* canadien?
_____ couleurs sont deux des couleurs du drapeau des États-Unis.

VIDÉO-REPRISE

Les Stagiaires

In *Épisode 3* of *Les Stagiaires,* Amélie considers rooming with Céline, the Technovert marketing director, who has been looking for someone to share her apartment for a while. Before you watch the episode, review what you learned in *Chapitre 3* by doing these exercises in which Céline discusses her apartment with other prospective apartment mates.

A **Quelques questions.** Une amie pose des questions à Céline parce qu'elle pense peut-être habiter chez elle. Complétez les questions avec **du, de la, de l', des** ou **de (d').**

1. Est-ce que tu habites près ou loin _____ centre-ville?

2. Tu habites près _____ université?

3. Y a-t-il un arrêt de bus près _____ appartement?

4. Qu'est-ce qu'il y a en face _____ chez toi, de l'autre côté _____ rue?

5. Est-ce qu'il y a une salle de bains à côté _____ chambres?

Maintenant, posez ces questions à un(e) partenaire pour parler de sa maison, de son appartement ou de sa résidence universitaire.

B **L'appartement de Céline.** Céline décrit son appartement. Complétez le paragraphe suivant avec les expressions indiquées.

porte d'entrée

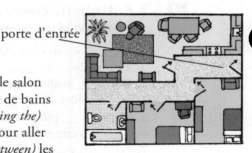

Quand on entre dans mon appartement, la cuisine et le salon sont __1__ *(to the right)* et les deux chambres et la salle de bains sont __2__ *(to the left).* La porte du salon est __3__ *(facing the)* porte d'entrée. Il faut *(One must)* passer par le salon pour aller à la cuisine et il y a une petite salle à manger __4__ *(between)* les deux pièces. La salle de bains est __5__ *(at the end of the)* couloir, __6__ *(next to the)* deuxième chambre.

C **Encore des questions.** Une amie voudrait passer chez Céline pour voir son appartement. Quelles questions avec **quel/quelle/quels/quelles** est-ce qu'elle pose à Céline pour obtenir les réponses suivantes?

> **EXEMPLE** Le nom de la rue, c'est *rue du Stade.*
> **Quel est le nom de la rue?**

1. L'adresse exacte de l'immeuble, *c'est le 125 rue du Stade.*

2. C'est l'appartement *numéro 12.*

3. Mon numéro de téléphone, c'est *le 06 35 42 89 95.*

4. Je rentre chez moi *vers six heures et demie* ce soir.

D Qu'est-ce que tu as? Céline parle à une amie. Complétez les phrases suivantes en traduisant les mots entre parenthèses.

> **EXEMPLE** J'ai un nouveau portable. *(I have a new cell phone).* **Mon** *(My)* numéro de téléphone, c'est le 06 35 42 89 95.

1. _____ *(I have a modern apartment)* dans le centre-ville. _____ *(My)* adresse, c'est le 125 rue du Stade, appartement 12.

2. _____ *(The neighborhood has a lot of good restaurants).* C'est un quartier très agréable et j'aime beaucoup _____ *(its)* ambiance.

3. Quelquefois, je passe le week-end chez mes parents. _____ *(They have a big house)* en banlieue. _____ *(Their)* jardin *(yard)* est très joli.

4. Chez moi, _____ *(I have a little dog).* _____ *(My)* chien est sympa, mais il aboie *(barks)* toujours quand quelqu'un s'approche de *(someone approaches)* la porte.

5. _____ *(The only problem)* chez moi, c'est que dans le parking de mon immeuble, _____ *(we don't have)* assez de places pour _____ *(our)* voitures.

Maintenant, changez les phrases pour décrire votre situation.

E C'est combien? Céline cherche du mobilier *(furnishings)* pour son appartement sur *Craigslist*. Donnez le prix de chaque objet comme dans l'exemple. Utilisez **ce, cet, cette** ou **ces**.

> **EXEMPLE**
>
> | TABLE, 6 CHAISES 450 € |
> | Tél: 06 96 78 26 65 |
>
> **Cette table et ces chaises coûtent** *(cost)* **quatre cent cinquante euros.**

1. TABLE, 6 CHAISES
laquées noires, très propres
1 150 €
Tél: 06 53 44 94 95

2. FAUTEUIL, CANAPÉ
fleuris 550 €
Tél: 06 31 42 51 15

3. TÉLÉ Sony,
état neuf 700 €
Tél: 06 12 21 49 14

4. LIT «king» complet:
base, lit en pin, matelas,
le tout en très bon état 150 €
Tél: 06 11 09 07 67

5. TABLE D'ORDINATEUR
blanche, 3 tiroirs, en bon
état 115 €
Tél: 06 89 85 10 11

6. ORDINATEUR Toshiba,
excellente condition 495 €
Tél: 06 55 64 69 94

Access the Video *Les Stagiaires* online.

▶ **Épisode 3: Un nouvel appartement**

AVANT LA VIDÉO

Dans cet épisode, Céline demande à Amélie si elle veut *(wants)* être sa colocataire. Avant de regarder l'épisode, pensez à trois questions qu'on pose souvent à un(e) colocataire potentiel(le).

APRÈS LA VIDÉO

Regardez le clip et notez trois questions qu'Amélie pose à Céline à propos de l'appartement et de ses habitudes.

LECTURE

POUR MIEUX LIRE:
Previewing content

Looking at the title of an article and thinking about the topic can help you anticipate its content and read it more easily. You are going to read an article by an interior decorator in Quebec about how colors can change your moods. Before you begin to read, look at the title of the article. What is it about? What feelings do you associate with the following colors?

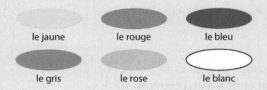

le jaune   le rouge   le bleu

le gris   le rose   le blanc

Associations. Quelle(s) couleur(s) associez-vous le plus aux choses suivantes?

1. la passion
2. la dépression
3. la concentration
4. l'énergie
5. la relaxation
6. la pureté
7. l'appétit
8. l'irritation

© Artazum/Shutterstock.com

Les couleurs et leurs effets sur la nature humaine

Les couleurs changent nos **humeurs** et reflètent notre personnalité. **Pour mieux vous faire connaître** les effets qu'ont les couleurs sur la nature humaine, nous avons préparé un guide qui va vous aider à choisir les couleurs pour votre maison ou appartement.

Les couleurs chaudes: le rouge et le jaune

Le rouge stimule le métabolisme, le rythme cardiaque et la température **corporelle.** Le rouge est une couleur agressive, vitale et passionnante. **Puisque** c'est une couleur qui stimule l'appétit, le rouge est souvent utilisé pour les salles à manger et les restaurants.

Le jaune stimule la mémoire, le mouvement, la coordination et le système digestif. Le jaune et le rouge sont considérés comme «énergiques». Mais **faites attention,** le jaune dans une chambre de bébé **peut rendre** l'enfant irritable.

Les couleurs froides: le bleu et le vert

Le bleu encourage la concentration, **fait ralentir** le rythme cardiaque et la respiration et **fait baisser** la température du **corps.** Cette couleur est très recommandée dans un bureau.

Le vert augmente la relaxation. Le corps et **l'esprit se détendent** dans une atmosphère verte. Il est **donc parfait** pour une chambre à coucher.

---

humeurs *moods*   **Pour mieux vous faire connaître** *To inform you better about*   **corporelle** *body*   **Puisque** *Since*   **faites attention** *be careful* **peut rendre** *can make*   **froides** *cold*   **fait ralentir** *slows down* **fait baisser** *lowers*   **corps** *body*   **l'esprit** *the mind*   **se détendent** *relax* **donc** *therefore*   **parfait** *perfect*

Les couleurs neutres: le blanc, le gris et le noir

Le blanc stimule les fonctions vitales, par conséquent **le sommeil** n'est pas aussi **bénéfique** dans une chambre blanche. Le blanc est aussi associé à la pureté et à l'honnêteté.

Le gris incite à la dépression et à l'indifférence. Il est préférable de l'utiliser comme accent plutôt que couleur dominante dans votre décor.

Le noir est une couleur distincte, audacieuse et classique. Le noir est un fond idéal **pour faire ressortir** les autres couleurs, mais il peut être **étouffant** en trop grande quantité.

© Kate Macrae

---

le sommeil *sleep*　**bénéfique** *beneficial*　**pour faire ressortir** *to make stand out*　**étouffant** *stifling*

Compréhension

Quelles couleurs? Complétez les phrases suivantes en indiquant les couleurs appropriées d'après la lecture du texte.

1. Si vous désirez manger moins, évitez *(avoid)* le _____ pour décorer votre salle à manger.
2. Pour mieux vous concentrer, étudiez dans une pièce _____.
3. Si votre bébé pleure *(cries)* beaucoup, utilisez le _____ dans sa chambre et évitez le _____.
4. Si vous souffrez de dépression, évitez le _____ dans votre décor.
5. Si vous avez souvent froid *(often feel cold)* chez vous, utilisez le _____ et évitez le _____.

COMPOSITION

Brainstorming on a topic before writing about it can help you organize your thoughts. To brainstorm, first think about what general sections you want to include in your writing, then jot down as many notes for each section as you can. Finally, use these sections to organize your writing.

Organisez-vous. Imagine that you are responding to a roommate ad in Quebec. What would you want to know about the apartment and its occupant? Jot down as many words and phrases in French as you can under each heading in this chart, using a separate piece of paper.

location	rooms and furnishings	roommate's personality/ habits

Un mail

You are moving to Quebec and respond to an ad for a roommate. Write an e-mail in which you introduce yourself and tell the sort of place you are looking for. Then, write three paragraphs asking about the apartment's location, the rooms and furnishings, and what the roommate is like. Begin with **Cher monsieur / Chère madame** and end the e-mail with **En attendant votre réponse.** Don't forget to sign your name.

LE QUÉBEC D'AUJOURD'HUI

Le Québec est, **à bien des égards,** une société distincte à l'intérieur du Canada. Dans cette province où le français est la langue officielle, le français est la langue maternelle de 78 % de la population, l'anglais de 8 % de la population et 14 % parle d'autres langues.

En 1534, l'explorateur français Jacques Cartier fonde une colonie **appelée** la Nouvelle-France. Les Français et les Anglais **se battent** pour le contrôle de cette région jusqu'en 1763, quand la France cède ses territoires canadiens aux Anglais. **Pendant** 200 **ans,** les Québécois **vivent** sous la domination anglophone.

Dans les années 1960, les Québécois prennent conscience de leur identité francophone et un mouvement appelé «la Révolution tranquille» se développe pour défendre la culture francophone au Québec. En 1976, **une loi** pour la défense du français est votée et oblige **les immigrés à apprendre** le français. Aujourd'hui, un Québécois sur huit est immigré.

à bien des égards *in many regards*   **appelé(e)** *called*   **se battent** *fight*   **Pendant** *For, During*   **ans** *years*   **vivent** *live*   **Dans les années 1960** *In the sixties*
une loi *a law*   **les immigrés à apprendre** *immigrants to learn*

Le Québec d'aujourd'hui est une société multi-ethnique avec des contributions de ses immigrés, de ses peuples indigènes (les Inuits et les Amérindiens) et de **ses racines** françaises et anglaises. **Pourtant,** le Québec **maintient surtout** un attachement profond à son héritage français.

Compréhension

1. Au Québec, 78 % de la population parle _____ comme langue maternelle, 8 % parle _____ et 14 % parle d'_____. Quelle est la situation linguistique dans votre région?

2. Au cours du 17ᵉ et du 18ᵉ siècles, les _____ et les _____ se battent pour le contrôle du Canada. En 1763, les _____ gagnent la guerre *(war)*. Comment est-ce que l'histoire de votre région influence sa situation linguistique?

3. «La _____» est un mouvement pour la protection de la culture francophone au Canada qui commence dans les années 1960. Est-ce qu'il y a des mouvements pour protéger des cultures minoritaires dans votre région?

4. Le Québec d'aujourd'hui est une société multi-ethnique avec des contributions de ses _____, ses peuples _____ et de ses racines _____ et _____. Quelles cultures ont influencé votre société?

---

ses racines *its roots* **Pourtant** *However* **maintient surtout** *maintains especially*

RÉSUMÉ DE GRAMMAIRE

cent   = *one hundred*
mille   = *one thousand*
un million = *one million*
un million d'habitants

300	trois cents
301	trois cent un
3 000	trois mille
3 100 000	trois millions cent mille

Ma rue, c'est la première (deuxième, troisième, quatrième, cinquième, sixième, septième, huitième, neuvième, dixième, onzième...) rue à droite.

—J'**ai** un appartement. Et toi? Tu **as** une maison?
—Ma famille **a** une petite maison. J'habite chez mes parents.

un tableau → des tableaux
un bureau → des bureaux
un animal → des animaux
un DVD → des DVD

Je rentre **de l'**université à cinq heures.

Ma résidence est **près d'**ici, **derrière** la bibliothèque et **à côté de** la librairie.

Je n'aime pas habiter dans la résidence universitaire parce qu'elle est loin **du** parking et ma chambre est en face **des** ascenseurs, à côté **de** l'escalier et loin **de la** salle de bains!

NUMBERS ABOVE 100

- Use **un** in **un million,** but not before the words **cent** and **mille.** The word **million(s)** is followed by **de (d')** when followed directly by a noun.
- **Million** takes an **s** when plural. **Cent** generally only takes an **s** when plural if not followed by another number. Never add an **s** to **mille.**

ORDINAL NUMBERS

Use **premier (première)** to say *first.* To form the other ordinal numbers *(second, third, fourth . . .),* add the suffix **-ième** to the cardinal numbers **(deux, trois, quatre...).** Drop a final **e** of cardinal numbers before adding **-ième.** Note the spelling changes in **cinquième** *(fifth)* and **neuvième** *(ninth).*

AVOIR

The verb **avoir** *(to have)* is irregular.

AVOIR *(to have)*	
j'**ai**	nous ‿ **avons**
tu **as**	vous ‿ **avez**
il/elle/on **a**	ils/elles ‿ **ont**

PLURALS ENDING WITH -*X* AND PLURALS OF ACRONYMS

In the plural, most words ending in **-eau, -au,** or **-eu** end in **-x** rather than **-s,** and the ending **-al** becomes **-aux.** Acronyms, such as **DVD** and **CD** do not add an **-s** in plural forms.

PREPOSITIONS

When used alone, the preposition **de** means *of, from,* or *about.* **De** is also used in some of the following prepositions.

sur	*on*	**près (de)**	*near*
sous	*under*	**loin (de)**	*far (from)*
entre	*between*	**à côté (de)**	*next to, beside*
dans	*in*	**à droite / gauche (de)**	*to the right / left (of)*
devant	*in front of*	**en face (de)**	*across (from), facing*
derrière	*behind*	**dans le coin (de)**	*in the corner (of)*

De contracts with the articles **le** and **les,** but not with **la** or **l'.**

CONTRACTION:			NO CONTRACTION:		
de + le	→	du	de + la	→	de la
de + les	→	des	de + l'	→	de l'

ADJECTIVE PLACEMENT

Adjectives generally are placed *after* the nouns they describe. However ordinal and cardinal numbers and the following adjectives go *before* nouns.

beau (belle)	jeune	bon (bonne)	grand(e)	autre
joli(e)	vieux (vieille)	mauvais(e)	petit(e)	même
	nouveau (nouvelle)	meilleur(e) gentil(le)	gros(se)	seul(e)

The adjectives **beau, nouveau,** and **vieux** have irregular forms. The alternate singular forms **bel, nouvel,** and **vieil** are used before masculine singular nouns beginning with a vowel sound. When the plural indefinite article **des** is followed directly by an adjective that precedes a plural noun, it changes to **de.**

POSSESSION

De is used instead of *'s* to indicate possession and relationship. The possessive adjectives also indicate possession.

	MASCULINE SINGULAR	FEMININE SINGULAR (+ consonant sound)	FEMININE SINGULAR (+ vowel sound)	PLURAL
my	**mon** vélo	**ma** voiture	**mon** adresse	**mes** meubles
your (sing. fam.)	**ton** vélo	**ta** voiture	**ton** adresse	**tes** meubles
his/her/its	**son** vélo	**sa** voiture	**son** adresse	**ses** meubles
our	**notre** vélo	**notre** voiture	**notre** adresse	**nos** meubles
your (form./pl.)	**votre** vélo	**votre** voiture	**votre** adresse	**vos** meubles
their	**leur** vélo	**leur** voiture	**leur** adresse	**leurs** meubles

Use the forms **mon, ton,** and **son** rather than **ma, ta,** and **sa** before feminine nouns beginning with vowel sounds.

CE (CET)/CETTE/CES AND QUEL/QUELLE/QUELS/QUELLES

Use the demonstrative adjective **ce (cet)/cette/ces** to say both *this/these* and *that/those.* The masculine **ce** becomes **cet** before masculine singular nouns beginning with a vowel sound.

	SINGULAR	PLURAL
MASCULINE (+ consonant sound)	ce chien	ces chiens
MASCULINE (+ vowel sound)	cet animal	ces animaux
FEMININE	cette étagère	ces étagères

Use **quel/quelle/quels/quelles** to say *which* or *what* directly before a noun or the verbs **est** and **sont** followed by a noun. It agrees with the gender and number of the noun it modifies.

	MASCULINE	FEMININE
SINGULAR	quel pays	quelle ville
PLURAL	quels pays	quelles villes

un appartement moderne
des murs blancs

la première rue
au deuxième étage

un joli parc
le meilleur quartier

un bel immeuble
un nouvel immeuble
un vieil immeuble

de bons colocataires
de nouveaux meubles

—C'est la porte **de la** salle de bains?
—Non, c'est la porte **du** placard.

—Tu habites encore chez **tes** parents?
—Non, j'habite chez **mon** frère.
—Où est **sa** maison?
—Pas loin de chez **nos** parents.
—Dans quelle rue est la maison de **vos** parents?
—**Leur** adresse, c'est le 435, rue Martin.

son quartier = *his/her/its neighborhood*
sa porte = *his/her/its door*
ses murs = *his/her/its walls*

Mon amie s'appelle Marion.

—Tu habites dans **cette** rue?
—Oui, j'aime beaucoup **ce** quartier. Mon appartement est dans **cet** immeuble.
—Mon appartement est derrière **ces** arbres.

—Dans **quelle** ville habites-tu?
—J'habite à Sherbrooke.
—**Quelle** est ton adresse?
—C'est le 1202, rue Galt.
—**Quel** est ton numéro de téléphone?
—C'est le (819) 569-1208.

VOCABULAIRE

Talking about where you live

NOMS MASCULINS

un appartement	an apartment
un arrêt de bus	a bus stop
un ascenseur	an elevator
le centre-ville	downtown
un colocataire	a co-renter, a housemate, an apartment mate
un dollar	a dollar
un escalier	stairs, a staircase
un étage	a floor
un immeuble	an apartment building
le logement	lodging, housing
le loyer	the rent
le rez-de-chaussée	the ground floor
un salon	a living room
un sous-sol	a basement

NOMS FÉMININS

la banlieue	the suburbs
la campagne	the country(side)
une chambre	a bedroom
une colocataire	a co-renter, a housemate, an apartment mate
une cuisine	a kitchen
une fenêtre	a window
une maison	a house
une pièce	a room
une porte	a door
une salle à manger	a dining room
une salle de bains	a bathroom
des toilettes	a restroom, a toilet
une ville	a city

ADJECTIFS

cher (chère)	expensive
confortable	comfortable
moderne	modern
pratique	practical, convenient

DIVERS

à la campagne	in the country(side)
À quel étage?	On what floor?
au premier (deuxième...) étage	on the first / second (second / third . . .) floor
au rez-de-chaussée	on the ground / first floor
au sous-sol	in the basement
cent	a/one hundred
dans le centre-ville	downtown
en banlieue	in the suburbs
en ville	in town
Je n'ai pas de...	I don't have (any) . . .
loin (de)	far (from)
mille	a/one thousand
un million (de)	a/one million
par mois	per month
penser	to think
premier (première)	first
(tout) près (de)	(very) near
trop	too (much/many)
il/elle va	he/she is going, he/she goes

*Pour **les nombres ordinaux,** voir la page 116.*

Talking about your possessions

NOMS MASCULINS

un animal (*pl* des animaux)	an animal
un canapé	a couch
un CD	a CD
un chat	a cat
un chien	a dog
un DVD	a DVD
un fauteuil	an armchair
un lecteur CD/DVD/Blu-ray	a CD/DVD/Blu-ray player
un (ordinateur) portable	a laptop (computer)
un (téléphone) portable	a cell phone
un problème	a problem
un smartphone	a smartphone
un tableau (*pl* des tableaux)	a painting
un tapis	a rug
un vélo	a bicycle
des vêtements	clothes

NOMS FÉMININS

une chaîne hi-fi	an audio system
une chaise	a chair
une chose	a thing
une console de jeux	a game console
une lampe	a lamp
une plante	a plant
une table	a table
une télé	a TV
une voiture	a car

PRÉPOSITIONS

à côté (de)	next to, beside
à droite (de)	to the right (of)
à gauche (de)	to the left (of)
dans	in
dans le coin (de)	in the corner (of)
de	of, from, about
derrière	behind
devant	in front of
en face (de)	across from, facing
entre	between
loin (de)	far (from)
près (de)	near
sous	under
sur	on

VERBES

avoir	to have
chercher	to look for
fumer	to smoke
partager	to share
téléphoner (à)	to phone

DIVERS

combien (de)	how many, how much
embêtant(e)	annoying
en ordre	in order, orderly
non plus	neither
partout	everywhere
Pas de problème.	No problem.
peut-être	maybe, perhaps
(bien) rangé(e)	neat, put away, straightened up
ton/ta/tes	your (sing. fam.)
tout	everything, all

Describing your room

NOMS MASCULINS

un adjectif	*an adjective*
un bureau (*pl* des bureaux)	*a desk*
un couloir	*a hall, a corridor*
un lit	*a bed*
des meubles	*furniture, furnishings*
un mur	*a wall*
un placard	*a closet*
un poster	*a poster*
un rideau (*pl* des rideaux)	*a curtain*

NOMS FÉMININS

une commode	*a dresser, a chest of drawers*
une couleur	*a color*
une couverture	*a (bed)cover, a blanket*
une étagère	*a bookcase, a shelf*
une vue	*a view*

ADJECTIFS POSSESSIFS

mon/ma/mes	*my*
ton/ta/tes	*your*
son/sa/ses	*his, her, its*
notre/nos	*our*
votre/vos	*your*
leur/leurs	*their*

EXPRESSIONS VERBALES

Ça a l'air bien.	*It seems nice.*
Ça te plaît.	*You like it.*
comme tu vois	*as you see*
espérer	*to hope*
indiquer	*to indicate*
laisser	*to leave* (something somewhere)
montrer	*to show*
Viens voir!	*Come see!*

LES COULEURS

De quelle couleur est...?	*What color is . . . ?*
De quelle couleur sont...?	*What color are . . . ?*
beige	*beige*
blanc(he)	*white*
bleu(e)	*blue*
gris(e)	*gray*
jaune	*yellow*
marron	*brown*
noir(e)	*black*
orange	*orange*
rose	*pink*
rouge	*red*
vert(e)	*green*
violet(te)	*purple*

DIVERS

à sa place	*in its place*
au bout (de)	*at the end (of)*
chaque	*each*
en désordre	*in disorder, disorderly*
justement	*as a matter of fact, precisely, exactly*
par terre	*on the floor, on the ground*
préféré(e)	*favorite*
propre	*clean*
sale	*dirty*
seul(e)	*only, alone*

Giving your address and phone number

NOMS MASCULINS

un code postal	*a zip code*
un État	*a state*
les États-Unis	*the United States*
un nom (de famille)	*a (sur)name, a (last) name, a noun*
un numéro de téléphone	*a telephone number*
un pays	*a country*
un prénom	*a first name*
des renseignements	*information*

NOMS FÉMININS

une adresse (mail)	*an (e-mail) address*
la Louisiane	*Louisiana*
une nationalité	*a nationality*
une province	*a province*
une rue	*a street*

DIVERS

ce (cet)/cette	*this, that*
ces	*these, those*
il/elle doit...	*he/she must . . .*
partagé(e) (entre)	*shared, divided (among, between)*
poser une question	*to ask a question*
quel/quelle/quels/quelles	*which, what*
s'inscrire	*to register*
suivant(e)	*following*

En famille

 Pair work

 Group work

Class work

 Video

 Audio

© Melanie Stetson Freeman/Christian Science Monitor/Getty Images

LE MONDE FRANCOPHONE

Géoculture et Vidéo-voyage: En Amérique: En Louisiane

COMPÉTENCE

1 Describing your family
Ma famille

Describing feelings and appearance
*Les expressions avec **avoir***

Stratégies et Compréhension auditive
- **Pour mieux comprendre:** *Asking for clarification*
- **Compréhension auditive:** *La famille de Robert*

2 Saying where you go in your free time
Le temps libre

Saying where you are going
*Le verbe **aller**, la préposition **à** et le pronom **y***

Giving directions and making suggestions
L'impératif

3 Saying what you are going to do
Le week-end prochain

Saying what you are going to do
Le futur immédiat

Saying when you are going to do something
Les dates

4 Planning how to get there
Les moyens de transport

Deciding how to get there and come back
*Les verbes **prendre** et **venir** et les moyens de transport*

Vidéo-reprise: *Les Stagiaires*

Lecture et Composition
- **Pour mieux lire:** *Using your knowledge of the world*
- **Lecture:** *Deux mots*
- **Pour mieux écrire:** *Visualizing your topic*
- **Composition:** *Ma famille*

Comparaisons culturelles: *L'histoire des Cadiens*

Résumé de grammaire

Vocabulaire

GÉOCULTURE ET VIDÉO-VOYAGE:
EN AMÉRIQUE: EN LOUISIANE

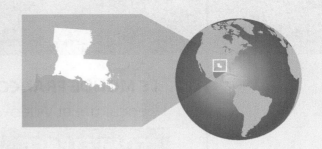

 LA LOUISIANE

NOMBRE D'HABITANTS:
4 600 000 (les Louisianais) (Un peu moins de 195 000 parlent français, cadien [cajun] ou créole et parmi eux [among them] 180 000 parlent ces langues à la maison.)

La ville de Lafayette est au cœur de la région cadienne, l'Acadiane, 22 paroisses dans la partie sud de la Louisiane. La Nouvelle-Orléans est au cœur de la région créole.

Les Cadiens et les Créoles aiment bien manger et ils sont **fiers** de leurs cuisines. La cuisine cadienne est une cuisine **campagnarde** des bayous. La cuisine créole **tire ses racines** des familles aristocrates européennes de La Nouvelle-Orléans. Les deux cuisines sont similaires et beaucoup de **plats** sont à base d'une sauce appelée «un roux» (composée de **beurre** et de **farine**), de **riz** et de «la sainte trinité»: l'oignon, **le poivron vert** et le céleri. En général, les plats sont très **épicés** comme **les écrevisses** ou **les crevettes à l'étouffée,** le jambalaya, le gombo, **l'andouille** et **le boudin.**

Que savez-vous de la Louisiane francophone et de ses traditions? **Connaissez-vous** la cuisine ou la musique de cette région?

Il y a deux traditions francophones en Louisiane, **les Cadiens** et les Créoles. Les Cadiens sont les descendants des Acadiens déportés du Canada par les Anglais après 1755. Les Créoles sont les descendants des premiers **colons** français et européens, d'**immigrés** des îles caraïbes **ou encore** d'**esclaves échappés** de cette région.

© Ian Cook/Photolibrary/Getty Images

Les Cadiens et les Créoles sont fiers de leur cuisine.

Que savez-vous de *What do you know about*   **Connaissez-vous** *Are you familiar with*   **les Cadiens** *the Cajuns*   **colons** *settlers, colonists*   **immigrés** *immigrants*   **ou encore** *as well as*   **esclaves échappés** *escaped slaves*   **au cœur de** *in the heart of*   **paroisses** *parishes*   **la partie sud** *the southern part*   **fiers** *proud*   **campagnarde** *country style*   **tire ses racines** *gets its roots*   **plats** *dishes*   **beurre** *butter*   **farine** *flour*   **riz** *rice*   **le poivron vert** *green bell pepper*   **épicés** *spicy*   **les écrevisses** *crawfish*   **les crevettes** *shrimp*   **à l'étouffée** *smothered*   **l'andouille** *andouille (a smoked pork sausage with garlic)*   **le boudin** *blood sausage*

Les Cadiens et les Créoles aiment aussi la musique et la danse. Le zydeco et le swamp pop sont deux genres de musique originaires de la Louisiane. Dérivé du blues, de la musique country et du swing, le zydeco a pour instruments traditionnels le violon, l'accordéon, la guitare, l'harmonica et **le frottoir.** Le swamp pop est **un mélange** de zydeco, de rock et de boogie.

Le frottoir et l'accordéon sont deux instruments traditionnels du zydeco.

Un «**fais dodo**» est une soirée dansante cadienne. Le nom «fais dodo» **vient de la berceuse:** *Fais dodo Colas mon p'tit frère.* **On chantait cette chanson pour que les enfants dorment pendant que** les parents dansaient et chantaient **aux bals** avec leurs amis.

Un fais dodo est une soirée dansante cadienne.

Le savez-vous?

Que savez-vous de la Louisiane francophone? Avez-vous visité la Louisiane? Quel mot de la liste va avec chaque définition?

> le zydeco   la sainte trinité   les Créoles
> les Cadiens   Lafayette   La Nouvelle-Orléans
> un fais dodo   un roux   le frottoir   l'Acadiane

1. les descendants des habitants de la Louisiane avant son annexion par les États-Unis, principalement d'origines européennes et africaines
2. les descendants des francophones expulsés du Canada par les Anglais au dix-huitième siècle *(century)*
3. la ville au cœur de la région créole
4. la ville au cœur de la région cadienne
5. les 22 paroisses de la région cadienne au sud de la Louisiane
6. un genre de musique influencé par le blues, la musique country et le swing qui est souvent joué à l'accordéon
7. un instrument du zydeco
8. une sauce qui est la base des cuisines cadienne et créole
9. trois ingrédients de nombreux *(numerous)* plats cadiens et créoles: l'oignon, le poivron vert et le céleri
10. une soirée dansante cadienne

Laissez les bons temps rouler!

---

le frottoir *the rubboard*   un mélange *a mix*   fais dodo *go to sleep*   vient de la berceuse *comes from the lullaby*   On chantait cette chanson pour que les enfants dorment pendant que *People used to sing this song so the children would sleep while*   aux bals *at dances*   Laissez les bons temps rouler! *Let the good times roll!* (regional)

AVANT LA VIDÉO

Vous allez voir une vidéo sur la culture francophone dans le sud de la Louisiane. Pour vous aider à mieux comprendre, complétez ces descriptions avec les mots logiques de chaque liste.

marécage fluvial	*river marsh*
rempli	*full*
serpentants	*winding*

1. Notre pays est _____ de bayous _____, de lacs tranquilles, de prairies tremblantes et du plus grand _____ en Amérique.

doigts	*fingers*
écrevisses	*crawfish*
festin	*feast*

2. Regardez toutes ces _____! Attention aux _____! Ça va être un vrai _____.

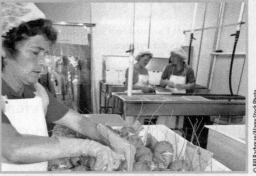

ciel	*sky*
oiseaux	*birds*
ours	*bears*

3. On trouve des alligators, des chats-tigres *(wildcats)* et des _____ sur nos terres *(lands)* et 270 espèces d' _____ qui survolent *(fly over)* notre _____.

frottoir	*rubboard*
gigue	*Irish two-step, jig*
zydeco	*zydeco*

4. La musique de chez nous est une fusion complexe de cultures pour le rythme cajun et le staccato du _____. On fait de la musique avec le _____, le violon et l'accordéon. Nous autres, on danse la valse et la _____.

mélange	*mixture*
monde	*world*
roux	*roux (a mixture of butter and flour)*

5. Notre pays a une cuisine unique au _____. Notre cuisine est un _____ d'influences européennes, ainsi qu'afro-américaines et amérindiennes. On utilise des ingrédients comme le _____.

joie de vivre	*joy of living*
plancher	*dance floor*

6. Notre histoire et notre culture restent intactes aujourd'hui, et nous autres, on les fête avec une _____ incomparable. Les vieux et les jeunes dansent ensemble sur le _____.

marais	*swamp*
perdu	*lost*
prie	*pray*

7. Je _____ le Bon Dieu *(Lord)* de me guider si je suis _____ là-bas dans le _____.

▶ **EN REGARDANT LA VIDÉO**

Regardez la vidéo et indiquez dans quel ordre on parle des aspects de la culture louisianaise mentionnés dans la section *Avant la vidéo*.

▶ **APRÈS LA VIDÉO**

Regardez la vidéo une deuxième fois et complétez les phrases qui suivent avec un mot de la liste.

accordéon   céleri   cuisine   écrevisses   françaises   nature

1. La culture cadienne vient de ses racines *(roots)* _____, espagnoles, africaines et amérindiennes.

2. La musique et la _____ sont deux emblèmes de cette riche culture.

3. Le roux et la sainte trinité [le _____, l'oignon et le poivron vert *(green bellpepper)*] sont trois ingrédients de la cuisine cadienne.

4. On mange aussi beaucoup de poisson *(fish)*, de crevettes *(shrimp)* et d'_____.

5. On fait de la musique avec le frottoir, le violon et l'_____.

6. L'histoire cadienne est l'histoire de l'homme et de la _____.

Describing your family

MA FAMILLE

Vocabulaire supplémentaire

adopté(e) *adopted*
un beau-frère *a brother-in-law*
une belle-sœur *a sister-in-law*
l'aîné (l'aînée) *the oldest child*
le cadet (la cadette) *the middle child, the younger child*
le benjamin (la benjamine) *the youngest child (of more than two)*
un demi-frère (une demi-sœur) *a stepbrother, a half-brother (a stepsister, a half-sister)*
un ex-mari (une ex-femme) *an ex-husband (an ex-wife)*
un fils unique (une fille unique) *an only child*
des petits-enfants (un petit-fils, une petite-fille) *grandchildren (a grandson, a granddaughter)*
porter des lentilles (f) *to wear contact lenses*

Note *de vocabulaire*

Use **avoir l'air** *(+ adjective)* to say someone *looks young, happy...*
Il a l'air sympa. *(He looks nice.)*. Use **ressembler à** to say a person *looks like* someone: **Je ressemble à ma mère.** *(I look like my mother.)*

Robert et ses amis **ont l'intention de** passer une semaine de **vacances** *(f)* chez **le père** de Robert à Lafayette. Robert parle de sa famille.

Voici ma famille. Mes parents sont divorcés maintenant. Ils ont quatre **enfants,** trois **garçons** et **une fille.**

(mes grands-parents)

mon grand-père (Il est **décédé** maintenant.) ma grand-mère

 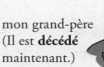  

(mes parents)

ma mère

mon père   mon oncle ma tante

moi   mes frères   ma sœur   son mari   mon cousin   ma cousine

le **fils** et la fille de ma sœur (mon neveu et ma nièce)

Mon père s'appelle Luke.
Il **a (environ) 50 ans** *(m)*.
Il est **encore** jeune, mais il **a l'air** plus âgé.
Il est **de taille moyenne.**
Il **a les cheveux courts** et gris.

Il **a les yeux** *(m)* marron.
Il a **une barbe** grise et une moustache.
Il **porte des lunettes** *(f)*.

Et vous? Comment êtes-vous?

J'ai les yeux **noirs** / marron / **noisette** / verts / bleus / gris.
J'ai les cheveux courts / **mi-longs** / longs et noirs / **bruns** / **châtains** / auburn / blonds / gris / blancs / **roux.**

🔊 4-1

Robert parle de sa famille avec Adam.

ADAM: Vous êtes combien dans ta famille?

ROBERT: Nous sommes sept: mon père, **ma belle-mère,** ma mère, mes deux frères, ma sœur et moi. Ma sœur est mariée et elle habite à La Nouvelle-Orléans.

ADAM: Elle est plus jeune ou **plus âgée que** toi? Quel âge a-t-elle?

ROBERT: Elle a 28 ans.

ADAM: Comment s'appelle-t-elle?

ROBERT: Elle s'appelle Sarah.

A La famille. Donnez l'équivalent féminin.

EXEMPLE le frère   **la sœur**

1. le père   **3.** le garçon   **5.** le beau-père   **7.** le fils
2. l'oncle   **4.** le neveu   **6.** le cousin   **8.** le grand-père

B Généalogie. Complétez les phrases.

EXEMPLE Les parents de mon père, ce sont **mes grands-parents.**

1. Le père de mon père, c'est _____. Sa femme, c'est _____.
2. La sœur de ma mère, c'est _____. Son mari, c'est _____. Leurs enfants sont _____. Leur fils, c'est _____ et leur fille, c'est _____.
3. Le fils de ma sœur, c'est _____. Sa fille, c'est _____.

C Mon meilleur ami. Changez les mots en italique pour décrire votre meilleur ami.

1. Il s'appelle *Emmitt / Chuong / ???* et il a *18 / 25 / 38 / 45 / ???* ans.
2. Il est *grand / petit / de taille moyenne.*
3. Il a les cheveux *longs / mi-longs / courts* et *blonds / noirs / ???.*
4. Il a les yeux *marron / gris / ???.*
5. Il a l'air *intellectuel / sportif / jeune / ???.*

D Entretien. Posez ces questions à votre partenaire. Ensuite, changez de rôles.

1. Vous êtes combien dans ta famille? Tu as des frères et sœurs? (Ils sont plus âgés ou moins âgés que toi?)
2. Avec quel membre de ta famille préfères-tu passer du temps? Comment s'appelle-t-il/elle? Quel âge a-t-il/elle? Il/Elle est grand(e), petit(e) ou de taille moyenne? Il/Elle a les yeux de quelle couleur? Il/Elle a les cheveux longs, mi-longs ou courts? Il/Elle a les cheveux de quelle couleur? Il/Elle a l'air plutôt sportif (sportive) ou plutôt intellectuel(le)? Il/Elle porte des lunettes?

À VOUS!

Avec un(e) partenaire, relisez à haute voix la conversation entre Adam et Robert. Ensuite, adaptez la conversation pour parler d'un membre de votre famille.

You can access the audio of the active vocabulary of this **Compétence** online.

---

une belle-mère (un beau-père, des beaux-parents) *a stepmother / a mother-in-law (a stepfather / a father-in-law, stepparents / in-laws)* **plus âgé(e) que** *older than*

DESCRIBING FEELINGS AND APPEARANCE

✔ *Pour vérifier*

1. How do you say *I'm hungry? I'm thirsty? I'm hot? I'm cold? I'm sleepy? I'm afraid? I'm right? I'm never wrong? I need to stay home? I feel like staying home? I intend to stay home?*

2. How do you say *How old is he? He's 24? He has short black hair and brown eyes? He seems nice? He has a black beard, a mustache, and glasses?*

Note *de vocabulaire*

1. Use **les** when talking about someone's hair and eyes. **Les cheveux** and **les yeux** are both masculine plural, so follow them with an adjective in the masculine plural form. **Ma sœur a les cheveux bruns et les yeux verts.** Auburn, **marron,** and **noisette,** however, are invariable.

2. Brown eyes can be **noirs** *(almost black or dark brown)* or **marron** *(light to medium brown).* Brown hair can be **bruns** *(dark or medium brown)* or **châtains** *(light to medium brown).* The words **brun, roux, auburn,** and **châtain** are mainly used to describe someone's hair.

3. You can say that someone is *blond* or *a blond, brunette* or *a brunette,* or *red-headed* or *a red-head,* using **blond(e), brun(e),** or **roux (rousse). Elle est rousse, mais sa sœur est blonde.** *She's a red-head, but her sister's a blonde.*

4. To say you are *very* hot / cold / hungry . . . use **très. J'ai *très* chaud.**

Les expressions avec **avoir**

1. Use these expressions with **avoir** to describe people or say how they feel.

avoir (environ)... ans	*to be (around) ... years old*	avoir faim	*to be hungry*
avoir l'air...	*to look ..., to seem ...*	avoir soif	*to be thirsty*
avoir une barbe / une moustache / des lunettes	*to have a beard / a mustache / glasses*	avoir froid	*to be cold*
		avoir chaud	*to be hot*
avoir les yeux bleus / verts...	*to have blue / green ... eyes*	avoir raison	*to be right*
		avoir tort	*to be wrong*
avoir les cheveux longs / roux...	*to have long / red ... hair*	avoir peur (de)	*to be afraid (of)*
		avoir sommeil	*to be sleepy*

— Mon fils **a peur** des chiens.   — *My son is afraid of dogs.*
— Quel **âge** a-t-il? Il **a l'air** très jeune.   — *How old is he? He looks very young.*
— Tu **as raison.** Il **a** quatre ans.   — *You're right. He's four.*

2. Notice these three expressions that also use **avoir** in French.

avoir besoin de (d') + noun or infinitive	*to need* + noun or infinitive
avoir envie de (d') + noun or infinitive	*to feel like* + noun or verb
avoir l'intention de (d') + infinitive	*to intend* + infinitive

J'**ai besoin de** la voiture.   *I need the car.*
J'**ai envie de** sortir.   *I feel like going out.*
J'**ai l'intention de** rentrer à midi.   *I intend to return at noon.*

Tu **as besoin de** manger?   *Do you need to eat?*
Tu **as envie de manger** un sandwich?   *You feel like eating a sandwich?*

Vocabulaire supplémentaire

avoir un tatouage / un piercing
avoir un bouc *to have a goatee*
avoir des pattes *(f) to have sideburns*
être chauve *to be bald*
avoir la tête rasée *to have a shaved head*

Sélection musicale. Search for the song **"J'ai besoin d'un chum"** by Céline Dion online to enjoy a musical selection containing structures and vocabulary from this **Compétence.**

A **Comment est-il?** Répondez aux questions pour faire une description du meilleur ami de Robert.

1. Comment s'appelle-t-il? Quel âge a-t-il?
2. Il a les cheveux de quelle couleur? Il a les cheveux longs ou courts? Il a les yeux de quelle couleur?
3. Il a une barbe? Il porte des lunettes? Il a l'air sympa?

Maintenant, changez la description précédente d'Antoine pour parler de vous.

Antoine, 20 ans

EXEMPLE Je m'appelle Pat. J'ai 25 ans. J'ai les cheveux...

B **Les activités de Robert.** Quelles sont les activités que Robert a probablement envie de faire? Quelles sont les activités qu'il a probablement besoin de faire?

> **EXEMPLES** faire ses devoirs **Il a besoin de faire ses devoirs.**
> regarder la télé **Il a envie de regarder la télé.**

1. aller au cinéma
2. aller prendre un verre
3. aller travailler
4. étudier
5. sortir avec des amis
6. faire la lessive *(the laundry)*

 Maintenant, circulez dans la classe et trouvez quelqu'un qui a l'intention de faire les activités mentionnées ce week-end.

> **EXEMPLE** faire tes devoirs
> — **As-tu l'intention de faire tes devoirs ce week-end?**
> — **Oui, j'ai l'intention de faire mes devoirs dimanche soir.**

C **Moi, j'ai…** Utilisez une expression avec **avoir** de la liste à la page précédente. Faites attention au contexte.

> **EXEMPLE** Je voudrais aller prendre un verre. **J'ai soif.**

1. Brrrr… Fermez la fenêtre.
2. Ah! C'est un serpent!
3. Voilà. Ma réponse est correcte.
4. J'ai envie de manger quelque chose.
5. Je voudrais un coca.
6. J'ai besoin de dormir.

D **Qu'est-ce qu'ils ont?** Aujourd'hui, la fille d'une amie fête ses cinq ans *(is celebrating her fifth birthday)*. Que dit sa mère? Utilisez une expression avec **avoir**.

1. Ma fille… aujourd'hui.

2. Ses amis…

3. Mon frère…

4. Mes cousins…

5. Mon mari et moi, nous…

6. Moi, j'…

7. Le chien de mon fils…

8. Tu… de faire ça au chien!

E **Entretien.** Interviewez votre partenaire.

1. Qu'est-ce que tu as envie de faire ce week-end? Qu'est-ce que tu as besoin de faire? Qu'est-ce que tu as l'intention de faire dimanche soir?
2. Tu as faim maintenant? Tu as soif? Est-ce que tu as l'intention de manger quelque chose après le cours? As-tu sommeil maintenant? As-tu l'intention de dormir après le cours?

STRATÉGIES ET COMPRÉHENSION AUDITIVE

POUR MIEUX COMPRENDRE: *Asking for clarification*

When you do not understand something, it is useful to be able to ask for clarification. You already know three ways to do this: by asking for something to be repeated, by asking what a word means, or by asking how a word is spelled.

Comment? Répétez, s'il vous plaît.
Je ne comprends pas. Que veut dire **belle-sœur**?
Ça s'écrit comment?

🔊 **A** **Je ne comprends pas.** Listen to three conversations. In each, which
4-2 method is used to ask for clarification: **a, b,** or **c**?

a. asking for something to be repeated (**Comment? Répétez, s'il vous plaît.**)

b. asking the meaning of a word (**Qu'est-ce que ça veut dire...?**)

c. asking the spelling of a word (**Ça s'écrit comment?**)

🔊 **B** **Comment?** Listen to these three other scenes, in which one of the speakers
4-3 is having difficulty understanding. In each case, what could he or she say to ask for
clarification?

Compréhension auditive: *La famille de Robert*

🔊
4-4 Robert is describing his family to a friend who is studying French. Use what you know and your ability to guess logically to help you understand what he says. The first time, listen only for the number of times his friend asks for clarification.

A **La famille de Robert.** Écoutez encore une fois *(again)* la description de la famille de Robert et complétez l'arbre généalogique *(family tree)* avec les prénoms des membres de sa famille.

Robert

B **C'est qui?** Écoutez encore une fois la description de la famille de Robert et répondez aux questions.

1. Qui habite à Lafayette?
2. Qui habite à Atlanta?
3. Qui habite à La Nouvelle-Orléans?
4. Qui est marié?
5. Qui est divorcé?
6. Comment dit-on **pédiatre** en anglais?
7. Dans la famille de Robert, qui est pédiatre?
8. Quelle est la profession du père de Robert?

Saying where you go in your free time

LE TEMPS LIBRE

Vocabulaire supplémentaire

à la synagogue
à la mosquée
au temple *to church* (Protestant), *to temple*
au lac *to the lake*
au bar

Chez vous, où est-ce qu'**on va** pour passer **son temps libre**?

On aime beaucoup les activités culturelles et **de temps en temps,** on va...

au musée pour voir **une exposition**

au théâtre pour voir **une pièce**

à un concert ou à un festival de musique

On aime aussi **les activités de plein air** et on va souvent...

au parc pour courir

à la piscine pour nager

à la plage pour **prendre un bain de soleil**

Pour **retrouver des amis,** on va...

à un match de basket

en boîte

à l'église

Pour faire du shopping, on va...

Et pour **acheter** des livres, on va...

au centre commercial

dans les petits magasins

à la librairie

---

on va *one goes*   **son temps libre** *one's free time*   **de temps en temps** *from time to time*   **une exposition** *an exhibit*
une pièce *a play*   **les activités de plein air** *outdoor activities*   **prendre un bain de soleil** *to sunbathe*
retrouver des amis *to meet friends*   **acheter** *to buy*

🔊
4-5

Robert et Gabriel parlent de leurs projets *(m)* pour ce soir.

GABRIEL: **On sort** ce soir?

ROBERT: D'accord. On va au cinéma?

GABRIEL: Ah, non, je préfère **connaître** un peu la région. **On dit que** la cuisine **cadienne** est **extra**! Allons **plutôt** au restaurant.

ROBERT: D'accord. Allons dîner au restaurant Préjean. C'est un très bon restaurant où **on sert** les spécialités de la région, et il y a un orchestre cadien. Ça te dit?

GABRIEL: Oui, bonne idée. Allons au restaurant et après, allons écouter de la musique zydeco.

ROBERT: Pas de problème. **On peut** toujours **trouver** des concerts ici!

🔁 **A** **Où va-t-on pour...** Demandez à un(e) partenaire où on va pour faire les choses suivantes.

EXEMPLE lire
— **Où est-ce qu'on va pour lire?**
— **On va à la bibliothèque.**

1. dîner
2. voir une pièce
3. retrouver des amis
4. prendre un verre
5. faire du shopping

6. nager
7. voir une exposition
8. prendre un bain de soleil
9. acheter des livres
10. courir

| au restaurant |
| au musée |
| à la piscine |
| au café |
| au centre commercial |
| à l'église |
| au parc |
| au théâtre |
| à la plage |
| à la librairie |
| à la bibliothèque |

🔁 **B** **Entretien.** Interviewez votre partenaire.

1. Où aimes-tu passer ton temps libre? Qu'est-ce que tu aimes faire après les cours? le week-end?
2. Où aimes-tu retrouver tes amis? Où aimez-vous aller ensemble? Aimez-vous les activités de plein air? Préférez-vous aller à la plage, à la piscine ou au parc? Aimes-tu nager? prendre un bain de soleil?
3. Aimes-tu faire du shopping? Préfères-tu acheter des vêtements, des livres, des DVD ou des CD? Dans quel magasin aimes-tu faire du shopping? Ce magasin est au centre commercial? C'est un magasin cher? Aimes-tu faire des achats en ligne *(buy things online)*?
4. Aimes-tu les activités culturelles? Préfères-tu aller au musée, au théâtre ou à un concert? Préfères-tu aller voir une pièce, une exposition ou un film?

🔁 **À VOUS!**

Avec un(e) partenaire, relisez à haute voix la conversation entre Gabriel et Robert. Ensuite, imaginez que vous êtes chez un(e) ami(e) dans une autre ville et que vous parlez de vos projets pour ce soir. Décidez ensemble d'un type de cuisine (mexicaine, italienne, française, japonaise, chinoise...) et d'un genre de musique (du rock, du jazz, du hip-hop...) populaire dans votre région et refaites la conversation pour parler de vos projets.

You can access the audio of the active vocabulary of this *Compétence* online.

On sort...? *How about going out . . . ?* **connaître** *to know, to get to know* **On dit que** *They say that* **cadien(ne)** *Cajun* **extra(ordinaire)** *great* **plutôt** *instead, rather* **on sert** *they serve* (**servir** *to serve*) **On peut** *One can* (**pouvoir** *can, may, to be able*) **trouver** *to find*

SAYING WHERE YOU ARE GOING

✔ *Pour vérifier*

1. What are the forms of **aller**?

2. With which forms of the definite article does **à** contract? What are the contracted forms? With which forms does it not contract? How do you say *to the café? to the library? to the university? to the students?*

3. What does the word **y** mean and how do you pronounce it? What happens to words like **je** and **ne** before **y**?

4. Where do you place **y** in a sentence where there is a verb followed by an infinitive? Where do you place it otherwise?

*Le verbe **aller,** la préposition **à** et le pronom **y***

1. To talk about going places, use the irregular verb **aller** *(to go)*.

ALLER *(to go)*	
je **vais**	nous ᶻallons
tu **vas**	vous ᶻallez
il/elle/on **va**	ils/elles **vont**

2. Use the preposition **à** *(to, at, in)* to say where you are going. When **à** falls before **le** or **les,** the two words contract to **au** and **aux.**

PREPOSITION À + LE, LA, L', LES	
à + le → au	Je vais **au** cinéma.
à + la → à la	Je vais **à la** librairie.
à + l' → à l'	Gabriel va **à l'**université.
à + les → aux	Robert va **aux** festivals de musique de la région.

3. The pronoun **y** *(there)* is used to avoid repeating the name of the place where one is going. Pronounce it like the French letter **i.** Treat **y** as a vowel sound and use elision and liaison before it.

Je vais **au parc.** J'**y** vais avec mes cousins. Nous ᶻ**y** allons à trois heures.

Y is generally placed *immediately* before the verb. It goes before the infinitive if there is one. If not, it goes before the conjugated verb.

— Il voudrait aller **au cinéma**?   — Ils vont **au musée**?
— Oui, il voudrait **y** aller.   — Oui, ils **y** vont.

In the negative, **y** remains *immediately* before the infinitive or the conjugated verb.

— Tu voudrais aller **au parc**?   — Tu **y** vas aujourd'hui?
— Non, je n'ai pas envie d'**y** aller.   — Non, je n'**y** **vais** pas aujourd'hui.

Whenever you use **aller** to talk about going somewhere and don't name the place you are going, use **y** even when the word *there* would not be stated in English.

On **y** va? *Shall we go (there)?*   J'**y** vais. *I'm going (there).*

PRONONCIATION

*Les lettres **a, au** et **ai***
4-6

- Pronounce **a** or **à** with the mouth wide open as in the word *father,* but with the tongue slightly higher and closer to the front of the mouth.

  Ton *a*mi v*a à* P*a*ris.   Tu v*a*s *à* P*a*ris *a*vec t*a* c*a*mar*a*de?

- Pronounce **au** like the **o** in **nos.**

  Ton beau-père va *au* rest*au*rant?   Les *au*tres y vont *au*ssi?

- Pronounce the **ai** of **je vais** like the **ais** of **français.** Be sure to distinguish this sound from the **a** of **tu vas** or **il va.**

  Je v*ai*s au café.   Tu n'y vas jam*ai*s?

A Prononcez bien! D'abord, pratiquez la prononciation des formes de la préposition **à** dans la troisième colonne. Ensuite, formez des phrases logiques en vous servant d'un élément de chaque colonne.

EXEMPLE Mon ami a envie de voir un film. Il va au cinéma.

Mon ami a envie de voir un film. Il...		piscine
Toi, tu as envie de nager. Tu...	allez	arrêt de bus
Nous avons soif. Nous...	vais	au	librairie
Mes amis vont en cours. Ils...	va	à la	café
Vous voudriez acheter un livre. Vous...	allons	à l'	université
Mon frère aime écouter de la	vas	aux	cinéma
musique. Il...	vont		concerts de ses
Je prends *(am taking)* le bus ce			artistes préférés
matin. Je...			

B On sort. Robert parle avec Adam de ses amis et de sa famille. Complétez ses phrases. Utilisez la forme convenable du verbe **aller** et de la préposition **à (au, à la, à l', aux)**.

EXEMPLE Je **vais à la piscine.**

la piscine

la piscine
1. Toi et moi, nous...

l'église
2. Mes cousins...

la bibliothèque
3. Toi, tu...

l'université
4. Ma sœur...

le musée
5. Gabriel et son frère...

la librairie
6. Mon père...

le parc
7. Notre chien...

les matchs de basket de l'université
8. Le week-end, mes amis...

C Où aiment-ils aller? Demandez à votre partenaire si ces personnes aiment aller aux endroits indiqués. Il/Elle va utiliser le pronom **y** dans ses réponses et va aussi dire si les personnes y vont souvent, rarement...

EXEMPLE tu: au musée
— **Tu aimes aller au musée?**
— **Oui, j'aime y aller. J'y vais souvent / quelquefois...**
Non, je n'aime pas y aller. Je n'y vais jamais.

1. tu: à l'opéra, à un match de basket

2. tes amis et toi: en boîte, au centre commercial

3. ton meilleur ami (ta meilleure amie): au parc, à l'église

4. tes parents: à la piscine, à un concert de musique hip-hop

GIVING DIRECTIONS AND MAKING SUGGESTIONS

✔ Pour vérifier

1. How do you form the imperative (commands)? With which verbs do you drop the final **s** in the **tu** form of the imperative?

2. What are the command forms of **avoir** and **être**? How do you tell a friend: *Be on time! Be good! Let's be ready! Have confidence! Let's have patience!*

3. How do you translate suggestions made using **on**? What form of the verb do you use with **on**?

Sélection musicale. Search for the song "**Toi plus moi**" by Grégoire online to enjoy a musical selection containing these structures.

L'impératif

1. To give instructions, or to tell someone to do something, use either the **tu** form of the verb or the **vous** form of the verb, as appropriate, without the pronouns **tu** and **vous**. In **tu** form commands, drop the final **s** of **-er** verbs and of **aller**.

Va à la bibliothèque! / **Allez** à la bibliothèque!	*Go to the library!*
Ne **mange** pas ça! / Ne **mangez** pas ça!	*Don't eat that!*
Écoute! / **Écoutez!**	*Listen!*

2. Verbs that do not end in **-er** do not drop the **s** in commands. Here are the command forms of some other verbs you have seen. You learned many of these **vous** form commands in the *Chapitre préliminaire*.

TU FORM COMMAND	*VOUS* FORM COMMAND	
Apprends les verbes!	**Apprenez** les verbes!	*Learn the verbs!*
Prends ces papiers!	**Prenez** ces papiers!	*Take these papers!*
Lis la phrase!	**Lisez** la phrase!	*Read the sentence!*
Écris la réponse!	**Écrivez** la réponse!	*Write the answer!*
Fais tes devoirs!	**Faites** vos devoirs!	*Do your homework!*

3. To make suggestions with *Let's . . .* , use the **nous** form of the verb, without the pronoun **nous**.

Allons au cinéma!	*Let's go to the movies!*
Ne **restons** pas à la maison!	*Let's not stay home!*

4. You can also propose doing something with someone (*How about . . .? Shall we . . .?*) by asking a question with **on**. Remember to use the **il/elle** form of verbs with **on,** no matter how it is translated.

On va au cinéma?	*How about going to the movies?*
Qu'est-ce qu'**on fait** ce soir?	*What shall we do this evening?*

5. The verbs **être** and **avoir** have irregular command forms.

ÊTRE (be . . .)		AVOIR (have . . .)	
Sois sage!	*Be good!*	**Aie** confiance!	*Have confidence!*
Soyons prêts!	*Let's be ready!*	**Ayons** de la patience!	*Let's have patience!*
Soyez à l'heure!	*Be on time!*	**Ayez** confiance!	*Have confidence!*

A **Pour réussir.** Donnez des conseils à un groupe de nouveaux étudiants. Utilisez l'impératif à l'affirmatif ou au négatif.

> **EXEMPLE** étudier avec d'autres étudiants
> **Étudiez avec d'autres étudiants.**
> **N'étudiez pas avec d'autres étudiants.**

1. aller à tous les cours
2. être souvent absents
3. être à l'heure
4. avoir confiance
5. faire tous les devoirs
6. copier sur un autre étudiant
7. lire les explications du livre
8. apprendre le vocabulaire
9. aller en boîte tous le soirs
10. avoir peur de parler au prof

B **Des parents difficiles.** Des parents disent à leur fils adolescent qu'il doit faire *(must do)* l'une des choses indiquées et qu'il ne doit pas faire l'autre. Qu'est-ce qu'ils lui disent? Utilisez l'impératif et soyez logique!

> **EXEMPLE** arrêter *(to stop)* de fumer / fumer dans la maison
> **Arrête de fumer. Ne fume pas dans la maison.**

1. être plus propre / laisser tes vêtements partout
2. rester au lit tout le temps / être plus dynamique
3. être paresseux / faire quelque chose de ta vie *(life)*
4. prendre la vie au sérieux / être irresponsable
5. jouer à des jeux vidéo toute la journée / avoir un peu d'ambition
6. lire un livre / regarder la télé tout le temps
7. aller au café tous les jours / faire tes devoirs
8. écouter nos conseils *(advice)* / avoir cette attitude négative

C **Qu'est-ce qu'on fait?** Suggérez quelque chose de logique de la liste à un(e) ami(e) qui dit les choses suivantes.

> | aller danser | rentrer pour faire une sieste | jouer au basket |
> | aller au café | aller au centre commercial | aller au cinéma |
> | aller à la piscine | manger quelque chose | aller à la librairie |

> **EXEMPLE** J'ai soif.
> **Allons au café! / On va au café?**

1. J'ai faim.
2. J'ai envie de voir un film.
3. Je voudrais sortir en boîte.
4. J'ai envie d'acheter un livre.
5. Je voudrais prendre un bain de soleil.
6. J'ai besoin de faire de l'exercice.
7. J'ai envie de faire du shopping.
8. J'ai sommeil.

D **On...?** Un(e) ami(e) vous invite *(invites you)* à faire ces choses. Répondez à ses suggestions selon vos goûts *(according to your tastes)*.

> **EXEMPLE**—On joue à des jeux vidéo?
> —D'accord. Jouons à des jeux vidéo.
> Non, ne jouons pas à des jeux vidéo.
> Regardons plutôt un DVD.

1.
2.
3.
4.

E **Une sortie.** Vous allez sortir ce week-end avec un(e) ami(e) et vous faites des projets *(are making plans)* ensemble. Avec un(e) autre étudiant(e), préparez une conversation dans laquelle *(in which)* vous suggérez plusieurs *(several)* activités. Vous choisissez deux choses que vous allez faire ensemble et vous décidez quel jour et à quelle heure. Utilisez l'impératif dans votre conversation.

Saying what you are going to do

LE WEEK-END PROCHAIN

Robert va passer le week-end prochain à La Nouvelle-Orléans. Et vous? Qu'est-ce que vous allez faire?

Je vais... / Je ne vais pas...

quitter la maison **tôt**

partir pour le week-end

visiter une autre ville

faire un tour de la ville

aller **boire** quelque chose au café

rentrer **tard**

4-7

Robert et Adam **font des projets** *(m)* pour le week-end prochain.

ADAM: Qu'est-ce qu'on fait ce week-end?

ROBERT: J'ai beaucoup de projets pour ce week-end. Jeudi matin, on va partir très tôt pour La Nouvelle-Orléans. **D'abord,** on va visiter la ville. **Ensuite,** on va **aller voir** ma sœur. On va **passer la soirée** chez elle. Vendredi, on va faire un tour du **Vieux Carré.** On va rentrer à Lafayette assez tard.

ADAM: Et samedi?

ROBERT: À midi, on va déjeuner au restaurant Prudhomme. C'est un restaurant célèbre pour sa cuisine régionale. **Et puis,** le soir, on va aller à Eunice, une petite ville pas loin de Lafayette. Il y a une soirée de musique et de folklore cadiens tous les samedis.

ADAM: **Génial!**

Le week-end prochain *Next weekend* **quitter** *to leave* **tôt** *early* **partir** *to leave* **boire** *to drink* **tard** *late* **faire des projets** *to make plans* **D'abord** *First* **Ensuite** *Then, Next* **aller voir** *to go see, to visit* (a person) **passer la soirée** *to spend the evening* **le Vieux Carré** *the French Quarter* **Et puis** *And then* **Génial!** *Great!*

A **Le week-end prochain.** Est-ce que vous allez faire les choses suivantes samedi prochain?

EXEMPLE rester à la maison

Je vais rester à la maison. / Je ne vais pas rester à la maison.

1. quitter la maison tôt
2. partir pour la journée
3. faire un tour de la ville
4. visiter une autre ville
5. aller voir des amis
6. retrouver des amis en ville

7. aller boire quelque chose
8. dîner au restaurant
9. rentrer tard
10. passer la soirée à la maison
11. inviter des amis à la maison
12. regarder des DVD

B **Entretien.** Interviewez votre partenaire.

1. Quel(s) jour(s) est-ce que tu quittes la maison tôt? D'habitude, à quelle heure est-ce que tu quittes la maison le lundi? le mardi? Est-ce que tu rentres tard quelquefois? (Quels jours est-ce que tu rentres tard?) À quelle heure est-ce que tu rentres?
2. Est-ce que tu aimes partir quelquefois pour le week-end? Est-ce que tu aimes aller voir des amis qui habitent dans une autre ville? Quelle ville aimes-tu visiter? Qu'est-ce que tu aimes faire dans cette ville?
3. Vas-tu souvent au café? Qu'est-ce que tu aimes boire le matin? Et quand tu as très soif? Et quand tu as froid? Et quand tu as chaud?
4. En général, quel(s) jour(s) est-ce que tu passes la journée à la maison? Et la soirée? Est-ce que tu passes toute la journée chez toi de temps en temps?

Au Vieux Carré à La Nouvelle-Orléans

À VOUS!

Avec un(e) partenaire, relisez à haute voix la conversation entre Adam et Robert. Ensuite, imaginez qu'un(e) ami(e) passe le week-end chez vous et que vous parlez de vos projets pour vendredi, samedi et dimanche.

You can access the audio of the active vocabulary of this *Compétence* online.

SAYING WHAT YOU ARE GOING TO DO

Le futur immédiat

Sélection musicale. Search for the song "**Je vais changer le monde**" by Jean-François Bastien online to enjoy a musical selection containing this structure.

1. To say what you *are going to do,* use a form of **aller** followed by an infinitive.

je vais étudier	nous allons rentrer
tu vas travailler	vous allez sortir
il/elle/on va lire	ils/elles vont nager

—Qu'est-ce que tu **vas faire** demain?

—Je **vais sortir.**

—*What **are you going to do** tomorrow?*

—*I'm going to go out.*

2. In the negative, put the **ne... pas** around the conjugated form of **aller.**

Je **ne vais pas** sortir ce soir.   *I'm not going to go out tonight.*

3. Place the pronoun **y,** when needed, *immediately before* the infinitive.

Ma sœur va aller en boîte, mais moi, je **ne vais pas y aller.**

4. **Il y a** becomes **il va y avoir** when saying *there is/are going to be.*

Il va y avoir un concert demain. **Il ne va pas y avoir** de film.

5. Use these expressions to tell when you are going to do something.

maintenant *now*	**plus tard** *later*
aujourd'hui *today*	**demain** *tomorrow*
ce matin *this morning*	**demain matin** *tomorrow morning*
cet après-midi *this afternoon*	**demain après-midi** *tomorrow afternoon*
ce soir *tonight / this evening*	**demain soir** *tomorrow night / evening*
lundi *Monday*	**lundi prochain** *next Monday*
ce week-end *this weekend*	**le week-end prochain** *next weekend*
cette semaine *this week*	**la semaine prochaine** *next week*
ce mois-ci *this month*	**le mois prochain** *next month*
cette année *this year*	**l'année prochaine** *next year*

A **Que vont-ils faire?** Dites ou demandez si ces personnes vont faire les choses indiquées aux moments donnés.

EXEMPLE Ce soir, moi, je **vais** travailler.
Ce soir, moi, je **ne vais pas** travailler.

1. Ce soir, je _____ rentrer tard.

2. Demain matin, je _____ quitter la maison tôt.

3. Samedi prochain, mes amis et moi _____ passer la soirée ensemble.

4. Le week-end prochain, mon meilleur ami (ma meilleure amie) _____ aller voir sa famille.

5. La semaine prochaine, en cours de français, nous _____ avoir un (d')examen.

6. Les cours universitaires _____ se terminer *(to end)* le mois prochain.

7. *[au professeur]* L'année prochaine, vous _____ continuer à travailler ici?

8. *[à un(e) autre étudiant(e)]* L'année prochaine, tu _____ étudier ici?

B **Et ensuite?** Qu'est-ce que ces personnes vont faire **d'abord** et qu'est-ce qu'elles vont faire **ensuite**?

EXEMPLE moi, je: manger / préparer le dîner

D'abord, moi, je vais préparer le dîner et ensuite, je vais manger.

1. nous: travailler tout l'après-midi / aller prendre un verre
2. moi, je: dormir / rentrer à la maison
3. mon frère: retrouver sa copine en ville / dîner au restaurant avec elle
4. vous: dîner au restaurant / sortir danser
5. mes amis: préparer le dîner / aller au supermarché *(supermarket)*
6. toi, tu: faire cet exercice-ci / commencer l'exercice suivant

C **Projets.** Demandez à votre partenaire si ces personnes vont faire les choses indiquées aux moments donnés.

EXEMPLE tes amis et toi / jouer à des jeux vidéo ce soir
— **Tes amis et toi, vous allez jouer à des jeux vidéo ce soir?**
— **Oui, nous allons jouer à des jeux vidéo ce soir. Non, nous n'allons pas jouer à des jeux vidéo ce soir.**

1. tu / rester au lit demain matin
2. tu / retrouver des amis au café ce week-end
3. tes amis et toi / aller en boîte samedi prochain
4. nous / avoir des devoirs de français ce soir

D **Pourquoi y vont-ils?** Robert dit où ces personnes vont aller ce week-end et ce qu'elles vont y faire. Complétez ce qu'il dit.

EXEMPLE moi, je / musée

Moi, je vais aller au musée ce week-end. Je vais y voir une exposition.

1. moi, je / au centre commercial
2. mes amis / à la piscine
3. nous / au cinéma
4. Gabriel / à la salle de gym
5. mes amis et moi / à la librairie
6. mon père et ma belle-mère / au théâtre

E **Entretien.** Interviewez un(e) partenaire avec les questions suivantes.

1. Avec qui est-ce que tu vas passer l'après-midi, samedi? (Qu'est-ce que vous allez faire ensemble?)
2. Est-ce que tu vas retrouver des amis en ville samedi soir? (Où? Qu'est-ce que vous allez faire ensemble?)
3. Où est-ce que tu vas passer la journée, dimanche? Qu'est-ce que tu vas faire l'après-midi et le soir?
4. Quand est-ce que tu vas étudier ce week-end? Avec qui est-ce que tu vas étudier?

SAYING WHEN YOU ARE GOING TO DO SOMETHING

✔ **Pour vérifier**

1. Do you generally use cardinal or ordinal numbers to give dates in French? What is the exception?

2. In what two ways can the year 1789 be expressed in French? How do you say the year 2019?

3. How do you say *in* with months and years? How do you say *in January*? *in 2017*?

4. What are these dates in French: 15/3/1951 and 11/1/2022?

Vocabulaire supplémentaire

LES FÊTES ET LES OBSERVANCES RELIGIEUSES
un anniversaire de mariage
   a wedding anniversary
la fête des Mères / la fête des Pères
la fête nationale *the national holiday*
Hanoukka *(f)*
le (réveillon du) jour de l'An *New Year's (Eve)*
Noël *(m) Christmas*
Pâques *(f) Easter*
la pâque juive *Passover*
le ramadan
la Saint-Valentin
Yom Kippour
Bon anniversaire! *Happy Birthday!*
Bonne année! *Happy New Year!*
Joyeux Noël! *Merry Christmas!*

Vocabulaire sans peine!

The word **anniversaire** means both *birthday* and *anniversary* in French. Note the cognate pattern *-ary* = **-aire.**

le contraire = *the contrary*
révolutionnaire = *revolutionary*
nécessaire = *necessary*

How would you say the following in French?

commentary
imaginary
ordinary

Les dates

1. To express the date in French, use **le** and the cardinal numbers **(deux, trois...),** except for *the first* of the month. For *the first,* use the ordinal number: **le premier (1ᵉʳ).**

—Quelle est la date aujourd'hui? / C'est quelle date aujourd'hui?
—C'est **le premier... le deux... le trois... le quatre...**

janvier	avril	juillet	octobre
février	mai	août	novembre
mars	juin	septembre	décembre

—Quelle est la date de la fête *(holiday)* nationale française?
—C'est le 14 (quatorze) juillet.

Note that the day goes before the month in French.

14/7/1789 = le quatorze juillet dix-sept cent quatre-vingt-neuf

2. You can express the years 1100–1999 in French in either of two ways. Years starting at 2000 are only expressed using the word **mille.**

1945: mille neuf cent quarante-cinq / dix-neuf cent quarante-cinq
2019: deux mille dix-neuf

3. Use **en** to say *in* what month or year. Use **le** when saying *on* a certain date.

—Ton anniversaire *(birthday),* c'est quand?
—C'est **en** novembre. C'est **le** 18 novembre *([on] November 18ᵗʰ).* Je vais faire une fête **le** 16 novembre *(I am going to have a party [on] November 16ᵗʰ).*

—**En** quelle année vas-tu finir tes études?
—**En** 2022.

A **Quel mois?** Regardez la liste de fêtes dans la marge de cette page et complétez ces phrases avec le nom du mois correspondant.

EXEMPLE Le jour de l'An, c'est en **janvier.**

1. Le réveillon du jour de l'An, c'est en...
2. L'année scolaire commence en...   Elle finit en...
3. La fête nationale française, c'est en...   Notre fête nationale, c'est en...
4. La fête des Mères, c'est en...   La fête des Pères, c'est en...
5. Thanksgiving, c'est en...

B **Encore des dates.** Demandez à votre partenaire la date des jours indiqués.

aujourd'hui	demain	de lundi	de ton anniversaire
de notre fête nationale		de Noël	de Halloween
du jour de l'An *(New Year's Day)*			de la Saint-Valentin
	de ta fête préférée		

C **Votre anniversaire.** Les autres étudiants vont essayer de deviner *(will try to guess)* la date de votre anniversaire. Répondez **avant** ou **après** jusqu'à ce qu'ils devinent juste *(guess right)*.

> **EXEMPLE** — Ton anniversaire, c'est en mars?
> — Après.
> — C'est en mai?
> — Oui.
> — C'est le quinze mai?
> — Avant...

D **Comparaisons culturelles.** Lisez à haute voix ces dates importantes.

> **EXEMPLE** 4/7/1776 (le début de la Révolution américaine)
> **le quatre juillet mille sept cent soixante-seize**
> **(le quatre juillet dix-sept cent soixante-seize)**

1. 1/11/1718 (Bienville fonde La Nouvelle-Orléans.)
2. 14/7/1789 (la prise de la Bastille)
3. 30/4/1812 (La Louisiane devient *[becomes]* un État des États-Unis.)
4. 11/11/1918 (le jour de l'Armistice de la Première Guerre mondiale)
5. 6/6/1944 (le jour du débarquement en Normandie)

E **À quelle date?** Dites si ces personnes vont faire les choses indiquées aux dates données.

> **EXEMPLE** 25/12 je / aller voir mes parents
> **Le 25 décembre, je vais aller voir mes parents.**
> **Le 25 décembre, je ne vais pas aller voir mes parents.**

beaucoup de mes amis / faire un pique-nique
ma famille / aller voir des feux d'artifice *(fireworks)*
mes amis et moi / aller à la plage

1. 4/7

beaucoup de mes amis / dîner au restaurant
je / sortir avec un(e) ami(e) (des amis)
je / acheter des chocolats pour mes amis

2. 14/2

je / passer la soirée avec des amis
mes parents / aller voir des amis
mon meilleur ami (ma meilleure amie) / rentrer tard

3. 31/12

je / inviter des amis chez moi
mes amis et moi / faire une fête
je / avoir ?? ans

4. la date de votre anniversaire

F **Entretien.** Interviewez votre partenaire.

1. Quelle est la date aujourd'hui? Quelle est la date de ton anniversaire? Qu'est-ce que tu vas probablement faire ce jour-là *(that day)*? Quelle est la date de ta fête préférée? Qu'est-ce que tu aimes faire ce jour-là?
2. Quelle est la date du dernier *(last)* jour du cours de français? Qu'est-ce que tu vas faire après ton dernier cours ce semestre / trimestre? Est-ce que tu vas continuer à étudier ici l'année prochaine?

Planning how to get there

LES MOYENS *(m)* DE TRANSPORT

Robert et ses amis vont aller à La Nouvelle-Orléans en voiture. Et vous? Comment préférez-vous voyager?

Pour visiter une autre ville, je préfère y aller...

en avion *(m)*   en train *(m)*   en bateau *(m)*   en car / en autocar *(m)*

Il y a d'autres possibilités pour aller en ville. Comment **venez-vous** en cours?

Je viens en cours...

à pied *(m)*   à vélo *(m)*   en taxi *(m)*

en voiture *(f)*   en métro *(m)*   en bus / en autobus *(m)*

4-8

C'est mercredi soir et Robert parle à Adam du voyage à La Nouvelle-Orléans.

ROBERT: Bon, demain matin, on va à La Nouvelle-Orléans. Tout est prêt?

ADAM: Oui. On y va en car?

ROBERT: Non, on va **louer** une voiture, c'est plus pratique.

ADAM: C'est loin? **Ça prend combien de temps pour y aller?**

ROBERT: Ça prend environ deux heures et demie en voiture, **pas plus.**

ADAM: Et **on revient** quand?

ROBERT: On revient **après-demain.**

Les moyens de transport *Means of transportation*   **vous venez / Je viens (venir** *to come)*   **louer** *to rent*   **Ça prend combien de temps pour y aller?** *How long does it take to go there?*   **pas plus** *no more*   **on revient (revenir** *to come back)*   **après-demain** *the day after tomorrow*

A Moyens de transport. Complétez les phrases pour parler de vous.

> en avion   en train   en car   en bateau   en voiture
> à pied   à vélo   en taxi   en métro   en bus

1. Pour faire un long voyage, je préfère voyager...
2. Je n'aime pas beaucoup voyager...
3. Je ne voyage presque jamais...
4. Je préfère aller en ville...
5. D'habitude, je viens en cours...
6. Je ne viens presque jamais en cours...

B On y va comment? Dites où chacun va et comment.

EXEMPLE Ils **vont à La Nouvelle-Orléans en voiture.**

1. Je...

2. Ils...

3. Vous...

4. Nous...

5. Elle...

C Entretien. Interviewez votre partenaire.

1. Quelle ville est-ce que tu visites souvent? Comment est-ce que tu préfères y aller? (en voiture? en train? en avion?) Ça prend combien de temps pour y aller?
2. Tu voyages souvent en avion? Tu as peur de voyager en avion? Pour aller de chez toi à l'aéroport, ça prend combien de temps? Qu'est-ce que tu aimes faire pendant *(during)* les longs voyages en avion? (dormir? lire? parler?...)
3. Quels jours est-ce que tu viens en cours? Comment préfères-tu venir en cours? Comment viens-tu en cours, d'habitude? Comment est-ce que tu rentres chez toi?

À VOUS!

Avec un(e) partenaire, relisez à haute voix la conversation entre Robert et Adam. Ensuite, adaptez la conversation pour parler d'un voyage que vous allez faire ensemble pour visiter une autre ville. Parlez de comment vous allez voyager et de combien de temps ça va prendre pour y aller.

You can access the audio of the active vocabulary of this *Compétence* online.

DECIDING HOW TO GET THERE AND COME BACK

*Les verbes **prendre** et **venir** et les moyens de transport*

✔ **Pour vérifier**

1. What are the forms of **venir**? of **prendre**? What two verbs are conjugated like **venir**? like **prendre**? What verb do you use to say you are *having* something to eat or drink? When is **apprendre** followed by **à**?

2. In what forms of the verbs **venir** and **prendre** are the vowels nasal? **Je viens / tu viens / il vient** rhyme with what word? **Je prends / tu prends / il prend** rhyme with what word? How do you pronounce the **ils/elles viennent** form? the **ils/elles prennent** form?

1. The conjugations of **prendre** *(to take)* and **venir** *(to come)* are irregular.

PRENDRE *(to take)*		VENIR *(to come)*	
je **prends**	nous **prenons**	je **viens**	nous **venons**
tu **prends**	vous **prenez**	tu **viens**	vous **venez**
il/elle/on **prend**	ils/elles **prennent**	il/elle/on **vient**	ils/elles **viennent**

2. Prendre means *to take*.

Je **prends** des notes en cours.   **Prenons** le métro!

Use **prendre** to say that you are *taking* a means of transportation. Remember that you can also use **aller, venir,** or **voyager** and the preposition **en** (or **à** with **vélo**) to say that you are *going, coming,* or *traveling **by*** a particular means of transportation. To say *on foot*, use **à pied.**

Je **prends** le métro.   Je **prends** l'avion.
J'y **vais** en métro.   Je **voyage** en avion.   Je **viens** en cours **à pied.**

3. Use **prendre** as *to have* when talking about *having* something to eat or drink.

Je vais **prendre** un sandwich et une eau minérale.

4. Comprendre *(to understand)* and **apprendre** *(to learn)* are conjugated like **prendre.** When **apprendre** is followed by an infinitive, the infinitive is preceded by **à.**

J'**apprends à** parler français. Ma sœur **apprend** le français aussi. Tu **comprends**?

5. Use **venir** to say *to come*. **Revenir** *(to come back)* and **devenir** *(to become)* are conjugated like **venir.**

Vous **revenez** tard et il **devient** impatient.

Note *de vocabulaire*

1. Use **en** with **aller, venir,** or **voyager** to say you are traveling *by* a means of transportation. **Je viens *en* bus, *en* taxi, *en* train...**

2. Use **prendre** to say what means of transportation you are *taking*. In this case, you can generally use the same article with the noun that you would in English: *I take **the** bus, **a** cab, **the** train ...* **Je prends *le* bus, *un* taxi, *le* train...**

3. Note that you do not use **prendre** in French to say *to take a class* (**suivre un cours**) or *to take an exam* (**passer un examen**).

Sélection musicale. Search for the songs "La liberté de penser" by Florent Pagny and "Où aller" by Kathleen online to enjoy musical selections containing these structures.

PRONONCIATION

*Les verbes **prendre** et **venir***   4-9

In the **je, tu,** and **il/elle/on** forms of the verb **venir,** the vowel combination **ie** has the nasal sound [jɛ̃]. The consonants after **ie** are all silent. All three forms rhyme with the word **bien.** In the **ils/elles viennent** form, however, the **ie** is not nasal and the **nn** is pronounced.

je viens   **tu viens**   **il vient**   **ils viennent**   **elles viennent**

Similarly, the **e** in the **je, tu,** and **il/elle/on** forms of the verb **prendre** is nasal and the consonants after the vowel are silent. All three forms rhyme with the word **quand.** In the **ils/elles prennent** form, however, the **e** is not nasal. It is pronounced like the **è** in **mère** and the **nn** is pronounced.

je prends   **tu prends**   **il prend**   **ils prennent**   **elles prennent**

The **e** in the **nous** and **vous** forms of both verbs is pronounced like the **e** in **je.**

nous venons   **vous venez**   **nous prenons**   **vous prenez**

4-10 **A** **Prononcez bien!** D'abord, écoutez les phrases et indiquez pour chacune si on parle d'**une personne** ou de **plus d'une personne**. Après, écrivez deux phrases avec le verbe **prendre** et deux phrases avec le verbe **venir**. Lisez-les à un(e) partenaire qui va dire si vous parlez **d'une personne** ou de **plus d'une personne**.

B **Qu'est-ce qu'on fait?** Conjuguez les verbes entre parenthèses et posez les questions à votre partenaire.

1. Quels jours est-ce que tu *(venir)* en cours? Est-ce que tu *(prendre)* le bus pour venir en cours? Est-ce que tu *(venir)* en cours à pied ou à vélo quelquefois?
2. Est-ce que les autres étudiants du cours de français *(venir)* toujours en cours? Est-ce qu'ils *(comprendre)* bien le français? Est-ce que nous *(apprendre)* beaucoup en cours?
3. Est-ce que le cours de français *(devenir)* plus difficile? Est-ce que le (la) prof *(devenir)* impatient(e) quand les étudiants *(ne pas apprendre)* le vocabulaire?
4. Est-ce que tu *(revenir)* à cette université l'année prochaine? Est-ce que tu *(apprendre)* beaucoup ici?

C **Que font-ils?** Faites une phrase logique à partir de chaque sujet donné pour parler de votre cours de français.

EXEMPLE Moi, je ne viens pas en cours en bus.

				des/de notes en cours
				bien le professeur
		prendre		beaucoup de verbes
moi, je		apprendre		beaucoup de vocabulaire
le (la) prof	(ne/n')	comprendre	(pas)	à l'université le week-end
nous		venir		impatient(e)(s)
les étudiants		revenir		paresseux (paresseuse[s])
		devenir		le bus pour venir en cours
				en cours à pied
				en cours en bus

D **La santé.** Votre ami voudrait être en meilleure santé *(health)*. Donnez-lui des conseils. Utilisez l'impératif.

EXEMPLE Je prends un coca ou un jus d'orange?
Prends un jus d'orange! Ne prends pas de coca!

1. Je prends une bière ou une eau minérale?
2. Je viens en cours en voiture ou à vélo?
3. Je prends une salade ou des frites?
4. Je vais au parc ou je reste à la maison?
5. Je vais au parc en voiture ou à pied?
6. Je prends un bain de soleil ou je nage?

Prenons les vélos!

VIDÉO-REPRISE

Les Stagiaires

Rappel!
Dans le dernier *(last)* épisode de la vidéo, Amélie et Céline ont décidé d'être colocataires et d'habiter ensemble dans l'appartement de Céline.

See the *Résumé de grammaire* section at the end of each chapter for a review of all the grammar presented in the chapter.

Dans l'***Épisode 4,*** Céline et Amélie parlent de la famille d'Amélie et de celle de *(that of)* Christophe. Avant de regarder l'épisode, faites ces exercices pour réviser ce que vous avez appris dans le ***Chapitre 4.***

A **La famille de Christophe.** Rachid parle à Christophe de sa famille. Complétez leur conversation avec les mots logiques.

RACHID: Alors, Christophe, c'est vrai que M. Vieilledent est ton __1__?
CHRISTOPHE: Oui, c'est vrai.
RACHID: Tu as une grande __2__? Tu as des __3__ et sœurs?
CHRISTOPHE: Moi, je suis le seul __4__, mais j'ai deux __5__, Léa et Emma.
RACHID: Elles sont plus __6__ ou plus jeunes que toi?
CHRISTOPHE: Je suis le plus jeune. Elles __7__ vingt-six et vingt-quatre __8__.
RACHID: Et ta __9__, elle s'appelle comment?
CHRISTOPHE: Elle s'appelle Pauline, mais mes parents ne sont plus ensemble. Ils sont __10__.

Maintenant, préparez une conversation avec un(e) partenaire dans laquelle *(in which)* vous parlez de vos familles.

B **Aujourd'hui.** Utilisez des expressions avec **avoir** pour dire comment l'équipe *(team)* de Technovert se sent *(feels)* aujourd'hui.

EXEMPLE M. Vieilledent voudrait des croissants parce qu'il **a faim.**

1. Camille voudrait boire quelque chose parce qu'elle _____.
2. Matthieu voudrait enlever son pull *(to take off his sweater)* parce qu'il _____.
3. Amélie a besoin d'un pull parce qu'elle _____.
4. Christophe voudrait faire la sieste *(to take a nap)* parce qu'il _____.
5. Rachid _____ d'étudier parce qu'il a un examen demain.

C **Les anniversaires.** Les résultats du trimestre sont tellement *(so)* bons que M. Vieilledent pense donner un bonus à chaque employé(e) pour son anniversaire. Donnez la date de l'anniversaire de chacun.

EXEMPLE Camille: 25/1
L'anniversaire de Camille, c'est le vingt-cinq janvier.

1. Céline: 30/3   3. Matthieu: 21/8   5. Amélie: 14/2
2. Christophe: 16/5   4. Rachid: 1/6

D **Pauvre Matthieu.** Matthieu voudrait sortir avec Amélie, mais il n'a pas le courage de lui parler *(to talk to her)* parce qu'il est trop timide. Est-ce que Camille dit *(tells)* à Matthieu de faire ou de ne pas faire les choses suivantes pour l'encourager *(to encourage him)*? Utilisez l'impératif des verbes suivants à la forme affirmative ou négative pour former des phrases logiques.

EXEMPLE être timide
Ne sois pas timide!

1. avoir un peu de courage
2. être ridicule
3. avoir peur de parler à Amélie
4. aller dans son bureau sans rien dire *(without saying anything)*
5. regarder Amélie tout le temps sans parler
6. parler avec elle de temps en temps
7. prendre l'initiative de parler à Amélie
8. inviter Amélie au nouveau restaurant du quartier

E Parlons ensemble.

M. Vieilledent parle aux stagiaires de leur travail. Complétez les phrases suivantes avec l'impératif des verbes entre parenthèses. Mettez l'un des verbes à la forme de vous et l'autre à la forme de nous pour faire des phrases logiques.

EXEMPLE Rachid et Amélie, **venez** (venir) avec moi, s'il vous plaît.
Allons (aller) dans mon bureau.

1. S'il vous plaît, _____ (entrer) dans mon bureau, tous les deux, et asseyez-vous *(have a seat)*, je vous en prie. Si vous voulez bien, _____ (prendre) un peu de temps pour parler de votre travail à Technovert.

2. _____ (commencer) par vos responsabilités. _____ (ne pas hésiter) à poser des questions si vous ne comprenez pas quelque chose.

3. _____ (venir) me voir *(to see me)* s'il y a un problème et _____ (trouver) une solution ensemble.

4. _____ (partager) vos idées et vos opinions avec moi. _____ (être) toujours ouverts et francs les uns avec les autres.

5. _____ (travailler) tous ensemble! _____ (ne pas avoir) peur de faire des suggestions. Ma porte est toujours ouverte.

F Le week-end.

Rachid pose des questions à Amélie. Complétez chaque question avec la forme correcte du verbe logique entre parenthèses.

1. (aller, venir) Le week-end, est-ce que tu _____ plus souvent chez tes amis ou est-ce que tes amis _____ plutôt chez toi?

2. (aller, prendre) Qui _____ sa voiture généralement quand tes amis et toi _____ en ville le week-end?

3. (aller, avoir) Est-ce que tu _____ envie de sortir samedi soir ou est-ce que tu _____ rester chez toi?

4. (aller, avoir) Et dimanche, qu'est-ce que tu _____ l'intention de faire? Tu _____ étudier?

5. (avoir, devenir) Est-ce que tu _____ une page sur Facebook? On _____ amis sur Facebook?

Maintenant, utilisez ces questions pour interviewer un(e) partenaire.

Access the Video *Les Stagiaires* online.

▶ Épisode 4: Vive la famille!

AVANT LA VIDÉO

Dans cet épisode, Céline parle de la famille de Christophe et pose des questions à Amélie au sujet de sa famille. Avant de regarder l'épisode, imaginez une des questions que Céline pose à Amélie.

APRÈS LA VIDÉO

Regardez l'épisode et notez une chose au sujet de la famille de Christophe et une chose au sujet de la famille d'Amélie.

LECTURE ET COMPOSITION

LECTURE

POUR MIEUX LIRE:
Using your knowledge of the world

You are going to read the poem *Deux mots* by Jean Gentil that appeared in 1878 in *Le Louisianais,* a newspaper published in the town of Convent in the Saint James Parish of Louisiana. In this poem, Jean Gentil expresses the importance of the freedom of religion. Using what you already know about different religions of the world will help you understand as you read. Before reading it, do this activity to make your reading easier.

Associations. À quelle religion de la liste associez-vous les choses ou les personnes suivantes?

le catholicisme	le protestantisme
le judaïsme	l'islam

1. Rome et le pape
2. le Pater noster
3. Martin Luther
4. un rabbin
5. le Talmud
6. le Coran

Deux mots

Homme, sois catholique,
Si ça te fait plaisir;
Sois **aristotélique,**
Si c'est là ton désir;
Jure par le pape et Rome,
En disant ton Pater,
Ou bien proteste comme
A protesté Luther;
Suis le Talmud **lui-même,**
En rabbin révérend,
Ou bien, si ton **cœur** l'aime,
Obéis au Coran;
Bien plus, si tu préfères
Les Kings et **le Chou-King,**
Ce sont là **tes affaires,**
Et j'aime assez Péking.
Chacun de nous est libre,
Et **croit comme il l'entend:**
Je prends mon équilibre;
Tu peux en faire autant.
Aussi, petits bonhommes
De trois ou quatre jours,
Étant ce que nous sommes,
Respectons-nous toujours.
Mais si **l'apostasie**
Est une indignité,
Certes, l'hypocrisie
Est **une lâcheté.**

Source: Jean Gentil, "Deux mots" in *Le Louisianais,* June 1878

Si ça te fait plaisir *If that makes you happy*   **aristotélique** *(someone who follows the philosophy of Aristotle)*   **Jure par** *Swear by*   **En disant** *By saying*   **Suis** *Follow*   **lui-même** *itself*   **cœur** *heart*   **Obéis** *Obey*   **le Chou-King** *(a Chinese dynasty)*   **tes affaires** *your business*   **Chacun** *Each one*   **croit comme il l'entend** *believes as he thinks best*   **Tu peux en faire autant** *You can do the same*   **Étant ce que** *Being what*   **l'apostasie** *apostasy (abandoning your beliefs)*   **Certes** *Certainly*   **une lâcheté** *a cowardly act*

Lou...

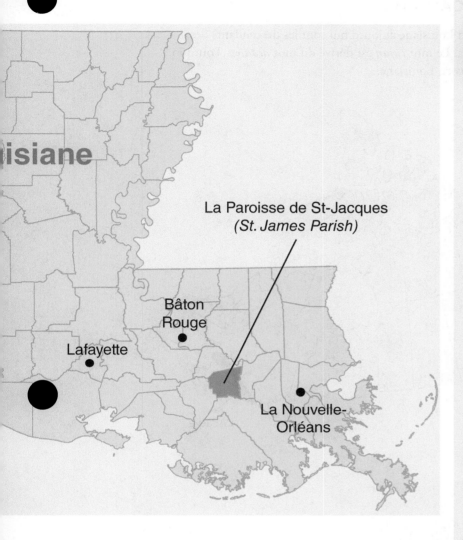

La Paroisse de St-Jacques
(St. James Parish)

Bâton Rouge

Lafayette

La Nouvelle-Orléans

POUR MIEUX ÉCRIRE:
Visualizing your topic

Sometimes it is easier to write a description of people or things if you visualize or look at images of them. Using an image such as a family photo or a family tree helps structure a description.

Organisez-vous. Vous allez écrire une description de votre famille. D'abord, dessinez *(draw)* un arbre généalogique de votre famille. À côté de chaque membre de votre famille sur l'arbre généalogique, écrivez tous les mots que vous associez à cette personne: son âge, sa profession, son apparence physique, son caractère et ses activités.

Compréhension

Deux mots. Lisez le poème et répondez aux questions suivantes.

1. De quelles religions ou philosophies est-ce que Jean Gentil parle dans le poème?
2. Dans le poème, il dit «Je prends mon équilibre, Tu peux en faire autant.» Qu'est-ce que ça veut dire?
3. Que pense-t-il de l'hypocrisie?
4. Est-ce que vous trouvez le message de ce poème publié en 1878 tout aussi valable *(just as pertinent)* aujourd'hui?

Ma famille

Faites une description écrite détaillée de votre famille. Basez votre description sur l'arbre généalogique que vous venez de créer *(that you just created)*.

COMPARAISONS CULTURELLES

L'HISTOIRE DES CADIENS

La majorité des Cadiens en Louisiane aujourd'hui sont les descendants des Acadiens **venus** du Canada. Le mot *cajun* est dérivé du mot *acadien*. Pourquoi ces Acadiens **sont-ils venus** en Louisiane?

En 1604, les Français **fondent** une colonie dans **la partie est** du Canada qu'ils appellent l'Acadie.

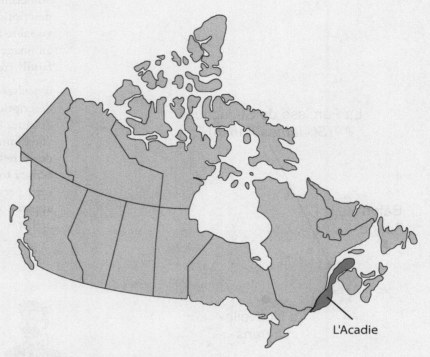

L'Acadie

Courtesy of Claude Picard and the Grand-Pré National Historic Site, Nova Scotia

En 1713, les Anglais prennent possession de l'Acadie. Les Acadiens prospèrent et, en 1755, ils sont au nombre de 15 000. Cela **inquiète** les autorités anglaises, qui commencent alors à déporter les Français. Cette expulsion des Acadiens est **appelée** «le Grand Dérangement».

venus *who came*　**sont-ils venus** *did they come*　**fondent** *found*　**la partie est** *the eastern part*　**inquiète** *worries*
appelée *called*

Après une période noire **pendant laquelle** beaucoup d'Acadiens **meurent,** certains groupes d'Acadiens viennent **s'établir dans la partie sud** de la Louisiane. **En raison de** l'inaccessibilité de la région, ces francophones restent **isolés pendant** plus de 200 ans, et leur culture et leur langue restent dominantes dans le sud de la Louisiane.

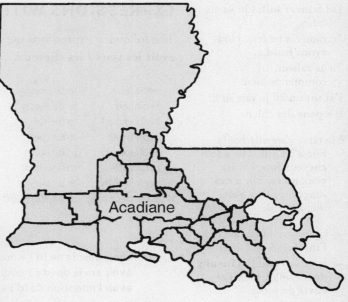

Acadiane

No French to be spoken in school. Oil on Canvas © 1984 Georges Rodrigue

Vers la fin du 19e siècle, des vagues d'anglophones commencent à arriver dans la région. En 1916, l'État de Louisiane **exige que la scolarité se fasse** en anglais et l'anglais devient de ce **fait** la langue prédominante chez les jeunes. L'usage du français en Louisiane **diminue.**

En 1968, la Louisiane **met** en place le CODOFIL, le Conseil pour le développement du français en Louisiane, pour **protéger** la langue et la culture françaises. Et en 1971, l'État crée la région d'Acadiane, **comprenant 22 paroisses** francophones dans la partie sud de l'État.

Compréhension

1. La majorité des Cadiens en Louisiane sont les descendants de quel groupe?

2. Qu'est-ce que «le Grand Dérangement»?

3. Pourquoi est-ce que l'anglais devient la langue prédominante après 1916?

4. Quel est le but *(goal)* du CODOFIL? Que pensez-vous de cette idée de créer une agence pour la défense de la langue et de la culture d'une minorité? Est-ce qu'il y a des organisations publiques dans votre région qui protègent la langue ou la culture d'une minorité?

CODOFIL

AGENCE DES AFFAIRES FRANCOPHONES

www.codofil.org

---

pendant laquelle *during which*   **meurent** *die*   **s'établir dans la partie sud** *establish themselves in the southern part*
En raison de *Because of*   **isolés pendant** *isolated for*   **Vers la fin du 19e siècle, des vagues** *Towards the end of the 19th century,*
waves   **exige que la scolarité se fasse** *requires that education be done*   **fait** *act, deed, fact*   **diminue** *diminishes*   **met** *puts*
protéger *to protect*   **comprenant 22 paroisses** *including 22 parishes* (equivalent of counties)

RÉSUMÉ DE GRAMMAIRE

J'**ai faim** et **soif**. On va au café?

Fermons la fenêtre! Nous **avons froid.**

Tu **as raison.** Tu comprends bien!

J'**ai sommeil**! Je vais au lit.

Il **a peur des** chiens.

Ma tante s'appelle Sonia. Elle **a 34 ans.** Elle **a les cheveux longs** et les **yeux noirs.** Elle **a des lunettes.** Elle **a l'air** intellectuelle.

—Qu'est-ce que tu **as l'intention de** faire?

—Je ne sais pas. J'**ai besoin de** travailler, mais j'**ai envie de** sortir.

—Où **vas**-tu cet après-midi?

—Je **vais au** cinéma. Mes parents **vont aux** nouvelles expositions de deux artistes de la ville et ma sœur **va à la** bibliothèque. Et vous deux, où **allez**-vous?

—Nous **allons à** l'église.

—Je vais à l'université. Tu voudrais **y** aller avec moi?

—Non, je n'**y** vais pas aujourd'hui.

Va au restaurant Préjean et **mange** les spécialités de la maison.

Mangez bien. **Ne mangez pas** de dessert.

—**On sort** ce soir?

—D'accord. **Allons** au cinéma.

—Non, **n'allons pas** au cinéma. **Dînons** plutôt au restaurant.

EXPRESSIONS WITH *AVOIR*

The following expressions use **avoir.** Note the use of the definite article with **avoir les yeux / les cheveux.**

avoir faim	*to be hungry*	avoir... ans	*to be ... years old*
avoir soif	*to be thirsty*	avoir les cheveux longs	*to have long hair*
avoir chaud	*to be hot*	avoir les yeux marron	*to have brown eyes*
avoir froid	*to be cold*	avoir l'air...	*to look ..., to seem ...*
avoir raison	*to be right*	avoir une barbe /	*to have a beard /*
avoir tort	*to be wrong*	une moustache /	*a mustache /*
avoir sommeil	*to be sleepy*	des lunettes	*glasses*
avoir peur (de)	*to be afraid (of)*		

avoir besoin de (d') + noun or infinitive	*to need* + noun or infinitive
avoir envie de (d') + noun or infinitive	*to feel like* + noun or verb
avoir l'intention de (d') + infinitive	*to intend* + infinitive

THE VERB *ALLER*, THE PREPOSITION *À*, AND THE PRONOUN *Y*

Use the verb **aller** and the preposition **à** *(to, at, in)* to say where someone is going. When **à** falls before **le** or **les,** the two words contract to **au** and **aux.**

ALLER *(to go)*	
je **vais**	nous‿**allons**
tu **vas**	vous‿**allez**
il/elle/on **va**	ils/elles **vont**

Use the pronoun **y** to mean *there,* even when *there* is only implied in English. Place it *immediately before* the infinitive if there is one. Otherwise, place it *immediately before* the conjugated verb. Treat **y** as a vowel for purposes of elision and liaison.

COMMAND FORMS (*L'IMPÉRATIF*)

To tell someone to do something, use the **tu** or **vous** form of the verb, as appropriate, without the pronoun **tu** or **vous.** In **tu** form commands, drop the final **s** of **-er** verbs and **aller.**

You can invite someone to do something with you by asking a question with **on** (*Shall we . . . ? / How about . . . ?*). To say *Let's . . . ,* use the **nous** form of the appropriate verb without the pronoun **nous.**

Avoir and **être** have irregular command forms.

ÊTRE (be . . .)	AVOIR (have . . .)
sois	aie
soyons	ayons
soyez	ayez

THE IMMEDIATE FUTURE (*LE FUTUR IMMÉDIAT*)

To talk about what someone *is going to do,* use a conjugated form of the verb **aller** followed by an infinitive. To say what someone is *not* going to do, place **ne... pas** around the conjugated form of **aller**. **Il y a** becomes **il va y avoir.**

DATES

To tell the date, use **le** and the cardinal numbers (**deux, trois, quatre...**), except for *the first* (**le premier**). The day goes *before* the month: **30/9/2015.**

You can express the years 1100–1999 in two ways. Years from 2000 on are only expressed using the word **mille.** Use **en** to say *in* what year or month. Do not use a word to say *on* with a date.

THE VERBS *PRENDRE* AND *VENIR* AND MEANS OF TRANSPORTATION

Prendre *(to take)* and **venir** *(to come)* are irregular.

PRENDRE *(to take)*		VENIR *(to come)*	
je **prends**	nous **prenons**	je **viens**	nous **venons**
tu **prends**	vous **prenez**	tu **viens**	vous **venez**
il/elle/on **prend**	ils/elles **prennent**	il/elle/on **vient**	ils/elles **viennent**

Prendre means *to take.* You can also use it as *to have* when talking about having something to eat or drink. **Comprendre** *(to understand)* and **apprendre** *(to learn)* are conjugated like **prendre.**

Revenir *(to come back)* and **devenir** *(to become)* are conjugated like **venir.**

Use the preposition **en** (or **à** with **vélo**) to say *by* what means you are traveling with verbs like **aller, venir,** and **voyager.** When using **prendre** to say what means of transportation you are taking, you can often use the same article with the noun that you would in English.

Sois à l'heure pour tes cours.

N'aie pas peur! **Aie** confiance!

N'ayons pas peur! **Soyons** prêts!

Ayez de la patience! **Ne soyez pas** impatients!

—Qu'est-ce que tu **vas faire** ce soir? Tu **vas sortir**?

—Non, je **ne vais pas sortir.** Je **vais rester** à la maison. **Il va y avoir** un match de foot à la télé.

—Quelle est la date, aujourd'hui? C'est **le trente septembre**?

—Non, c'est **le premier octobre.**

1910 **mille neuf cent dix / dix-neuf cent dix**

Mon anniversaire, c'est **en mars.** Je vais faire une fête le 15 mars.

Je vais finir mes études **en 2022 (deux mille vingt-deux).**

—**Venez**-vous à l'université **en voiture**?

—Non, je ne **viens** pas en cours en voiture. Je **prends** mon vélo. **Prenez**-vous votre voiture?

Le matin, il **prend** un café et un croissant.

Tu **comprends**?

Nous **apprenons** beaucoup dans ce cours.

Ses fils **reviennent** de plus en plus tard à la maison et le père **devient** impatient.

D'habitude, ils **voyagent en avion,** mais aujourd'hui ils **prennent le train.**

VOCABULAIRE

COMPÉTENCE 1

Describing your family

LA FAMILLE

des beaux-parents / un beau-père / une belle-mère	stepparents, in-laws / a stepfather, a father-in-law / a stepmother, a mother-in-law
un(e) cousin(e)	a cousin
un(e) enfant	a child
un fils / une fille	a son / a daughter
un frère / une sœur	a brother / a sister
un garçon / une fille	a boy / a girl
des grands-parents / un grand-père / une grand-mère	grandparents / a grandfather / a grandmother
un neveu (pl des neveux) / une nièce	a nephew / a niece
un oncle / une tante	an uncle / an aunt
des parents / un père / une mère	parents / a father / a mother

NOMS FÉMININS

une barbe	a beard
des lunettes	glasses
une moustache	a mustache
des vacances	vacation

ADJECTIFS

âgé(e)	old
auburn (inv)	auburn
blond(e)	blond(e)
brun(e)	medium / dark brown (with hair)
châtain	light / medium brown (with hair)
court(e)	short
décédé(e)	deceased
long(ue)	long
mi-longs	shoulder-length (with hair)
noir(e)	black, very dark brown (with eyes)
noisette (inv)	hazel (with eyes)
roux (rousse)	red (with hair)

EXPRESSIONS VERBALES

avoir besoin de	to need
avoir chaud / froid	to be hot / cold
avoir envie de	to feel like, to want
avoir faim / soif	to be hungry / thirsty
avoir l'air...	to look . . ., to seem . . .
avoir les cheveux / les yeux...	to have . . . hair / eyes
avoir l'intention de	to intend to
avoir peur (de)	to be afraid (of)
avoir raison / tort	to be right / wrong
avoir sommeil	to be sleepy
Comment s'appelle-t-il/elle? Il/Elle s'appelle...	What is his/her name? His/Her name is . . .
porter	to wear, to carry
Quel âge a...? avoir (environ)... ans	How old is . . . ? to be (about) . . . years old
Vous êtes combien dans votre (ta) famille? Nous sommes...	How many people are there in your family? There are . . . of us.

DIVERS

de taille moyenne	of medium height
encore	still
environ	about
La Nouvelle-Orléans	New Orleans

COMPÉTENCE 2

Saying where you go in your free time

NOMS MASCULINS

un centre commercial	a shopping mall
un concert	a concert
un festival	a festival
un magasin	a store
un musée	a museum
un orchestre	an orchestra, a band
un parc	a park
des projets	plans
le temps libre	free time
un théâtre	a theater

NOMS FÉMININS

une activité (de plein air)	an (outdoor) activity
la cuisine	cooking, cuisine
une église	a church
une exposition	an exhibit
une librairie	a bookstore
la musique zydeco	Zydeco music
une pièce (de théâtre)	a play
une piscine	a swimming pool
une plage	a beach
une région	a region
une spécialité	a specialty

EXPRESSIONS VERBALES

acheter	to buy
aie, ayons, ayez	have, let's have, have
aller (à)	to go (to)
avoir confiance	to have confidence
avoir de la patience	to have patience
connaître	to know, to get to know, to be acquainted / familiar with
prendre un bain de soleil	to sunbathe
retrouver	to meet
servir	to serve
sois, soyons, soyez	be, let's be, be
trouver	to find

DIVERS

à l'heure	on time
bonne idée	good idea
cadien(ne)	Cajun
culturel(le)	cultural
de temps en temps	from time to time
extra(ordinaire)	great
On...?	Shall we . . . ?, How about . . . ?
on dit que	they say that
on peut	one can
plutôt	rather, instead
pour	in order to
prêt(e)	ready
sage	good, well-behaved
y	there

COMPÉTENCE 3

Saying what you are going to do

NOMS MASCULINS

un anniversaire	*a birthday*
le folklore	*folklore*

NOMS FÉMININS

une fête	*a holiday, a party*
la soirée	*the evening*

EXPRESSIONS VERBALES

aller voir	*to go see, to visit* (a person)
boire	*to drink*
faire une fête	*to have a party*
faire des projets	*to make plans*
faire un tour	*to take a tour, to go for a ride*
il va y avoir	*there is / are going to be*
partir (pour le week-end)	*to go away, to leave (for the weekend)*
quitter	*to leave*
visiter	*to visit* (a place)

LES DATES

En quelle année?	*In what year?*
Quelle est la date?	*What is the date?*
C'est quelle date?	*What is the date?*
C'est le premier (deux, trois...)	*It's the first (second, third . . .) of*
janvier / février / mars / avril / mai / juin / juillet / août / septembre / octobre / novembre / décembre	*January / February / March / April / May / June / July / August / September / October / November / December*

EXPRESSIONS ADVERBIALES

ce matin	*this morning*
ce mois-ci	*this month*
ce soir	*tonight, this evening*
ce week-end	*this weekend*
cet après-midi	*this afternoon*
cette année	*this year*
cette semaine	*this week*
d'abord	*first*
demain matin / après-midi / soir	*tomorrow morning / afternoon / evening*
ensuite	*then, afterwards*
l'année prochaine	*next year*
la semaine prochaine	*next week*
le mois prochain	*next month*
le week-end prochain	*next weekend*
lundi (mardi...) prochain	*next Monday (Tuesday . . .)*
plus tard	*later*
(et) puis	*(and) then*
tard	*late*
tôt	*early*

DIVERS

célèbre	*famous*
génial(e) (*m pl* géniaux)	*great*
national(e) (*m pl* nationaux)	*national*
prochain(e)	*next*
régional(e) (*m pl* régionaux)	*regional*
le Vieux Carré	*the French Quarter*

COMPÉTENCE 4

Planning how to get there

NOMS MASCULINS

un (auto)bus	*a bus* (in a city)
un (auto)car	*a bus* (between cities)
un avion	*a plane*
un bateau	*a boat*
le métro	*the subway*
un moyen de transport	*a means of transportation*
un taxi	*a cab, a taxi*
un train	*a train*
un voyage	*a trip*

NOMS FÉMININS

des notes	*notes*
une possibilité	*a possibility*

EXPRESSIONS VERBALES

aller à pied	*to go on foot*
à vélo	*by bike*
en (auto)bus	*by bus*
en (auto)car	*by bus*
en avion	*by plane*
en bateau	*by boat*
en métro	*by subway*
en taxi	*by taxi*
en train	*by train*
en voiture	*by car*
apprendre	*to learn*
comprendre	*to understand*
devenir	*to become*
louer	*to rent*
prendre	*to take*
revenir	*to come back*
venir	*to come*

DIVERS

après-demain	*the day after tomorrow*
Ça prend combien de temps?	*How long does it take?*
Ça prend...	*It takes . . .*
impatient(e)	*impatient*
pas plus	*no more*

À Paris

Les projets

 Pair work   Video

Group work   Audio

Class work

5

LE MONDE FRANCOPHONE
Géoculture et Vidéo-voyage: Les régions de la France

© iStock.com/Jankowski

GÉOCULTURE ET VIDÉO-VOYAGE:
LES RÉGIONS DE LA FRANCE

France

 LA FRANCE
(La République française)

NOMBRE D'HABITANTS: **65 350 000 (les Français)**

Quelles images viennent à l'**esprit** quand vous pensez à la France? Paris et la tour Eiffel? des plages de la Méditerranée? les Alpes? En réalité, la France est un pays riche en diversité géographique et culturelle. Les contrastes entre la vie urbaine et la vie rurale sont les plus marqués. **Alors que** la France **était autrefois** traditionnellement un pays agricole, aujourd'hui quatre personnes sur cinq **vivent** dans des zones urbaines.

Il y a de grandes villes et…

des régions agricoles, avec leurs petits villages et leur vie pastorale.

Dans le **sud**, il y a des plages et des cafés **inondés** de soleil.

Dans certaines parties du **nord**, on voit des plaines et des **collines**.

---

esprit *mind* **Alors que** *While* **était autrefois** *was formerly* **vivent** *live* **sud** *south* **inondés** *flooded* **nord** *north* **collines** *hills*

Il y a des différences dans les coutumes et les habitudes de vie entre le nord et le sud du pays. Dans le sud, par exemple, la vie **se déroule** à l'extérieur, sur la place principale de la ville, dans les cafés, dans les marchés. Mais dans le nord, on **privilégie** la **vie privée** et l'espace personnel.

Dans certains **endroits, on entend même** des langues régionales à côté du français. **Celles** parlées dans le nord **appartiennent** au groupe des langues d'oïl, **tandis que** les langues du sud appartiennent au groupe des langues d'oc, tous les deux nommés d'après le mot local signifiant «oui». Ces langues sont en général **en voie de disparition** et la majorité d'entre elles sont à présent parlées presque exclusivement par des personnes âgées.

© Christophe Boisvieux/AGE Fotostock

Il existe une diversité presque inimaginable d'une région de la France à l'autre. Chacune a son propre héritage historique et culturel qui se révèle dans ses traditions, sa cuisine et sa musique.

La France est, bien sûr, un pays **uni,** et les Français partagent une histoire, une langue et un **patrimoine** riche en culture et tradition. **Pourtant,** dans un sens, c'est précisément sa diversité, plus que toute autre chose, qui définit la France.

Le savez-vous?

Complétez ces phrases.

oui	traditions	rurale	d'oïl	nord
l'espace personnel	d'oc	urbaine	urbaines	à l'extérieur
sud	voie de disparition			

1. Aujourd'hui, la majorité des Français vivent dans des zones _____.
2. Il y a un contraste marqué entre la vie _____ et la vie _____. Il y a aussi un contraste entre la vie dans le _____ et dans le _____ du pays.
3. Dans le nord, les gens privilégient _____ et dans le sud, la vie se déroule (takes place) _____.
4. Chaque région a aussi ses propres _____.
5. Les langues régionales du nord du pays appartiennent au groupe des langues _____ et celles du sud appartiennent au groupe des langues _____. Ces noms viennent du mot local signifiant «_____».
6. Beaucoup de langues régionales sont aujourd'hui en _____.

---

se déroule *unfolds, takes place* **privilégie** *favor* **vie privée** *private life* **endroits** *places* **on entend même** *one even hears* **Celles** *Those* **appartiennent** *belong*
tandis que *while* **en voie de disparition** *disappearing* **uni** *united* **patrimoine** *heritage* **Pourtant** *However* **propre** *own*

AVANT LA VIDÉO

Vous allez visiter la France à travers la vidéo. En 2016, la France a réorganisé ses régions administratives. Pour vous aider à mieux comprendre, regardez ces images et complétez les descriptions avec une option de la liste.

13	**économies urbaines**	**châteaux**	**menhirs** (*menhirs*
22	**cigogne** (*stork*)	**marchés de Noël**	[stone megaliths])

Avant 2016, il y avait (*there were*) __1__ régions administratives en France métropolitaine.

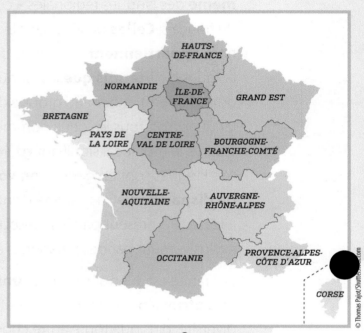

Depuis (*Since*) 2016, il y a __2__ régions.

L'Île-de-France (la région parisienne) est le centre économique de la France. Avec 25 % du produit intérieur brut (*gross domestic product*), c'est une des __3__ les plus importantes du monde.

La ville de Lille dans les Hauts-de-France est connue *(known)* pour ses __4__.

La __5__ est un des symboles de l'Alsace.

La Dordogne est réputée pour ses 1001 __6__.

Les 2934 __7__ de la commune de Carnac en Bretagne datent d'entre 3300 et 4500 ans avant notre ère *(BCE)*.

▶ EN REGARDANT LA VIDÉO

Regardez la vidéo et indiquez si les phrases suivantes sont vraies ou fausses.

1. Les contrastes entre la vie urbaine et la vie rurale ne sont pas très marqués en France.
2. La moitié *(half)* des Français habitent dans une zone rurale.
3. La région parisienne est une des économies urbaines les plus importantes dans le monde *(world)*.
4. Les langues régionales sont en voie de disparation *(disappearing)* en France.

▶ APRÈS LA VIDÉO

Regardez la vidéo une deuxième fois et répondez aux questions suivantes.

1. Quelle est une des différences entre la vie dans le sud et la vie dans le nord?
2. Comment s'appelle le groupe de langues régionales parlées dans le nord? Comment s'appelle le groupe de langues régionales parlées dans le sud? Le breton et l'alsacien appartiennent *(belong)* à quel groupe? Et le provençal, l'auvergnat, le limousin et le languedocien?
3. Qu'est-ce qu'on voit *(see)* dans la vidéo quand on mentionne les endroits suivants *(following places)*: l'Alsace, la Lorraine, la Picardie, la Dordogne, Limoges dans le Limousin, la Bretagne?

Saying what you did

LE WEEK-END DERNIER

Vocabulaire sans peine!

Remember that the French ending **-é** is often the equivalent of the English past participle ending *-ed* or of other English past participles such as *spoken, sung,* etc. As in English, such words can be used as part of the past tense and also as adjectives.

-é = *-ed*

continué = *continued*

How would you complete the second expression in French?

they divorced **ils ont divorcé**

a divorced man **un homme...**

Alice Pérez, **femme d'affaires** américaine **travaillant** à Paris, parle de ses activités de **samedi dernier.** Et vous?

Où est-ce que vous êtes allé(e)? Qu'est-ce que vous avez fait?

Samedi matin,...

je ne suis pas sortie,
je suis restée chez moi.

J'ai dormi jusqu'à 10 heures.

J'ai **pris** mon **petit déjeuner.**

Samedi après-midi,...

je suis allée en ville.

Je n'ai pas travaillé.

J'ai retrouvé un ami au café.

Samedi soir,...

je suis sortie.

J'ai dîné avec une amie et j'ai bien mangé.

J'ai vu un film **étranger**.

Après le film,...

je suis rentrée chez moi.

J'ai lu le journal.

Je **n'**ai **rien** fait.

Le week-end dernier *Last weekend*   **une femme d'affaires (un homme d'affaires)** *a businesswoman (a businessman)*
travaillant *working*   **samedi dernier** *last Saturday*   **Où est-ce que vous êtes allé(e)?** *Where did you go?*   **Qu'est-ce que vous avez fait?** *What did you do?*   **prendre son petit déjeuner** *to have one's breakfast*   **étranger (étrangère)** *foreign*
ne... rien *nothing*

Sélection musicale. Search for the song **"Champs-Élysées"** by Joe Dassin and sung by Soma Riba online to enjoy a musical selection related to this theme.

5-1

C'est lundi et Cathy, la fille d'Alice, parle avec un ami des activités du week-end dernier.

CATHY: Tu as passé un bon week-end?

JÉRÉMY: Oui, pas mal. Samedi matin, j'**ai révisé** mes cours et samedi après-midi, j'ai joué au foot avec des amis.

CATHY: Qu'est-ce que tu as fait samedi soir?

JÉRÉMY: Je suis sorti. Je suis allé en boîte et j'ai beaucoup dansé.

CATHY: Et **hier**?

JÉRÉMY: Hier matin, j'**ai fait une promenade** sur les Champs-Élysées. Et **hier soir,** j'ai regardé la télé.

A Activités logiques. **Formez des phrases logiques. Complétez chaque début de phrase à gauche avec la fin de phrase logique à droite.**

Je suis resté(e) au lit et...	j'ai pris un verre.
J'ai retrouvé des amis au café où...	j'ai dormi.
J'ai dîné au restaurant où...	j'ai beaucoup dansé.
Je suis allé(e) au cinéma où...	je n'ai pas gagné.
Je suis allé(e) en boîte où...	j'ai vu un film étranger.
J'ai joué au tennis avec une amie, mais...	j'ai très bien mangé.
Je suis allé(e) au parc où...	j'ai fait une promenade.

B Et vous? **Complétez les phrases pour indiquer comment vous avez passé la journée d'hier.**

1. J'ai dormi jusqu'à *8 heures / 10 heures / ???*.
2. J'ai pris le petit déjeuner *chez moi / au café / chez une amie / ???. (Je n'ai pas pris de petit déjeuner.)*
3. J'ai lu *le journal / un livre / un blog / un article sur Internet / ???. (Je n'ai rien lu.)*
4. J'ai déjeuné *chez moi / chez des amis / au restaurant / ???. (Je n'ai pas déjeuné.)*
5. *J'ai travaillé. / Je n'ai pas travaillé.*
6. J'ai dîné *chez moi / chez mes parents / ???. (Je n'ai pas dîné.)*
7. J'ai *beaucoup / peu* mangé. *(Je n'ai pas mangé.)*
8. Le soir, *je suis resté(e) chez moi / je suis sorti(e)*.

Hier, j'ai fait une promenade au jardin des Tuileries.

À VOUS!

Avec un(e) partenaire, relisez à haute voix la conversation entre Cathy et Jérémy. Ensuite, adaptez la conversation pour parler de votre week-end passé. *Note: You may not know how to say everything you did. Pick two or three things that you know how to say or ask your instructor for help.*

You can access the audio of the active vocabulary of this ***Compétence*** online.

---

réviser *to review*   **hier** *yesterday*   **faire une promenade** *to take a walk*   **hier soir** *last night, yesterday evening*

SAYING WHAT YOU DID

✔ **Pour vérifier**

1. The **passé composé** always has two parts. What are they called?

2. What verb is usually used as the auxiliary verb? Do you conjugate it?

3. How do you form the past participle of all **-er** and most **-ir** verbs? Which verbs that you know have irregular past participles? What are their past participles?

4. What are the three possible English translations of **j'ai mangé**?

5. In the **passé composé**, where do you place adverbs like **souvent** or **bien**?

6. How is the negative of verbs formed in the **passé composé**? How do you say *I did nothing / I didn't do anything*?

Le passé composé avec **avoir**

1. To say what happened in the past, put the verb in the **passé composé.** It is composed of two parts, the auxiliary verb and the past participle. The auxiliary verb, usually **avoir,** is conjugated in the present tense. The past participle of all **-er** verbs ends in **-é,** and that of most **-ir** verbs ends in **-i.**

PARLER		DORMIR	
j'**ai parlé**	nous **avons parlé**	j'**ai dormi**	nous **avons dormi**
tu **as parlé**	vous **avez parlé**	tu **as dormi**	vous **avez dormi**
il/elle/on **a parlé**	ils/elles **ont parlé**	il/elle/on **a dormi**	ils/elles **ont dormi**

2. Many irregular verbs have irregular past participles that must be memorized.

avoir	j'ai **eu**, tu as **eu...**	**être**	j'ai **été**, tu as **été...**
il y a	il y a **eu**	**faire**	j'ai **fait**, tu as **fait...**
boire	j'ai **bu**, tu as **bu...**	**écrire**	j'ai **écrit**, tu as **écrit...**
courir	j'ai **couru**, tu as **couru...**	**prendre**	j'ai **pris**, tu as **pris...**
lire	j'ai **lu**, tu as **lu...**	**apprendre**	j'ai **appris...**
voir	j'ai **vu**, tu as **vu...**	**comprendre**	j'ai **compris...**

3. The **passé composé** can be translated in a variety of ways in English.

I took the bus.
I have taken the bus. } J'ai pris le bus.
I did take the bus.

4. Adverbs indicating *how often* (**toujours, souvent...**) and *how well* (**bien, mal...**) are usually placed between the two parts of the verb. To put a verb in the negative form, place **ne** directly after the subject, and place **pas, jamais,** or **rien** just after the auxiliary verb.

J'ai **beaucoup** travaillé hier matin. Après, je **n'**ai **rien** fait.

Note *de grammaire*

Some verbs expressing *going, coming,* and *staying,* such as **aller, sortir, rentrer,** and **rester,** have **être,** not **avoir,** as their auxiliary verb. You will learn about them in the next **Compétence.** For now, remember to use **je suis allé(e), je suis sorti(e), je suis resté(e),** and **je suis rentré(e)** if you want to say *I went, I went out, I stayed,* and *I returned.* (If you are a female, add the extra **e** to the past participle of these verbs, just as you do with adjectives. Do not add this feminine **e** to the verbs you are learning to conjugate with the auxiliary **avoir** in this **Compétence.**)

A **La journée de Cathy.** Voici les activités de Cathy hier. Est-ce qu'elle a fait les choses suivantes?

EXEMPLE Hier matin, Cathy... quitter la maison tôt

Hier matin, Cathy n'a pas quitté la maison tôt.

Hier matin, Cathy...

1. dormir
2. passer la matinée chez elle
3. faire une promenade
4. travailler tôt

Hier soir, Cathy et ses amis...

5. voir un film
6. prendre un café
7. beaucoup parler
8. faire du sport

B **Qu'avez-vous fait?** Dites si ces personnes ont fait les choses suivantes la dernière fois que *(the last time)* vous êtes allé(e) en cours de français.

> **EXEMPLE** Moi, je (j') / dormir jusqu'à 10 heures
>
> **Moi, j'ai dormi jusqu'à 10 heures.**
>
> **Moi, je n'ai pas dormi jusqu'à 10 heures.**

AVANT LE COURS

Moi, je (j')...

1. être dans un autre cours
2. passer la matinée chez moi
3. lire le journal

Mon (Ma) meilleur(e) ami(e)...

4. boire un café avec moi
5. manger avec moi
6. passer la matinée avec moi

EN COURS

Les étudiants...

7. dormir en cours
8. bien comprendre la leçon
9. beaucoup apprendre

Nous...

10. avoir un examen
11. faire beaucoup d'exercices
12. voir un film français

C **Entretien.** Posez ces questions à votre partenaire sur ce qu'il/elle a fait hier.

> **EXEMPLE** — **À quelle heure est-ce que tu as quitté la maison hier?**
>
> — **J'ai quitté la maison vers 9 heures.**
>
> **Je n'ai pas quitté la maison hier.**

1. Jusqu'à quelle heure est-ce que tu as dormi?
2. Quand est-ce que tu as quitté la maison?
3. Où est-ce que tu as pris ton petit déjeuner?
4. Avec qui est-ce que tu as déjeuné?
5. Qu'est-ce que tu as étudié?
6. Qu'est-ce que tu as fait hier soir?

Après, décrivez la journée de votre partenaire à la classe.

> **EXEMPLE** **Rachel a dormi jusqu'à sept heures. Elle a quitté la maison...**

D **Devinez!** Dites à votre partenaire combien des choses suivantes vous avez faites récemment *(recently)* avec des ami(e)s. Votre partenaire va deviner lesquelles *(guess which ones)*.

> boire un café   parler sur Skype   voir un bon film
> visiter une autre ville   faire une promenade
> prendre un verre   déjeuner
> prendre le petit déjeuner   faire du vélo

On a joué au frisbee à la plage.

> **EXEMPLE** — **Mes amis et moi, on a fait cinq choses de la liste récemment.**
>
> — **Vous avez bu un café ensemble?**
>
> — **Oui, on a bu un café. / Non, on n'a pas bu de café.**
>
> — **Vous avez parlé sur Skype?...**

STRATÉGIES ET LECTURE

1. You can often guess the meaning of unfamiliar verbs in a narrative by thinking about what actions would occur together and in what order. For example, when taking the bus, you wait for the bus first, get on the bus, then get off at your destination. Learn to read a whole sentence or paragraph, rather than one word at a time.
2. Notice that the prefix **re-** means that an action in a sequence is done again, as in English (*do* and *redo, read* and *reread*).
3. You will also notice that prepositions can indicate relationships between actions. **Pour** means *in order to* when it is followed by a verb. **Sans,** meaning *without,* can also be followed by an infinitive.

A **Devinez!** Use the sequence of events in this passage to guess the meaning of the boldfaced words.

Cathy **a ouvert** une enveloppe et elle **a sorti** une feuille de papier. Elle **a lu** les instructions sur la feuille, mais elle n'a pas compris. Alors, elle **a relu** les instructions et elle **a remis** la feuille de papier dans l'enveloppe.

Cathy **a attendu** le bus devant son appartement. Quand il est arrivé, elle **est montée** dedans, et elle **est descendue** quand elle est arrivée à sa destination. Elle **est entrée** dans un café et a commandé un coca. Elle a bu son coca, elle **a payé l'addition** et elle **est repartie.**

Elle est entrée dans une station de métro où elle a acheté un ticket **au guichet,** mais elle n'a pas pris le métro. Elle **a mis** le ticket dans son enveloppe et elle a quitté la station.

Devant un magasin de vélos, Cathy a admiré un vélo rouge dans **la vitrine.** Elle est entrée dans le magasin et a demandé **le prix** du vélo.

B **Dans l'ordre logique.** Mettez les activités suivantes de Cathy dans l'ordre logique. La première et la dernière *(last)* sont indiquées.

_____ Elle est allée vers la porte.
_____ Elle a lu les instructions sur la feuille de papier.
__**1**__ Cathy a vu une enveloppe sur la table.
_____ Elle a sorti une feuille de papier de l'enveloppe.
_____ Elle a ouvert l'enveloppe.
__**7**__ Elle a ouvert la porte et elle est sortie.
_____ Elle a remis la feuille dans l'enveloppe.

C **Quel verbe?** Complétez ces phrases logiquement. N'oubliez pas *(Don't forget)* que **pour** veut dire *in order to* et **sans** veut dire *without.*

1. Cathy a quitté l'appartement sans… (boire son café, ouvrir la porte).
2. Elle a pris le bus pour… (rester à la maison, aller en ville).
3. Elle a retrouvé des amis pour… (passer le week-end seule, aller au cinéma).
4. Elle est allée au guichet pour… (acheter des tickets, boire un coca).
5. Elle est rentrée à la maison sans… (quitter le café, prendre le bus).

🔊 Lecture: *Qu'est-ce qu'elle a fait?*

5-2

Seule dans son appartement, Cathy Pérez avait l'air un peu agitée. Elle a pris une enveloppe qui était sur la table et en a sorti une feuille de papier. Elle a lu les instructions et a remis la feuille dans l'enveloppe. Elle a pris l'enveloppe et a quitté son appartement.

Cathy est entrée dans un café où elle a commandé un coca et ensuite, elle a demandé l'addition. Quand l'addition est arrivée, elle a payé. Elle a ouvert l'enveloppe, a relu les instructions, a mis l'addition dans l'enveloppe et a quitté le café sans boire son coca. C'est bien bizarre! Pourquoi avait-elle l'air si agitée?

Ensuite, Cathy est allée à la station de métro. Elle est entrée dans la station et sans regarder le plan, est allée au guichet et a demandé un ticket. Quand on lui a donné son ticket, elle l'a mis dans l'enveloppe, a remonté l'escalier et a quitté la station de métro. Pourquoi a-t-elle acheté un ticket sans prendre le métro? Tout cela est fort bizarre!

Cathy a continué sa route jusqu'à un magasin de vélos. Elle a regardé un vélo rouge qui était dans la vitrine. Elle est entrée dans le magasin et elle a demandé le prix du vélo. Elle a écrit le prix du vélo sur une feuille de papier et elle a mis la feuille de papier dans l'enveloppe. Ensuite, elle est sortie du magasin.

Cathy est allée au coin de la rue pour attendre l'autobus. Quand l'autobus est arrivé, elle l'a pris, et puis elle est descendue à l'université. Elle avait l'air un peu plus calme. Pourquoi a-t-elle fait tout ça? Pourquoi a-t-elle mis ces choses dans l'enveloppe? Pourquoi est-elle plus calme maintenant?

A **Comprenez-vous?** Dites ce que Cathy a fait d'abord et ce qu'elle a fait ensuite.

1. Elle a sorti une feuille de papier de l'enveloppe. / Elle a lu les instructions.
2. Elle a quitté son appartement. / Elle est allée au café.
3. Elle a commandé un coca. / Elle est partie sans boire son coca.
4. Elle a payé le serveur. / Elle a demandé l'addition.
5. Elle a demandé un ticket de métro. / Elle est allée au guichet.

B **Maintenant... c'est à vous!** Est-ce que vous trouvez les actions de Cathy plutôt bizarres? Pourquoi est-ce qu'elle a fait tout ça? Imaginez une explication.

Est-ce qu'elle... est agent de police ou détective privé? souffre d'amnésie? travaille pour la CIA? est espionne comme James Bond? collectionne des souvenirs de Paris? fait un exercice pour son cours de français?

Réponse:
Il y a une explication simple et logique! Cathy suit *(is taking)* un cours de français pour étrangers à Paris. Ses devoirs, consistent à prouver au professeur qu'elle est capable de commander quelque chose à boire au café, de demander le prix d'un vélo et d'acheter un ticket de métro. Elle doit rapporter *(needs to bring back)* l'addition, le prix du vélo et le ticket de métro à son professeur.

Telling where you went

JE SUIS PARTI(E) EN VOYAGE

La dernière fois que vous êtes parti(e) en voyage, où est-ce que vous êtes allé(e)? Qu'est-ce que vous avez fait?

Je suis allé(e)	à Denver.	**J'y suis allé(e)**	en avion.
	à New York.		en train.
	???		en autocar.
			en voiture **(de location).**
Je suis parti(e)	en mars.	Je suis arrivé(e)	le même jour.
	le matin.		trois heures plus tard.
	vers trois heures.		**le lendemain.**
	???		???
Je suis descendu(e)	à l'hôtel.	Je suis resté(e)	**une nuit.**
			le week-end.
Je suis allé(e)	dans un camping.		trois jours.
Je suis resté(e)	chez des amis.		
	chez **des parents.**		
Je suis allé(e)	à la plage.	Je suis rentré(e)	trois jours après.
	à un concert.		la semaine suivante.
	en boîte.		deux semaines plus tard.

5-3

Alice est partie en week-end. Le mardi suivant, elle parle avec son amie Claire du voyage qu'elle a fait le week-end passé.

CLAIRE: Qu'est-ce que tu as fait le week-end dernier?
ALICE: J'ai pris le train pour aller à Deauville.
CLAIRE: Quand est-ce que tu es partie?
ALICE: Je suis partie samedi matin et je suis rentrée hier soir.
CLAIRE: Tu as trouvé un bon hôtel?
ALICE: Je suis descendue dans un petit hôtel confortable, pas trop loin de la plage.
CLAIRE: **Quelle chance!** Moi aussi, j'ai envie de visiter Deauville.

A **En week-end.** Décrivez la dernière fois que vous êtes parti(e) en voyage.

1. Je suis allé(e) à (Chicago, Houston, ???).
2. J'y suis allé(e) (en avion, en train, ???).
3. Je suis parti(e) (le soir, vers cinq heures, ???).
4. Je suis arrivé(e) (une heure, trois jours, ???) plus tard.
5. Je suis resté(e) (à l'hôtel, chez des amis, ???).
6. Je suis resté(e) (deux jours, une semaine, ???).

La dernière fois *The last time* **J'y suis allé(e)** *I went there* **de location** *rental* **le lendemain** *the next day, the following day* **Je suis descendu(e) (descendre [dans / à / de])** *I stayed (to stay [at], to descend, to come down, to get off / out [of] [a vehicle])* **une nuit** *one night* **des parents** *some relatives* **Quelle chance!** *What luck!*

B **Un tour de Paris.** Alice et sa famille adorent visiter Paris et la région parisienne. Regardez les photos et complétez les phrases avec une expression de la colonne de droite.

1. Son mari, Vincent, est allé à la Sainte-Chapelle pour...
2. Ses enfants sont allés à Versailles pour...
3. Ils sont allés à Notre-Dame pour...
4. Ils sont allés au musée d'Orsay pour...
5. Ils sont allés au café sur les Champs-Élysées pour...

voir une nouvelle exposition.
prendre un café.
voir son architecture gothique.
admirer les vitraux *(stained-glass windows)*.
visiter le château.

la Sainte-Chapelle

le château de Versailles

Notre-Dame

le musée d'Orsay

 **À VOUS!**

Avec un(e) partenaire, relisez à haute voix la conversation entre Claire et Alice. Ensuite, adaptez la conversation pour parler de la dernière fois que vous êtes parti(e) en week-end.

You can access the audio of the active vocabulary of this ***Compétence*** online.

TELLING WHERE YOU WENT

✔ *Pour vérifier*

1. Which verbs have **être** as the auxiliary in the **passé composé**? What do you have to remember to do with the past participle of these verbs that you don't do with verbs that have **avoir** as their auxiliary?

2. How do you say *to enter*? What preposition do you use with it? How do you say *to go out*? *to go out of*?

3. What preposition do you use with **partir** to say *to leave from*? What is the difference between **partir** and **quitter**? between **rentrer** and **retourner**?

4. How do you say *to go/come down, to descend*? *to get out of/down from/ off of*? *to stay at*? How do you say *to go up*? *to get on/in*?

*Le passé composé avec **être***

1. The following verbs, many of which have to do with coming and going, have **être** as their auxiliary verb in the **passé composé**. The past participle of these verbs agrees with the subject in number and gender. Do not make this agreement when **avoir** is the auxiliary.

Elle est *partie* hier.   **Elle a *pris* le train.**

ALLER → ALLÉ		SORTIR → SORTI	
je **suis allé(e)**	nous **sommes allé(e)s**	je **suis sorti(e)**	nous **sommes sorti(e)s**
tu **es allé(e)**	vous **êtes allé(e)(s)**	tu **es sorti(e)**	vous **êtes sorti(e)(s)**
il **est allé**	ils **sont allés**	il **est sorti**	ils **sont sortis**
elle **est allée**	elles **sont allées**	elle **est sortie**	elles **sont sorties**
on **est allé(e)(s)**		on **est sorti(e)(s)**	

aller	je suis allé(e)	*I went*
venir /	je suis venu(e) /	*I came /*
devenir / revenir	devenu(e) / revenu(e)	* became / came back*
arriver	je suis arrivé(e)	*I arrived*
rester	je suis resté(e)	*I stayed, I remained*
entrer (dans)	je suis entré(e) (dans)	*I entered, I went in*
sortir (de)	je suis sorti(e) (de)	*I went out / came out (of)*
partir (de)	je suis parti(e) (de)	*I left*
passer (par/	je suis passé(e) (par/	*I passed (by [. . .'s house])*
chez/devant)	chez/devant)	
rentrer	je suis rentré(e)	*I came home, I returned*
retourner	je suis retourné(e)	*I returned, I went back*
monter (dans)	je suis monté(e) (dans)	*I went up, I got on/in*
descendre	je suis descendu(e)	*I came down, I got out (of) /*
(de/dans/à)	(de/dans/à)	* off (of) (a vehicle),*
		* I stayed (at)*
tomber	je suis tombé(e)	*I fell (down)*
naître	je suis né(e)	*I was born*
mourir	il/elle est mort(e)	*he/she died*

2. In the **passé composé**, place **y** *(there)* immediately before the auxiliary verb.

J'**y** suis allé(e).   Je n'**y** suis pas allé(e).

Note *de grammaire*

1. When **on** means *we*, its past participle may either be left in the masculine singular form (**On est sorti.**) or it may agree (**On est sorti[e]s**). Either is correct.

2. Passer takes **être** in the **passé composé** when it means *to pass by*. **Je suis passé(e) chez toi.** It takes **avoir** when it means *to spend time*. **J'ai passé la soirée avec mes amis.**

3. Rentrer means *to return/go back home* (or to the place you are staying). Use **retourner** for *to return* in most other cases.

4. Partir and **quitter** both mean *to leave*. **Partir** has **être** as its auxiliary, but **quitter** takes **avoir** and *must* have a direct object: **Elle est partie tôt. Elle *a quitté la maison* à 6h.**

PRONONCIATION

*Les verbes auxiliaires **avoir** et **être***
5-4

As you practice when to use **avoir** and when to use **être** to form the **passé composé,** be careful to pronounce the forms of these auxiliary verbs distinctly.

tu as parlé / tu es parti(e)   il a parlé / il est parti   ils ᶻont parlé / ils sont partis

◀)) **🔁** **A** **Prononcez bien!** Écoutez les questions suivantes et écrivez les verbes
5-5   auxiliaires que vous entendez *(hear)*. Ensuite, posez les questions à un(e) partenaire.

1. Est-ce que tes parents _____ allés à l'université? Est-ce qu'ils
_____ étudié le français? Est-ce qu'ils _____ fait du sport?

2. Où est-ce que ta mère _____ née? Où est-ce qu'elle _____ passé
sa jeunesse *(youth)*? Dans quelles villes est-ce qu'elle _____ habité?

🔁 **B** **Tu es parti(e) en week-end?** Pensez à la dernière fois que vous êtes
parti(e) en week-end. Votre partenaire va vous poser des questions au sujet de ce
week-end.

EXEMPLE où / aller
— **Où est-ce que tu es allé(e)?**
— **Je suis allé(e) à Deauville.**

1. quand / partir   3. quand / arriver   5. combien de temps / rester
2. comment / y aller   4. où / descendre   6. quand / rentrer

Maintenant, posez ces mêmes questions au professeur.

EXEMPLE — **Où est-ce que vous êtes allé(e)?**
— **Je suis allé(e) à Rome.**

🔁 **C** **Qu'est-ce que tu as fait?** Posez ces questions à votre partenaire au sujet
de la dernière fois qu'il/qu'elle a mangé au restaurant avec un(e) ami(e) ou avec des
amis.

EXEMPLE — **Avec qui est-ce que tu es sorti(e)?**
— **Je suis sorti(e) avec Thomas et Karima.**

1. Avec qui est-ce que tu es sorti(e)?
2. Vous êtes allé(e)s à quel restaurant?
3. Vers quelle heure est-ce que vous êtes arrivé(e)s au restaurant?
4. Combien de temps est-ce que vous êtes resté(e)s au restaurant?
5. Vers quelle heure est-ce que tu es rentré(e)?

D **Le week-end dernier.** Regardez les illustrations et formez des phrases
pour dire qui a fait chacune des choses indiquées: **Cathy, Evan** ou **Vincent et Alice.**
Attention! Certains verbes sont conjugués avec **avoir**, mais d'autres prennent **être.**

EXEMPLE aller à Nice   **Cathy est allée à Nice.**
voir des amis   **Vincent et Alice ont vu des amis.**

Cathy

Evan

Vincent et Alice

1. sortir en couple
2. aller ensemble chez des amis
3. arriver à l'hôtel du Vieux Nice en taxi
4. faire du ski
5. descendre à l'hôtel du Vieux Nice
6. avoir un accident de ski

7. tomber en faisant du ski
   (while skiing)
8. aller à l'hôpital
9. prendre un verre chez des amis
10. rentrer la jambe cassée
    (with a broken leg)

TELLING WHEN YOU DID SOMETHING

✔ Pour vérifier

1. How do you say *last month? last week? last year? the last time?* How do you say *last?* What is the feminine form? Does it go before or after the noun in most of these expressions? What is the exception? Most of the expressions with **dernier (dernière)** are preceded by **le** or **la.** Which one is not?

2. How do you say that you did something *yesterday? yesterday morning? yesterday evening / last night?*

3. How would you say *for two hours?* How do you say *for* when talking about time in the past?

4. How do you say *ago?* How do you say *a year ago? a long time ago?*

5. What do **déjà** and **ne... pas encore** mean? Where do you place them?

Les expressions qui désignent le passé et reprise du passé composé

1. The following expressions are useful when talking about the past.

hier (matin, après-midi)	*yesterday (morning, afternoon)*
hier soir	*last night, yesterday evening*
lundi (mardi...) dernier	*last Monday (Tuesday . . .)*
le week-end dernier	*last weekend*
la semaine dernière	*last week*
le mois dernier	*last month*
l'année dernière	*last year*
la dernière fois	*the last time*
récemment	*recently*
Pendant combien de temps?	*For how long?*
pendant deux heures (longtemps)	*for two hours (a long time)*
Il y a combien de temps?	*How long ago?*
il y a trois jours (cinq ans, quelques semaines, deux minutes, trois secondes...)	*three days (five years, a few weeks, two minutes, three seconds . . .) ago*
déjà	*already, ever*
ne... pas encore	*not yet*

Note *de vocabulaire*

1. Use **an** *(m)* instead of **année** *(f)* after a number: **il y a trois ans.**

2. To say *a week ago,* people in France often use **il y a huit jours;** and to say *two weeks ago,* **il y a quinze jours.**

2. Most of these time expressions go at the beginning or end of a clause or sentence. However, **déjà** is placed between the two parts of the verb in the **passé composé.** When using **ne... pas encore,** place **ne** immediately after the subject and **pas encore** between the two parts of the verb.

— Tu as **déjà** fait tes devoirs?	— *Have you **already** done your homework?*
— Non, je **n'**ai **pas encore** fait mes devoirs.	— *No, I haven**'t** done my homework **yet.***
— Moi, j'ai fait mes devoirs **il y a trois heures.**	— *I did my homework **three hours ago.***

A **Quand?** Voici le calendrier de Cathy. Quand est-ce qu'elle a fait les choses indiquées? Aujourd'hui, c'est le 14 novembre.

EXEMPLE beaucoup travailler (la semaine dernière, le mois dernier)
   Cathy a beaucoup travaillé le mois dernier.

1. dîner chez une amie (il y a trois jours, le mois dernier)
2. aller au Louvre (il y a un mois, il y a deux semaines)
3. préparer un examen (la semaine dernière, hier)
4. passer *(to take)* l'examen (la semaine dernière, hier)
5. faire du shopping (il y a une semaine, le week-end dernier)
6. passer le week-end à Deauville (il y a une semaine, le week-end dernier)

OCTOBRE

L	M	M	J	V	S	D
						1
2	3 Dîner chez Brigitte	4 travailler	5	6	7	8
9	10 travailler	11	12	13	14 Louvre	15
16	17	18 travailler	19	20	21	22
23	24	25 travailler	26	27	28	29
30	31					

NOVEMBRE

L	M	M	J	V	S	D
			1	2	3	4	5
6	7 Shopping	8	9 Préparer l'examen	10	11 Deauville	12
13 examen	14	15	16	17	18	19
20	21	22	23	24	25	26
27	28	29	30			

B **Déjà?** Demandez à un(e) partenaire s'il/si elle a déjà fait ces choses. Utilisez **ne... pas encore** pour les réponses négatives.

EXEMPLE faire ses devoirs aujourd'hui
— **Tu as déjà fait tes devoirs aujourd'hui?**
— **Oui, j'ai déjà fait mes devoirs.**
Non, je n'ai pas encore fait mes devoirs.

1. aller au bureau du / de la prof ce semestre / trimestre
2. apprendre tout le vocabulaire de ce chapitre
3. être absent(e) ce mois
4. travailler en groupes avec tous les autres étudiants

C **Et toi?** Circulez parmi vos camarades de classe et posez des questions pour trouver quelqu'un qui a fait chacune des choses suivantes récemment. Après, dites à la classe qui a fait chaque chose et quand il/elle l'a faite.

EXEMPLE voir un bon film
— **Sam, tu as vu un bon film récemment?**
— **Non, je n'ai pas vu de bon film récemment.**
— **Lisa, tu as vu un bon film récemment?**
— **Oui, j'ai vu un bon film hier soir.**

Après, à la classe: **Lisa a vu un bon film hier soir...**

> voir un bon film   faire de l'exercice   partir en week-end   être malade *(sick)*
> aller au café avec des amis   sortir avec des amis
> arriver en cours en retard *(late)*   rentrer à la maison après minuit

D **Entretien.** Posez ces paires de questions à votre partenaire.

EXEMPLE tu / aller au café ce matin
tu / prendre un café ce matin
— **Tu es allé(e) au café ce matin?**
— **Non, je ne suis pas allé(e) au café.**
— **Tu as pris un café?**
— **Oui, j'ai pris un café chez moi.**

1. tu / aller au cinéma récemment
   tu / voir un bon film récemment
2. tu / venir en cours la semaine dernière
   tu / bien comprendre la leçon sur le passé composé
3. tes amis et toi, vous / sortir ensemble le week-end dernier
   vous / prendre un verre ensemble récemment
4. tu / étudier ici l'année dernière
   tu / venir étudier ici à l'université il y a combien de temps
5. tu / dormir jusqu'à quelle heure ce matin
   tu / partir de chez toi à quelle heure ce matin
6. tu / rester chez toi samedi dernier
   tu / réviser tes cours pendant combien de temps samedi dernier

Discussing the weather and your activities

LE TEMPS ET LES PROJETS

Vocabulaire supplémentaire

Il fait bon. *The weather's nice.*
Il fait humide. *It's humid.*
Il y a des nuages. / C'est nuageux.
   It's cloudy.
Il y a du brouillard. *It's foggy.*
Il y a du verglas. *It's icy.*
Il grêle. *It's hailing.*
Il y a un orage. *There's a storm.*
C'est orageux. *It's stormy.*
Le ciel est couvert. *The sky is overcast.*

Quel temps fait-il aujourd'hui?

Il fait froid.

Il fait **frais.**

Il fait chaud.

Il fait beau.

Il fait mauvais.

Il fait (du) soleil.

Il fait / Il y a du vent.

Il pleut.

Il neige.

Quelle **saison** préférez-vous? Qu'est-ce que vous faites **pendant** cette saison? Est-ce que vos projets **dépendent du temps qu'il fait**?

J'adore **l'été** *(m)*. En été,...

je vais à la plage.
je fais du bateau et
   du ski nautique.

J'aime l'automne *(m)*. En automne,...

je fais du camping.
je **fais du VTT.**

J'aime beaucoup **l'hiver** *(m)*.
   En hiver,...

je vais à la
   montagne.
je fais du ski.

J'adore **le printemps.**
   Au printemps,...

je vais au parc.
je **fais des
   randonnées.**

Quel temps fait-il? *What is the weather like?*   **frais** *cool*   **la saison** *the season*   **pendant** *during, for*   **dépendre de** *to depend on*   **le temps qu'il fait** *what the weather is like*   **l'été** *summer*   **faire du VTT (vélo tout terrain)** *to go all-terrain biking*   **l'hiver** *winter*   **le printemps** *spring*   **faire une randonnée (faire des randonnées)** *to go for a hike (to go hiking, to hike)*

5-6

C'est vendredi après-midi et Alice et Cathy parlent de leurs projets pour le week-end.

ALICE: **S'il** fait beau demain, je vais faire une promenade au jardin du Luxembourg. J'ai besoin de faire de l'exercice. Et toi, qu'est-ce que tu as l'intention de faire?

CATHY: S'il fait beau, j'ai envie de faire du jogging.

ALICE: Et s'il fait mauvais?

CATHY: S'il fait mauvais, je ne vais rien faire de spécial.

Note *de grammaire*

The use of **si** *(if)* clauses is as common in French as it is in English. As in English, when the verb in the *if* clause is in the present tense, the verb in the second clause may be in the present tense, the immediate future, or the imperative.

S'il pleut, j'aime rester chez moi.

S'il pleut demain, je vais rester chez moi.

S'il pleut demain, reste chez toi.

A **Et chez vous?** Chez vous, en quelle saison fait-il le temps indiqué?

EXEMPLE Il neige.
Ici, il neige souvent (rarement, quelquefois) en hiver.
Ici, il ne neige jamais.

1. Il fait frais.
2. Il fait du vent.
3. Il fait mauvais.
4. Il fait très beau.
5. Il fait froid.
6. Il fait chaud.
7. Il fait du soleil.
8. Il pleut.
9. Il neige.

B **Et vous?** Complétez les phrases.

1. Quand il fait beau, j'aime...
2. S'il fait beau ce week-end, j'ai l'intention de...
3. Quand il pleut, je préfère...
4. S'il fait mauvais ce week-end, je vais...
5. À la montagne, j'aime...
6. À la plage, j'aime...

Quel temps fait-il aujourd'hui?

C **Quel temps fait-il?** Demandez à un(e) partenaire quel temps il fait aux moments indiqués. Il/Elle doit répondre en utilisant au moins *deux* expressions pour décrire le temps.

EXEMPLE en automne
— **Quel temps fait-il en automne?**
— **Il fait beau et il fait frais.**

1. en hiver
2. en été
3. en automne
4. au printemps
5. aujourd'hui

D **Entretien.** Posez ces questions à votre partenaire.

1. Aimes-tu l'été? Aimes-tu aller à la plage? Aimes-tu nager? Préfères-tu faire du bateau ou faire du ski nautique?
2. Aimes-tu l'hiver? Aimes-tu aller à la montagne? Préfères-tu faire des randonnées ou faire du ski? Aimes-tu faire du camping? du VTT?
3. Qu'est-ce que tu aimes faire quand il fait chaud? Et quand il fait froid? Et quand il neige?
4. Quelle saison préfères-tu? Quel temps fait-il d'habitude? Qu'est-ce que tu aimes faire pendant cette saison?

À VOUS!

Avec un(e) partenaire, relisez à haute voix la conversation entre Alice et Cathy. Ensuite, adaptez la conversation pour parler de vos projets pour le week-end.

You can access the audio of the active vocabulary of this *Compétence* online.

S'il *If it* (**si** *if*)

TALKING ABOUT THE WEATHER AND WHAT YOU DO

✔ **Pour vérifier**

1. What is the present tense of **faire**? How is the **vous** form of this verb different from the usual **vous** form of a verb? What does the verb mean?

2. How do you say that you are doing *nothing*?

3. How do you say *What is the weather like? The weather is nice? It is raining? It is snowing?* How do you say *What is the weather going to be like? It is going to be nice? It is going to rain? It is going to snow?* How do you say *What was the weather like? It was nice? It rained? It snowed?*

4. How do you say *I like snow? I like rain?*

Le verbe **faire,** l'expression **ne... rien** et les expressions pour décrire le temps

1. To say *to make* or *to do,* use the irregular verb **faire.**

FAIRE *(to make, to do)*	
je **fais**	nous **faisons**
tu **fais**	vous **faites**
il/elle/on **fait**	ils/elles **font**
PASSÉ COMPOSÉ: **j'ai fait**	

— Qu'est-ce que tu **fais** ce soir?
— Je reste à la maison. Je **fais** mes devoirs.

— Qu'est-ce que papa **fait** dans la cuisine?
— Il **fait** des sandwichs.

2. To say that you do *nothing* or you do *not* do *anything,* use **ne... rien.** This expression can be the subject or object of the verb, or the object of a preposition. Place **rien** in the position of the subject, of the object, or after the preposition, as appropriate, and always place **ne (n')** before the verb.

Rien n'est prêt.	Je **n'**achète **rien.**	Je **n'**ai besoin de **rien.**
Nothing is ready.	*I'm not buying anything.*	*I don't need anything.*

3. When negating an infinitive, place both parts of the negative expression before it.

Je préfère **ne pas** sortir ce soir.   Je voudrais **ne rien** faire demain soir.

4. The verb **faire** is used in many, but not all, weather expressions. You will also need the infinitives and past participles **pleuvoir** *(to rain)* → **plu** and **neiger** *(to snow)* → **neigé.** Use **la pluie** to say *(the) rain* and **la neige** to say *(the) snow.*

AUJOURD'HUI	DEMAIN	HIER
Quel temps fait-il?	Quel temps va-t-il faire?	Quel temps a-t-il fait?
Il fait beau / du vent...	Il va faire beau / du vent...	Il a fait beau / du vent...
Il pleut.	Il va pleuvoir.	Il a plu.
Il neige.	Il va neiger.	Il a neigé.

Note *de prononciation*

The **ai** in **fais** and **fait** rhymes with the **ai** in **français.** The **ai** in **faites** rhymes with the **ai** in **française,** but the **ai** in **faisons** rhymes with the **e** in **je.**

Aimez-vous faire du camping?

A **Que faites-vous?** Dites ou demandez si ces personnes font les choses indiquées.

1. Moi, je...
   faire beaucoup de choses seul(e)
   faire beaucoup de choses le soir

2. Mon meilleur ami (Ma meilleure amie)...
   faire beaucoup de choses pour moi
   faire souvent du VTT

3. En cours, nous...
   faire beaucoup d'exercices ensemble
   faire les devoirs en ligne

4. Mes parents...
   faire beaucoup de choses ensemble
   faire souvent du sport

5. *[au professeur]* Est-ce que vous...?
   faire souvent du camping
   faire souvent du bateau

B **Quel temps va-t-il faire?** Voilà la météo *(weather forecast)* pour certaines régions de France pour demain. Pour chaque région, dites quel temps il va faire. Utilisez deux expressions pour chaque région.

EXEMPLE Demain, en Bretagne, il va faire frais et....

1. Demain, en Bretagne...
2. Demain, dans les Alpes...
3. Demain, sur la Côte d'Azur...

Maintenant, imaginez qu'hier dans ces régions, il a fait le même temps qu'il va faire demain. Dites quel temps il a fait dans chaque région.

EXEMPLE Hier, en Bretagne, il a fait frais et...

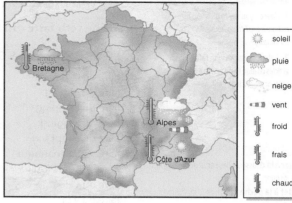

☀	soleil
☁	pluie
☁	neige
💨	vent
🌡	froid
🌡	frais
🌡	chaud

C **Qu'est-ce qu'ils ont fait?** Alice parle des activités récentes de sa famille et du temps qu'il a fait ce jour-là. Complétez ses phrases. Utilisez deux expressions pour décrire le temps.

EXEMPLE Hier, j'**ai lu un livre.** Il **a fait mauvais et il a plu** toute la journée.

EXEMPLE Hier, j'...
Il... toute la journée.

1. À Deauville, nous...
Il...

2. Vendredi dernier, Vincent et moi...
Il...

3. À Chamonix, les enfants... Il...

4. Hier, Vincent...
Il...

5. Ce matin, Vincent et notre fils... Il...

D **Entretien.** Interviewez votre partenaire.

1. Qu'est-ce que tu aimes faire le vendredi soir? le samedi soir? Qu'est-ce que tu fais d'habitude le dimanche matin?
2. Quel temps va-t-il faire ce week-end? Qu'est-ce que tu as envie de faire s'il fait beau? Qu'est-ce que tu as l'intention de faire s'il fait mauvais? Qu'est-ce que tu vas faire samedi soir? Est-ce que tu préfères ne rien faire quelquefois?

Note *de grammaire*

Questions asked with **faire** are often answered with a different verb.
— **Qu'est-ce que tu fais le samedi matin?**
— **Je regarde la télé.**

TALKING ABOUT ACTIVITIES

✔ *Pour vérifier*

1. How do you say *to go camping? to take a trip? to do housework? to do laundry?*

2. In the expressions with **faire**, which articles change to **de (d')** in a negative sentence? Which do not?

Vocabulaire supplémentaire

aller à la chasse / chasser *to go hunting / to hunt*

aller à la pêche / pêcher *to go fishing / to fish*

faire de la muscu(lation) *to do body building*

faire de la varappe / de l'escalade *to go rock climbing*

faire du cheval / de l'équitation *to go horseback riding*

faire du patin (à glace) *to go (ice-) skating*

faire du roller *to go rollerblading*

faire du snowboard *to go snowboarding*

faire la fête *to party*

faire de la marche *to go walking*

Les expressions avec faire

1. The verb **faire** can have a variety of meanings in idiomatic expressions.

LE SPORT ET LES DISTRACTIONS	LE MÉNAGE ET LES COURSES
faire de l'exercice	faire des courses *(to run errands)*
faire du bateau	faire les courses *(to buy groceries)*
faire du camping	faire du jardinage *(to garden)*
faire du jogging	faire la cuisine *(to cook)*
faire du shopping	faire la lessive *(to do laundry)*
faire du ski (nautique)	faire la vaisselle *(to do the dishes)*
faire du sport (du tennis, du hockey,...)	faire le ménage *(to do housework)*
faire du vélo	
faire du VTT	
faire une promenade	
faire une randonnée	
faire un voyage *(to take a trip)*	

2. The **un, une, des, du, de la,** and **de l'** in the expressions with **faire** become **de (d')** when the verb is negated. The definite article (**le, la, l', les**) does not change.

Je ne fais pas **de** jogging en hiver.   Nous ne faisons pas **la** cuisine le matin.

A **Un besoin ou une envie?** Commencez ces phrases logiquement avec **J'ai envie de...** ou **J'ai besoin de...**

EXEMPLE   faire des devoirs   **J'ai besoin de faire des devoirs.**
              faire du ski   **J'ai envie de faire du ski.**

1. faire des courses
2. faire du bateau
3. faire la lessive
4. faire du vélo
5. faire le ménage
6. faire la cuisine
7. faire la vaisselle
8. rester à la maison et ne rien faire

Aimez-vous faire du snowboard?

B **Préférences.** Écrivez les activités suivantes dans l'ordre de vos préférences. Votre partenaire va vous poser des questions pour déterminer l'ordre des activités sur votre feuille de papier.

faire du jogging	faire des randonnées	faire du jardinage
faire la cuisine	faire du vélo	ne rien faire

EXEMPLE — Préfères-tu faire du jogging ou ne rien faire?
            — Je préfère ne rien faire.
            — Préfères-tu ne rien faire ou faire la cuisine?...

C Que font-ils? Éric parle des projets de la famille pour aujourd'hui. Complétez ses phrases avec une expression avec **faire**.

1. Maman... ce matin.

2. Maman et Michel...

3. Papa... cet après-midi.

4. Papa et maman...

5. Cathy et moi, nous...

6. Moi, je...

D Activités. Complétez les phrases avec une expression avec **faire**. Ensuite, dites si c'est vrai pour vos amis et vous. Corrigez les phrases fausses.

1. Je _____ au centre commercial le samedi.

2. Mes amis et moi aimons jouer au tennis et au basket. Nous _____ ensemble tous les week-ends.

3. Mes parents ont un joli jardin. Ils aiment _____.

4. Chez moi, tout est toujours propre parce que je _____ tous les week-ends.

5. Je vais _____ aujourd'hui après les cours. J'ai besoin d'aller au bureau de poste et à la banque.

faire la cuisine
faire du sport
faire du jardinage
faire la lessive
faire du shopping
faire des courses
faire une promenade
faire le ménage
faire la vaisselle
faire du vélo
faire les courses

E Conseils. Donnez des conseils à un ami. Utilisez une expression avec **faire** et mettez le verbe à l'impératif.

EXEMPLE — La vaisselle est sale.
— **Eh bien, fais la vaisselle!**

1. J'ai faim.

2. Tous mes vêtements sont sales.

3. J'ai envie de faire de l'exercice.

4. J'ai besoin d'acheter de nouveaux vêtements.

5. Mon appartement est très sale.

6. Il n'y a pas de café, de fromage ou de lait à la maison!

Deciding what to wear and buying clothes

LES VÊTEMENTS

Vocabulaire supplémentaire

un blouson *a windbreaker, a jacket*
une casquette *a cap*
une ceinture *a belt*
un chapeau *a hat*
des chaussettes *(f) socks*
un col roulé *a turtleneck*
un débardeur *a tank top*
un legging *leggings*
un pyjama *pajamas*
des sous-vêtements *(m) underwear*
un sweat-shirt *a sweatshirt*
un tailleur *a woman's suit*
des hauts talons *(m) high heels*
une tunique *a tunic*
une veste *a sports coat*

Qu'est-ce que vous **mettez** pour aller en cours? pour sortir le soir?
Qu'est-ce que vous **avez mis** ce matin? hier soir?

Je mets souvent...   Je mets **parfois**...   Ce matin, j'ai mis...

un jean   un short   un pantalon   une jupe

un pull   un polo ou un tee-shirt   une chemise et une cravate   un chemisier

un survêtement   une robe   un costume   des chaussures *(f)*, des baskets *(f)*, des bottes *(f)*, des sandales *(f)* ou des tongs *(f)*

un anorak   un imperméable   un manteau   un maillot de bain ou un bikini

J'emporte...   Je porte...

un parapluie   un sac ou un portefeuille   une montre   des lunettes de soleil

Note *de vocabulaire*

Porter means *to carry* or *to wear* and **mettre** *to put, to put on,* or *to wear.* They can both be used to say what one wears in general, although **mettre** is more commonly used in this case and in the **passé composé. Il porte/met souvent un jean. Il a mis un jean hier.** Use **porter** to say what someone is wearing at a particular moment. **Aujourd'hui, il porte un pantalon blanc.**

The forms of **mettre** are:

je **mets**	nous **mettons**
tu **mets**	vous **mettez**
il/elle/on **met**	ils/elles **mettent**

PASSÉ COMPOSÉ: **j'ai mis**

The verb **essayer** means both *to try* and *to try on.* It is a **-yer** spelling-change verb, like **envoyer.**

The forms of **essayer** are:

j' **essaie**	nous **essayons**
tu **essaies**	vous **essayez**
il/elle/on **essaie**	ils/elles **essaient**

PASSÉ COMPOSÉ: **j'ai essayé**

Sélection musicale. Search for the song **"Je vends des robes"** by Nino Ferrer online to enjoy a musical selection related to this vocabulary.

mettez (mettre *to put, to put on***)**   **avez mis (mettre** past participle: **mis)**   **parfois** *sometimes*   **emporter** *to take (along), to carry (away)*

5-7

Alice Pérez cherche un nouveau maillot de bain. Elle entre dans un magasin.

LA VENDEUSE:	Bonjour, madame. **Je peux vous aider?**
ALICE:	Je cherche un maillot de bain.
LA VENDEUSE:	**Quelle taille faites-vous?**
ALICE:	**Je fais du** 42.
LA VENDEUSE:	Nous avons **ces** maillots-**ci.** Ils sont très jolis et ils sont **en solde.**
ALICE:	J'aime bien ce maillot noir. **Je peux l'essayer?**
LA VENDEUSE:	**Bien sûr,** madame. **La cabine d'essayage** est **par ici.**

Alice sort de la cabine d'essayage.

LA VENDEUSE:	Alors, **qu'en pensez-vous?**
ALICE:	**Il me plaît** beaucoup. Il **coûte** combien?
LA VENDEUSE:	**Voyons,** c'est 65 euros.
ALICE:	C'est bien. Alors, je **le** prends.

A **Préférences.** Complétez ces phrases pour parler de vos préférences.

1. Quand il fait froid, je préfère mettre *un pantalon et un pull / un survêtement / un manteau ou un anorak.*
2. Quand il fait chaud, je préfère mettre *un jean / un pantalon / un short / un maillot de bain et un polo / un tee-shirt / une chemise / un chemisier.*
3. Pour aller à la plage, je mets le plus souvent *un bikini / un maillot de bain / un short.*
4. Quand il fait du soleil, *je mets / je ne mets pas* souvent des/de lunettes de soleil.
5. Quand il pleut, je préfère *emporter un parapluie / mettre un imperméable.*
6. Je porte *souvent / rarement* une montre. *(Je préfère regarder l'heure sur mon téléphone portable.)*
7. Comme chaussures, je préfère mettre *des baskets / des bottes / des sandales / des tongs.*
8. Normalement, je mets mon argent dans *un sac / un portefeuille / ma poche* (pocket).

B **Entretien.** Interviewez votre partenaire.

1. Tu aimes faire du shopping? Tu préfères acheter des vêtements, des CD, des DVD, des jeux vidéo ou des livres?
2. Tu préfères acheter tes vêtements au centre commercial, dans les petits magasins, dans un magasin d'occasion *(second-hand store)* ou sur Internet?
3. Pour aller à un mariage ou à un entretien *(interview)*, qu'est-ce que tu préfères mettre?

À VOUS!

Avec un(e) partenaire, relisez à haute voix la conversation entre la vendeuse et Alice. Après, adaptez la conversation pour acheter un jean, un anorak ou un manteau. Jouez le rôle d'Alice et votre partenaire va jouer le rôle du vendeur (de la vendeuse). Ensuite, échangez les rôles.

---

une vendeuse (un vendeur) *a salesclerk* **Je peux vous aider?** *Can I help you?* **Quelle taille faites-vous?** *What size do you wear?* **Je fais du...** *I wear size...* **ces... -ci / -là** *these / those ... over here / over there* **en solde** *on sale* **Je peux l'essayer? (essayer)** *Can I try it on? (to try, to try on)* **Bien sûr** *Of course* **La cabine d'essayage** *The fitting room* **par ici** *this way* **qu'en pensez-vous?** *what do you think about it?* **Il me plaît. (plaire)** *I like it. / It pleases me. (to please)* **coûter** *to cost* **Voyons** *Let's see* **le (l')** *it, him* **(la, l')** *it, her*

You can access the audio of the active vocabulary of this *Compétence* online.

AVOIDING REPETITION

✔ Pour vérifier

1. How do you say the direct object pronouns *him, her, it,* and *them* in French?

2. Where do you place the direct object pronouns and **y** when there is an infinitive? in the **passé composé**? Where do you place them otherwise? Where do you place them in a negative sentence?

Les pronoms **le, la, l'** *et* **les**

1. Use the direct object pronouns **le, la, l',** and **les** to replace a person, animal, or thing that is the direct object of the verb. Use **le** *(him, it)* to replace masculine singular nouns, **la** *(her, it)* to replace feminine singular nouns, and **les** *(them)* to replace all plural nouns. **Le** and **la** become **l'** when the following word begins with a vowel or silent **h.**

   — Tu prends ce maillot?   — Tu prends cette robe aussi?
   — Oui, je **le** prends.   — Oui, je **la** prends.

   — Tu achètes cette chemise?   — Tu achètes ces bottes?
   — Oui, je **l'**achète.   — Oui, je **les** achète.

	BEFORE A CONSONANT SOUND	BEFORE A VOWEL OR SILENT *H*
him, it (masculine)	le	l'
her, it (feminine)	la	l'
them	les	les

2. Like **y,** these pronouns are generally placed *immediately before* the verb, even in the negative.

   — Tu aimes **cette chemise**?   — Tu vas **au centre commercial**?
   — Oui, je **l'**aime bien.   — Oui, j'**y** vais.
     Non, je ne **l'**aime pas.   Non, je n'**y** vais pas.

   Place them *immediately before* an infinitive, if there is one in the clause.

   — Tu vas acheter **cette chemise**?
   — Oui, je vais **l'**acheter. / Non, je ne vais pas **l'**acheter.

3. In the **passé composé,** direct object pronouns and **y** are placed *immediately before* the auxiliary verb (the conjugated form of **avoir** or **être).**

   Je **l'**ai fait.   J'**y** suis allé(e).
   Je ne **l'**ai pas fait.   Je n'**y** suis pas allé(e).

   Generally, in the **passé composé,** the past participle agrees in gender and number with the subject when the auxiliary verb is **être,** but not when it is **avoir.** However, the past participle used with **avoir** will agree with *direct objects,* but only if they *precede* the verb, as they do with direct object pronouns.

   Éric a acheté **cette chemise.** Il **l'**a achetée hier.

   Cathy a acheté **ces pulls.** Elle **les** a achetés ce matin.

A   Au magasin de vêtements.   Alice et Vincent sont au magasin de vêtements. Complétez ce que chacun dit avec le pronom qui convient (**le, la, l', les**).

1. J'aime ce maillot de bain. Je peux _____ essayer?
2. J'aime ces bottes. Je _____ prends.
3. Je n'aime pas ce bikini. Je ne _____ prends pas.
4. Comment trouves-tu cette robe? Voudrais-tu _____ essayer?
5. Je n'aime pas cet anorak. Je ne vais pas _____ prendre.
6. Regarde cette belle cravate! Je _____ trouve super!

B **À Paris.** Dites si vous reconnaissez *(recognize)* ces sites parisiens. Utilisez **Je reconnais...** *(I recognize . . .)* et le pronom qui convient **(le, la, l', les)**.

EXEMPLE Cette avenue?
Oui, je la reconnais. C'est les Champs-Élysées.
Non, je ne la reconnais pas.

EXEMPLE Cette avenue?

1. Cette cathédrale?

2. Ce musée?

3. Cette tour?

4. Cette place?

5. Ce fleuve *(river)*?

C **Le samedi.** Dites si vous faites ou ne faites pas souvent ces choses. Remplacez les mots en italique avec **le, la, l'** ou **les**.

EXEMPLE écouter souvent *la radio* dans la voiture
Oui, je l'écoute souvent dans la voiture.

1. faire souvent *le ménage* le samedi
2. passer souvent *le samedi soir* à la maison
3. regarder souvent *la télé* le matin
4. inviter souvent *mon meilleur ami (ma meilleure amie)* chez moi
5. faire souvent *les courses* le week-end
6. prendre souvent *le petit déjeuner* dans un café
7. réviser souvent *mes cours* le samedi soir

D **Intentions.** Un(e) ami(e) voudrait savoir ce que vous allez faire avec les choses suivantes. Répondez en utilisant un pronom **(le, la, l', les)** et un verbe logique. Jouez les deux rôles avec un(e) partenaire.

EXEMPLE ces frites
— **Qu'est-ce que tu vas faire avec ces frites?**
— **Je vais les manger!**

1. ces vêtements   **4.** cette chemise   **7.** ce journal
2. ce DVD   **5.** ces bottes   **8.** ce CD
3. ce jus de fruit   **6.** cette eau minérale **9.** ce sandwich

E **Et vous?** Avez-vous fait ces choses le week-end dernier? Répondez en employant le pronom qui convient: **y, le, la, l'** ou **les.**

> **EXEMPLE** Vous avez regardé *la télé* le week-end dernier?
> **Oui, je l'ai regardée.**
> **Non, je ne l'ai pas regardée.**

1. Vous êtes resté(e) *chez vous* tout le week-end?
2. Vous avez fait *le ménage*?
3. Vous avez fait *la lessive*?
4. Vous avez lu *le livre de français*?
5. Vous avez fait *vos devoirs*?
6. Vous avez dîné *au restaurant*?
7. Vous êtes allé(e) *au cinéma*?

F **Le week-end des Pérez.** Regardez les explications de ce que les Pérez ont fait le week-end dernier et complétez les réponses. Utilisez **y, le, la, l'** ou **les.**

> **EXEMPLE** Qui est allé *au Quartier latin?*
> Éric et Michèle **y sont allés.**

1. Quand est-ce qu'ils sont allés *au Quartier latin*?

   Ils _____ vendredi après-midi.

2. Qui a commandé *les spaghettis à la carbonara*?

   Éric _____.

3. Qui a acheté *le nouveau livre de Jérôme Ferrari*?

   Michèle _____.

4. Où est-ce qu'ils ont retrouvé *leurs amis*?

   Ils _____ dans un café du quartier.

5. Avec qui est-ce qu'ils ont pris *leur café*?

   Ils _____ avec des amis.

6. Où est-ce qu'Éric et Michèle ont vu *le film avec Jean Reno*?

   Ils _____ au cinéma du Panthéon.

Vendredi après-midi, Éric et sa copine Michèle sont allés au Quartier latin, où ils ont mangé dans un restaurant italien. Michèle a mangé des raviolis et Éric a commandé des spaghettis à la carbonara. Après le repas, ils sont allés dans une librairie où Michèle a acheté un livre de Jérôme Ferrari. Après ça, ils ont retrouvé des amis dans un café du quartier et ils ont pris un café ensemble en terrasse. Plus tard, Éric et Michèle sont allés au cinéma du Panthéon pour voir le nouveau film avec Jean Reno.

© Bill Ross/Corbis/Getty Images

7. Quand est-ce qu'Alice est allée *au musée d'Orsay*?

   Elle _____ samedi matin.

8. Où est-ce qu'elle a vu *la nouvelle exposition sur Cézanne*?

   Elle _____ au musée d'Orsay.

9. Elle a vu *les autres expositions du musée*?

   Non, elle _____.

10. Elle est allée *au cinéma* après le musée?

    Non, elle _____.

11. Où est-ce qu'elle a retrouvé *Vincent*?

    Elle _____ dans un restaurant du quartier.

Samedi matin, Alice est allée au musée d'Orsay, où elle a vu la nouvelle exposition sur Cézanne. Elle n'a pas eu le temps de voir les autres expositions parce qu'elle est allée acheter une jupe dans un magasin de vêtements. Vers une heure et demie, elle a retrouvé Vincent dans un restaurant du quartier.

G Préférences. Répondez aux questions de votre ami(e) en remplaçant les mots en italique par le pronom qui convient. Jouez les rôles avec un(e) partenaire.

EXEMPLE — **Je révise *mes leçons* tous les jours. Et toi?**
— **Moi aussi, je les révise tous les jours.**
Moi non, je ne les révise pas tous les jours.

1. Je regarde souvent *la télé* le week-end. Et toi?
2. J'ai envie de regarder *la télé* ce soir. Et toi?
3. J'invite souvent *mes parents* à la maison. Et toi?
4. Ce week-end, j'ai l'intention de voir *mes parents*. Et toi?
5. Je trouve *mes cours* plutôt difficiles. Et toi?
6. Ce soir, je vais préparer *le prochain examen de français*. Et toi?
7. Samedi soir, je vais faire *mes devoirs*. Et toi?
8. Samedi dernier, je suis allé(e) *au cinéma*. Et toi?
9. Dimanche dernier, j'ai fait *mes devoirs*. Et toi?
10. Hier soir, j'ai regardé *la télé*. Et toi?

H Entretien. Interviewez votre partenaire. Utilisez **y** ou un pronom complément d'objet direct pour remplacer les mots en italique dans vos réponses.

1. Est-ce que tu achètes *tes vêtements* au centre commercial? Dans quel magasin est-ce que tu achètes *tes vêtements* le plus souvent? Où est-ce que tu as acheté *les vêtements que tu portes maintenant*?

2. Chez toi, dans quelle pièce préfères-tu regarder *la télé*? Aimes-tu faire tes devoirs *dans cette pièce* aussi? Vas-tu passer beaucoup de temps *dans cette pièce* ce soir?

3. Invites-tu souvent *tes amis* chez toi? Où préfères-tu retrouver *tes amis*? La dernière fois que tu es sorti(e) avec des amis, où est-ce que tu as retrouvé *tes amis*?

4. Où aimes-tu passer *ton temps libre*? Où est-ce que tu as passé *la soirée* hier? Est-ce que tu vas passer la soirée *chez toi* ce soir?

VIDÉO-REPRISE

Les Stagiaires

Dans l'*Épisode 5,* Matthieu parle à Christophe d'une soirée que Christophe, Rachid et Amélie ont passée ensemble. Avant de regarder l'épisode, faites ces exercices pour réviser ce que vous avez appris dans le *Chapitre 5.*

Rappel!

Matthieu, l'informaticien timide à Technovert, est amoureux fou d'Amélie *(crazy about Amélie)* mais trop timide pour le lui dire *(to tell her).* Il parle aux autres pour découvrir tout ce qu'il peut *(to discover all that he can)* à son sujet.

See the *Résumé de grammaire* section at the end of each chapter for a review of all the grammar presented in the chapter.

A **Samedi dernier.** Un ami pose des questions à Christophe sur ce qu'il a fait samedi dernier. Complétez ses questions en mettant les verbes au passé composé.

EXEMPLE Tu **es sorti** (sortir) avec des amis ou ils **sont venus** (venir) chez toi?

1. Avec qui est-ce que tu _____ (sortir)?

2. Tu _____ (retrouver) les autres en ville ou vous y _____ (aller) tous ensemble?

3. Tu _____ (prendre) ta voiture?

4. Quel temps est-ce qu'il _____ (faire)? Il _____ (pleuvoir)?

5. Quels vêtements est-ce que tu _____ (mettre) pour sortir?

6. Qu'est-ce que vous _____ (faire)? Vous _____ (dîner) ensemble? Vous _____ (aller) danser? Vous _____ (voir) un film au cinéma?

7. De quoi *(About what)* est-ce que vous _____ (parler)?

8. Tu _____ (rentrer) vers quelle heure?

9. Vous _____ (partir) tous en même temps ou les autres _____ (rester) plus longtemps?

Maintenant, utilisez les questions précédentes pour interviewer un(e) partenaire sur la dernière fois qu'il/elle est sorti(e) avec des amis.

B **Je veux tout savoir.** Céline pose des questions à Amélie sur une soirée qu'elle a passée avec Christophe et Rachid. Complétez les réponses d'Amélie en remplaçant les mots en italique par le pronom qui convient: **le, la, l', les** ou **y.** Utilisez le verbe de la question dans la réponse.

EXEMPLE — Alors, Christophe et toi avez passé *la soirée* ensemble l'autre jour?
— Oui, on **l'a passée** ensemble samedi dernier.

1. — Est-ce que tu as retrouvé *Christophe* en ville ou vous y êtes allés ensemble?
— Je _____ en ville.

2. — Vous êtes allés *en ville* seuls tous les deux?
— Non, Rachid _____ avec nous.

3. — Comment est-ce que tu trouves *Rachid*?
— Je _____ très sympa.

4. — Comment est-ce que tu as trouvé *le restaurant* où vous avez dîné?
— On a dîné dans le restaurant marocain *(Moroccan)* de la sœur de Rachid et moi, je _____ excellent.

5. — Vous êtes allés *en boîte* aussi?
— Oui, on _____ après le dîner.

6. — Tu vas voir *Christophe et Rachid* le week-end prochain, aussi?
— Pour l'instant, je n'ai pas l'intention de _____ le week-end prochain, mais on ne sait jamais *(you never know).*

C Qui fait quoi? Amélie dîne avec Rachid et Christophe dans le restaurant de la sœur de Rachid. Complétez ses phrases avec une expression logique de la liste. Mettez la forme correcte du verbe **faire** dans le premier espace et le reste de l'expression dans le deuxième espace.

> faire les courses   faire le ménage   faire la vaisselle
> faire la cuisine   faire une promenade

EXEMPLE Ta sœur et toi, vous **faites** toujours **les courses** pour le restaurant très tôt tous les matins, non? Où est-ce que vous trouvez tous les produits pour ces plats marocains *(Moroccan)*?

1. Ta sœur _____ très bien _____. Mon plat *(dish)* est excellent.

2. Céline et moi _____ toujours _____ immédiatement après le dîner parce qu'elle a peur d'avoir des insectes dans la cuisine.

3. Notre appartement est toujours très propre. Céline _____ souvent _____.

4. Je _____ souvent _____ après le dîner si je mange beaucoup pour faciliter la digestion.

D Quel temps fait-il? Au dîner, Rachid parle du temps qu'il fait au Maroc au cours de l'année. Complétez ses phrases.

1.    **2.**    **3.**

1. En été, il fait du _____ et il fait souvent très _____.

2. Quelquefois en hiver, il fait _____, mais il ne _____ presque jamais.

3. Il fait souvent du _____, mais il ne _____ pas beaucoup.

Access the Video *Les Stagiaires* online.

© Cengage Learning

▶ **Épisode 5: Qu'est-ce que vous avez fait?**

AVANT LA VIDÉO

Dans cet épisode, Matthieu parle à Christophe d'une soirée que Christophe et Rachid ont passée avec Amélie. Avant de regarder l'épisode, pensez à des activités qu'on fait quand on passe une soirée en ville avec des amis.

APRÈS LA VIDÉO

Regardez l'épisode et répondez aux questions suivantes.

- Où est-ce que Christophe, Rachid et Amélie sont allés?
- Qu'est-ce qu'ils ont fait?
- De quoi *(About what)* ont-ils parlé?

LECTURE ET COMPOSITION

LECTURE

POUR MIEUX LIRE:
Using visuals to make guesses

Before reading a text, scan it and use the title and any accompanying visuals (photos, charts, etc.) to help you anticipate content and read more easily.

Un blog. Regardez le texte et les photos. Quel genre de blog est-ce? Quelle sorte de renseignements est-ce que vous pensez y trouver?

Je blogue donc je suis

Les blogs **font** de plus en plus **partie des** loisirs des Français, et la France est devenue championne du **monde** du nombre de blogs par **internaute.** Bloguer est surtout populaire chez les jeunes, surtout les jeunes politiquement engagés, mais **chacun** a sa **propre** raison de bloguer. Pour certains, c'est le désir de faire partie d'une communauté. Pour d'autres, c'est le besoin de mettre en mots ses sentiments, **promouvoir** ses idées ou **décrire** ses expériences. Les blogs de voyage sont **parmi** les plus populaires. Lisez le blog de voyage **qui suit.**

Mon week-end à Paris

Je suis allé passer un week-end à Paris avec des amis. Arrivés le vendredi vers 18h, on a profité de la première soirée pour visiter Montmartre. J'ai trouvé la vue de Paris de là-haut inoubliable.

Le lendemain, on a fait une promenade le long des Champs-Élysées et ensuite, on a longé les quais de la Seine. Après, on a visité Notre-Dame. J'ai admiré la façade avec toutes ses statues et j'ai pris beaucoup de photos.

Le dimanche matin, on a vu une exposition d'art moderne au Centre Pompidou avant de quitter Paris.

Paris, c'est sans doute la plus belle ville du monde!

---

font partie de *are part of* **le monde** *the world* **internaute** *Internet user*
chacun *each one* **propre** *own* **promouvoir** *to promote* **décrire** *to describe*
parmi *among* **qui suit** *that follows*

© Directphoto/AGE Fotostock

COMPOSITION

To write well, you first need to organize your ideas. You can sometimes base your organization on a document you already have or can easily create. For example, to describe a book you have read, you can use the table of contents to organize your thoughts. To talk about a trip you have taken, you can use your itinerary, and when writing a blog, you can look at how other blogs are organized.

Organisez-vous. Vous allez écrire un blog sur une semaine imaginaire en France. D'abord, sur une feuille de papier, créez votre itinéraire.

1.
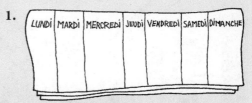

2. Sous chaque jour, écrivez des phrases pour décrire *(describe)* une progression logique de votre séjour *(your stay)*. Dites:

   - quand vous êtes parti(e), et avec qui et comment vous avez voyagé
   - où et à quelle heure vous êtes arrivé(e) en France et dans quelle sorte d'hôtel(s) vous êtes descendu(e)
   - ce que *(what)* vous avez fait chaque jour
   - quand vous avez quitté la France

Compréhension

1. Est-ce que les Français aiment bloguer? Quel groupe blogue le plus?
2. Pourquoi est-ce qu'on blogue?
3. Dans ce blog de voyage, quels endroits à Paris est-ce que le blogueur mentionne?

Un voyage en France

En vous basant sur votre itinéraire, écrivez un blog sur votre voyage imaginaire.

   EXEMPLE **L'été dernier, je suis allé(e) en France avec...**

COMPARAISONS CULTURELLES

LE SPORT ET LE TEMPS LIBRE DES FRANÇAIS

Les Français passent souvent leur temps libre chez eux où ils aiment regarder la télé, écouter de la musique, passer du temps sur Internet et lire.

Les Français aiment beaucoup les activités culturelles aussi et ils consacrent beaucoup de temps à ces activités, **allant** souvent au cinéma, à des expositions d'art, au théâtre, à des concerts... De nombreux festivals et fêtes qui permettent d'avoir accès à l'art, à la musique, **au monde du septième art** et à leur **patrimoine** montrent **l'engouement** des Français pour la culture.

Pourtant, selon une enquête récente **auprès des Français,** l'activité **dite** la plus satisfaisante (après passer du temps entre amis), est faire du sport, et beaucoup d'entre eux pratiquent une activité sportive **plusieurs** fois par mois.

À l'école, le sport est obligatoire et il est **enseigné** comme les autres **matières.** Pourtant, **les élèves ne peuvent pas** pratiquer de sports à l'école après les cours. Ils **doivent** s'inscrire dans un club. Les clubs de football, de tennis et d'**équitation** sont les plus souvent choisis.

allant *going*   **au monde du septième art** *to the world of the seventh art* (cinema)   **patrimoine** *heritage*   **l'engouement** *enthusiasm*   **Pourtant, selon une enquête** *However, according to a survey*   **auprès des Français** *with the French*   **dite** *said*   **plusieurs** *several*   **À l'école** *At school*   **enseigné** *taught*   **matières** *subjects*   **les élèves** *the students*   **ne peuvent pas** *can't*   **doivent** *have to*   **équitation** *horseback riding*

Beaucoup de Français **ne font pas partie de** clubs, mais ils pratiquent une activité sportive seuls. Ils font du jogging, **de la marche, de la natation** ou du cyclisme. À Paris, tous les week-ends, **les berges** de la Seine sont fermées pour permettre aux cyclistes de se promener; et le vendredi soir, **grâce à** l'association sportive «Pari roller», les Parisiens **peuvent traverser la ville en roller** sur un circuit **interdit à la circulation automobile.**

Les sports d'hiver (**le patin à glace,** le ski, le snowboard), les sports d'été (la natation, **la voile, la planche à voile**) aussi bien que les sports «d'aventure» (**l'escalade, le parapente,** le canoë-kayak) sont aussi très appréciés!

Et chez vous, quels sont les sports les plus populaires dans votre région?

© RAYMOND ROIG/AFP/Getty Images

Compréhension

1. Qu'est-ce que les Français aiment faire chez eux pendant leur temps libre? Est-ce que ce sont les mêmes activités que celles *(those)* qui sont populaires chez vous?

2. Quelles sont les activités culturelles les plus populaires en France? Et chez vous?

3. Est-ce que le sport fait partie du cursus scolaire *(school curriculum)* d'un(e) élève français(e)? Et des élèves dans votre région? Qu'est-ce que les jeunes doivent faire *(have to do)* pour participer à des activités sportives après les cours? Est-ce que c'est similaire ou différent dans votre région?

4. Quelles activités sportives sont populaires chez les Français? Et chez vous?

---

ne font pas partie de *don't belong to*   **de la marche** *walking*   **de la natation** *swimming*   **les berges** *the banks* (of a river)
grâce à *thanks to*   **peuvent traverser la ville en roller** *can skate across the city*   **interdit à la circulation automobile** *closed to traffic*   **le patin à glace** *ice-skating*   **la voile** *sailing*   **la planche à voile** *windsurfing*   **l'escalade** *rock climbing*
le parapente *paragliding*

RÉSUMÉ DE GRAMMAIRE

PASSÉ COMPOSÉ

J'ai mangé.
I ate.
I have eaten.
I did eat.

Ils n'ont pas beaucoup dormi.
They didn't sleep much.
They haven't slept much.

To say what happened in the past, put the verb in the **passé composé.** It may be translated in a variety of ways. The **passé composé** is composed of an auxiliary verb and a past participle. For most verbs the auxiliary verb is **avoir,** but for a few verbs it is **être.** All **-er** verbs have past participles with **-é** (**parler: j'ai parlé**) and most **-ir** verbs with **-i** (**dormir: j'ai dormi**).

PARLER → PARLÉ	
j'**ai parlé**	nous **avons parlé**
tu **as parlé**	vous **avez parlé**
il/elle/on **a parlé**	ils/elles **ont parlé**

These verbs conjugated with **avoir** have irregular past participles.

avoir:	j'ai eu	mettre:	j'ai mis	être:	j'ai été
il y a:	il y a eu	prendre:	j'ai pris	faire:	j'ai fait
boire:	j'ai bu	apprendre:	j'ai appris	écrire:	j'ai écrit
courir:	j'ai couru	comprendre:	j'ai compris		
lire:	j'ai lu				
pleuvoir:	il a plu				
voir:	j'ai vu				

— Qu'est-ce que tu **as fait** hier soir?
— J'**ai vu** un film avec des amis et après, on **a pris** un verre au café.

A few verbs have **être** as their auxiliary. With these verbs, the past participle agrees with the subject for gender and plurality.

ALLER → ALLÉ	
je **suis allé(e)**	nous **sommes allé(e)s**
tu **es allé(e)**	vous **êtes allé(e)(s)**
il **est allé**	ils **sont allés**
elle **est allée**	elles **sont allées**
on **est allé(e)(s)**	

— Est-ce que ta mère et ta tante **sont allées** à Paris avec toi?
— Oui, elles ont fait le voyage avec moi, mais je **suis restée** plus longtemps. Elles **sont rentrées** une semaine avant moi.

Here are some verbs that have **être** as their auxiliary verb. Use **être** with **passer** only when it means *to pass by* and not when it means *to spend time.*

aller:	je suis allé(e)	monter:	je suis monté(e)
arriver:	je suis arrivé(e)	descendre:	je suis descendu(e)
rester:	je suis resté(e)	venir:	je suis venu(e)
entrer:	je suis entré(e)	revenir:	je suis revenu(e)
sortir:	je suis sorti(e)	devenir:	je suis devenu(e)
partir:	je suis parti(e)	naître:	je suis né(e)
passer:	je suis passé(e)	mourir:	il/elle est mort(e)
rentrer:	je suis rentré(e)	tomber:	je suis tombé(e)
retourner:	je suis retourné(e)		

— Tu as **déjà** dîné?
— Non, je **n'**ai **pas encore** mangé.

— Qu'est-ce que ton mari et toi avez fait l'année dernière pour les vacances?
— On **n'**a **rien** fait.

— J'ai **toujours bien** mangé dans ce restaurant. J'y suis **souvent** allé(e).

To negate a verb in the **passé composé,** place **ne** immediately after the subject and **pas, rien** *(nothing),* or **jamais** after the auxiliary verb. Use **ne... pas encore** to say *not yet* and **déjà** to say *already* or *ever.* **Déjà** and adverbs indicating *how often* (**toujours, souvent...**) and *how well* (**bien, mal...**) are usually placed between the auxiliary verb and the past participle.

The following adverbs indicate when something happened in the past. They may be placed at the beginning or end of a clause.

hier (matin, après-midi, soir)	récemment
le week-end (le mois) dernier	pendant deux heures (longtemps)
la semaine (l'année) dernière	il y a quelques secondes (cinq minutes, cinq ans...)
la dernière fois	

FAIRE

The verb **faire** *(to do, to make)* is irregular.

FAIRE *(to do, to make)*	
je **fais**	nous **faisons**
tu **fais**	vous **faites**
il/elle/on **fait**	ils/elles **font**
PASSÉ COMPOSÉ: **j'ai fait**	

Faire is also used in many weather expressions, as well as the expressions listed on page 206.

The **un, une, des, du, de la,** and **de l'** in the expressions with **faire** become **de (d')** when the verb is negated. The definite article (**le, la, l', les**) does not change.

NE... RIEN

Ne... rien means *nothing* or *not anything*. This expression can be the subject or object of the verb, or the object of a preposition.

When negating an infinitive, place both parts of the negative expression before it.

DIRECT OBJECT PRONOUNS

The direct object pronouns are **le, la, l',** and **les.** Use **le** *(him, it)* to replace masculine singular nouns and **la** *(her, it)* to replace feminine singular nouns. **Les** *(Them)* replaces all plural nouns. **Le** and **la** become **l'** when the following word begins with a vowel or silent **h.**

	BEFORE A CONSONANT	BEFORE A VOWEL OR SILENT *H*
him, it (masculine)	le	l'
her, it (feminine)	la	l'
them	les	les

These pronouns are generally placed *immediately before* the verb. They go before the infinitive if there is one. If not, they go before the conjugated verb. In the negative, the pronoun remains *immediately before* the conjugated verb or the infinitive.

In the **passé composé,** direct object pronouns are placed just before the auxiliary verb (the conjugated form of **avoir**), and the past participle agrees with them for gender and plurality by adding **-e, -s,** or **-es.**

— Tu es parti en vacances **pendant combien de temps?**
— **Pendant** quinze jours.
— Tu es rentré **il y a combien de temps?**
— Je suis rentré **mardi dernier.**

Je ne **fais** rien ce week-end.
Qu'est-ce que tu **fais?**
On **fait** quelque chose ensemble?
Faisons quelque chose avec mes amis.
Que **faites**-vous généralement?
Mes amis **font** beaucoup de sport.

— Quel temps **fait**-il?
— Il **fait** beau (mauvais, froid, chaud, frais, [du] soleil, du vent).
Ils **font** la cuisine et nous **faisons** la vaisselle.

Je ne fais jamais **d'**exercice.
Mon colocataire ne fait jamais **le** ménage.

Rien n'est en solde?
Tu **n'**achètes **rien?**
Je **n'**ai besoin de **rien.**
Je préfère **ne rien** acheter.

— Tu prends ce sac?
— Oui, je **le** prends.
— Tu aimes cette robe aussi?
— Oui, je **l'**aime bien.
— Tu achètes tes vêtements ici?
— Oui, je **les** achète souvent ici.

Je **les** achète.
Je ne **les** achète pas.
Je vais **les** acheter.
Je ne vais pas **les** acheter.

— A-t-il acheté les chaussures?
— Oui, il **les** a acheté**es.**
Non, il ne **les** a pas acheté**es.**

VOCABULAIRE

Saying what you did

NOMS MASCULINS

un homme d'affaires	*a businessman*
le journal	*the newspaper*
le petit déjeuner	*breakfast*

NOM FÉMININ

une femme d'affaires	*a businesswoman*

EXPRESSIONS ADVERBIALES

hier	*yesterday*
hier soir	*last night, yesterday evening*
samedi dernier	*last Saturday*
le week-end dernier	*last weekend*

DIVERS

dernier (dernière)	*last*
étranger (étrangère)	*foreign*
faire une promenade	*to take a walk*
ne... rien	*nothing, not anything*
prendre son petit déjeuner	*to have one's breakfast*
réviser	*to review*
travaillant	*working*

Telling where you went

NOMS MASCULINS

un an	*a year*
un camping	*a campground*
un hôtel	*a hotel*
le lendemain	*the next day, the following day*
des parents	*relatives*

NOMS FÉMININS

la chance	*luck*
une heure	*an hour*
une minute	*a minute*
une nuit	*a night*
une seconde	*a second* (in time)
une voiture de location	*a rental car*

EXPRESSIONS VERBALES

descendre (de/à/dans)	*to descend, to come down, to get off/out (of) (a vehicle), to stay (at)*
entrer (dans)	*to enter*
faire un voyage	*to take a trip*
monter (dans)	*to go up, to get on/in*
mourir (mort[e])	*to die (dead)*
naître (né[e])	*to be born (born)*
partir en voyage	*to leave on a trip*
partir en week-end	*to go away for the weekend*
passer (chez/devant/par)	*to pass (by [. . . 's house])*
retourner	*to return, to go back*
tomber	*to fall*

EXPRESSIONS ADVERBIALES

l'année dernière	*last year*
déjà	*already, ever*
la dernière fois	*the last time*
hier (matin, après-midi)	*yesterday (morning, afternoon)*
hier soir	*last night, yesterday evening*
Il y a combien de temps?	*How long ago?*
il y a quelques secondes	*a few seconds ago*
longtemps	*a long time*
lundi (mardi...) dernier	*last Monday (Tuesday . . .)*
le mois dernier	*last month*
ne... pas encore	*not yet*
Pendant combien de temps?	*For how long?*
pendant deux heures	*for two hours*
récemment	*recently*
la semaine dernière	*last week*
le week-end dernier	*last weekend*
le week-end passé	*the past weekend*

DIVERS

Quelle chance!	*What luck!*
quelques	*some, a few*

Discussing the weather and your activities

NOMS MASCULINS

l'automne (en automne)	autumn/fall (in autumn/in the fall)
l'été (en été)	summer (in summer)
l'hiver (en hiver)	winter (in winter)
un jardin	a garden
le printemps (au printemps)	spring (in spring)
le temps	the weather, time

NOMS FÉMININS

des distractions	entertainment
la neige	snow
la pluie	rain
une saison	a season

EXPRESSIONS VERBALES

adorer	to love, to adore
aller à la montagne	to go to the mountains
dépendre (de)	to depend (on)
faire de l'exercice	to exercise
faire des courses	to run errands
faire du bateau	to go boating
faire du camping	to go camping
faire du jardinage	to garden
faire du jogging	to go jogging
faire du shopping	to go shopping
faire du ski (nautique)	to (water)ski
faire du sport (du tennis, du hockey...)	to play sports (tennis, hockey . . .)
faire du vélo	to go bike-riding
faire du VTT	to go all-terrain biking
faire la cuisine	to cook
faire la lessive	to do laundry
faire la vaisselle	to do the dishes
faire le ménage	to do housework
faire les courses	to buy groceries
faire une promenade	to take a walk
faire une randonnée (faire des randonnées)	to take a hike, to hike (to go hiking, to hike)
faire un voyage	to take a trip
neiger	to snow
pleuvoir (Il a plu.)	to rain (It rained.)

DIVERS

ne... rien (de spécial)	nothing, not anything (special)
pendant	during, for
Quel temps fait-il?	What's the weather like?
Il fait beau / chaud / frais / froid / mauvais / (du) soleil / du vent.	It's nice / hot / cool / cold / bad / sunny / windy.
Il y a du vent.	It's windy.
Il pleut.	It is raining., It rains.
Il neige.	It is snowing., It snows.
Quel temps va-t-il faire?	What's the weather going to be like?
Il va faire...	It's going to be . . .
Il va pleuvoir / neiger.	It's going to rain / to snow.
si	if

Deciding what to wear and buying clothes

NOMS MASCULINS

un anorak	a ski jacket
un bikini	a bikini
un chemisier	a blouse
un costume	a suit (for a man)
un imperméable	a raincoat
un jean	jeans
un maillot de bain	a swimsuit
un manteau	a coat, an overcoat
un pantalon	pants
un parapluie	an umbrella
un polo	a knit shirt
un portefeuille	a wallet
un pull	a pullover sweater
un sac	a purse, a sack, a bag
un short	shorts
un survêtement	a jogging suit
un tee-shirt	a T-shirt
un vendeur	a salesclerk

NOMS FÉMININS

des baskets	tennis shoes, sneakers
des bottes	boots
une cabine d'essayage	a fitting room
des chaussures	shoes
une chemise	a shirt
une cravate	a tie
une jupe	a skirt
des lunettes (de soleil)	(sun)glasses
une montre	a watch
une robe	a dress
des sandales	sandals
des tongs	flip-flops
une vendeuse	a salesclerk

EXPRESSIONS VERBALES

coûter	to cost
emporter	to take (along), to carry (away)
essayer	to try, to try on
Il/Elle me plaît.	I like it.
mettre (je mets, vous mettez) (j'ai mis)	to wear, to put, to put on (I wore, put, put on)
porter	to wear

DIVERS

Bien sûr!	Of course!
ce (cet, cette, ces)...-ci/-là	this/that/these/those . . . over here/ over there
en solde	on sale
Je peux vous aider?	May I help you?
le (l') / la (l')	him, it / her, it
les	them
parfois	sometimes
par ici	this way
Quelle taille faites-vous?	What size do you wear?
Je fais du...	I wear size . . .
Qu'en pensez-vous?	What do you think about it?
voyons	let's see

BIENVENUE EN EUROPE FRANCOPHONE

En Europe, le français est une langue officielle dans quatre pays et **une principauté:** la France, la Belgique, la Suisse, le Luxembourg et Monaco. **Lesquels aimeriez-vous** visiter?

Fondée en 963, la ville de Luxembourg offre la possibilité de voir plus de mille ans d'histoire.

Le **Grand-Duché** du Luxembourg est un des plus petits États d'Europe. Il y a trois langues officielles au Luxembourg: le français, le luxembourgeois et l'allemand.

Grâce à sa forte immigration, **surtout venant** des pays de l'Union européenne, le Luxembourg est devenu un microcosme de l'Europe moderne.

Bienvenue Welcome   **une principauté** a principality   **Lesquels aimeriez-vous** Which ones would you like
Grand-Duché Grand Duchy   **Grâce à** Thanks to   **surtout venant** especially coming

La Suisse a quatre langues officielles: l'allemand, le français, l'italien et le romanche, et **chacun de** ces groupes linguistiques a **ses propres coutumes** et traditions. Les Suisses sont très **fiers de** leur culture et de leur diversité multiculturelle.

La Suisse offre de très belles vues.

Qu'aimeriez-vous faire en Suisse: du ski, des randonnées en montagne ou de l'alpinisme?

---

chacun de *each of*   **ses propres coutumes** *its own customs*   **fiers de** *proud of*   **Qu'aimeriez-vous** *What would you like*
de l'alpinisme *mountain climbing*

La Belgique est connue pour la variété de son architecture, pour la beauté de ses **paysages** et pour ses **nombreux** châteaux.

Les trois régions qui forment la Belgique, la Région **flamande,** la Région **wallonne** et la Région de Bruxelles (la capitale) donnent à la Belgique une riche diversité culturelle. Les Flamands (approximativement 60 % de la population) parlent **néerlandais.** Les Wallons (à peu près **un tiers** de la population) parlent français. **Parmi** le reste, il y a une minorité (moins de 1 %) qui parle allemand et, bien sûr, des gens qui parlent d'autres langues et des gens bilingues.

On peut aller sur la Grand-Place à Bruxelles pour admirer son architecture baroque et gothique, prendre un café et faire du shopping.

Monaco est célèbre pour le tourisme, le luxe et pour ses casinos, **ainsi que** pour son fameux Grand Prix de Formule 1.

Monaco est **une principauté** et une monarchie constitutionnelle. Le français y est la langue officielle, mais on y parle aussi l'anglais et l'italien. Près de 5 000 personnes parlent **monégasque,** un dialecte dérivé de l'italien.

---

flamande Flemish   **wallonne** French-speaking, Walloon   **néerlandais** Dutch   **un tiers** one-third   **Parmi** Among
paysages landscapes, countryside   **nombreux** numerous   **une principauté** a principality   **monégasque** Monegasque
(language native to Monaco)   **ainsi que** as well as

La France **comprend la France métropolitaine** et **plusieurs** collectivités et départements et régions **d'outre-mer, tels que** la Guadeloupe (dans la mer des Caraïbes, près de l'Amérique centrale), Mayotte (près de l'Afrique) et la Polynésie française (dans le Pacifique). Regardez la carte du monde francophone **à la fin du** livre. Quelle partie de la France **aimeriez-vous** visiter?

Dans les villes françaises, comme ici à Strasbourg, on peut visiter les parties historiques de la ville.

En sortant des grandes villes, on trouve de beaux paysages et de petits villages fascinants.

Aimeriez-vous mieux visiter un des départements et régions d'outre-mer, comme Mayotte?

Le savez-vous?

Quel État francophone correspond à chaque description?

la France	**la Belgique**	**le Luxembourg**
Monaco	**la Suisse**	

1. Ce pays est fier de sa diversité et chacun de ses quatre groupes linguistiques principaux a ses propres coutumes.
2. Ce pays est un grand-duché et il y a trois langues officielles.
3. Les habitants de la région francophone de ce pays s'appellent les Wallons.
4. Cette monarchie constitutionnelle est connue (known) pour le luxe et pour sa beauté.
5. Ce pays a plusieurs collectivités et départements et régions d'outre-mer.

---

comprend *includes*   **la France métropolitaine** *metropolitan France (the part of France in Europe)*   **plusieurs** *several*
d'outre-mer *overseas*   **tels que** *such as*   **à la fin du** *at the end of the*   **aimeriez-vous** *would you like*   **on peut** *one can*
En sortant des *By leaving the*

À Paris

Les sorties

Pair work	Video	
Group work	Audio	
Class work		

6

LE MONDE FRANCOPHONE
Géoculture et Vidéo-voyage: À Paris

COMPÉTENCE

1 Inviting someone to go out
Une invitation

Issuing and accepting invitations
*Les verbes **vouloir**, **pouvoir** et **devoir***
Stratégies et Compréhension auditive
• **Pour mieux comprendre:** *Noting the important information*
• **Compréhension auditive:** *On va au cinéma?*

2 Talking about how you spend and used to spend your time
Aujourd'hui et dans le passé

Saying how things used to be
L'imparfait
Talking about activities
*Les verbes **sortir**, **partir** et **dormir***

3 Talking about the past
Une sortie

Telling what was going on when something else happened
L'imparfait et le passé composé
Telling what happened and describing the circumstances
Le passé composé et l'imparfait

4 Narrating in the past
Les contes

Narrating what happened
Le passé composé et l'imparfait (reprise)

Vidéo-reprise: *Les Stagiaires*

Lecture et Composition
• **Pour mieux lire:** *Using standard formats*
• **Lecture:** *Deux films français*
• **Pour mieux écrire:** *Using standard formats*
• **Composition:** *Un film à voir*

Comparaisons culturelles: *Le cinéma: les préférences des Français*

Résumé de grammaire
Vocabulaire

© Brigitte Merle/Photononstop/Getty Images

GÉOCULTURE ET VIDÉO-VOYAGE:
À PARIS

PARIS

NOMBRE D'HABITANTS: **2 235 000 (avec la région parisienne: plus de 12 089 500) (les Parisiens)**

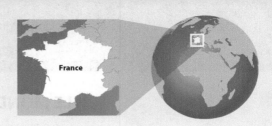

France

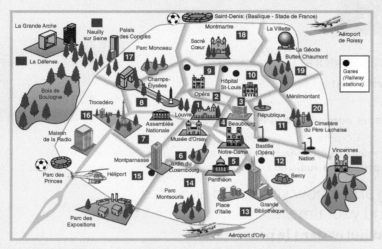

Paris est une des plus belles villes **du monde**!

Mais **que serait Paris** sans la Seine? La Seine sépare la ville en deux parties, **la rive** gauche et la rive droite. Les deux îles situées **au milieu de** la Seine sont l'île de la Cité et l'île Saint-Louis. La ville de Paris est née sur l'île de la Cité il y a plus de 2000 ans quand les Parisii **(une tribu gauloise)** y **ont établi** un village.

Depuis, la ville a prospéré et s'est organisée **autour du fleuve. C'est ainsi que** beaucoup de sites **parmi** les plus célèbres de Paris **se trouvent au bord de** la Seine.

Faisons donc un tour en bateau-mouche! Les tours en bateau-mouche sont parmi les plus populaires à Paris. En réalité, ces bateaux **sont originaires de** la ville de Lyon, pas de Paris, où, **au départ, ils servaient** au transport de marchandises. **Construits** dans les **ateliers** du quartier de la Mouche, ils **ont été appelés** «bateaux-mouches».

Aujourd'hui, Paris compte **pas moins de** 37 **ponts qui traversent** la Seine. Beaucoup de ces ponts sont **des ouvrages d'art** très riches en histoire.

© Evannovostro/Shutterstock.com

Commandé par Napoléon 1er, le pont des Arts est le premier pont métallique de Paris. Avec sa belle vue sur la Seine, il a eu un grand succès le jour de son inauguration avec 64 000 visiteurs.

© anyaivanova/Shutterstock.com

Le pont des Arts est un lien entre deux **lieux** d'art, d'un côté l'Institut de France, de l'autre, le Louvre.

du monde *in the world*	que serait Paris *what would Paris be*	la rive *the bank (of a river)*	au milieu de *in the middle of*	une tribu gauloise *a Gallic tribe*

du monde *in the world*　que serait Paris *what would Paris be*　la rive *the bank (of a river)*　au milieu de *in the middle of*　une tribu gauloise *a Gallic tribe*
ont établi *established*　Depuis *Since*　autour du fleuve *around the river*　C'est ainsi que *It's because of this*　parmi *among*　se trouvent *are located*
au bord de *next to*　sont originaires de *originated in*　au départ, ils servaient *they originally served*　Construits *Built, Constructed*　ateliers *workshops*
ont été appelés *were called*　pas moins de *no less than*　ponts qui traversent *bridges that cross*　des ouvrages d'art *works of art*　un lien *a link*　lieux *places*

Le pont **Neuf**, construit en 1607, est aujourd'hui le plus ancien pont de Paris.

Le Louvre, **anciennement un palais royal** et aujourd'hui l'un des plus grands musées du monde, fait presqu'un kilomètre de long. Devenu un musée en 1791, c'est aujourd'hui un des musées les plus visités du monde.

Les ponts construits avant la construction du pont Neuf étaient très souvent **surmontés d'habitations.** Le pont Neuf a été construit sans maisons. Alors, les Parisiens **se rassemblaient** sur ce pont comme sur **une place.** On y trouvait **des filous,** des charlatans, **des arracheurs de dents, des vendeurs d'onguent.** C'était très **vivant**!

Le Louvre, Notre-Dame de Paris et la tour Eiffel **se voient de** la Seine.

Le savez-vous?

Quel site touristique correspond à chaque description?

> **Notre-Dame de Paris   le Louvre   la Seine   le pont des Arts   le pont Neuf   l'île de la Cité   les bateaux-mouches**

1. Ce fleuve sépare Paris en deux parties, la rive droite et la rive gauche.
2. Entre 260 et 200 BCE, une tribu gauloise, les Parisii, y ont établi un village et c'est ainsi que *(and thus)* la ville de Paris est née.
3. Ce musée, anciennement un palais royal, est un des musées les plus visités du monde.
4. Ce pont relie *(links)* l'Institut de France au Louvre.
5. À l'époque de sa construction, les gens se rassemblaient sur ce pont comme sur une place.
6. Il a fallu *(It took)* plus de 100 ans pour construire cette cathédrale gothique.
7. Ces bateaux sont à Paris ce que *(what)* les gondoles sont à Venise.

Notre-Dame de Paris se trouve sur l'île de la Cité. Excellent exemple du style gothique, la construction de cette cathédrale a commencé en 1163 et s'est achevée en 1272.

Neuf *New*   **surmontés d'habitations** *built with dwellings on top*   **se rassemblaient** *gathered, assembled*   **une place** *a public square*   **des filous** *crooks*
des arracheurs de dents *tooth pullers*   **des vendeurs d'onguent** *ointment sellers*   **vivant** *lively*   **se voient de** *can be seen from*
anciennement un palais royal *formerly a royal palace*   **s'est achevée** *was completed*

AVANT LA VIDÉO

Vous allez visiter la ville de Paris à travers la vidéo. Pour vous aider à mieux comprendre, relisez les pages 230–231. Ensuite, regardez ces photos et complétez les descriptions.

Le pont Neuf	**la Seine**	**une place**
le premier pont métallique	**promenades touristiques**	**ouvrages d'art**
nom	**La tour Eiffel**	**trente-sept**
maisons	**Napoléon 1ᵉʳ**	

© MarinaDa/Shutterstock.com

1. Pour beaucoup, Paris est la plus belle ville du monde. Oui, mais que serait Paris sans _____? La ville a prospéré et s'est organisée tout autour du fleuve.

© Viacheslav Lopatin/Shutterstock.com

2. _____ se voit de la Seine. Et pour une vue panoramique de la Seine et de la ville de Paris, montez en haut de cette tour.

© Rudy Balasko/Shutterstock.com

3. Paris compte pas moins de _____ ponts. Les ponts sont des _____ très riches en histoire.

5. _____, c'est le plus ancien pont de Paris aujourd'hui. À l'époque, c'était vraiment le pont moderne, construit sans _____, donc les Parisiens s'y rassemblaient comme sur _____.

4. Le pont des Arts, c'est _____ de Paris, commandé par _____.

6. À l'origine, ces bateaux étaient construits dans les ateliers du quartier de la Mouche à Lyon: d'où leur _____! Au départ, ils servaient au transport de marchandises jusqu'à ce que Jean Bruel, le fondateur de la compagnie des bateaux-mouches, ait l'excellente idée de proposer des _____ sur la Seine.

▶ EN REGARDANT LA VIDÉO

Regardez la vidéo et indiquez dans quel ordre on parle de ces sites ou attractions touristiques à Paris: **les bateaux-mouches, le pont Neuf, le pont des Arts.**

▶ APRÈS LA VIDÉO

Regardez la vidéo une deuxième fois et complétez les phrases qui suivent.

1. Le grand fleuve qui traverse *(crosses)* Paris s'appelle _____.

2. Les deux ponts décrits dans la vidéo sont: le pont _____, qui est le plus ancien, et le pont _____ qui est le premier pont métallique.

3. Au commencement, les bateaux-mouches servaient au transport de marchandises dans la ville de _____.

4. Il n'y a pas moins de _____ ponts qui traversent *(cross)* la Seine à Paris.

Inviting someone to go out

UNE INVITATION

Pour inviter **quelqu'un** à sortir, **vous pouvez dire...**

À UN(E) AMI(E)	À UNE AUTRE PERSONNE OU À UN GROUPE DE PERSONNES
Tu veux...?	Vous voulez...?
Tu voudrais...?	Vous voudriez...?
Je t'invite à...	Je voudrais vous inviter à...

Si **quelqu'un vous invite,** vous pouvez répondre...

POUR DIRE OUI	POUR DIRE NON
Oui, je veux bien... / **nous voulons** bien...	Je regrette, mais... / Nous regrettons, mais...
Quelle bonne idée!	je ne suis pas libre. / nous ne sommes pas libres.
Avec plaisir!	**je ne peux** (vraiment) **pas.** / **nous ne pouvons** (vraiment) **pas.**
D'accord!	**je dois** étudier... / **nous devons** étudier...
	je suis **occupé(e).** / nous sommes occupé(e)s.

POUR SUGGÉRER UNE AUTRE ACTIVITÉ

Je préfère...   J'aime mieux...   Allons plutôt à...

Les Français **utilisent** l'heure officielle pour tous **les horaires** *(m)* (le train, le cinéma, **les heures d'ouverture...**). Pour lire l'heure officielle, on utilise uniquement des nombres. Aux États-Unis, on **appelle** cette **façon** de lire l'heure *military time*.

L'HEURE OFFICIELLE		L'HEURE FAMILIÈRE
0h05	zéro heure cinq	minuit cinq
1h15	une heure quinze	une heure et quart (du matin)
12h20	douze heures vingt	midi vingt
13h30	treize heures trente	une heure et demie (de l'après-midi)
20h40	vingt heures quarante	neuf heures moins vingt (du soir)
20h45	vingt heures quarante-cinq	neuf heures moins le quart (du soir)

THÉÂTRE DE PARIS

CLAUDE BRASSEUR
PATRICK CHESNAIS

Chantal NEUWIRTH

LE TARTUFFE
MOLIÈRE

MARION BIERRY

© Théâtre de Paris/EFL/B. Richebé

Séances: du lundi au jeudi à 19h30 | vendredi à 19h00 et à 22h00 | samedi à 19h00 et à 21h30 | dimanche à 13h30 et à 18h30

---

quelqu'un *someone*   **vous pouvez (pouvoir** *can, may, to be able)*   **dire** *to say*   **Tu veux / Vous voulez (vouloir** *to want)*
quelqu'un vous invite *someone invites you*   **nous voulons (vouloir** *to want)*   **je ne peux pas / nous ne pouvons pas**
(pouvoir *can, may, to be able)*   **je dois / nous devons (devoir** *must, to have to)*   **occupé(e)** *occupied, busy*   **utiliser** *to use,*
to utilize   **un horaire** *a schedule*   **les heures d'ouverture** *business hours*   **appeler** *to call*   **une façon** *a way*

🔊
6-1

Éric téléphone à sa copine Michèle.

MICHÈLE:	**Allô?**
ÉRIC:	Salut, Michèle. C'est moi, Éric. Ça va?
MICHÈLE:	Oui, très bien. Et toi?
ÉRIC:	Moi, ça va. Écoute, tu es libre ce soir? Tu voudrais sortir?
MICHÈLE:	Oui, je veux bien. Qu'est-ce que tu as envie de faire?
ÉRIC:	**Je pensais** aller voir la nouvelle comédie qu'on **passe** au cinéma Gaumont.
MICHÈLE:	Tu sais, moi, je n'aime pas **tellement** les comédies. Je préfère les films d'**amour** *(m)*. Allons plutôt voir le nouveau film d'amour au cinéma Rex.
ÉRIC:	Bon, je veux bien. À quelle heure?
MICHÈLE:	Il y a **une séance** à vingt heures quarante-cinq.
ÉRIC:	Alors, je passe chez toi vers huit heures?
MICHÈLE:	D'accord. Alors, au revoir.
ÉRIC:	**À tout à l'heure,** Michèle.

A Invitations. Circulez dans la classe et utilisez différentes expressions pour inviter d'autres étudiants à faire les choses suivantes. Ils vont accepter ou refuser chaque invitation ou proposer une autre activité.

INVITEZ UN(E) AMI(E) À...

1. aller danser samedi soir
2. dîner au restaurant ce soir
3. aller voir une exposition demain
4. aller prendre un verre aujourd'hui après les cours

INVITEZ UN GROUPE D'AMIS À...

5. aller voir un film d'amour demain
6. réviser ensemble ce soir
7. faire du vélo ce week-end
8. aller au match de football américain / de basket ce week-end

B Je regrette, mais... Préparez la conversation suivante avec un(e) partenaire.

Un ami téléphone à Éric pour l'inviter à sortir, mais Éric préfère ne rien faire et il refuse. L'ami insiste. Éric est très imaginatif dans ses excuses. Jouez les deux rôles avec un(e) partenaire.

C À quelle heure? Regardez la liste des séances de la pièce de théâtre *Le Tartuffe* à la page précédente. Exprimez l'heure de chaque séance de deux façons. Ensuite, préparez une conversation avec un(e) partenaire dans laquelle vous l'invitez à voir la pièce et vous choisissez une séance.

EXEMPLE 19h30

> **Du lundi au jeudi, il y a une séance à dix-neuf heures trente; c'est-à-dire** *(that is to say)* **à sept heures et demie du soir.**

À VOUS!

Avec un(e) partenaire, relisez à haute voix la conversation entre Michèle et Éric. Ensuite, adaptez la conversation pour faire des projets pour aller au cinéma ensemble. Servez-vous du *Vocabulaire supplémentaire* et parlez de quel(s) genre(s) de film vous aimez, de quel film vous voudriez voir et de comment et où vous allez vous retrouver *(you are going to meet up)*.

Vocabulaire supplémentaire
LES FILMS

une comédie romantique
un dessin animé *a cartoon*
un drame
un film d'animation
un film d'aventure
un film d'horreur
un film de science-fiction
un film fantastique
un film policier

POUR SE RETROUVER

Je passe chez toi / chez vous. *I'll come by your place.*
Passe / Passez chez moi. *Come by my place.*
Rendez-vous à... *Let's meet at ...*

You can access the audio of the active vocabulary of this *Compétence* online.

Allô *Hello* (on the telephone)   **Je pensais** *I was thinking*   **passer (un film)** *to show (a movie)*   **tellement** *so much*
l'amour *love*   **une séance** *a showing*   **À tout à l'heure.** *See you in a little while.* (the same day)

ISSUING AND ACCEPTING INVITATIONS

✔ *Pour vérifier*

1. What does **vouloir** mean? What are three meanings of **pouvoir**? What are the meanings of **devoir**? What are the conjugations of these three verbs?

2. The **nous** and **vous** forms have the same vowels in the stem as the infinitive. What vowels do the other forms have?

3. What auxiliary verb do you use to form the **passé composé** of these three verbs? What are their past participles?

Sélection musicale. Search for the songs "**Tu peux compter sur moi**" by Bénabar and "**Je ne veux pas travailler**" by Pink Martini online to enjoy musical selections with these verbs.

Les verbes **vouloir**, **pouvoir** et **devoir**

1. The verbs **vouloir** *(to want)*, **pouvoir** *(can, may, to be able)*, and **devoir** *(must, to have to)* are useful for issuing and accepting or declining invitations. They have similar conjugations. Note that **devoir** also means *to owe*.

VOULOIR (to want)	POUVOIR (can, may, to be able)	DEVOIR (must, to have to, to owe)
je **veux**	je **peux**	je **dois**
tu **veux**	tu **peux**	tu **dois**
il/elle/on **veut**	il/elle/on **peut**	il/elle/on **doit**
nous **voulons**	nous **pouvons**	nous **devons**
vous **voulez**	vous **pouvez**	vous **devez**
ils/elles **veulent**	ils/elles **peuvent**	ils/elles **doivent**
PASSÉ COMPOSÉ: **j'ai voulu**	PASSÉ COMPOSÉ: **j'ai pu**	PASSÉ COMPOSÉ: **j'ai dû**

Je **veux** sortir, mais je **ne peux pas.** Je **dois** travailler. Je **dois** 100 euros à mes parents.

*I **want** to go out, but I **can't**. I **have to** work. I **owe** my parents 100 euros.*

2. In the **passé composé**, **devoir** can mean that someone *had* to do something or *must have* done something. Context will clarify the meaning.

Michèle n'est pas chez elle. Elle **a dû** partir.
*Michèle isn't home. She **had to** leave. / She **must have** left.*

Il n'a pas pu sortir parce qu'il a dû travailler.
*He wasn't able to go out because he **had to** work.*

PRONONCIATION

Les verbes **vouloir**, **pouvoir** et **devoir** 6-2

In the **je, tu,** and **il/elle/on** forms of **vouloir** and **pouvoir**, the vowel combination **eu** sounds like the **eu** in the word **deux**.

deux: je veux, tu veux, il veut, je peux, tu peux, il peut

In the plural **ils/elles** forms of these verbs, the vowel combination **eu** has the slightly more open sound as in the word **heure**.

heure: il veulent, ils peuvent

The **e** in the stem of **nous devons** and **vous devez** sounds like the **e** in **le**, and the **oi** in the forms, **je dois, tu dois, il doit** and **ils doivent** sounds like the **oi** in **moi**.

Note that you can hear a difference between the third-person singular and plural forms of **vouloir, pouvoir,** and **devoir**.

il veut / ils veulent   **il peut / ils peuvent**   **il doit / ils doivent**

A **Prononcez bien!** Dites si ces personnes **veulent, peuvent** et **doivent** ou **ne doivent pas** faire chaque chose indiquée en cours de français.

> **EXEMPLE** je / boire une bière en cours
> **Je veux / ne veux pas boire une / de bière en cours.**
> **Je ne peux pas boire de bière.**
> **Je ne dois pas boire de bière.**

1. je / fumer en cours

   je / sortir avant la fin du cours

2. le prof / toujours parler français

   le prof / insulter les étudiants

3. les étudiants / toujours écouter en cours

   les étudiants / utiliser les livres pendant les examens

4. nous / dormir en cours

   nous / parler au téléphone

B **Entretien.** Posez ces questions à un(e) partenaire.

1. À quelle heure finit ton dernier cours aujourd'hui? Est-ce que tu peux rentrer après ton dernier cours ou est-ce que tu dois faire quelque chose?

2. Qu'est-ce que tu veux faire aujourd'hui après les cours? Est-ce que tu peux faire ce que *(what)* tu veux?

3. Qu'est-ce que tu veux faire ce week-end? Qu'est-ce que tu dois faire? Est-ce que tu peux sortir avec des amis?

C **On veut...** Aujourd'hui, les Pérez ne peuvent pas faire ce qu'ils veulent. Jouez le rôle d'Alice et expliquez ce que chacun veut et doit faire.

> **EXEMPLE** **Moi, je veux dormir, mais je dois sortir le chien.**

Moi...

1. Éric...

2. Éric et Cathy...

3. Vincent...

4. Nos amis...

5. Michel...

Plus tard, Alice dit que chacun n'a pas pu faire ce qu'il voulait *(wanted)* et elle explique ce qu'ils ont dû faire. Qu'est-ce qu'elle dit? Utilisez le passé composé.

> **EXEMPLE** **Moi, je n'ai pas pu dormir. J'ai dû sortir le chien.**

POUR MIEUX COMPRENDRE: *Noting the important information*

When making plans, we often jot down important information for later reference. If a friend invited you to do something, what sort of information would you want to remember? Look at the following invitation and think about what information is given.

Nous vous attendons
le _samedi 18 novembre_
à _19_ heures.
Notre adresse:
85 boulevard St-Michel

Téléphone: 02-43-29-69-50

R.S.V.P.

🔊 6-3 **A Prenez des notes.** Trois amis invitent Éric à faire quelque chose. Écoutez chaque invitation et prenez des notes en français. Qu'est-ce qu'ils vont faire? Où? Quel jour? À quelle heure?

B À vous. Éric demande à Michèle de l'accompagner. Utilisez vos notes de l'exercice précédent pour jouer les rôles d'Éric et de Michèle avec un(e) partenaire.

EXEMPLE — Je vais jouer au tennis avec Marc demain à... Est-ce que tu voudrais jouer avec nous?
— Oui, je veux bien!

🔊 Compréhension auditive: *On va au cinéma?*

6-4

Vincent demande à Alice si elle voudrait aller au cinéma. Lisez les questions de l'exercice suivant. Ensuite, écoutez la conversation et notez les détails importants sur une feuille de papier.

A **Quel film?** Écoutez encore une fois la conversation entre Vincent et Alice et répondez aux questions suivantes.

1. Comment est-ce qu'Alice trouve les films de science-fiction?
2. Quel genre *(type)* de film est-ce qu'ils décident d'aller voir?
3. À quelle séance est-ce qu'ils vont aller?

B **Vos notes.** Utilisez vos notes pour recréer *(to recreate)* la conversation entre Alice et Vincent avec un(e) partenaire.

C **Tu veux sortir?** Invitez votre partenaire à aller voir un film avec vous. Choisissez une séance et décidez à quelle heure vous allez passer chez votre ami(e).

10:35 ▮ 13:20 ▮ 16:05 ▮ 19:00 ▮ 21:45

11:50 ▮ 14:40 ▮ 17:25 ▮ 20:05

Talking about how you spend and used to spend your time

AUJOURD'HUI ET DANS LE PASSÉ

Michèle compare sa **vie** quand **elle était** au **lycée** avec sa vie d'aujourd'hui.

Quand j'étais au lycée...　　　**Maintenant...**

J'avais 15 ans.

J'étais **lycéenne**.

J'habitais avec ma famille.

J'avais cours du lundi au vendredi.

Je n'aimais pas beaucoup **l'école** *(f)*.

Je rentrais souvent à la maison pour déjeuner.

Le week-end, j'étais toujours fatiguée et **je dormais** beaucoup.

Le vendredi soir, je passais du temps avec ma famille ou **je sortais** avec des copains. On allait au cinéma, au café ou à une fête.

Le samedi, je faisais du sport avec des amis: on jouait au foot ou **on faisait du roller.**

J'ai 21 ans.

Je suis étudiante à l'université.

J'habite avec ma famille.

J'ai cours du lundi au vendredi.

J'aime l'université.

En général, je déjeune au **resto U.**

Le week-end, je suis souvent fatiguée et je dors beaucoup.

Le vendredi soir, **je sors** souvent avec des copains. On va au cinéma, en boîte ou à **une soirée.**

Tous les samedis, je joue au tennis avec des amis et je fais aussi souvent du roller.

dans le passé *in the past*　　**la vie** *life*　　**elle était** *she was*　　**le lycée** *high school*　　**Quand j'étais au lycée** *When I was in high school*　　**J'avais 15 ans.** *I was fifteen.*　　**un(e) lycéen(ne)** *a high school student*　　**J'habitais** *I lived, I used to live*　　**J'avais cours** *I had class, I used to have class*　　**l'école** *school*　　**le resto U** *the university cafeteria*　　**je dormais** *I slept, I used to sleep*　　**je sors (sortir)** *I go out (to go out)*　　**je sortais** *I went out, I used to go out*　　**une soirée** *a party*　　**on faisait du roller** *we went in-line skating, we used to go in-line skating*

Michèle demande à Éric **ce qu'**il faisait quand il était au lycée aux États-Unis.

6-5

MICHÈLE: Qu'est-ce que tu aimais faire quand tu étais au lycée?

ÉRIC: J'aimais passer mon temps avec des copains. Le vendredi soir, on allait aux matchs de football américain ou de basket au lycée.

MICHÈLE: Et le samedi?

ÉRIC: Le samedi matin, je travaillais. Le samedi après-midi, on faisait du skateboard. Le samedi soir, je sortais avec ma copine. On allait au cinéma.

MICHÈLE: Et qu'est-ce que tu faisais le dimanche?

ÉRIC: Le dimanche, je ne faisais rien de spécial. Je restais à la maison. Je regardais la télé.

A **Maintenant ou dans le passé?** Est-ce que Michèle parle de sa vie maintenant ou de sa vie quand elle avait 15 ans? Commencez chaque phrase avec **Quand j'avais 15 ans...** ou **Maintenant...**

1. J'étais lycéenne.
2. J'ai cours du lundi au vendredi.
3. Je n'aimais pas beaucoup l'école.
4. Je déjeune souvent au resto U.
5. Je sors beaucoup le week-end.
6. Mes copains et moi, on aimait aller au café.
7. On faisait souvent du sport ensemble.

B **Et vous?** Dites si vous faites ces choses maintenant et si vous faisiez ces choses quand vous aviez 10 ans.

EXEMPLES Maintenant, j'habite avec ma famille.
Maintenant, j'habite avec ma famille.
Maintenant, je n'habite pas avec ma famille.

Quand j'avais 10 ans, j'habitais avec ma famille.
Quand j'avais 10 ans, j'habitais avec ma famille.
Quand j'avais 10 ans, je n'habitais pas avec ma famille.

1. Maintenant, j'ai cours tous les jours.
   Quand j'avais 10 ans, j'avais cours tous les jours.
2. Maintenant, j'aime mes études.
   Quand j'avais 10 ans, j'aimais l'école.
3. Maintenant, mes copains (copines) et moi, on fait souvent du sport ensemble.
   Quand j'avais 10 ans, on faisait souvent du sport ensemble.
4. Maintenant, je sors souvent le samedi soir.
   Quand j'avais 10 ans, je sortais souvent le samedi soir.
5. Maintenant, je suis souvent fatigué(e) le dimanche.
   Quand j'avais 10 ans, j'étais souvent fatigué(e) le dimanche.
6. Maintenant, je dors beaucoup le week-end.
   Quand j'avais 10 ans, je dormais beaucoup le week-end.

À VOUS!

Avec un(e) partenaire, relisez à haute voix la conversation entre Michèle et Éric. Ensuite, adaptez la conversation pour parler de ce que vous faisiez *(what you used to do)* quand vous étiez au lycée. Si vous voulez utiliser des verbes que vous n'avez pas encore appris dans cette forme du passé, demandez à votre professeur comment les conjuguer.

You can access the audio of the active vocabulary of this *Compétence* online.

ce que *what*

SAYING HOW THINGS USED TO BE

✔ *Pour vérifier*

1. Which form of the present tense do you use to create the stem for all verbs in the imperfect, except for **être**? What is the stem for **être**?

2. You use the **passé composé** to talk about a specific occurrence in the past. When do you use the **imparfait**?

3. Which imperfect endings are pronounced alike? What single letter distinguishes the **nous** and **vous** forms of the imperfect from the present?

Note *de grammaire*

1. Note that verbs like **étudier** retain the **i** of the stem before the **imparfait** endings.

j'étud**i**ais	nous étud**i**ions
vous étud**i**iez	ils étud**i**aient

2. Note the stem for the **imparfait** of **sortir, partir, dormir,** and **courir**.

je **sort**ais	nous **sort**ions
je **part**ais	nous **part**ions
je **dorm**ais	nous **dorm**ions
je **cour**ais	nous **cour**ions

L'imparfait

1. Use the **passé composé** to talk about what happened on a specific occasion. To tell what things used to be like, or what happened over and over, use the **imparfait** *(imperfect)*. The **imparfait** can be translated in a variety of ways in English.

I was working mornings.
I used to work mornings. ⎫
I worked mornings. ⎬ Je travaillais le matin.
I would work mornings. ⎭

2. All verbs except **être** form this tense by dropping the **-ons** from the present tense **nous** form and adding the endings you see below. The stem for **être** is **ét-**.

	PARLER (nous parl~~ons~~ → parl-)	FAIRE (nous fais~~ons~~ → fais-)	PRENDRE (nous pren~~ons~~ → pren-)	ÊTRE (ét-)
je (j')	parl**ais**	fais**ais**	pren**ais**	ét**ais**
tu	parl**ais**	fais**ais**	pren**ais**	ét**ais**
il/elle/on	parl**ait**	fais**ait**	pren**ait**	ét**ait**
nous	parl**ions**	fais**ions**	pren**ions**	ét**ions**
vous	parl**iez**	fais**iez**	pren**iez**	ét**iez**
ils/elles	parl**aient**	fais**aient**	pren**aient**	ét**aient**

3. Spelling changes in the present tense **nous** form of verbs like **manger** and **commencer** occur in the **imparfait** *only before endings beginning with an **a***.

MANGER	COMMENCER
je mang**e**ais	je commen**ç**ais
tu mang**e**ais	tu commen**ç**ais
il/elle/on mang**e**ait	il/elle/on commen**ç**ait
nous mangions	nous commencions
vous mangiez	vous commenciez
ils/elles mang**e**aient	ils/elles commen**ç**aient

4. Also learn these expressions in the imperfect.

c'est → c'était   il y a → il y avait   il pleut → il pleuvait   il neige → il neigeait

PRONONCIATION

Les terminaisons de l'imparfait
6-6

The **-ais, -ait,** and **-aient** endings of the imperfect are all pronounced alike. The **nous** and **vous** endings of the imperfect, **-ions** and **-iez,** are distinguished from the present only by the vowel **i** in the ending.

Ils travaillaient pour IBM.   *They worked for IBM.*
Nous allions à la plage.   *We used to go to the beach.*

A **Prononcez bien!** Une amie parle de sa vie maintenant et de sa vie quand elle était au lycée. D'abord, pratiquez la prononciation de chaque phrase. Ensuite, lisez à haute voix une phrase de chaque paire. Votre partenaire va dire si vous parlez du **présent** ou du **passé**.

Maintenant	**Quand j'étais au lycée**
1. J'ai cours tous les jours.	J'avais cours tous les jours.
2. J'étudie beaucoup.	J'étudiais beaucoup.
3. Mon meilleur ami aime le sport.	Mon meilleur ami aimait le sport.
4. Il joue au basket.	Il jouait au basket.
5. Nous aimons sortir ensemble.	Nous aimions sortir ensemble.
6. Nous allons souvent au cinéma.	Nous allions souvent au cinéma.
7. Mes parents travaillent beaucoup.	Mes parents travaillaient beaucoup.
8. Ils sont souvent fatigués.	Ils étaient souvent fatigués.

Maintenant, changez chaque phrase pour parler de vous.

EXEMPLE **Maintenant, j'ai cours le mardi et le jeudi. Quand j'étais au lycée, j'avais cours du lundi au vendredi.**

B **La jeunesse.** Interviewez un(e) partenaire pour savoir ce qu'il/elle faisait quand il/elle était au lycée

EXEMPLE fumer / ne pas aimer ça
— **Tu fumais quand tu étais au lycée ou tu n'aimais pas ça?**
— **Je fumais. / Je n'aimais pas ça.**

1. aller presque toujours en cours / être souvent absent(e)
2. avoir beaucoup de copains / passer beaucoup de temps seul(e)
3. faire souvent du sport / préférer faire autre chose
4. pouvoir sortir tard / devoir rentrer tôt
5. aimer dormir tard le week-end / avoir beaucoup d'énergie le matin

Maintenant, avec votre partenaire, préparez six questions pour votre professeur. Demandez ce qu'il/elle faisait quand il/elle était étudiant(e) à l'université.

Quand j'avais dix ans, j'aimais jouer avec mon chien.

C **Chez nous.** Que faisaient ces personnes quand vous aviez dix ans? Dites au moins trois choses pour chacune.

EXEMPLE Mon père...
Mon père était très patient. Il travaillait souvent le week-end et il rentrait tard. Il n'était pas souvent à la maison.

1. Mes parents...	**3.** Ma mère...	**5.** Dans ma famille, nous...
2. Mes amis…	**4.** Mon père...	**6.** Mes copains et moi...

avoir beaucoup d'amis / un chien	arriver à l'école à... heures
être patient(e)(s) / impatient(e)(s)	rentrer à... heures
travailler le week-end	jouer au golf / à des jeux vidéo...
aimer lire / dormir…	faire souvent du roller / du sport...
être à la maison le week-end	voyager souvent
faire le ménage / du shopping...	aller souvent voir mes cousins...
aimer les maths / les sciences...	aller à la plage / au cinéma...

Sélection musicale. Search for the songs **"Comme toi"** by Jean-Jacques Goldman, **"J'aimais mieux avant"** by Christophe Cerillo, or **"Michèle"** by Gérard Lenorman online to enjoy musical selections with this structure.

TALKING ABOUT ACTIVITIES

Les verbes *sortir, partir et dormir*

✔ **Pour vérifier**

1. What are the conjugations of **sortir, partir,** and **dormir**? Which auxiliary verb is used with each one in the **passé composé**?

2. How do you say *to go out of*? *to leave from*? *to leave for*?

3. How do you say *to leave for the weekend*? *to leave on vacation*? *to leave on a trip*?

4. What is the difference in pronunciation between **il sort** and **ils sortent**?

1. The verbs **sortir, partir,** and **dormir** have similar patterns of conjugation.

SORTIR *(to go out)*	PARTIR *(to leave)*	DORMIR *(to sleep)*
je **sors**	je **pars**	je **dors**
tu **sors**	tu **pars**	tu **dors**
il/elle/on **sort**	il/elle/on **part**	il/elle/on **dort**
nous **sortons**	nous **partons**	nous **dormons**
vous **sortez**	vous **partez**	vous **dormez**
ils/elles **sortent**	ils/elles **partent**	ils/elles **dorment**
P.C. **je suis sorti(e)**	P.C. **je suis parti(e)**	P.C. **j'ai dormi**
IMP. **je sortais**	IMP. **je partais**	IMP. **je dormais**

Note *de vocabulaire*

Remember that **quitter** means *to leave* a person or a place and is *always* used with a direct object. In the **passé composé**, it is conjugated with **avoir**. Whereas you must use **de** after **partir** and **sortir** before the name of a place you are leaving, **quitter** is not followed by **de**.

Je suis parti(e) en week-end avec un ami.

J'ai quitté la maison à neuf heures.

On est sortis le samedi.

2. You have already seen that **sortir** can mean *to go out,* in the sense of going out with friends. It can also mean *to go / come out of,* in the sense of going out of a place. It is the opposite of **entrer.** Use **de** to say *of.*

Je suis sorti **de** l'appartement en pyjama pour aller chercher le journal.

3. **Partir** means *to leave* in the sense of *to go away.* It is the opposite of **arriver.** Some common expressions with **partir** are: **partir en week-end, partir en vacances, partir en voyage.** To name the place you are leaving, use **partir de.** To say where you are leaving *for,* use **partir pour.**

Il part en vacances aujourd'hui. Il est parti **de** son bureau à trois heures et il est parti **pour** l'aéroport vers cinq heures.

PRONONCIATION

Les verbes *sortir, partir et dormir*
6-7

You can distinguish aurally between the **il/elle** singular and **ils/elles** plural forms of verbs like **sortir, partir,** and **dormir.** Compare these sentences.

ALICE	**ALICE ET SA FILLE**
Elle dort bien.	Elles dorment bien.
Elle sort ce soir.	Elles sortent ce soir.
Elle part demain.	Elles partent demain.

When a word ends with a pronounced consonant sound in French, it must be released. Note that when you pronounce the boldfaced consonants in the following English phrases, your tongue or lips do not have to move back and release them.

What par**t**?   What sor**t**?   In the dor**m**.

Compare how the boldfaced consonants in the following plural verb forms are released.

Ils par**t**ent.   Ils sor**t**ent.   Ils dor**m**ent.

◄))
6-8

A Prononcez bien! Pour chaque phrase que vous entendez, dites si Alice parle **d'Éric** ou **d'Éric et de Cathy.**

B Entretien. Complétez ces questions avec la forme correcte des verbes indiqués au présent et interviewez un(e) partenaire.

> **EXEMPLE** —Est-ce que tu **sors** (sortir) souvent en semaine *(during the week)* avec tes amis?
> — **Je sors quelquefois le mercredi soir.**

1. Est-ce que ton meilleur ami (ta meilleure amie) _____ (sortir) souvent avec toi le week-end? Est-ce que vous _____ (sortir) quelquefois en semaine?
2. Quand tu _____ (sortir) avec tes amis le samedi soir, jusqu'à quelle heure est-ce que tu _____ (dormir) le dimanche?
3. Est-ce que tes amis _____ (sortir) souvent pendant la semaine sans toi? Est-ce qu'ils _____ (dormir) quelquefois pendant leurs cours?
4. Est-ce que tu _____ (partir) souvent en week-end? Généralement, où vas-tu quand tu _____ (partir) pour quelques jours?

Maintenant, mettez les verbes à l'imparfait pour parler de ce que votre partenaire et ses amis faisaient quand il/elle était lycéen(ne).

> **EXEMPLE** —Quand tu étais au lycée, est-ce que tu **sortais** (sortir) souvent en semaine avec tes amis?
> — **Non, je ne sortais jamais en semaine.**

C Vos habitudes. Formez des phrases pour parler de ce que vous faites les jours du cours de français et quand vous sortez avec des amis. Circulez dans la classe et trouvez quelqu'un qui fait la même chose que vous.

> **EXEMPLES** Les jours du cours de français, je / dormir jusqu'à... heures.
> — **Les jours du cours de français, je dors jusqu'à 7 heures. Et toi? Tu dors jusqu'à 7 heures aussi?**
> — **Non, je dors jusqu'à 8 heures.**

1. Les jours du cours de français, je / dormir jusqu'à... heures.
2. Aujourd'hui, je / sortir de mon dernier cours à... heures.
3. Mes amis et moi / sortir le plus souvent le... soir.
4. D'habitude, je / dormir jusqu'à... le dimanche.
5. Je / partir le plus souvent en vacances au mois de...

Maintenant, dites à la classe qui fait les mêmes choses que vous.

> **EXEMPLES** Les jours du cours de français, Courtney dort jusqu'à 7 heures, comme moi.
> Luis et ses amis sortent le plus souvent le samedi soir, comme mes amis et moi.

D Toujours des questions! Parlez avec votre partenaire de la dernière fois qu'il/elle est sorti(e) avec des amis. Posez les questions indiquées. Utilisez le passé composé.

> **EXEMPLE** quand / sortir ensemble
> — **Quand est-ce que vous êtes sortis ensemble?**
> — **On est sortis ensemble hier.**

1. quand / sortir ensemble
2. où / aller ensemble
3. qu'est-ce que / faire

4. à quelle heure / partir de la maison
5. jusqu'à quelle heure / dormir le lendemain

Talking about the past

UNE SORTIE

Cathy parle de la dernière fois qu'elle a dîné avec des amis. Et vous? La dernière fois que vous êtes sorti(e) avec des ami(e)s, comment était la soirée? **Qu'est-ce qui s'est passé?**

Quand j'ai quitté l'appartement, il pleuvait.

Il était sept heures et demie quand je suis arrivée au restaurant.

On n'avait pas très faim et on n'a pas mangé **tout de suite.**

Le repas était **délicieux** et j'ai beaucoup mangé.

Après le repas, nous sommes partis parce que nous étions fatigués.

Quand je suis rentrée chez moi, il était environ dix heures.

Le lendemain, c'était dimanche et je suis restée au lit jusqu'à dix heures.

Qu'est-ce qui s'est passé? *What happened?*   **tout de suite** *right away*   **Le repas** *The meal*   **délicieux (délicieuse)** *delicious*

🔊 6-9 Cathy et une amie parlent de leurs activités du week-end dernier.

MANON: Je suis allée au restaurant avec des copines ce week-end.

CATHY: Vous êtes allées où?

MANON: Au Bistro Romain.

CATHY: **Ça t'a plu?**

MANON: Beaucoup. C'était délicieux. On a bien mangé et on a beaucoup parlé. C'était vraiment bien!

CATHY: Et qu'est-ce que tu as fait après?

MANON: **Rien du tout.** J'étais fatiguée et je suis rentrée. Et toi, qu'est-ce que tu as fait ce week-end?

CATHY: Moi aussi, je suis sortie avec des copains. On est allés au cinéma.

A **Au restaurant.** La dernière fois que vous êtes allé(e) au restaurant, qu'est-ce qui s'est passé? Changez les mots en italique pour parler de votre sortie.

1. Quand j'ai quitté *la maison*, il était *huit heures* et il *faisait froid.*
2. Quand je suis arrivé(e) au restaurant, il était *neuf heures.*
3. On *avait très faim* et on *a mangé tout de suite.*
4. Le repas était vraiment *médiocre* et j'ai *peu* mangé.
5. Après le repas, nous avions envie de *continuer la soirée* et nous *sommes allés en boîte.*
6. Quand je suis rentré(e), il était *onze heures* et j'*étais fatigué(e).*
7. Le lendemain, c'était *dimanche* et je *suis resté(e) au lit.*

Note *de grammaire*

You usually answer a question in the same tense in which it is asked.

B **La journée d'Alice.** Décrivez la journée d'Alice vendredi dernier.

1. Alice était seule quand elle a quitté l'appartement? Quelle heure était-il? Est-ce qu'il pleuvait? Est-ce qu'il faisait froid? Quels vêtements est-ce qu'elle portait?
2. Alice était seule au café? Elle a mangé quelque chose? Elle a bu quelque chose?
3. Quelle heure était-il quand elle est rentrée chez elle?

🔁 **À VOUS!**

Avec un(e) partenaire, relisez à haute voix la conversation entre Manon et Cathy. Ensuite, adaptez la conversation pour parler de la dernière fois que vous avez mangé avec des copains.

You can access the audio of the active vocabulary of this *Compétence* online.

Ça t'a plu? *Did you like it?*   **Rien du tout.** *Nothing at all.*

TELLING WHAT WAS GOING ON WHEN SOMETHING ELSE HAPPENED

✔ *Pour vérifier*

1. With a sequence of events that happen one after another, are the verbs in the **passé composé** or the **imparfait**?

2. If one action interrupts another one that is already in progress, which one is in the **passé composé** and which one is in the **imparfait**?

L'imparfait et le passé composé

In French, the **passé composé** and the **imparfait** convey different meanings. In English, the use of different past tenses also changes a message. Is the message the same in these sentences?

When her husband came home, they kissed.
When her husband came home, they were kissing.

Use the **passé composé** for a sequence of events that happened one after another.

Ce matin, **j'ai quitté** la maison à midi et **je suis arrivé** à l'université à midi vingt.

When saying what was going on when something else occurred, use the **imparfait** for the action in progress and use the **passé composé** to say what happened, interrupting it.

ACTIONS IN PROGRESS	INTERRUPTING ACTIONS
IMPARFAIT	PASSÉ COMPOSÉ
Le professeur parlait...	quand je suis entré(e) dans la salle de cours.
On jouait au foot...	quand Pierre est arrivé.

PRONONCIATION

Le passé composé et l'imparfait 6-10

Since the use of the **passé composé** or the **imparfait** imparts a different message, it is important that you pronounce each tense distinctly. Listen to these pairs of sentences. Where do you hear a difference?

Je travaillais.	Elle mangeait.	Tu parlais.	Il allait.
J'ai travaillé.	Elle a mangé.	Tu as parlé.	Il est allé.

 6-11 **A** **Prononcez bien!** Indiquez si vous entendez la phrase de la colonne A ou de la colonne B.

A L'IMPARFAIT: *(WHAT WAS GOING ON)*	**B** LE PASSÉ COMPOSÉ: *(WHAT HAPPENED)*
1. Je travaillais.	J'ai travaillé.
2. Mon mari téléphonait.	Mon mari a téléphoné.
3. Mon fils était malade.	Mon fils a été malade.
4. J'allais chez moi.	Je suis allée chez moi.
5. J'entrais.	Je suis entrée.
6. Tous mes amis commençaient à chanter «Bon anniversaire».	Tous mes amis ont commencé à chanter «Bon anniversaire».
7. Ils étaient chez moi pour une surprise-partie.	Ils ont été chez moi pour une surprise-partie.
8. On dansait toute la soirée.	On a dansé toute la soirée.
9. Ils restaient jusqu'à minuit.	Ils sont restés jusqu'à minuit.

B **Quand ils sont rentrés...** Deux couples ont laissé leurs enfants avec une nouvelle baby-sitter le week-end dernier. Qui faisait les choses suivantes quand ils sont rentrés?

EXEMPLE porter les vêtements de sa mère
Annick portait les vêtements de sa mère quand ils sont rentrés.

1. embrasser *(to kiss)* son copain
2. parler au téléphone
3. fumer
4. jouer dans l'escalier
5. jouer à des jeux vidéo
6. manger quelque chose sur la table
7. dormir sur le canapé
8. être surpris(e)

C **Que faisaient-ils?** Expliquez ce qui s'est passé.

EXEMPLE Alice (lire un livre) / quand sa fille (arriver)
Alice lisait un livre quand sa fille est arrivée.

1.

Cathy (étudier) / quand un ami (téléphoner)

2.

Vincent (jouer au golf) / quand il (commencer à pleuvoir)

3.

Michèle (embrasser *[to kiss]* un copain) / quand Éric (arriver)

4.

Quand le chien (entrer) / le chat (dormir)

5.

Alice (faire la cuisine) / quand le chat (voir le chien)

6.

Quand Vincent (rentrer) / Alice (nettoyer *[to clean]* la cuisine)

TELLING WHAT HAPPENED AND DESCRIBING THE CIRCUMSTANCES

✔ *Pour vérifier*

1. Do you generally use the **passé composé** or the **imparfait** to say what happened at a specific moment, for a specific duration, or a specific number of times? to describe how things were or used to be or to talk about actions in progress?

2. Which would you use to talk about how you were feeling? to describe a change in a mental or physical state?

3. Which tense do you use to say what was going to happen?

Note *de grammaire*

You generally use the verb **vouloir** in the **imparfait** to say what someone wanted to do.

Je *voulais* aller voir un film.
I wanted to go see a movie.

Use **pouvoir** in the **imparfait** to say what people could do if they might have wanted to, but use it in the **passé composé** to say what they managed to do on an occasion when they tried.

Ma copine *pouvait* sortir.
My girlfriend could go out.

J'*ai pu* persuader une autre amie d'y aller aussi.
I was able to persuade another friend to go also.

Use **devoir** in the **imparfait** to say what one was supposed to do, but in the **passé composé** for what one must have done, or had to do on a specific occasion.

Il *devait* déjà être ici.
He was supposed to be here already.

Il *a dû* travailler tard.
He had to work late. / He must have worked late.

Sélection musicale. Search for the songs **"Il avait les mots"** by Sheryfa Luna or **"On savait"** by La Grande Sophie online to enjoy musical selections with these structures.

Le passé composé et l'imparfait

You know to use the **imparfait** to tell how things used to be or what was going on when something else occurred. The **imparfait** is used to describe continuing actions or states, whereas the **passé composé** is used for actions that happened and were finished.

USE THE *IMPARFAIT* TO SAY:	USE THE *PASSÉ COMPOSÉ* TO SAY:
1. HOW THINGS USED TO BE OR WHAT USED TO HAPPEN • continuing actions, states, or situations • repeated or habitual actions of an unspecified duration	**1. WHAT HAPPENED AT A PRECISE MOMENT OR FOR A SPECIFIC DURATION OR NUMBER OF TIMES** • completed actions • actions that occurred for a specific duration or a specific number of times

Notre amie habitait à côté de chez nous.
Our friend lived next to us.
Elle invitait toujours des amis chez elle.
She always invited friends over.

Elle a fait une soirée le mois dernier.
She had a party last month.
Nous sommes allées à cinq de ses soirées.
We went to five of her parties.

USE THE *IMPARFAIT* TO SAY:	USE THE *PASSÉ COMPOSÉ* TO SAY:
2. WHAT THINGS WERE LIKE OR HOW SOMEONE FELT • physical or mental states	**2. WHAT CHANGED** • changes in states

Tout le monde allait bien, mais moi, j'étais fatiguée.
Everyone was doing fine, but I was tired.

Tout à coup, j'ai eu peur.
All of a sudden, I got frightened.

Watch for words like **tout d'un coup** (*all at once*), **tout à coup** (*all of a sudden*), **soudain** (*suddenly*), **une fois** (*once*), and **un jour** (*one day*) indicating changes in states.

3. WHAT SOMEONE WAS GOING TO DO	**3. WHAT SOMEONE WENT TO DO**

On allait partir.
We were going to leave.

Je suis allée chercher mon sac.
I went to get my purse.

A **Pourquoi?** Expliquez pourquoi Cathy a fait ou n'a pas fait ces choses. Quel verbe doit être au passé composé et lequel *(which one)* doit être à l'imparfait?

EXEMPLE Cathy **était** (être) malade, alors elle **n'a pas travaillé** (ne pas travailler).

1. Cathy _____ (ne pas sortir) parce qu'elle _____ (être) malade.
2. Elle _____ (être) trop fatiguée, alors elle _____ (ne pas faire) ses devoirs.
3. Elle _____ (faire) du shopping parce qu'elle _____ (vouloir) acheter une nouvelle robe.
4. Elle _____ (mettre) un pull parce qu'elle _____ (avoir) froid.
5. Elle _____ (avoir) besoin d'étudier, alors elle _____ (ne pas sortir) avec ses amis.

B **Ce matin chez les Pérez.** Alice Pérez décrit la journée de sa famille. Qu'est-ce qu'elle dit? Mettez les verbes au passé composé ou à l'imparfait.

EXEMPLE Moi, j'ai couru ce matin. Je voulais dormir.

1.

2.

Moi...	Éric et Cathy...
courir ce matin	préparer le déjeuner aujourd'hui
vouloir dormir	vouloir faire du shopping
avoir sommeil	déjeuner avant de sortir
ne pas avoir envie de sortir	aller au centre commercial à une heure
sortir à sept heures	avoir l'intention d'acheter des vêtements
rentrer une heure plus tard	rentrer vers cinq heures
avoir besoin d'un bain *(bath)*	avoir faim
aller dans la salle de bains	retrouver des amis au restaurant
prendre un long bain	rentrer à neuf heures

C **Entretien.** Parlez à votre partenaire de la dernière fois qu'il/elle est allé(e) au restaurant avec des amis.

La dernière fois que tu es allé(e) au restaurant avec des amis,...

1. Quel temps faisait-il? Qu'est-ce que tu as mis pour sortir? un jean? une robe?
2. Quelle heure était-il quand tu es arrivé(e) au restaurant?
3. Avais-tu très faim? As-tu mangé tout de suite? Comment était le repas?
4. Qu'est-ce que tu as fait après le repas?
5. Quelle heure était-il quand tu es rentré(e)? Étais-tu fatigué(e)? Est-ce que tu es allé(e) tout de suite au lit? As-tu bien dormi?
6. Le lendemain, jusqu'à quelle heure es-tu resté(e) au lit?

Narrating in the past

LES CONTES (m)

Vocabulaire sans peine!

Most nouns referring to people that end with *-tor* in English are similar in French, but end with **-teur** in the masculine and **-trice** in the feminine.

actor = **acteur / actrice**
educator = **éducateur / éducatrice**

How would you say these words in French?

protector
procrastinator

Most English adjectives ending with *-ible* are similar in French.

horrible = **horrible**
terrible = **terrible**

How would you say these words in French?

accessible
compatible

Éric et Michèle sont allés voir le film classique *La Belle et la Bête* de Jean Cocteau. **Connaissez-vous** ce film? Connaissez-vous **le conte de fées** sur **lequel** ce film est basé?

© Hulton Archive/Moviepix/Getty Images

Il était une fois un vieux **marchand** qui avait trois filles. Sa plus jeune fille, Belle, était très jolie, **douce** et **gracieuse.**

Un jour, la Bête a emprisonné le marchand. Belle **a promis** à la Bête de venir prendre la place de son père.

Le monstre était horrible! Il était grand et laid et il avait l'air **féroce. Au début,** Belle avait très peur de lui. Mais elle était toujours gentille et patiente avec lui.

Petit à petit, les choses ont changé. Belle et la Bête ont commencé à **se parler.** La Bête a beaucoup changé et Belle a appris à apprécier le monstre. Finalement, Belle **est tombée amoureuse de** lui! Et la Bête a aussi appris à aimer.

À suivre...

Cathy parle à son frère de ses activités du week-end dernier.

6-12

CATHY:	Tu es sorti ce week-end?
ÉRIC:	Oui, je suis allé au cinéclub avec Michèle.
CATHY:	Quel film est-ce que vous avez vu?
ÉRIC:	Nous avons vu *La Belle et la Bête* de Cocteau.
CATHY:	C'est un classique! **Ça t'a plu?**
ÉRIC:	Oui, ça m'a beaucoup plu. Les acteurs **ont bien joué, les effets spéciaux** étaient excellents **pour l'époque** et il n'y avait pas **trop de** violence.

---

un conte *a story* (for children)   ***La Belle et la Bête*** *Beauty and the Beast*   **Connaissez-vous...?** *Do you know...?*   **un conte de fées** *a fairy tale*   **lequel (laquelle)** *which*   **Il était une fois...** *Once upon a time there was...*   **un marchand** *a merchant, a shopkeeper*   **doux (douce)** *sweet, soft, gentle*   **gracieux (gracieuse)** *gracious*   **a promis (promettre** *to promise* [past participle **promis**])   **féroce** *ferocious*   **Au début** *At the beginning*   **se parler** *to talk to each other*   **tomber amoureux (amoureuse) de** *to fall in love with*   **À suivre** *To be continued*   **Ça t'a plu?** *Did you like it?*   **bien jouer** *to act well* (in movies and theater)   **les effets spéciaux** *the special effects*   **pour l'époque** *for that time (period)*   **trop de** *too much*

A **C'est qui?** Décidez lequel des personnages les adjectifs suivants décrivent: **le père de Belle**, **Belle** ou **la Bête**. N'oubliez pas d'utiliser l'imparfait pour faire une description!

EXEMPLE douce **Belle était douce.**

1. jolie   **2.** grande et laide   **3.** vieux   **4.** gracieuse   **5.** horrible

Maintenant, dites qui a fait les choses suivantes. N'oubliez pas d'utiliser le passé composé pour décrire le déroulement de l'action *(sequence of events)*!

EXEMPLE promettre de venir prendre la place de son père
Belle a promis de venir prendre la place de son père.

1. emprisonner le marchand
2. prendre la place de son père
3. commencer à parler avec la Bête
4. apprendre à apprécier la Bête
5. tomber amoureuse de Belle
6. beaucoup changer

B **Contes de fées.** En 1697, l'écrivain *(the writer)* français Charles Perrault a publié les contes de fées suivants dans son livre *Histoires ou contes du temps passé*. Choisissez la forme correcte des verbes entre parenthèses pour compléter les descriptions qui suivent. Ensuite, dites quel titre de la liste correspond à chacune.

Le Chat botté   Le Petit Chaperon rouge   La Belle au bois dormant   Cendrillon

1. Les parents d'une princesse (n'ont pas invité / n'invitaient pas) une vieille fée à la fête pour le baptême de leur fille. Vexée, la vieille fée (a jeté / jetait) un sort *(cast a spell)* à la princesse.

2. Une petite fille qui (a porté / portait) toujours un chaperon *(hood)* rouge (a traversé / traversait) *(was crossing)* la forêt pour aller voir sa grand-mère quand elle (a rencontré / rencontrait) un grand méchant loup *(wolf)*.

3. Un homme pauvre *(poor)* (a laissé / laissait) un chat à son fils comme seul héritage *(inheritance)*. Mais le chat (a eu / avait) des pouvoirs magiques *(magical powers)* et, avec son aide, le jeune homme (est devenu / devenait) riche.

4. Comme son père était mort, une belle jeune fille vivait *(lived)* avec sa belle-mère et ses deux demi-sœurs. Sa belle-mère (a été / était) cruelle et ses demi-sœurs (ont été / étaient) laides. Le prince (a invité / invitait) les filles des alentours *(surrounding area)* à un bal magnifique.

C **Une sortie au cinéma.** Alice parle du week-end à une amie. Complétez la conversation en mettant les verbes au passé composé ou à l'imparfait. Ensuite, adaptez la conversation pour parler de votre week-end avec un(e) partenaire.

— Tu **_1_** (passer) un bon week-end?
— Assez bon. Mon amie **_2_** (vouloir) aller voir un film, alors je **_3_** (aller) au cinéma avec elle et je **_4_** (rentrer) tard.
— Quelle heure **_5_** (être)-il quand tu **_6_** (rentrer)?
— On **_7_** (rester) au cinéma jusqu'à 10h30 et après, on **_8_** (avoir) faim, alors on **_9_** (aller) manger quelque chose. Il y **_10_** (avoir) beaucoup de gens au restaurant et on **_11_** (devoir) attendre pour avoir une table. Il **_12_** (être) environ 1h00 quand on **_13_** (partir) du restaurant.

À VOUS!

Avec un(e) partenaire, relisez à haute voix la conversation entre Cathy et Éric. Ensuite, adaptez la conversation pour parler d'un film que vous avez vu récemment.

You can access the audio of the active vocabulary of this **Compétence** online.

NARRATING WHAT HAPPENED

✔ Pour vérifier

If you were describing a play that you saw, would you use the **passé composé** or the **imparfait** to describe the setting and what was happening on stage when the curtain went up? Which tense would you use to explain the actions of the actors that advanced the story?

For a chart summarizing all of the uses of the **passé composé** and the **imparfait,** see the **Résumé de grammaire** on page 263.

Sélection musicale. Search for the songs **"Nathalie"** by Gilbert Bécaud or **"La Rua Madureira"** by Nino Ferrer online to enjoy musical selections with these structures.

Le passé composé et l'imparfait (reprise)

When telling a story in the past, you use both the **passé composé** and the **imparfait.**

USE THE *IMPARFAIT* TO SAY:	USE THE *PASSÉ COMPOSÉ* TO SAY:
WHAT WAS ALREADY GOING ON	**WHAT HAPPENED NEXT / WHAT CHANGED**
• descriptions of the scene / setting • background information about the characters • interrupted actions in progress	• sequence of events that advance the storyline • actions interrupting something in progress

If you were telling the old French tale **Cendrillon** *(Cinderella),* you might begin . . .

Il **était** une fois une belle jeune fille qui **s'appelait** Cendrillon. Son père **était** mort et elle **habitait** avec sa belle-mère et ses deux demi-sœurs. Sa belle-mère **était** cruelle et ses demi-sœurs **étaient** laides et très gâtées *(spoiled).* C'**était** Cendrillon qui **faisait** tout le travail, mais elle **était** toujours belle et gracieuse. Un jour, le prince **a décidé** de donner un bal au palais et un messager **est allé** chez Cendrillon avec une invitation.

There are only two events that occur advancing the story: the prince decided to give a ball and the messenger went to Cinderella's house. These two verbs are in the **passé composé.** All the rest of the paragraph is background information, setting the scene, so the verbs are in the **imparfait.**

When deciding whether to put a verb in the **passé composé** or the **imparfait,** learn to ask yourself whether you are talking about background information or something that was already in progress **(imparfait),** or the next thing that happened in the story **(passé composé).**

A **La journée d'Alice.** Alice parle de sa journée. Décidez si chaque phrase décrit la scène / la situation ou raconte le déroulement de l'action *(sequence of events)*. Décidez dans quelle colonne va chaque phrase.

Il est sept heures. Il pleut. Je quitte la maison. Il y a beaucoup de voitures sur la route. J'arrive au bureau en retard. Mon patron *(boss)* n'est pas content. Je travaille beaucoup. Je ne déjeune pas. Je rentre à cinq heures. Je suis fatiguée. Il n'y a rien à manger. Nous allons au restaurant. Nous rentrons. Je prends un bain. Il est 11 heures. Je vais au lit.

EXEMPLE

LA SCÈNE / LA SITUATION	LE DÉROULEMENT DE L'ACTION
Il est sept heures.	Je quitte la maison.

Maintenant, réécrivez le paragraphe en mettant les verbes qui présentent le déroulement de l'action au passé composé et les verbes qui décrivent la scène ou la situation à l'imparfait.

B **Il était une fois...** Réécrivez le début de l'histoire de *La Belle et la Bête* au passé en mettant les verbes en caractères gras à l'imparfait ou au passé composé.

EXEMPLE Il y **avait** un marchand très riche...

Il y (**1**) **a** un marchand très riche qui (**2**) **a** trois filles. Ils (**3**) **habitent** tous ensemble dans une belle maison en ville. Mais un jour, des voleurs *(thieves)* (**4**) **prennent** toute sa fortune et le marchand et ses filles (**5**) **doivent** aller habiter dans une petite maison à la campagne.

Ses deux filles aînées (**6**) **sont** très malheureuses *(unhappy)*. Elles (**7**) **parlent** constamment des choses qu'elles (**8**) **veulent.** Belle (**9**) **est** la plus jeune de ses filles. Elle (**10**) **est** très jolie et aussi très douce. Elle (**11**) **accepte** sa nouvelle vie et elle (**12**) **est** heureuse *(happy)*.

Un jour, le marchand (**13**) **part** pour la ville voisine *(neighboring)*. Il (**14**) **neige** et il (**15**) **fait** très froid et en route, il ne (**16**) **peut** rien voir dans la forêt. Le marchand (**17**) **pense** qu'il (**18**) **va** mourir quand, soudain, il (**19**) **trouve** un château. La porte du château (**20**) **est** ouverte et il (**21**) **décide** d'entrer. Il (**22**) **remarque** [remarquer *to notice*] une grande table couverte de plats délicieux. Il (**23**) **mange,** puis il (**24**) **fait** une sieste *(nap)*.

Après sa sieste, il (**25**) **sort** dans le jardin où il (**26**) **trouve** une jolie rose qu'il (**27**) **veut** rapporter *(to bring back)* à Belle. À ce moment-là, un monstre horrible (**28**) **arrive** et (**29**) **commence** à crier *(to shout)* qu'il (**30**) **veut** que Belle vienne habiter chez lui, sinon *(otherwise)*, la Bête (**31**) **va** tuer *(to kill)* le marchand.

C **La Belle et la Bête.** Continuez l'histoire de *La Belle et la Bête* en mettant les verbes entre parenthèses au passé composé ou à l'imparfait.

Quand le marchand __1__ (rentrer), il __2__ (raconter *[to recount]*) ses aventures à ses filles et Belle __3__ (décider) d'aller habiter chez la Bête. Quand elle __4__ (arriver) au château, elle __5__ (trouver) tout ce dont *(that)* elle __6__ (avoir) besoin. Chaque jour, elle __7__ (avoir) tout ce qu'elle __8__ (vouloir). Mais pendant les cinq premiers jours, elle __9__ (ne pas voir) la Bête.

Un jour, elle le (l') __10__ (voir) pour la première fois pendant *(while)* qu'elle __11__ (faire) une promenade dans le jardin. Elle le (l') __12__ (trouver) horrible et elle __13__ (crier). Belle __14__ (avoir) peur et elle __15__ (ne pas pouvoir) regarder la Bête dans les yeux, mais elle __16__ (aller) faire une promenade avec lui. La conversation __17__ (être) agréable. Quand la Bête __18__ (demander) à Belle de faire une promenade deux jours plus tard, elle __19__ (accepter).

Après ce jour-là, ils __20__ (faire) une promenade chaque après-midi. Ils __21__ (parler) de tout. Au début, Belle __22__ (avoir) très peur de la Bête mais, finalement, Belle __23__ (apprendre) à avoir confiance en lui. Après un certain temps, Belle __24__ (commencer) à aimer le monstre et un jour, elle l' __25__ (embrasser *[to kiss]*). Tout à coup, le visage *(face)* de la Bête __26__ (changer) et il __27__ (devenir) un beau et jeune prince.

VIDÉO-REPRISE

Les Stagiaires

Rappel!
Dans l'épisode précédent de la vidéo, Matthieu et Christophe ont parlé d'une soirée que Christophe avait passée avec Amélie et Rachid, et Matthieu lui a posé *(asked him)* beaucoup de questions au sujet d'Amélie et de ce qu'elle aimait faire.

See the *Résumé de grammaire* section at the end of each chapter for a review of all the grammar presented in the chapter.

Dans *l'Épisode 6*, Matthieu essaie de dominer sa timidité pour inviter Amélie à sortir avec lui. Avant de regarder l'épisode, faites ces activités pour réviser ce que vous avez appris dans le *Chapitre 6.*

A **Invitations.** Matthieu voudrait inviter Amélie à sortir avec lui. Comment est-ce qu'on invite un(e) ami(e) à aller quelque part *(to go somewhere)*? Invitez un(e) partenaire à faire les choses suivantes. Il/Elle va accepter une de vos invitations, refuser une de vos invitations et suggérer une autre activité pour la troisième. Utilisez des expressions variées.

> **EXEMPLE** aller au cinéma demain
> **— Tu voudrais aller au cinéma demain?**
> **— Oui, d'accord.**

1. aller prendre un verre après les cours
2. aller danser samedi soir
3. aller voir une exposition au musée dimanche après-midi

B **On ne peut pas toujours faire ce qu'on veut!** Camille explique ce que ses collègues ont envie de faire et ce qu'ils ont besoin de faire. Répétez ce qu'elle dit, en utilisant les verbes **vouloir, pouvoir** et **devoir.**

> **EXEMPLE** Christophe a envie de lire un manga, mais il a besoin de faire des photocopies pour son père.
> **Christophe veut lire un manga, mais il ne peut pas parce qu'il doit faire des photocopies pour son père.**

1. M. Vieilledent a envie de boire du café, mais il a besoin de réduire *(reduce)* sa consommation de caféine.
2. Rachid et Amélie ont envie de partir tôt du bureau aujourd'hui, mais ils ont besoin de finir leur travail.
3. J'ai envie de prendre une longue pause pour le déjeuner *(lunch break)* aujourd'hui pour faire du shopping, mais j'ai besoin de rentrer au bureau.
4. Nous avons tous envie de moins travailler, mais nous avons besoin de terminer *(to finish)* ce projet pour des clients.

C **Au bureau.** Camille décrit les habitudes de ses collègues. Complétez chaque phrase en mettant le verbe donné à la forme correcte du présent. Ensuite, dites si les autres personnes indiquées font la même chose.

> **EXEMPLE** Le lundi matin, M. Vieilledent **part** (partir) pour le travail avant huit heures. Et vous?
> **Moi aussi, je pars pour le travail avant huit heures le lundi matin.**

1. Céline _____ (partir) souvent en week-end. Et vous? Et vos amis?
2. Christophe _____ (dormir) souvent jusqu'à midi le week-end. Et vous? Et vos amis?
3. Rachid et Amélie _____ (sortir) souvent danser le samedi soir. Et vos amis et vous?
4. Amélie _____ (sortir) souvent avec ses amis. Et vous?
5. Amélie ne _____ (dormir) jamais en cours. Et le professeur de français? Et les autres étudiants et vous?

D Hier soir.

Matthieu parle de ce qu'il a fait hier soir. Complétez ce qu'il dit en mettant les verbes donnés au passé composé ou à l'imparfait.

J'aime beaucoup faire la cuisine et hier, j' **1** (inviter) des amis à dîner chez moi. Vers quatre heures, je **2** (sortir) pour aller faire les courses. J' **3** (acheter) tout ce dont *(that)* j' **4** (avoir) besoin et je **5** (rentrer). Je/J' **6** (commencer) à préparer le repas *(meal)* quand le téléphone **7** (sonner *[to ring]*). C' **8** (être) un de mes amis qui **9** (vouloir) me dire *(to tell me)* qu'ils **10** (aller) arriver un peu en retard *(late)*. Il **11** (être) déjà huit heures quand ils **12** (arriver) et nous **13** (avoir) tous très faim, alors, nous **14** (commencer) à manger tout de suite. Après, nous **15** (jouer) à des jeux vidéo jusqu'à minuit. Quand mes amis **16** (partir), j' **17** (être) fatigué et je/j' **18** (aller) au lit.

E Quelle soirée!

Amélie est allée à une fête chez des amis, les Fédor. Par petits groupes, regardez l'illustration et racontez *(tell)* ce qui s'est passé à la fête. Utilisez **le voleur** pour *the thief,* **voler** pour *to steal* et **entrer par la fenêtre** pour *to come in through the window.* Avant de commencer, réfléchissez *(think)* aux questions suivantes.

- What night was it?
- What time was it?
- What was the weather like?
- How many people were in the Fédors' living room?

- Why were they there?
- What was each person doing?
- What was in the bedroom?
- What happened?
- What happened next?

le voleur

Les Dupont   Hassan Amélie   Les Fédor

Access the Video *Les Stagiaires* online.

▶ Épisode 6: Je t'invite…

AVANT LA VIDÉO

Dans cet épisode, Matthieu invite Amélie à sortir avec lui. Avant de regarder l'épisode, faites une liste de trois phrases qu'on peut utiliser pour inviter quelqu'un.

APRÈS LA VIDÉO

Regardez l'épisode pour déterminer quand Matthieu et Amélie vont sortir ensemble et où ils vont aller.

LECTURE ET COMPOSITION

LECTURE

POUR MIEUX LIRE:
Using standard formats

You are going to read summaries of the two French movies that are so far the biggest box-office hits in France. Such summaries generally have similar formats. There is a presentation of the characters; a description of a conflict or a struggle between characters, cultures, or with oneself; and a resolution. Most movie plots can be categorized into one of the following categories: 1) a triumph of good over evil (a villain or a monster), 2) a rags to riches story, 3) a comically awkward attempt to acquire or get rid of something, 4) a quest for an object or a place, 5) a spiritual journey or a rebirth, or 6) a tragic spiral towards death or destruction. Can you think of movies that fit in each of these categories? How would you categorize the last three movies you saw? Keeping these common formats in mind will help you understand better as you watch or read about movies in French.

Intrigues. Lisez les résumés des films français *Bienvenue chez les Ch'tis* et *Intouchables* et décidez si on peut les classer *(categorize)* comme: 1) un triomphe du bien sur le mal, 2) une histoire d'ascension de la pauvreté à la richesse, 3) une comédie où quelqu'un veut obtenir ou se débarrasser de *(to get rid of)* quelque chose, 4) la quête d'un objet ou d'un endroit, 5) une quête spirituelle ou une renaissance ou 6) une spirale tragique vers la mort ou la destruction.

Deux films français

Résumé du film *Bienvenue chez les Ch'tis*

Philippe Abrams est directeur d'un bureau de poste et il veut **se faire muter** sur la Côte d'Azur. **De façon à** être prioritaire pour **la mutation,** il essaie de se faire passer pour un handicapé. **Découvrant sa supercherie,** l'administration l'envoie dans le Nord pour une mutation disciplinaire de deux ans. **Croyant** que le Nord est une région froide et inhospitalière, sa femme, Julie, décide de rester dans le Sud avec leur fils, et Philippe part seul pour son nouveau poste chez les «Ch'tis», les habitants du Nord. **Contre toute attente,** Philippe trouve les «Ch'tis» **chaleureux** et charmants. **En outre,** il considère la séparation temporaire positive pour sa relation avec sa femme et il essaie de **lui faire croire** que la vie dans la petite ville du Nord est **un cauchemar** pour la dissuader de venir le rejoindre. Persuadée que son mari est **déprimé,** Julie annonce finalement qu'elle va aller le voir. Avec la complicité de ses amis, Philippe essaie de faire croire à Julie que tous les clichés qu'elle a sur les gens du Nord sont vrais. Découvrant **les mensonges** de son mari et vexée, Julie retourne dans le Sud. Finalement, Philippe redescend dans le Sud pour lui demander de venir le rejoindre dans le Nord. Deux ans plus tard, Philippe doit quitter les «Ch'tis» parce qu'il est muté dans le Sud.

---

se faire muter *to be transferred*   **De façon à** *In order to*   **la mutation** *the transfer*   **Découvrant sa supercherie** *Discovering his deception*   **Croyant** *Believing*   **Contre toute attente** *Unexpectedly*   **chaleureux** *warm*   **En outre** *Moreover*   **lui faire croire** *to make her believe*   **un cauchemar** *a nightmare*   **déprimé** *depressed*   **les mensonges** *the lies*

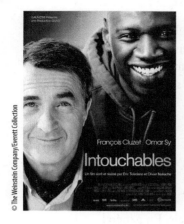

Résumé du film *Intouchables*

Après six mois de prison, Driss, un jeune homme d'origine sénégalaise de la banlieue parisienne, trouve du travail comme **aide à domicile** chez Philippe, un riche aristocrate devenu **tétraplégique** après un accident de **parapente.** Driss **n'a aucune formation,** mais sa confiance, sa manière franche et spontanée de parler et son énergie impressionnent Philippe, qui est fatigué de la pitié de ses anciens aides. Les différences entre les univers des deux hommes **donnent lieu** à des situations pleines d'humour, et **une amitié inattendue** entre les deux hommes **naît.** Ce film est basé sur une histoire vraie.

---

aide à domicile *personal assistant, home helper* **tétraplégique** *quadriplegic*
parapente *paragliding* **n'a aucune formation** *has no training*
donnent lieu *give rise* **une amitié inattendue** *an unexpected friendship* **naît** *is born*

Compréhension

A Répondez aux questions suivantes.

1. Dans quelle catégorie classez-vous ces deux films?

2. Qui sont les personnages *(characters)* du film *Bienvenue chez les Ch'tis*? Quels conflits surgissent *(arise)* dans ce film? Comment est-ce que le film finit?

3. Qui sont les personnages du film *Intouchables*? Quels conflits de culture y a-t-il entre les deux hommes? Est-ce qu'ils deviennent amis? Pourquoi est-ce qu'on pourrait dire *(might you say)* qu'il y a «une renaissance *(a rebirth)*» des personnages?

4. Voudriez-vous plutôt voir *Bienvenue chez les Ch'tis* ou *Intouchables*? Pourquoi?

B On peut résumer un film au présent ou au passé. Changez ces résumés du présent au passé en mettant les verbes au passé composé ou à l'imparfait.

COMPOSITION

POUR MIEUX ÉCRIRE:
Using standard formats

You are going to write a brief summary of one of your favorite films using the **passé composé** and the **imparfait.** Such summaries usually begin with one or two sentences introducing the characters and setting the scene; a few sentences stating the main events that create a conflict or a struggle; and a sentence or two explaining how it is (or is not) resolved. Following this format will help you organize a clear and concise summary.

Organisez-vous. Suivez les étapes *(steps)* suivantes pour organiser votre résumé.

1. Écrivez une ou deux phrases pour présenter les personnages *(characters)* et la situation. Allez-vous utiliser le passé composé ou l'imparfait pour décrire les personnages et la scène?

2. Faites une liste des actions les plus importantes des personnages. Allez-vous utiliser le passé composé ou l'imparfait pour décrire le déroulement de l'action *(the sequence of events)*?

3. Écrivez une ou deux phrases pour expliquer comment le film se termine *(ends)*. Commencez par **À la fin...**

Un film à voir!

Utilisez les phrases que vous avez préparées dans la section ***Organisez-vous*** pour écrire un résumé du film que vous avez choisi.

LE CINÉMA: LES PRÉFÉRENCES DES FRANÇAIS

Le cinéma, **que ce soit** les films vus au cinéma, à la télévision, en DVD, ou sur ordinateur ou téléphone, occupe une place centrale dans le temps libre des Français. Avant de lire les renseignements **qui suivent** sur le cinéma en France, essayez de **deviner** comment compléter les phrases. Est-ce que la situation du cinéma en France est comparable à la situation dans votre région?

LES FILMS

Les Français préfèrent...

❏ les films français.   ❏ les films étrangers.

Les Français aiment **autant** les films étrangers **que** les films français. En général, les films français représentent à peu près 40 % des entrées au cinéma.

Comme films étrangers, ils préfèrent...

❏ les films américains.   ❏ les films européens.

Parmi les films étrangers, ce sont les films américains qui sont les plus populaires. Des dix films les plus populaires en France depuis 1945, sept sont des productions américaines.

Comme genre, les Français préfèrent...

❏ les drames.   ❏ les films d'aventure.

Ce sont les films qui **attirent** un public jeune qui sont les plus populaires en France: films d'aventure, d'horreur... Les Français aiment aussi les comédies et les films à grand spectacle et on assiste à la popularité **croissante** des films à message social et des films d'amour.

D'après les Français, **les cinéastes** français font les meilleurs...

❏ films à grand spectacle   ❏ films comiques et satires sociales

tandis que les Américains font les meilleurs...

❏ films à grand spectacle.   ❏ films comiques et satires sociales.

D'après les sondages auprès des Français, les cinéastes français font les meilleures comédies et satires sociales et les Américains sont plus forts pour le grand spectacle.

LES SPECTATEURS

La majorité des spectateurs...

❏ ont plus de 50 ans.   ❏ ont entre 25 et 34 ans.   ❏ ont moins de 25 ans.

The Artist, un film français muet en noir et blanc, est un hommage aux films muets hollywoodiens des années 1920. Au Festival de Cannes en 2011, l'acteur Jean Dujardin obtient le Prix d'interprétation masculine *(best leading actor).* Le film remporte aussi trois Golden Globes, sept BAFTA, six Césars, un Goya et cinq Oscars.

---

que ce soit *whether it be*   **qui suivent** *that follow*   **deviner** *to guess*   **autant que** *as much as*   **attirent** *attract*   **croissante** *growing*   **D'après** *According to*   **les cinéastes** *film-makers*   **tandis que** *whereas*   **D'après les sondages auprès des** *According to surveys of the*

Les moins de 25 ans représentent 35 % des spectateurs et deux-tiers (2/3) des gens qui vont au cinéma au moins une fois par mois.

En général, les Français vont au cinéma...

❏ pendant la semaine.   ❏ le week-end.   ❏ le mercredi, jour de sortie en salle des nouveaux films.

❏ en hiver.   ❏ en été.   ❏ de façon égale en toute saison.

En France, la saison du cinéma est l'hiver et on y va le plus souvent le week-end.

Source: Gérard Mermet, *Francoscopie*, Éditions Larousse.

Voici une liste des dix films les plus vus au cinéma en France depuis 1945. Qu'est-ce que vous remarquez?

Les plus grands succès du cinéma en France depuis 1945, en millions d'entrées.	
TITANIC (ÉTATS-UNIS)	21,77
BIENVENUE CHEZ LES CH'TIS (FRANCE)	20,49
INTOUCHABLES (FRANCE)	19,44
BLANCHE-NEIGE ET LES SEPT NAINS (ÉTATS-UNIS)	18,32
LA GRANDE VADROUILLE (FRANCE, G.-B.)	17,27
AUTANT EN EMPORTE LE VENT (ÉTATS-UNIS)	16,72
IL ÉTAIT UNE FOIS DANS L'OUEST (ÉTATS-UNIS)	14,86
AVATAR (ÉTATS-UNIS)	14,77
LE LIVRE DE LA JUNGLE (ÉTATS-UNIS)	14,70
LES 101 DALMATIENS (ÉTATS-UNIS)	14,66

Source: www.jpbox-office.com

Compréhension

1. Qu'est-ce que vous pouvez dire au sujet des spectateurs français et de leurs préférences en matière de *(with regards to)* films? Quelles sont les préférences des gens là où vous habitez?

2. Combien de films du tableau ci-dessus *(chart above)* sont américains? français? Certains Français trouvent qu'il y a trop d'influence américaine dans les salles de cinéma en France et que la culture française est menacée *(is threatened)*. Est-ce que ce sentiment est justifié? Quel est le rôle du gouvernement dans la préservation de la culture? Est-ce qu'il doit y avoir une censure? des quotas? des subventions *(subsidies)*?

3. D'après la majorité des Français, quels genres de films est-ce que les cinéastes français font le mieux? Et les cinéastes américains? Est-ce que l'industrie cinématographique d'un pays est un reflet de *(a reflection of)* sa culture? Si oui, quelles comparaisons culturelles peut-on faire entre les Français et les Américains?

RÉSUMÉ DE GRAMMAIRE

Je **veux** sortir ce soir, mais je ne **peux** pas. Je **dois** travailler.

THE VERBS *VOULOIR, POUVOIR,* AND *DEVOIR*

Here are the conjugations of **vouloir** *(to want)*, **pouvoir** *(can, may, to be able)*, and **devoir** *(must, to have to, to owe)*.

VOULOIR	POUVOIR	DEVOIR
je **veux**	je **peux**	je **dois**
tu **veux**	tu **peux**	tu **dois**
il/elle/on **veut**	il/elle/on **peut**	il/elle/on **doit**
nous **voulons**	nous **pouvons**	nous **devons**
vous **voulez**	vous **pouvez**	vous **devez**
ils/elles **veulent**	ils/elles **peuvent**	ils/elles **doivent**
P.C. **j'ai voulu**	P.C. **j'ai pu**	P.C. **j'ai dû**
IMP. **je voulais**	IMP. **je pouvais**	IMP. **je devais**

Nous **voulions** partir en vacances, mais nous n'**avons** pas **pu.** Nous **avons dû** travailler.

You generally use the verb **vouloir** in the **imparfait** to say what someone wanted. Use **pouvoir** in the **imparfait** to say what people could do if they might have wanted to, but use it in the **passé composé** to say what they managed to do on an occasion when they tried. Use **devoir** in the **imparfait** to say what one was supposed to do, but in the **passé composé** for what one must have done, or had to do on a specific occasion.

Elle **a dû** quitter la maison très tôt. Elle **devait** arriver à sept heures.
She must have left / had to leave the house very early. She was supposed to arrive at seven o'clock.

THE VERBS *SORTIR, PARTIR,* AND *DORMIR*

Here are the conjugations of **sortir** *(to go out)*, **partir** *(to leave)*, and **dormir** *(to sleep)*.

Je **dors** jusqu'à sept heures et je **pars** pour l'université à huit heures.

SORTIR	PARTIR	DORMIR
je **sors**	je **pars**	je **dors**
tu **sors**	tu **pars**	tu **dors**
il/elle/on **sort**	il/elle/on **part**	il/elle/on **dort**
nous **sortons**	nous **partons**	nous **dormons**
vous **sortez**	vous **partez**	vous **dormez**
ils/elles **sortent**	ils/elles **partent**	ils/elles **dorment**
P.C. **je suis sorti(e)**	P.C. **je suis parti(e)**	P.C. **j'ai dormi**
IMP. **je sortais**	IMP. **je partais**	IMP. **je dormais**

Ce matin, j'**ai dormi** jusqu'à sept heures et demie et je **suis partie** pour l'université en retard *(late).*

Avant, je **sortais** souvent avec des amis, mais nous ne **sommes** pas **sortis** le week-end dernier.

Sortir means *to go out* both in the sense of going out with friends and going out of a place. Use **partir** to say *to leave* in the sense of *to go away.* **Quitter** means *to leave* a person or a place and *must* be used with a direct object.

Il **quitte** Paris pour aller travailler à Nice. Il **part** demain.

Use these prepositions with these verbs:

Je **sors de** mon cours à midi.

to come / go out (of) = **sortir (de)**

Je **pars de** chez moi à huit heures.

to leave (from) = **partir (de)**

Je **pars pour** Nice demain.

to leave (for) = **partir (pour)**

L'IMPARFAIT AND *LE PASSÉ COMPOSÉ*

All verbs except **être** form the **imparfait** by dropping the **-ons** from the present tense **nous** form and adding these endings. The stem for **être** is **ét-**.

	PARLER (nous parl~~ons~~ → parl-)	**FAIRE** (nous fais~~ons~~ → fais-)	**PRENDRE** (nous pren~~ons~~ → pren-)	**ÊTRE** (ét-)
je (j')	parl**ais**	fais**ais**	pren**ais**	ét**ais**
tu	parl**ais**	fais**ais**	pren**ais**	ét**ais**
il/elle/on	parl**ait**	fais**ait**	pren**ait**	ét**ait**
nous	parl**ions**	fais**ions**	pren**ions**	ét**ions**
vous	parl**iez**	fais**iez**	pren**iez**	ét**iez**
ils/elles	parl**aient**	fais**aient**	pren**aient**	ét**aient**

Quand j'**avais** 16 ans, j'**allais** au lycée. Je **passais** beaucoup de temps avec mes copains. On **aimait** faire du roller.

Verbs with spelling changes in the present tense **nous** form, like **manger** and **commencer,** retain the spelling changes in the **imparfait** only before endings beginning with an **a.**

Note these expressions in the **imparfait**:

il y a	→	il y avait
il pleut	→	il pleuvait
il neige	→	il neigeait

Nous **mangions** bien, mais je **mangeais** peu.

Vous **commenciez** vos cours à midi, mais moi, je **commençais** mes cours à 11 heures.

Il y avait du vent, il **pleuvait** et **il faisait** froid, mais **il** ne **neigeait** pas.

When talking about the past, you use both the **passé composé** and the **imparfait.** Note their uses:

USE THE *IMPARFAIT* TO SAY:	USE THE *PASSÉ COMPOSÉ* TO SAY:
1. **HOW THINGS USED TO BE OR WHAT USED TO HAPPEN** • continuous actions or states • repeated or habitual actions of an unspecified duration	1. **WHAT HAPPENED AT A PRECISE MOMENT, FOR A SPECIFIC DURATION, OR A SPECIFIC NUMBER OF TIMES** • completed actions • actions within a specific duration • actions done a specific number of times
2. **WHAT WAS GOING ON** • scene or setting • interrupted actions in progress	2. **WHAT HAPPENED NEXT** • sequence of events • actions interrupting something in progress
3. **WHAT THINGS WERE LIKE OR HOW SOMEONE FELT** • physical or mental states	3. **WHAT CHANGED** • changes in states
4. **WHAT SOMEONE WAS GOING TO DO**	4. **WHAT SOMEONE WENT TO DO**

Cendrillon **pleurait** *(was crying)* quand sa marraine *([fairy] godmother)* **est arrivée.** La marraine **a aidé** Cendrillon et Cendrillon **est allée** au bal du prince. Le prince **est** immédiatement **tombé** amoureux de Cendrillon. Ils **ont dansé** et ils **ont** beaucoup **parlé.** À minuit, Cendrillon **est partie** sans dire au prince qui elle **était,** mais elle **a laissé** tomber *(dropped)* une de ses chaussures.

VOCABULAIRE

Inviting someone to go out

NOMS MASCULINS

l'amour	*love*
un film d'amour	*a romantic movie, a love story*
un groupe	*a group*
un horaire	*a schedule*

NOMS FÉMININS

une comédie	*a comedy*
une façon	*a way*
l'heure officielle	*official time*
les heures d'ouverture	*business hours*
une idée	*an idea*
une invitation	*an invitation*
une personne	*a person*
une séance	*a showing*

EXPRESSIONS VERBALES

appeler	*to call*
devoir	*must, to have to, to owe*
dire	*to say, to tell*
passer un film	*to show a movie*
pouvoir	*can, may, to be able*
regretter	*to regret, to be sorry*
répondre (à)	*to answer, to respond (to)*
suggérer	*to suggest*
téléphoner (à)	*to phone*
utiliser	*to use, to utilize*
vouloir	*to want*

DIVERS

allô	*hello* (on the telephone)
À tout à l'heure.	*See you later.* (the same day)
avec plaisir	*gladly, with pleasure*
Je pensais	*I was thinking*
Je t'invite...	*I'm inviting you …*
Je voudrais vous inviter...	*I'd like to invite you …*
occupé(e)	*occupied, busy*
Quelle bonne idée!	*What a good idea!*
quelqu'un	*someone, somebody*
tellement	*so much, so*
uniquement	*uniquely, only*
Vous voudriez...?	*Would you like … ?*

Talking about how you spend and used to spend your time

NOMS MASCULINS

un lycée	*a high school*
un lycéen	*a high school student*
un resto U	*a university cafeteria*

NOMS FÉMININS

une école	*a school*
une lycéenne	*a high school student*
une soirée	*a party*
la vie	*life*

EXPRESSIONS VERBALES

avoir cours	*to have class*
comparer	*to compare*
dormir	*to sleep*
faire du roller	*to go in-line skating*
faire du skateboard	*to skateboard*
partir (de/pour)	*to leave (from/for), to go away (from/to)*
partir en vacances	*to leave on vacation*
partir en voyage	*to leave on a trip*
partir en week-end	*to go away for the weekend*
quitter	*to leave*
sortir (de)	*to go out (of)*

DIVERS

ce que	*what*
dans le passé	*in the past*
rien de spécial	*nothing special*

COMPÉTENCE 3

Talking about the past

NOMS MASCULINS

un bistro	*a pub, a restaurant*
un repas	*a meal*

NOMS FÉMININS

une fois	*once, one time*
une sortie	*an outing*

EXPRESSIONS ADVERBIALES

un jour	*one day*
soudain	*suddenly*
tout à coup	*all of a sudden*
tout de suite	*right away*
tout d'un coup	*all at once*

DIVERS

Ça t'a plu?	*Did you like it?*
délicieux (délicieuse)	*delicious*
Qu'est-ce qui s'est passé?	*What happened?*
rien du tout	*nothing at all*
tout le monde	*everybody, everyone*

COMPÉTENCE 4

Narrating in the past

NOMS MASCULINS

un acteur	*an actor*
un bal	*a ball*
un classique	*a classic*
un conte	*a story* (for children)
un conte de fées	*a fairy tale*
les effets spéciaux	*special effects*
un marchand	*a merchant, a shopkeeper*
un messager	*a messenger*
un monstre	*a monster*
un palais	*a palace*
le travail	*work*

NOMS FÉMININS

une actrice	*an actress*
une bête	*a beast*
une demi-sœur	*a stepsister*
une époque	*a time (period)*
une marchande	*a merchant, a shopkeeper*
une messagère	*a messenger*
la violence	*violence*

EXPRESSIONS VERBALES

apprécier	*to appreciate*
à suivre	*to be continued*
changer	*to change*
Connaissez-vous...?	*Do you know . . . ?*
décider	*to decide*
emprisonner	*to imprison*
jouer	*to act* (in movies and theater)
se parler	*to talk to each other*
prendre la place de	*to take the place of*
promettre (promis)	*to promise (promised)*
tomber amoureux (amoureuse) de	*to fall in love with*

ADJECTIFS

amoureux (amoureuse) (de)	*in love (with)*
basé(e) (sur)	*based (on)*
cruel(le)	*cruel*
doux (douce)	*sweet, soft, gentle*
excellent(e)	*excellent*
féroce	*ferocious*
gâté(e)	*spoiled*
gracieux (gracieuse)	*gracious*
horrible	*horrible*
patient(e)	*patient*

DIVERS

au début (de)	*at the beginning (of)*
Ça t'a plu?	*Did you like it?*
Ça m'a plu.	*I liked it.*
finalement	*finally, in the end*
Il était une fois...	*Once upon a time there was . . .*
lequel (laquelle)	*which, which one*
petit à petit	*little by little*
trop de	*too much*

 Pair work

 Group work

Class work

 Video

 Audio

© Boris Stroujko/Shutterstock.com

7

LE MONDE FRANCOPHONE
Géoculture et Vidéo-voyage: En Bretagne

COMPÉTENCE

1 Describing your daily routine
La vie de tous les jours

Describing your daily routine
Les verbes réfléchis au présent

Stratégies et Lecture
- **Pour mieux lire:** *Using word families and watching out for* **faux amis**
- **Lecture:** *Il n'est jamais trop tard!*

2 Talking about relationships
La vie sentimentale

Saying what people do for each other
Les verbes réciproques au présent et les verbes réfléchis et réciproques au futur immédiat

Talking about activities
Les verbes en **-re**

3 Talking about what you did and used to do
Les activités d'hier

Saying what people did
Les verbes réfléchis et réciproques au passé composé

Saying what people did and used to do
Les verbes réfléchis et réciproques à l'imparfait et reprise de l'usage du passé composé et de l'imparfait

4 Describing traits and characteristics
Les traits de caractère

Specifying which one
Les pronoms relatifs **qui, que** *et* **dont**

Vidéo-reprise: *Les Stagiaires*

Lecture et Composition
- **Pour mieux lire:** *Recognizing conversational style*
- **Lecture:** *Conte pour enfants de moins de trois ans*
- **Pour mieux écrire:** *Organizing a paragraph*
- **Composition:** *Le matin chez moi*

Comparaisons culturelles: *L'amour et le couple*

Résumé de grammaire

Vocabulaire

deux cent soixante-sept | **267**

GÉOCULTURE ET VIDÉO-VOYAGE:
EN BRETAGNE

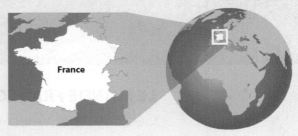

France

LA BRETAGNE
NOMBRE D'HABITANTS: **3 259 000 (les Bretons)**
CAPITALE: **Rennes**

La Bretagne, c'est la beauté…

de ses **falaises rocheuses,** de ses ports, de ses **villages de pêcheurs** et des îles **le long de** ses 200 kilomètres de **côtes,** aussi bien que de ses beaux **paysages** et des villages pittoresques de son **arrière-pays.**

La Bretagne, c'est une identité culturelle aux **racines** celtiques…

qui se révèle dans ses fêtes traditionnelles et **qui s'entend** dans **le breton.** La langue officielle de la région est, bien sûr, le français, mais le breton est sa langue régionale.

La Bretagne, c'est des grandes villes historiques…

comme la ville de Vannes et comme sa capitale, Rennes, avec ses **maisons à colombages** et ses nombreux bars et cafés de sa célèbre rue de la Soif.

La Bretagne Brittany   **falaises rocheuses** rocky cliffs   **villages de pêcheurs** fishing villages   **le long de** along   **côtes** coasts, coastlines   **paysages** landscapes, countryside   **arrière-pays** interior   **racines** roots   **qui s'entend** which is heard   **le breton** the Breton language   **maisons à colombages** half-timbered houses

La Bretagne, c'est des sites préhistoriques…

comme les alignements de Carnac, une des plus importantes collections mégalithiques du monde.

comme les mégalithes de l'Île-aux-Moines, la plus grande île dans le golfe du Morbihan.

La Bretagne, c'est la légende…

comme celle du roi Arthur et de la quête du Graal, centrée dans la forêt mythique de Brocéliande, **sans doute inspirée de** la forêt de Paimpont.

Le savez-vous?

Quel site ou chose correspond à chaque description?

> **Rennes**
> **les falaises rocheuses**
> **la forêt de Brocéliande**
> **les alignements de Carnac**
> **ses racines celtiques**
> **le breton**

1. Ces attractions naturelles font partie de la beauté des côtes de la Bretagne.

2. Le français est la langue officielle de cette région, mais cette langue est sa langue régionale.

3. Cet aspect de l'identité culturelle de la région se révèle dans ses fêtes traditionnelles et dans sa langue régionale.

4. Cette ville est la capitale de la Bretagne et elle est connue pour ses maisons à colombages.

5. C'est une des plus importantes collections mégalithiques du monde.

6. C'est la forêt mythique de la légende du roi Arthur.

---

sans doute inspirée de *most likely inspired by*

Vous allez visiter la Bretagne à travers la vidéo. Pour vous aider à mieux comprendre, regardez ces photos et complétez les descriptions.

Concerts   **mégalithes**   **la vieille ville**

Soif   **surfer**

1. Réveil matinal *(Early rising)* pour aller chercher la vague *(wave)* sur la Pointe de la Torche. Eh oui, on peut aussi _____ en Bretagne!

2. À l'heure du déjeuner, prenez le temps de souffler *(to breathe)* à Vannes, dans _____, avant d'embarquer pour l'Île aux Moines.

3. Sur l'Île aux Moines, c'est vélo de rigueur *(required)* pour découvrir *(to discover)* les _____. À moins que vous ne préfériez le farniente *(to do nothing)* sur la plage.

4. Rejoignez *(Reach)* Rennes et pour bien terminer la journée, posez-vous en terrasse dans la célèbre rue de la _____.

5. Si vous passez en Bretagne en juillet, ne ratez surtout pas *(be sure not to miss)* le festival des Vieilles Charrues. _____ à gogo et artistes internationaux au programme.

▶ **EN REGARDANT LA VIDÉO**

Regardez la vidéo et indiquez lesquelles *(which)* de ces activités on y voit.

faire du ski	**faire du vélo**
faire du surf	**aller au café**
écouter de la musique	**faire du kayak**
nager	**jouer au tennis**

▶ **APRÈS LA VIDÉO**

Regardez la vidéo une deuxième fois et répondez aux questions.

1. Quelle ville est la capitale de la Bretagne?
2. Pour quel sport la Pointe de la Torche est-elle célèbre?
3. Qu'est-ce qu'on peut voir à l'Île aux Moines?
4. À quel endroit la légende du roi Arthur est-elle associée?
5. Qu'est-ce qu'on trouve dans la rue de la Soif?

Describing your daily routine

LA VIE DE TOUS LES JOURS

Note *de grammaire*

1. When saying that people are doing something to a part of their body, you generally use the definite article (**le, la, l', les**) in French, rather than a possessive adjective as in English.

   Je me lave **les** mains.
   *I'm washing **my** hands.*

2. After the expression **avant de,** use an infinitive rather than a conjugated verb.

   Before I eat (Before eating), I wash my hands.
   Avant de manger, je me lave les mains.

Quelle est votre routine *(f)* **quotidienne**?

D'habitude le matin...

Je me réveille vers six heures.

Je me lève tout de suite et je **fais ma toilette.**

Je me lave **la figure** et **les mains** *(f)*.

Je prends un bain ou **une douche.**

Je me brosse les cheveux.

Je me brosse les dents.

Je me maquille **avant de m'habiller.**

Je m'habille.

Le soir...

Quelquefois, **je me repose.**

D'autres fois, je m'amuse avec des amis.

Parfois, quand je suis seule, **je m'ennuie.**

Je me déshabille.

Je me couche et **je m'endors** facilement.

---

quotidien(ne) *daily* **faire sa toilette** *to wash up* **la figure** *the face* **les mains** *the hands* **une douche** *a shower*
avant de m'habiller *before I dress, before dressing* **je me repose (se reposer** *to rest)* **D'autres fois** *Other times*
je m'ennuie (s'ennuyer *to be bored, to get bored)* **je m'endors (s'endormir** *to fall asleep)*

7-1

Rosalie Toulouse-Richard, d'origine française, habite à Atlanta **depuis** son mariage avec un Américain. **Veuve** maintenant, elle retourne en France avec sa **petite-fille** Rose, qui ne **connaît** pas du tout la France. **Comme** elles partagent une chambre **pendant** leur **séjour** *(m)*, elles parlent de leurs routines le matin.

ROSALIE: Tu te lèves vers quelle heure d'habitude?

ROSE: Entre six heures et six heures et demie. Je fais **vite** ma toilette, je m'habille et puis je me maquille. Je suis prête en une demi-heure.

ROSALIE: C'est parfait. Moi, je prends quelquefois une douche le matin, mais je préfère prendre mon bain le soir. Je peux très bien **attendre** jusqu'à sept heures pour faire ma toilette.

ROSE: Et moi, je ne quitte jamais la maison avant huit heures et demie. Alors si tu veux, on peut prendre le petit déjeuner ensemble tous les matins.

A **Et ensuite...** Trouvez la suite logique pour compléter chaque phrase.

Je me lève...   avec des amis.
Je me brosse...   je me couche.
Je prends...   vers huit heures.
L'après-midi, je m'amuse...   les dents.
Je me déshabille et puis...   une douche ou un bain.
Je me couche et...   je m'endors.

B **Ma routine.** Complétez les phrases avec une expression de la liste.

EXEMPLE Je me réveille avant six heures.
Je me réveille rarement avant six heures.
Je ne me réveille jamais avant six heures.

toujours	ne... jamais
souvent	tous les jours
quelquefois	le lundi, le mardi...
de temps en temps	le matin, l'après-midi, le soir
rarement	une (deux...) fois par jour (semaine...)

1. Je me réveille après neuf heures.
2. Je me lève tout de suite.
3. Je prends une douche ou un bain.
4. Je me lave les mains.
5. Je me lave les cheveux.
6. Je me brosse les dents.
7. Je m'habille vite.
8. Je m'ennuie.
9. Je me repose.
10. Je m'amuse bien.
11. Je me couche tard.
12. Je m'endors sur le canapé.

Note *de grammaire*

To form the negative of a reflexive verb, place **ne** directly after the subject and **pas, jamais,** or **rien** directly after the verb. Remember that **toujours, souvent,** and **rarement** go right after the verb, but the other adverbial phrases listed go at the end of the sentence.

À VOUS!

Avec un(e) partenaire, relisez à haute voix la conversation entre Rosalie et Rose. Ensuite, imaginez que vous voyagez ensemble et adaptez la conversation pour parler de votre routine le matin.

You can access the audio of the active vocabulary of this *Compétence* online.

depuis *since*   **Veuve (Veuf)** *Widow (Widower)*   **une petite-fille (un petit-fils)** *a granddaughter (a grandson)*   **elle connaît (connaître** *to know)*   **Comme** *Since, As*   **pendant** *during*   **un séjour** *a stay*   **vite** *quickly, fast*   **attendre** *to wait (for)*

DESCRIBING YOUR DAILY ROUTINE

✔ *Pour vérifier*

1. What is the difference in usage between the reflexive verb **se laver** and the non-reflexive verb **laver**?

2. What are the different reflexive pronouns that are used with each subject pronoun when you conjugate a reflexive verb like **se laver**?

3. Where do you place **ne... pas** when negating reflexive verbs?

4. How is **s'endormir** conjugated?

5. In which forms do verbs like **se lever, s'appeler,** and **s'ennuyer** have spelling changes? What are the changes? Which forms do not have spelling changes?

Les verbes réfléchis au présent

1. You can do something to or for yourself or to or for another person or thing. When someone performs an action on or for himself/herself, a reflexive verb is generally used in French. Compare these sentences.

REFLEXIVE   **NON-REFLEXIVE**

Je me lave les mains.   Je lave la voiture.

2. The infinitive of reflexive verbs is preceded by the reflexive pronoun **se.** When you conjugate these verbs, change the reflexive pronoun according to the subject. In the negative, place **ne** directly after the subject and **pas** after the conjugated verb.

SE LAVER *(to wash [oneself])*		NE PAS SE LAVER	
je me lave	nous nous lavons	je ne me lave pas	nous ne nous lavons pas
tu te laves	vous vous lavez	tu ne te laves pas	vous ne vous lavez pas
il/elle/on se lave	ils/elles se lavent	il/elle/on ne se lave pas	ils/elles ne se lavent pas

3. **Me, te,** and **se** change to **m', t',** and **s'** before a vowel sound: **je m'habille, tu t'habilles, elle s'habille, ils s'habillent.**

4. Here are some reflexive verbs you can use to talk about your daily life:

s'amuser	*to have fun*
s'appeler	*to be named*
se brosser (les cheveux, les dents)	*to brush (one's hair, one's teeth)*
se coucher / se recoucher	*to go to bed / to go back to bed*
s'endormir	*to fall asleep*
s'ennuyer	*to be bored, to get bored*
s'habiller / se déshabiller	*to get dressed / to get undressed*
se laver (les mains, la figure)	*to wash (one's hands, one's face)*
se lever	*to get up*
se maquiller	*to put on make-up*
se raser	*to shave*
se reposer	*to rest*
se réveiller	*to wake up*

5. The verb **s'endormir** is conjugated like **dormir.**

S'ENDORMIR *(to fall asleep)*	
je m'endors	nous nous endormons
tu t'endors	vous vous endormez
il/elle/on s'endort	ils/elles s'endorment

6. Remember that in verbs ending in **-yer,** such as **s'ennuyer,** the letter **y** changes to **i** in all forms except those of **nous** and **vous.**

S'ENNUYER *(to be bored, to get bored)*	
je m'ennuie	nous nous ennuyons
tu t'ennuies	vous vous ennuyez
il/elle/on s'ennuie	ils/elles s'ennuient

7. There is an accent spelling change in the conjugation of **se lever.** Its conjugation is similar to that of **acheter. S'appeler** changes its spelling by doubling the final consonant of the stem in all present tense forms except those of **nous** and **vous.**

SE LEVER *(to get up)*	
je me **lè**ve	nous nous levons
tu te **lè**ves	vous vous levez
il/elle/on se **lè**ve	ils/elles se **lè**vent

S'APPELER *(to be named)*	
je m'appe**ll**e	nous nous appelons
tu t'appe**ll**es	vous vous appelez
il/elle/on s'appe**ll**e	ils/elles s'appe**ll**ent

A Équivalents. Trouvez le verbe réfléchi correspondant à chaque définition.

> s'endormir   s'ennuyer
> se reposer   se lever
> s'habiller   s'amuser
> se coucher   se maquiller

1. aller au lit

2. sortir du lit

3. mettre des vêtements

4. faire quelque chose d'amusant

5. faire quelque chose d'ennuyeux

6. ne rien faire

7. commencer à dormir

8. mettre du mascara

B D'abord... Indiquez l'ordre logique des activités données.

EXEMPLE prendre un bain / se lever
> **D'abord, on se lève et puis on prend un bain.**

1. se réveiller / se lever

2. se laver la figure / se maquiller

3. s'habiller / prendre un bain ou une douche

4. quitter la maison / s'habiller

5. se reposer / rentrer à la maison après les cours

6. s'amuser / retrouver des amis

7. se déshabiller / se coucher

8. s'endormir / se coucher

Mes amis et moi, on s'amuse toujours bien le week-end.

C **Un samedi typique.** Voilà la routine de Rose le samedi. Qu'est-ce qu'elle fait?

EXEMPLE Le samedi matin,... vers 9h.
Le samedi matin, **elle se réveille** vers 9h.

EXEMPLE **1.** **2.** **3.**

1. ... tout de suite.

2. ... la figure et les mains.

3. ... avant le petit déjeuner.

4. **5.** **6.** **7.**

4. Après le petit déjeuner,...

5. ... les cheveux juste avant de quitter la maison.

6. Le samedi soir,... avec des amis.

7. ... vers deux heures du matin et... facilement.

D **Et vous?** Regardez les illustrations de **C. Un samedi typique.** Est-ce que vous faites les mêmes choses le samedi?

EXEMPLE  ... vers 9h
Je me réveille vers 9h.
Je ne me réveille pas vers 9h.
Je me réveille vers 10h.

E **Ma routine.** Complétez ces phrases pour parler de vous.

1. En semaine *(During the week),* je me réveille...

2. Je me lève...

3. Mes amis et moi, nous nous amusons beaucoup quand...

4. Nous nous ennuyons quand...

5. En semaine, je me couche...

6. Je m'endors...

F **Questions.** Travaillez en groupes pour préparer autant de questions que possible à poser au professeur au sujet de sa routine quotidienne. Utilisez les éléments donnés ou d'autres expressions logiques. Le groupe avec le plus grand nombre de questions logiques gagne.

> s'amuser   s'ennuyer   se réveiller   se lever
> se coucher   s'endormir   se laver la figure et les mains
> se brosser les dents / les cheveux

> à quelle heure   tôt / tard   facilement   tout de suite
> combien de fois par jour   avant / après le petit déjeuner   quand

EXEMPLE Est-ce que vous vous couchez tôt d'habitude?

G **Beaucoup de questions!** Circulez parmi les étudiants. Posez chaque paire de questions à un(e) étudiant(e) différent(e). Notez leurs réponses et ensuite, dites à la classe ce que vous avez appris.

EXEMPLE —Eva, à quelle heure est-ce que tu te réveilles le samedi matin?
—Je me réveille vers 10h.

Après, à la classe: **Eva se réveille vers 10h le samedi matin.**

> À quelle heure est-ce que tu te réveilles le samedi matin?
> Est-ce que tu te lèves tout de suite?

> Quand est-ce que tu te reposes?
> Tu te couches tôt pendant la semaine?

> Tu t'amuses ou tu t'ennuies quand tu es seul(e) le soir?
> Quand est-ce que tu t'amuses?

> Tu préfères prendre un bain ou une douche?
> Est-ce que tu prends ton bain ou ta douche le matin ou le soir?

> Vers quelle heure est-ce que tu te couches le samedi soir?
> Est-ce que tu t'endors tout de suite?

H **Vous faites du baby-sitting.** Imaginez que vous allez faire du baby-sitting pour les deux enfants d'un(e) ami(e). Demandez ces renseignements à votre ami(e). Votre partenaire va jouer le rôle de votre ami(e) et imaginer ses réponses. Préparez une scène à présenter à la classe.

Find out . . .

EXEMPLE *what time they wake up*
—À quelle heure est-ce qu'ils se réveillent?
—Ils se réveillent vers huit heures.

1. *if they get up right away*
2. *if they take a bath or a shower in the morning or the evening*
3. *if they rest in the afternoon*
4. *at what time they eat dinner*
5. *at what time they go to bed*
6. *if they fall asleep easily*

POUR MIEUX LIRE: *Using word families and watching out for **faux amis***

Recognizing words that belong to the same word family can make reading easier. Can you supply the missing meanings below?

la vie	**vivre**	**se marier**	**le mariage**
life	*to live*	*to marry*	*marriage*
l'arrêt	**s'arrêter**	**espérer**	**l'espoir**
the stop	*???*	*to hope*	*???*

Using cognates and word families can help you understand new texts more easily. However, beware of **faux amis,** words that look like cognates but have different meanings. For example, **rester** does not mean *to rest,* but *to stay.* Use cognates, but if a word does not seem right in the context, look it up.

A Familles de mots. Vous allez voir ces mots dans l'histoire qui suit. Servez-vous du sens des mots donnés pour déterminer le sens des autres mots.

rêver	**un rêve**	**dire**	**dit(e)**
to dream	*a dream*	*to say, to tell*	*said, told*
se souvenir de	**des souvenirs**	**connaître**	**connu(e)**
to remember	*???*	*to know*	*???*
saluer	**une salutation**	**reconnaître**	**reconnu(e)**
to greet	*???*	*to recognize*	*???*

B Faux amis. Donnez le sens des faux amis en caractères gras selon le contexte.

M. Dupont se repose dans un fauteuil au jardin quand une jolie jeune fille qui passe **attire** son attention. Il la **salue** et lui dit bonjour. Cette fille ressemble à quelqu'un qu'il connaissait dans le passé et il commence à rêver. Il a de beaux **souvenirs** du temps où il était jeune. Il aimait une jeune fille et il **garde** toujours l'espoir de la revoir un jour.

Lecture: *Il n'est jamais trop tard!*

🔊
7-2

Rosalie Toulouse-Richard, qui habite à Atlanta depuis son mariage avec un Américain, retourne à Quimper avec sa petite-fille Rose. Son vieil ami, André Dupont, ne sait pas encore que Rosalie est à Quimper.

André Dupont a toujours aimé passer des heures à travailler dans son jardin. Il a une passion pour les roses et depuis des années, il plante des rosiers de toutes les variétés et de toutes les couleurs dans son jardin.

Ses rosiers font l'admiration de tous les gens du quartier et beaucoup d'entre eux passent devant chez lui pour regarder son beau jardin. Aujourd'hui, trois jeunes filles s'arrêtent devant son jardin et lui disent bonjour. Il reconnaît deux d'entre elles, ce sont les petites-filles de son ami Jean Toulouse, mais c'est la troisième qui attire son attention. Il ne l'a jamais vue, et pourtant il a l'impression de la connaître! Elle ressemble à quelqu'un... quelqu'un qu'il a connu il y a très longtemps.

Les souvenirs lui reviennent, comme si c'était hier. C'était il y a longtemps, il avait dix-huit ans et il était amoureux fou d'une jolie jeune fille de son âge. Elle s'appelait Rosalie...! Il voulait lui dire combien il l'aimait, mais il n'en avait pas le courage. Il était trop timide. Un beau jour, il s'est décidé à tout lui dire. Il a choisi des fleurs de son jardin pour en faire un bouquet, il a pris son vélo et il est allé chez Rosalie. Mais en arrivant, il a trouvé Rosalie en compagnie d'un jeune Américain et elle regardait ce jeune homme d'un regard de femme amoureuse. André, lui, est rentré chez lui sans jamais parler à Rosalie.

Quelques mois après, Rosalie s'est mariée avec le jeune Américain et ils sont partis vivre aux États-Unis. De temps en temps, André avait des nouvelles, car le frère de Rosalie et lui étaient de bons amis. Il savait qu'elle habitait à Atlanta, qu'elle avait eu trois enfants, et il y a trois ans, il a appris que son mari était mort. Il gardait toujours l'espoir de la revoir, mais les années passaient et elle ne revenait toujours pas.

—Vos rosiers sont magnifiques, monsieur!
C'est Rosalie qui parle! En un instant, André Dupont revient au présent et ouvre les yeux. C'est la jeune fille qui parle... celle qu'il ne connaît pas.
—Rosalie???
—Moi, monsieur? Non, je m'appelle Rose. Rosalie, c'est ma grand-mère.
—Ta grand-mère?
—Oui. Vous connaissez ma grand-mère?
—Rosalie Toulouse? Oui, je la connais, mais...
—Eh bien, venez la voir, elle est chez son frère Jean! Je suis sûre qu'elle sera contente de revoir un ami d'ici! Allez, venez donc avec nous!

Quoi? C'est trop beau! Est-ce qu'il rêve? Rosalie, ici! Comme la vie est à la fois belle et bizarre! Va-t-elle le reconnaître? A-t-il le courage de lui dire qu'il l'aime toujours, après toutes ces années? André Dupont choisit les plus belles roses de son jardin et en fait un magnifique bouquet. Il va enfin pouvoir les offrir à la femme pour qui il a planté tous ces rosiers au cours des années.

Qui parle? Qui parle: **André**, **Rosalie** ou **Rose**?

1. J'adore les fleurs et j'aime faire du jardinage.
2. J'ai eu trois enfants et mon mari est mort il y a trois ans.
3. Je suis passée devant une maison où il y avait des roses splendides.
4. Un monsieur m'a parlé. Il connaît ma grand-mère mais il ne l'a pas vue depuis longtemps.
5. J'ai invité ce monsieur à venir nous voir.
6. Je me suis mariée avec un Américain et je suis allée vivre aux États-Unis.
7. J'étais amoureux de Rosalie mais je n'ai jamais eu le courage de le lui dire.
8. Je garde toujours l'espoir de dire à Rosalie que je l'aime.

Talking about relationships

LA VIE SENTIMENTALE

André va chez les Toulouse et André et Rosalie **se rencontrent** pour la première fois depuis des années. Voilà **ce qui se passe.**

André et Rosalie se regardent.

Ils s'embrassent. C'est **le coup de foudre**!

Ils se parlent pendant des heures.

Ils se quittent vers sept heures.

Pendant les semaines qui **suivent,** André et Rosalie passent beaucoup de temps ensemble. Ils **se souviennent de** leur **jeunesse** *(f)* ensemble. C'est **le grand amour**!

Ils se retrouvent en ville chaque après-midi.

Quelquefois, ils se disputent.

Mais **la plupart du temps, ils s'entendent** bien.

Enfin, André et Rosalie **prennent une décision.** Ils vont se marier et vont **s'installer à** Quimper. Ils vont être très **heureux.**

🔊 7-3

Un soir, Rosalie parle à sa petite-fille Rose de sa relation avec André.

ROSE:	Alors, **mamie,** tu as passé une bonne journée?
ROSALIE:	Oui. André et moi, nous sommes allés visiter les mégalithes de Carnac.
ROSE:	Alors, vous vous entendez bien?
ROSALIE:	Très bien. Nous nous retrouvons tous les jours, nous passons des heures ensemble et nous parlons de tout.
ROSE:	**Formidable!** Moi, je **rêve d'une telle** relation.
ROSALIE:	Et ton copain et toi, ça va?
ROSE:	Pas très bien. On ne s'entend pas très bien. On se dispute souvent.
ROSALIE:	**C'est dommage!**

---

se rencontrer *to meet each other* (by chance), *to run into each other*   **ce qui** *what*   **se passer** *to happen*   **le coup de foudre** *love at first sight*   **suivent (suivre** *to follow)*   **se souvenir de** *to remember*   **la jeunesse** *youth*   **le grand amour** *true love*   **la plupart du temps** *most of the time*   **s'entendre** *to get along*   **Enfin** *Finally*   **prendre une décision** *to make a decision*   **s'installer (à / dans)** *to settle (in), to move (into)*   **heureux (heureuse)** *happy*   **mamie** *grandma*   **Formidable!** *Great!*   **rêver (de)** *to dream (of, about)*   **un(e) tel(le)** *such a*   **C'est dommage!** *That's too bad!*

A **Test.** Faites ce test pour savoir si vous êtes romantique.

Êtes-vous romantique?

I. Indiquez vos opinions sur ces sujets.

1 Pensez-vous que le grand amour...
- **a.** arrive une fois dans la vie?
- **b.** n'existe pas?
- **c.** est sans importance?

2 Pensez-vous qu'un couple peut s'aimer pour toujours?
- **a.** Certainement.
- **b.** Je ne sais pas, on peut essayer.
- **c.** Probablement pas: la vie est trop longue.

3 Au restaurant, **vous voyez** des amoureux qui se regardent dans les yeux pendant tout le dîner. Vous trouvez ça...
- **a.** assez charmant.
- **b.** ridicule.
- **c.** adorable.

II. Comment êtes-vous en couple?

1 Vous vous rencontrez **par hasard** et c'est le coup de foudre. Que pensez-vous?
- **a.** C'est juste **une attirance** physique.
- **b.** C'est peut-être l'amour.
- **c.** **Attention!**

2 Vous vous disputez. Quelle est la meilleure manière de vous réconcilier?
- **a.** Nous devons nous embrasser.
- **b.** Nous devons essayer de parler calmement du problème.
- **c.** Nous devons nous quitter pendant un certain temps.

3 Vous vous adorez. Vous voulez...
- **a.** essayer de vous voir tous les jours.
- **b.** vous téléphoner tous les jours et vous voir trois ou quatre fois par semaine.
- **c.** vous retrouver le week-end, si vous n'avez pas d'autres projets.

SCORE: **Partie I.** 1. a–2 points 2. a–2 points, b–1 point 3. c–2 points, a–1 point
   Partie II. 1. b–2 points, a–1 point 2. a–2 points, b–1 point 3. a–2 points, b–1 point

- Si vous avez entre 10 et 12 points, vous êtes une personne très (peut-être même un peu trop?) romantique. Attention! **Ne perdez pas votre temps** à attendre un amour parfait. Essayez d'être un peu plus réaliste, quand même.
- Si vous avez entre 6 et 9 points, vous êtes romantique, mais vous n'exagérez pas. Vous êtes prêt(e) à aimer quand le bon moment arrivera, mais vous ne perdez pas votre temps à chercher l'amour idéal partout.
- Si vous avez entre 0 et 5 points, vous êtes réaliste, cynique même! Ne voulez-vous pas mettre un peu plus de poésie dans votre vie?

B **En couple.** Est-ce qu'on fait ces choses **dans un couple heureux** ou **dans un couple malheureux** (unhappy)?

EXEMPLE On se dispute rarement.
On se dispute rarement **dans un couple heureux.**

1. On se dispute tout le temps.
2. On se parle de tout.
3. On ne s'entend pas bien du tout.
4. On s'amuse ensemble.
5. On s'ennuie ensemble.
6. On s'embrasse tout le temps.

À VOUS!

Avec un(e) partenaire, relisez à haute voix la conversation entre Rose et Rosalie. Ensuite, adaptez la conversation pour parler de votre relation avec votre mari, votre femme, votre copain, votre copine, votre meilleur(e) ami(e) ou votre colocataire.

You can access the audio of the active vocabulary of this **Compétence** online.

---

vous voyez you see   **par hasard** by chance   **une attirance** an attraction   **Attention!** Watch out!   **Ne perdez pas votre temps** Don't waste your time

SAYING WHAT PEOPLE DO FOR EACH OTHER

✔ *Pour vérifier*

1. When do you use a reciprocal verb?

2. What verbs can be made into reciprocal verbs? How would you say *to look at each other* or *to listen to each other*?

3. When a reflexive or reciprocal verb is used in the infinitive, does the reflexive pronoun change with the subject? How would you say *I am going to get up at 7:00? I am not going to get up at 6:00?*

Note *de grammaire*

Note that although the verbs **se fiancer** and **se marier** are reflexive, **divorcer** is not.

Les verbes réciproques au présent et les verbes réfléchis et réciproques au futur immédiat

1. You have seen that reflexive verbs are used when someone is doing something to or for himself/herself. You use similar verbs to describe reciprocal actions; that is, to indicate that people are doing something to or for each other. Here are some reflexive and reciprocal verbs commonly used to describe relationships:

s'aimer	*to like each other, to love each other*
se détester	*to hate each other*
se disputer	*to argue*
s'embrasser	*to kiss each other, to embrace each other*
s'entendre (bien / mal)	*to get along (well / badly) with each other*
se fiancer	*to get engaged*
se marier	*to get married*
se quitter	*to leave each other*
se réconcilier	*to make up*
se regarder	*to look at each other*
se rencontrer	*to meet* (for the first time), *to run into each other* (by chance)
se retrouver	*to meet* (by design)
se téléphoner	*to telephone each other*

2. The verb **s'entendre** *(to get along)* is a regular **-re** verb. You will learn how to conjugate other **-re** verbs in the next section on page 286. The forms of **s'entendre** are:

S'ENTENDRE *(to get along)*	
je m'entends	nous nous entendons
tu t'entends	vous vous entendez
il/elle/on s'entend	ils/elles s'entendent

3. Most verbs indicating actions done to other people can be used reciprocally.

retrouver quelqu'un *(to meet someone)*	Je retrouve **Jim** au café.
se retrouver *(to meet each other)*	Nous **nous** retrouvons souvent au café.

4. As with other verbs, use **aller** + an infinitive to form the immediate future of reflexive and reciprocal verbs. When reflexive or reciprocal verbs are used in the infinitive, the pronoun is placed before the infinitive, and it matches the subject. In the negative, place **ne** after the subject and **pas, jamais,** or **rien** after the first verb.

SE LEVER *(to get up)*	
je vais me lever	nous allons nous lever
tu vas te lever	vous allez vous lever
il/elle/on va se lever	ils/elles vont se lever

Je ne vais pas **me** lever tôt.   **Nous** aimons **nous** retrouver au café.

Sélection musicale. Search for the songs **"C'est quoi, c'est l'habitude"** by Isabelle Boulay and **"Ils s'aiment"** by the Lost Fingers online to hear musical selections related to this vocabulary and structure.

A Une histoire d'amour.
Isabelle, la cousine de Rose, rencontre Luc et ils tombent amoureux. Qu'est-ce qui se passe?

> se regarder se rencontrer au parc se marier
> s'embrasser s'installer dans une maison se fiancer
> se réconcilier se disputer

EXEMPLE

Ils se rencontrent au parc.

1.

2.

3.

4.

5.

6.

7.

B Questions.
Un(e) ami(e) veut en savoir plus *(to know more)* sur Isabelle et Luc. Avec un(e) partenaire, posez ses questions et imaginez les réponses qu'Isabelle lui donne.

EXEMPLE s'aimer beaucoup
> —**Est-ce que vous vous aimez beaucoup?**
> —**Oui, nous nous aimons beaucoup.**
> **Oui, on s'aime beaucoup.**

1. se téléphoner tous les jours
2. se disputer souvent
3. se réconcilier facilement
4. s'entendre mal quelquefois
5. s'envoyer des textos plusieurs *(several)* fois par jour

C Isabelle et Luc.
Tout va très bien entre Isabelle et Luc. Ils se retrouvent en ville tous les jours. Est-ce qu'ils vont faire les choses suivantes demain?

EXEMPLE se disputer
> **Non, ils ne vont pas se disputer.**

1. se téléphoner
2. se retrouver en ville
3. se parler de tout
4. bien s'entendre
5. s'ennuyer ensemble
6. s'embrasser

D **Et demain chez Rose.** Dites ce que Rose va faire demain d'après les illustrations.

EXEMPLE

... vers neuf heures.

Elle va se réveiller vers neuf heures.

1. ... tout de suite.

2. ... la figure et les mains.

3. ... les cheveux.

4. ... avant de manger.

5. ... vers deux heures du matin.

E **Ce week-end.** Dites si ces personnes vont probablement faire ces choses ce week-end.

EXEMPLE Moi, je... (se lever tôt)

Moi, je vais me lever tôt. / Moi, je ne vais pas me lever tôt.

1. Samedi matin, moi, je...
se réveiller tard
se lever tout de suite
rester au lit quelques minutes

2. Samedi matin, mon meilleur ami (ma meilleure amie)...
se réveiller tôt
se lever facilement
prendre son petit déjeuner avec moi

3. Ce week-end, cet(te) ami(e) et moi, nous...
se retrouver en ville
s'amuser
s'ennuyer
s'entendre bien

F **Partons en week-end.** Vous allez partir avec un groupe d'amis ce week-end. Travaillez avec un petit groupe d'étudiants et faites des projets. Ensuite, dites à la classe ce que vous allez faire. Dites:

- si vous allez à la campagne, à la montagne ou à la plage
- à quelle heure vous allez partir
- comment vous allez voyager
- si vous allez faire du camping, descendre à l'hôtel ou rester chez des parents / amis
- si vous allez vous lever tôt ou tard tous les jours
- ce que vous allez faire pendant la journée pour vous amuser
- quand vous allez vous reposer
- ce que vous allez faire le soir
- à quelle heure vous allez vous coucher

EXEMPLE On va aller à la plage. On va partir vers 8h.

G **Beaucoup de questions!** Circulez parmi les étudiants et posez les questions suivantes pour trouver quelqu'un qui fait la même chose que vous. Après, dites à la classe ce que vous avez en commun avec d'autres étudiants.

**EXEMPLE —Eva, à quelle heure est-ce que tu te réveilles en semaine?
—Je me réveille vers 8h.**

Après, à la classe:

Eva et moi, nous nous réveillons vers 8h. / Eva et moi, on se réveille vers 8h.

À quelle heure est-ce que tu te réveilles en semaine?	À quelle heure est-ce que tu vas te réveiller demain?	Est-ce que tu préfères te lever tôt ou tard?
Après les cours, est-ce que tu préfères te reposer ou t'amuser avec des amis?	Est-ce que tu vas te reposer aujourd'hui après les cours?	À quelle heure est-ce que tu vas te coucher ce soir?

H **Entretien.** Posez ces questions à votre partenaire au sujet de ses relations avec son meilleur ami (sa meilleure amie).

1. Est-ce que vous vous parlez tous les jours? Est-ce que vous préférez vous téléphoner ou vous envoyer des textos?

2. Combien de fois par semaine est-ce que vous vous retrouvez? Où aimez-vous vous retrouver?

3. Qu'est-ce que vous faites ensemble pour vous amuser? Est-ce que vous vous ennuyez quelquefois ensemble?

4. Est-ce que vous vous entendez toujours bien? Est-ce que vous vous disputez de temps en temps?

TALKING ABOUT ACTIVITIES

✔ **Pour vérifier**

1. What ending do you add for each subject pronoun after dropping the **-re** from the infinitive of these verbs? What is the conjugation of **perdre**?

2. Which **-re** verbs are conjugated with **être** in the **passé composé**?

Note *de vocabulaire*

1. Use **rendre visite à** or **aller voir** to say that you visit a person, but use **visiter** to say that you visit a place.

Je visite Tulsa.

Je rends visite à ma sœur.

Je vais voir ma sœur.

2. Note this information about prepositions.

- Do *not* use **pour** after **attendre** to say *for* whom or what you are waiting.
  J'attends des amis.
  I'm waiting for friends.

- Use **à** after **rendre visite** to say whom you are visiting.
  Je rends visite à ma famille.

- Use **à** after **répondre** to say whom or what you are answering.
  Je réponds **au** prof / **à la** question / **au** téléphone.

- Use **de** after **descendre** to say what you get off *of*, down *from*, or out *of*.
  Je descends **du** train à Rennes.

Les verbes en -re

1. Many verbs that end in **-re** follow a regular pattern of conjugation.

ATTENDRE (to wait for)	
j'attend**s**	nous attend**ons**
tu attend**s**	vous attend**ez**
il/elle/on attend	ils/elles attend**ent**

PASSÉ COMPOSÉ: **j'ai attendu**   IMPARFAIT: **j'attendais**

2. The following are some common **-re** verbs. Notice the difference in meaning between the reflexive and non-reflexive forms of **perdre** *(to lose)* / **se perdre** *(to get lost)* and **entendre** *(to hear)* / **s'entendre** *(to get along)*.

attendre	*to wait (for)*
descendre (de) (à)	*to go down, to get off (of), to stay (at)*
entendre	*to hear*
s'entendre (bien / mal) avec	*to get along (well / badly) with*
perdre	*to lose, to waste*
se perdre	*to get lost*
rendre quelque chose à quelqu'un	*to return something to someone, to turn in something to someone*
rendre visite à quelqu'un	*to visit someone*
répondre (à)	*to answer, to respond (to)*
vendre / revendre	*to sell / to sell back, to resell*

3. In the **passé composé, descendre** and the reflexive verbs are conjugated with **être** as the auxiliary verb. The other verbs in this list are all conjugated with **avoir.**

J'ai rendu visite à une amie à Paris.   Je suis descendu(e) à l'hôtel Étoile.

PRONONCIATION

Les verbes en -re 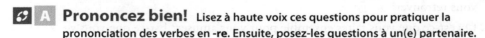 7-4

The endings of the singular forms of **-re** verbs are silent, as is the consonant that precedes them. In the plural forms, this consonant is pronounced, and you hear a difference between the **il/elle** singular and **ils/elles** plural forms.

je ren~~ds~~   tu ren~~ds~~   il/elle/on ren~~d~~   nous ren**d**ons   vous ren**d**ez   ils/elles ren**d**ent

Sélection musicale. Search for the song **"J'attends l'amour"** by Jenifer online to enjoy a musical selection related to this vocabulary.

🔁 **A** **Prononcez bien!** Lisez à haute voix ces questions pour pratiquer la prononciation des verbes en **-re**. Ensuite, posez-les questions à un(e) partenaire.

1. Est-ce que le/la prof attend l'arrivée de tous les étudiants avant de commencer le cours? / Est-ce que les étudiants attendent le/la prof s'il / si elle arrive en retard *(late)*?

2. Est-ce qu'on entend bien dans cette salle de cours? / Est-ce que les étudiants entendent bien le professeur?

3. Le/La prof s'entend bien avec les étudiants? / Les étudiants s'entendent bien?

4. Le/La prof répond toujours aux questions des étudiants? / Les étudiants répondent bien aux questions du/de la prof?

B **La routine de Rose.** En vous servant des illustrations et des phrases proposées, décrivez la routine de Rose quand elle est à Atlanta.

EXEMPLE Rose: attendre le bus le matin / aller en cours à pied
Rose attend le bus le matin. Elle ne va pas en cours à pied.

1.  **2.**  **3.**  **4.**

1. Rose: perdre patience quand le bus est en retard *(late)* / attendre patiemment
2. Rose: perdre son temps dans le bus / préférer lire
3. Rose: descendre chez un ami / descendre à l'université
4. Rose: s'entendre bien avec ses profs / s'entendre mal avec ses profs

5.  **6.**  **7.**  **8.**

5. Les étudiants: travailler bien en cours / perdre leur temps
6. Les étudiants: perdre leurs devoirs / rendre leurs devoirs au professeur
7. Après les cours, Rose: rentrer chez elle / rendre visite à son ami Daniel
8. Rose et son ami: s'entendre mal / s'entendre bien

C **Et toi?** Choisissez le verbe logique et complétez les questions. Ensuite, posez les questions à votre partenaire. Utilisez le présent ou le passé composé comme indiqué.

AU PRÉSENT

1. Tu _____ souvent visite à tes parents? (rendre, entendre) Ta famille et toi, vous _____ bien la plupart du temps? (perdre, s'entendre) Est-ce que tu _____ souvent patience avec tes parents? (perdre, répondre) Est-ce qu'ils _____ souvent patience avec toi? (perdre, répondre)
2. Tu _____ tes prochaines vacances avec impatience? (attendre, entendre) Tu _____ facilement quand tu es dans une autre ville? (se perdre, vendre) Quand tu voyages avec des amis, vous _____ quelquefois dans un hôtel de luxe? (vendre, descendre)

AU PASSÉ COMPOSÉ

3. Tu _____ visite à tes parents récemment? (revendre, rendre) La dernière fois que tu as vu tes parents, est-ce qu'ils _____ patience avec toi? (perdre, vendre)
4. La dernière fois que vous êtes partis en week-end ensemble, est-ce que vous _____ à l'hôtel? (descendre, entendre)

Talking about what you did and used to do

LES ACTIVITÉS D'HIER

Rose parle de ce qu'elle a fait hier.

Le réveil a sonné et je me suis réveillée.

Je me suis levée.

J'ai pris un bain.

Je me suis brossé les dents.

Je me suis peignée.

Je me suis habillée.

J'ai passé le reste de la journée avec ma cousine et son nouvel ami.

Nous nous sommes promenés.

Nous nous sommes arrêtés au restaurant pour manger.

Nous nous sommes bien amusés.

Nous nous sommes quittés vers 10 heures et je me suis couchée vers 11 heures.

Le réveil *The alarm clock*   **sonner** *to ring*   **se promener** *to go for a walk*   **s'arrêter** *to stop*

🔊 7-5 Rose parle à sa cousine, Isabelle, qui **raconte** comment elle a rencontré son ami, Luc.

ROSE: Alors, Luc et toi, vous vous êtes rencontrés où?

ISABELLE: J'étais au parc et Luc était à côté de moi. On s'est vus et on s'est parlé un peu. Quelques jours plus tard, il était dans une librairie où j'achetais un livre et **on s'est reconnus.** Il m'a demandé si je voulais aller prendre un verre et j'ai accepté son invitation. On a passé le reste de la journée ensemble.

ROSE: Vous vous êtes bien entendus, **donc**?

ISABELLE: **Parfaitement** bien. On s'est très bien amusés et on s'est retrouvés le lendemain pour aller au cinéma. Depuis, on s'est téléphoné ou on s'est vus presque tous les jours.

A Récemment. Quand avez-vous fait ces choses?

ce matin	hier soir	il y a deux semaines
cet après-midi	hier matin	il y a un mois
???	lundi dernier	il y a longtemps

1. Le réveil a sonné et je me suis levé(e) tout de suite...

2. J'ai pris un bain / une douche...

3. Je me suis brossé les cheveux / Je me suis peigné(e)...

4. Mes amis et moi, nous nous sommes bien amusés ensemble...

5. Nous nous sommes promenés en ville...

6. Je me suis arrêté(e) dans un fast-food pour manger...

7. Je me suis couché(e) après minuit...

B Ils se sont retrouvés. Décrivez la première fois que Rosalie et André se sont revus après toutes ces années en mettant ces phrases dans l'ordre logique.

_____ Ils se sont embrassés.

___1___ André et Rosalie se sont vus.

_____ Ils se sont quittés.

_____ Ils se sont reconnus.

_____ Ils se sont parlé pendant plusieurs heures et ils se sont souvenus du passé.

♻ À VOUS!

Avec un(e) partenaire, relisez à haute voix la conversation entre Rose et Isabelle. Ensuite, parlez avec votre partenaire de comment vous avez rencontré votre meilleur(e) ami(e) ou votre copain (copine).

You can access the audio of the active vocabulary of this ***Compétence*** online.

---

raconter *to tell* **on s'est reconnus (passé composé** of **se reconnaître** *to recognize each other***) donc** *then, thus, so*
Parfaitement *Perfectly*

SAYING WHAT PEOPLE DID

Les verbes réfléchis et réciproques au passé composé

✔ *Pour vérifier*

1. Do you use **être** or **avoir** as the auxiliary verb with reflexive and reciprocal verbs in the **passé composé**?

2. Where are reflexive pronouns placed with respect to the auxiliary verb? How do you conjugate **s'amuser** in the **passé composé**?

3. Where do you place **ne... pas** in the negative? How do you say *I didn't wake up early*?

4. When does the past participle agree with the reflexive pronoun and subject? When does it not agree? What are four verbs that you know that do not have agreement?

1. All reflexive and reciprocal verbs have **être** as the auxiliary verb in the **passé composé.** Always place the reflexive pronoun directly before the auxiliary verb.

SE LEVER	
je me suis levé(e)	nous nous sommes levé(e)s
tu t'es levé(e)	vous vous êtes levé(e)(s)
il s'est levé	ils se sont levés
elle s'est levée	elles se sont levées
on s'est levé(e)(s)	

2. To negate a reflexive or reciprocal verb in the **passé composé,** place **ne** directly after the subject and **pas** or **jamais** directly after the conjugated form of **être.**

Je me suis réveillé(e) tôt mais je **ne** me suis **pas** levé(e) tout de suite.

3. In the **passé composé,** the past participle agrees in gender and number with the reflexive pronoun (and the subject) when it is the direct object of the verb.

Rosalie **s**'est lev**ée** tôt.   André et Rosalie **se** sont marié**s.**

In this chapter, make the past participle agree except in these cases:

Note *de grammaire*

1. Remember that the past participles of regular **-er** verbs end in **-é (je me suis ennuyé[e]),** those of regular **-ir** verbs end in **-i (je me suis endormi[e]),** and those of regular **-re** verbs end in **-u (nous nous sommes entendu[e]s).**

2. The past participle of **écrire** is **écrit.**

3. When **on** means *we,* its verb may either be left in the masculine singular form **(on s'est levé)** or it may agree **(on s'est levé[e][s]).** Either form is considered correct.

- There is no agreement when a reflexive verb is followed by a noun that is the direct object of the verb. Past participles of verbs like **se laver, se maquiller,** or **se brosser** do not agree with the subject when they are followed by the name of a part of the body.

  Rose et Rosalie se sont lav**ées.**   BUT   Rose et Rosalie se sont lavé **les mains.**
  Rose s'est maquill**ée.**   Rose s'est maquillé **les yeux.**

- With the verbs **se parler, se téléphoner, s'envoyer (des textos),** and **s'écrire** *(to write to each other),* there is no agreement because the reflexive pronoun is an *indirect* object, not a *direct* object.

  Ils se sont parlé.   Nous nous sommes téléphoné.   Ils se sont écrit.

Sélection musicale. To enjoy a musical selection illustrating the use of this structure, search online for the song **"Une belle histoire"** by Michel Fugain, which has been sung by numerous artists, including Charles Benevuto.

A **Hier chez Henri et Patricia.** Voilà ce que Patricia, la cousine de Rose, a fait hier. Qu'est-ce qu'elle a fait?

EXEMPLE Patricia **s'est réveillée à six heures.**

EXEMPLE Patricia...   **1.** Elle...   **2.** Son mari Henri et elle...

3. Ils... **4.** Patricia... **5.** Patricia et Henri...

B Qu'est-ce qu'ils ont fait? Travaillez avec un groupe d'étudiants pour créer autant de *(create as many)* questions que possible au sujet de ce que Patricia et Henri ont fait hier. Basez vos questions sur les illustrations dans *A. Hier chez Henri et Patricia.* Chaque groupe gagne 1 point pour chaque question bien formée et 1 point chaque fois que les étudiants du groupe répondent correctement à la question d'un autre groupe.

EXEMPLE À quelle heure est-ce que Patricia s'est réveillée?

C Et toi? Demandez à votre partenaire s'il/si elle a fait les choses suivantes hier.

EXEMPLE se lever tôt
—**Tu t'es levé(e) tôt hier?**
—**Oui, je me suis levé(e) tôt hier.**
Non, je ne me suis pas levé(e) tôt hier.

1. se réveiller tôt **5.** se reposer
2. se lever tout de suite **6.** s'ennuyer
3. prendre un bain ou une douche **7.** s'amuser
4. passer la soirée à la maison **8.** se coucher tard

D Je veux tout savoir. Utilisez les verbes suivants pour poser des questions à votre partenaire sur ses interactions avec son meilleur ami (sa meilleure amie) cette semaine.

EXEMPLE se téléphoner
—**Est-ce que vous vous êtes téléphoné cette semaine?**
—**Oui, on s'est téléphoné hier.**
Non, on ne s'est pas téléphoné cette semaine.

se retrouver en ville	se disputer
se promener au parc	s'envoyer des textos
beaucoup se voir	s'amuser ensemble

E Entretien. Posez ces questions à votre partenaire.

1. À quelle heure est-ce que tu t'es couché(e) hier soir? Tu as bien dormi? Tu as dormi jusqu'à quelle heure ce matin? Tu t'es levé(e) facilement?

2. Avec qui est-ce que tu es sorti(e) récemment? Où est-ce que vous vous êtes retrouvé(e)s? Qu'est-ce que vous avez fait? Vous vous êtes bien amusé(e)s?

SAYING WHAT PEOPLE DID AND USED TO DO

✔ *Pour vérifier*

1. How do you form the **imparfait** of all verbs except **être**? What is the **imparfait** of **je m'amuse**? of **je ne m'amuse pas**?

2. Do you use the **imparfait** or the **passé composé** to say what happened on a specific occasion? to say how things used to be?

Note *de grammaire*

Before doing the exercises in this section, review the specific uses of the **passé composé** and the **imparfait** on page 263.

Les verbes réfléchis et réciproques à l'imparfait et reprise de l'usage du passé composé et de l'imparfait

1. As with all other verbs (except **être**), the **imparfait** of reflexive verbs is formed by dropping the **-ons** from the present tense **nous** form and adding the endings shown.

SE LEVER	NE PAS SE LEVER
je me lev**ais**	je ne me lev**ais** pas
tu te lev**ais**	tu ne te lev**ais** pas
il/elle/on se lev**ait**	il/elle/on ne se lev**ait** pas
nous nous lev**ions**	nous ne nous lev**ions** pas
vous vous lev**iez**	vous ne vous lev**iez** pas
ils/elles se lev**aient**	ils/elles ne se lev**aient** pas

2. Remember to use the **imparfait** to tell *what things were like in general* or *what was going on when something else happened* and the **passé composé** to tell *what happened on specific occasions* or to recount *a sequence of events.*

Ce matin, **je me suis levé(e)** à 6h.

Quand j'étais au lycée, **je me levais** à 7h.

A **À 16 ans.** Parlez de votre routine quotidienne à l'âge de 16 ans.

> **EXEMPLE** se réveiller souvent tôt
> **À l'âge de 16 ans, je me réveillais souvent tôt.**
> **Je ne me réveillais pas souvent tôt.**

1. se réveiller souvent avant 6h

2. se lever facilement

3. prendre un bain / une douche le matin

4. se laver les cheveux tous les jours

5. prendre toujours le petit déjeuner

6. aller toujours en cours

7. sécher mes cours *(to cut class)* quelquefois

8. s'ennuyer quelquefois en cours

© Robert Fried/Alamy Stock Photo

B **Et hier?** Utilisez les verbes de l'exercice précédent pour parler de ce que vous avez fait hier.

> **EXEMPLE** se réveiller tôt
> **Hier, je me suis réveillé(e) tôt.**
> **Hier, je ne me suis pas réveillé(e) tôt.**

C Alors? Rosalie parle de ce qui s'est passé hier. Complétez ses phrases logiquement en mettant les verbes donnés au passé composé ou à l'imparfait.

EXEMPLE Hier matin, j' _____ (être) fatiguée, alors je _____ (rester) au lit.
Hier matin, j'**étais** fatiguée, alors je **suis restée** au lit.

1. Je (J') _____ (vouloir) préparer le petit déjeuner, alors je _____ (se laver) les mains.
2. Vers midi, André et moi, nous _____ (avoir) faim, alors on _____ (se préparer) des sandwichs.
3. Nous _____ (boire) deux bouteilles d'eau minérale aussi parce que nous _____ (avoir) très soif.
4. Après, André _____ (se coucher) une demi-heure parce qu'il _____ (être) fatigué.
5. Il _____ (se lever) vers trois heures parce qu'il _____ (vouloir) travailler un peu dans le jardin.
6. Il _____ (faire) très beau, alors nous _____ (se promener) dans le quartier.
7. Quand nous _____ (rentrer), Rose et ses copains _____ (être) à la maison.
8. Nous _____ (se quitter) assez tôt parce que nous _____ (vouloir) nous lever tôt le lendemain pour aller à Carnac.

D Le mariage d'André et de Rosalie. André et Rosalie se sont enfin mariés. Décrivez le jour de leur mariage en mettant les verbes donnés au passé composé ou à l'imparfait.

Le jour de son mariage, Rosalie __1__ (se lever) tôt. André __2__ (arriver) vers 9h mais, tout de suite après, il __3__ (se souvenir) d'une course qu'il __4__ (devoir) faire et il __5__ (repartir). Il __6__ (aller) acheter une nouvelle cravate.

Il __7__ (être) 3h quand André __8__ (revenir). La cérémonie __9__ (commencer) à 4h. Tous les invités *(guests)* __10__ (être) dans le jardin. Il __11__ (faire) beau et Rosalie et André __12__ (être) contents. Rosalie __13__ (porter) une jolie robe beige et André __14__ (porter) un costume noir. Rosalie __15__ (être) très jolie! Après la cérémonie, les amis __16__ (rester) et ils __17__ (manger) du gâteau *(cake)*. Ils __18__ (s'amuser) bien quand tout d'un coup il __19__ (commencer) à pleuvoir, alors ils __20__ (rentrer) dans la maison.

André __21__ (partir) et il __22__ (revenir) avec assez de chaises pour tout le monde. Vers 8h, les invités __23__ (partir). André et Rosalie __24__ (se regarder) et ils __25__ (commencer) à sourire *(to smile)*. Ils __26__ (être) fatigués mais très, très heureux.

E Entretien. Interviewez votre partenaire.

1. Est-ce que tu te réveillais facilement quand tu étais ado *(teenager)*? À quelle heure est-ce que tu te réveillais pour aller au lycée? Tu prenais l'autocar *(schoolbus)*, une voiture ou tu y allais à pied? Tu y arrivais souvent en retard *(late)*?
2. Quand tu étais lycéen(ne), tu t'ennuyais ou tu t'amusais la plupart du temps *(most of the time)*? Qu'est-ce que tu faisais pour t'amuser le week-end? Comment s'appelait ton meilleur ami (ta meilleure amie)? Qu'est-ce que vous aimiez faire ensemble?
3. À quelle heure est-ce que tu t'es réveillé(e) ce matin? Tu t'es levé(e) tout de suite? Qu'est-ce que tu as fait ensuite?
4. La dernière fois que tu es sorti(e) avec des amis, est-ce que tu t'es bien amusé(e) ou est-ce que tu t'es un peu ennuyé(e)? Qu'est-ce que vous avez fait ensemble?

Describing traits and characteristics

LES TRAITS DE CARACTÈRE

Sélection musicale. Search for the song **"À nos actes manqués"** by M. Pokora online to enjoy a musical selection related to this vocabulary.

Vocabulaire sans peine!

English words ending in *-ance*, *-ence*, or *-ion* often have corresponding cognates in French. Such nouns are often feminine.

-ance = **-ance**
arrogance = **l'arrogance**
-ence = **-ence**
indifference = **l'indifférence**
-ion = **-ion**
comprehension = **la compréhension**

How would you say these words in French?

ignorance
indulgence
assertion

Rencontres en ligne: Test de compatibilité

Rangez chaque groupe de réponses de 1 (la réponse qui **exprime** le mieux vos sentiments) à 4 (la réponse qui exprime le moins bien vos sentiments).

Je préfère partager la vie avec quelqu'un qui **s'intéresse...**

1 2 3 4   à l'art
1 2 3 4   au sport
1 2 3 4   à la politique
1 2 3 4   à la nature

Je préfère quelqu'un qui **cultive...**

1 2 3 4   sa spiritualité
1 2 3 4   son **corps**
1 2 3 4   son **esprit** *(m)*
1 2 3 4   sa vie professionnelle

Le trait de caractère que j'apprécie le plus chez un(e) partenaire, c'est...

1 2 3 4   un bon sens de l'humour
1 2 3 4   la passion
1 2 3 4   la beauté
1 2 3 4   **la tendresse**

Un **défaut** que je ne **supporte** pas chez une autre personne, c'est...

1 2 3 4   l'indécision *(f)*
1 2 3 4   l'inflexibilité *(f)*
1 2 3 4   **l'insensibilité** *(f)*
1 2 3 4   la vanité, l'arrogance *(f)*

Ce que je supporte le moins dans une relation, c'est...

1 2 3 4   la jalousie
1 2 3 4   l'indifférence *(f)*
1 2 3 4   l'infidélité *(f)*
1 2 3 4   la violence

Chez un(e) partenaire, ce qui a le moins d'importance pour moi, c'est...

1 2 3 4   son argent
1 2 3 4   sa profession
1 2 3 4   sa religion
1 2 3 4   son **aspect** *(m)* **physique**

---

ranger *to arrange, to order*   **exprimer** *to express*   **s'intéresser à** *to be interested in*   **cultiver** *to cultivate*   **le corps** *the body*   **l'esprit** *the mind, the spirit*   **la tendresse** *tenderness, softness, affection*   **un défaut** *a fault*   **supporter** *to bear, to tolerate, to put up with*   **l'insensibilité** *insensitivity*   **l'aspect physique** *physical appearance*

Rose parle à sa cousine, Isabelle, de son copain, Luc.

ROSE: Alors, tu as trouvé **le bonheur** avec ton nouvel ami, Luc? Il est comment?

ISABELLE: Il a un bon sens de l'humour et il est sympa. Son seul défaut, c'est qu'il est un peu **jaloux** si je ne passe pas tout mon temps avec lui.

ROSE: Vous vous intéressez aux mêmes choses?

ISABELLE: Oui et non. On aime plus ou moins la même musique et les mêmes films et il s'intéresse à la politique comme moi, mais il est **de droite** et moi, tu sais, je suis plutôt **de gauche.**

A **Et vous?** Changez les mots en italique pour parler de vous.

1. J'ai beaucoup d'amis qui s'intéressent *au sport / à la nature / à la politique...*
2. Je ne m'intéresse pas du tout *à la politique / au sport / à l'art...*
3. Je préfère cultiver *mon esprit / mon corps et mon aspect physique / ma spiritualité...*
4. Chez un(e) partenaire, ce qui a le plus d'importance pour moi, c'est *sa beauté / son intelligence / sa religion...*
5. Chez un(e) partenaire, je ne supporte pas *la vanité / l'indécision / l'inflexibilité...*
6. Dans une relation, je ne supporterai jamais *(will never tolerate) la jalousie / la violence / l'infidélité...*

B **Entretien.** Interviewez votre partenaire.

1. Tu t'intéresses au sport? à l'art? au cinéma? à la politique? à la philosophie? Est-ce que tu t'ennuies si quelqu'un parle de ces choses-là?
2. Tu passes plus de temps à cultiver ton corps, ton esprit, ta spiritualité ou ta vie professionnelle? Qu'est-ce que tu fais pour le (la) cultiver?

C **Test de compatibilité.** Travaillez en groupes pour écrire deux questions pour un nouveau test de compatibilité. Ensuite, utilisez les questions de tous les groupes pour créer *(to create)* le nouveau test.

EXEMPLE **Quelle activité aimez-vous le moins faire avec une autre personne?**

1 2 3 4   **faire la cuisine**
1 2 3 4   **faire de l'exercice**
1 2 3 4   **faire du shopping**
1 2 3 4   **voyager**

À VOUS!

Avec un(e) partenaire, relisez à haute voix la conversation entre Rose et Isabelle. Ensuite, adaptez la conversation pour parler d'un(e) ami(e), de votre copain (copine) ou de votre mari ou femme. Commencez la conversation en disant: **Alors, tu passes beaucoup de temps avec...** (au lieu de dire *[instead of saying]*: **Alors, tu as trouvé le bonheur avec...**).

You can access the audio of the active vocabulary of this *Compétence* online.

---

le bonheur *happiness*   **jaloux (jalouse)** *jealous*   **de droite** *conservative*   **de gauche** *liberal*

Les pronoms relatifs **qui, que** et **dont**

1. A relative clause gives more information about a person or object you are talking about in a sentence. A relative clause begins with a relative pronoun, a word like *who, that,* or *which* that refers back to the noun being described.

Je sors avec une femme
$\begin{cases} \textbf{qui} \text{ est beaucoup plus âgée que moi.} \\ \textbf{que} \text{ j'ai rencontrée pendant mes vacances.} \\ \textbf{dont} \text{ je suis amoureux.} \end{cases}$

I'm going out with a woman
$\begin{cases} \textbf{\textit{who}} \textit{ is a lot older than I am.} \\ \textbf{\textit{whom}} \textit{ I met during my vacation.} \\ \textbf{\textit{with whom}} \textit{ I'm in love.} \end{cases}$

2. The relative pronouns **qui, que,** and **dont** are all used for both people and things. The choice depends on how the pronoun functions in the relative clause.

3. Note how relative pronouns are used to combine two sentences talking about the same thing. The relative clause is placed immediately after the noun it describes.

- Use **qui** for both people or things when they are the *subject* of the relative clause. Since **qui** is the subject, it is followed by a verb and it can mean *that, which,* or *who.* Note that **qui** does not make elision before a vowel sound.

  Comment s'appelle ton ami? **Ton ami** habite à New York.
  Comment s'appelle ton ami **qui** habite à New York?

- Use **que (qu')** for people or things when they are the *direct object* in the relative clause. **Que (qu')** can mean *that, which,* or *whom,* or the relative pronoun may be omitted in English. Note that the pronoun **que** makes elision **(qu')** before a vowel sound.

  Comment s'appelle ton ami? Tu as invité **cet ami** hier.
  Comment s'appelle ton ami **que** tu as invité hier?

  Since past participles agree with preceding direct objects, they will agree with the noun that **que** represents.

  Je sors avec une femme **que** j'ai rencontré**e** pendant mes vacances.

- Use **dont** to replace the preposition **de** + *a person or thing* in relative clauses with verbs such as the following. It can mean *whom, of (about, with) whom, whose, that,* or *of (about, with) which.*

avoir besoin de	se souvenir de
avoir envie de	parler de
avoir peur de	rêver de
être amoureux (amoureuse) de	tomber amoureux (amoureuse) de
être jaloux (jalouse) de	faire la connaissance de (*to make the acquaintance of, to meet* [for the first time])

  Comment s'appelle ton ami? Ta sœur parlait **de cet ami** hier.
  Comment s'appelle ton ami **dont** ta sœur parlait hier?

A **Préférences.** Complétez ces phrases comme dans les exemples. Pour chaque section, utilisez le pronom relatif indiqué.

Utilisez le pronom relatif qui et conjuguez le verbe.

EXEMPLE Je préfère les personnes... (avoir un bon sens de l'humour, avoir beaucoup d'argent)
Je préfère les personnes qui ont un bon sens de l'humour.

1. Je préfère un(e) colocataire... (sortir tout le temps, rester souvent à la maison)
2. Je préfère les films... (avoir beaucoup d'action, avoir peu de violence)
3. Je préfère un(e) partenaire... (cultiver son corps, cultiver son esprit)

Utilisez le pronom relatif que (qu').

EXEMPLE Je préfère les personnes... (je rencontre en cours, je rencontre en boîte)
Je préfère les personnes que je rencontre en boîte.

1. Je préfère les personnes... (on rencontre dans une salle de gym, on rencontre à la bibliothèque)
2. Je préfère les activités... (je fais seul[e], je fais en groupe)
3. Je préfère la musique... (on fait maintenant, on faisait il y a vingt ans)

Utilisez le pronom relatif dont.

EXEMPLE L'argent est une chose... (j'ai très envie, je n'ai pas très envie)
L'argent est une chose dont je n'ai pas très envie.

1. L'amour est quelque chose... (j'ai très besoin dans ma vie, je n'ai pas vraiment besoin pour le moment)
2. La ville où je suis né(e) est un endroit *(place)*... (je me souviens bien, je ne me souviens pas bien)
3. Ma vie amoureuse, c'est une chose... (j'aime bien parler, je n'aime pas beaucoup parler)

B **Identification.** Complétez les descriptions suivantes avec **qui, que** ou **dont**. Ensuite, donnez les renseignements demandés.

EXEMPLE Un film _____ j'aime beaucoup, c'est...
Un film **que** j'aime beaucoup, c'est *Le Maître*.

1. Un film _____ a gagné beaucoup d'Oscars, c'est...
2. Un film _____ j'ai vu plusieurs fois, c'est...
3. Un film _____ on parle beaucoup en ce moment, c'est...

4. Un acteur (Une actrice) _____ je trouve beau (belle), c'est...
5. Un acteur (Une actrice) _____ tout le monde parle souvent, c'est...
6. Un acteur (Une actrice) _____ n'a vraiment pas de talent, c'est...

7. Une émission *(program)* de télévision _____ est à la télé depuis longtemps, c'est...
8. Une émission de télévision de mon enfance *(childhood)* _____ je me souviens, c'est...
9. Une émission de télévision _____ j'aime beaucoup regarder, c'est...

VIDÉO-REPRISE

Les Stagiaires

Rappel!
Dans l'épisode précédent de la vidéo, Matthieu a enfin dominé sa timidité et a invité Amélie à sortir.

See the **Résumé de grammaire** section at the end of each chapter for a review of all the grammar presented in the chapter.

Dans l'*Épisode 7* de la vidéo *Les Stagiaires,* Amélie et Céline parlent de la soirée qu'Amélie a passée avec Matthieu. Avant de regarder l'épisode, faites ces exercices pour réviser ce que vous avez appris dans le *Chapitre 7.*

A **Au bureau.** Amélie parle à une amie de ses collègues et de son travail à Technovert. Complétez chaque phrase avec la forme correcte du verbe logique entre parenthèses.

EXEMPLE Technovert **vend** (perdre / vendre) des produits technologiques verts.

1. Je prends le bus pour aller au travail et je _____ (descendre / entendre) juste en face du bureau.

2. M. Vielledent est le directeur, mais son assistante Camille _____ (s'entendre / répondre) à toutes nos questions sur le fonctionnement de l'entreprise.

3. Christophe est un peu paresseux et il _____ (rendre / attendre) toujours le dernier moment pour faire son travail.

4. Camille et Céline _____ (perdre / vendre) souvent patience avec Christophe.

5. Je (J') _____ (entendre / s'entendre) souvent Camille parler de ses frustrations concernant le travail de Christophe.

6. Il _____ (perdre / descendre) beaucoup de temps au bureau en lisant *(reading)* des mangas.

7. J'habite avec la directrice de marketing, Céline. Nous _____ (entendre / s'entendre) bien. Il n'y a jamais de problèmes entre nous.

8. Céline _____ (attendre / rendre) souvent visite à ses parents le week-end, alors je suis seule dans l'appartement.

B **Chez Christophe.** Christophe parle de ses parents. Complétez les phrases suivantes avec la forme correcte du verbe réfléchi ou réciproque indiqué entre parenthèses.

EXEMPLE Je **m'entends** *(get along)* mieux avec mon père qu'avec ma mère.

1. Ma mère et moi, on _____ *(argue)* souvent.

2. Mon père et moi, nous ne _____ *(talk to each other)* pas beaucoup.

3. Le week-end, mon père est toujours très occupé. Il ne _____ *(rests)* jamais.

4. Mon père _____ *(wakes up)* à 6h le samedi.

5. Moi, je _____ *(get up)* vers midi.

6. Le samedi soir, mes amis et moi, on _____ *(meet one another)* presque toujours en ville.

7. Je _____ *(get bored)* si je reste à la maison le week-end.

8. Je _____ *(have fun)* plus avec mes amis qu'avec ma famille.

Maintenant changez les phrases précédentes pour décrire votre situation.

EXEMPLE Je m'entends aussi bien avec mon père qu'avec ma mère.
Je m'entends bien avec ma mère, mais je m'entends moins bien avec mon père.

C Conseils. Matthieu pose des questions à un ami à propos des relations sociales. Complétez ses questions avec le pronom relatif (**qui, que, dont**) approprié.

1. Quand tu sors avec des amis, quels sont les sujets de conversation _____ vous parlez le plus souvent?

2. As-tu plus d'amis _____ s'intéressent à l'art, au sport ou à la politique?

3. Tu penses que c'est une bonne idée de sortir en couple avec quelqu'un _____ on a rencontré au travail?

4. Est-ce que tu as beaucoup d'amis _____ sont mariés?

5. Est-ce qu'on doit se marier avec la première personne _____ on tombe amoureux?

6. Est-ce que le mariage est quelque chose _____ tu trouves important ou _____ n'est pas important pour toi?

Maintenant interviewez un(e) autre étudiant(e) en utilisant les questions précédentes.

D Hier soir. Après sa soirée avec Amélie, Matthieu parle à son ami. Complétez le paragraphe suivant en mettant les verbes entre parenthèses au passé composé ou à l'imparfait.

Amélie et moi, on __1__ (se retrouver) au restaurant. J' __2__ (être) déjà au restaurant quand elle __3__ (arriver). Au début, quand j' __4__ (attendre), j' __5__ (être) nerveux, mais après, on __6__ (commencer) à parler et j'ai découvert *(discovered)* qu'elle aimait les mêmes choses que moi. Après le dîner, on __7__ (se promener) un peu et on __8__ (s'arrêter) dans un café pour prendre un verre. Il __9__ (être) assez tard quand on __10__ (se quitter).

Access the Video ***Les Stagiaires*** online.

▶ **Épisode 7: Vous vous êtes amusés?**

AVANT LA VIDÉO
Dans cet épisode, Céline parle à Amélie de son rendez-vous d'hier soir avec Matthieu. Avant de le regarder, imaginez trois choses dont Amélie et Matthieu ont peut-être parlé.

APRÈS LA VIDÉO
Regardez l'épisode et répondez aux questions suivantes:
• De quoi est-ce que Matthieu et Amélie ont parlé?
• Vers quelle heure est-ce qu'ils se sont quittés?

LECTURE ET COMPOSITION

POUR MIEUX LIRE:
Recognizing conversational style

You are going to read a story by Eugène Ionesco (1912–1994), in which a father finds himself alone one morning with his two- or three-year-old daughter.

Sometimes a writer uses language that is not completely "correct" to portray how someone speaks. To appreciate this style and how it tells something about the character who is speaking, you can compare this conversational language with the more "correct" version of the language. In Ionesco's story, the author modifies his language to represent the way a little girl would speak or how someone might speak to a young child.

Du vocabulaire enfantin. Regardez ces phrases. Comment dit-on la même chose d'une façon plus correcte?

1. Tu laves ta figure.
2. Je rase ma barbe.
3. Tu laves ton «dérère» *(backside)*.

Conte pour enfants de moins de trois ans

Ce matin, comme d'habitude, Josette **frappe** à la porte de la chambre à coucher de ses parents. Papa n'a pas très bien dormi. Maman est partie à la campagne pour quelques jours. Alors papa a profité de cette absence pour manger beaucoup de **saucisson,** pour boire de la bière, pour manger du **pâté de cochon** et beaucoup d'autres choses que maman **l'empêche de** manger parce que c'est pas bon pour **la santé.** Alors, voilà, papa **a mal au foie, il a mal à l'estomac, il a mal à la tête,** et ne voudrait pas se réveiller. Mais Josette frappe toujours à la porte. Alors, papa **lui dit** d'entrer. Elle entre, elle va chez son papa. Il n'y a pas maman. Josette demande:

—*Où elle est maman?*

Papa répond: *Ta maman est allée se reposer à la campagne chez sa maman à elle.*

Josette répond: *Chez Mémée?*

Papa répond: *Oui, chez Mémée.*

—*Écris à maman,* dit Josette. *Téléphone à maman,* dit Josette.

Papa dit: **Faut pas** *téléphoner. Et puis papa dit pour **lui-même:** Parce qu'elle est peut-être **autre part...**

Josette dit: **Raconte** *une histoire avec maman et toi, et moi.*

—*Non,* dit papa, *je vais aller au travail. Je me lève, je vais m'habiller.*

---

frappe *knocks* **saucisson** *salami* **pâté de cochon** *pork pâté* **l'empêche de** *keeps him from* **la santé** *health*
a mal au foie, il a mal à l'estomac, il a mal à la tête *has indigestion, he has a stomachache, he has a headache*
lui dit *tells her* **Faut pas** *We must not* **lui-même** *himself* **autre part** *somewhere else* **Raconte** *Tell*

Et papa se lève. Il met **sa robe de chambre** rouge, **par dessus** son pyjama, il met les **pieds** dans ses **pantoufles.** Il va dans la salle de bains. Il ferme la porte de la salle de bains. Josette est à la porte de la salle de bains. Elle frappe avec ses petits **poings,** elle **pleure.**

Josette dit: *Ouvre-moi la porte.*

Papa répond: *Je ne peux pas. Je suis **tout nu,** je me lave, après je me rase.*

Josette dit: *Et tu fais pipi-caca.*

—*Je me lave,* dit papa.

Josette dit: *Tu laves ta figure, tu laves tes **épaules,** tu laves tes **bras,** tu laves ton **dos,** tu laves ton «dérère», tu laves tes pieds.*

—*Je rase ma barbe,* dit papa.

— *Tu rases ta barbe avec **du savon,** dit Josette. Je veux entrer. Je veux voir.*

Papa dit: *Tu ne peux pas me voir, parce que je **ne** suis **plus** dans la salle de bains.*

Josette dit (derrière la porte): *Alors, où tu es?*

Papa répond: *Je ne sais pas, va voir. Je suis peut-être dans la salle à manger, va me chercher.*

Josette **court** dans la salle à manger, et papa commence sa toilette. Josette court avec ses petites **jambes,** elle va dans la salle à manger. Papa est tranquille, mais pas pour longtemps. Josette arrive **de nouveau** devant la porte de la salle de bains, elle **crie à travers** la porte:

Josette dit: *Je t'ai cherché. Tu n'es pas dans la salle à manger.*

Papa dit: *Tu n'as pas bien cherché. Regarde sous la table.*

Josette retourne dans la salle à manger. Elle revient.

Elle dit: *Tu n'es pas sous la table.*

Papa dit: *Alors va voir dans le salon. Regarde bien si je suis sur le fauteuil, sur le canapé, derrière les livres, à la fenêtre.*

Josette s'en va. Papa est tranquille, mais pas pour longtemps.

Josette revient.

Elle dit: *Non, tu n'es pas dans le fauteuil, tu n'es pas à la fenêtre, tu n'es pas sur le canapé, tu n'es pas derrière les livres, tu n'es pas dans la télévision, tu n'es pas dans le salon.*

Papa dit: *Alors, va voir si je suis dans la cuisine.*

Josette dit: *Je vais te chercher dans la cuisine.*

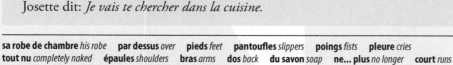

sa robe de chambre *his robe* **par dessus** *over* **pieds** *feet* **pantoufles** *slippers* **poings** *fists* **pleure** *cries*
tout nu *completely naked* **épaules** *shoulders* **bras** *arms* **dos** *back* **du savon** *soap* **ne... plus** *no longer* **court** *runs*
jambes *legs* **de nouveau** *again* **crie à travers** *yells through*

Josette court à la cuisine. Papa est tranquille, mais pas pour longtemps. Josette revient.

Elle dit: *Tu n'es pas dans la cuisine.*

Papa dit: *Regarde bien, sous la table de la cuisine, regarde bien si je suis dans le buffet, regarde bien si je suis dans **les casseroles,** regarde bien si je suis dans **le four** avec le poulet.*

Josette va et vient. Papa n'est pas dans le four, papa n'est pas dans les casseroles, papa n'est pas dans le buffet, papa n'est pas sous **le paillasson,** papa n'est pas dans **la poche** de son pantalon, dans la poche du pantalon il y a **seulement le mouchoir.**

Josette revient devant la porte de la salle de bains.

Josette dit: *J'ai cherché partout. Je ne t'ai pas trouvé. Où tu es?*

Papa dit: *Je suis là.*

Et papa, qui a eu le temps de faire sa toilette, qui s'est rasé, qui s'est habillé, ouvre la porte.

Il dit: *Je suis là.*

Il prend Josette **dans ses bras,** et voilà aussi la porte de la maison qui s'ouvre, **au fond** du couloir, et c'est maman qui arrive. Josette **saute** des bras de son papa, elle **se jette** dans les bras de sa maman, elle l'embrasse, elle dit:

*Maman, j'ai cherché papa sous la table, dans l'armoire, sous le tapis, derrière **la glace,** dans la cuisine, dans **la poubelle,** il n'était pas là.*

Papa dit à maman: **Je suis content que tu sois revenue.** *Il faisait beau à la campagne? Comment va ta mère?*

Josette dit: *Et Mémée, elle va bien? On va chez elle?*

Eugène Ionesco, *Conte No 4* © Éditions GALLIMARD, www.gallimard.fr

---

les casseroles *the pans*   **le four** *the oven*   **le paillasson** *the doormat*   **la poche** *the pocket*   **seulement le mouchoir** *only the handkerchief*   **dans ses bras** *in his arms*   **au fond** *at the end*   **saute** *jumps*   **se jette** *throws herself*   **la glace** *the mirror*   **la poubelle** *the trash can*   **Je suis content que tu sois revenue.** *I'm glad you came back.*

Avez-vous des enfants? Si non *(If not)*, voulez-vous avoir des enfants un jour? Pourquoi ou pourquoi pas?

COMPOSITION

You know how to use words like **d'abord, ensuite, alors,** and **et puis** to connect your sentences into a well-ordered paragraph. Another way to link ideas is to use **pour** to say *in order to*. In this case, **pour** is followed by an infinitive.

> **Je pars à 7h pour arriver à 8h.**
> *I leave at 7:00 (in order) to arrive at 8:00.*

To say that you do something *before* you do something else, use **avant de** followed by an infinitive.

> **Avant de m'habiller, je mange.**
> *Before I get dressed (Before getting dressed), I eat.*

Organisez-vous. Vous allez décrire votre routine matinale. Avant de commencer, traduisez les phrases qui suivent.

1. *I'm tired in the morning, so I don't wake up easily.*
2. *First, I eat breakfast. Next, I take a shower. Then, I get dressed. And then, I leave.*
3. *I eat quickly in order to be on time.*
4. *Before I eat, I get dressed.*
5. *I take a bath before I dress.*

Compréhension

1. Pourquoi est-ce que le père de Josette a mal à la tête et à l'estomac?
2. Quel jeu invente-t-il pour pouvoir faire sa toilette?
3. Dans quelles pièces est-ce que la petite fille cherche son papa?
4. Où est-ce qu'elle le cherche dans la cuisine?
5. Qui rentre à la fin du conte? Quelle est la réaction du papa?

Le matin chez moi

Décrivez votre routine du matin. Utilisez des mots comme **d'abord, ensuite** et **avant de** pour indiquer l'ordre de vos actions.

> **EXEMPLE** **Le matin, je me lève vers six heures. D'abord...**

L'AMOUR ET LE COUPLE

Voici les résultats de **sondages** d'opinion des Français sur l'amour et le couple. **Qu'est-ce qui vous surprend?** Quelles sont vos opinions?

Question: Êtes-vous amoureux (amoureuse) en ce moment? Avez-vous été amoureux (amoureuse)? Combien de fois avez-vous été amoureux (amoureuse)?

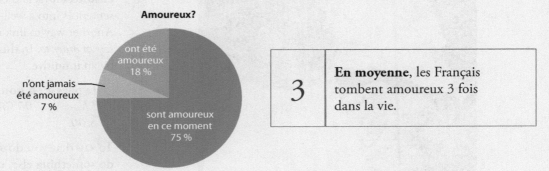

Amoureux?

- ont été amoureux 18 %
- n'ont jamais été amoureux 7 %
- sont amoureux en ce moment 75 %

| 3 | **En moyenne**, les Français tombent amoureux 3 fois dans la vie. |

Question: Croyez-vous au grand amour? Croyez-vous en l'amour pour la vie?

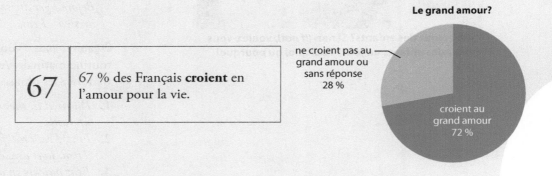

| 67 | 67 % des Français **croient** en l'amour pour la vie. |

Le grand amour?

- ne croient pas au grand amour ou sans réponse 28 %
- croient au grand amour 72 %

Question: Est-ce que votre vie sentimentale est quelque chose dont vous êtes très ou assez satisfait(e)? dont vous êtes peu satisfait(e)? dont vous n'êtes pas satisfait(e)?

Et votre vie sexuelle?

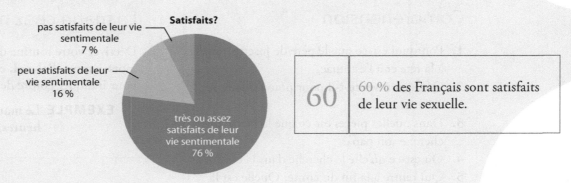

Satisfaits?

- pas satisfaits de leur vie sentimentale 7 %
- peu satisfaits de leur vie sentimentale 16 %
- très ou assez satisfaits de leur vie sentimentale 76 %

| 60 | 60 % des Français sont satisfaits de leur vie sexuelle. |

---

sondages *polls*   **Qu'est-ce qui vous surprend?** *What surprises you?*   **En moyenne** *On average*   **Croyez-vous…?** *Do you believe…?*   **croient** *believe*

Question: Dans un couple, est-il plus important de tout partager ou de garder son jardin secret? **Changeriez-vous** de travail et/ou de ville pour l'amour?

Tout partager?

sans réponse
2 %

On doit tout partager.
34 %

On doit conserver son jardin secret.
64 %

74	**Pourtant,** 74 % des Français **changeraient** leur vie (travail, ville…) pour l'autre.

Question: Quelles sont les qualités qui **vous séduisent** le plus chez l'autre?

Qualités les plus séduisantes			
Pour les femmes		**Pour les hommes**	
honnêteté	60 %	tendresse	51 %
fidélité	48 %	honnêteté	48 %
tendresse	47 %	intelligence	42 %
intelligence	39 %	fidélité	38 %
humour	39 %	humour	27 %

23	Pour 23 % des hommes en France, la beauté est une des qualités les plus importantes, contre 8 % pour les femmes.

Compréhension

A Vrai ou faux?

1. Plus de la moitié *(More than half)* des répondants sont amoureux en ce moment.
2. La majorité changerait de travail ou de ville pour l'autre.
3. La majorité croit au grand amour.
4. La plupart croient en l'amour pour la vie.
5. Plus de la moitié des répondants sont satisfaits de leur vie sentimentale et de leur vie sexuelle.
6. La plupart préfèrent tout partager.
7. Pour la majorité des répondants, la beauté est la qualité la plus séduisante chez l'autre.

B Comparaisons. Discutez des questions suivantes.

1. Dans les réponses des Français au sondage, qu'est-ce qui vous surprend? Qu'est-ce qui ne vous surprend pas? Pourquoi?
2. Dans un sondage sur ce sujet fait dans votre pays, quelles autres questions est-ce qu'on poserait *(would one ask)*? Est-ce qu'il y a des questions qu'on ne poserait probablement pas? Voyez-vous des attitudes différentes sur ce sujet?

© Bill Bachmann/Alamy Stock Photo

Changeriez-vous…? *Would you change…?*   **Pourtant** *However*   **changeraient** *would change*
vous séduisent *attract you*

RÉSUMÉ DE GRAMMAIRE

Je **me** réveille à six heures et puis, je réveille mes enfants à sept heures.
*I wake (**myself**) up at six o'clock, and then I wake up my children at seven.*

Mon fils de trois ans **s'**habille tout seul.
My three-year-old son dresses all by himself.

—Tu **ne** t'ennuies **pas** dans ce cours?

—Non, mes camarades et moi, nous **ne** nous y ennuyons **jamais**!

—Comment vous appelez-vous?

—Je m'appe**ll**e Catherine Faure.

—À quelle heure est-ce que vous vous **le**vez?

—Je me **lè**ve très tôt.

Mon père **s'**achète une nouvelle voiture chaque année.
*My father buys **himself** a new car each year.*

Je me brosse **les** dents trois fois par jour.
*I brush **my** teeth three times a day.*

Vous **vous** retrouvez après les cours?
*Do you meet **each other** after class?*

Mes voisins ne **se** parlent pas.
*My neighbors don't talk **to one another.***

—**Vous** voulez **vous** marier?

—Oui, et **nous** allons **nous** installer dans un petit appartement.

REFLEXIVE VERBS

Reflexive verbs are used to say that people do something to or for themselves. In French, the reflexive pronoun corresponding to the subject is placed before the verb.

SE COUCHER *(to go to bed)*	
je **me** couche	nous **nous** couchons
tu **te** couches	vous **vous** couchez
il/elle/on **se** couche	ils/elles **se** couchent

The reflexive pronouns **me, te,** and **se** become **m', t',** and **s'** before vowel sounds. Also note the spelling changes with **s'ennuyer, s'appeler,** and **se lever.** Remember that all verbs ending with **-yer,** such as **envoyer, essayer,** and **payer,** follow the same pattern as **s'ennuyer. Se promener** is conjugated like **se lever.**

S'ENNUYER *(to be / get bored)*	S'APPELER *(to be named)*	SE LEVER *(to get up)*
je m'ennuie	je m'appelle	je me lève
tu t'ennuies	tu t'appelles	tu te lèves
il/elle/on s'ennuie	il/elle/on s'appelle	il/elle/on se lève
nous nous ennuyons	nous nous appelons	nous nous levons
vous vous ennuyez	vous vous appelez	vous vous levez
ils/elles s'ennuient	ils/elles s'appellent	ils/elles se lèvent

To negate reflexive verbs, place **ne** directly after the subject and **pas** or **jamais** directly after the conjugated verb.

Verbs that are reflexive in English, such as *to amuse **oneself*** or *to buy **oneself** something* will generally also be reflexive in French. Many other verbs that are reflexive in French are not in English. Consult the end-of-chapter vocabulary list to find all the reflexive verbs learned in this chapter.

Verbs indicating that people are doing something to their own body are generally reflexive in French. After such verbs, in French, you generally use the definite article (**le, la, l', les**) with a body part, rather than the possessive adjective *(my, your, his . . .)*.

RECIPROCAL VERBS

Reciprocal verbs indicate that two or more people do something to or for one another. Most verbs expressing something one person might do to another can be made reciprocal by adding a reciprocal pronoun.

aimer	*to love*	s'aimer	*to love each other*
détester	*to hate*	se détester	*to hate each other*
regarder	*to look at*	se regarder	*to look at each other*

When reflexive / reciprocal verbs are used in the infinitive, the reflexive / reciprocal pronoun changes to match the subject of the conjugated verb.

PAST TENSES OF REFLEXIVE AND RECIPROCAL VERBS

All reflexive / reciprocal verbs are conjugated with **être** in the **passé composé.** The past participle agrees in gender and number with the reflexive / reciprocal pronoun (and the subject) when it is the *direct* object of the verb.

S'AMUSER	
je me suis amusé(e)	nous nous sommes amusé(e)s
tu t'es amusé(e)	vous vous êtes amusé(e)(s)
il s'est amusé	ils se sont amusés
elle s'est amusée	elles se sont amusées
on s'est amusé(e)(s)	

—Tous tes amis se sont retrouvé**s** chez toi?
—Oui, et on s'est bien amusé**s** jusqu'à très tard. Mon amie Rose s'est endormi**e** sur le canapé.

With negated verbs, place **ne** directly after the subject and **pas** after the conjugated form of **être.**

Past participles do not agree with reflexive / reciprocal pronouns that are *indirect* objects. For this reason, there is no agreement with **se parler, se téléphoner, s'écrire, s'envoyer des textos,** or when a reflexive verb is followed directly by a noun that is the direct object of the verb, such as a part of the body.

—Vous **ne** vous êtes **pas** vus hier?
—Non, mais nous nous sommes téléphoné trois fois.

Ma petite sœur s'est maquillé**e.**
Ma petite sœur s'est maquillé **les yeux.**

As with all verbs except **être,** form the imperfect of reflexive verbs by dropping the **-ons** from the **nous** form of the verb and adding the imperfect endings: **-ais, -ais, -ait, -ions, -iez, -aient.**

—Tu te levais plus tôt l'année dernière?
—Oui, je me levais à six heures.

REGULAR *-RE* VERBS

The following verbs are conjugated like **répondre: descendre, entendre, s'entendre (bien / mal) (avec), perdre, se perdre, rendre visite à quelqu'un, rendre quelque chose à quelqu'un, vendre, revendre.** They all take **avoir** in the **passé composé** except **descendre** and the reflexive verbs.

—Tu ne rends jamais visite à ton ex-copine?
—Non, on a perdu contact. On ne s'entend pas très bien. Si je téléphone chez elle, elle ne répond pas au téléphone.

RÉPONDRE *(to answer)*	
je répon**ds**	nous répond**ons**
tu répon**ds**	vous répond**ez**
il/elle/on répon**d**	ils/elles répond**ent**

PASSÉ COMPOSÉ: **j'ai répondu**
IMPARFAIT: **je répondais**

RELATIVE PRONOUNS

A relative clause is a phrase that describes a noun. The word that begins the phrase, referring back to the noun described is a relative pronoun. The relative pronouns **qui, que,** and **dont** are all used for both people and things. The choice of relative pronoun depends on the pronoun's function in the relative clause. **Qui** replaces the subject of the relative clause, **que (qu')** replaces the direct object, and **dont** replaces the preposition **de** and its object.

Place relative clauses directly after the noun they describe. When **que** is the object of a verb in the **passé composé,** the past participle agrees in number and gender with the noun it represents.

La femme **qui** habite à côté est française. (= La femme est française. **Cette femme** habite à côté.)
La femme **que** j'ai invitée est française. (= La femme est française. J'ai invité **cette femme.**)
La femme **dont** je parle souvent est française. (= La femme est française. Je parle souvent **de cette femme.**)

VOCABULAIRE

COMPÉTENCE 1

Describing your daily routine

NOMS MASCULINS

un bain	*a bath*
le mariage	*marriage*
un petit-fils	*a grandson*
un séjour	*a stay*
un veuf	*a widower*

NOMS FÉMININS

une demi-heure	*a half hour*
les dents	*the teeth*
une douche	*a shower*
la figure	*the face*
la main	*the hand*
une petite-fille	*a granddaughter*
une routine	*a routine*
une veuve	*a widow*

EXPRESSIONS VERBALES

s'amuser	*to have fun*
s'appeler	*to be named / called*
attendre	*to wait (for)*
se brosser (les cheveux / les dents)	*to brush (one's hair / one's teeth)*
connaître	*to be familiar with, to be acquainted with, to know*
se coucher / se recoucher	*to go to bed / to go back to bed*
s'endormir	*to fall asleep*
s'ennuyer	*to be bored, to get bored*
faire sa toilette	*to wash up*
s'habiller / se déshabiller	*to get dressed / to get undressed*
se laver (la figure / les mains)	*to wash (one's face / one's hands)*
se lever	*to get up*
se maquiller	*to put on makeup*
prendre un bain / une douche	*to take a bath / a shower*
se raser	*to shave*
se reposer	*to rest*
se réveiller	*to wake up*

DIVERS

avant de (+ infinitive)	*before (. . . ing)*
comm	*since, as*
d'autres fois	*other times*
depuis	*since (then), for*
d'origine...	*of . . . origin*
facilement	*easily*
parfait(e)	*perfect*
pendant	*during*
quotidien(ne)	*daily*
vite	*quick(ly), fast*

COMPÉTENCE 2

Talking about relationships

NOMS MASCULINS

le coup de foudre	*love at first sight*
le grand amour	*true love*

NOMS FÉMININS

la jeunesse	*youth*
une relation	*a relationship*

EXPRESSIONS VERBALES

s'aimer	*to like each other, to love each other*
descendre	*to go down, to get off, to stay (at a hotel)*
se détester	*to hate each other*
se disputer	*to argue*
s'embrasser	*to kiss each other, to embrace each other*
entendre	*to hear*
s'entendre (bien / mal) (avec)	*to get along (well / badly) (with)*
se fiancer	*to get engaged*
s'installer (dans / à)	*to move (into), to settle (in)*
se marier (avec)	*to get married (to)*
se parler	*to talk to each other*
se passer	*to happen*
perdre	*to lose*
se perdre	*to get lost*
prendre une décision	*to make a decision*
se quitter	*to leave each other*
se réconcilier	*to make up with each other*
se regarder	*to look at each other*
se rencontrer	*to meet each other (by chance, for the first time), to run into each other*
rendre quelque chose à quelqu'un	*to return something to someone*
rendre visite à quelqu'un	*to visit someone*
répondre (à)	*to answer, to respond (to)*
se retrouver	*to meet each other (by design)*
revendre	*to sell back / resell*
rêver (de)	*to dream (of, about)*
se souvenir de	*to remember*
suivre	*to follow*
se téléphoner	*to phone each other*
vendre	*to sell*

DIVERS

ce qui	*what*
C'est dommage!	*That's too bad!*
enfin	*finally*
formidable	*great*
heureux (heureuse)	*happy*
la plupart du temps	*most of the time*
mamie	*grandma*
sentimental(e) (*mpl* sentimentaux)	*sentimental, emotional*
un(e) tel(le)	*such a*

Talking about what you did and used to do

NOMS MASCULINS

le reste (de)	*the rest (of)*
un réveil	*an alarm clock*

EXPRESSIONS VERBALES

accepter	*to accept*
s'arrêter	*to stop*
se peigner	*to comb one's hair*
se promener	*to go walking*
raconter	*to tell*
se reconnaître	*to recognize each other*
sonner	*to ring*
se voir	*to see each other*

DIVERS

ce que	*what*
donc	*then, so, thus, therefore*
parfaitement	*perfectly*

Describing traits and characteristics

NOMS MASCULINS

l'aspect physique	*physical appearance*
le bonheur	*happiness*
le corps	*the body*
un défaut	*a fault*
l'esprit	*the mind, the spirit*
un groupe	*a group*
un partenaire	*a partner*
un sens de l'humour	*a sense of humor*
un sentiment	*a feeling*
un test	*a test*
un trait (de caractère)	*a (character) trait*

NOMS FÉMININS

l'arrogance	*arrogance*
la beauté	*beauty*
la compatibilité	*compatibility*
l'importance	*the importance*
l'indécision	*indecision*
l'indifférence	*indifference*
l'infidélité	*infidelity*
l'inflexibilité	*inflexibility*
l'insensibilité	*insensitivity*
la jalousie	*jealousy*
la nature	*nature*
une partenaire	*a partner*
la passion	*passion*
la politique	*politics*
la profession	*the profession*
la religion	*religion*
une rencontre	*an encounter*
la spiritualité	*spirituality*
la tendresse	*tenderness, affection*
la vanité	*vanity*

VERBES

cultiver	*to cultivate*
exprimer	*to express*
faire la connaissance de	*to make the acquaintance of, to meet (for the first time)*
s'intéresser à	*to be interested in*
ranger	*to arrange, to order*
supporter	*to bear, to tolerate, to put up with*

DIVERS

chez (une personne)	*with, in (a person)*
de droite	*conservative*
de gauche	*liberal*
dont	*whom, of (about, with) whom, whose, that, of (about, with) which*
jaloux (jalouse)	*jealous*
le mieux	*the best*
professionnel(le)	*professional*
que	*that, which, whom*
qui	*that, which, who*

 Pair work

 Group work

 Class work

 Video

Audio

© Algol/AGF Srl/Alamy Stock Photo

LE MONDE FRANCOPHONE

Géoculture et Vidéo-voyage: La cuisine régionale

COMPÉTENCE

GÉOCULTURE ET VIDÉO-VOYAGE: LA CUISINE RÉGIONALE

France

LA BRETAGNE

NOMBRE D'HABITANTS: **3 259 000 (les Bretons)**
CAPITALE: **Rennes**

Il est **d'usage de dire, «Dis-moi** ce que tu manges, **je te dirai** qui tu es!» En effet, en France, vous pouvez beaucoup apprendre sur la région et **le patrimoine** d'une personne **en regardant** ce qu'elle mange.

La cuisine française est très diversifiée et **chaque** région a ses plats traditionnels. Ce qu'on mange dans chaque région dépend en effet de l'héritage culturel et des produits **disponibles.** Ce qui est disponible dépend de **la terre** et du climat, qui varient d'une région de la France à une autre.

Les cultures **voisines** laissent aussi leur marque sur la cuisine d'une région.

L'Alsace **se trouve** à **la frontière allemande** et faisait **autrefois** partie **de l'Allemagne.** Sa cuisine bénéficie d'une forte influence allemande. Voudriez-vous **goûter** ces plats alsaciens: **la choucroute garnie,** les spaetzle, la tarte flambée?

Les spaetzle

La tarte aux pommes normande

Dans le nord-ouest, à côté de l'Atlantique, **les produits laitiers** et **les pommes** sont **parmi** les produits agricoles les plus importants. Ici, on apprécie **le poisson** et **les fruits de mer,** la cuisine à base de crème et de **beurre** et les desserts aux pommes.

---

d'usage de dire commonly said   **Dis-moi** Tell me   **je te dirai** I will tell you   **le patrimoine** patrimony, cultural heritage   **en regardant** by looking at **chaque** each   **disponibles** available   **la terre** soil   **voisines** neighboring   **se trouve** is located   **la frontière allemande** the German border **autrefois** formerly   **de l'Allemagne** of Germany   **goûter** to taste   **la choucroute garnie** sauerkraut and sausage   **les produits laitiers** dairy products **les pommes** apples   **parmi** among   **le poisson** fish   **les fruits de mer** seafood   **beurre** butter

Dans le sud, la cuisine est influencée par la cuisine méditerranéenne. Le poisson et les fruits de mer, **l'huile** d'olive, les herbes et les tomates sont à la base de la plupart des plats.

La morue à la provençale

La ratatouille

Certaines spécialités régionales sont devenues des plats de référence française, notamment le pot-au-feu, le coq au vin, le confit de canard et le bœuf bourguignon. **Lorsqu'il s'agit de** desserts, toute la France aime les crêpes, la crème brûlée et les profiteroles. Mais même ces **recettes** communes varient d'une région à l'autre. Par exemple, la recette originale du coq au vin se fait avec du vin rouge, mais dans le nord, c'est avec de la bière et dans le nord-ouest avec du cidre qu'elle se prépare.

Mais **quoiqu'ils mangent,** tous les Français apprécient **une nourriture** de bonne qualité. **Les repas** sont accompagnés de **pain,** de vin, de fromages, de café et… d'amis! Les repas sont des moments **conviviaux.**

Le savez-vous?

1. Quelles sont trois choses qui influencent la cuisine d'une région?

2. Qu'est-ce qui *(What)* détermine les produits disponibles dans une région?

3. La cuisine alsacienne est influencée par la cuisine de quel pays? Pourquoi?

4. La cuisine du sud est influencée par quelle cuisine? Quels ingrédients y trouve-t-on *(are found in it)*?

5. Quels ingrédients sont souvent à la base de la cuisine du nord-ouest de la France?

6. Qu'est-ce que les Français apprécient dans un repas?

7. Un repas est souvent accompagné de quoi?

---

l'huile oil   **Lorsqu'il s'agit de** *When talking about*   **recettes** *recipes*   **quoiqu'ils mangent** *whatever they eat*   **une nourriture** *food*   **Les repas** *Meals*
pain *bread*   **conviviaux** *convivial, among friends*

Dans cette vidéo, vous allez découvrir la diversité de la cuisine de la France métropolitaine et aussi la diversité de la cuisine d'autres régions francophones. Pour vous aider à mieux comprendre, regardez ces photos et indiquez quelle image représente chacune des phrases suivantes.

> **EXEMPLE** Dans les Caraïbes françaises, vous trouverez un étonnant mélange *(astonishing mixture)* de traditions françaises, créoles et d'influences asiatiques comme dans les accras *(fritters)*.
>
> **e**

1. En Louisiane, il y a le gombo créole et certaines spécialités cajuns, comme le boudin.

2. Les moules frites *(mussels and fries)* sont le symbole de la Belgique.

3. Les pays voisins d'Afrique du Nord apportent *(bring)* aussi leur contribution à la cuisine française avec de nombreux plats maghrébins *(from the Maghreb region)*, comme le couscous berbère.

4. Le Québec est célèbre pour la poutine – des frites et des tortillons au fromage *(cheese curds)* recouverts de sauce *(covered with gravy)*.

a.

b.

c.

d.

e.

▶ EN REGARDANT LA VIDÉO

Regardez la vidéo et indiquez les sujets mentionnés.

1. ☐ ce qui influence la cuisine d'une région
2. ☐ les spécialités ou les ingrédients à la base de la cuisine de plusieurs régions de la France
3. ☐ l'histoire de la cuisine créole de la Louisiane
4. ☐ des plats communs à toute la France, comme le pot-au-feu
5. ☐ un plat typique de la Suisse
6. ☐ une recette du coq au vin
7. ☐ une exposition au Louvre sur l'histoire de la cuisine

▶ APRÈS LA VIDÉO

Regardez la vidéo une deuxième fois et répondez à ces questions.

1. Qu'est-ce que vous avez appris au sujet de la cuisine française? Citez au moins quatre choses.
2. Est-ce qu'il y a autant de *(as much)* diversité culinaire dans votre région? Pourquoi ou pourquoi pas?
3. Quels plats français avez-vous déjà goûtés *(tasted)*? Est-ce que vous voudriez goûter la cuisine d'une des régions ou un des plats montrés dans la vidéo?

Marché en plein air à Rennes, Bretagne

Ordering at a restaurant

AU RESTAURANT

Note de grammaire

1. The article you see in front of many of these nouns is called the partitive. It expresses the idea of *some* or *any*. Why are there four different forms?

du pâté *some pâté*
de la soupe *some soup*
de l'eau *some water*
des œufs *some eggs*

You will learn how to use the partitive article in the next section. For now, learn the new vocabulary with the partitive.

2. Notice the difference in meaning between **entrée** in French and *entrée* in English.

3. The word **hors-d'œuvre** is invariable; that is, it does not change in the plural: **un hors-d'œuvre / des hors-d'œuvre**.

4. The final **f** of the singular word **œuf** [œf] is pronounced, but it is not pronounced in the plural form: **œufs** [ø]. Note the pronunciation of the word **yaourt** [jauRt].

5. The irregular verb **servir** (*to serve*) is conjugated like **sortir**: **je sers, tu sers, il/elle/on sert, nous servons, vous servez, ils/elles servent;** PASSÉ COMPOSÉ: **j'ai servi;** IMPARFAIT: **je servais.**

Les Français aiment bien les grands repas traditionnels.

On commence par **une entrée** ou **un hors-d'œuvre:**

de la soupe à l'oignon   du pâté   des œufs (m) durs à la mayonnaise   **des crudités** (f)

de la salade de tomates   des escargots (m)

Sur la table, il y a aussi...

du sel et du poivre   du pain   de l'eau minérale

Pour le plat principal, **on sert:**

DE LA VIANDE   **DU POISSON**

du rosbif   une côte de porc   **du thon**

un bifteck   **du saumon**

DE LA VOLAILLE   **DES FRUITS (m) DE MER**

du poulet   **des moules** (f)   **du homard**

du canard   **des huîtres** (f)   **des crevettes** (f)

---

une entrée *a first course*   **un hors-d'œuvre** *an appetizer*   **des crudités** *raw vegetables*   **on sert** (**servir** *to serve*)
de la viande *meat*   **du poisson** *fish*   **du thon** *tuna*   **du saumon** *salmon*   **de la volaille** *poultry*   **du canard** *duck*
des fruits de mer *shellfish*   **des moules** *mussels*   **du homard** *lobster*   **des huîtres** *oysters*   **des crevettes** *shrimp*

Le plat principal **comprend** aussi **du riz** et **des légumes** (m):

des haricots (m) verts

des pommes (f) de terre

des petits pois (m)

On sert généralement la salade verte après le plat principal. On sert le fromage après ou avec la salade.

une salade

du fromage

On finit le repas avec des fruits (m) – ou un dessert.

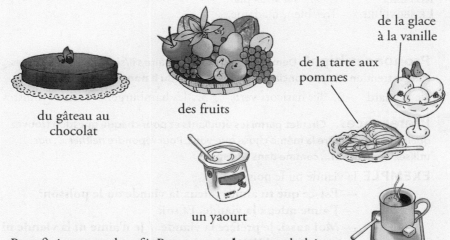

du gâteau au chocolat

des fruits

de la glace à la vanille

de la tarte aux pommes

un yaourt

Pour finir, on sert le café. Prenez-vous **du sucre,** du lait ou de la crème dans votre café?

du café

Vocabulaire sans peine!

Most foreign names of food items borrowed into English from other languages will be the same words in French. They tend to be masculine, unless they are borrowed from another romance language such as Spanish and Italian and end with **-a,** or sometimes **-e.** Italian pasta dishes ending with **-i** are plural, as in Italian.

du sushi	**une enchilada**
du curry	**des spaghetti**
un baklava	

How would you say the following in French?
a taco   *tofu*
chow mein   *macaroni*

Vocabulaire supplémentaire

bleu(e) *very rare*
saignant(e) *rare*
à point *medium*
bien cuit(e) *well-done*
végétarien(ne) *vegetarian*
végétalien(ne) *vegan*
D'AUTRES PLATS (DISHES):
   de l'agneau (m) *lamb*
   du bifteck haché *ground meat*
   des coquilles St-Jacques (f) *scallops*
   de la dinde *turkey*
   des pâtes (f) *pasta, noodles*
   du rôti de porc *pork roast*
   de la sole *sole*
   de la truite *trout*
   du veau *veal*
POUR METTRE LA TABLE (TO SET THE TABLE):
   une assiette *a plate*
   un bol *a bowl*
   un couteau *a knife*
   une cuillère / cuiller *a spoon*
   une fourchette *a fork*
   une nappe *a tablecloth*
   une serviette *a napkin*
   une tasse *a cup*
   un verre *a glass*

Pour une liste de fruits et de légumes, voir la page 327.

PRONONCIATION

*Le **h** aspiré*
8-1

In French, **h** is never pronounced and there is usually liaison or elision before it.

J'aime les_ᶻ huîtres.   Il y a beaucoup **d'**huile *(oil)* dans la salade.

Before a few words beginning with **h,** there is no liaison or elision, even though the **h** is silent. These words are said to begin with **h aspiré.** In vocabulary lists, they are indicated by an asterisk (*). English words that begin with *h* often have an **h aspiré** when used in French. The following words have **h aspiré:**

   le homard   **les haricots**   **les hors-d'œuvre**   **les hot-dogs**   **les hamburgers**

One hears **haricots verts** both with and without **h aspiré.**

---

comprend (comprendre *to include)*   **du riz** *rice*   **des légumes** *vegetables*   **du sucre** *sugar*

André a invité Rosalie au restaurant du quartier. Regardez **la carte** de ce restaurant aux pages 320–321.

8-2

LE SERVEUR:	Bonsoir, monsieur. Bonsoir, madame. Aimeriez-vous **un apéritif** avant de commander?
ANDRÉ:	Rosalie?
ROSALIE:	Non, merci, pas ce soir.
ANDRÉ:	Pour moi non plus.
LE SERVEUR:	Et pour dîner? Est-ce que vous avez décidé?
ANDRÉ:	Nous allons prendre le menu à 25 euros.
LE SERVEUR:	Très bien, monsieur. Et qu'est-ce que vous désirez **comme** entrée?
ANDRÉ:	Pour madame, le saumon fumé, s'il vous plaît. Et pour moi, les huîtres.
LE SERVEUR:	Et comme plat principal?
ROSALIE:	**La raie** pour moi, s'il vous plaît.
ANDRÉ:	Et pour moi, **le pavé de saumon.**
LE SERVEUR:	Bien, monsieur. Et comme boisson?
ANDRÉ:	Une carafe de vin blanc et **une bouteille d'**eau minérale.
LE SERVEUR:	Évian ou Perrier?
ROSALIE:	Évian, s'il vous plaît.
LE SERVEUR:	Très bien, madame.

A Prononcez bien! Demandez à votre partenaire s'il/si elle aime ces choses. Faites attention à la prononciation du **h aspiré** et du **h non-aspiré**.

1. *le homard   2. *les haricots verts   3. *les hamburgers   4. les‿huîtres

B Préférences. Circulez parmi les étudiants et pour chaque question trouvez quelqu'un qui préfère la même chose que vous. Pour répondre *neither . . . nor . . . ,* utilisez **ne... ni... ni...** comme dans l'exemple.

EXEMPLE la viande ou le poisson

— **Est-ce que tu aimes mieux la viande ou le poisson?**
— **J'aime mieux la viande. Et toi?**
— **Moi aussi, je préfère la viande. / Je n'aime ni la viande ni le poisson. / J'aime les deux.**

1. la viande rouge ou la volaille
2. les légumes ou la viande
3. le poisson ou les fruits de mer
4. les crudités ou la salade verte
5. les pommes de terre ou le riz
6. les haricots verts ou les petits pois
7. les escargots ou les œufs durs
8. les crevettes ou le homard

C Catégories logiques. Quel mot ne va pas logiquement avec les autres? Pourquoi?

EXEMPLE le thé, le jus de fruit, le sel, le lait, l'eau
Le sel, parce que ce n'est pas une boisson.

1. le pain, les petits pois, les pommes de terre, les haricots verts
2. le gâteau au chocolat, le poivre, la tarte aux pommes, la glace
3. la salade de tomates, le pâté, la soupe à l'oignon, le rosbif
4. le déjeuner, le dîner, le petit déjeuner, le sel
5. le homard, le rosbif, les crevettes, les huîtres, les moules
6. les pommes de terre, les petits pois, les haricots verts, le gâteau

---

la carte *the menu*   **un apéritif** *a before-dinner drink*   **comme** *for, as a(n)*   **la raie** *skate, rayfish*   **le pavé de saumon** *the salmon steak*   **une bouteille de** *a bottle of*

D **Aujourd'hui on sert...** Regardez la liste et indiquez ce qu'il y a par catégorie.

> de l'eau minérale   du vin   du canard   du thon
> du saumon   des crevettes   des huîtres
> des petits pois   des pommes de terre   du gâteau
> de la tarte aux pommes   des côtes de porc
> du bifteck   du pâté   des œufs durs   du poulet

EXEMPLE viande
Comme viande, il y a des côtes de porc et...

1. entrée
2. volaille
3. viande
4. poisson
5. dessert
6. légume
7. boisson
8. fruits de mer

E **Comparaisons culturelles.** Pour chaque catégorie, est-ce que vous préférez la même chose que les Français (indiquée par un X)?

1. Je préfère...
   X le café noir ou avec du sucre.
   __ le café au lait.
   __ le café vanille ou le café noisette *(hazelnut)*.

2. Je préfère prendre la salade...
   __ avant le plat principal.
   __ avec le plat principal.
   X après le plat principal.

3. Pour terminer un repas, je préfère...
   __ du gâteau ou de la tarte.
   __ un fruit.
   X un yaourt ou un fromage blanc.

4. Comme glace, je préfère...
   X la glace à la vanille.
   __ la glace au chocolat.
   __ la glace à la fraise *(strawberry)*.

F **Un dîner.** Voici ce que Rosalie a mangé hier soir. Qu'est-ce qu'elle a mangé? Dans quel ordre? Utilisez **du** *(m. sing.)*, **de la** *(f. sing.)* ou **des** *(pl.)* pour dire *some* ou **un(e)** pour dire *a* avant chaque substantif *(noun)*.

À VOUS!

Avec deux autres étudiant(e)s, relisez à haute voix la conversation au restaurant. Ensuite, imaginez que vous dînez au restaurant Au vieux Breton avec un(e) ami(e). Commandez un repas complet. Le (La) troisième étudiant(e) va jouer le rôle du serveur (de la serveuse).

Sélection musicale. Search for the song **"Les cornichons"** by Nino Ferrer online to enjoy a musical selection containing food vocabulary.

You can access the audio of the active vocabulary of this **Compétence** online.

RESTAURANT
AU VIEUX BRETON

NOS MENUS
service compris

Nos menus sont uniquement composés de produits frais de saison. Nos poissons et fruits de mer sont d'arrivage journalier et certains plats peuvent nous manquer. Nous vous remercions de votre compréhension.

Le vieux Breton – 20 €

Entrées
entrée du jour
rillette de sardines
pressé de fromage de chèvre
œufs pochés à la bretonne
velouté de chou-fleur

Plats
plat du jour
choucroute de poissons
émincé de porc sauce moutarde
galette complète
poulet-frites

Desserts
dessert du jour
crêpe du jour
coupe de glace – 2 boules
riz au lait
crème caramel
mousse au chocolat

Menu du pêcheur – 25 €

Entrées
entrée du jour
rillette de sardines
petite terrine bretonne maison
soupe de poissons
saumon fumé
6 huîtres + suppl.
plateau de fruits de mer + suppl.

Plats
poisson du jour
brochette de poissons
choucroute de poissons
moules de pays, frites
aile de raie au beurre
pavé de saumon

Desserts
dessert du jour
crêpe au choix
coupe de glace – 2 boules
far breton
poires caramélisées
gâteau aux pommes

LA CARTE
service compris

Entrées
entrée du jour **6,50 €**
rillette de sardines **6,50 €**
pressé de fromage de chèvre **6,50 €**
velouté de chou-fleur **6,50 €**
œufs pochés à la bretonne **7 €**
huîtres fines de claires no 3
   les 6 **13 €**   les 9 **18 €**   les 12 **25€**
saumon fumé **7,50€**
soupe de poissons **7,50 €**
petite terrine bretonne maison **8 €**
foie gras maison **12 €**
plateau de fruits de mer **25 €**

Poissons et fruits de mer
poisson du jour selon l'arrivage **15 €**
brochette de poisson au beurre **15 €**
choucroute de poissons **15 €**
moules de pays, frites **15 €**
aile de raie au beurre **15 €**
pavé de saumon **15 €**
araignée de mer **17 €**
Saint-Jacques à la bretonne **17 €**
homard breton **40 €**

Viandes et volailles
plat du jour **12,50 €**
émincé de porc **12,50 €**
galette complète **12,50 €**
poulet-frites **12,50 €**
confit de canard **15 €**
lapin maison **15 €**
ris de veau **16 €**
carré d'agneau **18 €**
tournedos de bœuf **18 €**

Crêpes
crêpe du jour **5,50 €**
crêpes au choix:
   sucre confiture citron **6 €**
   caramel chocolat **6,50 €**

Desserts
dessert du jour **5,50 €**
coupe de glace (2 boules) **5,50 €**
riz au lait **5,50 €**
mousse au chocolat **5,50 €**
crème caramel **5,50 €**
far breton **6,50 €**
gâteau aux pommes **6,50 €**
tarte tatin **7 €**
poires caramélisées **7 €**

TALKING ABOUT WHAT YOU EAT

✔ *Pour vérifier*

1. How do you express the idea of *some* in French? What are the forms of the partitive and when do you use each? Can you drop the word for *some* or *any* in French, as you can in English?

2. In what two circumstances do you use **de** instead of the partitive?

Le partitif

1. To express the idea of *some* or *any*, use the partitive article (**du, de la, de l', des**).

MASCULINE SINGULAR BEFORE A CONSONANT SOUND	FEMININE SINGULAR BEFORE A CONSONANT SOUND	SINGULAR BEFORE A VOWEL SOUND	PLURAL
du pain	de la glace	de l'eau	des fruits

Note *de grammaire*

Remember to use the definite article immediately after verbs that express general likes, dislikes, and preferences.
J'aime beaucoup *le* café.

2. The words *some* or *any* may be left out in English, but the partitive article must be used in French.

Je voudrais **du café.**	*I'd like **(some) coffee.***
Tu as **du temps libre**?	*Do you have **(some) free time**?*

3. The partitive article becomes **de (d'):**

- after negated verbs (except after the verb **être**).

Tu **ne** veux **pas de café**?	*Don't you want **(any) coffee**?*
Je n'ai **pas de temps libre.**	*I don't have **(any) free time.***

- after expressions of quantity like **beaucoup, combien,** and **trop.**

J'ai acheté **trop de café.**	*I bought **too much coffee.***
J'ai **peu de temps libre.**	*I have **little free time.***

A **Je prends...** Complétez les espaces avec la forme correcte de l'article partitif. Ensuite, demandez à un(e) partenaire s'il/si elle prend souvent ces choses le soir.

EXEMPLE du vin
— Est-ce que tu prends souvent du vin le soir?
— Oui, je prends souvent du vin.
Je prends du vin quelquefois.
Non, je ne prends jamais de vin.

1. ___ pain
2. ___ œufs
3. ___ eau minérale
4. ___ viande rouge
5. ___ crevettes
6. ___ poisson
7. ___ volaille
8. ___ soupe

B **Comparaisons culturelles.** Indiquez si les Français prennent souvent ces choses **comme entrée, comme plat principal, comme boisson, comme dessert** ou **comme légume.** Ensuite, dites si vous faites souvent la même chose.

EXEMPLE pâté
Les Français prennent souvent du pâté comme entrée.
Moi aussi, je prends souvent du pâté comme entrée.
Moi, je ne prends jamais de pâté comme entrée.

1. salade de tomates
2. eau minérale
3. petits pois
4. saumon
5. canard
6. tarte
7. gâteau
8. vin
9. pâté

C **Sur la table.** Rose est invitée à une fête où il y a beaucoup à manger et à boire. Voici la table de la salle à manger et la table de la cuisine. Travaillez en groupes pour faire des comparaisons entre les deux.

EXEMPLE Il y a des chips dans la cuisine et dans la salle à manger.
Il y a de l'eau minérale dans la salle à manger mais il n'y a pas d'eau minérale dans la cuisine.

la salle à manger   la cuisine

D **Entretien.** Complétez les questions avec l'article qui convient: **du, de la, de l', des** ou **de**. Ensuite, utilisez ces questions pour interviewer un(e) partenaire.

1. Qu'est-ce que tu préfères faire quand tu as _____ temps libre: faire _____ sport, écouter _____ musique, faire _____ shopping, faire _____ jardinage ou jouer à _____ jeux vidéo? Est-ce que tu as beaucoup _____ temps libre ou est-ce que tu as beaucoup _____ travail? Tu invites souvent _____ amis à dîner chez toi?

2. Est-ce que tu prends beaucoup _____ repas au restaurant avec tes amis? Quand tu vas au restaurant, tu commandes plus souvent _____ viande, _____ poisson, _____ légumes ou _____ fruits de mer? Tu prends _____ vin quelquefois avec tes repas? Tu manges beaucoup _____ légumes? Est-ce que tu prends plus souvent _____ glace, _____ tarte ou _____ gâteau comme dessert?

E **Préparatifs.** Vous allez inviter des amis pour un grand repas traditionnel à la française. Avec un(e) partenaire, faites des projets pour ce dîner.

Parlez de:

- quand et où vous allez faire ce dîner et qui vous allez inviter.
- ce que vous allez servir. (Imaginez que tout le monde n'aime pas les mêmes choses et proposez au moins trois possibilités pour l'entrée, le plat principal, le dessert et la boisson.)

STRATÉGIES ET COMPRÉHENSION AUDITIVE

POUR MIEUX COMPRENDRE: *Planning and predicting*

Since no two cultures are identical, you may sometimes find yourself lacking the cultural knowledge to understand what you hear in French. For example, if the waiter asks «**Évian ou Perrier?**», you will not be able to answer unless you recognize that these are brand names of French mineral waters. In such situations, try to infer what is being asked from the context. Also, when possible, prepare and predict from previous experiences what might be asked or said. For example, before ordering mineral water, glance at the menu to see what kinds are sold.

🔊 **A** **Pendant le repas.** Vous êtes au restaurant. Est-ce qu'on vous dit les choses
8-3   que vous entendez **avant le repas** ou **à la fin du repas**?

B **Questions.** Faites une liste de trois questions qu'un(e) client(e) pose souvent au serveur ou à la serveuse dans un restaurant.

Compréhension auditive: *Au restaurant*

🔊 Deux touristes sont dans un restaurant français. Écoutez leur conversation.
8-4   Qu'est-ce qu'ils commandent? Nommez au moins quatre choses.

Que demandent-ils? Écoutez encore une fois la conversation au restaurant et écrivez deux questions que les clients posent à la serveuse.

© Markus Kirchgessner/laif/Redux

Buying food

LES COURSES

Note *culturelle*

Dans le passé, les Français faisaient leurs courses presque tous les jours chez les petits commerçants. Aujourd'hui, certains Français font leurs achats *(purchases)* dans les hard-discount *(discount supercenters)*, d'autres dans les hypermarchés *(supercenters)* et supermarchés et d'autres encore chez les petits commerçants et au marché. Les supérettes (les petits supermarchés) deviennent aussi de plus en plus populaires. Ces habitudes varient en partie selon les ressources financières, le niveau d'éducation, la situation géographique (milieu urbain ou rural) et l'attitude envers la nourriture *(towards food)*. Combien de fois par semaine faites-vous vos courses? Où préférez-vous les faire?

De plus en plus de Français font leurs courses dans les supermarchés et **les grandes surfaces** où on vend de tout. Mais beaucoup préfèrent aller chez les petits **commerçants** du quartier où le service est plus personnalisé.

À la boulangerie-pâtisserie, on peut acheter du pain et **des pâtisseries** *(f)*:

une baguette   un pain au chocolat   **un pain complet**   une tarte aux **cerises** *(f)*   une tartelette aux **fraises** *(f)*

À la boucherie, on achète de la viande:

du poulet   du bœuf   du porc

À la charcuterie, on achète **de la charcuterie** et **des plats préparés:**

du saucisson   du jambon   des saucisses *(f)*   des plats préparés

On achète du poisson et des fruits de mer à la poissonnerie.

Et on va à **l'épicerie** *(f)* pour acheter des fruits, des légumes, **des conserves** *(f)* et des produits *(m)* **surgelés.**

Vocabulaire supplémentaire

la confiserie *the candy shop, the confectioner's shop*
la fromagerie *the cheese shop*
le marchand de fruits et légumes *the fruit and vegetable market*
le traiteur *the caterer*

Sélection musicale. Search for the song **"Sur la table"** by Charles Aznavour online to enjoy a musical selection related to this vocabulary.

---

une grande surface *a superstore*   **un(e) commerçant(e)** *a shopkeeper*   **une pâtisserie** *a pastry*   **un pain complet** *a loaf of whole-grain bread*   **une cerise** *a cherry*   **une fraise** *a strawberry*   **de la charcuterie** *deli meats, cold cuts*   **un plat préparé** *a ready-to-serve dish*   **l'épicerie** *the grocery store*   **des conserves** *canned goods*   **surgelé(e)** *frozen*

Beaucoup de Français **disent** que pour avoir un bon **choix** de légumes et de fruits vraiment **frais, il faut** aller au marché.

© Courtesy of Esther Marshall

Au marché, on peut acheter:

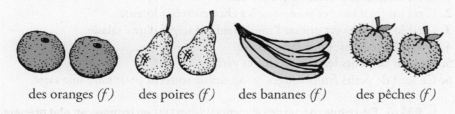

des oranges *(f)*   des poires *(f)*   des bananes *(f)*   des pêches *(f)*

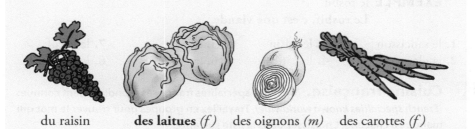

du raisin   **des laitues** *(f)*   des oignons *(m)*   des carottes *(f)*

Vocabulaire supplémentaire

LÉGUMES
un artichaut *an artichoke*
des asperges *(f) asparagus*
une aubergine *an eggplant*
du brocoli
des champignons *(m) mushrooms*
du chou *cabbage*
du chou-fleur *cauliflower*
des choux de Bruxelles *(m) Brussels sprouts*
un concombre *a cucumber*
une courgette *a zucchini*
des épinards *(m) spinach*
du maïs *corn*
un radis *a radish*

FRUITS
un abricot *an apricot*
un ananas *a pineapple*
des bleuets *(m) blueberries (Canada)*
un citron vert *a lime*
des framboises *(f) raspberries*
un kiwi
une mandarine *a tangerine*
un melon
des myrtilles *(f) blueberries (France)*
une nectarine
un pamplemousse *a grapefruit*
une pastèque *a watermelon*
une prune *a plum*
un pruneau *a prune*
des raisins secs *(m) raisins*

---

disent (dire *to say, to tell*)   **un choix** *a choice*   **frais (fraîche)** *fresh*   **il faut** *it is necessary, one needs, one must*
une laitue *a head of lettuce*

Rosalie fait ses courses au marché.

ROSALIE:	Bonjour, monsieur.
LE MARCHAND:	Bonjour, madame. **Qu'est-ce qu'il vous faut aujourd'hui?**
ROSALIE:	Euh... voyons... un kilo de pommes de terre, **une livre** de tomates... Vous avez des haricots verts?
LE MARCHAND:	Non, madame, pas aujourd'hui. Mais j'ai des petits pois. Regardez comme ils sont beaux.
ROSALIE:	Non, merci, pas de petits pois aujourd'hui.
LE MARCHAND:	Alors, qu'est-ce que je peux vous proposer d'autre?
ROSALIE:	Donnez-moi aussi 500 grammes de fraises.
LE MARCHAND:	Et voilà, 500 grammes. Et avec ça?
ROSALIE:	C'est tout, merci. Ça fait combien?
LE MARCHAND:	Voilà... Alors, un kilo de pommes de terre – 1,40 €, une livre de tomates – 1,36 € et 500 grammes de fraises – 3,50 €. Ça fait 6,26 €.
ROSALIE:	Voici 7 euros.
LE MARCHAND:	Et voici votre monnaie. Merci, madame, et à bientôt!
ROSALIE:	Merci. Au revoir, monsieur.

A **Devinettes.** Qu'est-ce que c'est?

EXEMPLE C'est un fruit rond, orange et plein de vitamine C.
C'est une orange.

1. C'est le légume préféré de Bugs Bunny.
2. C'est un fruit long et jaune que les chimpanzés adorent.
3. C'est le légume vert qui est l'ingrédient principal d'une salade.
4. On utilise ce fruit pour faire du vin.
5. Ce sont de petits légumes ronds et verts.
6. Ce sont de petits fruits rouges qu'on utilise souvent pour faire une tarte.

B **C'est...** Est-ce que chacun des aliments suivants est **un légume, un plat préparé, une viande, un fruit, de la charcuterie, un fruit de mer** ou **un produit surgelé**?

EXEMPLE le rosbif
Le rosbif, c'est une viande.

1. le saucisson	3. le raisin	5. le porc	7. le bœuf
2. la glace	4. le pâté	6. la laitue	8. le homard

C **Cuisine française.** Voici des spécialités françaises mondialement connues *(French specialties known worldwide)*. Travaillez en groupes pour trouver le mot qui manque à chacune. Choisissez dans la liste suivante.

EXEMPLE un **pain** au chocolat

> bœuf canard chocolat crème oignon pain quiche salade vin

1. de la mousse au _____
2. du coq au _____
3. de la _____ lorraine
4. de la _____ brûlée

5. une _____ niçoise
6. du _____ à l'orange
7. de la soupe à l'_____
8. du _____ bourguignon

Qu'est-ce qu'il vous faut aujourd'hui? *What do you need today?*   **une livre** *half a kilo (≈ a pound)*

D **Un dîner.** Votre classe va préparer un dîner. Qu'est-ce que vous allez servir? Chaque étudiant doit répéter de mémoire les choses déjà mentionnées et ajouter *(add)* quelque chose.

EXEMPLE Étudiant 1: **On va servir du pain.**
Étudiant 2: **On va servir du pain et du pâté.**
Étudiant 3: **On va servir du pain, du pâté et du bifteck...**

Maintenant travaillez en groupes pour dire ce que vous allez acheter de cette liste dans chaque magasin. Vous allez faire les courses chez les petits commerçants au lieu d'aller au supermarché. Le premier groupe à compléter la liste de courses gagnera.

EXEMPLE **À la boulangerie-pâtisserie, on va acheter du pain...**

À la charcuterie

E **Entretien.** Interviewez votre partenaire.

1. Aimes-tu faire les courses? Combien de fois par semaine est-ce que tu fais les courses? Où est-ce que tu fais tes courses d'habitude? Est-ce que tu achètes quelquefois des choses chez les petits commerçants?
2. Aimes-tu les fruits? les légumes? Préfères-tu les fruits ou les légumes? Quels légumes préfères-tu? Quels légumes est-ce que tu n'aimes pas? Quels fruits préfères-tu? Quels fruits est-ce que tu n'aimes pas?

À VOUS!

Avec un(e) partenaire, relisez à haute voix la conversation entre Rosalie et le marchand. Ensuite, imaginez que vous êtes à la boulangerie-pâtisserie. Achetez au moins trois choses.

You can access the audio of the active vocabulary of this *Compétence* online.

SAYING HOW MUCH

✔ Pour vérifier

What word follows quantity expressions before nouns? Do you use **de** or **des** after a quantity expression followed by a plural noun?

Les expressions de quantité

1. Use these expressions to specify how much you want at the market or in a restaurant.

un verre de	*a glass of*	une boîte de	*a box of, a can of*
un litre de	*a liter of*	un pot de	*a jar of*
une carafe de	*a carafe of*	un paquet de	*a bag of, a sack of*
une bouteille de	*a bottle of*	une douzaine de	*a dozen*
une tranche de	*a slice of*	300 grammes de	*300 grams of*
un morceau de	*a piece of*	un kilo (et demi) de	*a kilo (and a half) of*
		une livre de	*a half a kilo (1.1 pounds) of*

2. After quantity expressions like those above, use **de (d')** before a noun instead of **du, de la, de l'**, or **des**.

   J'ai acheté un pot **de** crème et un kilo **de** viande.

3. Also use **de (d')** before a noun after less specific quantities such as:

combien de	*how much, how many*
(un) peu de	*(a) little*
assez de	*enough*
beaucoup de	*a lot of*
trop de	*too much, too many*
beaucoup trop de	*much too much, way too many*
plus de	*more*
moins de	*less*

   J'ai acheté beaucoup **de** légumes!

A **C'est assez?** Dans chaque situation, est-ce que la quantité indiquée est suffisante?

EXEMPLE Vous prenez le petit déjeuner seul(e) le matin et il y a un verre de lait dans le réfrigérateur.
Il y a trop de lait. / Il y a assez de lait. / Il y a trop peu de lait.

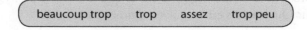

beaucoup trop   trop   assez   trop peu

1. Vous êtes quatre au restaurant et il y a une demi-bouteille d'eau.
2. Vous allez préparer une salade de tomates pour deux personnes. Vous avez un kilo de tomates.
3. Vous allez faire une omelette pour deux personnes et vous avez un seul œuf.
4. C'est le matin et il y a un verre de lait dans le réfrigérateur chez vous.
5. Vous dînez seul(e) au restaurant et il y a trois carafes d'eau.
6. Vous voulez préparer des carottes pour six personnes et vous avez deux carottes.

B Je voudrais... Complétez de façon logique chaque quantité proposée.

> | thon | cerises | jambon | vin | tomates | fromage |
> |------|---------|--------|-----|---------|---------|
> | jus de fruit | rosif | lait | sel | sucre | riz |

Je voudrais...

1. une bouteille de
2. un paquet de
3. une boîte de
4. une livre de
5. deux kilos de
6. un morceau de
7. un litre de
8. dix tranches de

Je voudrais six tranches de jambon, s'il vous plaît.

C Donnez-moi... Demandez les quantités indiquées des produits suivants.

EXEMPLE Une bouteille de vin, s'il vous plaît.

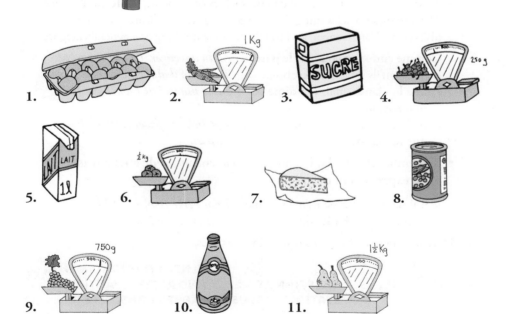

D Ces courses. Avec un(e) partenaire, faites une liste de choses qu'on achète dans les endroits suivants. Utilisez une expression de quantité logique avec chacune.

EXEMPLE à la charcuterie

> **une tranche de pâté, une livre de jambon, trois cents grammes de saucisson, un kilo de saucisses**

1. à la boucherie
2. au marché de fruits et légumes

Maintenant, préparez une conversation avec un(e) commerçant(e) dans laquelle vous achetez trois choses d'une de ces listes.

TALKING ABOUT FOODS

✔ *Pour vérifier*

1. Which article do you use to say *a* in French? Which articles do you use to express the idea of *some* or *any*?

2. Which article do you use to say *the*? to talk about likes, dislikes, and preferences? to make statements about entire categories?

3. Which articles change to **de**? When do they make this change? Which articles do not change to **de**?

L'usage des articles

1. Each article you use with a noun conveys a different meaning.

Vous voulez **de la** tarte?
*Do you want **(some)** pie?*
(This refers to a portion.)

Vous voulez **une** tarte?
*Do you want **a** pie?*
(This refers to a whole pie.)

- To say *a* or talk about a whole, use **un** or **une.** To say *some* or *any,* use **du, de la, de l',** or **des.**

  J'ai acheté **un croissant** et **du thé.**   *I bought **a croissant** and **(some) tea.***

- Remember that after a negative or an expression of quantity, **un, une, du, de la, de l',** and **des** all change to **de (d').**

  Elle ne mange jamais **de viande.**   *She never eats **meat.***
  Elle mange beaucoup **de légumes.**   *She eats a lot **of vegetables.***

- To say *the* or refer to a specific item, such as on a menu, use **le, la, l',** or **les.** Also use these articles immediately after verbs that indicate general likes, dislikes, and preferences, and to talk about something as a general category.

  Comme entrée, je voudrais **le pâté.**   *As an appetizer, I'd like **the pâté.***
  Le pâté qu'ils servent ici est bon.   ***The pâté** that they serve here is good.*
  J'aime **la viande** mais je n'aime pas   *I like **meat,** but I don't like **fish.***
    le poisson.
  Mais **le poisson** a moins de calories   *But **fish** has fewer calories than*
    que **la viande.**   **meat.**

- Remember that **le, la, l',** and **les** do *not* change to **de** after a negative or an expression of quantity.

  Je n'aime pas **le poisson,** mais j'aime   *I don't like **fish,** but I like*
    beaucoup **les fruits de mer.**   **shellfish** a lot.

2. Here is a review of how to use various articles.

	IN AFFIRMATIVE STATEMENTS, USE:	IN NEGATIVE STATEMENTS AND AFTER QUANTITY EXPRESSIONS, USE:
To say *a* or to talk about a whole:	**un, une** (J'achète **une** tarte.)	**de (d')** (Je n'achète pas **de** tarte.) (Je mange trop **de** tarte.)
To say *some* or *any:*	**du, de la, de l', des** (J'achète **du** lait.)	**de (d')** (Je n'achète pas **de** lait.) (J'achète beaucoup **de** lait.)
To say *the,* to name things someone likes or dislikes, or to make generalizations about categories:	**le, la, l', les** (**Le** thon est bon.) (J'aime **le** thon.) (**Le** thon est un poisson.)	**le, la, l', les** (**Le** thon n'est pas bon.) (Je n'aime pas **le** thon.) (**Le** thon n'est pas une viande.) (Je n'aime pas trop **le** thon.)

Note *de grammaire*

Note that **je voudrais** expresses a want or desire, not a preference, and is often followed by a partitive article: **Je voudrais du** jambon et **des** légumes.

A Manges-tu bien? Demandez à votre partenaire s'il/si elle mange souvent les choses suivantes.

EXEMPLE pâté

— **Manges-tu souvent du pâté?**
— **Je mange rarement du pâté. / Je ne mange jamais de pâté.**

1. escargots
2. tarte
3. légumes
4. viande rouge
5. poulet
6. crudités
7. glace
8. tarte aux pommes
9. carottes

Maintenant, demandez à votre partenaire s'il/si elle aime ces mêmes choses.

EXEMPLE pâté

— **Aimes-tu le pâté?**
— **J'aime assez le pâté. / Je n'aime pas le pâté.**

B Vos préférences. Dites si vous achetez souvent les choses suivantes et expliquez pourquoi.

EXEMPLE café

J'achète souvent du café parce que j'aime le café.
Je n'achète jamais de café parce que je n'aime pas le café.

1. fromage
2. bananes
3. viande rouge
4. raisin
5. eau minérale
6. jambon
7. huîtres
8. jus de fruit
9. crevettes

C Vos goûts. Complétez les phrases suivantes avec le nom d'un aliment (food) ou d'une boisson logique. Utilisez les articles appropriés.

1. Moi, j'adore...
2. J'aime bien...
3. Comme viande, je mange souvent...
4. Chez moi, il n'y a jamais...
5. Pour le déjeuner, je prends souvent...

D Ce soir. Rosalie parle du dîner qu'elle va préparer ce soir. Complétez ses phrases avec l'article qui convient: **un, une, du, de la, de l', des, le, la, l', les** ou **de (d')**.

Ce soir, je vais servir __1__ soupe de légumes, __2__ poulet, __3__ riz et __4__ petits pois. Et comme dessert, je pense préparer __5__ tarte aux cerises. Moi, je préfère __6__ gâteau, mais André aime beaucoup __7__ tarte! Cet après-midi, je dois aller acheter __8__ sucre, 500 grammes __9__ cerises et beaucoup __10__ légumes. Il y a un marché tout près où __11__ légumes sont toujours très frais! Je ne mets pas __12__ oignons dans la soupe parce qu'André n'aime pas __13__ oignons. C'est dommage parce que __14__ oignons sont bons pour la santé (health).

E Entretien. Interviewez votre partenaire.

1. Quels fruits de mer aimes-tu? Quelles viandes? Est-ce que tu manges plus de fruits de mer ou plus de viande?
2. Manges-tu plus souvent des fruits ou des légumes? Quel fruit préfères-tu? Quel légume préfères-tu? Quels fruits et légumes est-ce que tu n'aimes pas? Est-ce que tu achètes plus de légumes surgelés, frais ou en conserve?

Talking about meals

LES REPAS

En France, le petit déjeuner est généralement un repas **léger.** On prend:

du café au lait   du thé

des tartines *(f)* ou des croissants *(m)*

du chocolat   du beurre    de la confiture

De plus en plus de Français, **surtout** les jeunes, prennent aussi des céréales le matin.

Les Américains et les Canadiens prennent souvent un petit déjeuner plus **copieux.** Ils prennent:

   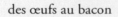

des œufs au bacon   des céréales *(f)*   du pain grillé   des fruits

À midi, certains Français prennent un déjeuner complet. D'autres prennent un repas rapide. Dans les cafés, les fast-foods et les self-services, on peut manger:

une soupe	une salade	une pizza
une omelette	un hamburger	un sandwich
un steak-frites		

Les gens qui prennent un repas rapide à midi mangent souvent un repas plus complet le soir. **Ceux** qui mangent un repas plus copieux à midi mangent **seulement** de la soupe, des légumes, de la charcuterie, une salade, du fromage ou une omelette comme dîner.

---

léger (légère) *light*   **une tartine** *bread with butter and jelly*   **surtout** *especially*   **copieux (copieuse)** *copious, large*
un steak-frites *steak and fries*   **Ceux (Celles)** *Those*   **seulement** *only*

Rose prépare le petit déjeuner avec sa cousine Lucie.

LUCIE: Tu as faim? Je peux te faire des œufs au bacon si tu veux – un vrai petit déjeuner à l'américaine.

ROSE: Merci, c'est gentil, mais je mange très peu le matin. **Pourtant, je prendrais bien** des céréales et du thé si tu **en** as.

LUCIE: Ah, je suis **désolée**... il **n'**y a **plus** de thé. Mais il y a du café. Tu en veux?

ROSE: Oui, je veux bien. Et toi? Qu'est-ce que tu vas prendre?

LUCIE: Le matin, **je bois** toujours du chocolat chaud et quelquefois je prends des tartines.

ROSE: Oh, regarde! **Il n'y a presque plus** de pain.

LUCIE: Mais **si**! Il y a **encore** une baguette, **là.**

Vocabulaire supplémentaire

des gaufres *(f) waffles*
des muffins *(m)* **anglais**
des pancakes *(m)*
des petites saucisses *breakfast sausages*
du sirop d'érable *maple syrup*
du porridge d'avoine *oatmeal*
une barre de céréales *a granola bar*
du pain perdu *French toast*

A **Vrai ou faux?** Est-ce que ces phrases sont vraies ou fausses?

1. En France, on prend plus souvent des œufs le soir ou à midi que le matin.
2. Les Français prennent un repas copieux le matin.
3. Beaucoup de Français prennent seulement du pain et du café le matin.
4. Certains, surtout les jeunes, aiment prendre des céréales.

B **Chez nous.** Aux États-Unis et au Canada, à quel(s) repas mange-t-on le plus souvent ces choses: **au petit déjeuner, au déjeuner** ou **au dîner**?

EXEMPLE une omelette
On mange plus souvent une omelette au petit déjeuner.

1. des croissants
2. des céréales
3. du poisson
4. un hamburger
5. de la soupe
6. du pain grillé
7. du saumon
8. des œufs au bacon
9. des légumes

C **Comparaisons culturelles.** Avec d'autres étudiant(e)s, devinez comment le plus grand nombre de Français ont répondu aux questions suivantes dans des sondages *(polls)*. Après, faites un sondage parmi *(among)* les étudiants de votre classe.

1. Combien de temps prenez-vous pour le petit déjeuner tous les matins? (moins de 10 minutes / de 10 à 15 minutes / plus de 15 minutes / Je ne prends pas de petit déjeuner.)
2. Que mangez-vous au petit déjeuner? (des céréales / du pain ou des biscottes *[melba toast]* / des viennoiseries *[pastries]* / des œufs / rien)
3. Quelle est votre confiture préférée? (cerises / oranges / fraises / abricots / framboises *[raspberry]*)
4. Qu'est-ce que vous aimez manger quand vous avez un peu faim entre les repas? (un fruit / des chips / du fromage / des biscuits *[cookies, crackers]* / du yaourt)

🔄 **À VOUS!**

Avec un(e) partenaire, relisez à haute voix la conversation entre Rose et Lucie. Ensuite, imaginez que vous passez des vacances avec un(e) ami(e) français(e). Parlez de ce que vous mangez d'habitude le matin.

You can access the audio of the active vocabulary of this *Compétence* online.

Pourtant *However*   **je prendrais bien** *I would gladly have*   **en** *some, any*   **désolé(e)** *sorry*   **ne... plus** *no more, no longer*   **je bois (boire** *to drink)*   **Il n'y a presque plus** *There is almost no more*   **si** *yes* (in response to a question / statement in the negative)   **encore** *still, again, more*   **là** *there*

SAYING WHAT YOU EAT AND DRINK

✔ *Pour vérifier*

1. In what three instances do you use the pronoun **en**? How is **en** usually translated in English? Can you omit **en** in French as you often can its equivalent in English?

2. How do you say *to drink* in French? What is the conjugation of this verb? How do you say *I drank some coffee this morning? I used to drink a lot of coffee?*

Le pronom en et le verbe boire

1. Use the pronoun **en** *(some, any, of it, of them)* to replace a noun preceded by a partitive article, an expression of quantity, **un, une, des,** or a number. Although the equivalent expression may be omitted in English, **en** is always used in French.

— Tu veux un croissant? — *Do you want a croissant?*
— Oui, j'**en** veux un. — *Yes, I want one (of them).*

2. **En** is placed *immediately* before the verb. It goes before the infinitive if there is one. If not, it goes before the conjugated verb. In the **passé composé,** it is placed before the auxiliary verb.

— Tu prends du gâteau?
— Oui, je vais **en** prendre. / Oui, j'**en** prends. / Non, merci, j'**en** ai déjà pris.

3. Use **en** to replace:

- a noun preceded by **du, de la, de l', des,** or **de (d').**

— Tu veux **du café**? — *Do you want some coffee?*
— Non merci, je n'**en** veux pas. — *No thanks, I don't want any.*

- a noun preceded by an expression of quantity. (In this case, repeat the expression of quantity in the sentence containing **en,** unless it is negative.)

— Vous voulez un kilo **de cerises**? — *Do you want a kilo of cherries?*
— Oui, j'**en** veux un kilo. — *Yes, I want a kilo (of them).*
Non, je n'**en** veux pas. — *No, I don't want any.*

- a noun preceded by **un, une,** or a number. (In this case, include **un, une,** or the number in the sentence containing **en,** unless it is negative.)

— Tu as mangé **une tartelette**? — *You ate a tart?*
— Oui, j'**en** ai mangé une. — *Yes, I ate one (of them).*
Non, je n'**en** ai pas mangé. — *No, I didn't eat any (of them).*

4. Use the irregular verb **boire** *(to drink)* to talk about what you drink.

BOIRE *(to drink)*	
je **bois**	nous **buvons**
tu **bois**	vous **buvez**
il/elle/on **boit**	ils/elles **boivent**

PASSÉ COMPOSÉ: j'**ai bu**
IMPARFAIT: je **buvais**

Vous avez bu du vin hier soir?   Je buvais du lait quand j'étais petit.

⟳ A **À table.** Un(e) ami(e) vous propose les choses suivantes au petit déjeuner. Comment répondez-vous? Utilisez le pronom **en** dans vos réponses.

EXEMPLE du café
— **Tu veux du café?**
— **Non merci, je n'en veux pas. / Oui, j'en veux bien.**

1. du café   **3.** des œufs   **5.** des tartines
2. du thé   **4.** de l'eau   **6.** des céréales

Sélection musicale. Search for the song **"Bois ton café"** by L'Affaire Louis' trio online to enjoy a musical selection containing the verb **boire**.

B Des courses. Voici la liste de Rosalie pour les courses. Combien va-t-elle acheter de chaque chose? Utilisez le pronom **en** dans vos réponses.

> **EXEMPLE** du sucre
> **Elle va en acheter un paquet.**

1. des pommes
2. du bœuf
3. du lait
4. des œufs

5. du vin rouge
6. des cerises
7. du pâté
8. des céréales

un paquet de sucre
6 pommes
un kilo de bœuf
2 litres de lait
une douzaine d'œufs
une bouteille de vin rouge
500 grammes de cerises
300 grammes de pâté
une boîte de céréales

C Et toi? Posez ces questions à un(e) partenaire pour savoir s'il/si elle fait attention à sa santé. Il/Elle va répondre avec le pronom **en.**

> **EXEMPLE** —**Tu manges des œufs?**
> —**Oui, j'en mange trop / beaucoup / assez.**
> **Oui, mais je n'en mange pas assez.**
> **Non, je n'en mange pas.**

1. Tu bois de l'eau?
2. Tu manges des desserts?
3. Tu fais de l'exercice?
4. Tu manges des fruits?

5. Tu manges du poisson?
6. Tu fumes des cigarettes?
7. Tu manges des légumes?
8. Tu manges de la viande?

D Boissons. Complétez les phrases logiquement en utilisant le verbe **boire.**

> **EXEMPLE** Le matin, je **bois du lait.**

1. Au petit déjeuner, les Français...
2. Au petit déjeuner, les Américains / Canadiens...
3. Le matin, je...
4. Quand j'étais jeune, le matin, je...
5. Ce matin, j'...
6. Avec un hamburger, on...
7. Dans cette région, quand il fait chaud, nous...
8. Quand j'ai très soif, je...
9. *[À un(e) autre étudiant(e)]* À une fête, qu'est-ce que tu...?
10. *[Au professeur]* Est-ce que vous... beaucoup de café?

E Entretien. Interviewez votre partenaire. Utilisez le pronom **en** dans les réponses.

1. Manges-tu souvent des légumes? Est-ce que tu en as déjà mangé aujourd'hui? Manges-tu souvent de la viande rouge? En manges-tu tous les jours? Est-ce que tu vas en manger aujourd'hui ou demain?

2. Fais-tu souvent de l'exercice? Combien de fois par semaine est-ce que tu en fais?

3. Est-ce que tu bois du café? En bois-tu trop? Quand est-ce que tu en bois? Et tes amis, est-ce qu'ils en boivent souvent?

TALKING ABOUT CHOICES

✔ *Pour vérifier*

1. How do you find the stem of a regular **-ir** verb? What are the endings? What is the conjugation of **grandir**? of **grossir**?

2. What auxiliary verb do you use in the **passé composé** with the verbs listed here, except with the reflexive verb **se nourrir**? How do you form the past participle? How do you say *I finished*? What is the conjugation of **-ir** verbs in the imperfect?

3. How do you pronounce an initial **s**? a single **s** between vowels? How do you pronounce double **ss**? How can you hear the difference between the singular and plural forms of **-ir** verbs in the present tense?

Les verbes en **-ir**

1. To conjugate regular **-ir** verbs in the present tense, drop the **-ir** and add the following endings. All **-ir** verbs presented here form the **passé composé** with **avoir**, except the reflexive verb **se nourrir**.

CHOISIR *(to choose)*	
je chois**is**	nous chois**issons**
tu chois**is**	vous chois**issez**
il/elle/on chois**it**	ils/elles chois**issent**

PASSÉ COMPOSÉ: j'**ai choisi**
IMPARFAIT: je **choisissais**

2. Here are some common **-ir** verbs.

choisir (de faire)	*to choose (to do)*
finir (de faire)	*to finish (doing)*
grandir	*to grow (up), to grow taller*
grossir	*to get fatter*
maigrir	*to get thinner, to slim down*
(se) nourrir	*to feed, to nourish, to nurture (oneself)*
obéir (à quelqu'un / à quelque chose)	*to obey (somebody / something)*
réfléchir (à)	*to think (about)*
réussir (à)	*to succeed (at), to pass (a test)*

Note *de vocabulaire*

Notice that some **-ir** verbs are based on a related adjective: (**gros** → **grossir**, **grand** → **grandir**).

PRONONCIATION

La lettre **s** et les verbes en **-ir** 8-7

To remember whether to spell words like **choisir** and **réussir** with one **s** or two, it is helpful to know the rules for pronouncing the letter **s**.

Pronounce an **s** as [s] when it is the first letter of the word, it is followed by a consonant, or it appears as a double **s** between two vowels, as in **réussir**.

s̆alade   s̆eulement   s̆urtout   s̆teak   res̆taurant   s̆port   des̆s̆ert   réus̆s̆ir   gros̆s̆ir

Pronounce an **s** as [z] when it appears in liaison or as a single **s** between two vowels, as in **choisir**.

les̆ apéritifs   mes̆ enfants   les̆ entrées   serveus̆e   chois̆ir   copieus̆e

Notice that in the present tense, an **s** sound in the ending of **-ir** verbs indicates that you are talking about more than one person.

il grandit / ils grandissent   elle finit / elles finissent   il choisit / ils choisissent

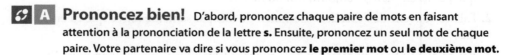 **A   Prononcez bien!**   D'abord, prononcez chaque paire de mots en faisant attention à la prononciation de la lettre **s**. Ensuite, prononcez un seul mot de chaque paire. Votre partenaire va dire si vous prononcez **le premier mot** ou **le deuxième mot**.

1. basse / base
2. coussin / cousin
3. croissant / croisant
4. poisson / poison
5. dessert / désert
6. il grossit / ils grossissent
7. il réussit / ils réussissent
8. il choisit / ils choisissent

🔊 8-8 Maintenant, écoutez les phrases et dites si on parle **du professeur** ou **des étudiants**.

EXEMPLE Ils réussissent toujours à comprendre.
On parle des étudiants.

B **Une histoire d'amour.** Complétez cette description de la relation de Rosalie et d'André avec la forme correcte des verbes indiqués au présent.

Rosalie est réaliste et elle répète toujours qu'on ne __1__ (se nourrir) pas d'amour et d'eau fraîche. Cependant *(However)*, elle __2__ (réfléchir) beaucoup à sa vie sentimentale et elle __3__ (réussir) à trouver le grand amour avec André. Leur amour __4__ (se nourrir) des plus petites choses, une caresse ou un mot doux *(sweet)*, et André __5__ (choisir) toujours de petits cadeaux *(gifts)* parfaits pour Rosalie. Cet amour __6__ (grandir) de jour en jour et ils __7__ (finir) par se marier. Ils ne __8__ (réfléchir) pas trop aux défauts de l'autre et ils __9__ (réussir) toujours à garder *(to keep)* leur sens de l'humour. Ils __10__ (finir) leur vie ensemble à l'âge de presque cent ans et tous les matins pendant toutes ces années, André __11__ (choisir) des roses de son jardin pour en faire un bouquet pour Rosalie.

C **Il y a cinq ans.** Demandez à votre partenaire s'il/si elle fait les choses suivantes maintenant ou s'il/si elle les faisait plutôt il y a cinq ans.

EXEMPLE réfléchir plus à ton avenir *(future)*
— **Tu réfléchis plus à ton avenir maintenant ou est-ce que tu réfléchissais plus à ton avenir il y a cinq ans?**
— **Je réfléchis plus à mon avenir maintenant.**
Je réfléchissais plus à mon avenir il y a cinq ans.

1. réfléchir plus à tes problèmes
2. réussir mieux à contrôler le stress
3. finir la journée plus tôt
4. choisir mieux tes priorités
5. te nourrir mieux
6. obéir plus aux autres

D **Un repas.** Interviewez votre partenaire avec les questions suivantes.

1. Quand tu sors dîner avec ton meilleur ami (ta meilleure amie), qui choisit le restaurant en général? Quel genre de cuisine choisissez-vous le plus souvent? Si vous buvez du vin au restaurant, choisissez-vous quelquefois un vin français?

2. Quand tu choisis un plat principal au restaurant, est-ce que tu réfléchis aux calories? Est-ce que tu finis le repas par un dessert? Et ton meilleur ami (ta meilleure amie)? Qu'est-ce que tu choisis le plus souvent comme dessert?

3. Si tu ne réussis pas à tout manger est-ce que tu demandes à emporter les restes chez toi *(ask for a doggy bag)*?

Maintenant, adaptez les questions précédentes en mettant les verbes au passé composé pour interviewer votre partenaire sur la dernière fois qu'il/elle a dîné avec son meilleur ami (sa meilleure amie) au restaurant.

Choosing a healthy lifestyle

LA SANTÉ

Faites-vous attention à votre santé? **À votre avis** *(m)*, qu'est-ce qu'il faut faire pour rester en bonne santé?

Pour rester en bonne santé, est-ce qu'**on devrait...**

manger des plats **sains** et légers?

manger plus de produits **bio**?

manger moins de **matières grasses** *(f)*?

manger plus **lentement**?

prendre des vitamines?

éviter l'alcool et le tabac?

contrôler le stress? (faire du yoga ou de la méditation, parler avec des ami[e]s...)

Pour être en forme et pour devenir plus **fort,** est-ce qu'on devrait...

marcher et faire des randonnées?

faire de l'aérobic?

faire de la muscu(lation)?

Patricia demande **des conseils** *(m)* à Rosalie.

PATRICIA: **Je me sens** toujours fatiguée ces jours-ci. J'ai besoin d'être en meilleure santé. Toi, tu as l'air toujours en forme. **Tu pourrais** me donner des conseils?

ROSALIE: Tu dors assez la nuit?

PATRICIA: Je me couche assez tôt, mais je dors très mal. Je me réveille **plusieurs** fois pendant la nuit. Si je pouvais mieux dormir, **je serais** contente.

ROSALIE: Tu devrais boire moins de café pendant la journée. **Tu ferais mieux de** bien manger aussi et de faire de l'exercice régulièrement.

PATRICIA: J'aime bien marcher. Si j'avais plus de temps libre, **j'aimerais** bien faire du sport tous les jours.

ROSALIE: Si tu marchais tous les jours et si tu mangeais mieux, **tu te sentirais sans doute** mieux. Et **n'oublie pas** de boire moins de café et plus d'eau!

La santé *Health*   **faire attention (à)** *to pay attention (to), to watch out (for)*   **À votre avis** *In your opinion*
on devrait *one should*   **sain(e)** *healthy*   **bio (biologiques)** *organic*   **les matières grasses** *fats*   **lentement** *slowly*
éviter *to avoid*   **fort(e)** *strong*   **marcher** *to walk*   **faire de la muscu(lation)** *to do weight training, to do bodybuilding*
des conseils *advice*   **Je me sens (se sentir** *to feel)*   **Tu pourrais...?** *Could you...?*   **plusieurs** *several*
je serais *I would be*   **Tu ferais mieux de** *You would do better to*   **j'aimerais** *I would like*   **tu te sentirais** *you would feel*
sans doute *without doubt, doubtless*   **n'oublie pas** *don't forget* **(oublier** *to forget)*

A **Des conseils.** C'est **un bon conseil** ou **un mauvais conseil** pour la santé?

1. Il faut faire de l'exercice plusieurs fois par semaine.
2. On devrait manger plus de viande rouge et moins de légumes.
3. Il est important de faire de l'aérobic.
4. On devrait éviter les matières grasses.
5. Les plats sains et légers sont bons pour la santé.
6. On peut devenir plus fort si on fait de la muscu.
7. On devrait manger plus vite pour éviter de trop manger.
8. On devrait manger des produits bio.
9. On ferait mieux de rester très stressé, ça donne de l'énergie.
10. Si vous voulez être en bonne santé, n'oubliez pas de boire assez d'eau.

B **Habitudes.** Deux amis parlent de ce qu'ils font pour être en meilleure santé. Mettez chaque verbe entre parenthèses à la forme correcte dans l'espace qui convient.

> **EXEMPLE** Je **maigris** parce que je **choisis** des plats sains et légers. (choisir, maigrir)

1. Les enfants _____ si on les _____ mal. (grossir, nourrir)
2. Je _____ à ne pas fumer, mais je _____ parce que je mange quand j'ai envie d'une cigarette. (réussir, grossir)
3. Mon meilleur ami _____ parce qu'il _____ toujours des desserts avec beaucoup de sucre. (choisir, grossir)
4. Dans notre famille, nous _____ beaucoup à notre régime *(diet)*: on _____ bien et on _____ rarement le dîner par un dessert. (réfléchir, finir, se nourrir)
5. Nos enfants _____ toujours et ils _____ tous leurs légumes. (obéir, finir)
6. Tu ne _____ pas à contrôler ton stress parce que tu _____ trop à tes problèmes. (réussir, réfléchir)

C **Entretien.** Interviewez votre partenaire.

1. Est-ce que tu te sens souvent fatigué(e)? Dors-tu assez?
2. Fais-tu attention à ta santé? Que fais-tu pour ta santé?
3. Manges-tu bien? Manges-tu beaucoup de fruits et de légumes? beaucoup de plats sains et légers? beaucoup de produits bio? Est-ce que tu prends des vitamines?
4. Est-ce que tu évites l'alcool ou est-ce que tu en bois? Est-ce que tu fumes?
5. Es-tu stressé(e)? Que fais-tu pour contrôler le stress?
6. Aimes-tu faire de l'exercice? Fais-tu de l'aérobic? de la muscu? des randonnées?

À VOUS!

Avec un(e) partenaire, relisez à haute voix la conversation entre Rosalie et Patricia. Ensuite, imaginez que vous voulez faire plus attention à votre santé. Demandez des conseils à votre partenaire.

You can access the audio of the active vocabulary of this *Compétence* online.

SAYING WHAT YOU WOULD DO

✔ Pour vérifier

1. What other verb tense has the same endings as the conditional? What is the stem for the conditional of most verbs? What are 14 verbs with irregular stems in the conditional? What is the stem of each? Do they use the regular conditional endings?

2. How do you say *there would be? it would rain? it would be necessary?*

3. How do you express *could* and *should* in French?

4. When do you use the conditional?

Note *de prononciation*

An unaccented **e** is usually not pronounced if you can drop it without bringing three pronounced consonants together (**samẹdi**). This is called **e caduc** and often occurs in the pronunciation of conditional verb forms (**j'habitẹrais**).

This occurs in many words in English, as in the words *refẹrence, diffẹrence,* and *revẹrence.*

Sélection musicale. Search online for the songs **"Mourir demain"** by Natasha St Pier and Pascal Obispo and **"Si tu n'existais pas"** performed by Willy Denzey online to enjoy musical selections containing verbs in the conditional form.

Le conditionnel

1. To say what one ***would*** do, use the conditional form of the verb.

> To say ***would*** + verb, use the conditional form of the verb.

I would like to lose weight.   **J'aimerais** maigrir.
If he cooked, *he'd eat* better.   S'il faisait la cuisine, **il mangerait** mieux.

2. The verb stem used to form the conditional of all regular and most irregular verbs is the verb's infinitive. If an infinitive ends in **-e,** the **e** is dropped. The endings are identical to those used in the **imparfait: -ais, -ais, -ait, -ions, -iez, -aient.**

REGULAR -*ER* VERBS	REGULAR -*IR* VERBS	REGULAR -*RE* VERBS
je parler**ais**	je finir**ais**	je perdr**ais**
tu parler**ais**	tu finir**ais**	tu perdr**ais**
il/elle/on parler**ait**	il/elle/on finir**ait**	il/elle/on perdr**ait**
nous parler**ions**	nous finir**ions**	nous perdr**ions**
vous parler**iez**	vous finir**iez**	vous perdr**iez**
ils/elles parler**aient**	ils/elles finir**aient**	ils/elles perdr**aient**

3. All regular and most irregular verbs follow this same pattern.

> dormir → je dormirais...   prendre → je prendrais...   boire → je boirais...

4. Spelling change verbs like **acheter, appeler,** and **payer** have spelling changes in *all* forms of the conditional; but verbs like **préférer** or **répéter** do not change their accent marks in any conditional form.

j'achèterais / nous achèterions   je préférerais / nous préférerions
j'appellerais / nous appellerions   je répéterais / nous répéterions
je paierais / nous paierions

5. The following verbs have irregular stems in the conditional. The endings are regular.

STEM ENDS WITH *R*		STEM ENDS WITH *DR / VR*		STEM ENDS WITH *RR*	
aller	**ir-**	venir	**viendr-**	voir	**verr-**
avoir	**aur-**	revenir	**reviendr-**	envoyer	**enverr-**
être	**ser-**	devenir	**deviendr-**	pouvoir	**pourr-**
faire	**fer-**	vouloir	**voudr-**	mourir	**mourr-**
		devoir	**devr-**	courir	**courr-**

6. Also note these conditional forms:

il y a	→	**il y aurait**	*there would be*
falloir	→	**il faudrait**	*it would be necessary*
il pleut	→	**il pleuvrait**	*it would rain*

7. In the conditional, use **devoir** to say what one ***should*** do and **pouvoir** to say what one ***could*** do.

> To say ***should*** + verb, use the conditional of **devoir** plus an infinitive.
> To say ***could*** + verb, use the conditional of **pouvoir** plus an infinitive.

You should eat more vegetables.   **Tu devrais manger** plus de légumes.
You could eat better.   **Tu pourrais** mieux **manger.**

8. Use the conditional:

- to make polite requests or offers.

  Pourrais-tu me passer le sel?   ***Could you*** *pass me the salt?*
  Voudriez-vous du café?   ***Would you like*** *some coffee?*

- to say what someone would do if circumstances were different (to make hypothetical or contrary-to-fact statements).

  Si je faisais la cuisine, **je mangerais** mieux.
  If I cooked, ***I would eat*** *better.*

In statements such as the one above, the **si** clause is in the imperfect and the result clause is in the conditional. Note that either clause can come first.

si + imperfect → conditional

Si **nous avions** plus de temps libre, **nous nous reposerions** plus.
If ***we had*** *more free time,* ***we would rest*** *more.*

Nous nous reposerions plus si **nous avions** plus de temps libre.
We would rest *more if* ***we had*** *more free time.*

PRONONCIATION

*La consonne **r** et le conditionnel* 8-10

The conditional stem of all verbs in French ends in **-r.** To pronounce a French **r,** arch the back of the tongue firmly in the back of the mouth, as if to pronounce a *g,* and pronounce a strong English *h* sound.

je pourrais   tu trouverais   nous serions   il reviendrait   ils devraient

A   **Prononcez bien!**   Dites ce que les personnes indiquées feraient dans les circonstances données. Faites attention à la prononciation de la consonne **r.**

1. Si j'avais plus de temps,...
je mangerais / je ne mangerais pas mieux.
je me reposerais / je ne me reposerais pas plus.
je dormirais / je ne dormirais pas plus.

2. Si mes amis et moi pouvions passer plus de temps ensemble,...
nous dînerions / nous ne dînerions pas plus au restaurant.
nous ferions / nous ne ferions pas plus d'exercice ensemble.
nous irions / nous n'irions pas danser ensemble.

3. Si on voulait être en meilleure santé,...
on éviterait / on n'éviterait pas le tabac.
on irait / on n'irait pas souvent à la salle de gym.
on devrait / on ne devrait pas manger plus de légumes.

B **Scrupules.** Que feriez-vous dans ces circonstances?

1. Si vous voyiez *(saw)* la fiancée de votre frère embrasser un autre garçon, est-ce que vous...
   a. le diriez *(would tell)* à votre frère?
   b. ne feriez rien?
   c. demanderiez 50 dollars à sa fiancée pour garder le silence?

2. Si vous voyiez une copie de l'examen de fin de semestre / trimestre sur le bureau du prof deux jours avant l'examen, est-ce que vous...
   a. la prendriez?
   b. ne feriez rien?
   c. liriez l'examen tout de suite?

3. Si vous trouviez un chien perdu dans la rue, est-ce que vous...
   a. téléphoneriez à la Société protectrice des animaux?
   b. prendriez le chien et chercheriez son maître *(owner)*?
   c. ne feriez rien?

4. Si vous ne veniez pas en cours le jour d'un examen important parce que vous n'étiez pas préparé(e), est-ce que vous...
   a. expliqueriez *(would explain)* la situation au professeur?
   b. diriez au professeur que vous étiez malade?
   c. accepteriez d'avoir un zéro à l'examen?

5. Si vous voyiez quelqu'un qui attaquait votre professeur de français, est-ce que vous...
   a. téléphoneriez à la police?
   b. resteriez là pour aider votre professeur?
   c. resteriez là pour aider l'agresseur?

C **Temps libre.** Demandez à votre partenaire s'il/si elle ferait les choses suivantes s'il/si elle avait plus de temps libre.

EXEMPLE préparer plus souvent des plats sains
— **Si tu avais plus de temps libre, préparerais-tu plus souvent des plats sains?**
— **Oui, je préparerais plus souvent des plats sains.**
Non, je ne préparerais pas plus souvent des plats sains.

1. dormir plus
2. être moins stressé(e)
3. pouvoir plus te reposer
4. partir souvent en week-end
5. aller plus souvent au parc
6. faire plus d'exercice
7. voir plus souvent tes amis
8. rendre plus souvent visite à ta famille

D **Une interview.** Un journaliste vous interviewe. Comment lui répondez-vous? Jouez les deux rôles avec votre partenaire.

1. Si vous habitiez dans une autre ville, où voudriez-vous habiter?
2. Si vous étiez un animal, quel animal seriez-vous: un chien, un chat, un poisson, un rat ou un oiseau *(a bird)*?
3. Si vous étiez une saison, quelle saison seriez-vous: l'hiver, l'été, le printemps ou l'automne?
4. Si votre vie était un morceau de musique, est-ce que ce serait de la musique populaire, de la musique classique, du rock, du blues...?
5. Si votre vie était un film, est-ce que ce serait un drame, une comédie, un film d'horreur ou un film d'aventure?

E **Situations.** Qu'est-ce que ces gens feraient ou ne feraient pas dans les situations suivantes?

EXEMPLE Si nous n'avions pas cours aujourd'hui, mes amis et moi... (aller au parc)
Si nous n'avions pas cours aujourd'hui, nous irions au parc.
Si nous n'avions pas cours aujourd'hui, nous n'irions pas au parc.

1. Si nous n'avions pas cours aujourd'hui, mes amis et moi... (être ici, aller prendre un verre, passer l'après-midi ensemble, se reposer)

2. Si Rose voulait être en meilleure santé, elle... (fumer beaucoup, devoir faire plus d'exercice, prendre des vitamines, boire assez d'eau)

3. Si les étudiants voulaient mieux réussir en cours de français, ils... (faire tous les devoirs, aller à tous les cours, dormir en cours, boire plus de vin français)

4. Si mes parents avaient des vacances cette semaine, ils... (être contents, faire un voyage, rester chez eux, aller en France)

F **Décisions.** Qu'est-ce que ces gens feraient dans les circonstances données?

EXEMPLE Si je pouvais quitter le cours maintenant, **je rentrerais chez moi.**

1. Si je pouvais faire ce que je voulais en ce moment, je (j')...

2. Si j'avais des vacances la semaine prochaine, je (j')...

3. Si mon meilleur ami (ma meilleure amie) pouvait faire ce qu'il/elle voulait en ce moment, il/elle...

4. S'il/Si elle gagnait au loto *(the lottery),* il/elle...

5. Si nous pouvions sortir ensemble ce soir, nous...

6. Si nous avions envie de faire de l'exercice, nous...

7. Si mes parents gagnaient au loto, ils...

8. S'ils pouvaient partir en vacances maintenant, ils...

9. Si le professeur nous disait *(told us)* qu'il n'y aurait plus d'examens dans ce cours, nous...

G **Par politesse.** Mettez ces phrases au conditionnel pour être plus poli(e) *(polite).*

EXEMPLE Veux-tu rester en forme?
Voudrais-tu rester en forme?

1. Tu veux faire de l'exercice?

2. Quand as-tu le temps d'aller à la salle de gym avec moi?

3. Peux-tu passer chez moi vers dix heures?

4. Ton amie veut venir aussi?

5. Qu'est-ce que vous voulez faire après?

6. On peut aller au restaurant végétarien?

7. Est-ce que vous voulez manger leur nouvelle salade?

VIDÉO-REPRISE

Les Stagiaires

Rappel!

Dans l'épisode précédent de la vidéo, Amélie a tout raconté *(told)* à Céline sur sa sortie avec Matthieu. Maintenant tout le monde semble *(seems)* être au courant *(aware)* de cette sortie.

See the *Résumé de grammaire* section at the end of each chapter for a review of all the grammar presented in the chapter.

Dans l'*Épisode 8,* Amélie parle à Rachid du restaurant où elle a dîné avec Matthieu. Avant de regarder la vidéo, faites ces activités pour réviser ce que vous avez appris dans le *Chapitre 8.*

A **Un grand dîner.** Matthieu va préparer un grand dîner avec un groupe d'amis. Qu'est-ce qu'ils pourraient servir? Travaillez avec un(e) partenaire pour nommer autant de choses que possible pour chaque catégorie.

EXEMPLE Comme entrée, **ils pourraient servir du pâté...**

Comme entrée...   Comme légumes...   Comme boisson...
Comme plat principal...   Comme dessert...

Matthieu fait les courses pour le dîner. Dites où il va aller pour acheter chacune des choses indiquées.

EXEMPLE Il va aller à l'épicerie pour acheter un pot de confiture.

1.   2.   3.   4.

B **La bonne santé.** Camille fait très attention à sa santé, mais elle n'arrive pas à convaincre *(she's not able to convince)* Monsieur Vieilledent de boire moins de café et de manger moins de croissants. Répondez à ces questions en employant le pronom **en.**

EXEMPLE Camille mange beaucoup *de pâtisseries*?
Non, elle n'en mange pas beaucoup.

1. Camille mange *de la viande rouge* tous les soirs?
2. Elle fait *de l'exercice* tous les jours?
3. Elle a bu beaucoup *de vin* hier soir?
4. Monsieur Vieilledent va boire moins *de café*?
5. Il va prendre *des croissants* ce matin?

C **Comparaisons culturelles.** Monsieur Vieilledent dîne avec un client américain. Son client parle des différences entre les habitudes alimentaires des Américains et les habitudes alimentaires des Français. Nommez autant de choses que possible pour chaque repas ou situation.

EXEMPLE au petit déjeuner
En France, au petit déjeuner, vous mangez des tartines ou des croissants et vous buvez du café. Chez nous, on mange...

1. au petit déjeuner
2. dans un fast-food
3. pour un dîner léger
4. pour un repas traditionnel

D **À table!** Continuez à faire des comparaisons culturelles en complétant ces phrases avec la forme correcte de l'article qui convient.

Ce qu'on mange varie d'une culture à l'autre. Aux États-Unis, par exemple, on prend __1__ petit déjeuner copieux. On mange souvent __2__ œufs au bacon et __3__ pain grillé. En France, __4__ petit déjeuner est un repas léger. On boit __5__ café au lait, __6__ thé ou __7__ chocolat chaud et on mange __8__ tartines.

À midi, on peut manger dans un café où on peut prendre __9__ omelette, __10__ salade ou __11__ sandwich avec __12__ vin ou __13__ eau minérale. __14__ vins français sont très bons, mais __15__ eau minérale est très populaire aussi. On peut finir son repas avec __16__ café avec un peu __17__ sucre ou un peu __18__ lait.

E **Qu'est-ce qu'ils font?** Amélie parle à Rachid des habitudes alimentaires des gens à Technovert. Complétez ses phrases de façon logique.

> **EXEMPLE** Je ne veux pas grossir. Alors, je (finir) tous mes repas par un dessert.
> Je ne veux pas grossir. Alors, je **ne finis pas** tous mes repas par un dessert.

1. Céline et moi faisons attention à notre santé. Alors, nous (choisir) des plats sains.
2. Céline et son chien (maigrir) parce qu'ils marchent tous les jours.
3. Toi, tu n'aimes pas les boissons alcoolisées. Alors, tu (boire) beaucoup de bière.
4. Camille et Céline veulent rester en bonne forme. Alors, elles (boire) très rarement de la bière.
5. Monsieur Vieilledent ne fait pas attention à sa santé. Il (boire) beaucoup de café et il (choisir) toujours des croissants au petit déjeuner.
6. Tes amis et toi, vous voulez rester en forme. Alors, vous (choisir) de bien manger et vous (boire) trop de café.

F **Si...** Amélie dit ce que tous les gens de Technovert feraient s'ils avaient plus de temps libre. Qu'est-ce qu'elle dit?

> **EXEMPLE** Monsieur Vieilledent (voyager plus, passer plus de temps avec ses enfants)
> **Si Monsieur Vieilledent avait plus de temps libre, il voyagerait plus et il passerait plus de temps avec ses enfants.**

1. Matthieu (inventer des jeux vidéo, apprendre à danser)
2. Moi, je (réfléchir plus à mon avenir, sortir plus souvent)
3. Camille et Céline (faire de l'exercice, se reposer plus)
4. Christophe (dormir plus, lire plus de mangas, aller plus souvent au cinéma)
5. Rachid et moi (réussir mieux à nos cours, être moins stressés)

Access the Video *Les Stagiaires* online.

 Épisode 8: Qu'est-ce qu'ils servent?

AVANT LA VIDÉO
Dans cet épisode, Amélie parle du restaurant où elle est allée avec Matthieu. Avant de le regarder, citez au moins trois choses qu'on sert dans un restaurant que vous aimez bien.

APRÈS LA VIDÉO
Regardez la vidéo et déterminez ce que Matthieu et Amélie ont commandé au restaurant.

LECTURE ET COMPOSITION

LECTURE

To appreciate a poem, it is important to read it with the right rhythm. Traditionally, French poems have verses with an even number of syllables, with regular pauses in the middle. Modern poets such as Jacques Prévert often use more irregular rhythms to create different moods. Prévert's poem *Déjeuner du matin* can be read in more than one way, creating different impressions. Do the following activity to help you read it.

Sentiments. Jacques Prévert (1900–1977), l'un des poètes les plus célèbres du vingtième siècle *(century)*, aimait parler de la vie de tous les jours dans sa poésie. Lisez les phrases suivantes du poème *Déjeuner du matin* en faisant une pause à la fin de chaque vers *(line)*. Ensuite, relisez les phrases sans pause. Pour vous, quels sentiments sont évoqués par les différentes manières de lire les vers?

l'hésitation	l'angoisse	le calme
la patience	la confusion	le désaccord
la décision	l'accord	???
l'indifférence	l'indécision	
l'impatience	la réflexion	

Il a mis
Son chapeau *(hat)* sur sa tête *(head)*

Il a fait des ronds *(rings)*
Avec la fumée *(smoke)*

Et moi, j'ai pris
Ma tête *(head)* dans ma main
Et j'ai pleuré *(cried)*

Déjeuner du matin

Jacques Prévert

Il a mis le café
Dans **la tasse**
Il a mis le lait
Dans la tasse de café
Il a mis le sucre
Dans le café au lait
Avec la petite **cuiller**
Il a tourné
Il a bu le café au lait
Et il a reposé la tasse
Sans me parler
Il a allumé
Une cigarette
Il a fait des ronds
Avec la fumée
Il a mis **les cendres**
Dans **le cendrier**
Sans me parler
Sans me regarder
Il s'est levé
Il a mis
Son **chapeau** sur sa **tête**
Il a mis
Son manteau de pluie
Parce qu'il pleuvait
Et il est parti
Sous la pluie
Sans **une parole**
Sans me regarder
Et moi j'ai pris
Ma tête dans ma main
Et **j'ai pleuré.**

© James Leynse/Getty Images

Jacques Prévert, "Déjeuner du matin" in *Paroles* © Éditions GALLIMARD
© Fatras / succession Jacques Prévert pour les droits électroniques réservés.

---

la tasse *the cup*   **cuiller** *spoon*   **les cendres** *the ashes*   **le cendrier** *the ashtray*
chapeau *hat*   **tête** *head*   **une parole** *a word*   **j'ai pleuré** *I cried*

Compréhension

Qu'est-ce qui s'est passé? Qu'est-ce qui s'est passé dans le poème?

1. Faites une liste des choses qu'il a faites.
2. Nommez deux choses qu'il n'a pas faites.
3. Quelle a été la réaction de l'autre personne?
4. Qui sont ces personnages? Sont-ils amis? parents? Sont-ils mariés, divorcés...?
5. Pourquoi est-ce qu'ils ne se parlent pas? Qu'est-ce qui s'est passé?

COMPOSITION

POUR MIEUX ÉCRIRE:
Finding the right word

You are going to write a review of a restaurant. When you write, try to use the most precise word possible to get your message across. Note how, in the following sentence, the word *small* can convey different messages.

It is a *small* restaurant with only fifteen tables.
Positive: It is a *cozy (intimate)* restaurant with only fifteen tables.
Negative: It is a *cramped (crowded)* restaurant with only fifteen tables.

To find the right word to express your meaning in French, you may need to use a synonym dictionary. Once you select a French word from an English-French dictionary, double check that you understand its use by looking it up in a French-English or French-French dictionary, or search for it on the Internet in the context in which you wish to use it.

Organisez-vous. Dans les phrases suivantes, voici quelques mots qu'on pourrait utiliser au lieu des mots en italique pour décrire un restaurant. Trouvez un mot supplémentaire pour chaque liste en cherchant dans un dictionnaire de synonymes sur Internet ou à la bibliothèque.

Le décor est *joli* (beau, charmant, harmonieux, pittoresque, ???).
Le décor est *laid* (atroce, hideux, grotesque, vulgaire, ???).
Le menu est *intéressant* (exotique, varié, extraordinaire, sensationnel, phénoménal, ???).
Le menu est *ennuyeux* (médiocre, ordinaire, limité, commun, insuffisant, banal, ???).
La cuisine est *bonne* (délicieuse, appétissante, savoureuse, délectable, exquise, succulente, ???).
La cuisine est *mauvaise* (insipide, déplorable, révoltante, fade, désastreuse, ???).
L'ambiance est *agréable* (sympathique, chaleureuse, intime, charmante, confortable, ???).
L'ambiance est *désagréable* (déplaisante, inhospitalière, froide, ???).
Le service est *bon* (rapide, animé, enthousiaste, immédiat, plaisant, gracieux, ???).
Le service est *mauvais* (lent, impoli, hostile, inconsistant, honteux, exaspérant, ???).

Une critique gastronomique

Écrivez une critique gastronomique d'un restaurant de votre ville. Parlez du décor, du menu, de la cuisine, de l'ambiance et du service.

COMPARAISONS CULTURELLES

À TABLE!

Ce qui est considéré «normal» ou «**poli**» diffère souvent d'une culture à l'autre. Chaque société a ses **propres coutumes,** ses plats préférés, et même sa propre **façon** de manger.

Par exemple, lorsqu'on est invité chez des Français, pour **éviter de venir les mains vides,** on offre généralement un bouquet de fleurs (mais pas de chrysanthèmes, qui sont des fleurs de cimetières en France) ou des chocolats. Il est préférable d'éviter d'**apporter** un dessert ou une bouteille de vin, **car** cela voudrait dire que votre hôte ou hôtesse a oublié ou les a peut-être mal choisis!

À table, **on garde** toujours les deux mains sur la table, mais on ne met pas **les coudes** sur la table. **Après avoir coupé** la viande, on garde sa **fourchette** dans la main gauche. On ne boit jamais de lait avec les repas comme le font certains Américains et le café est servi à la fin du repas, après le dessert. De nombreux restaurants et cafés acceptent que leurs clients viennent en compagnie de leur chien, du moment qu'il **se comporte** correctement.

Regardez ces photos. Qu'est-ce que vous **remarquez**?

poli *polite*   propres coutumes *own customs*   façon *way, manner*   éviter de venir les mains vides *to avoid coming empty-handed*   apporter *to bring, bringing*   car *because*   on garde *one keeps*   les coudes *elbows*   Après avoir coupé *After cutting*   fourchette *fork*   se comporte *behaves*   remarquez *notice*

Lisez ces phrases concernant les coutumes et les bonnes manières. Lesquelles sont vraies dans votre région? Et en France?

	CHEZ NOUS	EN FRANCE
1. On boit quelquefois du lait aux repas.	☐	☐
2. On mange souvent des œufs le matin.	☐	☐
3. On mange plus souvent des œufs le soir ou à midi.	☐	☐
4. On mange assez souvent dans des fast-foods.	☐	☐
5. La présentation est presque aussi importante que la saveur (taste) d'un plat.	☐	☐
6. Le pain est presque indispensable à tous les repas.	☐	☐
7. Le pain se mange généralement sans beurre, sauf le matin.	☐	☐
8. On fait assez souvent les courses chez les petits commerçants.	☐	☐
9. On mange beaucoup de choses avec les mains.	☐	☐
10. On mange très peu de choses avec les mains et certains mangent même les fruits avec un couteau et une fourchette.	☐	☐
11. Quand on mange, on garde toujours les deux mains sur la table.	☐	☐
12. On met le pain directement sur la table, pas sur l'assiette (plate).	☐	☐
13. Au restaurant, on peut commander à la carte ou on peut choisir un menu à prix fixe.	☐	☐
14. La carte est toujours affichée (posted) à l'extérieur d'un restaurant.	☐	☐

> Pour la France – Vrai: 3, 4, 5, 6, 7, 8, 10, 11, 12, 13, 14

Compréhension

1. Quelles différences est-ce qu'il y a entre ce qu'on fait chez vous et ce qu'on fait en France? Quelles ressemblances?
2. Les opinions des Français ne sont pas toujours reflétées (reflected) dans leur vie de tous les jours. Comment pouvez-vous expliquer ce contraste entre ce que les Français pensent et ce qu'ils font?

Opinions	Actions
Manger, c'est un art et un plaisir et les qualités esthétiques d'un plat (dish) (son apparence, sa présentation, sa fraîcheur,...) sont presque aussi importantes que sa saveur (taste).	Aujourd'hui, les Français se contentent de menus plus simples et passent moins de temps à table. On passe de moins en moins de temps à préparer les repas en se servant (using) de produits tout prêts, de produits surgelés et du four à micro-ondes (microwave).
Les repas sont un moment pour se retrouver en famille ou entre amis et pour apprécier la bonne cuisine.	Les repas sont pris moins souvent en famille et plus souvent devant la télé.
Le service et la qualité sont meilleurs chez les petits commerçants que dans les grandes surfaces.	On fait de plus en plus souvent les courses dans les grandes surfaces.

RÉSUMÉ DE GRAMMAIRE

Je vais acheter **de l'**eau, **du** pain, **de la** crème et **des** légumes.

I'm going to buy (some) water, (some) bread, (some) cream, and (some) vegetables.

— Je vais prendre **un** sandwich et **des** frites.
— Je **ne** prends **pas de** frites parce qu'elles ont **trop de** calories.

— Tu **n'**aimes **pas les** frites?
— Mais si, j'aime **beaucoup les** frites, mais **le** riz est meilleur pour **la** santé.
— Mais **les** frites qu'ils servent ici sont délicieuses.

Le matin, je **bois** du thé mais mon mari **boit** du café. À midi, nous **buvons** de l'eau.

Qu'est-ce que tu **as bu** ce matin?

Qu'est-ce qu'il tu **buvais** quand tu étais petit?

Les étudiants **réussissent** toujours aux examens. Tu **réussis** à tes examens?

J'**ai fini** mes devoirs.

Je ne **réfléchissais** pas beaucoup à mon avenir *(future)* quand j'étais jeune.

— Tu veux **de l'**eau?
— Oui, j'**en** veux bien. Non merci, je n'**en** veux pas.

— Tu prends un **sandwich**?
— Oui, j'**en** prends **un.** Non, j'**en** prends **deux.** Non, je n'**en** prends pas.

— Tu as acheté un kilo **de carottes**?
— Oui, j'**en** ai acheté **un kilo.** Non, j'**en** ai acheté **une livre.** Non, je n'**en** ai pas acheté.

THE PARTITIVE AND REVIEW OF ARTICLE USE

In French, use the partitive to convey the idea of *some* or *any,* even when *some* or *any* can be omitted in English.

MASCULINE SINGULAR BEFORE A CONSONANT SOUND	FEMININE SINGULAR BEFORE A CONSONANT SOUND	SINGULAR BEFORE A VOWEL SOUND	PLURAL
du pain	de la glace	de l'eau	des fruits

Un and **une** mean *a* and **du, de la, de l',** and **des** express the idea of *some* or *any.* All of these forms change to **de (d')** after most negated verbs and after expressions of quantity. (See page 330 for a list of quantity expressions.)

Use the definite article **(le, la, l', les)** to say *the,* to express likes, dislikes, and preferences, or to make statements about entire categories. The definite article does *not* change to **de** after a negative or quantity expression.

THE VERB *BOIRE* AND REGULAR *-IR* VERBS

The verb **boire** *(to drink)* is irregular.

BOIRE *(to drink)*	
je **bois**	nous **buvons**
tu **bois**	vous **buvez**
il/elle/on **boit**	ils/elles **boivent**
PASSÉ COMPOSÉ: **j'ai bu**	
IMPARFAIT: **je buvais**	

The stem for the present tense of regular **-ir** verbs is obtained by dropping the **-ir.** Add the following endings for the present tense.

RÉUSSIR *(to succeed)*	
je réuss**is**	nous réuss**issons**
tu réuss**is**	vous réuss**issez**
il/elle/on réuss**it**	ils/elles réuss**issent**
PASSÉ COMPOSÉ: **j'ai réussi**	
IMPARFAIT: **je réussissais**	

See page 338 for a list of common **-ir** verbs. All **-ir** verbs presented in this chapter form the **passé composé** with **avoir,** except the reflexive verb **se nourrir.**

THE PRONOUN *EN*

En replaces a noun preceded by a partitive article, an expression of quantity, **un, une,** or a number. When replacing a noun preceded by **un, une,** a number, or an expression of quantity, repeat the **un, une,** number, or expression of quantity in the sentence containing **en,** unless it's negative. In English, **en** is usually translated by *some, any, of it,* or *of them.* Although the equivalent expression may be omitted in English, **en** is always used in French.

En is placed *immediately* before the verb. It goes before the infinitive if there is one. If not, it goes before the conjugated verb. In the **passé composé,** place it before the auxiliary verb.

Je vais **en** prendre.
J'**en** prends.
J'**en** ai pris.

THE CONDITIONAL (*LE CONDITIONNEL*)

Use the conditional to say what someone *would, could,* or *should* do. To form the conditional of most verbs, add the same endings as the **imparfait** to the infinitive of the verb. If an infinitive ends in **-e,** drop the **e** before adding the endings.

PARLER	FINIR	PERDRE
je parler**ais**	je finir**ais**	je perdr**ais**
tu parler**ais**	tu finir**ais**	tu perdr**ais**
il/elle/on parler**ait**	il/elle/on finir**ait**	il/elle/on perdr**ait**
nous parler**ions**	nous finir**ions**	nous perdr**ions**
vous parler**iez**	vous finir**iez**	vous perdr**iez**
ils/elles parler**aient**	ils/elles finir**aient**	ils/elles perdr**aient**

Si j'avais plus de temps, **j'étudierais** plus. **Je finirais** tous mes devoirs et **le prof perdrait** moins souvent patience avec moi.

Most irregular verbs follow this same pattern.

dormir → je dormirais, tu dormirais…
prendre → je prendrais, tu prendrais…
boire → je boirais, tu boirais…

Si tu voulais être en forme, **tu dormirais** plus, **tu prendrais** des vitamines et **tu boirais** assez d'eau.

Spelling-change verbs like **se lever, appeler,** and **payer** have spelling changes in *all* forms of the conditional; but verbs like **préférer** or **répéter** do not change their accent marks in any conditional form.

The following verbs have irregular stems in the conditional. The endings are regular.

Si nous étions en vacances, **nous nous lèverions** plus tard. **Mon ami préférerait** se lever vers neuf heures.

aller → j'irais, tu irais…
avoir → j'aurais, tu aurais…
être → je serais, tu serais…
faire → je ferais, tu ferais…
devoir → je devrais, tu devrais…
vouloir → je voudrais, tu voudrais…
venir → je viendrais, tu viendrais…
devenir → je deviendrais, tu deviendrais…
revenir → je reviendrais, tu reviendrais…
voir → je verrais, tu verrais…
envoyer → j'enverrais, tu enverrais…
pouvoir → je pourrais, tu pourrais…
courir → je courrais, tu courrais…
mourir → je mourrais, tu mourrais…

Si j'avais plus de temps libre, **je ferais** beaucoup de choses. **J'irais** plus souvent au parc, **je verrais** plus souvent mes amis et **je serais** content!

Also learn the following:

il y a → il y aurait	il pleut → il pleuvrait	il faut → il faudrait

Si tu visitais la Bretagne au printemps, **il y aurait** du vent et **il pleuvrait. Il** te **faudrait** un parapluie!

To say *should,* use the conditional of **devoir** plus an infinitive. To say *could,* use the conditional of **pouvoir** plus an infinitive.

Use the conditional:
- to make polite requests or offers.
- to say what someone would do if circumstances were different.

— **Pourrais-tu** me donner des conseils pour rester en bonne santé?
— **Tu devrais** bien manger et faire de l'exercice.

Voudrais-tu y aller avec moi?

S'il faisait la cuisine, **il mangerait** mieux.

VOCABULAIRE

Ordering at a restaurant

NOMS MASCULINS

un apéritif	a before-dinner drink
un dessert	a dessert
un fruit	a fruit
des fruits de mer	shellfish, crustaceans
*des haricots (verts)	(green) beans
*un hors-d'œuvre	an hors d'œuvre, an appetizer
du lait	milk
des légumes	vegetables
un menu à prix fixe	a set-price menu
du pain	bread
un pavé (de)	a thick slice (of)
des petits pois	peas
le plat (principal)	the (main) dish
du poisson (fumé)	(smoked) fish
du poivre	pepper
un repas	a meal
du riz	rice
du sel	salt
du sucre	sugar

NOMS FÉMININS

une bouteille (de)	a bottle (of)
une carafe (de)	a carafe (of)
la carte	the menu
de la crème	cream
une entrée	a first course
une pomme	an apple
une pomme de terre	a potato
de la raie	rayfish, skate
une salade	a salad
de la viande	meat
de la volaille	poultry

DIVERS

Aimeriez-vous...?	Would you like ...?
comme	for, as (a)
comprendre	to include
décider	to decide
du, de la, de l', des	some, any
finir	to finish
fumé(e)	smoked
généralement	generally
servir	to serve
traditionnel(le)	traditional

Pour les noms des différentes sortes d'entrées, voir la page 316.
Pour les noms des différentes sortes de viandes, de volailles, de poissons et de fruits de mer, voir la page 316.
Pour voir les différentes possibilités pour finir un repas, voir la page 317.

Buying food

NOMS MASCULINS

du bœuf	beef
un choix	a choice
un commerçant	a shopkeeper
un marché	a market
un oignon	an onion
un pain au chocolat	a chocolate-filled croissant
un pain complet	a loaf of whole-grain bread
un plat préparé	a ready-to-serve dish
du porc	pork
un produit	a product
du raisin	grapes
du saucisson	salami
le service personnalisé	personal service
un supermarché	a supermarket

NOMS FÉMININS

une baguette	a loaf of French bread
une banane	a banana
la boucherie	the butcher's shop
la boulangerie-pâtisserie	the bakery-pastry shop
une calorie	a calorie
une carotte	a carrot
une cerise	a cherry
la charcuterie	the deli
de la charcuterie	deli meats, cold cuts
une commerçante	a shopkeeper
des conserves	canned goods
l'épicerie	the grocery store
une fraise	a strawberry
une grande surface	a superstore
une laitue	a head of lettuce
une orange	an orange
une pâtisserie	a pastry
une pêche	a peach
une poire	a pear
la poissonnerie	the fish market
des saucisses	sausages
une tartelette (aux fraises / aux cerises)	a (strawberry / cherry) tart

DIVERS

C'est tout.	That's all.
de plus en plus (de)	more and more (of)
dire	to say, to tell
frais (fraîche)	fresh
il faut	it is necessary, one needs, one must
Qu'est-ce que je peux vous proposer d'autre?	What else can I get you?
Qu'est-ce qu'il vous faut?	What do you need?
surgelé(e)	frozen

Pour les expressions de quantité, voir la page 330.

COMPÉTENCE 3

Talking about meals

NOMS MASCULINS

du bacon	*bacon*
du beurre	*butter*
du chocolat	*chocolate*
un croissant	*a croissant*
le déjeuner	*lunch*
le dîner	*dinner*
*un hamburger	*a hamburger*
du pain grillé	*toast*
un self-service	*a self-service restaurant*
un steak-frites	*a steak and fries*

NOMS FÉMININS

des céréales	*cereal*
de la confiture	*jelly*
une omelette	*an omelet*
une pizza	*a pizza*
une tartine	*bread with butter and jelly*

EXPRESSIONS VERBALES

boire	*to drink*
choisir (de faire)	*to choose (to do)*
finir (de faire)	*to finish (doing)*
grandir	*to grow, to grow up, to get taller*
grossir	*to get fatter*
maigrir	*to get thinner, to slim down*
(se) nourrir	*to feed, to nourish, to nurture (oneself)*
obéir (à)	*to obey*
réfléchir (à)	*to think (about)*
réussir (à)	*to succeed (at, in), to pass* (a test)

DIVERS

à l'américaine	*American-style*
certains	*some (people)*
ceux (celles)	*those*
complet (complète)	*complete*
copieux (copieuse)	*copious, large*
désolé(e)	*sorry*
en	*some, any, of it, of them*
encore	*still, again, more*
grillé(e)	*toasted, grilled*
je prendrais	*I would have, I would take*
là	*there*
léger (légère)	*light*
ne... plus	*no more, no longer*
pourtant	*however*
rapide	*rapid, fast, quick*
seulement	*only*
si	*yes (in response to a question or statement in the negative)*
surtout	*especially*
vrai(e)	*true*

COMPÉTENCE 4

Choosing a healthy lifestyle

NOMS MASCULINS

l'alcool	*alcohol*
des conseils	*advice*
des produits bio	*organic products*
le stress	*stress*
le tabac	*tobacco*

NOMS FÉMININS

des matières grasses	*fats*
la santé	*health*
des vitamines	*vitamins*

EXPRESSIONS VERBALES

contrôler	*to control*
éviter	*to avoid*
faire attention (à)	*to pay attention (to), to watch out (for)*
faire de l'aérobic	*to do aerobics*
faire de la méditation	*to meditate*
faire de la muscu(lation)	*to do weight training, to do bodybuilding*
faire du yoga	*to do yoga*
faire mieux (de)	*to do better (to)*
marcher	*to walk*
on devrait	*one should*
oublier	*to forget*
se sentir	*to feel*

DIVERS

à votre avis	*in your opinion*
content(e)	*content, happy*
en forme	*in shape*
fort(e)	*strong*
lentement	*slowly*
plusieurs	*several*
régulièrement	*regularly*
sain(e)	*healthy*
sans doute	*without doubt, doubtless*

Aux Antilles
En vacances

Pair work	▶ Video
Group work	🔊 Audio
Class work	

© GUIZIOU Franck/hemis.fr/Getty Images

9

LE MONDE FRANCOPHONE

Géoculture et Vidéo-voyage: La France d'outre-mer

COMPÉTENCE

1 Talking about vacation
Les vacances

Talking about how things will be
Le futur

Stratégies et Lecture
- **Pour mieux lire:** *Recognizing compound tenses*
- **Lecture:** *Quelle aventure!*

2 Preparing for a trip
Les préparatifs

Communicating with people
*Les verbes **dire**, **lire** et **écrire***

Avoiding repetition
*Les pronoms compléments d'objet indirect **(lui, leur)** et reprise des pronoms compléments d'objet direct **(le, la, l', les)***

3 Buying your ticket
À l'agence de voyages

Saying what people know
*Les verbes **savoir** et **connaître***

Indicating who does what to whom
*Les pronoms **me, te, nous** et **vous***

4 Deciding where to go on a trip
Un voyage

Saying where you are going
Les expressions géographiques

Vidéo-reprise: *Les Stagiaires*

Lecture et Composition
- **Pour mieux lire:** *Understanding words with multiple meanings*
- **Lecture:** *Ma grand-mère m'a appris à ne pas compter sur les yeux des autres pour dormir*
- **Pour mieux écrire:** *Revising what you write*
- **Composition:** *Un itinéraire*

Comparaisons culturelles: *La culture créole aux Antilles*

Résumé de grammaire

Vocabulaire

GÉOCULTURE ET VIDÉO-VOYAGE:
La France d'outre-mer

LA GUADELOUPE

NOMBRE D'HABITANTS:
472 000 (les Guadeloupéens)

CHEF-LIEU *(ADMINISTRATIVE CENTER)*: **Basse-Terre**

LA GUYANE

NOMBRE D'HABITANTS:
285 550 (les Guyanais)

CHEF-LIEU: **Cayenne**

LA MARTINIQUE

NOMBRE D'HABITANTS:
396 000 (les Martiniquais)

CHEF-LIEU: **Fort-de-France**

MAYOTTE

NOMBRE D'HABITANTS:
251 100 (les Mahorais)

CHEF-LIEU: **Dzaoudzi (siège du conseil départemental: Mamoudzou)**

LA RÉUNION

NOMBRE D'HABITANTS: **842 800 (les Réunionnais)**

CHEF-LIEU: **Saint-Denis**

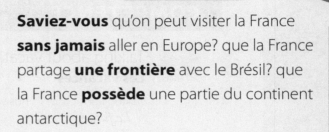

Saviez-vous qu'on peut visiter la France **sans jamais** aller en Europe? que la France partage **une frontière** avec le Brésil? que la France **possède** une partie du continent antarctique?

En effet, la République française **comprend:**

- la France métropolitaine (la France en Europe plus l'île de Corse)
- cinq départements et régions d'outre-mer (les DROM)
- plusieurs collectivités d'outre-mer (les COM)
- les **Terres australes** et antarctiques françaises et l'île de Clipperton

Les cinq DROM – la Guadeloupe, la Martinique, la Guyane, La Réunion et Mayotte – **font partie de** la France **tout comme** Hawaï fait partie des États-Unis.

La Guadeloupe et la Martinique sont les deux plus grandes îles françaises des Caraïbes. Leur beauté naturelle attire un grand nombre de touristes.

© Danita Delimont/Gallo Images/Getty Images

La Réunion est le département et région français d'outre-mer le plus peuplé, avec une société multiethnique.

© Tibor Bognar/age fotostock

---

d'outre-mer *overseas*   **Saviez-vous** *Did you know*   **sans jamais** *without ever*   **une frontière** *a border*   **possède** *possesses*   **En effet** *In fact*   **comprend** *includes*   **Terres australes** *Southern Lands*   **font partie de** *are part of*   **tout comme** *just as*   **attire** *attracts*   **le plus peuplé** *the most populous*

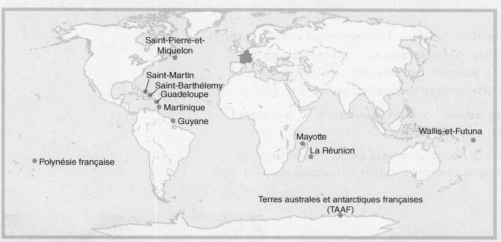

Les Outre-mer

Les collectivités d'outre-mer – la Polynésie française, Wallis-et-Futuna, Saint-Pierre-et-Miquelon, Saint-Barthélemy et Saint-Martin – sont comparables aux territoires américains de Porto Rico et Guam.

L'ancien territoire de la Nouvelle-Calédonie a voté sur l'indépendance en 2018.

La Guyane est caractérisée par sa biodiversité. Le tourisme vert s'y développe, mais l'économie se base surtout sur l'industrie spatiale.

Le savez-vous?

Quelles régions de la République française voudriez-vous visiter? Servez-vous de la carte *(map)*, des photos et des renseignements donnés sur ces pages pour compléter les phrases qui suivent.

**Guyane   collectivités d'outre-mer
départements et régions d'outre-mer
Guadeloupe   Martinique   Réunion**

1. Les _____ font partie de la France, tout comme Hawaï fait partie des États-Unis. Les _____ sont comparables aux territoires américains de Porto Rico et Guam.

2. La _____ et la _____ sont deux îles dans la mer des Caraïbes. La majorité des habitants de ces deux départements et régions d'outre-mer sont des descendants d'esclaves africains amenés *(African slaves brought)* dans ces îles pour travailler dans les plantations.

3. La _____, en Amérique du Sud, est connue *(known)* pour sa beauté naturelle et pour sa base du programme spatial français.

4. La _____ est située dans l'océan Indien près de Madagascar. C'est le département et région d'outre-mer le plus peuplé, avec une société multiethnique: des Africains, des Européens, des Indiens, des Chinois et des Malgaches *(inhabitants of Madagascar)*.

L'ancien *The former*   se base surtout sur *is largely based on*

AVANT LES VIDÉOS

Pour voir la biodiversité des départements et régions d'outre-mer français, vous allez regarder deux vidéos, l'une sur la Guyane française, en Amérique du Sud, et l'autre sur La Réunion, située à 700 kilomètres à l'est de Madagascar, dans l'océan Indien. Pour vous aider à mieux comprendre, regardez ces images et complétez les descriptions avec une option de la liste.

demeure *(dwelling, house)* **forêt équatoriale** **orchidées**
paresseux *(sloths)* **pollinisation**

Depuis quelques années, le nouveau mot à la mode, c'est biodiversité, et en France, la championne de diversité naturelle des organismes vivants, c'est la Guyane.

1. Coincée *(Wedged)* entre l'immense Brésil et le Surinam, la Guyane est couverte à 96 % d'une _____ qui reste parmi les plus riches et les moins écologiquement fragmentées du monde.

2. Tortues *(Turtles)* marines, échassiers *(wading birds)*, _____ et jaguars, les animaux sont davantage *(more)* chez eux en Guyane que les humains, et les plus dangereux ne sont pas ceux *(those)* que l'on pense!

Pour voir l'immense biodiversité des départements et régions d'outre-mer français, il faut aussi visiter La Réunion.

3. Le domaine du Grand Hazier est un bon exemple de la générosité de la terre réunion-naise. Cette grande _____ créole avec ses dépendances au cœur *(in the heart)* d'un immense parc avec jardin, verger *(orchard)* créole et potager *(vegetable garden)* est inscrit à l'inventaire des Monuments historiques.

4. Au domaine du Grand Hazier, on peut faire un tour de la vanilleraie, où on produit une des meilleures vanilles du monde. Saviez-vous que la vanille fait partie de la famille des _____?

5. En 1841, Edmond Albius, un jeune esclave *(slave)* âgé de douze ans, a découvert le procédé de _____ manuelle de la vanille encore utilisé de nos jours. Grâce à *(Thanks to)* lui, la vanille a connu un développement de grande ampleur sur l'île de La Réunion.

▶ **EN REGARDANT LES VIDÉOS**

Regardez les vidéos et indiquez dans quelle(s) vidéo(s) on voit les choses suivantes, celle *(the one)* sur la Guyane, celle sur La Réunion ou les deux?

1. une carte *(a map)* de l'Amérique du Sud

2. une carte de l'Afrique

3. la côte et l'océan

4. un singe *(a monkey)*

5. de vieux meubles et de vieilles photos d'une époque passée

6. un paysage tropical

▶ **APRÈS LES VIDÉOS**

Répondez aux questions suivantes d'après les vidéos.

1. Quel est le plus grand département et région français d'outre-mer?

2. Quel pourcentage du territoire de la Guyane est couvert de forêt équatoriale?

3. À la fin de la vidéo sur la Guyane, on dit que les animaux sont davantage chez eux en Guyane que les humains, et que les plus dangereux ne sont pas ceux que l'on pense. À votre avis, qui sont les plus dangereux?

4. Quelle orchidée cultivée à La Réunion est la seule orchidée dont le fruit est comestible *(edible)*?

5. D'où sont venus les premiers vanilliers plantés à La Réunion?

6. Aimeriez-vous mieux visiter la Guyane ou La Réunion? Pourquoi?

Talking about vacation

LES VACANCES

Vocabulaire supplémentaire

faire de la plongée avec masque et tuba *to go snorkeling*
faire de la plongée sous-marine *to go scuba diving*
faire de la planche à voile *to go windsurfing*
faire du wakeboard *to go wakeboarding*

Sélection musicale. Search for the song **"Tes vacances avec moi"** by Sonia Dersion from Martinique online to enjoy a musical selection related to this vocabulary.

Lucas, un jeune Parisien, va passer ses vacances en Guadeloupe. Et vous? Où aimez-vous passer vos vacances?

dans un pays étranger ou exotique
   sur une île tropicale ou **à la mer**
   dans une grande ville
   à la montagne

Qu'est-ce qu'on peut faire dans chaque **endroit** (m)?

admirer **les paysages** (m)
   visiter des sites (m) historiques et touristiques
   profiter des activités culturelles (aller à l'opéra, au ballet…)

bronzer ou courir sur la plage
   goûter la cuisine locale **assis** à la terrasse d'un restaurant
   faire des randonnées

Lucas parle à son ami Alex de ses prochaines vacances en Guadeloupe.

9-1

LUCAS:	Je vais bientôt partir en vacances.
ALEX:	Et tu vas où?
LUCAS:	Je vais en Guadeloupe.
ALEX:	En Guadeloupe? Quelle chance! Tu pars quand?
LUCAS:	Je pars le 20 juillet et je **compte** y passer trois semaines.
ALEX:	Génial! J'espère que **ça te plaira**!

à la mer *at the coast, by the sea*   **un endroit** *a place*   **les paysages** *the scenery, the landscape*   **bronzer** *to tan*
goûter *to taste*   **assis(e)** *seated*   **compter** *to plan on, to count on*   **ça te plaira** *you'll like it*

A **Activités.** Lesquelles des activités nommées fait-on normalement à l'endroit indiqué?

EXEMPLE dans une grande ville: faire du shopping / faire des randonnées / profiter des activités culturelles

Dans une grande ville, on fait du shopping et on profite des activités culturelles. On ne fait pas de randonnées.

1. sur une île tropicale: manger beaucoup de fruits de mer / courir sur la plage / faire du snowboard
2. à la montagne: profiter des activités culturelles / faire des randonnées / admirer les paysages
3. dans un pays étranger: visiter des sites historiques et touristiques / goûter la cuisine locale / voyager sans passeport
4. à la mer: faire du ski / bronzer / nager

B **Que feriez-vous?** Imaginez où vous iriez et ce que vous feriez si vous aviez assez d'argent pour faire un beau voyage. Choisissez une des destinations données et indiquez trois choses que vous y feriez.

> à la montagne   à la campagne   dans un pays étranger
> sur une île tropicale   dans une grande ville   chez moi

EXEMPLE Si j'avais assez d'argent, je passerais mes vacances **sur une île tropicale** où **je bronzerais, je nagerais et je prendrais beaucoup de photos.**

Maintenant, circulez dans la classe et demandez à plusieurs personnes où elles iraient et ce qu'elles feraient si elles pouvaient faire un beau voyage.

EXEMPLE —**Si tu pouvais faire un beau voyage, où passerais-tu tes vacances et qu'est-ce que tu ferais?**
—**Je passerais mes vacances sur une île tropicale où je bronzerais, je nagerais et je prendrais beaucoup de photos. Et toi?**
—**Moi, je…**

Après, dites à la classe ce que vous avez appris.

EXEMPLE **Clarence passerait ses vacances sur une île tropicale où il…**

C **Entretien.** Interviewez votre partenaire.

1. Préférerais-tu visiter une île tropicale ou visiter une grande ville? aller à la mer ou à la montagne? faire une randonnée ou faire du ski? faire de l'exercice à l'hôtel ou courir sur la plage? bronzer ou nager?
2. Où est-ce que tu aimerais passer tes prochaines vacances? Qu'est-ce qu'on peut faire dans cette région? Où est-ce que tu as passé tes meilleures vacances? Pourquoi as-tu trouvé ces vacances agréables? Qu'est-ce que tu as fait?

Au parc national de la Guadeloupe, on peut profiter de tous les loisirs de la nature: randonnées, promenades, VTT...

À VOUS!

Avec un(e) partenaire, relisez à haute voix la conversation entre Lucas et Alex. Ensuite, imaginez que vous allez faire le voyage de vos rêves *(dreams)* et changez la conversation pour dire où vous allez, avec qui, quand et combien de temps vous comptez rester.

You can access the audio of the active vocabulary of this *Compétence* online.

TALKING ABOUT HOW THINGS WILL BE

✔ *Pour vérifier*

1. What do most verbs have as the stem in the future tense? Which verbs have irregular stems? What other verb form has the same stem as the future?

2. What endings do you use to form the future tense in French?

3. In French, what verb tense is used in clauses with **quand** referring to the future? How do you say *When I finish, I'll go home*?

Note *de grammaire*

The future/conditional stem always ends with **-r.** Do you remember these irregular ones?

aller	ir-
avoir	aur-
être	ser-
faire	fer-
devoir	devr-
vouloir	voudr-
venir	viendr-
revenir	reviendr-
devenir	deviendr-
voir	verr-
envoyer	enverr-
pouvoir	pourr-
mourir	mourr-
courir	courr-

Note these forms in the future:

il y a	il y aura
il faut	il faudra
il pleut	il pleuvra
c'est	ce sera

As in the conditional, verbs like **se lever, payer,** and **appeler** have spelling changes in *all* forms of the future (**je me lèverai, je paierai, j'appellerai**). Those like **préférer** do not (**je préférerai**).

Note *de prononciation*

As in the conditional forms, an unaccented **e** is usually not pronounced in future tense forms if you can drop it without bringing together three pronounced consonants (**j'habit̮erai, nous invit̮erons**).

Sélection musicale. Search for the song **"Mon île"** by Sonia Dersion online to enjoy a musical selection illustrating the use of this structure.

Le futur

1. You have used **aller** + *infinitive* to say what someone *is going* to do. You can use the future tense to say what someone *will* do. Form the future tense by adding the boldfaced endings below to the same stem you use for the conditional.

PARLER	ÊTRE	VENIR
je parler**ai**	je ser**ai**	je viendr**ai**
tu parler**as**	tu ser**as**	tu viendr**as**
il/elle/on parler**a**	il/elle/on ser**a**	il/elle/on viendr**a**
nous parler**ons**	nous ser**ons**	nous viendr**ons**
vous parler**ez**	vous ser**ez**	vous viendr**ez**
ils/elles parler**ont**	ils/elles ser**ont**	ils/elles viendr**ont**

2. The future is generally used in French as it is in English. However, one difference is its use in clauses with **quand** referring to the future. English has the present in such clauses.

> **quand** + future → future

Quand j'**arriverai** en Guadeloupe, je **prendrai** un taxi pour aller à l'hôtel.
*When I **arrive** in Guadeloupe, I'**ll take** a taxi to go to the hotel.*

3. As in English, use the future tense to say what will happen if another event occurs. Use the present tense in the clause with **si.**

> **si** + present → future

Si je **peux** visiter la Martinique, je **serai** vraiment content!
*If I **can** visit Martinique, I **will be** really happy!*

A **Boule de cristal.** Vous pouvez voir l'avenir *(the future)* dans une boule de cristal. Comment sera la vie des personnes suivantes dans cinq ans?

EXEMPLE Moi, je... (être riche)
Je serai riche. / Je ne serai pas riche.

1. Moi, je (j')...
   habiter ici
   avoir mon diplôme
   devoir travailler
   aller souvent en France
   faire souvent des voyages

2. Mon meilleur ami
   (Ma meilleure amie)...
   venir souvent me voir
   réussir dans la vie
   sortir souvent avec moi
   être marié(e)

3. La personne de mes rêves
et moi, nous...
se marier
avoir des enfants
acheter une maison
faire beaucoup de voyages
ensemble

4. Tous les membres de ma famille...
s'entendre bien
se rendre souvent visite
se voir souvent
voyager souvent ensemble

5. *[à un(e) autre étudiant(e)]*
Toi, tu...
finir tes études
trouver un bon travail
apprendre beaucoup
avoir beaucoup de problèmes

6. *[au professeur]*
Vous...
avoir toujours cours à 7 heures du matin
pouvoir prendre votre retraite *(retirement)*
travailler toujours *(still)* ici
être heureux (heureuse)

B **Je... quand...** Lucas parle à un ami avant de partir en Guadeloupe. Complétez la phrase suivante en mettant les deux actions dans l'ordre logique. Mettez les deux verbes au futur.

Je... quand...

EXEMPLE partir en vacances / pouvoir se reposer
Je pourrai me reposer quand je partirai en vacances.

1. aller en Guadeloupe / être dans l'avion pendant onze heures
2. arriver / envoyer des textos à mes amis
3. s'amuser / être en Guadeloupe
4. faire des excursions / ne pas être à la plage
5. visiter les sites touristiques / voir des choses intéressantes
6. aller voir le volcan la Soufrière / prendre beaucoup de photos
7. écrire un blog de voyage sur ma page Internet / rentrer à l'hôtel chaque soir
8. faire le blog / mettre mes photos sur Facebook

C **Si...** Complétez logiquement ces phrases.

EXEMPLE S'il pleut ce week-end, je **resterai à la maison.**

1. S'il fait beau ce week-end, je (j')...
2. S'il fait mauvais ce week-end, je (j')...
3. Si je sors avec des amis ce week-end, on...
4. Si je peux partir en vacances cette année, je (j')...
5. Si un jour je peux visiter la France, je (j')...
6. Si mes amis et moi décidons de visiter une autre ville, nous...

D **Entretien.** Pensez à un voyage (réel ou imaginaire) que vous ferez pendant les prochaines vacances. Votre partenaire vous posera des questions au sujet de ce voyage. Après, changez de rôles.

1. Où iras-tu? Comment est-ce que tu voyageras?
2. Quand est-ce que tu partiras? Quand est-ce que tu reviendras?
3. Qui fera le voyage avec toi? Quels vêtements est-ce que vous devrez emporter?
4. Où descendrez-vous?
5. Qu'est-ce que vous ferez pendant le voyage? Qu'est-ce que vous verrez d'intéressant? Quels sites touristiques est-ce que vous visiterez?

Visiterez-vous la Martinique ou la Guadeloupe un jour?

POUR MIEUX LIRE: *Recognizing compound tenses*

French has other compound tenses, like the **passé composé,** which are formed with the auxiliary verb **avoir** or **être** and a past participle (**dansé, mangé, vu,** etc.). To translate these tenses, change the auxiliary verb *have* in English to the same tense as in French (imperfect, future, conditional): *They had (will have, would have) arrived.*

In the **passé composé,** where the auxiliary verb is in the *present* tense, translate it as the simple past or as *has/have + past participle.*

J'**ai** commencé.	Elle **est** rentrée.
*I began. / I **have** begun.*	*She returned. / She **has** returned.*

If the auxiliary verb is in the *imperfect,* translate it as *had + past participle.*

J'**avais** déjà commencé.	Il **n'était pas** encore rentré.
*I **had** already begun.*	*He **hadn't** returned yet.*

If the auxiliary verb is in the *conditional,* translate it as *would have + past participle.*

J'**aurais** déjà commencé.	Nous **ne serions pas** encore rentré(e)s.
*I **would have** already begun.*	*We **wouldn't have** returned yet.*

If it is in the *future,* translate it as *will have + past participle.*

J'**aurai** déjà commencé.	Tu **ne seras pas** encore rentré(e).
*I **will have** already begun.*	*You **will not have** returned yet.*

Note *de grammaire*

Note the names of these compound tenses.

plus-que-parfait: auxiliary verb in the *imperfect* + *past participle*
J'avais fini. *I had finished.*

conditionnel passé: auxiliary verb in the *conditional* + *past participle*
J'aurais fini. *I would have finished.*

futur antérieur: auxiliary verb in the *future* + *past participle*
J'aurai fini. *I will have finished.*

A **Et vous?** Traduisez les phrases suivantes en anglais.

1. J'ai déjà visité la Guadeloupe.
2. L'année dernière, j'y suis resté un mois.
3. Avant de partir en vacances, j'avais réservé une chambre d'hôtel.
4. J'ai visité la Martinique aussi. J'y étais déjà allé(e) deux fois avant.
5. Si j'avais eu assez d'argent, j'aurais passé mes vacances en Europe.
6. Mes vacances auraient été plus agréables s'il n'avait pas plu tout le temps.
7. Après ce voyage, j'aurai visité la Martinique trois fois.
8. J'aurai fini quatre semestres de français avant d'y aller.

B **Le temps des verbes.** Dans le texte qui suit, traduisez tous les verbes *en italique.*

Lecture: *Quelle aventure!*

🔊 9-2 Lucas, un jeune Parisien qui passe ses vacances en Guadeloupe, raconte ses aventures dans un mail à son ami Alex.

Salut Alex,

Je passe des vacances formidables ici en Guadeloupe! *Je t'aurais écrit* plus tôt si *je n'avais pas été* si occupé. Ici, tout est à mon goût... la cuisine, le paysage, les femmes! En fait, j'ai rencontré une jeune Guadeloupéenne très sympa. Elle s'appelle Anaïs et nous passons beaucoup de temps ensemble depuis notre rencontre assez comique au parc naturel.

J'étais allé au parc pour faire l'escalade de la Soufrière, un énorme volcan en repos... mais comme j'allais bientôt le comprendre, pas si «en repos» que ça! En montant vers le volcan, *j'avais remarqué* qu'il y avait un peu de vapeur qui sortait du cratère, mais *je n'avais pas fait trop attention.* Quand j'étais presque au sommet du volcan, je me suis assis par terre pour me reposer un peu et c'est là que la scène comique a commencé. Là où j'étais assis, la terre était toute chaude, mais vraiment chaude, et je voyais des jets de vapeur qui sortaient du sommet! J'ai pensé que le volcan allait exploser!

La Soufrière

J'ai commencé à crier aux autres touristes: «Attention! Attention! Le volcan entre en éruption, il va exploser!» Heureusement, Anaïs était parmi le groupe et elle nous a expliqué calmement: «Mais non, mais non... calmez-vous! C'est tout à fait normal. Le volcan est en repos, il n'y a pas de danger!» Si *elle n'avait pas été* avec nous, *on aurait* tous *commencé* à courir, paniqués.

Sur le moment, j'ai eu l'impression d'être complètement ridicule! Mais cette impression n'a pas duré. On a commencé à parler et nous avons continué l'escalade du volcan ensemble. Arrivés au sommet, nous avons découvert une vue impressionnante... la lave..., les fissures..., l'odeur... C'était un paysage presque irréel. Pendant un instant, j'ai eu l'impression d'être sur une autre planète!

Alors, tout est bien qui finit bien. Si *je n'avais pas fait* cette bêtise, *Anaïs et moi n'aurions jamais commencé à parler* et je n'aurais pas fait la connaissance de cette femme extraordinaire. Elle est super sympa et nous passons presque tous les soirs ensemble!

À bientôt,
Lucas

Compréhension. Répondez aux questions suivantes d'après la lecture.

1. Quel site touristique est-ce que Lucas visitait quand il a rencontré Anaïs?
2. Qu'est-ce que Lucas avait vu avant de commencer à crier que le volcan allait exploser?
3. Qu'est-ce que tous les touristes auraient fait si Anaïs n'avait pas été là pour les calmer?
4. Pourquoi est-ce que Lucas dit que «tout est bien qui finit bien»?

Preparing for a trip

LES PRÉPARATIFS

Avant de faire un voyage **à l'étranger,** il faut faire beaucoup de préparatifs *(m)*.

Avant **le départ,** il faut…

obtenir votre passeport *(m)* (bien à l'avance!) et acheter votre **billet** *(m)* **d'avion.**

vous informer sur la région sur Internet ou lire **un guide.**

réserver une chambre d'hôtel.

dire à votre famille où vous allez.

demander à **vos voisins** de **donner à manger à** votre chien.

faire vos valises *(f)*.

À votre **arrivée** *(f)*, vous devez…

montrer votre passeport.

passer **la douane.**

changer de l'argent.

Pour rester en contact pendant le voyage, vous pouvez…

envoyer des textos ou téléphoner à vos amis par Skype.

leur écrire des cartes postales.

mettre vos photos sur Facebook ou écrire un blog.

Les préparatifs *Preparations*   **à l'étranger** *in another country, abroad*   **le départ** *the departure*   **obtenir** *to obtain*   **un billet d'avion** *a plane ticket*   **s'informer** *to find out information*   **un guide** *a guidebook, a guide*   **dire** *to say, to tell*   **un(e) voisin(e)** *a neighbor*   **donner à manger à** *to feed*   **faire une valise** *to pack a suitcase*   **l'arrivée** *the arrival*   **la douane** *customs*   **leur** *them, to them*

🔊 9-3 Alex parle à sa femme d'**un mail** qu'**il a reçu** de son ami Lucas.

CATHERINE:	Qu'est-ce que **tu lis**?
ALEX:	C'est un mail que j'ai reçu de Lucas. Il **m'**écrit de la Guadeloupe où il passe ses vacances.
CATHERINE:	Et **ça lui plaît,** la Guadeloupe?
ALEX:	Ça lui plaît beaucoup.
CATHERINE:	La Guadeloupe, ça doit être beau. J'aimerais bien voir les plages et les paysages tropicaux.
ALEX:	Lucas dit qu'il aime beaucoup le paysage, la cuisine et le climat. Il me parle aussi d'une «jeune femme extraordinaire» qu'il a rencontrée **là-bas**.

A **Avant le départ ou après l'arrivée?** Quand on voyage à l'étranger, est-ce qu'il faut faire les choses suivantes **avant le départ** ou **après l'arrivée**?

EXEMPLE acheter un billet d'avion
Il faut acheter un billet d'avion avant le départ.

1. passer la douane
2. obtenir un passeport
3. s'informer sur Internet
4. réserver une chambre
5. montrer son passeport
6. lire des guides
7. faire ses valises
8. mettre des photos sur Facebook
9. demander à un ami de donner à manger à son chien

B **Et vous?** Quelle sorte de voyageur (voyageuse) êtes-vous? Dites ce que vous feriez si vous voyagiez à l'étranger.

1. J'achèterais mon billet d'avion *sur Internet / dans une agence de voyages*.
2. Pour préparer le voyage, *je m'informerais sur Internet / je lirais un guide / je ne m'informerais pas beaucoup avant de partir.*
3. J'obtiendrais mon passeport *bien à l'avance / au dernier moment.*
4. Je réserverais ma chambre *par téléphone / sur Internet.*
5. *Je dirais / Je ne dirais pas* à ma famille où j'allais.
6. Je ferais ma valise *bien à l'avance / au dernier moment.*
7. Je changerais de l'argent *avant mon départ / à l'arrivée.*
8. Pour rester en contact avec mes amis, *j'écrirais un blog / je leur enverrais des textos / je leur téléphonerais / je leur parlerais par Skype.*
9. Je mettrais les photos du voyage sur Facebook *pendant le voyage / après mon retour (return). (Je ne mettrais pas mes photos sur Facebook.)*

🔁 **À VOUS!**

Avec un(e) partenaire, relisez à haute voix la conversation entre Alex et Catherine. Ensuite, imaginez que vous recevez un mail d'un(e) ami(e) qui visite une autre région francophone. Parlez avec votre partenaire de vos impressions de cette région et dites pourquoi vous voudriez ou ne voudriez pas y aller.

You can access the audio of the active vocabulary of this *Compétence* online.

---

un mail *an email*   **il a reçu (recevoir** *to receive)*   **tu lis (lire** *to read)*   **me (m')** *me, to me*
ça lui plaît? (plaire *to please) does he like it?*   **là-bas** *over there*

COMMUNICATING WITH PEOPLE

✔ *Pour vérifier*

1. What are the conjugations of **dire, lire,** and **écrire**? What do you need to remember about the **vous** form of **dire**? What are the future and conditional stems of these verbs?

2. Which two of these verbs have similar past participles? What are they? What is the past participle of **lire**?

Les verbes *dire, lire* et *écrire*

1. You have already seen the verbs **dire** *(to say, to tell)*, **lire** *(to read)*, and **écrire** *(to write)*. Here are their conjugations. The verb **décrire** *(to describe)* is conjugated like **écrire.**

DIRE *(to say, to tell)*	LIRE *(to read)*	ÉCRIRE *(to write)*
je **dis**	je **lis**	j' **écris**
tu **dis**	tu **lis**	tu **écris**
il/elle/on **dit**	il/elle/on **lit**	il/elle/on **écrit**
nous **disons**	nous **lisons**	nous **écrivons**
vous **dites**	vous **lisez**	vous **écrivez**
ils/elles **disent**	ils/elles **lisent**	ils/elles **écrivent**
PASSÉ COMPOSÉ: j'**ai dit**	PASSÉ COMPOSÉ: j'**ai lu**	PASSÉ COMPOSÉ: j'**ai écrit**
IMPARFAIT: je **disais**	IMPARFAIT: je **lisais**	IMPARFAIT: j'**écrivais**
CONDITIONNEL: je **dirais**	CONDITIONNEL: je **lirais**	CONDITIONNEL: j'**écrirais**
FUTUR: je **dirai**	FUTUR: je **lirai**	FUTUR: j'**écrirai**

2. Here are some things you might want to read or write.

un article *an article*	**une lettre** *a letter*
une carte postale *a postcard*	**un magazine** *a magazine*
un mail *an e-mail*	**un poème** *a poem*
une histoire *a story*	**une rédaction** *a composition*
un journal (*pl* **des journaux**) *a newspaper*	**un roman** *a novel*

A **En cours de français.** Est-ce que ces personnes font souvent les choses indiquées en cours de français?

> souvent   quelquefois   rarement   ne... jamais

EXEMPLE je / écrire des poèmes
> **Je n'écris jamais de poèmes en cours de français.**

1. le professeur / écrire au tableau
2. les étudiants / écrire au tableau
3. je / écrire quelque chose dans mon cahier
4. les autres étudiants et moi / s'écrire des mails après le cours
5. je / lire le journal
6. le professeur / lire des poèmes à la classe
7. nous / lire des phrases à haute voix *(aloud)*
8. les étudiants / lire des romans en français

Maintenant, dites si ces personnes ont fait ces choses en cours la semaine dernière.

EXEMPLE je / écrire des poèmes
> **Je n'ai pas écrit de poèmes en cours de français la semaine dernière.**

Sélection musicale. Search for the song **"Dis-moi pourquoi"** by the Guadeloupean Jane Fostin online to enjoy a musical selection illustrating the use of this structure.

B **Qu'est-ce qu'on dit?** Dites si ces personnes font les choses indiquées.

EXEMPLE je / dire «merci» quand le professeur me rend mes devoirs

Je (ne) dis (pas) «merci» quand le professeur me rend mes devoirs.

1. le prof / dire «bonjour» quand il arrive en cours
2. les autres étudiants et moi / se dire «bonjour» en cours
3. les étudiants / dire la vérité *(the truth)* au prof
4. nous / se dire «au revoir» quand nous quittons la classe
5. je / dire «merci» au prof

Maintenant, dites si ces personnes ont dit les choses indiquées pendant le dernier cours.

EXEMPLE je / dire «merci» quand le professeur me rend mes devoirs

J'ai dit (Je n'ai pas dit) «merci» quand le professeur m'a rendu mes devoirs.

C **En vacances.** Vous faites le voyage de vos rêves avec un(e) ami(e). Avec un(e) partenaire, faites des phrases logiques en utilisant un élément de chaque colonne. Faites au moins deux phrases pour chaque sujet.

EXEMPLE **Je lis des guides.**

Je... Nous... L'agent de voyages *(The travel agent)*...	dire écrire lire	un blog sur le voyage des mails un mail pour réserver une chambre des guides à des voisins de donner à manger aux animaux «au revoir» à nos amis le nom de notre hôtel à ma famille le prix *(price)* du voyage

D **Entretien.** Interviewez votre partenaire.

1. Est-ce que tu écris plus de textos ou plus de mails? Est-ce que tu as écrit un mail ce matin? À qui? Quand tu voyages, est-ce que tu écris des cartes postales? un blog? Est-ce que tu envoies des textos ou des mails? Tu mets tes photos sur Facebook?
2. Lis-tu le journal tous les jours? Est-ce que tu lis un journal en ligne? Quel journal préfères-tu lire? Le liras-tu ce soir? Est-ce que tu l'as lu ce matin? Quel magazine lis-tu le plus souvent? Est-ce que tu l'as lu ce mois-ci?
3. Lis-tu beaucoup de romans? Quel est le dernier roman que tu as lu? Quand est-ce que tu l'as lu?

AVOIDING REPETITION

✔ *Pour vérifier*

1. What are the French direct object pronouns for *him, her, it, them*? What are the indirect object pronouns for *(to) him, (to) her, (to) them*?

2. How can you often recognize a noun that is an indirect object in French? What types of verbs are frequently followed by indirect objects?

3. Where do you place the object pronoun when there is an infinitive in the same clause? Where does it go otherwise?

4. Where do you place the object pronoun in the **passé composé**? When does the past participle agree with an object pronoun?

Note *de grammaire*

In French, a noun that is a direct object generally follows the verb directly, whereas a noun that is an indirect object is preceded by a preposition, usually **à**.

J'invite **mes amis** chez moi. (direct object)
Je **les** invite chez moi.
Je téléphone **à mes amis**. (indirect object)
Je **leur** téléphone.

*Les pronoms compléments d'objet indirect (**lui, leur**) et reprise des pronoms compléments d'objet direct (**le, la, l', les**)*

1. In **Chapitre 5,** you learned that you can replace the direct object of the verb with the direct object pronouns **le, la, l',** and **les.**

—Tu fais **ta valise** maintenant?   —Tu as acheté **ton billet**?
—Oui, je **la** fais.   —Oui, je **l'**ai acheté.

2. Replace the indirect object of the verb with the indirect object pronouns **lui** (*[to] him, [to] her*) and **leur** (*[to] them*). Generally, indirect objects in French can only be people or animals, not places or things. You can recognize a noun that is an indirect object because it is usually preceded by the preposition **à** (**à, au, à la, à l', aux**).

Verbs indicating communication or exchanges, such as **parler à, téléphoner à, dire à, écrire à, demander à, rendre visite à,** and **donner à,** are often followed by indirect objects.

—Tu écris **à ta mère**?   —Tu vas rendre visite **à tes parents**?
—Oui, je **lui** écris un mail.   —Oui, je vais **leur** rendre visite ce week-end.

DIRECT OBJECT PRONOUNS		INDIRECT OBJECT PRONOUNS	
le (l')	*him, it (m)*	**lui**	*(to) him*
la (l')	*her, it (f)*	**lui**	*(to) her*
les	*them*	**leur**	*(to) them*

3. Indirect object pronouns follow the same placement rules as direct object pronouns. Generally, place them *immediately* before the verb. They go before the infinitive if there is one in the same clause. If not, they go before the conjugated verb. In the **passé composé,** they go before the auxiliary verb.

—Lucas va téléphoner **à Anaïs**?   —*Is Lucas going to call Anaïs?*
—Oui, il va **lui** téléphoner.   —*Yes, he's going to call **her**.*

—Il écrit **à son ami**?   —*Is he writing (**to**) **his friend**?*
—Oui, il **lui** écrit.   —*Yes, he is writing (**to**) **him**.*

—Il a parlé **à ses parents**?   —*Has he talked **to his parents**?*
—Non, il ne **leur** a pas parlé.   —*No, he hasn't talked **to them**.*

In negated sentences, place **ne** immediately after the subject and **pas, rien,** or **jamais** immediately after the first verb.

Je **ne** veux **pas lui** écrire.
Je **ne lui** écris **jamais.**
Je **ne lui** ai **pas** écrit.

4. In the **passé composé,** the past participle agrees with direct object pronouns, but not with indirect objects.

Lucas a invité Anaïs.   Lucas a téléphoné à Anaïs.
Lucas **l'**a invité**e.**   Lucas **lui** a téléphoné.

A **En voyage.** Quel genre de voyageur (voyageuse) êtes-vous? Formez des phrases pour parler de vos habitudes en voyage. Utilisez les pronoms **le, la, l', les.**

> **EXEMPLE** Je réserve *ma chambre* (sur Internet / par téléphone).
> **Je la réserve sur Internet.**

1. J'achète *mon billet* (dans une agence de voyages [*travel agency*] / sur Internet).
2. Je fais *ma valise* (au dernier moment / à l'avance).
3. Je lis *mon guide* (avant de partir / à l'hôtel au dernier moment).
4. Je visite *les sites touristiques* (avec un guide / sans guide).

Maintenant, utilisez les pronoms **lui** et **leur** pour remplacer les noms compléments d'objet indirect.

5. Je dis (toujours / quelquefois / rarement) *à mes parents* où je vais.
6. J'écris (souvent / quelquefois / rarement) des mails *à mes amis.*
7. (Je téléphone / Je ne téléphone pas) *à mon meilleur ami (à ma meilleure amie).*
8. (J'envoie / Je n'envoie pas) mes photos *à mon meilleur ami (à ma meilleure amie).*

B **La prochaine fois.** Refaites les phrases de *A. En voyage* pour parler de ce que vous allez probablement faire la prochaine fois que vous partirez en voyage.

> **EXEMPLE** Je réserve *ma chambre* (sur Internet / par téléphone).
> **La prochaine fois, je vais la réserver sur Internet.**

Maintenant, refaites ces mêmes phrases au passé composé pour dire ce que vous avez fait la dernière fois que vous êtes parti(e) en voyage.

> **EXEMPLE** Je réserve *ma chambre* (sur Internet / par téléphone).
> **La dernière fois, je l'ai réservée sur Internet.**

Aimez-vous faire de l'écotourisme?

C **Habitudes de voyage.** Parlez de vos voyages en répondant à ces questions. Utilisez **le, la, l', les, lui** ou **leur.**

> **EXEMPLE** Vous demandez de l'argent *à vos parents?*
> **Non, je ne leur demande pas d'argent.**

En général...

1. Vous réservez *votre chambre d'hôtel* sur Internet?
2. Vous achetez *votre billet* sur Internet ou dans une agence de voyages *(travel agency)?*
3. Vous proposez *à vos parents* de partir en vacances avec vous?
4. Vous demandez *à votre meilleur(e) ami(e)* de donner à manger à votre chien ou à votre chat?
5. Vous lisez *le magazine de la compagnie aérienne* dans l'avion?

Et la dernière fois que vous êtes parti(e) en voyage...

6. Vous avez téléphoné *à votre mère* pendant le voyage?
7. Vous avez envoyé des textos *à votre meilleur(e) ami(e)?*
8. Vous avez passé *vos soirées* à l'hôtel?
9. À votre retour *(return)*, vous avez parlé du voyage *à vos parents?*
10. Vous avez mis *vos photos* sur Facebook?

Buying your ticket

À L'AGENCE DE VOYAGES

Pour voyager à l'étranger, il faut avoir...

un passeport
un billet d'avion
une carte de crédit
(une carte bleue)
une carte bancaire

Il faut aussi **savoir...**

le numéro du **vol**
l'heure de départ
l'heure d'arrivée

Aimez-vous préparer vos voyages à l'avance? Il faut lire des infos *(f)* sur Internet pour mieux **connaître...**

l'histoire, la géographie et la culture régionale

le réseau de **transports** *(m)* **en commun**

Avant son voyage, Lucas achète son billet à l'agence de voyages.

LUCAS:	Bonjour, monsieur. Je voudrais acheter un billet Paris – Pointe-à-Pitre.
L'AGENT DE VOYAGES:	Très bien, monsieur. Vous voulez un billet aller-retour ou un aller simple?
LUCAS:	Un billet aller-retour.
L'AGENT DE VOYAGES:	À quelle date est-ce que vous voulez partir?
LUCAS:	Le 20 juillet.
L'AGENT DE VOYAGES:	Quand est-ce que vous voulez rentrer?
LUCAS:	Le 12 août.
L'AGENT DE VOYAGES:	Vous voulez un billet en première classe ou en classe économique?
LUCAS:	En classe économique.
L'AGENT DE VOYAGES:	Très bien. Il y a un vol le 20 juillet, départ Paris-Orly à 15h15, arrivée à Pointe-à-Pitre à 17h30, heure locale. Pour le retour, il y a un vol qui part de Pointe-à-Pitre le 12 août à 20h15 et qui arrive à Paris-Orly à 10h15 le 13 août. **Ça vous convient?**
LUCAS:	Oui, c'est parfait. Combien coûte le billet?
L'AGENT DE VOYAGES:	C'est 759 euros.
LUCAS:	Bon. Alors, faites ma réservation. Voilà ma carte bancaire.

---

une carte bancaire *a bank/debit card*   **savoir** *to know*   **un vol** *a flight*   **connaître** *to know, to be familiar with, to be acquainted with*   **le réseau** *the network*   **les transports en commun** *public transportation*   **Ça vous convient?** *Is that good for you?*

A **Le voyage de Lucas.** Lisez le récapitulatif *(itinerary)* du voyage de Lucas et répondez à ces questions.

1. Est-ce que Lucas a acheté un billet aller-retour ou un aller simple?
2. Est-ce que Lucas voyagera en première classe ou en classe économique?
3. Quelle est la date de son départ? de son retour? De quel aéroport partira-t-il?
4. Il devra arriver à l'aéroport combien d'heures avant le départ?
5. À quelle heure est son départ de Paris? À quelle heure est son arrivée à Pointe-à-Pitre?
6. Est-ce qu'un repas sera servi en route?
7. Quelle est la date de son retour à Paris? C'est quel jour de la semaine?

RÉCAPITULATIF DE VOTRE VOYAGE

Passager: Moreau/Lucas

Aller: Mardi 20 juillet:

Départ de Paris-Orly	15h15
Air France-Vol 624	Classe économique
Arrivée à Pointe-à-Pitre	17h30

• Un repas et une collation seront servis en vol.

Retour: Jeudi 12 août:

Départ de Pointe-à-Pitre	20h15
Air France-Vol 625	Classe économique
Arrivée à Paris-Orly	10h15

• Un repas et une collation seront servis en vol.

Prix du billet aller-retour: 759€.

Prévoyez d'arriver à l'aéroport deux heures avant l'heure de départ et n'oubliez pas de reconfirmer votre retour 72 heures avant le départ.

BON VOYAGE!

B **Et vous?** Choisissez la phrase qui vous décrit le mieux quand vous voyagez.

1. **a.** Je préfère préparer mes voyages bien à l'avance.
   b. Je prépare tout quelques jours avant de partir.
   c. Je préfère voyager sans prévoir *(without planning)*.

2. **a.** J'arrive à l'aéroport bien à l'avance.
   b. J'arrive à l'aéroport au dernier moment.
   c. Je manque *(miss)* quelquefois mon vol.

3. **a.** Pendant le voyage, je préfère payer par carte de crédit.
   b. Je préfère payer par carte bancaire.
   c. Pendant le voyage, je préfère payer en espèces *(in cash)*.

4. **a.** Dans une grande ville comme Paris, j'utilise les moyens de transport en commun.
   b. Je prends toujours un taxi ou je loue une voiture.
   c. Je ne sors pas de l'hôtel.

5. **a.** J'aime lire un guide pour connaître l'histoire et la culture d'une région.
   b. J'aime mieux m'informer sur Internet pour connaître la région.
   c. Je préfère tout découvrir *(discover)* pendant le voyage.

À VOUS!

Avec un(e) partenaire, relisez à haute voix la conversation entre Lucas et l'agent de voyages. Ensuite, imaginez que vous êtes dans une agence de voyages d'une ville francophone et que vous achetez un billet pour rentrer chez vous. Votre partenaire jouera le rôle de l'agent de voyages.

You can access the audio of the active vocabulary of this **Compétence** online.

SAYING WHAT PEOPLE KNOW

Les verbes *savoir* et *connaître*

1. Both **savoir** and **connaître** mean *to know*. The verb **reconnaître** *(to recognize)* has the same conjugation as **connaître**.

✔ Pour vérifier

1. What is the conjugation of **savoir**? of **connaître**?

2. Do you use **savoir** or **connaître** when *to know* is followed by a verb? by a question word, **si**, **que**, or **ce que**? to say that one knows a language? if *to know* is followed by a noun that indicates a fact or information? by a noun that indicates that someone is familiar with a person, place or thing?

Note *de grammaire*

1. When saying what someone knows how to do, use **savoir** + *an infinitive*. Since **savoir** means *to know how*, you do not need to add a word for *how*.

    Il sait parler italien.
    Je sais jouer de la guitare.

2. Notice that in the conjugation of **connaître**, there is a circumflex on the **i** only when it appears before the letter **t**.

SAVOIR *(to know [how])*		**CONNAÎTRE** *(to know, to be familiar with, to be acquainted with)*	
je **sais**	nous **savons**	je **connais**	nous **connaissons**
tu **sais**	vous **savez**	tu **connais**	vous **connaissez**
il/elle/on **sait**	ils/elles **savent**	il/elle/on **connaît**	ils/elles **connaissent**

PASSÉ COMPOSÉ: j'**ai su** *(I found out)*
IMPARFAIT: je **savais** *(I knew)*
CONDITIONNEL: je **saurais**
FUTUR: je **saurai**

PASSÉ COMPOSÉ: j'**ai connu** *(I met)*
IMPARFAIT: je **connaissais** *(I knew)*
CONDITIONNEL: je **connaîtrais**
FUTUR: je **connaîtrai**

2. Use **savoir** to say you *know* . . .

FACTS OR INFORMATION:
Est-ce que tu **sais** la réponse?
Nous ne **savons** pas où ils sont.

A LANGUAGE:
Je **sais** le français.
Je ne **sais** pas l'espagnol.

HOW TO DO SOMETHING:
Je **sais** nager.
Je ne **sais** pas danser.

Use **connaître** to say you *know (of)* or *are familiar* or *acquainted with* . . .

PEOPLE:
Vous **connaissez** mon amie Anaïs?
Je la **connais** bien.

PLACES:
Tu **connais** bien la Guadeloupe?
Qui **connaît** ce quartier?

THINGS:
Je ne **connais** pas ce monument.
Tu **connais** l'histoire de la Guadeloupe?

Use **savoir** when *to know* is followed by a verb, a question word (**qui, où...**), or by **si, que,** or **ce que.** When *to know* is followed by a noun, use **savoir** to say one *knows a language, a fact, or information*, and **connaître** to say one *is familiar with a person, place, or thing.*

A **Quel pays?** Quels pays est-ce que ces personnes connaissent bien? Quelles langues savent-elles parler?

EXEMPLE Lucas habite à Paris.
           Il connaît bien la France. Il sait parler français.

> la France   l'Argentine   le Canada
> l'Espagne   les États-Unis   le Sénégal

> français   anglais   espagnol

Sélection musicale. Search for the song **"Je voudrais la connaître"** by Patricia Kaas online to enjoy a musical selection illustrating the use of this structure.

1. Sophie habite à Buenos Aires. Elle...
2. Ana et Luis habitent à Barcelone. Ils...
3. Édouard habite à Dakar. Il...
4. Nous habitons à *[votre ville]*. Nous...
5. *[au professeur]* Et vous, vous habitez à *[votre ville]*. Alors, vous...?

B **Qui sait faire ça?** Dites qui sait faire les choses suivantes dans votre famille. Dites **Personne ne sait...** pour dire *No one knows how to . . .*

EXEMPLE nager

Tout le monde sait nager dans ma famille.
Moi, je sais nager mais les autres ne savent pas nager.
Personne ne sait nager dans ma famille.

1. bien faire la cuisine
2. faire du ski
3. bien danser
4. jouer au tennis
5. bien chanter
6. parler français

Maintenant, circulez dans la classe et trouvez quelqu'un qui sait faire chacune de ces choses.

EXEMPLE nager

—**Marc, tu sais nager?**
—**Oui, je sais nager. / Non, je ne sais pas nager.**

C **Et vous?** Complétez ces phrases avec **je sais / je ne sais pas** ou avec **je connais / je ne connais pas** pour parler de vos connaissances.

1. _____ bien le campus. _____ où se trouvent *(is located)* la bibliothèque et d'autres endroits importants.
2. D'habitude, _____ répondre aux questions du prof. _____ très bien le français. _____ bien les conjugaisons des verbes que nous avons étudiés. _____ qu'il est très important de bien apprendre toutes les conjugaisons.
3. _____ le nom de tous les autres étudiants. _____ bien ces étudiants. _____ ce qu'ils vont tous faire après les cours aujourd'hui.
4. _____ bien la bibliothèque. _____ où se trouvent tous les livres en français.
5. _____ utiliser Internet pour trouver comment dire ce que je veux en français. _____ des / de sites Web avec de bons dictionnaires.

Connaissez-vous la Guadeloupe?
Savez-vous parler français?

D **Ici et en voyage.** Complétez chaque question avec la forme correcte de **connaître** ou de **savoir** et posez-la à votre partenaire.

1. _____-tu un bon agent de voyages? _____-tu une bonne agence de voyages dans notre ville?
2. _____-tu acheter un billet sur Internet? Est-ce que tu _____ combien coûte un billet d'ici à Paris? _____-tu s'il y a un vol direct d'ici à Paris? _____-tu combien de temps dure *(lasts)* un vol d'ici à Paris?
3. _____-tu la Guadeloupe? Est-ce que tu _____ quelle ville est le chef-lieu *(administrative center)* de la Guadeloupe? _____-tu bien l'histoire et la géographie de la Guadeloupe?
4. Tu parles français et anglais. _____-tu parler d'autres langues? Est-ce que tu _____ bien un pays étranger?

INDICATING WHO DOES WHAT TO WHOM

✔ *Pour vérifier*

What four pronouns are used for both direct and indirect objects? Where are they usually placed in a sentence with an infinitive in the same clause? Where are they placed otherwise?

Les pronoms **me, te, nous** *et* **vous**

1. The pronouns **me** *(me, to me)*, **te** *(you, to you)*, **nous** *(us, to us)*, and **vous** *(you, to you)* are used as both direct and indirect objects.

me (m')	*me, to me*	Tu ne **m'**attends pas?
te (t')	*you, to you* (familiar)	Nous **t'**avons attendu(e) une heure.
nous	*us, to us*	Tu peux venir **nous** chercher?
vous	*you, to you* (plural / formal)	Je **vous** téléphonerai plus tard.

2. All object pronouns go immediately before an infinitive if there is one in the same clause; otherwise they go before the conjugated verb. In the **passé composé,** they go before the auxiliary verb.

   Je vais **te** voir demain.   Il ne **nous** connaît pas bien.   Je **vous** ai vu(e)(s).

   In the **passé composé,** the past participle agrees with preceding *direct* objects, but not with *indirect* objects.

   Il **nous** a *vus* mais il ne **nous** a pas *parlé.*

3. The expression **il faut** followed by an infinitive generally means *it is necessary* or *one must.*

   Il faut arriver une heure à l'avance.
   It is necessary to arrive (One must arrive) one hour in advance.

   Use **il faut** with the indirect object pronouns **me, te, nous, vous, lui,** and **leur** to say that someone needs something or needs to do something.

   Il me faut aller au consulat. Il me faut un passeport.
   I need to go to the consulate. I need a passport.

A **Que voulez-vous?** Dites la même chose en utilisant une des expressions données.

> il me faut   il te faut   il lui faut   il nous faut   il vous faut   il leur faut

EXEMPLE J'ai besoin d'un passeport.
   Il me faut un passeport.

1. Tu as besoin d'une carte bancaire.
2. Nous avons besoin d'un guide.
3. Vous avez besoin d'un billet.
4. J'ai besoin d'un nouveau bikini.
5. Tu as besoin d'une pièce d'identité *(identification)*.
6. Vous avez besoin d'une réservation.
7. Il a besoin d'un passeport.
8. Ils ont besoin d'une carte d'embarquement *(boarding pass)*.

Sélection musicale. Search for the song **"Radiologie"** by Malajube online to enjoy a musical selection illustrating the use of this structure.

Maintenant, expliquez pourquoi chacun a besoin de ces choses.

EXEMPLE J'ai besoin d'un passeport.

Il me faut un passeport pour faire un voyage à l'étranger.

> changer de l'argent   avoir une chambre d'hôtel   faire un voyage à l'étranger
> payer le voyage   monter dans l'avion   préparer un itinéraire
> aller à la plage

B **Meilleurs amis.** Demandez à votre partenaire si son meilleur ami (sa meilleure amie) fait les choses suivantes. Utilisez le pronom **te (t')** dans vos questions.

EXEMPLE téléphoner souvent

—**Il/Elle te téléphone souvent?**

—**Non, il/elle ne me téléphone pas souvent.**

Oui, il/elle me téléphone souvent.

1. parler tous les jours
2. retrouver souvent en ville
3. écouter toujours
4. comprendre bien
5. rendre souvent visite
6. donner de l'argent

C **Je te promets!** Un jeune homme dit à sa fiancée qu'il fait ou qu'il va faire tout ce qu'elle veut. Elle lui pose les questions suivantes. Comment répond-il?

EXEMPLE Tu m'aimes vraiment beaucoup?

Oui, je t'aime vraiment beaucoup.

1. Tu m'adores?
2. Tu me trouves belle?
3. Tu me comprends?
4. Tu veux me voir tous les jours?
5. Tu vas venir me voir demain?
6. Tu vas m'abandonner?
7. Tu vas m'aimer pour toujours?

Est-ce que ton meilleur ami t'écoute quand tu lui parles?

D **Professeurs et étudiants.** En groupes, dites au professeur trois choses que les autres étudiants et vous faites pour lui et trois choses que le professeur fait pour vous. Faites deux listes sur une feuille de papier.

EXEMPLES **Nous vous écoutons...**

Vous nous donnez trop de devoirs...

E **Entretien.** Interviewez votre partenaire.

1. Est-ce que tes amis t'invitent souvent à partir en voyage avec eux?
2. As-tu des amis qui te téléphonent d'un autre pays de temps en temps?
3. De tous les endroits où tu as passé tes vacances, quelle ville est-ce que tu me recommandes de visiter? Pourquoi?

Deciding where to go on a trip

UN VOYAGE

Vocabulaire sans peine!

Most countries, states, or regions ending with *-ia* in English end with **-ie** in French (except *India* [**l'Inde**]) and are feminine. Also, the words for the nationalities of the people from these countries end with **-ien(ne)** (except *Russian* [**russe**]).

Australia = **l'Australie**
Australian = **australien(ne)**

How would you say the following in French?

Tunisia / Tunisian

Vocabulaire supplémentaire

EN AFRIQUE	l'Afrique *(f)* du Sud
	la Tunisie
EN ASIE	la Corée (du Nord / du Sud)
	l'Inde *(f)*
	l'Iran *(m)*
	l'Irak *(m)*
EN EUROPE	le Danemark
	la Pologne
	le Portugal
	la République tchèque

Lucas visite la Guadeloupe. Et vous? Quels continents et pays ou régions aimeriez-vous visiter?

Moi, j'aimerais visiter...

l'Afrique *(f)*: **le Maroc,** l'Algérie *(f)*, l'Égypte *(f)*, le Sénégal, la Côte d'Ivoire

L'Oued Saoura, Algérie

l'Asie *(f)* et **le Moyen-Orient:** la Chine, Israël *(m)*, le Japon, le Viêt Nam

l'Amérique *(f)* du Nord ou l'Amérique centrale: **les Antilles** *(f pl)*, le Canada, les États-Unis *(m pl)*, le Mexique

La Guadeloupe

l'Amérique *(f)* du Sud: l'Argentine *(f)*, le Brésil, le Chili, la Colombie, la Guyane, le Pérou

l'Océanie *(f)*: l'Australie *(f)*, la Nouvelle-Calédonie, la Polynésie française

Le Parlement européen, Bruxelles

l'Europe *(f)*: **l'Allemagne** *(f)*, la Belgique, la Croatie, l'Espagne *(f)*, la France, la Grèce, l'Irlande *(f)*, l'Italie *(f)*, **le Royaume-Uni,** la Russie, la Suisse

---

le Maroc *Morocco*   **le Moyen-Orient** *the Middle East*   **les Antilles** *the West Indies*   **l'Allemagne** *Germany*
le Royaume-Uni *the United Kingdom*

🔊 9-5 Lucas et Anaïs parlent des voyages qu'ils ont faits.

ANAÏS: Pourquoi es-tu venu tout seul en Guadeloupe? Tu aimes voyager?

LUCAS: Oui, j'adore ça!

ANAÏS: Quels pays as-tu visités?

LUCAS: J'ai visité les États-Unis, la Chine et le Canada. Et toi? Tu aimes voyager?

ANAÏS: Je n'ai jamais quitté la Guadeloupe, mais j'aimerais bien visiter l'Afrique un jour.

LUCAS: Où aimerais-tu aller en Afrique?

ANAÏS: Moi, j'aimerais surtout visiter le Sénégal et la Côte d'Ivoire.

A **Quel continent?** Où se trouvent *(are located)* ces pays et régions?

> en Amérique du Nord   en Afrique   en Amérique du Sud
> en Océanie   en Asie   en Europe

EXEMPLE la Chine
La Chine se trouve en Asie.

1. les États-Unis   3. le Japon   5. l'Allemagne   7. la Guyane
2. l'Algérie   4. l'Australie   6. le Sénégal   8. le Maroc

B **Quels pays?** Dites quels pays vous aimeriez visiter dans la région indiquée.

EXEMPLE en Europe
En Europe, j'aimerais visiter la France, l'Espagne...

1. en Asie et au Moyen-Orient   4. en Afrique
2. en Amérique du Nord et centrale   5. en Europe
3. en Amérique du Sud   6. en Océanie

C **Associations.** Travaillez avec deux autres étudiant(e)s pour trouver le pays ou la région de chaque groupe qui ne va pas avec les autres. Expliquez pourquoi.

EXEMPLE l'Allemagne, les États-Unis, la France, la Suisse
les États-Unis: Tous les autres sont en Europe.

1. le Canada, l'Argentine, l'Espagne, le Pérou, le Mexique
2. l'Australie, la Polynésie française, la Martinique, le Sénégal
3. la France, les États-Unis, l'Australie, le Royaume-Uni
4. le Sénégal, l'Égypte, le Brésil, l'Algérie, le Maroc
5. la France, la Belgique, le Sénégal, la Suisse, le Mexique

À VOUS!

Avec un(e) partenaire, relisez à haute voix la conversation entre Anaïs et Lucas. Ensuite, changez la conversation pour parler des régions et pays que vous avez visités et de ceux que vous aimeriez visiter.

You can access the audio of the active vocabulary of this *Compétence* online.

SAYING WHERE YOU ARE GOING

✔ Pour vérifier

1. With which one of the following do you generally not use a definite article when it is the subject or direct object of a verb: cities, states, provinces, countries, or continents? Would you use **le, la, l'**, or **les** before the following place names?

_____ Italie, _____ Antilles,

_____ Ohio, _____ Japon,

_____ France

2. Which countries, states, or provinces are generally feminine? masculine?

3. How do you say *to* or *in* with a city? with a feminine country? with a masculine country beginning with a vowel sound? with a masculine country beginning with a consonant? with plural countries?

Note *de grammaire*

1. You can also say **dans le** with most masculine states (**dans le Vermont**).

2. You say **(dans) l'état de New York** and **(dans) l'état de Washington** to clarify that you are talking about the states rather than the cities with the same names.

Les expressions géographiques

1. When a place name is used as the subject or object of a verb, you generally need to use the definite article with continents, countries, states, and provinces, but not with cities. Most continents, countries, states, and provinces ending in **-e** are feminine, whereas most others are masculine. There are exceptions, such as **le Mexique, le Nouveau-Mexique, le Maine, le Delaware, le New Hampshire,** and **le Tennessee.**

   J'adore l'Europe. **La** France est très belle. Nous allons visiter Londres, Paris et Nice. J'aimerais aussi voir **les** États-Unis: **la** Californie, **le** Texas et **la** Floride.

2. To say *to* or *in* with a geographical location, the preposition you use varies.

to / in		
à	with cities	**à** Paris
aux	with any plural country or region	**aux** États-Unis
en	with any feminine country or region and with any masculine one beginning with a vowel	**en** France **en** Ontario
au	with any masculine country or region beginning with a consonant	**au** Canada

A **C'est connu!** D'abord, mettez la forme convenable de l'article défini devant le nom de chaque pays. Ensuite, demandez à votre partenaire quel pays est connu *(known)* pour les choses indiquées.

_____ Royaume-Uni	_____ Égypte	_____ Suisse
_____ Colombie	_____ États-Unis	_____ France
_____ Mexique	_____ Italie	_____ Brésil

EXEMPLE —Quel pays est connu pour le café?
—La Colombie.

Quel pays est connu pour...?

1. le fromage et le vin	**3.** le chocolat	**5.** les spaghetti	**7.** la musique rock
2. le carnaval	**4.** le thé	**6.** les pyramides	**8.** le sphinx

B **Leçon de géographie.** Votre ami(e) n'est pas très fort(e) en géographie et il/elle vous pose des questions. Répondez-lui. D'abord, donnez la préposition convenable pour dire *to / in* avec chaque pays. Ensuite, jouez les deux rôles avec votre partenaire.

EXEMPLE Londres (_____ Royaume-Uni, _____ Canada)
—Londres se trouve *(is located)* au Royaume-Uni ou au Canada?
—Londres se trouve au Royaume-Uni.

1. Tokyo (_____ Chine, _____ Japon)
2. Mexico (_____ Mexique, _____ Pérou)
3. Moscou (_____ Italie, _____ Russie)
4. Berlin (_____ Croatie, _____ Allemagne)
5. Hanoï (_____ Viêt Nam, _____ Chine)
6. Alger (_____ Algérie, _____ Maroc)

Sélection musicale. Search for the song **"Sénégal fast-food"** by Amadou & Mariam online to enjoy a musical selection illustrating the use of this structure.

7. Le Caire (_____ Maroc, _____ Égypte)

8. Dakar (_____ Sénégal, _____ Côte d'Ivoire)

9. La Nouvelle-Orléans (_____ États-Unis, _____ Irlande)

10. Abidjan (_____ Côte d'Ivoire, _____ Sénégal)

C **C'est où?** Devinez où dans le monde francophone se trouvent *(are located)* ces sites touristiques.

EXEMPLE Le château de Versailles
Le château de Versailles se trouve à Versailles en France.

Dakar (Sénégal)	Versailles (France)
Bruxelles (Belgique)	Fès (Maroc)
Québec (Canada)	Papeete (Polynésie française)

Le château de Versailles

1.

La Grand-Place

4.

Le marché de Papeete

2.

Le Château Frontenac

5.

3.

La Médina

La Grande Mosquée

VIDÉO-REPRISE

Les Stagiaires

Rappel!
Dans l'épisode précédent de la vidéo, Amélie a parlé avec Rachid du restaurant où elle a dîné avec Matthieu.

See the **Résumé de grammaire** section at the end of each chapter for a review of all the grammar presented in the chapter.

Dans l'**Épisode 9** de la vidéo **Les Stagiaires,** M. Vieilledent fait des projets pour des vacances en Martinique. Avant de regarder l'épisode, faites ces exercices pour réviser ce que vous avez appris dans le **Chapitre 9.**

A **Qu'est-ce qu'on fait?** Avant de décider où aller en vacances, M. Vieilledent parle à ses amis de ce qu'il pourrait faire dans les différents endroits où il pense peut-être aller. Avec un(e) partenaire, faites une liste de ce qu'il pourrait faire dans les endroits suivants: **dans une grande ville, à la mer, à la montagne.**

EXEMPLE dans une grande ville
Dans une grande ville, il pourrait profiter des activités culturelles...

B **Destinations.** Tout le monde à Technovert parle des vacances. Complétez chaque espace avec la préposition appropriée (**en, au, aux**).

EXEMPLE Christophe veut aller **au** Japon parce qu'il adore les mangas.

1. Matthieu veut aller _____ États-Unis pour pratiquer son anglais.
2. Rachid est marocain. Il est né _____ Maroc. Il a déjà voyagé _____ Algérie et _____ Égypte.
3. Amélie aime passer les vacances d'hiver _____ Suisse.
4. M. Vieilledent va bientôt partir pour la Martinique, _____ Antilles.

C **En Martinique.** M. Vieilledent dit à Camille qu'il va partir en vacances. Complétez les phrases suivantes en mettant les verbes au futur dans l'espace le plus logique.

EXEMPLE (être, prendre) Je **prendrai** des vacances à la fin de ce mois, alors je ne **serai** pas au bureau.

1. (partir, rentrer) Je _____ pour la Martinique le quinze et je _____ le vingt-neuf.
2. (arriver, décider, visiter) Je _____ peut-être la Guadeloupe aussi, mais je _____ ça quand j'_____ en Martinique.
3. (être, faire) Céline _____ mon travail et elle _____ responsable du bureau pendant mon absence.
4. (pouvoir, lire) Je _____ mes mails pendant les vacances et vous _____ aussi me téléphoner.

D **Renseignements.** M. Vieilledent parle à Camille de son voyage en Martinique. Complétez chaque phrase avec la forme correcte du verbe **savoir** ou **connaître.**

1. Vous _____ dans quel hôtel je vais descendre en Martinique?
2. _____-vous un bon site Web où on peut comparer des hôtels?
3. Je ne _____ pas la région. Ce sera mon premier voyage aux Antilles.
4. Je _____ qu'il y a des plantations de café que je voudrais voir.
5. _____-vous combien d'heures dure *(lasts)* le vol d'ici en Martinique?

E **Un mail.** Lisez la conversation suivante entre Céline et Amélie et complétez-la avec la forme correcte du verbe indiqué entre parenthèses.

CÉLINE: Qu'est-ce que tu **1** (lire)?

AMÉLIE: C'est un mail de Matthieu.

CÉLINE: Vous **2** (s'écrire) beaucoup de mails, on dirait, non?

AMÉLIE: Oui, Matthieu m' **3** (écrire) souvent. Il est un peu timide quand on est face à face et il **4** (dire) plus facilement ce qu'il pense dans un mail.

CÉLINE: Alors, ça devient sérieux entre vous deux si vous **5** (se dire) tous vos secrets.

AMÉLIE: Je ne lui **6** (dire) pas encore tous mes secrets,… mais je le trouve sympa.

F **Interactions.** Matthieu pense souvent à Amélie et rêve de leur relation. Décrivez tout ce que Matthieu fait dans ses rêves en faisant des phrases avec les verbes suivants et le pronom convenable, **la (l')** ou **lui.**

EXEMPLES écouter avec attention quand elle parle
Il l'écoute avec attention quand elle parle.
envoyer beaucoup de textos
Il lui envoie beaucoup de textos.

1. parler de tout
2. téléphoner tous les jours
3. inviter à sortir le week-end
4. retrouver en ville
5. acheter des fleurs *(flowers)*
6. dire tous ses secrets

 Maintenant parlez à un(e) autre étudiant(e) de sa relation avec son meilleur ami (sa meilleure amie). Posez des questions avec les verbes précédents et le pronom **te (t')** comme dans l'exemple.

EXEMPLE écouter avec attention quand elle parle
—**Est-ce que ton meilleur ami (ta meilleure amie) t'écoute avec attention quand tu parles?**
—**Il/Elle m'écoute en général.**

Access the Video *Les Stagiaires* online.

 Épisode 9: J'ai acheté vos billets

AVANT LA VIDÉO
Dans ce clip, Camille aide M. Vieilledent à choisir un hôtel pour son voyage en Martinique et elle lui donne les renseignements sur les réservations pour son billet d'avion. Avant de regarder l'épisode, imaginez quel genre d'hôtel M. Vieilledent pourrait préférer et les services qu'il aimerait y trouver.

APRÈS LA VIDÉO
Regardez le clip et répondez aux questions suivantes:
- Quel genre d'hôtel est-ce que M. Vieilledent a choisi?
- À quelle heure partira son vol pour la Martinique et à quelle heure arrivera-t-il?

LECTURE ET COMPOSITION

LECTURE

POUR MIEUX LIRE:
Understanding words with multiple meanings

You are going to read an excerpt from a work by Dany Bébel-Gisler (1935–2003), whose stories depict the culture of the Antilles. As you will find in this reading, words often have more than one meaning. Learning to be flexible about the meanings of words will help you read more easily. Consider the multiple meanings of these words.

apprendre	*to learn*	*to teach*
la terre	*the ground*	*the earth*
serrer	*to squeeze*	*to wrap around*
une berceuse	*a lullaby*	*a rocking chair*
soigner	*to care for*	*to treat*
frais (fraîche)	*cool*	*fresh*
finir	*to finish*	**finir par** *to end up*
compter	*to count, to plan*	**compter sur** *to depend on, to count on*

Quel sens? Traduisez les phrases suivantes. Choisissez selon le contexte le sens le plus logique pour les mots en italique. Voir la liste ci-dessus. *(See the above list.)*

1. Ma grand-mère *m'a appris* à ne pas trop *compter sur* les autres.
2. Elle m'a appris le travail de *la terre,* à reconnaître les plantes qui *soignent* les maladies.
3. Je *serre* ma tête *(head)* avec ce madras [a type of Caribbean cloth].
4. Quand ma grand-mère avait la tête *fraîche,* elle s'asseyait *(used to sit)* dans sa *berceuse.*
5. Ils *finissaient par* devenir riches.

Ma grand-mère m'a appris à ne pas compter sur les yeux des autres pour dormir.

Je suis restée avec grand-mère moins longtemps qu'avec maman. Maman était en meilleure santé, elle ne buvait pas, mais grand-mère a plus fait pour moi que maman. Elle m'a beaucoup appris. Et surtout à ne pas compter sur les yeux des autres pour dormir.

Elle m'**a enseigné** le travail de la terre, à organiser un jardin, à planter des légumes. À reconnaître aussi les plantes qui soignent, celles qui sont bonnes pour **le ventre,** pour **la toux,** pour **les blessures.**

[Quand **j'ai très mal,** ma grand-mère m'avait donné **un mouchoir.** Alors je prends ce mouchoir – ce que l'on appelle un madras chez nous ici – et je serre **ma tête** avec ce madras et **je me sens très forte.**]

La nuit venue, quand grand-mère **était d'attaque, debout** sur ses deux pieds, la tête bien fraîche, elle s'asseyait dans sa berceuse et me lançait: *Yékrik!* Je répondais: *Yékrak!* et allais m'installer **sur ses genoux.** Ma petite main dans **la sienne, j'enfouissais** ma tête entre ses deux **seins.** Alors grand-mère me faisait voyager dans **un monde étrange, celui** des contes… J'aimais beaucoup les contes où les **enfants orphelins, pauvres, à force de lutter contre la misère,** de marcher, de marcher, de marcher, **d'employer la ruse comme Compère Lapin,** finissaient, une fois grands, par devenir riches et respectés par tous.

Dany Bébel-Gisler, À la recherche d'une odeur de grand-mère © Éditions Jasor, 2000.

---

a enseigné *taught*   **le ventre** *the belly*   **la toux** *coughing*   **les blessures** *injuries*   **j'ai très mal** *I hurt very badly*   **un mouchoir** *a handkerchief*   **ma tête** *my head*
je me sens très forte *I feel very strong*   **était d'attaque, debout** *was feeling fit, standing*   **Yékrik! Yékrak!** *a cry used to begin a story*   **sur ses genoux** *on her lap*
la sienne *hers*   **j'enfouissais** *I buried*   **seins** *breasts*   **un monde étrange, celui** *a strange world, the one*   **enfants orphelins, pauvres** *orphaned children, poor*
à force de lutter contre la misère *by fighting poverty*   **d'employer la ruse comme Compère Lapin** *using trickery like Compère Lapin* (equivalent of Brer Rabbit)

Compréhension

1. Avec qui est-ce que la petite fille aimait passer son temps? Pourquoi?
2. Qu'est-ce qu'elle a appris de sa grand-mère?
3. Quelle sorte de contes est-ce qu'elle aimait?

COMPOSITION

POUR MIEUX ÉCRIRE:
Revising what you write

Editing and revising what you write is an important final step in the writing process. Once you finish a composition, reread it and make sure you have an introductory and a concluding sentence and that your sentences and paragraphs are clear and well organized. Then, check each sentence against this checklist:

- Are the verbs in the proper form for the subject and the tense?
- Do all of your adjectives agree (masculine, feminine, singular, plural) with the nouns they modify?
- Are all the words spelled correctly (including accents) and do the nouns have the correct article **(un, une, le, du, de,...)**, possessive adjective **(mon, ton, ses,...)**,...?
- Did you use the correct forms of the prepositions **de (du, de la,...)** and **à (au, à la,...)**?

Révisons! Lisez ce paragraphe. D'abord, trouvez une phrase pour commencer le paragraphe et une autre pour le terminer. Ensuite, corrigez les 16 erreurs *(errors)* (marquées en italique) dans le paragraphe.

Philippe préfère *voyagé* à l'étranger, mais Marie préfère *reste* dans son propre *(own)* pays. Quand ils *voyage* ensemble, Philippe passe très peu *du* temps *au* hôtel mais Marie aime passer toutes les soirées dans *son* chambre. Philippe préfère visiter une *grand* ville et profiter *de les* activités culturelles. Marie préfère les activités de plein air et elle aime passer *sa* vacances à la *montange* ou à la *mère*. L'année *prochain*, ils visiteront Nice *ou* Philippe *iront au* musées et Marie passera *sa* temps à la plage.

Un itinéraire

Imaginez que votre classe de français va faire un voyage d'une semaine dans un pays francophone. Écrivez une description détaillée du voyage que la classe fera ensemble. Dans la description, donnez les renseignements suivants:

- où vous irez, quand vous partirez et quand vous reviendrez
- comment vous voyagerez et combien coûtera le voyage par personne
- où vous descendrez et où vous prendrez les repas
- ce que vous ferez chaque jour de la semaine

N'oubliez pas de relire votre composition et de la réviser si nécessaire.

© Stock Connection/Stock Connection/Superstock

COMPARAISONS CULTURELLES

LA CULTURE CRÉOLE AUX ANTILLES

La culture **antillaise** est une culture créole qui reflète l'histoire de ces îles et la diversité de leurs peuples. La majorité des habitants sont les descendants d'**esclaves africains amenés** dans ces îles pour travailler dans les plantations. Il y a aussi des Amérindiens, des Indiens, des Chinois, des békés (les descendants des premiers **colons** français), des métros (les Français plus récemment arrivés d'Europe) et bien d'autres.

Le français est la langue officielle des Antilles françaises mais la population locale parle aussi créole. Le créole antillais est **un mélange de** français, de langues **indigènes** et africaines, d'espagnol, de portugais, d'anglais et de hindi. À l'origine une langue orale, il y a de nos jours un fort mouvement littéraire créole et un mouvement de **créolité** pour encourager et protéger la langue et la culture créoles.

Aux Antilles, les fêtes traditionnelles sont nombreuses. Le Tour des Yoles Rondes au mois d'août est une fête très populaire en Martinique: une semaine de compétition sur les bateaux typiques de l'île. C'est aussi l'occasion de **déguster** des plats antillais accompagnés de rhum dans une ambiance de musique et de fête.

La cuisine créole antillaise est un délicieux mélange de fruits tropicaux, de poissons et fruits de mer, de rhum et d'**épices d'Inde,** avec des influences africaines et françaises.

La Fête des **Cuisinières** est une grande tradition guadeloupéenne. Au mois d'août, à l'occasion de la St-Laurent, **patron** des cuisinières, 200 cuisinières **vêtues** de leurs plus belles robes et **parées** de leurs plus beaux **bijoux,** se rendent en procession à la cathédrale de Pointe-à-Pitre. Elles portent des **paniers remplis de** plats typiquement créoles (**écrevisses, boudin…**) pour **les faire bénir.** Après **la messe, elles défilent** dans les rues, puis passent à table. La fête se termine le soir avec le Bal des Cuisinières.

---

antillaise of the Antilles   **esclaves africains amenés** African slaves brought   **colons** colonists   **un mélange de** a mixture of   **indigènes** indigenous   **créolité** "Creoleness"   **déguster** to savor   **épices d'Inde** Indian spices   **Cuisinières** Cooks   **patron** patron saint   **vêtues** dressed   **parées** adorned   **bijoux** jewels   **paniers remplis de** baskets filled with   **écrevisses** crawfish   **boudin** blood sausage   **les faire bénir** to have them blessed   **la messe** the mass   **elles défilent** they parade

Le créole, c'est plus qu'une langue, c'est «également **une façon de vivre**, et l'histoire d'un peuple, **évoquant à la fois** l'Afrique, **l'esclavage**, mais aussi la danse, la musique, les îles, la fête... »[1]

La musique et la danse antillaises, **dérivées d'**un mélange de **sons** et de rythmes européens, américains et africains, reflètent l'histoire des îles caraïbes et sont connues partout dans le monde: le zouk, le zouk-love, la biguine, la Cadence-lypso et d'autres. **Parmi** les artistes antillais les plus connus, il y a Expérience 7, Zouk Machine et Kassav'.

Compréhension

1. La majorité des habitants des Antilles sont de quelle origine?

2. Quelle est la langue officielle des Antilles françaises? Quelle autre langue est-ce que la population locale parle?

3. Par définition une langue créole est une langue formée d'une combinaison de plusieurs langues. Le créole antillais est un mélange de quelles langues?

4. Comment s'appelle le mouvement qui a pour but *(goal)* la préservation et le développement de la culture créole?

5. Aimeriez-vous mieux participer au Tour des Yoles Rondes ou à la Fête des Cuisinières? Pourquoi?

6. Comment est la cuisine créole?

7. La musique et la danse antillaises sont dérivées d'un mélange de sons et de rythmes de quelles origines?

8. Quelles sont les cultures importantes dans votre région? Est-ce qu'il y a des traditions, des fêtes, de la musique ou une cuisine que vous associez à chacune?

[1] http://www.webcaraibes.com/guadeloupe/culture.htm

---

une façon *a way*   **évoquant à la fois** *evoking at the same time*   **l'esclavage** *slavery*   **dérivées de** *derived from*
sons *sounds*   **Parmi** *Among*

RÉSUMÉ DE GRAMMAIRE

THE FUTURE TENSE (LE FUTUR)

Use the future tense to say what someone *will* do. Form it by adding the bold-faced endings below to the same stem that you used for the conditional. For most verbs, it is the infinitive, but drop the final **e** of infinitives ending with **-re.**

Je prendrai des vacances en été.

Tu resteras ici?

Tu partiras tout seul?

Mes parents voyageront avec moi.

VISITER	CONNAÎTRE	FINIR
je visiter**ai**	je connaîtr**ai**	je finir**ai**
tu visiter**as**	tu connaîtr**as**	tu finir**as**
il/elle/on visiter**a**	il/elle/on connaîtr**a**	il/elle/on finir**a**
nous visiter**ons**	nous connaîtr**ons**	nous finir**ons**
vous visiter**ez**	vous connaîtr**ez**	vous finir**ez**
ils/elles visiter**ont**	ils/elles connaîtr**ont**	ils/elles finir**ont**

The following verbs have irregular stems.

J'irai en Europe.

Combien de temps **serez-vous** en Europe?

On reviendra après trois semaines.

-r-		-vr- / -dr-		-rr-	
aller:	ir-	devoir:	devr-	voir:	verr-
être:	ser-	pleuvoir:	pleuvr-	pouvoir:	pourr-
faire:	fer-	vouloir:	voudr-	mourir:	mourr-
avoir:	aur-	venir:	viendr-	courir:	courr-
savoir:	saur-	devenir:	deviendr-	envoyer:	enverr-
		revenir:	reviendr-		
		obtenir	obtiendr-		

S'il peut, mon frère **ira** en vacances avec nous.

Il décidera quand **on saura** la date exacte de notre départ.

As in English, use the future tense in *if / then* sentences to say what will happen if something else occurs. Use the present tense in the clause with **si.** Unlike English, use the future in French in clauses with **quand** referring to the future. English has the present tense in such clauses.

THE VERBS *DIRE, LIRE,* AND *ÉCRIRE*

The verbs **dire, lire,** and **écrire** are irregular in the present tense and the **passé composé (j'ai dit, j'ai lu, j'ai écrit).** As with other verbs, use the stem for **nous** in the present tense to form the imperfect (**je disais, je lisais, j'écrivais**). Obtain the future / conditional stem by dropping the final **e** of the infinitive (**je dirai, je lirai, j'écrirai**).

Est-ce que **tu lis** tes mails quand tu voyages?

J'écris à mes amis et je leur montre des photos de mon voyage.

Mes parents disent que la Méditerranée est très jolie.

DIRE	LIRE	ÉCRIRE
je **dis**	je **lis**	j' **écris**
tu **dis**	tu **lis**	tu **écris**
il/elle/on **dit**	il/elle/on **lit**	il/elle/on **écrit**
nous **disons**	nous **lisons**	nous **écrivons**
vous **dites**	vous **lisez**	vous **écrivez**
ils/elles **disent**	ils/elles **lisent**	ils/elles **écrivent**

THE VERBS *SAVOIR* AND *CONNAÎTRE*

Savoir and **connaître** both mean *to know*. Use **savoir** when *to know* is followed by a verb, a question word (**qui, où...**), or by **si, que,** or **ce que,** or to say that one knows a language. When *to know* is followed by a noun, use **savoir** to say one *knows a fact or information*, and **connaître** to say one *is familiar with a person, place, or thing*.

SAVOIR	CONNAÎTRE
je **sais**	je **connais**
tu **sais**	tu **connais**
il/elle/on **sait**	il/elle/on **connaît**
nous **savons**	nous **connaissons**
vous **savez**	vous **connaissez**
ils/elles **savent**	ils/elles **connaissent**

PASSÉ COMPOSÉ:	j'**ai su** *(I found out)*	j'**ai connu** *(I met)*
IMPARFAIT:	je **savais** *(I knew)*	je **connaissais** *(I knew)*
CONDITIONNEL:	je **saurais**	je **connaîtrais**
FUTUR:	je **saurai**	je **connaîtrai**

Quelles langues **sais-tu**?
Je sais parler français et **mes parents savent** l'allemand.

Savez-vous si vous allez visiter l'Allemagne?
On ira à Berlin, où **mes parents connaissent** beaucoup de gens.

Je ne connais pas du tout l'Europe. Est-ce que **tu connais** bien l'histoire de la région?

DIRECT AND INDIRECT OBJECT PRONOUNS

Direct object pronouns replace nouns that are the direct object of the verb. Indirect object pronouns replace nouns that are the indirect object of the verb. Generally, indirect objects are people or animals, not things, and they follow the preposition **à**. They often are used with verbs indicating communication or exchanges (**parler à, téléphoner à, dire à, écrire à, demander à, rendre visite à, donner à**).

DIRECT OBJECT PRONOUNS				INDIRECT OBJECT PRONOUNS			
me (m')	*me*	**nous**	*us*	**me (m')**	*(to) me*	**nous**	*(to) us*
te (t')	*you*	**vous**	*you*	**te (t')**	*(to) you*	**vous**	*(to) you*
le (l')	*him, it (m)*	**les**	*them*	**lui**	*(to) him*	**leur**	*(to) them*
la (l')	*her, it (f)*			**lui**	*(to) her*		

Both direct and indirect object pronouns have the same placement rules. They go immediately before the infinitive if there is one in the same clause. If not, they go before the conjugated verb. In the **passé composé,** they go before the auxiliary verb. The past participle agrees with direct object pronouns, but not with indirect objects.

Est-ce que tu **m'**écriras si je **te** donne mon adresse mail?

Mon frère habite à Paris. Je vais **te** donner son numéro de téléphone et tu pourras **lui** téléphoner quand tu seras en France.

Les amis de mes parents **nous** ont demandé de **leur** rendre visite. Mes parents ne **les** ont pas vus depuis vingt ans, la dernière fois qu'ils **leur** ont rendu visite.

GEOGRAPHICAL EXPRESSIONS

Use the definite article with names of continents, countries, states, and provinces used as the subject or object of a verb, but not with cities. Most continents, countries, states, and provinces ending in **e** are feminine, whereas most others are masculine.

To say *to* or *in* with a geographical location, use . . .

à	with cities
aux	with any plural country or region
en	with any feminine country or region and with any masculine one beginning with a vowel sound
au	with any masculine country or region beginning with a consonant

Je voudrais visiter **les** États-Unis, **le** Canada et **la** Colombie.

Pendant notre voyage, on ira à Berlin **en** Allemagne, à Copenhague **au** Danemark, à Amsterdam **aux** Pays-Bas et à Paris et à Nice **en** France.

VOCABULAIRE

COMPÉTENCE 1

Talking about vacation

NOMS MASCULINS

le ballet	the ballet
un endroit	a place
l'opéra	the opera
un Parisien	a Parisian
le paysage	the landscape, the scenery
un site	a site, a spot

NOMS FÉMININS

une île	an island
la mer	the sea
une Parisienne	a Parisian
une terrasse	a terrace

EXPRESSIONS VERBALES

admirer	to admire
bronzer	to tan
compter	to count on, to plan on
goûter	to taste
profiter de	to take advantage of

ADJECTIFS

assis(e)	seated
exotique	exotic
historique	historic
local(e) (*mpl* locaux)	local
touristique	touristic
tropical(e) (*mpl* tropicaux)	tropical

DIVERS

Ça te plaira.	You'll like it.

COMPÉTENCE 2

Preparing for a trip

NOMS MASCULINS

un article	an article
un billet (d'avion)	a (plane) ticket
un blog	a blog
le climat	the climate
le départ	the departure
un guide	a guidebook, a guide
un magazine	a magazine
un mail	an email
un passeport	a passport
un poème	a poem
des préparatifs	preparations
un roman	a novel
un voisin	a neighbor

NOMS FÉMININS

une arrivée	an arrival
une carte postale	a postcard
la douane	customs
une histoire	a story
une lettre	a letter
une rédaction	a composition
une région	a region, an area
une valise	a suitcase
une voisine	a neighbor

EXPRESSIONS VERBALES

changer	to change, to exchange
décrire	to describe
dire	to say, to tell
donner à manger à	to feed
écrire	to write
faire sa valise	to pack one's bag
s'informer	to find out information
lire	to read
obtenir	to obtain
passer	to pass (through)
recevoir	to receive
réserver	to reserve

DIVERS

(bien) à l'avance	(well) in advance
à l'étranger	in another country, abroad
Ça lui plaît?	Does he/she like it?
en contact	in contact
extraordinaire	extraordinary, great
là-bas	over there
leur	(to) them
lui	(to) him, (to) her
me (m')	(to) me

COMPÉTENCE 3

Buying your ticket

NOMS MASCULINS

un agent de voyages	*a travel agent*
un aller simple	*a one-way ticket*
un billet aller-retour	*a round-trip ticket*
un réseau	*a network*
le retour	*the return*
les transports en commun	*public transportation*
un vol	*a flight*

NOMS FÉMININS

une agence de voyages	*a travel agency*
une carte bancaire	*a bank card, a debit card*
une carte de crédit (une carte bleue)	*a credit card*
la classe économique	*economy class, coach*
la culture	*the culture*
la géographie	*the geography*
l'heure d'arrivée	*the arrival time*
l'heure de départ	*the departure time*
l'heure locale	*local time*
des infos	*info*
la première classe	*first class*

EXPRESSIONS VERBALES

connaître	*to know, to be familiar with, to be acquainted with*
faire une réservation	*to make a reservation*
reconnaître	*to recognize*
savoir	*to know*

DIVERS

Ça te/vous convient?	*Does that work for you?*
il me (te/nous/vous/lui/ leur) faut	*I (you/we/you/he [she]/ they) need*
me	*(to) me*
nous	*(to) us*
te	*(to) you*
vous	*(to) you*

COMPÉTENCE 4

Deciding where to go on a trip

NOMS MASCULINS

le Brésil	*Brazil*
le Canada	*Canada*
le Chili	*Chile*
un continent	*a continent*
les États-Unis	*the United States*
Israël	*Israel*
le Japon	*Japan*
le Maroc	*Morocco*
le Mexique	*Mexico*
le Moyen-Orient	*the Middle East*
l'Ontario	*Ontario*
le Pérou	*Peru*
le Royaume-Uni	*the United Kingdom*
le Sénégal	*Senegal*
le Texas	*Texas*
le Viêt Nam	*Vietnam*

NOMS FÉMININS

l'Afrique	*Africa*
l'Algérie	*Algeria*
l'Allemagne	*Germany*
l'Amérique centrale	*Central America*
l'Amérique du Nord	*North America*
l'Amérique du Sud	*South America*
les Antilles	*the West Indies*
l'Argentine	*Argentina*
l'Asie	*Asia*
l'Australie	*Australia*
la Belgique	*Belgium*
la Californie	*California*
la Chine	*China*
la Colombie	*Colombia*
la Côte d'Ivoire	*Ivory Coast*
la Croatie	*Croatia*
l'Égypte	*Egypt*
l'Espagne	*Spain*
l'Europe	*Europe*
la Floride	*Florida*
la France	*France*
la Grèce	*Greece*
la Guyane	*French Guiana*
l'Irlande	*Ireland*
l'Italie	*Italy*
la Nouvelle-Calédonie	*New Caledonia*
l'Océanie	*Oceania*
la Polynésie française	*French Polynesia*
la Russie	*Russia*
la Suisse	*Switzerland*

DIVERS

adorer	*to adore, to love*

Aux Antilles
À l'hôtel

 Pair work

 Group work

 Class work

 Video

 Audio

© Christian Heeb/laif/Redux

10

LE MONDE FRANCOPHONE

Géoculture et Vidéo-voyage: Les Antilles

COMPÉTENCE

1 Deciding where to stay
Le logement

Giving general advice
Les expressions impersonnelles et l'infinitif

Stratégies et Compréhension auditive
- **Pour mieux comprendre:** *Anticipating a response*
- **Compréhension auditive:** *À la réception*

2 Going to the doctor
Chez le médecin

Giving advice to someone in particular
Les expressions impersonnelles et les verbes réguliers au subjonctif

Giving advice
Les verbes irréguliers au subjonctif

3 Running errands on a trip
Des courses en voyage

Expressing wishes and emotions
Les expressions d'émotion et de volonté et le subjonctif

Saying who you want to do something
Le subjonctif ou l'infinitif?

4 Giving directions
Les indications

Telling how to go somewhere
Reprise de l'impératif et les pronoms avec l'impératif

Vidéo-reprise: *Les Stagiaires*

Lecture et Composition
- **Pour mieux lire:** *Using word families*
- **Lecture:** *Avis de l'hôtel*
- **Pour mieux écrire:** *Making suggestions*
- **Composition:** *Suggestions de voyage!*

Comparaisons culturelles: *La musique francophone: les influences africaines et antillaises*

Résumé de grammaire

Vocabulaire

GÉOCULTURE ET VIDÉO-VOYAGE:
LES ANTILLES

Guadeloupe

Martinique

LA GUADELOUPE

NOMBRE D'HABITANTS:
472 000 (les Guadeloupéens)

CHEF-LIEU *(ADMINISTRATIVE CENTER):* **Basse-Terre**

LA MARTINIQUE

NOMBRE D'HABITANTS:
396 000 (les Martiniquais)

CHEF-LIEU: **Fort-de-France**

Les Antilles françaises **comprennent** la Martinique, la Guadeloupe et son **archipel** (l'archipel des Saintes, la Désirade et Marie-Galante), Saint-Barthélemy et Saint-Martin. La Guadeloupe et la Martinique sont des régions et des départements **d'outre-mer** de la France, ce qui donne à leurs **citoyens** tous les **droits** et toutes les responsabilités des citoyens français. Ces deux îles offrent donc aux visiteurs **un monde** caraïbe **à la française.** Est-ce que vous aimeriez les visiter? Qu'est-ce qu'un touriste pourrait y faire?

Fort-de-France, **le chef-lieu** de la Martinique, est une ville **pleine d'activité.**

La Martinique est connue pour la beauté de ses paysages et **la chaleur** de son peuple.

Saint-Pierre, son **ancien** chef-lieu, a été **détruit** par une éruption volcanique en 1902. Près de 30 000 personnes sont mortes. Un seul habitant a **survécu,** un prisonnier protégé par les murs de la prison. **Au milieu de** la ville d'aujourd'hui, on peut voir des ruines de l'ancienne ville.

---

comprennent *include*   **archipel** *archipelago*   **d'outre-mer** *overseas*   **citoyens** *citizens*   **droits** *rights*   **un monde** *a world*   **à la française** *French-style*
le chef-lieu *the administrative center*   **pleine de** *full of*   **la chaleur** *the warmth*   **ancien** *former*   **détruit** *destroyed*   **a survécu** *survived*   **Au milieu de** *In the middle of*

La Guadeloupe est composée de deux îles en forme de **papillon:** Grande-Terre et Basse-Terre.

Grande-Terre a un climat **sec** et aride. Ses plages sont **couvertes d'un sable** blanc comme **le marbre**. Cette île est **recouverte de** nombreuses plantations de **canne à sucre**.

Basse-Terre est montagneuse et volcanique. C'est une île au climat tropical recouverte de forêt dense et humide. Pour protéger sa biodiversité unique, un parc national a été **établi** en 1989. La Soufrière, un volcan actif, domine la partie **sud** de l'île.

Le savez-vous?

Complétez ces phrases en vous servant des noms et expressions donnés.

> **Basse-Terre   Grande-Terre   Fort-de-France départements et régions   Martinique Guadeloupe   une éruption volcanique Pointe-à-Pitre   la ville de Basse-Terre**

1. Les Antilles françaises comprennent la _____, la _____ et son archipel, Saint-Barthélemy et Saint-Martin.

2. Les citoyens de ces deux îles ont tous les droits et toutes les responsabilités des citoyens français parce que la Guadeloupe et la Martinique sont des _____ français.

3. _____ est aujourd'hui le chef-lieu de la Martinique. Son ancien chef-lieu a été détruit par _____.

4. La Guadeloupe est composée de deux îles. _____ est montagneuse et volcanique, mais _____ a un climat sec et aride.

5. _____ est la plus grande ville de la Guadeloupe, mais _____ est son chef-lieu.

Pointe-à-Pitre, la plus grande ville de la Guadeloupe, se trouve sur Grande-Terre.

---

papillon *butterfly*   **sec** *dry*   **couvertes d'un sable** *covered with a sand*   **le marbre** *marble*   **recouverte de** *covered with* **canne à sucre** *sugar cane*   **établi** *established*   **sud** *south*   **se trouve** *is located*

AVANT LA VIDÉO

Dans la vidéo, vous allez découvrir une fête qui s'appelle le «Jou a Tradisyon» et qui a lieu *(takes place)* dans une zone industrielle en Guadeloupe appelée Jarry. Pour vous aider à mieux comprendre, regardez ces images. Lisez les descriptions et utilisez le contexte pour déterminer quelle traduction de la liste correspond à chaque mot en caractères gras *(boldfaced)*.

a big crowd
aging
arts and crafts
drum
exhibitors
flowers
giant fair
honey
oil
skin
slaves
sound

Source: https://twitter.com/baienahault

Cette fête, c'est comme une **foire géante** où il y a de la gastronomie, de l'**artisanat,** des plantes, des **fleurs,** il y a de tout.

© Christian Goupi/age fotostock/Superstock

Il y a plus de cent cinquante **exposants** qui viennent de toutes les îles de Guadeloupe.

© DAMIEN MEYER/AFP/Getty Images

Il y a surtout beaucoup, beaucoup, **beaucoup de monde.**

Il y a des produits régionaux comme le **miel** ou l'**huile** la plus antioxydante au monde pour protéger les cellules de la **peau** contre le **vieillissement** cellulaire. Cette huile vient du fruit du galba, un arbre guadeloupéen.

Il y a de la musique traditionnelle. Le ka, c'est le **tambour** typique de la Guadeloupe, parce qu'il allie toutes les ethnies *(it brings together all the ethnicities)* d'**esclaves** qu'il y avait en Guadeloupe. C'est un **son** qui est vraiment typique de la Guadeloupe. C'est le rythme classique du léwos.

▶ **EN REGARDANT LA VIDÉO**

Regardez la vidéo et choisissez la définition qui correspond à chaque nom.

1. Jarry		**a.**	un arbre dont le fruit produit une huile anti-oxydante
2. le Jou a Tradisyon		**b.**	une fête traditionnelle
3. le ka		**c.**	un tambour typique de la Guadeloupe
4. le léwos		**d.**	un rythme typique de la musique guadeloupéenne
5. le galba		**e.**	une zone au nord de Basse-Terre en Guadeloupe

▶ **APRÈS LA VIDÉO**

Répondez aux questions suivantes d'après la vidéo.

1. Où est-ce que le Jou a Tradisyon a lieu *(takes place)*?

2. Qu'est-ce qu'on peut trouver au Jou a Tradisyon? (Nommez trois choses.)

3. Qu'est-ce qu'on goûte dans la vidéo?

4. Quel est l'instrument typique de la Guadeloupe vu dans la vidéo?

5. Qu'est-ce qu'on fait du fruit du galba?

Deciding where to stay

LE LOGEMENT

Quand vous êtes en vacances, est-ce que vous aimez mieux descendre dans...?

un hôtel (de luxe)   **une auberge de jeunesse**   un chalet à la montagne

Préférez-vous avoir une chambre...?

simple ou double avec balcon *(m)*   avec ou sans salle de bains et **W.-C.** *(m)*   avec mini-bar *(m)*, télé et accès *(m)* Wi-Fi **gratuit**

10-1

Préférez-vous **régler la note en espèces** *(m)*, par carte *(f)* bancaire ou par carte de crédit?

Lucas a quitté la Guadeloupe pour aller passer quelques jours en Martinique. Il arrive à la réception d'un hôtel.

LUCAS:	Bonjour, monsieur.
L'HÔTELIER:	Bonjour, monsieur.
LUCAS:	Avez-vous une chambre pour ce soir?
L'HÔTELIER:	Eh bien... nous avons une chambre avec salle de bains et W.-C. privés.
LUCAS:	C'est combien la nuit?
L'HÔTELIER:	108 euros, monsieur.
LUCAS:	Vous avez quelque chose de moins cher?
L'HÔTELIER:	Voyons... nous avons une chambre avec douche et **lavabo** à 88 euros, si vous préférez.
LUCAS:	Je préfère une chambre calme.
L'HÔTELIER:	Alors, **il vaut mieux** prendre la chambre avec douche. C'est **côté cour** et il y a moins de **bruit.**

---

une auberge de jeunesse *a youth hostel*   **une chambre simple** *a single room*   **un W.-C.** *a toilet, a restroom*   **gratuit** *free*
régler la note *to pay the bill*   **en espèces** *in cash*   **un lavabo** *a sink*   **il vaut mieux** *it's better*   **côté cour** *on the courtyard side*   **le bruit** *noise*

LUCAS:	Bon, d'accord. Le petit déjeuner est **compris**?
L'HÔTELIER:	Non, monsieur. Il y a un supplément de 6 euros. Il est servi entre sept heures et neuf heures dans la salle à manger.
LUCAS:	Eh bien, je vais prendre la chambre avec douche. Vous préférez que je vous paie maintenant?
L'HÔTELIER:	Non, monsieur. Vous pouvez régler la note à votre départ. Voici **la clé.** C'est la chambre 210. C'est au bout du couloir.
LUCAS:	Y a-t-il un restaurant dans le quartier?
L'HÔTELIER:	Je vous recommande Le Tropical.
LUCAS:	Est-ce qu'il faut réserver?
L'HÔTELIER:	Oui, il vaut mieux.
LUCAS:	Merci, monsieur.
L'HÔTELIER:	**Bon séjour.**

A **Auberges de jeunesse.** À votre avis, est-ce que chacun des aspects suivants de ce genre de logement est un avantage, un inconvénient *(disadvantage)* ou est-ce que ça vous est égal *(you don't care)*?

> C'est un (petit / gros) avantage.   Ça m'est égal.   C'est un (petit / gros) inconvénient.

Une auberge de jeunesse

EXEMPLE Il y a des douches en commun.
Pour moi, c'est un gros inconvénient. / Ça m'est égal.

1. Ce n'est pas cher.
2. D'habitude, on y rencontre des voyageurs du monde *(world)* entier.
3. On partage souvent une chambre avec des gens qu'on ne connaît pas.
4. Il y a souvent une atmosphère de fête.
5. Il y a quelquefois beaucoup de bruit.
6. On peut rencontrer beaucoup de jeunes célibataires.
7. Généralement, il y a le Wi-Fi gratuit.
8. La décoration et les meubles sont souvent vieillots *(outdated)*.

B **Votre chambre.** Un(e) ami(e) et vous allez passer six jours dans un hôtel en Martinique. Répondez aux questions de l'hôtelier selon vos goûts. Jouez les deux rôles avec un(e) partenaire.

1. Vous voulez une chambre pour combien de personnes?
2. C'est pour combien de nuits?
3. Vous voulez une chambre à deux lits ou avec un grand lit?
4. Vous préférez une chambre avec salle de bains à 125 euros ou sans salle de bains à 85?
5. Voulez-vous prendre le petit déjeuner? Il y a un supplément de 10 euros.
6. Comment voulez-vous régler?
7. C'est à quel nom?

À VOUS!

Avec un(e) partenaire, relisez à haute voix la conversation entre Lucas et l'hôtelier. Ensuite, imaginez que vous allez visiter la Martinique ensemble. Parlez de la sorte de chambre que vous voulez et comment vous allez régler la note.

You can access the audio of the active vocabulary of this *Compétence* online.

---

compris(e) *included*   **la clé** *the key*   **Bon séjour.** *Enjoy your stay.*

GIVING GENERAL ADVICE

✔ **Pour vérifier**

1. What are two ways to say *it is necessary*? How do you say *it's not necessary*? What does **il ne faut pas** mean? How do you say *it's better*? *it's important*? *it's good*? *it's bad*?

2. When offering general advice, what form of the verb do you use following these impersonal expressions? How do you negate an infinitive?

Les expressions impersonnelles et l'infinitif

Use the following expressions to give advice and state opinions. When making generalizations, follow them with an infinitive.

Notice that although **il faut** means *it is necessary*, **il ne faut pas** means *one should not* or *one must not*. Use **il n'est pas nécessaire** to say *it is not necessary*.

Il faut	Il faut réserver bien à l'avance.
Il ne faut pas	Il ne faut pas attendre jusqu'au dernier moment.
Il est essentiel (de)	Il est essentiel de vérifier les prix.
Il est nécessaire (de)	Il est nécessaire de confirmer la réservation.
Il n'est pas nécessaire (de)	Il n'est pas nécessaire de payer à l'avance.
Il vaut mieux	Il vaut mieux s'informer sur les hôtels avant.
Il est possible (de)	Il est possible de comparer les prix sur Internet.
Il est préférable (de)	Il est préférable d'être près des transports.
Il est important (de)	Il est important de ne pas perdre la clé.
Il est bon (de)	Il est bon de choisir une chambre calme.
C'est bien (de)	C'est bien de profiter de la piscine.
Il est mauvais (de)	Il est mauvais de faire trop de bruit.

Note *de grammaire*

1. Note that the expressions that have **être** (**Il est important / essentiel / bon…**) require the preposition **de** (**d'**) before an infinitive.

2. **C'est bien…** is less formal than **Il est bon…** and is more likely to be used when talking with a friend. You will also hear **C'est important / essentiel / bon…** in less formal conversation.

3. When negating an infinitive, remember to place both parts of a negative expression before it: **Il est important de ne pas perdre la clé.**

A **À l'étranger.** Qu'est-ce qu'on doit faire pour être un bon touriste quand on voyage à l'étranger? Complétez chaque phrase avec **il faut, il vaut mieux** ou **il ne faut pas.**

1. _____ apprendre quelques mots de la langue avant de partir.

2. _____ supposer que tout le monde parle sa langue.

3. _____ s'informer sur la culture avant de partir.

4. _____ s'adapter aux différences culturelles.

5. _____ toucher aux objets d'art dans les musées.

6. _____ utiliser le flash pour prendre une photo d'une peinture *(painting)* au musée.

7. _____ demander la permission avant de prendre des photos de quelqu'un.

8. _____ respecter les traditions.

9. _____ faire beaucoup de bruit dans les endroits sacrés *(sacred).*

10. _____ être poli(e).

B **Préparatifs.** Un ami fait les préparatifs pour un voyage que vous allez faire ensemble. Utilisez un élément de chaque colonne pour lui expliquer ce qu'il faut faire.

EXEMPLE **Il vaut mieux réserver une chambre à l'avance.**

Il faut	réserver une chambre à l'avance
Il vaut mieux	obtenir les passeports bien à l'avance
Il est bon de	oublier les billets
Il n'est pas bon de	savoir le numéro et l'heure de départ du vol
Il est important de	tout payer par carte de crédit
Il n'est pas important de	choisir une chambre côté rue / cour
Il ne faut pas	faire beaucoup de bruit dans l'hôtel

Sélection musicale. Search for the song **"Il faut tout oublier"** by the zouk artist Jamice online to enjoy a musical selection illustrating the use of this structure.

C **Forum de voyages.** Lisez le forum de voyages suivant dans lequel un Français demande des conseils pour un voyage à New York. Ensuite, complétez ces phrases avec des conseils qu'on lui donne.

1. Il vaut mieux....
2. Il est possible de... mais il est difficile de...
3. Il faut...

4. Il est préférable de...
5. Il est bon de...
6. C'est bien de...

Je pense passer un week-end à New York, peut-être vers la fin de l'année. Est-ce que je pourrai trouver un hôtel pas trop cher quand j'arriverai à New York ou est-ce que je ferais mieux de réserver une chambre à l'avance? Merci!

D'abord, un week-end, c'est trop court après un vol de 8 heures! Il vaut mieux rester une semaine (minimum!) – il y a un tas de choses à faire et à voir à NYC! On peut trouver un hôtel sur place, bien sûr, mais ce n'est pas facile, surtout en période de fêtes. En plus, à votre arrivée, l'immigration vous demandera quelle sera votre adresse pendant votre séjour. Il est donc préférable de trouver un hôtel avant votre départ pour ne pas rencontrer de problème. Faites votre réservation en ligne avant votre départ et tout sera réglé! Bon voyage et amusez-vous bien!

Pour un week-end, il est bon de réserver à l'avance pour ne pas perdre de temps en cherchant un hôtel et pour avoir un hôtel près de ce qui vous intéresse, et il vaut mieux réserver de France car toutes les taxes sont comprises = pas de surprise. C'est bien de trouver un hôtel vers Times Square. Si vous voulez visiter Manhattan, c'est parfaitement bien placé.

D **Conseils.** Donnez des conseils sur un forum pour des voyageurs francophones qui vont visiter votre région. Travaillez en petits groupes pour compléter les phrases suivantes. Ensuite, comparez vos suggestions à celles des autres groupes.

EXEMPLE Il est essentiel d'aller **au City Arts Museum.**

1. Il vaut mieux venir au mois de (d')...
2. Il ne faut pas venir au mois de (d')...
3. Il est essentiel de ne pas oublier...
4. Il est bon de descendre à l'hôtel...
5. Pour goûter la cuisine locale, il est bon d'aller au restaurant...
6. Il est essentiel de voir...

STRATÉGIES ET COMPRÉHENSION AUDITIVE

POUR MIEUX COMPRENDRE: *Anticipating a response*

When you cannot understand everything you hear, use what you can understand, as well as non-verbal cues such as circumstances, tone of voice, and written materials such as ads or signs to anticipate what someone will say. Read the two hotel ads at the bottom of this page and on the next page and list five things you learned about each hotel from its ad.

🔊
10-2
A **Quel hôtel?** On parle de l'hôtel de l'Anse Bleue ou de l'hôtel Belle Époque?

🔊
10-3
B **Le ton de la voix.** Écoutez le début de ces conversations dans un hôtel. Pour chacune, écoutez le ton de la voix *(tone of voice)* pour deviner la suite *(what follows)*, **a** ou **b**.

1. **a.** C'est bien. Nous allons prendre la chambre.
   b. Est-ce que vous avez quelque chose de moins cher?
2. **a.** Nous préférons une chambre avec salle de bains.
   b. Bon, c'est bien. Je vais prendre cette chambre.
3. **a.** Voici votre clé, monsieur. Vous avez la chambre numéro 385.
   b. Je regrette, mais nous n'avons pas de réservation à votre nom.

Compréhension auditive: *À la réception*

🔊
10-4
Deux touristes arrivent dans un hôtel. Écoutez cette conversation pour déterminer le prix de leur chambre.

À l'hôtel. Écoutez la conversation une seconde fois et répondez à ces questions.

1. Pourquoi est-ce que les touristes ne veulent pas la première chambre?
2. Combien coûte le petit déjeuner? Où est-ce qu'il est servi?
3. Quel est le numéro de leur chambre?

Bienvenue
à l'Hôtel Belle Époque

Charme colonial... services modernes.
À St-Anne, sur une des plus belles plages du monde:
un paradis tropical pour un séjour inoubliable!

- ☛ 2 restaurants proposant une cuisine internationale.
- ☛ 2 bars à côté de la piscine ou sur la plage.
- ☛ 132 chambres climatisées.
- ☛ 8 suites de luxe.
- ☛ toutes les chambres avec terrasse ou balcon et une vue magnifique.

INFORMATIONS - RÉSERVATIONS

Tél.: 05 87 55 11 91

Fax: 05 92 65 44 13

Hôtel Belle Époque

97180 SAINTE-ANNE

Photo: © Fausto Giaccone/Anzenberger/Redux; © Cengage Learning

Going to the doctor

CHEZ LE MÉDECIN

Vocabulaire sans peine!

Notice the cognate patterns for these endings used to name illnesses and types of doctors.

-ite *(f) = -itis*
l'appendicite *(f) appendicitis*
-ose *(f)= -osis*
la mononucléose *mononucleosis*
-ologue *(m / f) = -ologist*
le/la dermatologue *dermatologist*

How would you say the following in French?

*bronchitis, arthritis
tuberculosis, osteoporosis
neurologist, pychologist*

Lucas tombe **malade** pendant son séjour en Martinique. Savez-vous communiquer avec le médecin si vous tombez malade **au cours d'**un voyage?

— Où est-ce que vous **avez mal**?
— J'ai mal à la tête et au ventre.
— Quels autres symptômes avez-vous?

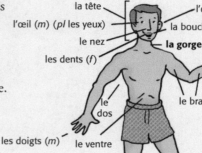

LE CORPS

la tête · l'oreille *(f)* · l'œil *(m)* *(pl* les yeux) · la bouche · le nez · **la gorge** · les dents *(f)* · la main · le dos · le bras · les doigts *(m)* · le ventre · la jambe · le pied · les doigts *(m)* de pied

— Je tousse.

— J'éternue.

— J'ai une indigestion et j'ai envie de vomir.

Avez-vous **la grippe**? **un rhume**? un virus? des allergies?
Êtes-vous **enceinte**?

10-5

Lucas va chez le médecin.

LE MÉDECIN:	Bonjour, monsieur. **Qu'est-ce qui ne va pas** aujourd'hui?
LUCAS:	Je ne sais pas exactement. Je me sens mal. Je tousse, j'**ai des frissons** et j'ai mal un peu partout.
LE MÉDECIN:	Vous avez mal à la gorge?
LUCAS:	Oui, très.
LE MÉDECIN:	Eh bien, vous avez tout simplement la grippe.
LUCAS:	Qu'est-ce que je dois faire?
LE MÉDECIN:	Je vais vous donner **une ordonnance.** Prenez ces médicaments trois fois par jour. Il est important que vous les finissiez tous. N'oubliez pas de boire beaucoup de liquides, mais ne buvez pas d'alcool. Et il est essentiel que vous restiez au lit.

le médecin *the doctor*   **malade** *sick*   **au cours de** *in the course of, during, while on*   **avoir mal (à)...** *one's ... hurts*
la gorge *the throat*   **la grippe** *the flu*   **un rhume** *a cold*   **enceinte** *pregnant*   **Qu'est-ce qui ne va pas?** *What's wrong?*
avoir des frissons *to have the shivers*   **une ordonnance** *a prescription*

A **J'ai mal partout!** Un hypocondriaque va voir son médecin. Selon lui *(According to him)*, il a mal partout, de la tête jusqu'aux pieds. De quoi se plaint-il? *(What does he complain about?)*

EXEMPLE Au secours *(Help)*, docteur! J'ai mal à la tête, j'ai mal aux yeux…

B **Associations.** Quelle(s) partie(s) du corps associez-vous aux verbes suivants?

EXEMPLE écrire **la main et les doigts**

1. fumer
2. se brosser
3. écouter
4. voir
5. éternuer
6. courir
7. toucher
8. embrasser

C **Qu'est-ce qui ne va pas?** Quels symptômes ont-ils?

EXEMPLE Il a mal aux yeux.

1.

2.

3.

4.

5.

D **Des symptômes.** Nommez autant de symptômes que possible pour chaque situation.

EXEMPLE Quand on a la grippe, **on a mal partout. On a des frissons et…**

1. Quand on a un rhume…
2. Quand on a un virus intestinal…

E **Entretien.** Posez ces questions à votre partenaire pour parler de la dernière fois qu'il/elle a été malade.

1. La dernière fois que tu as été malade, est-ce que tu avais mal à la tête? à la gorge? Est-ce que tu avais des frissons? Quels symptômes avais-tu? Qu'est-ce que tu avais? *(What was wrong?)*
2. Est-ce que tu es allé(e) chez le médecin? Est-ce que le médecin t'a donné une ordonnance? Est-ce que tu as pris des médicaments?

À VOUS!

Avec un(e) partenaire, relisez à haute voix la conversation entre Lucas et le médecin. Ensuite, imaginez que vous êtes malade et créez une conversation entre le médecin et vous.

Vocabulaire supplémentaire

un antibiotique *an antibiotic*
un antihistaminique *an antihistamine*
une aspirine *an aspirin*
des pastilles *(f)* **contre la toux** *cough drops*
du sirop contre la toux *cough syrup*
avoir de la fièvre *to have a fever*
avoir le nez bouché *to have a stuffy nose*
avoir le nez qui coule *to have a runny nose*
se brûler / se casser / se couper / se fouler la cheville *to burn / break / cut / sprain one's ankle*
faire une piqûre *to give a shot*

You can access the audio of the active vocabulary of this **Compétence** online.

GIVING ADVICE TO SOMEONE IN PARTICULAR

✔ Pour vérifier

1. When do you use the subjunctive?

2. For most verbs, the **nous** and **vous** forms of the subjunctive look like what other verb tense? How do you form them?

3. What do you use as the subjunctive stem for all verb forms other than **nous** and **vous**? What endings do you use?

Note *de grammaire*

1. The **de** in expressions like **il est important de** is replaced by **que** in these structures.

2. Remember that verbs ending in **-ier,** like **étudier** and **oublier,** will have two **i**'s in the **nous** and **vous** forms of the subjunctive, just as they did in the **imparfait: nous oubliions, vous étudiiez.**

Les expressions impersonnelles et les verbes réguliers au subjonctif

1. You know you can use impersonal expressions like **il faut** and **il est important de** followed by an infinitive to give general advice or state opinions. When talking to or about a particular person, you can use these same expressions followed by **que** and a second clause with a conjugated verb.

Il est important **de bien manger.**	Il est important **que tu manges mieux.**
*It's important **to eat well.***	*It's important **that you eat better.***

2. Up to now, you have used verbs in the present indicative mode to say what happens. Another verb mode called the subjunctive is generally used in the second clause of a sentence, when the first clause expresses a feeling, attitude, or opinion about what should or might be done, rather than simply stating what is happening. The present subjunctive is used after the following expressions, and it may imply either present or future actions.

Il faut que	Il vaut mieux que	Il est possible que
Il ne faut pas que	Il est préférable que	Il est bon que
Il est nécessaire que	Il est essentiel que	C'est bien que
Il n'est pas nécessaire que	Il est important que	Il est mauvais que

Il faut que tu te **reposes.**
Il vaut mieux que tu ne **sortes** pas.
Il est important que tu **finisses** ces médicaments.

3. For most verbs, the subjunctive is formed as follows:

- For **nous** and **vous,** the subjunctive looks like the imperfect. Drop the **-ons** ending of the **nous** form of the present indicative and use the endings: **-ions, -iez.**
- For the other forms, find the subjunctive stem by dropping the **-ent** ending of the **ils/elles** form of the present indicative and use the endings: **-e, -es, -e, -ent.**

	PARLER	FINIR	RENDRE
que je	parl**e**	finiss**e**	rend**e**
que tu	parl**es**	finiss**es**	rend**es**
qu'il/elle/on	parl**e**	finiss**e**	rend**e**
que nous	parl**ions**	finiss**ions**	rend**ions**
que vous	parl**iez**	finiss**iez**	rend**iez**
qu'ils/elles	parl**ent**	finiss**ent**	rend**ent**

Most irregular verbs follow the same rule.

connaître	que je connaiss**e**	que nous connaiss**ions**
dire	que je dis**e**	que nous dis**ions**
dormir	que je dorm**e**	que nous dorm**ions**
écrire	que j'écriv**e**	que nous écriv**ions**
lire	que je lis**e**	que nous lis**ions**
partir	que je part**e**	que nous part**ions**
sortir	que je sort**e**	que nous sort**ions**

These verbs follow the same rule, but have a different stem for the **nous** and **vous** forms.

acheter	que j'achèt**e**	que nous achet**ions**
boire	que je boiv**e**	que nous buv**ions**
devoir	que je doiv**e**	que nous dev**ions**
payer	que je pai**e**	que nous pay**ions**
prendre	que je prenn**e**	que nous pren**ions**
venir	que je vienn**e**	que nous ven**ions**

A **Précautions de santé.** Un guide touristique donne des conseils à des voyageurs pour éviter des problèmes de santé à l'étranger. Est-ce qu'il leur dit qu'**il faut** ou qu'**il ne faut pas** que les personnes suivantes fassent (do) les choses indiquées?

EXEMPLE vous: prendre des précautions / tomber malades pendant le voyage
Il faut que vous preniez des précautions.
Il ne faut pas que vous tombiez malades pendant le voyage.

1. les voyageurs: partir sans assurances (insurance) / vérifier leur couverture (coverage) à l'étranger
2. les voyageurs: oublier leurs médicaments / en apporter assez pour tout le voyage
3. nous: se reposer un peu à l'hôtel après le long vol / sortir trop fatigués
4. nous: essayer de trop faire tout de suite / s'adapter au décalage horaire (time difference)
5. vous: manger des plats légers / choisir des plats difficiles à digérer (to digest)
6. vous: risquer une infection gastro-intestinale / commander des plats bien cuits (cooked)
7. on: prendre trop d'alcool / boire beaucoup d'eau

B **Préparatifs.** Une amie va bientôt partir en vacances. Donnez-lui des conseils. Basez vos réponses sur les illustrations et utilisez une de ces expressions:

il (n')est (pas) essentiel / nécessaire / important / bon / mauvais que...

il vaut mieux que...   il faut que...   il ne faut pas que...

EXEMPLE  **Il vaut mieux que tu t'informes sur la région sur Internet.**

emporter des bagages légers
passer la douane
t'informer sur la région sur Internet
dire à tes parents où tu vas
lire des guides
téléphoner à l'hôtel pour confirmer ta réservation

1.  2.  3.  4.  5.

GIVING ADVICE

✔ **Pour vérifier**

1. What are seven verbs that are irregular in the subjunctive?

2. Which four of these verbs have a different stem for the **nous** and **vous** forms?

3. What are the conjugations of these seven verbs in the subjunctive?

4. What is the subjunctive of **il y a**? of **il pleut**?

Les verbes irréguliers au subjonctif

The following seven verbs are irregular in the subjunctive. Note that **être, avoir, aller,** and **vouloir** have a different stem for the **nous** and **vous** forms. All except **être** and **avoir** have the regular subjunctive endings.

	ÊTRE	AVOIR	ALLER	VOULOIR
	soi- / soy-	*ai- / ay-*	*aill- / all-*	*veuill- / voul-*
que je (j')	sois	aie	aille	veuille
que tu	sois	aies	ailles	veuilles
qu'il/elle/on	soit	ait	aille	veuille
que nous	soyons	ayons	allions	voulions
que vous	soyez	ayez	alliez	vouliez
qu'ils/elles	soient	aient	aillent	veuillent

	FAIRE	POUVOIR	SAVOIR
	fass-	*puiss-*	*sach-*
que je	fasse	puisse	sache
que tu	fasses	puisses	saches
qu'il/elle/on	fasse	puisse	sache
que nous	fassions	puissions	sachions
que vous	fassiez	puissiez	sachiez
qu'ils/elles	fassent	puissent	sachent

The subjunctive of **il y a** is **qu'il y ait.**
The subjunctive of **il pleut** is **qu'il pleuve.**

A **On a perdu mes bagages!** Pour ne pas perdre leurs bagages pendant un voyage en avion, vaut-il mieux que les passagers fassent ou qu'ils ne fassent pas les choses suivantes?

EXEMPLE avoir beaucoup de petites valises
Il vaut mieux que les passagers n'aient pas beaucoup de petites valises.

1. être à l'aéroport bien à l'avance
2. faire des correspondances de vol *(flight connections)* trop courtes
3. choisir des vols directs si possible
4. avoir un bagage à main dans l'avion pour les choses les plus importantes
5. pouvoir rapidement identifier leurs bagages
6. faire une marque sur les valises pour les rendre *(to make them)* uniques
7. savoir où aller pour reprendre les bagages à la fin du vol
8. aller directement à la zone de retrait des bagages *(baggage claim area)* après le vol

B **La grossesse.** Une femme enceinte parle avec son médecin. Lui dit-il qu'**il faut** ou qu'**il ne faut pas** qu'elle fasse les choses indiquées?

EXEMPLES **Il faut que vous mangiez bien.**
Il ne faut pas que vous fumiez.

Sélection musicale. Search for the song **"Il faut que tu t'en ailles"** by Marie-Mai online to enjoy a musical selection illustrating the use of this structure.

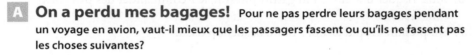

manger bien	fumer	se reposer assez	avoir beaucoup de stress
faire attention à votre santé		être très agitée	boire de l'alcool
savoir contrôler le stress		grossir beaucoup	prendre des vitamines

C Réactions. Une amie vous parle des habitudes de sa famille. Réagissez *(React)* à ce qu'elle dit avec **c'est bien que...** ou **ce n'est pas bien que...** Jouez les deux rôles avec un(e) partenaire.

> **EXEMPLE** — Je ne fume plus.
> — C'est bien que tu ne fumes plus.

1. Je veux mieux manger.
2. Je vais souvent à la salle de gym.
3. Mes enfants font très attention à leur santé.
4. Mon mari n'est pas en forme.
5. Il a souvent mal à la tête.
6. Le médecin ne sait pas pourquoi.
7. Mon mari ne veut pas arrêter de fumer.
8. Nous sommes stressés.
9. Nous avons beaucoup de problèmes.
10. Nous ne pouvons pas bien dormir la nuit.
11. Nous faisons des promenades ensemble.

D Encore des conseils. Avec un(e) partenaire, préparez des suggestions pour quelqu'un qui dit les choses suivantes. Utilisez des expressions qui exigent *(that require)* le subjonctif.

> **EXEMPLE** — Je suis toujours fatigué(e). Qu'est-ce que je devrais faire?
> — Il est important que tu... / Il ne faut pas que tu...

Je suis toujours fatigué(e).

Je mange mal et j'ai souvent mal au ventre.

Je prépare un voyage à l'étranger.

E L'ange et le diable. Un groupe de jeunes touristes fait un tour d'Europe. Donnez-leur des conseils dans les situations suivantes. Un(e) étudiant(e) jouera le rôle d'un ange *(angel)* et l'autre le rôle du diable *(devil)*. Utilisez des expressions telles que les suivantes: **Il faut que... / Il ne faut pas que... / Il vaut mieux que... / Il n'est pas bon que...,** etc.

> **EXEMPLE** Un très bel homme que je viens de rencontrer *(I just met)* m'a invitée au restaurant ce soir.
> **LE DIABLE:** Il faut que tu y ailles avec lui! Il est possible que ce soit le grand amour!
> **L'ANGE:** Il faut que tu fasses attention! Il vaut mieux que des amis y aillent avec toi.

1. Notre car touristique va partir dans dix minutes, mais je veux vite entrer dans ce magasin pour acheter des souvenirs.
2. Je veux monter sur cette statue pour une photo pendant que le policier ne regarde pas.
3. J'ai de la fièvre, mais je ne veux pas passer la journée à l'hôtel.
4. Je ne veux pas perdre mon temps avec le reste du groupe. Je veux faire un tour de la ville seul.
5. Mes amis veulent sortir en boîte ce soir, mais notre vol est à huit heures demain et je dois faire mes valises.

Running errands on a trip

DES COURSES EN VOYAGE

Note *culturelle*

En plus de la distribution du courrier *(mail),* la poste française offre des services supplémentaires comme, par exemple, dans les domaines des opérations bancaires, des sites Web et des téléphones portables. La Banque postale gère les comptes *(manages the accounts)* de plus de 11 millions de Français et est classée parmi les banques les moins chères du marché. La poste a un site Web: laposte.fr, qui inclut un Webmail, des pages d'actualités *(news)* et des sites d'e-commerce. Quels services offre la poste dans votre région?

Où va-t-on pour faire les choses suivantes en voyage? Il faut qu'on aille...

au **distributeur de billets** pour **retirer** de l'argent

à la banque ou au **bureau de change** pour changer de l'argent

à la pharmacie pour acheter de l'aspirine *(f)*

dans une boutique de **cadeaux** pour acheter un cadeau

au kiosque pour acheter le journal et une carte téléphonique

au bureau de poste pour envoyer des cartes postales et acheter **des timbres** *(m)*

Note *de grammaire*

1. Remember that **envoyer** is a spelling change verb (**j'envoie, nous envoyons**). The stem for the future and conditional is **enverr-**.
2. Remember that nouns ending in **-eau,** like **cadeau,** form their plurals with **-x (des cadeaux).**

🔊 10-6

Lucas quitte la Martinique pour retourner en Guadeloupe. Il parle au téléphone avec Anaïs.

ANAÏS:	Je suis contente que tu reviennes bientôt de Martinique. Quand penses-tu arriver en Guadeloupe?
LUCAS:	Je prends l'avion vendredi matin.
ANAÏS:	Voudrais-tu que j'**aille** te **chercher** à l'aéroport?
LUCAS:	Non, non, je ne veux pas que tu perdes ton temps à l'aéroport si l'avion arrive **en retard. J'aimerais autant** prendre **la navette.**
ANAÏS:	Mais non, j'insiste! L'avion arrive à quelle heure?
LUCAS:	À 10 heures.
ANAÏS:	Alors, je viendrai te chercher devant la porte principale de l'aéroport vers dix heures et quart. Et si tu n'as pas d'autres projets, nous pouvons passer la journée à Pointe-à-Pitre.
LUCAS:	Bonne idée! J'aimerais faire un tour de la ville.
ANAÏS:	Parfait. À demain, alors.
LUCAS:	Oui, au revoir, à demain.

---

un distributeur de billets *an ATM machine*   **retirer** *to withdraw*   **un bureau de change** *a currency exchange*   **un cadeau** *a gift*
un timbre *a stamp*   **aller / venir chercher** *to go / come pick up*   **en retard** *late*   **J'aimerais autant...** *I would just as soon...*
la navette *the shuttle*

A **Des courses.** Où dit-on les choses suivantes?

EXEMPLE C'est combien pour envoyer cette carte postale en Belgique?
au bureau de poste

1. Une carte téléphonique de dix euros, s'il vous plaît.
2. Qu'est-ce que vous recommandez contre les allergies? J'éternue beaucoup.
3. Je voudrais changer des dollars, s'il vous plaît.
4. C'est combien pour ces paniers *(baskets)* traditionnels? Je cherche un cadeau pour ma femme.
5. Avez-vous des magazines africains?
6. Trois timbres à 85 centimes, s'il vous plaît.

> à la banque
> au bureau de change
> dans un restaurant
> au distributeur de billets
> à la pharmacie
> au bureau de poste
> à la réception de l'hôtel
> à la boutique de cadeaux
> au kiosque
> à l'aéroport

B **Où faut-il aller?** Complétez ces phrases d'une façon logique.

EXEMPLE Notre vol va partir dans deux heures.
Il faut que nous **allions à l'aéroport.**

1. Vous voulez changer de l'argent. Il faut que vous...
2. Tu as perdu la clé de ta chambre? Il faut que tu...
3. Tes amis ont besoin d'acheter une carte téléphonique. Il faut qu'ils...
4. J'ai besoin de retirer de l'argent. Il faut que j'...
5. Nous voulons envoyer des cartes postales. Il faut que nous...
6. Lucas veut acheter de l'aspirine. Il faut qu'il...
7. Anaïs a besoin d'acheter des timbres. Il faut qu'elle...
8. Lucas veut acheter un cadeau pour Anaïs. Il faut qu'il...

C **Une journée chargée.** Pourquoi est-ce que Lucas est probablement allé aux endroits indiqués?

EXEMPLE Lucas est allé au marché pour **acheter des fruits.**

1. Lucas est allé au bureau de poste pour...
2. Il est allé à la pharmacie pour...
3. Il a cherché un distributeur de billets pour...
4. Il est allé à la banque pour...
5. Il est allé au restaurant pour...
6. Il est allé au kiosque pour...
7. Il est allé à l'agence de voyages pour...
8. Il est allé à la boutique de cadeaux pour...

© Christian Heeb/laif/Redux

À VOUS!

Avec un(e) partenaire, relisez à haute voix la conversation entre Lucas et Anaïs. Ensuite, imaginez qu'un(e) ami(e) va venir vous rendre visite. Créez une conversation dans laquelle vous parlez de quel jour il/elle va arriver, de l'endroit où vous allez vous retrouver et de ce que vous allez faire ensemble.

You can access the audio of the active vocabulary of this *Compétence* online.

EXPRESSING WISHES AND EMOTIONS

✔ *Pour vérifier*

1. What are eight expressions that indicate feelings that trigger the subjunctive? What expressions do you know that indicate desires, doubts, fears, opinions, and requests that trigger the subjunctive?

2. Do you use the subjunctive after the verb **espérer** *(to hope)*?

3. Does the present subjunctive always indicate present time?

Note *de grammaire*

1. Although most verbs that express desires trigger the subjunctive, **espérer** *(to hope)* does not.

J'espère que tu **es** heureuse ici.

2. Traditionally, **ne** was always used in a clause following the expression **avoir peur que.** This **ne explétif** does not change the meaning of the clause and is now optional.

J'ai peur qu'il **n'**arrive en retard.
= J'ai peur qu'il arrive en retard.
= *I'm afraid he'll arrive late.*

Les expressions d'émotion et de volonté et le subjonctif

1. The indicative mood is used to talk about reality. The subjunctive mood conveys subjectivity: feelings, desires, opinions, requests, doubts, and fears about what should or might happen.

You know to use the subjunctive to give advice and state opinions about someone in particular after impersonal expressions like **il faut que** and **il vaut mieux que.**

2. You also use the subjunctive in a second clause beginning with **que** when:

- the verb in the first clause "triggers" the subjunctive in the second clause by expressing a feeling, desire, doubt, fear, opinion, or request.
- the subject of the first clause is not the same as the subject of the second clause.

Verbal expressions such as these will "trigger" the subjunctive in the second clause.

FEELINGS	DESIRES
être content(e) que *to be glad that*	vouloir que *to want that*
être heureux (heureuse) que *to be happy that*	préférer que *to prefer that*
être furieux (furieuse) que *to be furious that*	aimer mieux que *to prefer that*
être surpris(e) que *to be surprised that*	souhaiter que *to wish that*
être étonné(e) que *to be astonished that*	**DOUBTS AND FEARS**
être triste que *to be sad that*	
être désolé(e) que *to be sorry that*	douter que *to doubt that*
regretter que *to regret that*	avoir peur que *to be afraid that*

OPINIONS	REQUESTS / DEMANDS
accepter que *to accept that*	insister pour que *to insist that*
c'est dommage que *it's too bad that*	
il est bon / mauvais, etc., que *it's good / bad, etc., that*	

Je suis désolé que votre chambre n'ait pas de vue sur la mer.
J'ai peur que le quartier de l'hôtel ne soit pas calme.
C'est dommage que votre lit ne soit pas confortable.
J'insiste pour que nous changions d'hôtel.

3. Remember that the present subjunctive refers to either the present or the future.

Je doute qu'elle soit ici.   *I doubt she **is / will be** here.*
Je doute qu'il arrive demain.   *I doubt he **will arrive** tomorrow.*

A **Écoutez la guide!** Anaïs guide un groupe de touristes au sommet du volcan la Soufrière. Dites si **elle veut** ou si **elle ne veut pas** que les touristes fassent les choses indiquées.

    EXEMPLE   rester près d'elle / se perdre
                    Elle veut qu'ils restent près d'elle.
                    Elle ne veut pas qu'ils se perdent.

Sélection musicale. Search for the song **"Je voudrais que tu me consoles"** by Julie Zenatti online to enjoy a musical selection illustrating the use of this structure.

1. se perdre / venir avec elle
2. rester avec le groupe / se promener seuls
3. s'amuser / s'ennuyer
4. avoir peur / rester calmes
5. être satisfaits du tour / avoir de mauvais souvenirs du tour

B Il se plaint! Un des touristes qui fait partie d'un groupe guidé par Anaïs se plaint de tout *(complains about everything)*. Donnez la réaction d'Anaïs à ce qu'il lui dit. Jouez les deux rôles avec un(e) partenaire.

> Je regrette que…
> C'est dommage que…
> Je suis désolée que…

EXEMPLE je / se sentir mal
> — **Je me sens mal.**
> — **C'est dommage que vous vous sentiez mal.**

EXEMPLE je / se sentir mal

1. je / avoir un rhume

2. notre chambre / être vraiment laide

3. le restaurant de l'hôtel / servir une cuisine très médiocre

4. on / ne pas pouvoir acheter de beaux cadeaux ici

5. le distributeur de billets / ne pas accepter notre carte bancaire

C Quel hôtel? Vous allez faire un voyage. Quelle sorte d'hôtel préférez-vous? Donnez votre réaction comme indiqué.

EXEMPLE l'hôtel / être près des sites touristiques
> **Je préfère que l'hôtel soit près des sites touristiques.**

> Je veux absolument que…
> Je préfère que…
> Il n'est pas important que…

1. quelqu'un de l'hôtel / aller nous chercher à l'aéroport
2. l'hôtel / avoir une piscine
3. le réceptionniste / parler anglais
4. l'hôtel / accepter les cartes de crédit
5. la chambre / être grande
6. la chambre / avoir un mini-bar et une télé HD
7. on / pouvoir acheter de beaux cadeaux dans la boutique

D Réactions. Vous êtes parti(e) en voyage organisé en Martinique et vous partagez votre chambre d'hôtel avec un(e) autre touriste. Donnez votre réaction à ce qu'il/elle vous dit. Jouez les deux rôles avec un(e) partenaire.

EXEMPLE — **Je parle français couramment** *(fluently)*.
> — **Je suis content(e) que vous parliez français couramment.**

1. Notre hôtel est tout près de la mer.
2. Notre chambre a un grand balcon.
3. Je ne dors pas bien la nuit.
4. Je tousse toute la nuit.
5. L'hôtel n'accepte pas les cartes de crédit.
6. Il n'y a pas de distributeur de billets à l'hôtel.
7. Je n'ai pas assez d'argent pour payer ma part de la chambre.

> Je (ne) suis (pas) content(e) que…
> Je suis furieux (furieuse) que…
> Je suis désolé(e) que…
> Je regrette que…

E Un voyage ensemble. Votre partenaire et vous pensez peut-être partir en voyage ensemble. Posez ces questions à votre partenaire pour parler de ses habitudes quand il/elle est en vacances. Réagissez chaque fois à sa réponse.

> **EXEMPLE** — Tu passes beaucoup de temps à l'hôtel?
> — Non, je ne passe pas beaucoup de temps à l'hôtel.
> — Je suis content(e) que tu ne passes pas beaucoup de temps à l'hôtel.

1. Tu préfères aller à la plage ou à la montagne?
2. Tu descends dans un hôtel de luxe ou dans un hôtel pas cher?
3. Tu sors souvent le soir ou tu restes à l'hôtel?
4. Tu préfères une chambre avec ou sans salle de bains?
5. Tu dînes dans un restaurant ou dans ta chambre?

F Un voyage en Afrique. Lucas veut qu'Anaïs et sa sœur fassent un voyage avec lui en Afrique. Qu'est-ce qu'il dit à Anaïs pour la persuader de l'accompagner? Commencez chaque phrase avec **j'aimerais que...** ou **je ne voudrais pas que...**

> **EXEMPLE** aller en vacances avec moi / me dire non
> **J'aimerais que vous alliez en vacances avec moi.**
> **Je ne voudrais pas que vous me disiez non.**

1. rater *(to lose out on)* cette occasion de voir l'Afrique / faire ce voyage avec moi
2. être timides / dire ce que vous voulez
3. visiter plusieurs pays africains avec moi / rentrer tout de suite en Guadeloupe
4. pouvoir rester au moins un mois en Afrique avec moi / prendre moins de quatre semaines de vacances
5. sortir seules dans la rue la nuit / être avec moi
6. avoir peur / se sentir à l'aise *(at ease)*
7. s'amuser / s'ennuyer
8. se souvenir de ce voyage / oublier notre voyage en Afrique

G Comparaisons culturelles. Voici les résultats de plusieurs sondages *(polls)* sur ce que les Françaises veulent chez les hommes. Complétez les phrases logiquement en mettant les verbes entre parenthèses au subjonctif.

1. (faire, être, avoir)
Pour la majorité des femmes, il est plus important qu'un homme _____ un bon sens de l'humour et qu'il les _____ rire *(laugh)*. Il est moins important qu'il _____ sexy.

2. (être, accepter)
Les femmes veulent qu'un homme _____ moderne et convaincu *(convinced)* des valeurs du féminisme, et qu'il _____ l'égalité sociale, politique et économique de la femme.

3. (avoir, montrer, payer)
Elles veulent aussi qu'il _____ des valeurs traditionnelles. Elles veulent encore qu'il _____ le chemin *(way)* et qu'il _____ l'addition au restaurant.

4. (être, avoir)

Pour 37 % (pour cent) des femmes, il faut absolument que leur partenaire _____ fidèle, mais 9 % acceptent sans problème qu'il _____ d'autres partenaires.

5. (se séparer, rester)

Si un couple avec un jeune enfant ne s'entend plus, 19 % des femmes pensent qu'il est nécessaire que le couple _____ ensemble mais 73 % disent qu'il vaut mieux que le couple _____.

6. (être, avoir)

La moitié *(half)* des Françaises veulent que leur partenaire _____ un côté spirituel, mais pour l'autre moitié il n'est pas important qu'il _____ religieux.

H **Et vous?** **Pour vous, quels sont les traits de caractère les plus importants chez un(e) partenaire? Exprimez vos opinions en vous servant des éléments donnés.**

j'insiste pour que je préfère que je ne voudrais pas que je souhaite que il n'est pas très important que je n'accepterais pas que	cette personne	être riche être intelligente avoir beaucoup d'ambition avoir les mêmes valeurs que moi fumer vouloir passer tout son temps avec moi

I **Un couple heureux.** **Travaillez avec un groupe d'étudiants pour expliquer ce qu'il faut faire pour être un couple heureux. Complétez les phrases suivantes. Quel groupe peut faire le plus grand nombre de phrases logiques?**

Il est très important qu'un couple / qu'une femme / qu'un homme...
Il est assez important qu'un couple / qu'une femme / qu'un homme...
Il n'est pas important qu'un couple / qu'une femme / qu'un homme...

© Yadid Levy/Alamy Stock Photo

SAYING WHO YOU WANT TO DO SOMETHING

✔ *Pour vérifier*

1. Do you use the infinitive or the subjunctive when people have feelings about what *others* should or might do? when they express feelings about what *they themselves* should or might do?

2. When do you use the infinitive after impersonal expressions such as **il faut**? When do you use the subjunctive?

Le subjonctif ou l'infinitif?

1. Use the subjunctive in a second clause when the first clause expresses feelings, desires, doubts, fears, requests, or opinions about what someone else does, might do, or should do. In this case, the subjunctive is used only when there are different subjects in the main and dependent clauses. When there is no change of subject, you normally use the infinitive.

FEELINGS ABOUT SOMEONE ELSE	FEELINGS ABOUT ONESELF
Je veux que tu le fasses. *I want you to do it.*	Je veux le faire. *I want to do it.*
Nous préférons qu'il soit à l'heure. *We prefer that he be on time.*	Nous préférons être à l'heure. *We prefer to be on time.*

Use **de** before an infinitive after the verb **regretter** or phrases that include the verb **être.**

Je regrette **de** partir demain.   Elle est contente **de** venir.

2. Remember to use an infinitive after expressions such as **il faut** or **il est important de** to talk about people in general, rather than someone specific.

TALKING ABOUT SOMEONE SPECIFIC	TALKING ABOUT PEOPLE IN GENERAL
Il faut que nous le fassions. *We have to do it.*	Il faut le faire. *It has to be done.*
Il est important qu'il y aille. *It's important for him to go there.*	Il est important d'y aller. *It's important to go there.*

A **De bons conseils.** Dites s'**il faut,** s'**il vaut mieux** ou s'**il ne faut pas** faire ces choses quand on voyage à l'étranger.

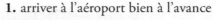

EXEMPLE prendre la photo d'un tableau avec un flash dans un musée
Il ne faut pas prendre la photo d'un tableau avec un flash dans un musée.

1. arriver à l'aéroport bien à l'avance
2. oublier son passeport
3. passer la sécurité
4. fumer dans l'avion
5. montrer son passeport à la douane
6. réserver une chambre avant de partir
7. faire beaucoup de bruit à l'hôtel
8. savoir parler un peu la langue

© Comstock/PhotoLibrary

Maintenant, imaginez que vous donnez ces mêmes conseils à un groupe de jeunes qui partent en voyage.

EXEMPLE prendre la photo d'un tableau avec un flash dans un musée
Il ne faut pas que vous preniez la photo d'un tableau avec un flash dans un musée.

B **Préférences.** Choisissez les mots entre parenthèses qui décrivent le mieux vos préférences quand vous voyagez. Conjuguez le verbe au subjonctif ou utilisez l'infinitif comme il convient.

1. Pour un long voyage, je préfère... (prendre l'avion, prendre le train, prendre ma voiture, ???)
2. Je préfère que mon vol... (être le matin, être l'après-midi, être le soir)
3. Pendant le vol, j'aime... (lire, voir le film, écouter de la musique, dormir, parler avec d'autres passagers, ???)
4. Je n'aime pas que les autres passagers près de moi... (parler tout le temps, avoir un petit bébé, se lever tout le temps, ???)
5. Je préfère que l'hôtel... (être près de tout, être beau mais pas trop cher, être dans une rue calme et tranquille, ???)
6. Je préfère que ma chambre d'hôtel... (avoir le Wi-Fi gratuit, être propre, avoir une belle vue, ???)
7. Généralement, j'aime... (dîner dans ma chambre d'hôtel, manger au restaurant de l'hôtel, sortir dîner dans un restaurant du quartier)
8. À l'hôtel, je préfère... (payer par carte bancaire, payer par carte de crédit, payer en espèces)

C **Des courses.** Anaïs et sa sœur se préparent pour aller voir leur oncle qui habite dans une autre ville. Anaïs préfère faire ce qu'il y a à faire à la maison et elle voudrait que sa sœur aille faire des courses. Que dit-elle à sa sœur de faire?

EXEMPLE faire le ménage / faire des courses
Je voudrais que tu fasses des courses.
Moi, je préfère faire le ménage.

1. aller retirer de l'argent au distributeur de billets / faire les valises
2. acheter un cadeau pour l'oncle Jean / lui faire un gâteau
3. écrire un mail à l'oncle Jean / envoyer ces lettres
4. téléphoner à l'hôtel / aller à la pharmacie
5. chercher des renseignements sur la région sur Internet / acheter un plan de la ville
6. aller en ville / rester à la maison

D **Entretien.** Interviewez votre partenaire sur un voyage qu'il/elle voudrait faire.

1. Où est-ce que tu voudrais faire un voyage? Quand est-ce que tu voudrais le faire? Est-ce que tu aimerais que ta famille ou que tes amis voyagent avec toi?
2. Est-ce que tu préfères que ton hôtel soit un hôtel de luxe ou un hôtel pas cher? Est-il important qu'il y ait une piscine? Aimes-tu nager dans la piscine d'un hôtel?
3. Aimes-tu voyager en avion? Aimes-tu parler avec les personnes à côté de toi dans l'avion ou préfères-tu dormir? Quand tu arrives, préfères-tu prendre la navette ou un taxi pour te rendre à ta destination ou préfères-tu que quelqu'un vienne te chercher?

Giving directions

LES INDICATIONS

Lucas et Anaïs visitent Pointe-à-Pitre. Ils sont à l'office de tourisme. Voici un plan du centre-ville. Qu'est-ce qu'il y a dans le quartier?

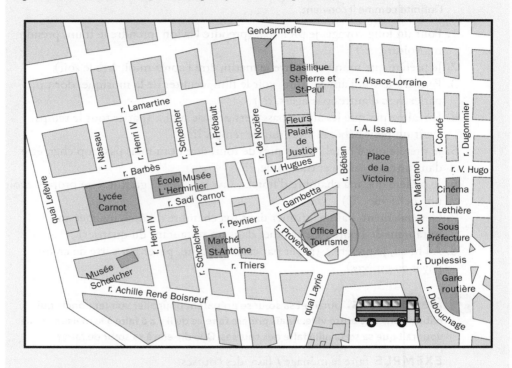

L'employé à l'office de tourisme va **expliquer** à Lucas et à Anaïs comment arriver au musée Schœlcher. Voici quelques expressions **utiles** pour **indiquer le chemin.**

Prenez la rue...	**Traversez la place...**
Continuez **tout droit jusqu'à...**	C'est dans la rue...
Tournez à droite.	sur le boulevard...
Tournez à gauche.	sur l'avenue...
Descendez la rue...	sur la place...
Montez la rue...	C'est **au coin de** la rue.

---

expliquer *to explain* **utile** *useful* **indiquer le chemin** *to give directions, to show the way* **tout droit jusqu'à...** *straight ahead until / as far as / up to . . .* **traverser** *to cross, to go across* **la place** *the square* **au coin de** *on the corner of*

Anaïs **se renseigne** à l'office de tourisme pour savoir comment aller au musée Schœlcher.

ANAÏS: S'il vous plaît, monsieur, pourriez-vous m'expliquer comment aller au musée Schœlcher?

L'EMPLOYÉ: Bien sûr, madame, il n'y a rien de plus simple. C'est tout près. Montez la rue Provence jusqu'à la rue Peynier. Tournez à gauche...

ANAÏS: À gauche dans la rue Peynier?

L'EMPLOYÉ: Oui, c'est ça. Continuez tout droit et le musée Schœlcher est sur votre gauche, juste après la rue Henri IV.

ANAÏS: Je vous remercie, monsieur.

L'EMPLOYÉ: Je vous en prie, madame.

Où allez-vous? Imaginez que vous êtes à l'office de tourisme avec Lucas et Anaïs. D'abord, complétez les explications suivantes en traduisant les mots entre parenthèses. Ensuite, regardez le plan à la page précédente et dites où vous arrivez.

1. _____ *(Go up)* la rue Provence _____ *(as far as)* la rue Peynier. _____ *(Turn left)*. _____ *(Continue straight ahead)* et il est sur votre gauche, juste après la rue Henri IV.

2. _____ *(Cross)* la place de la Victoire et prenez la rue Lethière. _____ *(Continue straight ahead)* jusqu'à la rue Condé et _____ *(turn left)*. Il est sur votre _____ *(right)* entre la rue Victor Hugo et la rue Lethière.

3. _____ *(Go up)* la rue Bébian _____ *(as far as)* la rue Alsace-Lorraine. _____ *(Turn left)*. Elle est juste devant vous.

© Stuart Cohen/The Image Works

4. _____ *(Go up)* la rue Provence, _____ *(turn left)* dans la rue Peynier. _____ *(Continue straight ahead)* et il est sur votre gauche, entre la rue Frébault et la rue Schœlcher.

À VOUS!

D'abord, avec un(e) partenaire, relisez à haute voix la conversation entre Anaïs et l'employé. Ensuite, votre partenaire va vous demander comment aller à votre restaurant préféré en partant de *(leaving from)* l'université. Expliquez-lui comment y aller. Il/Elle va dessiner un plan selon vos indications.

Vous pouvez aussi utiliser ces mots:

au feu *at the light*

au stop *at the stop sign*

Prenez l'autoroute 35. *Take freeway 35.*

Prenez la sortie 7. *Take exit 7.*

vers le nord / le sud / l'est / l'ouest *toward the north / the south / the east / the west*

You can access the audio of the active vocabulary of this *Compétence* online.

se renseigner *to inquire, to get information*

TELLING HOW TO GO SOMEWHERE

✔ *Pour vérifier*

1. How do you form the imperative of most verbs? Which verbs drop the final **s** in the **tu** form of the imperative? Which two verbs are irregular in the imperative and what are their forms?

2. Where do you place **y, en,** and object and reflexive pronouns in negative commands? Where do you place **y, en,** and object and reflexive pronouns in affirmative commands? What happens to **me** and **te** in an affirmative command?

3. When do you reattach the **s** to a **tu** form command?

Reprise de l'impératif et les pronoms avec l'impératif

1. You use the **impératif** (command) form of the verb to give directions. As you have seen, the imperative of most verbs is the **tu, vous,** or **nous** form of the verb without the subject pronoun.

Descends cette rue!	*Go down this street!*
Traversez la place!	*Cross the square!*
Allons à la banque!	*Let's go to the bank!*

Remember to drop the final **s** of **-er** verbs and of **aller,** but not of other verbs, in **tu** form commands.

Tourne à gauche!	*Turn left!*	Va en ville!	*Go to town!*
BUT: Prends la navette!	*Take the shuttle!*	Fais ta valise!	*Pack your bag!*

2. Review the irregular command forms of **être** and **avoir.**

Sois calme!	*Be calm!*	Aie de la patience!	*Have patience!*
Soyons gentils!	*Let's be nice!*	Ayons confiance!	*Let's have confidence!*
Soyez à l'heure!	*Be on time!*	Ayez pitié!	*Have pity!*

3. In negative commands, reflexive pronouns, direct and indirect object pronouns, **y,** and **en** are placed before the verb.

Ne te perds pas!	*Don't get lost!*
Ne les prends pas!	*Don't take them!*
N'y va pas!	*Don't go there!*

4. In affirmative commands, pronouns are attached to the end of the verb with a hyphen.

Attends-le à l'aéroport.	*Wait for him at the airport.*
Dis-lui que nous arriverons bientôt.	*Tell her that we will arrive soon.*

When **me** and **te** are attached to the end of the verb, they become **moi** and **toi.**

Attendez-moi!	*Wait for me!*	Lève-toi!	*Get up!*

When **y** or **en** follows a **tu** form command, the final **s** is reattached to the end of the verb and it is pronounced in liaison.

Vas-y!	*Go ahead!*	Manges-y!	*Eat there!*
Achètes-en!	*Buy some!*	Manges-en!	*Eat some!*

Sélection musicale. Search for the song **"Fais pas ci, fais pas ça"** by Jacques Dutronc online to enjoy a musical selection illustrating the use of this structure.

A **Le chemin.** Consultez le plan à la page 420 et expliquez comment aller...

- de l'office de tourisme à la gendarmerie (*police station*)
- de la gendarmerie au musée Schœlcher
- du musée Schœlcher à la sous-préfecture (*administrative building*)

B **Une drôle de touriste.** Une extraterrestre passe ses vacances ici. Dites-lui ce qu'il faut et ce qu'il ne faut pas faire pour s'adapter à la culture terrienne *(earthling).*

EXEMPLE Je m'habille avant de prendre une douche?
Non, ne t'habille pas avant de prendre une douche.
Habille-toi après.

1. Je me couche sur la table?
2. Je m'habille sur le balcon?
3. Je me couche à midi?
4. Je me lève à minuit?
5. Je me maquille le ventre?
6. Je me déshabille dans l'ascenseur?
7. Je me lave les mains avec du vin?
8. Je me brosse les dents avec l'eau de la piscine?

C **Lucas est amoureux.** Lucas est tombé amoureux d'Anaïs et il ne veut pas qu'elle l'oublie quand il sera rentré à Paris. Vous êtes son ami(e). Répondez à ses questions. Dites-lui de faire ou de ne pas faire chaque chose.

EXEMPLE — Est-ce que je devrais lui écrire des mails de Paris?
— Oui, écris-lui des mails.
Non, ne lui écris pas de mails. Téléphone-lui.

1. Est-ce que je devrais l'inviter à venir me voir l'été prochain?
2. Je devrais lui téléphoner deux fois par jour?
3. Est-ce que je devrais lui dire que je suis amoureux d'elle?
4. Est-ce que je devrais lui envoyer des fleurs *(flowers)*?
5. Est-ce que je devrais l'oublier?
6. Je ferais mieux de la quitter pour toujours?
7. Est-ce que je devrais l'embrasser avant de partir?

D **Anaïs aussi!** Anaïs aussi est amoureuse de Lucas. Est-ce qu'elle lui dirait de faire les choses indiquées dans **C. Lucas est amoureux**?

EXEMPLE Écris-moi des mails.
Ne m'écris pas de mails. Téléphone-moi.

E **Conseils.** Répondez aux questions d'un touriste. Utilisez l'impératif et le pronom convenable. Jouez les deux rôles avec un(e) partenaire.

EXEMPLE — Quand est-ce que je devrais confirmer mon vol?
— Confirmez-le 72 heures avant votre départ.

1. Quand est-ce que je règle la note de la chambre?
2. Comment est-ce que je peux régler la note?
3. Où est-ce que je peux prendre le petit déjeuner?
4. Où est-ce que je peux changer de l'argent?
5. Où est-ce que je peux acheter des timbres?
6. Où est-ce que je peux acheter un plan de la ville?
7. Comment est-ce que je peux aller à l'aéroport?
8. Où est-ce que je peux acheter de l'aspirine?

VIDÉO-REPRISE

Les Stagiaires

Rappel!
Dans l'épisode précédent de la vidéo, M. Vieilledent a fait des projets pour des vacances en Martinique.

See the ***Résumé de grammaire*** section at the end of each chapter for a review of all the grammar presented in the chapter.

Comme vous l'avez découvert dans l'épisode précédent de la vidéo, Monsieur Vieilledent va partir en voyage aux Antilles. Faites les exercices qui suivent pour en savoir un peu plus sur son voyage et pour réviser ce que vous avez appris dans ce chapitre avant de regarder le dernier épisode de la vidéo.

A **À l'étranger.** C'est le grand jour: Monsieur Vieilledent part en vacances! D'abord, dites ce qu'il vaut mieux faire en général quand on part en voyage.

EXEMPLE emporter beaucoup de choses ou emporter une seule valise
Il vaut mieux emporter une seule valise.

1. chercher un hôtel à l'arrivée ou réserver une chambre à l'avance
2. faire les valises à l'avance ou faire les valises au dernier moment
3. arriver à l'aéroport juste avant le départ ou être à l'aéroport au moins deux heures avant le départ
4. se souvenir de prendre ses médicaments ou oublier ses médicaments à la maison

Maintenant, dites à Monsieur Vieilledent ce qu'il vaut mieux qu'il fasse. Utilisez les phrases précédentes.

EXEMPLE **Il vaut mieux que vous emportiez une seule valise.**

B **Des préparatifs.** Vous aussi, vous partez à l'étranger avec un(e) ami(e) et vous faites les préparatifs. Dites à votre ami(e) ce que vous préférez faire et ce que vous préférez qu'il/elle fasse.

EXEMPLE choisir l'hôtel / choisir le vol
Je préfère choisir le vol et je préfère que tu choisisses l'hôtel.

1. faire les réservations d'hôtel / louer une voiture
2. lire le guide touristique / chercher des renseignements sur Internet
3. dormir dans le lit / dormir sur le canapé
4. acheter des timbres au bureau de poste / aller à la banque pour changer de l'argent
5. payer le voyage / ne rien payer

C **En voyage.** Votre ami(e) vous pose les questions suivantes pendant votre voyage. Répondez en utilisant l'impératif avec un pronom complément d'objet direct. Jouez les deux rôles avec un(e) partenaire.

EXEMPLE — **Je mets le réveil** *(set the alarm)* **pour six heures ou pour huit heures?**
—**Ne le mets pas pour six heures. Mets-le pour huit heures.**

1. Je paie l'hôtel avec ma carte de crédit ou avec ta carte de crédit?
2. Je fais le lit ou je le laisse pour la femme de chambre *(maid)*?
3. Je prends la clé avec moi ou je la laisse à la réception?
4. J'appelle le taxi une heure ou deux heures avant le vol?
5. J'écris ces cartes postales avant de partir ou je les écris dans l'avion?

D Il est malade! Monsieur Vieilledent tombe malade pendant son voyage. Il dit les choses suivantes à Camille au téléphone. Donnez les réactions de Camille à ce qu'il dit.

EXEMPLE Je me sens très malade et j'ai très mal à la tête.

Je suis désolée que vous vous sentiez très malade et que vous ayez très mal à la tête.

Je regrette que...	Je suis désolée que...	C'est dommage que...
Il est bon que...	Il n'est pas bon que...	Il est important que...

1. Je n'ai pas d'appétit et je ne mange presque rien.
2. Je reste au lit et je me repose.
3. L'hôtelier connaît un très bon médecin et il va lui téléphoner.
4. Je tousse toute la nuit et je ne peux pas dormir.
5. Je bois beaucoup de liquides et je prends de l'aspirine.

E Quelques ennuis. Monsieur Vieilledent se trouve dans les situations suivantes pendant son voyage. Avec un(e) partenaire, préparez une conversation pour chacun de ces scénarios.

Pauvre Monsieur Vieilledent! On a perdu sa réservation d'hôtel, alors il cherche un autre hôtel. Il discute des choses suivantes avec le (la) réceptionniste.

- *He says that he is looking for a room for two weeks.*
- *He describes what sort of room he is looking for.* [Use your imagination!]
- *They discuss the price, including breakfast.*

Monsieur Vieilledent est toujours malade. Préparez la conversation suivante entre le médecin et lui.

- *The doctor greets him and asks what is wrong.*
- *He says that he is coughing and has a sore throat and a headache.*
- *The doctor says he has the flu and gives him a prescription for medicine. The doctor says that it is important that he take it every morning and gives him other advice on what else to do.*

Monsieur Vieilledent va enfin mieux et il a décidé de passer deux ou trois jours en Guadeloupe. Il est perdu dans Pointe-à-Pitre. Consultez le plan de Pointe-à-Pitre à la page 420. Monsieur Vieilledent est à la gare routière dans la rue Dubouchage. (Cherchez le petit bus.) Il veut aller au marché St-Antoine et il demande son chemin à un(e) passant(e). Jouez la scène avec un(e) partenaire. Ensuite, changez de rôles. Cette fois, Monsieur Vieilledent voudrait aller de la gare routière au lycée Carnot.

Access the Video *Les Stagiaires* online.

▶ **Épisode 10: Au revoir et merci!**

AVANT LA VIDÉO

Dans ce dernier épisode, c'est le dernier jour de stage pour Rachid et Amélie. Monsieur Vieilledent, de retour de *(back from)* vacances, et tous leurs collègues de Technovert se réunissent *(get together)* pour leur dire au revoir. C'est surtout difficile pour Matthieu! Est-ce qu'il reverra Amélie?

Avant de regarder le clip, pensez à une chose que vous pourriez leur dire si vous étiez

Monsieur Vieilledent et à une chose que vous pourriez dire si vous étiez Amélie ou Rachid.

APRÈS LA VIDÉO

Regardez le clip et répondez aux questions qui suivent:

- Qu'est-ce que chaque personne dit à Rachid et Amélie à la fin de leur stage à Technovert?
- Qu'est-ce qui se passe – ou non – entre Matthieu et Amélie?

LECTURE ET COMPOSITION

LECTURE

When looking for a hotel for a trip, it is useful to read comments by former guests on Internet hotel booking services. You are going to read three opinions of former guests of a hotel in Guadeloupe.

Learning to recognize new words with the same root as vocabulary you already know will help you guess their meaning. Before reading the comments about the hotel, do the following activity to help make your reading easier.

Familles de mots. Servez-vous des mots donnés que vous avez déjà appris pour deviner les sens des mots en caractères gras.

1. vieille: La déco est un peu **vieillotte.**
2. vert: L'hôtel est à côté d'un parc **verdoyant.**
3. servir: Le personnel de l'hôtel est très **serviable.**
4. fraîche: L'hôtel a besoin d'un **rafraîchissement.**
5. le climat / un bruit: **La climatisation** était un peu **bruyante** dans la chambre.
6. propre / douter: La salle de bains était d'une **propreté douteuse.**

Avis de l'hôtel

J'ai passé huit jours dans cet hôtel. La déco est un peu vieillotte mais les chambres sont en bon état et propres. À proximité de belles plages, l'hôtel est très calme et tranquille et à côté d'un parc verdoyant. Le personnel de l'hôtel est sympa et très serviable. Il y a tout ce dont on a besoin: balcon pour chaque chambre, salle de sport, télé XXL, petit déjeuner copieux. Bref, un séjour très agréable.

Christophe: Caen, France

Les prix sont trop élevés pour un établissement à rénover. L'ensemble de l'hôtel est vieillot et a besoin d'un rafraîchissement. La déco de l'hôtel n'a aucun charme. La climatisation était bruyante et difficilement réglable. Par contre, son personnel est absolument charmant! Les femmes de ménage sont adorables! Sa situation géographique est excellente.

Florence: Liège, Belgique

L'hôtel n'avait pas notre réservation. Nous avons perdu beaucoup de temps à la réception dans une atmosphère de suspicion. Deux semaines avant notre nuitée, j'avais téléphoné pour demander une chambre avec vue sur la plage: «Oui, oui, c'est noté.» On a eu une chambre bruyante côté rue. La déco ancienne pourrait passer, mais la salle de bains était d'une propreté douteuse: odeur de toilettes dans la chambre.

Annick: Montréal, Canada

© Steve Heap/Shutterstock.com

COMPOSITION

When making suggestions in French or trying to persuade someone to do something, you can stress importance by using the imperative or certain expressions with the subjunctive (**il faut que..., il est essentiel que...**), or you can give less emphatic suggestions by using the conditional (**vous devriez..., vous pourriez...**) or other expressions with the subjunctive (**il vaut mieux que..., il est préférable que...**). Choosing the correct verb form sets the right tone for expressing the necessity of something.

Organisez-vous. Vous allez écrire des suggestions pour un blog pour des touristes français qui voudraient visiter votre pays. D'abord, complétez les phrases suivantes pour parler d'une région qu'ils devraient visiter et de ce qu'ils devraient faire dans cet endroit.

1. Visitez...
2. Allez voir...
3. Il faut absolument que vous...
4. Il est essentiel que vous...
5. Il vaut mieux que vous...
6. Il est préférable que vous...
7. Vous devriez...
8. Vous pourriez...

Compréhension

1. Quelles descriptions se répètent dans les avis de ces voyageurs?
2. D'après les descriptions, comment est la décoration de l'hôtel? le personnel? l'emplacement? la propreté?
3. Est-ce que vous voudriez descendre dans cet hôtel? Pourquoi (pas)?

Suggestions de voyage!

Écrivez une entrée pour un blog en français dans laquelle vous donnez des suggestions pour des voyageurs qui vont visiter une région de votre pays. Qu'est-ce qu'il faut absolument faire? Quelles autres choses les voyageurs pourraient-ils faire s'ils avaient le temps? Où est-ce qu'ils devraient loger *(to stay)* et manger? Qu'est-ce qu'ils devraient éviter?

COMPARAISONS CULTURELLES

LA MUSIQUE FRANCOPHONE: LES INFLUENCES AFRICAINES ET ANTILLAISES

Angélique Kidjo

En moyenne, un Français écoute au moins deux heures de musique par jour et la diversité **croissante** de la société française est reflétée dans la musique. La chanson française traditionnelle reste la musique préférée de la plupart des Français, mais la musique africaine et antillaise est de plus en plus populaire.

Youssou N'Dour

LA MUSIQUE FRANCOPHONE AFRICAINE

Dans la musique francophone d'Afrique, on trouve cinq genres d'influence régionale importants.

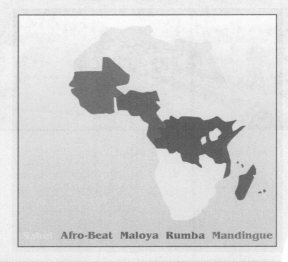

Sahel **Afro-Beat Maloya Rumba Mandingue**

la rumba

Pays francophones d'origine: la République démocratique du Congo, le Congo

Instruments typiques: **les tambours, les trompes,** les flûtes et les xylophones

Artistes: Papa Wemba, Zao, Tabu Ley Rochereau, Wendo Kolosoy

la musique Sahel

Pays francophones d'origine: le Sénégal, le Burkina Faso, la Mauritanie, le Mali, le Niger

Instruments typiques: les luths et les tambours

Artistes: Youssou N'Dour, Wasis Diop, Ismaël Lô, Ali Farka Touré

l'Afro-beat

Pays francophones d'origine: le Togo, le Bénin, le Cameroun, la République centrafricaine

Instruments typiques: les percussions

Artistes: Fela Kuti, Angélique Kidjo, Francis Bebey, Lapiro de Mbanga, Sally Nyolo

la musique Mandingue

Pays francophones d'origine: le Sénégal, la Côte d'Ivoire, la Guinée

Instruments typiques: **la kora, le balafon,** les percussions

Artistes: Amadou et Mariam, Tiken Jah Fakoly, Alpha Blondy, Salif Keïta

la musique Maloya

Pays francophones d'origine: Madagascar, l'Île Maurice, La Réunion, les Seychelles et les Comores

Instruments typiques: **la cithare** et l'accordéon

Artistes: René Lacaille, Danyel Waro, Abou Chihabi

---

croissante *growing*   **les tambours** *drums*   **les trompes** *horns*   **la kora** *the kora* (a 21 string harp lute)   **le balafon** *the balaphone* (an instrument similar to the xylophone)   **la cithare** *the zither*

LA MUSIQUE FRANCOPHONE ANTILLAISE

Quand on pense à la musique antillaise, on pense surtout au reggae et au zouk.

Le reggae, né en Jamaïque pendant les années 60, est devenu populaire auprès des Français. Dans un sondage sur les genres de musique les plus appréciés en France, 38 % des jeunes hommes de 15 à 24 ans mentionnent le reggae.

Le zouk, né en Guadeloupe et en Martinique dans les années 80, est chanté en français ou en créole et le verbe *zouker* est devenu un synonyme de *danser* dans la région. Comme beaucoup de musiques aux Caraïbes, ce genre possède des influences de la rumba africaine.

Le succès du reggae et des artistes du zouk antillais, comme Jocelyne Béroard, Sonia Dersion, Zouk Machine et surtout du groupe Kassav', a servi d'inspiration pour une renaissance de la musique populaire en Afrique. L'interaction artistique entre les Antilles et l'Afrique est signe des **liens** culturels forts entre leurs peuples.

Compréhension

1. Quels sont cinq genres de musique africaine qui ont influencé la musique francophone? Est-ce que la musique africaine a influencé la musique de votre pays? Quels genres de musique?
2. Quels sont deux genres de musique antillaise populaires en France? Dans lequel de ces genres est-ce qu'on trouve souvent des chansons en créole? Qui est Kassav'? Est-ce qu'on écoute ces genres de musique dans votre région?

Zouker, c'est danser!

Jean-Philippe Marthély avec le groupe Kassav' et Jocelyne Béroard.

---

liens *ties*

RÉSUMÉ DE GRAMMAIRE

IMPERSONAL EXPRESSIONS AND THE INFINITIVE

Use an infinitive after the following expressions to state general advice and opinions. Notice that **il faut** means *it is necessary,* **il ne faut pas** means *one should not / one must not* and **il n'est pas nécessaire** means *it is not necessary.*

Pour voyager à l'étranger, **il faut obtenir** un passeport.
Il vaut mieux réserver une chambre à l'avance.
Il ne faut pas attendre le dernier moment.

> Il faut... / Il ne faut pas...
> Il est nécessaire de... / Il n'est pas nécessaire de...
> Il vaut mieux...
> Il est essentiel / important / bon / mauvais / possible / préférable de...
> C'est bien de...

THE SUBJUNCTIVE *(LE SUBJONCTIF)*

The indicative mood expresses reality. The subjunctive mood conveys subjectivity; that is, feelings, desires, doubts, fears, opinions, and requests about what happens or might happen. The present subjunctive may imply either present or future actions.

The subjunctive is used in a second clause preceded by **que:**

S'il est malade, il faut **qu'il téléphone** au médecin.
J'ai peur **qu'il soit** très malade.
Je suis content **qu'il aille** chez le médecin.

- to give advice for someone in particular after impersonal expressions like those listed above. (In expressions like **il est bon de, que** replaces **de.**)
- when the verb in the first clause "triggers" the subjunctive in the second clause by expressing feelings, desires, doubts, fears, opinions, or requests; provided that the subject of the first clause is not the same as the subject of the second clause. (See page 414 for a list of such "trigger" verbs.)

For most verbs, form the subjunctive as follows.

- For **nous** and **vous,** the subjunctive looks like the imperfect. Form it by dropping the **-ons** ending of the **nous** form of the present indicative and use the endings: **-ions, -iez.**
- For the other forms, find the subjunctive stem by dropping the **-ent** ending of the **ils/elles** form of the present indicative and use the endings: **-e, -es, -e, -ent.**

Le médecin veut **qu'il reste** au lit et **qu'il finisse** tous ses médicaments.
Il vaut mieux **qu'il ne rende pas visite** à ses amis.

	PARLER	FINIR	RENDRE
que je	parle	finisse	rende
que tu	parles	finisses	rendes
qu'il/elle/on	parle	finisse	rende
que nous	parlions	finissions	rendions
que vous	parliez	finissiez	rendiez
qu'ils/elles	parlent	finissent	rendent

Most irregular verbs follow the same rule.

connaître	que je connaisse	que nous connaissions
dire	que je dise	que nous disions
dormir	que je dorme	que nous dormions
écrire	que j'écrive	que nous écrivions
lire	que je lise	que nous lisions
partir	que je parte	que nous partions
sortir	que je sorte	que nous sortions

These verbs follow the same rule, but have a different stem for the **nous** and **vous** forms.

acheter	que j'achète	que nous achetions
boire	que je boive	que nous buvions
devoir	que je doive	que nous devions
payer	que je paie	que nous payions
prendre	que je prenne	que nous prenions
venir	que je vienne	que nous venions

Only seven verbs are irregular in the subjunctive: **avoir, être, aller, faire, vouloir, savoir,** and **pouvoir.** Memorize their conjugations from the charts on page 410. The subjunctive of **il y a** is **qu'il y ait** and the subjunctive of **il pleut** is **qu'il pleuve.**

THE SUBJUNCTIVE OR THE INFINITIVE?

The subjunctive is used when there are different subjects in the main and dependent clauses. When there is no change of subject, you normally use the infinitive. Also remember to use an infinitive after expressions such as **il faut** or **il est important de** to talk about what should be done as a general rule, rather than what specific people should do. Use **de** before an infinitive after the verb **regretter** or phrases that include the verb **être.**

COMMANDS AND USING PRONOUNS WITH COMMANDS

The imperative (command form) of most verbs is the **tu, nous,** or **vous** form of the verb without the subject pronoun. Remember to drop the final **s** of -er verbs and of **aller,** but not of other verbs, in **tu** form commands.

Être and **avoir** have irregular command forms: **sois, soyons, soyez** and **aie, ayons, ayez.**

In negative commands, reflexive and object pronouns, **y,** and **en** are placed before the verb. In affirmative commands, pronouns are attached to the end of the verb with a hyphen, and **me** and **te** become **moi** and **toi.** When **y** or **en** follows a **tu** form command, the final **s** is reattached to the end of the verb.

Il ne veut pas **que je dise** à ses parents qu'il est malade.
Il faut **qu'il dorme** beaucoup. Il ne faut pas **qu'il sorte** ce soir.

Il faut **que nous achetions** ces médicaments à la pharmacie.
Il veut **que tu viennes** le voir.

Je regrette **qu'il soit** malade mais je suis content **qu'il aille** voir le médecin.

Je ne veux pas le **faire** seul. Je préfère **que tu** le **fasses** avec moi.

Prends la rue Provence, **va** jusqu'à la rue Thiers et **tourne** à gauche.
Prenons la rue Provence.
Prenez la rue Provence.
Sois à l'heure.
Aie de la patience.
Ne lui achète pas de cadeau dans la boutique de l'aéroport.
Achète-lui un cadeau au marché.
Réveille-toi tôt et **vas-y** le matin.

VOCABULAIRE

Deciding where to stay

NOMS MASCULINS

l'accès Wi-Fi	*Wi-Fi access*
un balcon	*a balcony*
un bruit	*a noise*
un chalet à la montagne	*a ski cabin*
un hôtelier	*a hotel manager*
un lavabo	*a washbasin, a sink*
le logement	*lodging*
un mini-bar	*a mini-bar*
un supplément	*an extra charge, a supplement*
un W.-C.	*a toilet*

NOMS FÉMININS

une auberge de jeunesse	*a youth hostel*
une chambre simple / double	*a single / double room*
une clé	*a key*
une hôtelière	*a hotel manager*
la réception	*the front desk*

EXPRESSIONS VERBALES

C'est bien de...	*It's good to . . .*
confirmer	*to confirm*
Il est bon de...	*It's good to . . .*
Il est essentiel de...	*It's essential to . . .*
Il est important de...	*It's important to . . .*
Il est mauvais de...	*It's bad to . . .*
Il est nécessaire de...	*It's necessary to . . .*
Il n'est pas nécessaire de...	*It's not necessary to . . .*
Il est possible de...	*It's possible to . . .*
Il est préférable de...	*It's preferable to . . .*
Il faut...	*One must . . . , It's necessary to . . .*
Il ne faut pas...	*One shouldn't . . . , One must not . . .*
Il vaut mieux...	*It's better to . . .*
recommander	*to recommend*
régler la note	*to pay the bill*
vérifier	*to check, to verify*

ADJECTIFS

calme	*calm*
compris(e)	*included*
gratuit(e)	*free*
privé(e)	*private*
servi(e)	*served*

DIVERS

Bon séjour!	*Enjoy your stay!*
côté cour	*on the courtyard side*
de luxe	*deluxe*
en espèces	*in cash*

Going to the doctor

NOMS MASCULINS

les frissons	*the shivers*
un liquide	*a liquid*
un médecin	*a doctor*
un médicament	*a medicine, a medication*
un rhume	*a cold*
un symptôme	*a symptom*
un virus	*a virus*

NOMS FÉMININS

une allergie	*an allergy*
la grippe	*the flu*
une indigestion	*indigestion*
une ordonnance	*a prescription*

LES PARTIES DU CORPS

la bouche	*the mouth*
le bras	*the arm*
le corps	*the body*
les dents *(f)*	*the teeth*
les doigts *(m)*	*the fingers*
les doigts *(m)* de pied	*the toes*
le dos	*the back*
la gorge	*the throat*
la jambe	*the leg*
la main	*the hand*
le nez	*the nose*
l'œil *(m)* (*pl* les yeux)	*the eye*
l'oreille *(f)*	*the ear*
le pied	*the foot*
la tête	*the head*
le ventre	*the stomach*

EXPRESSIONS VERBALES

avoir des frissons	*to have the shivers*
avoir mal à...	*one's . . . hurt(s)*
communiquer	*to communicate*
éternuer	*to sneeze*
tomber malade	*to get sick*
tousser	*to cough*
vomir	*to vomit, to throw up*

DIVERS

au cours de	*in the course of, during, while on*
enceinte	*pregnant*
exactement	*exactly*
Qu'est-ce qui ne va pas?	*What's wrong?*
tout simplement	*quite simply*

Running errands on a trip

NOMS MASCULINS

un aéroport	an airport
un bureau de change	a currency exchange
un bureau de poste	a post office
un cadeau (*pl* des cadeaux)	a present
un distributeur de billets	an ATM machine
un kiosque	a kiosk
un timbre	a stamp

NOMS FÉMININS

de l'aspirine	some aspirin
une banque	a bank
une boutique (de cadeaux)	a (gift) shop
une carte téléphonique	a telephone card
une navette	a shuttle
une pharmacie	a pharmacy

EXPRESSIONS VERBALES

accepter que...	to accept that...
aller / venir chercher quelqu'un	to go / come pick someone up
c'est dommage que...	it's too bad that...
douter que...	to doubt that...
être content(e) que...	to be happy that...
être désolé(e) que...	to be sorry that...
être étonné(e) que...	to be astonished that...
être furieux (furieuse) que...	to be furious that...
être heureux (heureuse) que...	to be happy that...
être surpris(e) que...	to be surprised that...
être triste que...	to be sad that...
insister pour que...	to insist that...
j'aimerais autant...	I would just as soon...
regretter que...	to regret that...
retirer de l'argent	to withdraw money
souhaiter que...	to wish that...

DIVERS

en retard	late
principal(e) (*mpl* principaux)	principal, main

Giving directions

NOMS MASCULINS

un employé	an employee
l'office de tourisme	the Tourist Office
un plan	a map

NOMS FÉMININS

une employée	an employee
une expression	an expression
les indications	the directions
une place	a (town) square, a plaza

EXPRESSIONS VERBALES

avoir pitié (de)	to have pity (on)
continuer (tout droit)	to continue (straight ahead)
descendre la rue...	to go down... Street
expliquer	to explain
indiquer le chemin	to give directions, to show the way
monter la rue...	to go up... Street
prendre la rue...	to take... Street
remercier	to thank
se renseigner	to inquire, to get information
tourner (à droite / à gauche)	to turn (right / left)
traverser	to cross, to go across

EXPRESSIONS PRÉPOSITIONNELLES

au coin de	on the corner of
dans la rue...	on... Street
jusqu'à	until, up to, as far as
sur l'avenue / le boulevard / la place...	on... Avenue / Boulevard / Square

DIVERS

juste	just
tout droit	straight (ahead)
utile	useful

LE FRANÇAIS est une langue importante dans plus de 20 pays d'Afrique et plus de 120 millions d'habitants de ce continent parlent français.

Allons visiter trois régions africaines francophones: la Côte d'Ivoire, le Maroc et l'île de La Réunion!

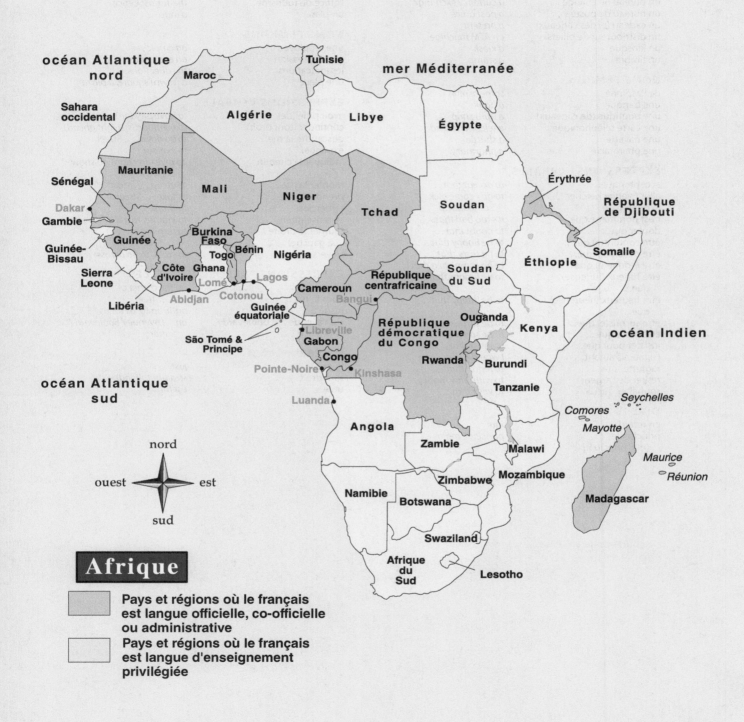

océan Atlantique nord

Tunisie

mer Méditerranée

Maroc

Sahara occidental

Algérie

Libye

Égypte

Mauritanie

Érythrée

Sénégal

Mali

Niger

Soudan

République de Djibouti

Dakar

Tchad

Gambie

Guinée-Bissau

Guinée

Burkina Faso

Bénin

Nigéria

Soudan du Sud

Somalie

Sierra Leone

Togo

Ghana

Côte d'Ivoire

Lomé

Lagos

Cameroun

République centrafricaine

Éthiopie

Libéria

Abidjan

Cotonou

Bangui

Guinée équatoriale

São Tomé & Principe

Libreville

Gabon

République démocratique du Congo

Ouganda

Kenya

océan Indien

Congo

Rwanda

Burundi

Seychelles

Pointe-Noire

Kinshasa

Tanzanie

Comores

Mayotte

Luanda

océan Atlantique sud

Angola

Zambie

Malawi

Maurice

Réunion

nord

Mozambique

ouest — est

Zimbabwe

Madagascar

Namibie

Botswana

sud

Swaziland

Afrique du Sud

Lesotho

Afrique

Pays et régions où le français est langue officielle, co-officielle ou administrative

Pays et régions où le français est langue d'enseignement privilégiée

La Côte d'Ivoire est un pays fascinant par sa diversité géographique et culturelle. Dans ce seul pays, vous pouvez voir des régions géographiques très variées.

Le long de la côte, il y a des plages et des falaises. Au centre, il y a la jungle et des forêts tropicales. Dans le nord, il y a la savane.

Soixante-huit ethnies différentes cohabitent en Côte d'Ivoire, chacune avec ses propres traditions.

En Afrique, on trouve le moderne juxtaposé au traditionnel. Abidjan, la plus grande ville ivoirienne, est une belle ville moderne qu'on appelait autrefois le «Paris de l'Afrique».

---

la côte *the coast*   **des falaises** *cliffs*   **ethnies** *ethnicities*   **chacune** *each one*   **propres** *own*   **autrefois** *in the past*

Le Maroc, aussi appelé «le pays du soleil couchant» *(al-Maghrib al-aqsa)*, est l'État le plus occidental de l'Afrique du Nord. Par sa situation entre la Méditerranée, l'Atlantique et le Sahara, le Maroc **appartient à la fois** au monde méditerranéen, occidental et berbère.

Composé de montagnes, de déserts, de plages, de côtes escarpées et de forêts, et doté de villes fascinantes (Rabat, Casablanca, Marrakech), le Maroc est un des plus beaux pays au monde.

Le Maroc est un trésor de sites historiques et archéologiques.

Encore plus attirante que la beauté de ses paysages, la culture marocaine est très riche car elle reflète l'histoire et les traditions du peuple marocain, tant d'origine arabe que berbère et saharienne.

---

appartient à la fois *belongs at the same time* **côtes escarpées** *rocky coasts* **doté de** *endowed with* **attirante** *attractive* **car** *because* **tant de (d')** *as much of*

La Réunion, **qui se trouve** près de Madagascar dans l'océan Indien et à plus de 10 000 kilomètres de Paris, est un département et une région de la France, tout comme Hawaï est un État des États-Unis.

La Réunion possède une société riche de différentes cultures: française, africaine, hindoue, **malaise**, chinoise, créole... toutes au parfum tropical! Cette diversité se révèle dans une variété de traditions, de styles architecturaux, de musique et de cuisine.

LE SAVEZ-VOUS?

Lequel de ces endroits d'Afrique francophone correspond à chaque description?

La Réunion   **la Côte d'Ivoire**   **le Maroc**

1. Il y a 68 ethnies différentes dans ce pays.
2. Ce pays fait partie du monde méditerranéen, occidental et berbère à la fois.
3. C'est un département et une région de la France, tout comme Hawaï est un État des États-Unis.
4. La population de cet endroit est composée de plusieurs cultures différentes: française, africaine, hindoue, malaise, chinoise et créole.
5. Autrefois, on appelait la plus grande ville de ce pays le «Paris de l'Afrique».

La Réunion offre aussi une grande variété géographique de villes, petits villages, **stations balnéaires**, plages, forêts...

---

qui se trouve *which is located*   **malaise** *Malaysian*   **stations balnéaires** *seaside resorts*

La vie moderne

  Pair work   Class work

Group work

© R. Ian Lloyd/Masterfile

CHAPITRE DE RÉVISION

Les profils en ligne

Ànous2

Faites-vous de nouveaux amis et cherchez des relations sentimentales sur notre site de rencontres.

MEMBRES

Email

Mot de passe

Je suis | un homme ▼ | de ☐ ans.
une femme

Je cherche | une femme ▼ | de ☐ à ☐ ans.
un homme

AHMAD LB13
35 ans
Salut, mon nom est Ahmad. Je suis un homme sincère, **sensible,** un peu geek. **Formation** en informatique. J'aime la musique, la nature et les animaux et les jeux vidéo. Recherche relation durable et honnête. Si tu aimes les promenades dans la nature et les dîners romantiques, contacte-moi.

ENZO JF77
25 ans
Salut! Je suis un homme sportif mais civilisé et romantique. Je suis éducateur. Je cherche une femme qui s'intéresse beaucoup au sport, surtout au foot. Vive les Bleus!

CASSANDRA SNS45
23 ans
Passionnée de musique, j'aime aussi le cinéma, la littérature et tous les arts, **surtout** la danse. J'aime sortir en boîte de nuit, danser, aller aux spectacles. Je cherche un homme avec qui **partager** mes intérêts.

LILOU JM100
32 ans
Je suis de nature indépendante, mais j'aimerais passer les beaux après-midi au parc avec un homme sympa qui aime la nature.

CHAN MP21
30 ans
Je suis calme et plutôt réservé. Cultivé, j'aime la littérature, le cinéma et les arts. Pourtant, je suis aussi sportif et j'aime surtout **la course à pied.** Je cherche une femme avec qui partager des moments tendres.

MONICA TTR38
20 ans
Jeune femme cool passionnée de musique. Profession: DJ. Contacte-moi si tu aimes sortir entre amis, aller prendre un verre et aller danser. Recherche relation sincère et sérieuse.

---

sensible *sensitive* **Formation** *Education* **partager** *to share* **surtout** *especially* **la course à pied** *running, racing*

AVANT DE LIRE

Mots apparentés. Regardez les six profils à la page précédente. Servez-vous des mots que vous connaissez, des mots apparentés et du contexte pour compléter le tableau suivant.

Review the reading strategy in the **Pour mieux lire** section on page 40 of **Chapitre 1** before beginning these activities.

	DESCRIPTIONS	ACTIVITÉS/ INTÉRÊTS	RECHERCHE
Ahmad			
Enzo			
Cassandra			
Lilou			
Chan			
Monica			

LECTURE ET COMPRÉHENSION

Comprenez-vous? Lisez les six profils à la page précédente. Décidez avec qui chacune des personnes décrites devrait prendre contact *(should get in touch)* et dites pourquoi.

> **EXEMPLE** Ahmad
>
> Ahmad devrait *(should)* contacter Lilou parce qu'ils aiment tous les deux la nature et il a 35 ans et elle a 32 ans. Je ne trouve pas *(I don't find)* de contact pour Ahmad.

Note *de vocabulaire*

To express someone's age, use **Il/Elle a... ans.** *He is 21.* **Il a 21 ans.**

À VOUS LA PAROLE!

Personnes célèbres. Recréez le formulaire suivant sur une feuille de papier. Ensuite, imaginez que vous êtes une personne célèbre et complétez le formulaire au nom de cette personne.

Nom: Antoine Beaujolais

Sexe: ● homme ○ femme

État civil: ○ célibataire ○ séparé(e) ● divorcé(e) ○ veuf/veuve
○ avec enfants ● sans enfants

Fumer: ○ fumeur ● non-fumeur

Intérêts: Sport, Musique, Politique, Associations caritatives, Bonne cuisine, Sorties

Données personnelles: Homme sportif et dynamique, j'aime le sport (surtout le basket) et la musique (surtout le rap et le hip-hop). Recherche une femme d'esprit ouvert qui aime la musique, le sport et l'humour.

Maintenant, toujours dans le rôle de votre célébrité, présentez-vous à la classe.

> **EXEMPLE** Bonjour, je suis Antoine Beaujolais et je suis... J'aime...

Review the *Résumé de grammaire* sections on pages 64–65 and 104–105 at the end of *Chapitre 1* and *Chapitre 2* before doing these activities.

PRATIQUE

A **Qui est-ce?** Complétez les descriptions suivantes avec **c'est** ou **il/elle est.** Ensuite, relisez les profils à la page 440 et identifiez la personne décrite.

> **EXEMPLE** **C'est** une femme qui aime tous les arts. **Elle est** passionnée de musique.
> **C'est Cassandra.**

1. _____ un homme réservé qui voudrait partager des moments tendres. _____ cultivé, mais _____ sportif aussi.

2. _____ un homme. _____ sportif. _____ éducateur.

3. _____ une femme qui voudrait une relation sincère. _____ passionnée de musique. _____ DJ.

4. _____ une personne indépendante. _____ une femme qui aime la nature.

B **Préférences.** Deux jeunes Français indiquent leurs préférences sur leurs profils en ligne. Que disent-ils? Complétez leurs phrases avec la forme correcte de l'adjectif donné. **Note:** La majorité des adjectifs suivent *(follow)* le nom qu'ils qualifient, mais certains adjectifs précèdent le nom. Dans cette activité, les blancs indiquent la position correcte de l'adjectif.

> **EXEMPLE** J'aime la littérature **classique.** *(classical)*

1. J'aime les activités *(f)* _____. *(intellectual)*
2. J'aime les loisirs _____. *(athletic)*
3. J'aime les amis _____. *(outgoing)*
4. J'aime les _____ restaurants. *(good)*
5. J'aime les _____ femmes. *(pretty)*
6. J'aime la cuisine _____. *(French)*
7. J'aime les _____ films. *(old)*
8. J'aime les femmes _____. *(athletic)*
9. J'aime les hommes _____. *(funny)*
10. J'aime les _____ hommes. *(handsome)*

C **Activités.** Utilisez le verbe **être** avec l'adjectif indiqué pour poser des questions à votre partenaire. Ensuite, demandez si ces personnes font souvent une activité logique de la liste.

> jouer au tennis et au foot   aimer lire   inviter des amis à la maison
> rester au lit jusqu'à midi   être seul(e)   aimer sortir
> jouer du piano ou de la guitare   envoyer des textos
> passer beaucoup de temps seul(e)

> **EXEMPLE** tu / sociable
> —**Tu es sociable? Tu envoies souvent des textos?**
> —**Je suis sociable, mais je n'envoie pas beaucoup de textos.**
> **Je préfère parler au téléphone.**

1. tes amis et toi / sportifs
2. tu / musicien(ne) *(musical)*
3. tes parents / sociables
4. ta meilleure amie / paresseuse
5. ton meilleur ami / timide
6. tes amis / intellectuels
7. tes amis et toi / très extravertis
8. tu / plutôt introverti(e)

À VOUS LA PAROLE!

A **Faisons connaissance!** D'abord, complétez la description suivante avec vos informations. Ensuite, interviewez votre partenaire pour compléter une description de lui/d'elle.

> **(avec) qui** **que (qu')** **quand** **où**
> **pourquoi** **comment** **quels jours** **jusqu'à quelle heure**

EXEMPLE — Qu'est-ce que tu étudies? / Qu'étudies-tu?
— J'étudie le français et...

MOI	MON/MA PARTENAIRE
EXEMPLE J'étudie **le français et les maths.**	**Il/Elle étudie le français et...**
J'étudie...	
Je suis en cours *[say which days]*...	
Le samedi, je reste au lit jusqu'à...	
J'aime sortir *[say when]*...	
Je préfère passer la soirée avec...	
J'aime passer mon temps avec lui/elle/ eux/elles parce que (qu')...	
Nous aimons aller *[say where]*...	

B **Mon profil.** Écrivez votre profil en français pour un site de correspondants *(penpals)* en ligne.

C **Des questions.** Avec un(e) partenaire, préparez une liste de 6–8 questions que vous voudriez poser à quelqu'un que vous rencontrez en ligne.

EXEMPLES Tu es célibataire, marié(e), divorcé(e) ou séparé(e)?
Tu habites seul(e)?

© lightpoet/Shutterstock.com

À VOUS!

Imaginez un premier rendez-vous au café entre deux des personnes décrites dans les profils à la page 440. En groupe de trois, préparez une conversation dans laquelle vous commandez quelque chose à boire et chacun pose trois ou quatre questions à l'autre. Un(e) étudiant(e) jouera *(will play)* le rôle du serveur/de la serveuse.

Vivre vert

Vivre vert est un jeu en ligne où vous gagnez des points pour chaque geste vert que vous faites dans la réalité. Recyclez, compostez, donnez, partagez... Bref! Vivez votre vie, gagnez des points, devenez plus **écolo** et amusez-vous! Comptez vos points et comparez votre score à celui de vos amis pour voir qui est le/la plus écolo!

---

1. Je recycle ma bouteille d'eau en plastique: 10 points

Recyclez le plastique ou le papier dans des containers spéciaux et gagnez des points facilement. Quand **on** ne **jette** pas tout à la poubelle, **on gaspille** moins.
   Une idée pour aller plus loin: Compostez! Réduisez la taille de votre poubelle, c'est bon pour l'environnement.

---

2. On échange des choses: 10 points

Donnez une deuxième vie à vos objets! Quand vous avez besoin de quelque chose, n'allez pas au centre commercial. Demandez à vos amis s'ils ont ce que vous cherchez.

   Une idée pour aller plus loin: Soyez créatifs et transformez les objets récupérés en œuvres d'art!

---

3. Je donne des vêtements à une famille dans le besoin: 25 points

Vous avez des vêtements **que vous ne mettez plus**? Donnez ces vêtements à une famille dans le besoin.
   Une idée pour aller plus loin: À chaque fois qu'on achète un vêtement, on donne un vêtement. Comme ça, notre placard est toujours en ordre!

---

4. Je n'utilise pas ma voiture: 50 points

Prenez le bus, le métro ou le train! Ou même mieux, allez en ville à vélo – arrivez à votre destination et faites de l'exercice en même temps.

   Une idée pour aller plus loin: Faites du covoiturage dans la semaine. Aller au travail avec un collègue, c'est sympa et c'est vert.

---

5. J'utilise des énergies renouvelables: 100 points

Avec les énergies renouvelables telles que l'énergie solaire, on préserve les ressources naturelles et on réduit les émissions de CO_2.
   Une idée pour aller plus loin: Achetez des appareils qui consomment moins d'électricité et qui ne gaspillent pas l'eau.

Vivre vert *Living green*   **écolo** *ecological*   **on jette** *one throws (away/out)*   **on gaspille** *one wastes*   **que vous ne mettez plus** *that you no longer wear*

AVANT DE LIRE

Review the reading strategies in the *Pour mieux lire* sections on pages 138 of *Chapitre 3* and 278 of *Chapitre 7* before beginning these activities.

A **Familles de mots.** Utilisez le vocabulaire en caractères gras *(boldface)* pour deviner le sens des mots en italique dans les phrases suivantes.

> **EXEMPLE** **vivre** *(to live): Vivez* votre *vie* de façon écologique!
> **Live your life in an ecological way!**

1. **amusant:** Jouez à ce jeu en ligne, *amusez-vous* et vivez une vie verte.
2. **la voiture:** Faites du *covoiturage* pour aller au travail.
3. **de taille moyenne:** Réduisez *la taille* de votre poubelle *(garbage container)*.
4. **le compost:** *Compostez* tout pour réduire la taille de votre poubelle.
5. **nouveau (nouvelle):** Utilisez les énergies *renouvelables* pour réduire les émissions de CO2.

Prendre le métro, c'est pratique et c'est vert!

B **Parcourez le texte!** Regardez la page précédente. Servez-vous des images, des phrases principales et de vos idées sur le thème de l'écologie pour prédire *(to predict)* si le programme *Vivre vert* vous proposerait *(would suggest)* de faire ces choses.

Pour être plus écologique, est-ce que le programme *Vivre vert* vous proposerait de (d')...?

	OUI	NON
EXEMPLE acheter de nouveaux vêtements		X
1. recycler vos bouteilles d'eau en plastique		
2. acheter beaucoup de nouvelles choses		
3. échanger des choses		
4. donner les vêtements que vous ne portez pas		
5. prendre votre vélo		
6. utiliser beaucoup de ressources naturelles		

LECTURE ET COMPRÉHENSION

Et vous? Lisez la page précédente. Quels gestes verts présentés sur le site *Vivre vert* est-ce que vous faites déjà et quels gestes est-ce que vous ne faites pas? Écrivez deux listes.

À VOUS LA PAROLE!

A **Entretien.** Interviewez votre partenaire sur les listes qu'il/elle a préparées.

1. Quel geste est-ce que tu fais le plus souvent?
2. Quel est un geste que tu ne fais pas, mais que tu voudrais faire?
3. Quel geste est le plus difficile à faire pour toi? Pourquoi?

B **Suggestions.** Travaillez en groupes pour créer une autre suggestion (avec une nouvelle image) pour le site *Vivre vert*. Servez-vous d'un dictionnaire (en ligne) si nécessaire. Ensuite, présentez vos idées à la classe.

Review the *Résumé de grammaire* sections on pages 142–143 and 180–181 at the end of *Chapitre 3* and *Chapitre 4* before doing these activities.

PRATIQUE

A Vivre vert! Complétez ce que dit un étudiant membre de *Vivre vert* en français avec l'expression avec **avoir** indiquée dans le premier espace et la forme convenable des autres verbes donnés en anglais dans les autres.

1. Quand j'_____ *(am thirsty)*, je n'_____ *(buy)* jamais de bouteille d'eau en plastique. Je _____ *(take)* de l'eau du robinet *(tap)*. Je _____ *(understand)* l'importance de protéger l'environnement.

2. Quand nous _____ *(need)* de recycler un vieil ordinateur, nous _____ *(go)* au centre de recyclage. Nous _____ *(learn)* tous les jours une nouvelle manière de recycler.

3. Beaucoup de gens _____ *(are cold)* en hiver. Alors, on _____ *(go)* au magasin d'une organisation caritative *(charitable organization)* pour donner des vêtements aux gens qui en ont besoin.

4. Beaucoup d'étudiants _____ *(feel like)* de vivre plus vert et ils _____ *(become)* plus écologiques parce qu'ils _____ *(understand)* l'importance de protéger l'environnement. Ils _____ *(come)* à la fac en bus ou à vélo.

5. Vous _____ *(are right)* de toujours prendre le métro ou le bus pour aller en ville. Comment est-ce que vous _____ *(come)* ici en cours? Est-ce que vous _____ *(take)* le bus?

6. Quand mon ami _____ *(is hungry)*, il _____ *(goes)* au restaurant d'à côté parce qu'il peut *(can)* y aller à pied. Il _____ *(understands)* l'importance de conserver nos ressources naturelles.

7. Tu _____ *(are wrong)* de gaspiller l'eau. Tu ne _____ *(understand)* pas l'importance de conserver l'eau!

B On échange? Vous êtes à une troc party *(swap party)*. Demandez à votre partenaire s'il/si elle préfère ses propres *(own)* choses ou les choses des gens indiqués. Utilisez les adjectifs donnés comme dans l'exemple.

EXEMPLE *this old blue bicycle* / Thomas
— **Tu préfères ton vélo ou ce vieux vélo bleu de Thomas?**
— **Je préfère mon vélo. / Je préfère son vélo. / Je n'ai pas de vélo.**

 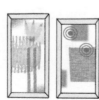

1. *this little red car* / l'ami de Sofia

2. *these other modern pictures* / Alain

3. *this new comfortable couch* / le frère de Gabriel

4. *this old practical bookcase* / les parents de Malika

Maintenant, utilisez **ce, cet, cette** ou **ces** pour dire comment vous trouvez ces choses.

EXEMPLE **Ce vélo est en bon état.**

élégant	laid	moderne	en bon état	un peu bizarre
très joli	trop vieux / petit...	???		

À VOUS LA PAROLE!

A **Des renseignements.** Imaginez que vous êtes québécois(e) et que vous désirez vous inscrire dans l'organisation *Vivre vert*. Créez votre nouvelle identité. Ensuite, votre partenaire va vous aider à vous inscrire. Il/Elle va vous poser des questions avec **quel/quelle** pour savoir: **votre nom, votre prénom, votre date de naissance, votre adresse mail** et **votre numéro de téléphone.**

> **EXEMPLE** — Quel est ton nom?
> — Mon nom, c'est Dupont.

B **Des solutions.** Utilisez l'impératif pour dire à un(e) ami(e) de faire ou de ne pas faire les choses suivantes pour vivre vert.

> **EXEMPLE** conserver l'eau / prendre de longues douches *(showers)*
> **Conserve l'eau! Ne prends pas de longues douches!**

1. prendre le bus ou le métro / venir toujours en ville en voiture
2. acheter beaucoup de choses / prendre seulement *(only)* les choses nécessaires
3. avoir peur de changer d'habitudes / apprendre à changer petit à petit
4. être pessimiste / comprendre que vivre vert, c'est facile

Maintenant, avec un(e) partenaire, créez trois autres conseils pour votre ami(e).

C **Ma vie verte.** Pour chaque activité, trouvez quelqu'un qui la fait déjà ou quelqu'un qui va la faire à l'avenir *(someone who already does it or someone who is going to do it in the future).*

> **EXEMPLE** — Austin, est-ce que tu utilises déjà des ampoules LED *(LED lightbulbs)* ou est-ce que tu vas utiliser des ampoules LED à l'avenir?
> — Je vais utiliser des ampoules LED à l'avenir.

	MAINTENANT	À L'AVENIR
utiliser des ampoules LED		*Austin*
acheter des produits régionaux		
venir en cours à pied ou à vélo		
aller sur Craigslist pour acheter des meubles		
composter		
acheter des cahiers en papier recyclé		
prendre des douches *(showers)* rapides		
recycler le papier et le plastique		

Ma vie, c'est une BD!

Lucile Gomez, auteur de BD et de blog

Lucile Gomez

Qui es-tu?

Lucile Gomez. Je suis une «mademoiselle» qu'on appelle de plus en plus souvent «madame». Je n'ai pas de chat et pourtant je parle avec lui. Je ne sais pas vraiment bien pourquoi mais j'aime bien tenir mon blog. :)

Peux-tu présenter ton blog?

Sur mon blog, je mets en scène un personnage que j'appelle mystérieusement «Mademoiselle». Ce personnage, ce n'est pas moi. C'est juste une fille de mon âge, avec les mêmes cheveux et souvent les mêmes problèmes. La Mademoiselle du blog a un chat noir nommé Méphistofélix. C'est son confident, sa conscience, son Jiminy Cricket...

Pourquoi as-tu commencé à bloguer?

On était au mois de janvier. À peine rentrée d'un voyage, j'ai dû rompre avec mon copain. Déboussolée, j'ai quitté l'appartement que je partageais avec «lui» et j'ai trouvé une toute petite chambre en ville. Bien qu'au 6ème étage, j'étais au fond du trou. Je pleurais dedans, il pleuvait dehors. Bref, la seule fenêtre qui m'offrait de la lumière était celle de mon ordinateur. À cette période, j'ai découvert beaucoup de blogs. Comme j'aimais dessiner, j'ai pensé: MONTRER DES DESSINS À DES GENS est peut-être une bonne façon de me changer les idées.

Où peut-on voir ton travail en dehors des blogs?

Dans le monde matériel, sur des cartes postales, jeux, petits livres illustrés... et puis dans mes albums de BD.

Parle-nous d'un truc qui n'a rien à voir avec la BD et que tu aimes.

J'aime faire du vélo en ville et chanter, boire des apéros entre amis, aller au cinéma, le chocolat, les voyages, la randonnée en montagne, les chats, les pistaches, le vin, les fleurs au printemps, l'été tout entier, le bruit de la pluie, mes baskets noires, boire du thé chez une copine, un expresso à une terrasse, observer les gens, mes amis, mon sac à dos, mon ordinateur, la musique, recevoir un gentil texto ou une carte postale, rire, faire rire, rire...

Ma vie *My life* **une BD (une bande dessinée)** *a comic (strip)* **on appelle** *one calls* **tenir** *to keep* **je mets en scène un personnage** *I present a character* **À peine** *Barely* **rompre avec** *to break up with* **Déboussolée** *Disoriented* **Bien que** *Although* **au fond du trou** *at the bottom of the hole* **Je pleurais dedans** *I was crying inside* **dehors** *outside* **de la lumière** *light* **j'ai découvert** *I discovered* **dessiner** *to draw* **des apéros** *drinks* **le bruit** *the noise* **rire** *to laugh*

AVANT DE LIRE

Review the reading strategy in the *Pour mieux lire* section on page 60 of *Chapitre 1* before beginning these activities.

Dans quel ordre? Avant de lire l'interview avec Lucile Gomez à la page précédente, parcourez *(scan)* le texte et regardez les questions qu'on lui pose pour déterminer dans quel paragraphe elle parle des choses suivantes: **le premier, le deuxième, le troisième, le quatrième** ou **le cinquième.**

1. Elle se présente dans le _____ paragraphe.
2. Elle parle de ce qui *(what)* l'a inspirée à bloguer dans le _____ paragraphe.
3. Elle parle de ses autres activités (en dehors de *[outside of]* son blog) dans le _____ paragraphe.
4. Elle parle de ses publications en dehors de l'Internet dans le _____ paragraphe.
5. Elle décrit *(describes)* son blog dans le _____ paragraphe.

LECTURE ET COMPRÉHENSION

Lucile et son blog. Lisez l'interview à la page précédente et répondez aux questions.

1. Qui est «Mademoiselle»?
2. Qui est Méphistofélix?
3. Qui était «lui»?
4. Qu'est-ce que Lucile voulait faire quand elle a commencé son blog?

À VOUS LA PAROLE!

Préférences. Relisez le dernier paragraphe de l'interview et indiquez quelque chose que Lucile aime bien dans chacune de ces catégories. Ensuite, pour ces mêmes catégories, indiquez quelque chose que vous aimez.

	LUCILE	MOI	MON/MA PARTENAIRE
quelque chose qu'on fait dehors			
quelque chose qu'on fait entre amis			
quelque chose qu'on mange ou qu'on boit			
quelque chose qu'on admire dans la nature			

Maintenant, interviewez un(e) autre étudiant(e) pour compléter la dernière colonne du tableau.

EXEMPLE — Qu'est-ce que tu aimes faire dehors?
— J'aime faire du vélo. Et toi?

Review the *Résumé de grammaire* sections on pages 220–221 and 262–263 at the end of *Chapitre 5* and *Chapitre 6* before doing these activities.

PRATIQUE

A On blogue! Comme Lucile, ces gens parlent de leur expérience sur les blogs. Complétez leurs phrases avec la forme correcte du verbe logique.

EXEMPLE Pourquoi est-ce que vous **faites** (partir/faire) un blog, vous?

1. Sur un blog, on _____ (sortir/devoir) de son silence. En général, les blogueurs écrivent *(write)* pour leurs amis et leur famille, mais certains _____ (vouloir/partir) aussi écrire pour le grand public.

2. Pendant que *(While)* le blogueur _____ (dormir/pouvoir), des gens de l'autre côté de la planète _____ (pouvoir/dormir) lire ses histoires *(stories)*.

3. Nous, les lecteurs *(readers)*, nous _____ (pouvoir/faire) aussi laisser des commentaires. Mais on ne _____ (devoir/partir) pas écrire des textes trop longs. Les gens préfèrent lire des commentaires plutôt courts.

4. Mon blog s'appelle: «Elle ne _____ (faire/dormir) rien!». Quand je _____ (partir/faire) en vacances, cela me donne de nouvelles idées de sujets pour bloguer. Ma sœur et moi, nous _____ (faire/pouvoir) aussi un blog ensemble. C'est génial!

B Une histoire personnelle. Dans son interview, Lucile raconte comment son blog est né. Utilisez le **passé composé** ou l'**imparfait** des verbes entre parenthèses pour compléter son histoire.

Lucile _____**1**_____ (partir) en voyage puis, quand elle _____**2**_____ (rentrer) à Paris en janvier, elle et son copain _____**3**_____ (avoir) une grosse rupture amoureuse *(break-up)*.

Lucile _____**4**_____ (devoir) quitter son appartement. Elle _____**5**_____ (louer) une petite chambre au 6ème étage.

Elle _____**6**_____ (commencer) son premier blog parce qu'elle _____**7**_____ (vouloir) montrer ses dessins à des gens. Avant de commencer à bloguer, elle _____**8**_____ (être) déprimée *(depressed)* et elle _____**9**_____ (passer) beaucoup de temps devant son ordinateur. Elle _____**10**_____ (ne pas sortir) beaucoup et elle _____**11**_____ (dormir) mal.

Peu après, son blog _____**12**_____ (avoir) du succès et sa nouvelle vie et sa carrière dans la BD _____**13**_____ (commencer)!

C Le monde de Lucile. À tour de rôle, posez les questions suivantes à un(e) partenaire. Utilisez un pronom complément d'objet direct dans la réponse.

EXEMPLE — Comment Lucile appelle-t-elle *le chat* de son blog?
           — Elle **l'appelle** Méphistofélix.

1. Est-ce que «Mademoiselle» écoute *son chat*?

2. Pourquoi est-ce que Lucile a commencé *son blog*?

3. Elle aime bien montrer *ses dessins* aux gens?

4. Où est-ce qu'on trouve *les dessins* de Lucile dans le monde matériel?

5. Où est-ce que Lucile a trouvé *sa nouvelle chambre* après sa rupture *(break-up)*?

6. Selon vous *(In your opinion)*, est-ce que Lucile va continuer *son blog*?

À VOUS LA PAROLE!

Le destin d'une lycéenne. Lisez la bande déssinée suivante de Lucile Gomez. Ensuite, en groupes, racontez l'histoire de cette lycéenne amoureuse en utilisant le **passé composé** et l'**imparfait.**

La vie saine

Le beurre de cacahuète, c'est pour les sportifs!

Le beurre de cacahuète: un super-aliment!

Le beurre de cacahuète est un super-aliment. Pourquoi? Parce qu'il est délicieux, nourrissant et bon pour la santé! Beaucoup de personnes l'évitent, parce qu'elles pensent qu'il est trop calorique. Mais nous allons vous montrer pourquoi on devrait tous en manger.

Ses bienfaits pour la santé

Ce super-aliment contient beaucoup de fibres. Il est aussi riche en minéraux et apporte du zinc (qui aide au bon fonctionnement immunitaire), du manganèse, du **cuivre,** du phosphore et du magnésium. En ce qui concerne les vitamines, il a aussi de la niacine (vitamine B3), de la vitamine E, de l'acide folique (vitamine B9) et de la vitamine B6.

Grâce à tous ces micronutriments, le beurre de cacahuète pourrait ainsi aider à **lutter** contre le cancer, le diabète de type 2 et les maladies cardiovasculaires!

Enfin, le beurre de cacahuète contient une bonne quantité de resvératrol, peut-être l'un des micronutriments les plus fascinants. C'est un antioxydant et un antimicrobien naturel qui protège contre les bactéries et les virus. On dit que le resvératrol serait à l'origine du fameux «paradoxe français». Sa présence dans le vin et le raisin expliquerait pourquoi les Français mangent plus gras que les Américains, mais ont moins de maladies cardiovasculaires.

Des protéines pour les sportifs

Pour les sportifs, le beurre de cacahuète est une excellente source de calories et de protéines, à la fois naturelle et pas chère. Deux **cuillères à soupe** de beurre de cacahuète (la quantité nécessaire pour faire une tartine de taille moyenne) contiennent environ sept grammes de protéines. Quelle bonne nouvelle pour les sportifs végétariens!

De bons acides gras

Les graisses présentes dans le beurre de cacahuète sont des acides gras insaturés: elles sont donc «bonnes» et ne produisent pas de mauvais cholestérol. Mais attention! Tous les beurres de cacahuète ne sont pas **égaux.** Quand on y **rajoute** des huiles végétales, ils produisent des acides gras trans, qu'il vaut mieux éviter. Choisissez donc de préférence des beurres non raffinés, c'est-à-dire naturels ou bio.

---

cacahuète *peanut*   **cuivre** *copper*   **Grâce à** *Thanks to*   **lutter** *to fight*   **cuillères à soupe** *soup spoonfuls*   **égaux** *equal*   **rajoute** *adds*

AVANT DE LIRE

Review the reading strategies in the *Pour mieux lire* sections on pages 60 of *Chapitre 1* and 138 of *Chapitre 3* before beginning these activities.

Mots apparentés. Les Français mangent très peu de beurre de cacahuète. Parcourez *(Scan)* l'article à la page précédente qui fait la promotion de cet aliment *(food)* et servez-vous des mots apparentés pour trouver les expressions indiquées ci-dessous *(below)*.

DANS LA SECTION	TROUVEZ:
Le beurre de cacahuète: un super-aliment!	deux mots qui indiquent pourquoi le beurre de cacahuète est un super-aliment *(food)*
Ses bienfaits pour la santé	• les noms de trois minéraux qu'on trouve dans le beurre de cacahuète • les noms de trois vitamines qu'on y trouve • les noms de trois types de maladies *(illnesses)* • le nom d'un antioxydant qui protège *(protects)* contre les virus
De bons acides gras	les deux différentes sortes de graisses *(fats)* mentionnées

LECTURE ET COMPRÉHENSION

Pourquoi le beurre de cacahuète? Une amie française ne connaît pas bien le beurre de cacahuète. Répondez à ses questions d'après le texte.

1. Ne devrait-on pas éviter le beurre de cacahuète parce qu'il a trop de calories?
2. Pourquoi est-ce que le beurre de cacahuète serait «un super-aliment»?
3. Quels minéraux est-ce que le beurre de cacahuète apporterait au régime *(diet)* de quelqu'un? Pourquoi est-ce que le zinc serait bon pour la santé? Quelles autres substances nutritives prendrait-on si on mangeait du beurre de cacahuète?
4. Contre quelles maladies est-ce que le beurre de cacahuète pourrait lutter?
5. Pourquoi est-ce que le beurre de cacahuète aiderait les sportifs?
6. Pourquoi faudrait-il choisir un beurre de cacahuète non raffiné?

À VOUS LA PAROLE!

Sport et nutrition. Posez ces questions à votre partenaire.

1. Est-ce que tu manges du beurre de cacahuète? Pourquoi est-ce que tu en manges? (Pourquoi est-ce que tu n'en manges pas?) Est-ce que tu conseillerais *(would advise)* à tous les sportifs de manger du beurre de cacahuète? Pourquoi (pas)?
2. Qu'est-ce que tu manges avant de faire du sport? Qu'est-ce que tu bois quand tu fais du sport? Qu'est-ce que tu ne bois pas ou ne manges pas avant de faire du sport?
3. D'après toi, qu'est-ce que les sportifs devraient manger ou boire parce que c'est bon pour eux? Qu'est-ce qu'ils devraient éviter?

À VOUS!

Vous êtes nutritionniste. Votre partenaire est un sportif (une sportive) qui n'a jamais entendu parler du *(has never heard of)* beurre de cacahuète. Préparez une conversation dans laquelle votre partenaire vous pose des questions à ce sujet et vous lui expliquez pourquoi il/elle devrait en manger. Est-ce que vous réussissez à le/la convaincre *(to convince)*?

Review the *Résumé de grammaire* sections on pages 306–307 and 352–353 at the end of *Chapitre 7* and *Chapitre 8* before doing these activities.

PRATIQUE

A **Que de bonnes choses!** Relisez l'article à la page 452. Ensuite, répondez aux questions en utilisant **en.**

EXEMPLE Est-ce qu'on trouve des protéines dans le beurre de cacahuète?
Oui, on en trouve.

1. Est-ce qu'il y a de la vitamine B6 dans le beurre de cacahuète?
2. Est-ce que le beurre de cacahuète a des minéraux?
3. Est-ce qu'on trouve de la vitamine C dans le beurre de cacahuète?
4. Est-ce que le beurre de cacahuète a du lactose?
5. Est-ce qu'il y a beaucoup de fibres dans le beurre de cacahuète?
6. Combien de grammes de protéines est-ce qu'il y a dans deux cuillères à soupe de beurre de cacahuète?

B **Une pub.** La pub *(ad)* suivante encourage les jeunes sportifs à manger plus de beurre de cacahuète. Complétez le texte de la pub avec **qui, que** ou **dont.**

«Quand je mange du beurre de cacahuète, je mange quelque chose ____**1**____ me fait du bien et _____**2**_____ les nutritionnistes recommandent aux sportifs comme moi. Tous les micronutriments _____**3**_____ le beurre de cacahuète contient sont bons pour ma santé!

Une tartine au goûter me donne les protéines _____**4**_____ mes muscles ont besoin pour se développer. Le beurre de cacahuète a aussi des fibres _____**5**_____ aident à la digestion et il n'a pas de mauvaises graisses _____**6**_____ pourraient me donner du mauvais cholestérol. Le beurre de cacahuète est un super-aliment _____**7**_____ toi aussi, tu devrais essayer!»

C **Un micro-trottoir *(Street interview)*.** Des Français dans la rue donnent leur avis *(opinion)* à un enquêteur *(interviewer)* sur le beurre de cacahuète. Complétez leurs déclarations en mettant un verbe au conditionnel et l'autre à l'imparfait.

EXEMPLE J'**achèterais** (acheter) du beurre de cacahuète si mon supermarché en **vendait** (vendre).

1. Je l'_____ (essayer), si je n'_____ (être) pas allergique aux cacahuètes.
2. Je _____ (pouvoir) mieux répondre à vos questions si je _____ (pouvoir) en goûter mais je ne sais pas ce que c'est.
3. J'en _____ (manger) souvent si le beurre de cacahuète _____ (avoir) moins de matières grasses.
4. Si on _____ (être) végétarien, le beurre de cacahuète _____ (être) peut-être un bon substitut à la viande.
5. Je _____ (préférer) manger du Nutella, même si le beurre de cacahuète _____ (être) meilleur pour la santé.
6. Moi, j'_____ (avoir) envie de vomir si je _____ (devoir) manger ça! Ça a l'air dégoûtant *(yucky, disgusting)*!
7. J'ai un ami américain qui _____ (mourir) de faim s'il n'y _____ (avoir) pas de beurre de cacahuète!

À VOUS LA PAROLE!

A **Entretien.** Complétez les questions suivantes avec **le, la, l', les, un, une, du, de la, de l', des** ou **de (d').**

1. Est-ce que tu aimes _____ beurre de cacahuète? Est-ce que tu manges beaucoup _____ beurre de cacahuète? Est-ce que tu aimes _____ tartines au beurre de cacahuète? Est-ce que tu préfères faire _____ tartine au beurre de cacahuète avec _____ confiture ou sans confiture? Est-ce que tu utilises _____ beurre de cacahuète pour faire _____ autres plats?

2. D'habitude, est-ce que tu bois _____ lait avec _____ tartine au beurre de cacahuète ou est-ce que tu préfères une autre boisson? Est-ce que tu aimes _____ lait? Est-ce que tu préfères _____ lait entier *(whole)* ou écrémé *(skim, low-fat)*? Est-ce que _____ lait a beaucoup _____ vitamine D? Est-ce que les Français boivent souvent _____ lait au déjeuner ou au dîner comme les Américains?

Maintenant, posez les questions à votre partenaire.

B **Conseils.** Vous êtes conseiller (conseillère) à l'université et vous aidez les étudiants qui sont souvent fatigués ou qui ont d'autres problèmes. Avec un(e) partenaire, préparez une liste de 6–8 questions que vous poseriez aux étudiants qui viennent vous demander des conseils. Utilisez les verbes en **-re** (p. 286), en **-ir** (p. 338), **boire** (p. 336) et les verbes réfléchis (p. 274) et réciproques (p. 282).

EXEMPLES **Est-ce que vous vous entendez bien avec vos colocataires? Est-ce que vous réfléchissez trop à des choses que vous ne pouvez pas changer?**

Maintenant, changez de partenaire et utilisez les questions que vous avez préparées pour interviewer votre nouveau (nouvelle) partenaire. Utilisez la forme familière.

EXEMPLES **— Est-ce que tu t'entends bien avec tes colocataires?**
— On s'entend bien en général, mais on se dispute de temps en temps.
— Est-ce que tu réfléchis trop à des choses que tu ne peux pas changer?
— Oui, je réfléchis souvent à des choses que je ne peux pas contrôler.

C **Le week-end dernier.** Avec un(e) partenaire, préparez 6–8 questions au passé composé ou à l'imparfait pour interviewer un(e) autre étudiant(e) sur ses activités du week-end dernier. Utilisez les verbes en **-ir**, les verbes en **-re**, **boire** et les verbes réfléchis et réciproques.

EXEMPLES **— Est-ce que tu t'es levé(e) tôt ou tard samedi?**
— Tes amis et toi, est-ce que vous vous êtes retrouvés en ville samedi soir?

Maintenant, changez de partenaire et utilisez les questions que vous avez préparées pour interviewer votre nouveau (nouvelle) partenaire. Ensuite, décrivez le week-end de votre partenaire à la classe.

EXEMPLE **Christine s'est levée vers onze heures samedi matin. Samedi soir, ses amis et elle se sont retrouvés au cinéma...**

L'écotourisme

Tours Guadeloupe Nature

Savez-vous comment **les Caraïbes des Petites Antilles** appelaient la Guadeloupe? *Karukera* ou «l'île aux belles eaux». Si vous venez faire de l'écotourisme en Guadeloupe, vous comprendrez pourquoi ce nom lui va si bien.

Les Chutes du Carbet

Venez avec nous faire des randonnées en pleine nature dans le Parc national de la Guadeloupe. Vous y observerez l'incroyable biodiversité de la forêt tropicale et vous verrez plusieurs sites naturels remarquables, comme les magnifiques Chutes du Carbet! Vous nagerez au pied de ces cascades, en pleine forêt tropicale, dans de petites piscines naturelles. Si la température est un peu trop fraîche, vous pourrez aussi essayer les sources d'eau chaude.

Les Bains jaunes

Au pied du volcan la Soufrière, vous trouverez les Bains jaunes, un petit bassin d'eau sulfureuse chaude et bien agréable à visiter avant ou après l'ascension du volcan.

Des cocotiers sur la plage du Gosier

Vous préférez la mer? Pas de problème! Nos guides vous feront visiter les plus belles plages de l'île, du sable blanc fin et des cocotiers de la plage du Gosier au sable noir volcanique de Grande-Anse. Et près de Port-Louis, vous pourrez faire de la plongée sous-marine.

Le soir? Nous voulons que vous finissiez votre journée en toute tranquillité. Nos bungalows sont dans un grand jardin botanique où vous serez au calme. Nous vous y proposons des massages relaxants et une délicieuse cuisine de plats antillais authentiques.

Alors, qu'attendez-vous? Il faut absolument que vous visitiez la Guadeloupe! Nous voulons que vous ayez une expérience formidable et que vous appreniez à connaître notre belle île. Faites-nous confiance. Vous verrez, vous ne le regretterez pas!

---

les Caraïbes *the Kalinagos* (an early Amerindian population of the Antilles)　　**des Petites Antilles** *of the Lesser Antilles*

AVANT DE LIRE

Devinez! Regardez la page précédente et utilisez les photos, le titre et l'organisation du texte pour répondre aux questions suivantes.

1. Le texte est une publicité pour quelle sorte de tourisme?
2. Qu'est-ce qu'on verra sur le tour proposé?
3. Quelles activités est-ce qu'on fera dans les endroits illustrés sur les photos?
4. En vous basant sur le thème de l'écotourisme et sur les photos à la page précédente, devinez le sens des mots et des expressions suivants.

> une chute   une source d'eau chaude   une cascade
> du sable blanc et des cocotiers   faire de la plongée sous-marine

Review the reading strategy in the *Pour mieux lire* section on page 216 of *Chapitre 5* before beginning these activities.

LECTURE ET COMPRÉHENSION

À mon avis. Lisez le texte, puis répondez aux questions.

1. Quel genre de paysages peut-on voir en Guadeloupe? Sont-ils variés?
2. Comprenez-vous pourquoi la Guadeloupe est parfois appelée «l'île aux belles eaux»?
3. Est-ce que la Guadeloupe est une bonne destination pour faire de l'écotourisme? Pourquoi (pas)?
4. Connaissez-vous des endroits qui ressemblent à *(look like)* la Guadeloupe?

À VOUS LA PAROLE!

A **Et toi?** Votre partenaire va visiter la Guadeloupe cet été avec Tours Guadeloupe Nature. Demandez-lui où il/elle ira et ce qu'il/elle fera. Est-ce qu'il y a des endroits où il/elle n'ira pas du tout? Des choses qu'il/elle n'essaiera pas? Posez-lui au moins cinq questions en utilisant des verbes au futur.

> **EXEMPLE** — Est-ce que tu iras à la plage?
> — Oui, j'irai voir le sable noir de Grande-Anse.

B **Itinéraire de voyage.** En groupes, identifiez un endroit que vous connaissez bien (votre quartier, votre campus, votre ville ou un autre endroit), puis créez un itinéraire de tourisme pour cet endroit.

- Faites une liste de sites naturels ou culturels à visiter.
- Décidez quelles sortes d'activités vous allez proposer aux touristes.

Finalement, créez la publicité pour votre voyage et présentez-la à la classe.

Review the *Résumé de grammaire* sections on pages 390–391 and 430–431 at the end of *Chapitre 9* and *Chapitre 10* before doing these activities.

PRATIQUE

A **On part bientôt!** Anna parle avec des amis de recherches qu'elle fait pour un séjour qu'ils vont tous faire en Guadeloupe. Complétez ses phrases avec le verbe logique au *présent*.

| dire | lire | écrire | connaître | savoir |

EXEMPLE Je **sais** qu'on peut faire de la plongée à Port-Louis.

1. Maintenant je _____ beaucoup mieux la culture guadeloupéenne parce que je _____ un bon guide sur la Guadeloupe.
2. Sur ce site de tourisme, ils _____ que les plages sont extraordinaires.
3. Vous ne _____ pas encore la cuisine créole? Je _____ préparer quelques plats.
4. Si nous _____ ensemble ces descriptions d'hôtels, nous pourrons trouver quelque chose qui plaira à tout le monde, d'accord?
5. Sur ce site, les voyageurs _____ des commentaires sur des hôtels.
6. Toi, tu _____ bien tes amis. Est-ce que tu _____ s'ils voudront aller à la plage tous les jours?

B **Tout est prêt?** Anna a donné à une amie une liste de choses à faire avant le voyage. Maintenant, elle demande à cette amie ce qu'elle a déjà fait. Avec un(e) partenaire, jouez les deux rôles en suivant les exemples. Utilisez un pronom complément d'objet direct ou indirect ou **en** dans les réponses.

obtenir ton passeport ✓
téléphoner à l'agent de voyages
acheter le billet ✓
réserver la chambre ✓
parler à papa ✓
parler aux voisins
acheter un guide pour moi
faire des recherches sur Internet
faire un itinéraire
confirmer l'heure du vol ✓

EXEMPLES obtenir *ton passeport*
— **Tu as obtenu ton passeport?**
— **Oui, je l'ai obtenu.**

téléphoner *à l'agent de voyages*
— **Tu as téléphoné à l'agent de voyages?**
— **Non, je ne lui ai pas encore téléphoné.**
— **Alors, téléphone-lui.**
— **Je lui téléphonerai demain.**

C **Réactions.** Anna parle de son voyage en Guadeloupe. Donnez votre réaction à ce qu'elle dit. Utilisez des expressions comme **il faut, il ne faut pas, il vaut mieux, c'est bien, ce n'est pas bien, c'est mauvais, c'est dommage…**

EXEMPLE Je m'amuse bien en Guadeloupe.
C'est bien que tu t'amuses bien en Guadeloupe.

1. Ma sœur ne mange pas la cuisine locale.
2. Je veux goûter la cuisine locale.
3. Ce monsieur fait des photos sans autorisation.
4. Le guide a beaucoup de patience.
5. Je ne dors pas bien.
6. On choisit de beaux souvenirs.
7. Nous nous levons très tôt.
8. Beaucoup de touristes ne savent pas respecter la nature.
9. Les enfants n'obéissent pas au guide.
10. Nous apprenons beaucoup sur la culture créole.

À VOUS LA PAROLE!

A Un voyage idéal. Vous allez faire le voyage de vos rêves avec quelques amis. Travaillez en petits groupes et déterminez les choses suivantes entre vous.

- quels pays / villes vous visiterez
- comment vous voyagerez
- quand vous partirez
- combien de temps vous resterez
- ce que vous ferez
- quand vous rentrerez
- quels préparatifs il vous faudra faire et qui fera chacun de ces préparatifs

EXEMPLE On ira en France, au Maroc et en Martinique.
On prendra l'avion et on partira...

B Conseils. Chaque groupe va présenter les détails du voyage qu'il a préparé dans *A. Un voyage idéal* à un autre groupe. L'autre groupe va donner au moins cinq réactions ou conseils.

EXEMPLE C'est bien que vous visitiez des pays étrangers.
Il faut que vous obteniez vos passeports bien à l'avance.
Il vaut mieux que...

Au Maroc, on goûtera la cuisine locale.

En Martinique, on nagera et on fera de la plongée.

En France, on visitera tous les sites touristiques et historiques comme la cathédrale de Chartres.

C Touristes responsables. En groupes, préparez une liste de 3–4 choses qu'il faut faire pour être un(e) touriste responsable et une autre liste de 3–4 choses qu'il ne faut pas faire.

EXEMPLES Il faut respecter la nature.
Il ne faut pas marcher sur les plantes dans les jardins.

Tableaux des verbes

VERBES AUXILIAIRES

VERBE		INDICATIF			CONDITIONNEL	SUBJONCTIF	
INFINITIF	PRÉSENT	PASSÉ COMPOSÉ	IMPARFAIT	FUTUR	PRÉSENT	PRÉSENT	IMPÉRATIF
avoir	ai	ai eu	avais	aurai	aurais	aie	
to have	as	as eu	avais	auras	aurais	aies	aie
	a	a eu	avait	aura	aurait	ait	
	avons	avons eu	avions	aurons	aurions	ayons	ayons
	avez	avez eu	aviez	aurez	auriez	ayez	ayez
	ont	ont eu	avaient	auront	auraient	aient	
être	suis	ai été	étais	serai	serais	sois	
to be	es	as été	étais	seras	serais	sois	sois
	est	a été	était	sera	serait	soit	
	sommes	avons été	étions	serons	serions	soyons	soyons
	êtes	avez été	étiez	serez	seriez	soyez	soyez
	sont	ont été	étaient	seront	seraient	soient	

VERBES RÉGULIERS

VERBE		INDICATIF			CONDITIONNEL	SUBJONCTIF	
INFINITIF	PRÉSENT	PASSÉ COMPOSÉ	IMPARFAIT	FUTUR	PRÉSENT	PRÉSENT	IMPÉRATIF
-er verbs							
parler	parle	ai parlé	parlais	parlerai	parlerais	parle	
to talk,	parles	as parlé	parlais	parleras	parlerais	parles	parle
to speak	parle	a parlé	parlait	parlera	parlerait	parle	
	parlons	avons parlé	parlions	parlerons	parlerions	parlions	parlons
	parlez	avez parlé	parliez	parlerez	parleriez	parliez	parlez
	parlent	ont parlé	parlaient	parleront	parleraient	parlent	
-ir verbs							
finir	finis	ai fini	finissais	finirai	finirais	finisse	
to finish	finis	as fini	finissais	finiras	finirais	finisses	finis
	finit	a fini	finissait	finira	finirait	finisse	
	finissons	avons fini	finissions	finirons	finirions	finissions	finissons
	finissez	avez fini	finissiez	finirez	finiriez	finissiez	finissez
	finissent	ont fini	finissaient	finiront	finiraient	finissent	
-re verbs							
vendre	vends	ai vendu	vendais	vendrai	vendrais	vende	
to sell	vends	as vendu	vendais	vendras	vendrais	vendes	vends
	vend	a vendu	vendait	vendra	vendrait	vende	
	vendons	avons vendu	vendions	vendrons	vendrions	vendions	vendons
	vendez	avez vendu	vendiez	vendrez	vendriez	vendiez	vendez
	vendent	ont vendu	vendaient	vendront	vendraient	vendent	

VERBES RÉFLÉCHIS

VERBE INFINITIF	INDICATIF PRÉSENT	PASSÉ COMPOSÉ	IMPARFAIT	FUTUR	CONDITIONNEL PRÉSENT	SUBJONCTIF PRÉSENT	IMPÉRATIF
se laver *to wash* *oneself*	me lave	me suis lavé(e)	me lavais	me laverai	me laverais	me lave	
	te laves	t'es lavé(e)	te lavais	te laveras	te laverais	te laves	lave-toi
	se lave	s'est lavé(e)	se lavait	se lavera	se laverait	se lave	
	nous lavons	nous sommes lavé(e)s	nous lavions	nous laverons	nous laverions	nous lavions	lavons-nous
	vous lavez	vous êtes lavé(e)(s)	vous laviez	vous laverez	vous laveriez	vous laviez	lavez-vous
	se lavent	se sont lavé(e)s	se lavaient	se laveront	se laveraient	se lavent	

VERBES À CHANGEMENTS ORTHOGRAPHIQUES

VERBE INFINITIF	INDICATIF PRÉSENT	PASSÉ COMPOSÉ	IMPARFAIT	FUTUR	CONDITIONNEL PRÉSENT	SUBJONCTIF PRÉSENT	IMPÉRATIF
préférer *to prefer*	préfère	ai préféré	préférais	préférerai	préférerais	préfère	
	préfères	as préféré	préférais	préféreras	préférerais	préfères	préfère
	préfère	a préféré	préférait	préférera	préférerait	préfère	
	préférons	avons préféré	préférions	préférerons	préférerions	préférions	préférons
	préférez	avez préféré	préfériez	préférerez	préféreriez	préfériez	préférez
	préfèrent	ont préféré	préféraient	préféreront	préféreraient	préfèrent	
acheter *to buy*	achète	ai acheté	achetais	achèterai	achèterais	achète	
	achètes	as acheté	achetais	achèteras	achèterais	achètes	achète
	achète	a acheté	achetait	achètera	achèterait	achète	
	achetons	avons acheté	achetions	achèterons	achèterions	achetions	achetons
	achetez	avez acheté	achetiez	achèterez	achèteriez	achetiez	achetez
	achètent	ont acheté	achetaient	achèteront	achèteraient	achètent	
appeler *to call*	appelle	ai appelé	appelais	appellerai	appellerais	appelle	
	appelles	as appelé	appelais	appelleras	appellerais	appelles	appelle
	appelle	a appelé	appelait	appellera	appellerait	appelle	
	appelons	avons appelé	appelions	appellerons	appellerions	appelions	appelons
	appelez	avez appelé	appeliez	appellerez	appelleriez	appeliez	appelez
	appellent	ont appelé	appelaient	appelleront	appelleraient	appellent	
essayer *to try*	essaie	ai essayé	essayais	essaierai	essaierais	essaie	
	essaies	as essayé	essayais	essaieras	essaierais	essaies	essaie
	essaie	a essayé	essayait	essaiera	essaierait	essaie	
	essayons	avons essayé	essayions	essaierons	essaierions	essayions	essayons
	essayez	avez essayé	essayiez	essaierez	essaieriez	essayiez	essayez
	essaient	ont essayé	essayaient	essaieront	essaieraient	essaient	
manger *to eat*	mange	ai mangé	mangeais	mangerai	mangerais	mange	
	manges	as mangé	mangeais	mangeras	mangerais	manges	mange
	mange	a mangé	mangeait	mangera	mangerait	mange	
	mangeons	avons mangé	mangions	mangerons	mangerions	mangions	mangeons
	mangez	avez mangé	mangiez	mangerez	mangeriez	mangiez	mangez
	mangent	ont mangé	mangeaient	mangeront	mangeraient	mangent	
commencer *to begin*	commence	ai commencé	commençais	commencerai	commencerais	commence	
	commences	as commencé	commençais	commenceras	commencerais	commences	commence
	commence	a commencé	commençait	commencera	commencerait	commence	
	commençons	avons commencé	commencions	commencerons	commencerions	commencions	commençons
	commencez	avez commencé	commenciez	commencerez	commenceriez	commenciez	commencez
	commencent	ont commencé	commençaient	commenceront	commenceraient	commencent	

VERBES IRRÉGULIERS

VERBE INFINITIF	INDICATIF PRÉSENT	INDICATIF PASSÉ COMPOSÉ	INDICATIF IMPARFAIT	INDICATIF FUTUR	CONDITIONNEL PRÉSENT	SUBJONCTIF PRÉSENT	IMPÉRATIF
aller	vais	suis allé(e)	allais	irai	irais	aille	
to go	vas	es allé(e)	allais	iras	irais	ailles	va
	va	est allé(e)	allait	ira	irait	aille	
	allons	sommes allé(e)s	allions	irons	irions	allions	allons
	allez	êtes allé(e)(s)	alliez	irez	iriez	alliez	allez
	vont	sont allé(e)s	allaient	iront	iraient	aillent	
s'asseoir	m'assieds	me suis assis(e)	m'asseyais	m'assiérai	m'assiérais	m'asseye	
to sit	t'assieds	t'es assis(e)	t'asseyais	t'assiéras	t'assiérais	t'asseyes	assieds-toi
(down)	s'assied	s'est assis(e)	s'asseyait	s'assiéra	s'assiérait	s'asseye	
	nous asseyons	nous sommes assis(es)	nous asseyions	nous assiérons	nous assiérions	nous asseyions	asseyons-nous
	vous asseyez	vous êtes assis(e)(s)	vous asseyiez	vous assiérez	vous assiériez	vous asseyiez	asseyez-vous
	s'asseyent	se sont assis(es)	s'asseyaient	s'assiéront	s'assiéraient	s'asseyent	
battre	bats	ai battu	battais	battrai	battrais	batte	
to beat	bats	as battu	battais	battras	battrais	battes	bats
	bat	a battu	battait	battra	battrait	batte	
	battons	avons battu	battions	battrons	battrions	battions	battons
	battez	avez battu	battiez	battrez	battriez	battiez	battez
	battent	ont battu	battaient	battront	battraient	battent	
boire	bois	ai bu	buvais	boirai	boirais	boive	
to drink	bois	as bu	buvais	boiras	boirais	boives	bois
	boit	a bu	buvait	boira	boirait	boive	
	buvons	avons bu	buvions	boirons	boirions	buvions	buvons
	buvez	avez bu	buviez	boirez	boiriez	buviez	buvez
	boivent	ont bu	buvaient	boiront	boiraient	boivent	
conduire	conduis	ai conduit	conduisais	conduirai	conduirais	conduise	
to drive	conduis	as conduit	conduisais	conduiras	conduirais	conduises	conduis
	conduit	a conduit	conduisait	conduira	conduirait	conduise	
	conduisons	avons conduit	conduisions	conduirons	conduirions	conduisions	conduisons
	conduisez	avez conduit	conduisiez	conduirez	conduiriez	conduisiez	conduisez
	conduisent	ont conduit	conduisaient	conduiront	conduiraient	conduisent	
connaître	connais	ai connu	connaissais	connaîtrai	connaîtrais	connaisse	
to be	connais	as connu	connaissais	connaîtras	connaîtrais	connaisses	connais
acquainted	connaît	a connu	connaissait	connaîtra	connaîtrait	connaisse	
with,	connaissons	avons connu	connaissions	connaîtrons	connaîtrions	connaissions	connaissons
to know	connaissez	avez connu	connaissiez	connaîtrez	connaîtriez	connaissiez	connaissez
	connaissent	ont connu	connaissaient	connaîtront	connaîtraient	connaissent	
courir	cours	ai couru	courais	courrai	courrais	coure	
to run	cours	as couru	courais	courras	courrais	coures	cours
	court	a couru	courait	courra	courrait	coure	
	courons	avons couru	courions	courrons	courrions	courions	courons
	courez	avez couru	couriez	courrez	courriez	couriez	courez
	courent	ont couru	couraient	courront	courraient	courent	
croire	crois	ai cru	croyais	croirai	croirais	croie	
to believe	crois	as cru	croyais	croiras	croirais	croies	crois
	croit	a cru	croyait	croira	croirait	croie	
	croyons	avons cru	croyions	croirons	croirions	croyions	croyons
	croyez	avez cru	croyiez	croirez	croiriez	croyiez	croyez
	croient	ont cru	croyaient	croiront	croiraient	croient	

VERBES IRRÉGULIERS (SUITE)

VERBE INFINITIF	PRÉSENT	PASSÉ COMPOSÉ	IMPARFAIT	FUTUR	CONDITIONNEL PRÉSENT	SUBJONCTIF PRÉSENT	IMPÉRATIF
		INDICATIF					
devoir	dois	ai dû	devais	devrai	devrais	doive	
must,	dois	as dû	devais	devras	devrais	doives	
to have to,	doit	a dû	devait	devra	devrait	doive	
to owe	devons	avons dû	devions	devrons	devrions	devions	
	devez	avez dû	deviez	devrez	devriez	deviez	
	doivent	ont dû	devaient	devront	devraient	doivent	
dire	dis	ai dit	disais	dirai	dirais	dise	
to say,	dis	as dit	disais	diras	dirais	dises	dis
to tell	dit	a dit	disait	dira	dirait	dise	
	disons	avons dit	disions	dirons	dirions	disions	disons
	dites	avez dit	disiez	direz	diriez	disiez	dites
	disent	ont dit	disaient	diront	diraient	disent	
dormir	dors	ai dormi	dormais	dormirai	dormirais	dorme	
to sleep	dors	as dormi	dormais	dormiras	dormirais	dormes	dors
	dort	a dormi	dormait	dormira	dormirait	dorme	
	dormons	avons dormi	dormions	dormirons	dormirions	dormions	dormons
	dormez	avez dormi	dormiez	dormirez	dormiriez	dormiez	dormez
	dorment	ont dormi	dormaient	dormiront	dormiraient	dorment	
écrire	écris	ai écrit	écrivais	écrirai	écrirais	écrive	
to write	écris	as écrit	écrivais	écriras	écrirais	écrives	écris
	écrit	a écrit	écrivait	écrira	écrirait	écrive	
	écrivons	avons écrit	écrivions	écrirons	écririons	écrivions	écrivons
	écrivez	avez écrit	écriviez	écrirez	écririez	écriviez	écrivez
	écrivent	ont écrit	écrivaient	écriront	écriraient	écrivent	
envoyer	envoie	ai envoyé	envoyais	enverrai	enverrais	envoie	
to send	envoies	as envoyé	envoyais	enverras	enverrais	envoies	envoie
	envoie	a envoyé	envoyait	enverra	enverrait	envoie	
	envoyons	avons envoyé	envoyions	enverrons	enverrions	envoyions	envoyons
	envoyez	avez envoyé	envoyiez	enverrez	enverriez	envoyiez	envoyez
	envoient	ont envoyé	envoyaient	enverront	enverraient	envoient	
faire	fais	ai fait	faisais	ferai	ferais	fasse	
to do,	fais	as fait	faisais	feras	ferais	fasses	fais
to make	fait	a fait	faisait	fera	ferait	fasse	
	faisons	avons fait	faisions	ferons	ferions	fassions	faisons
	faites	avez fait	faisiez	ferez	feriez	fassiez	faites
	font	ont fait	faisaient	feront	feraient	fassent	
falloir	faut	a fallu	fallait	faudra	faudrait	faille	
to be necessary							
lire	lis	ai lu	lisais	lirai	lirais	lise	
to read	lis	as lu	lisais	liras	lirais	lises	lis
	lit	a lu	lisait	lira	lirait	lise	
	lisons	avons lu	lisions	lirons	lirions	lisions	lisons
	lisez	avez lu	lisiez	lirez	liriez	lisiez	lisez
	lisent	ont lu	lisaient	liront	liraient	lisent	
mettre	mets	ai mis	mettais	mettrai	mettrais	mette	
to put (on),	mets	as mis	mettais	mettras	mettrais	mettes	mets
to place,	met	a mis	mettait	mettra	mettrait	mette	
to set	mettons	avons mis	mettions	mettrons	mettrions	mettions	mettons
	mettez	avez mis	mettiez	mettrez	mettriez	mettiez	mettez
	mettent	ont mis	mettaient	mettront	mettraient	mettent	

VERBES IRRÉGULIERS (SUITE)

VERBE INFINITIF	PRÉSENT	PASSÉ COMPOSÉ	IMPARFAIT	FUTUR	CONDITIONNEL PRÉSENT	SUBJONCTIF PRÉSENT	IMPÉRATIF
obtenir *to obtain*	obtiens	ai obtenu	obtenais	obtiendrai	obtiendrais	obtienne	
	obtiens	as obtenu	obtenais	obtiendras	obtiendrais	obtiennes	obtiens
	obtient	a obtenu	obtenait	obtiendra	obtiendrait	obtienne	
	obtenons	avons obtenu	obtenions	obtiendrons	obtiendrions	obtenions	obtenons
	obtenez	avez obtenu	obteniez	obtiendrez	obtiendriez	obteniez	obtenez
	obtiennent	ont obtenu	obtenaient	obtiendront	obtiendraient	obtiennent	
ouvrir *to open*	ouvre	ai ouvert	ouvrais	ouvrirai	ouvrirais	ouvre	
	ouvres	as ouvert	ouvrais	ouvriras	ouvrirais	ouvres	ouvre
	ouvre	a ouvert	ouvrait	ouvrira	ouvrirait	ouvre	
	ouvrons	avons ouvert	ouvrions	ouvrirons	ouvririons	ouvrions	ouvrons
	ouvrez	avez ouvert	ouvriez	ouvrirez	ouvririez	ouvriez	ouvrez
	ouvrent	ont ouvert	ouvraient	ouvriront	ouvriraient	ouvrent	
partir *to leave*	pars	suis parti(e)	partais	partirai	partirais	parte	
	pars	es parti(e)	partais	partiras	partirais	partes	pars
	part	est parti(e)	partait	partira	partirait	parte	
	partons	sommes parti(e)s	partions	partirons	partirions	partions	partons
	partez	êtes parti(e)(s)	partiez	partirez	partiriez	partiez	partez
	partent	sont parti(e)s	partaient	partiront	partiraient	partent	
pleuvoir *to rain*	pleut	a plu	pleuvait	pleuvra	pleuvrait	pleuve	
pouvoir *to be able, can*	peux	ai pu	pouvais	pourrai	pourrais	puisse	
	peux	as pu	pouvais	pourras	pourrais	puisses	
	peut	a pu	pouvait	pourra	pourrait	puisse	
	pouvons	avons pu	pouvions	pourrons	pourrions	puissions	
	pouvez	avez pu	pouviez	pourrez	pourriez	puissiez	
	peuvent	ont pu	pouvaient	pourront	pourraient	puissent	
prendre *to take*	prends	ai pris	prenais	prendrai	prendrais	prenne	
	prends	as pris	prenais	prendras	prendrais	prennes	prends
	prend	a pris	prenait	prendra	prendrait	prenne	
	prenons	avons pris	prenions	prendrons	prendrions	prenions	prenons
	prenez	avez pris	preniez	prendrez	prendriez	preniez	prenez
	prennent	ont pris	prenaient	prendront	prendraient	prennent	
recevoir *to receive*	reçois	ai reçu	recevais	recevrai	recevrais	reçoive	
	reçois	as reçu	recevais	recevras	recevrais	reçoives	reçois
	reçoit	a reçu	recevait	recevra	recevrait	reçoive	
	recevons	avons reçu	recevions	recevrons	recevrions	recevions	recevons
	recevez	avez reçu	receviez	recevrez	recevriez	receviez	recevez
	reçoivent	ont reçu	recevaient	recevront	recevraient	reçoivent	
rire *to laugh*	ris	ai ri	riais	rirai	rirais	rie	
	ris	as ri	riais	riras	rirais	ries	ris
	rit	a ri	riait	rira	rirait	rie	
	rions	avons ri	riions	rirons	ririons	riions	rions
	riez	avez ri	riiez	rirez	ririez	riiez	riez
	rient	ont ri	riaient	riront	riraient	rient	
savoir *to know*	sais	ai su	savais	saurai	saurais	sache	
	sais	as su	savais	sauras	saurais	saches	sache
	sait	a su	savait	saura	saurait	sache	
	savons	avons su	savions	saurons	saurions	sachions	sachons
	savez	avez su	saviez	saurez	sauriez	sachiez	sachez
	savent	ont su	savaient	sauront	sauraient	sachent	

VERBES IRRÉGULIERS (SUITE)

VERBE INFINITIF	PRÉSENT	INDICATIF PASSÉ COMPOSÉ	IMPARFAIT	FUTUR	CONDITIONNEL PRÉSENT	SUBJONCTIF PRÉSENT	IMPÉRATIF
sortir	sors	suis sorti(e)	sortais	sortirai	sortirais	sorte	
to go out	sors	es sorti(e)	sortais	sortiras	sortirais	sortes	sors
	sort	est sorti(e)	sortait	sortira	sortirait	sorte	
	sortons	sommes sorti(e)s	sortions	sortirons	sortirions	sortions	sortons
	sortez	êtes sorti(e)(s)	sortiez	sortirez	sortiriez	sortiez	sortez
	sortent	sont sorti(e)s	sortaient	sortiront	sortiraient	sortent	
suivre	suis	ai suivi	suivais	suivrai	suivrais	suive	
to follow	suis	as suivi	suivais	suivras	suivrais	suives	suis
	suit	a suivi	suivait	suivra	suivrait	suive	
	suivons	avons suivi	suivions	suivrons	suivrions	suivions	suivons
	suivez	avez suivi	suiviez	suivrez	suivriez	suiviez	suivez
	suivent	ont suivi	suivaient	suivront	suivraient	suivent	
venir	viens	suis venu(e)	venais	viendrai	viendrais	vienne	
to come	viens	es venu(e)	venais	viendras	viendrais	viennes	viens
	vient	est venu(e)	venait	viendra	viendrait	vienne	
	venons	sommes venu(e)s	venions	viendrons	viendrions	venions	venons
	venez	êtes venu(e)(s)	veniez	viendrez	viendriez	veniez	venez
	viennent	sont venu(e)s	venaient	viendront	viendraient	viennent	
vivre	vis	ai vécu	vivais	vivrai	vivrais	vive	
to live	vis	as vécu	vivais	vivras	vivrais	vives	vis
	vit	a vécu	vivait	vivra	vivrait	vive	
	vivons	avons vécu	vivions	vivrons	vivrions	vivions	vivons
	vivez	avez vécu	viviez	vivrez	vivriez	viviez	vivez
	vivent	ont vécu	vivaient	vivront	vivraient	vivent	
voir	vois	ai vu	voyais	verrai	verrais	voie	
to see	vois	as vu	voyais	verras	verrais	voies	vois
	voit	a vu	voyait	verra	verrait	voie	
	voyons	avons vu	voyions	verrons	verrions	voyions	voyons
	voyez	avez vu	voyiez	verrez	verriez	voyiez	voyez
	voient	ont vu	voyaient	verront	verraient	voient	
vouloir	veux	ai voulu	voulais	voudrai	voudrais	veuille	
to want,	veux	as voulu	voulais	voudras	voudrais	veuilles	veuille
to wish	veut	a voulu	voulait	voudra	voudrait	veuille	
	voulons	avons voulu	voulions	voudrons	voudrions	voulions	veuillons
	voulez	avez voulu	vouliez	voudrez	voudriez	vouliez	veuillez
	veulent	ont voulu	voulaient	voudront	voudraient	veuillent	

VOCABULAIRE français–anglais

This list contains words appearing in *Horizons,* except for absolute cognates. The definitions of active vocabulary words are followed by the number of the chapter where they are first presented. A (P) refers to the *Chapitre préliminaire.* When several translations, separated by commas, are listed before a chapter number, they are all considered active. Since verbs are sometimes introduced lexically in the infinitive before the conjugation of the present indicative is presented, consult the *Index* to find out the chapter where a conjugation is introduced. An *(m)*, *(f)*, or *(pl)* following a noun indicates that it is masculine, feminine, or plural. *Inv* means that a word is invariable. An asterisk before a word beginning with an **h** indicates that the **h** is aspirate.

A

à to, at, in (P); **À bientôt.** See you soon. **à cause de** due to, because of; **À ce soir.** See you tonight/this evening. (2); **à côté (de)** next to (3); **À demain.** See you tomorrow. (P); **à... heure(s)** at . . . o'clock (P); **à la campagne** in the country (3); **à la française** French-style; **à la maison** at home (P); **à la page...** on page . . . (P); **à l'avance** in advance (9); **à l'étranger** abroad (9); **à l'heure** on time (4); **à l'université** at the university (P); **à peu près** about; **à pied** on foot (4); **À plus (tard)!** See you later! (P); **À quelle heure?** At what time? (P); **à suivre** to be continued (6); **À tout à l'heure.** See you in a little while. (6); **au café** at the café (2); **au coin de** on the corner of (10); **au cours de** in the course of, during, while on (10); **au-dessus de** above; **au premier étage** on the first (second) floor (3); **Au revoir.** Good-bye. (P); **à votre avis** in your opinion (8); **café *(m)* au lait** coffee with milk (2); **du lundi au vendredi** from Monday to Friday *(every week)* (P); **j'habite à** *(+ city)* I live in *(+ city)* (P)
abandonner to abandon, to leave
abolir to abolish
abonnement *(m)* subscription
abonner: s'abonner à to subscribe to
abord: d'abord first (4)
abricot *(m)* apricot
abriter to shelter
absolument absolutely
Acadie *(f)* Acadia
accent *(m)* accent (P); **accent aigu / circonflexe / grave** acute / circumflex / grave accent (P); **Ça s'écrit avec ou sans accent?** That's written with or without an accent? (P)
accepter to accept (7)
accès *(m)* access (10); **accès Wi-Fi** *(m)* Wi-Fi access (10)
accessoire *(m)* accessory
accidentellement accidentally
accompagner to accompany
accomplir to accomplish
accord *(m)* agreement; **D'accord!** Okay! (2), Agreed!; **se mettre d'accord** to come to an agreement
accorder to give; **s'accorder** to grant each other
achat *(m)* purchase
acheter to buy (4)
acide gras (trans) *(m)* (trans) fatty acid
acteur *(m)* actor (6)
actif (active) active, working
activité *(f)* activity (2)
actrice *(f)* actress (6)
actuellement currently
adapter: s'adapter to adapt

addition *(f)* check, bill
adjectif *(m)* adjective (3)
administratif(-ive): centre administratif *(m)* administration building
admirer to admire (9)
adorer to adore, to love (5)
adresse *(f)* address (3); **adresse** *(f)* **mail** e-mail address (3)
aérien(ne) aerial
aérobic *(f)* aerobics: **faire de l'aérobic** to do aerobics (8)
aéroport *(m)* airport (10)
affaire *(f)* thing, belonging, business; **femme d'affaires** businesswoman (5); **homme d'affaires** businessman (5)
affiché(e) posted
africain(e) African
Afrique *(f)* Africa (9); **Afrique** *(f)* **du Sud** South Africa
âge *(m)* age (4); **Quel âge a... ?** How old is . . . ? (4)
âgé(e) old (4)
agence *(f)* **de voyages** travel agency (9)
agent *(m)* agent; **agent** *(m)* **de police** police officer; **agent** *(m)* **de voyages** travel agent (9)
agir to act, to take action
agité(e) agitated
agneau *(m)* lamb
agréable pleasant (1)
agricole agricultural
aider to help (5); **Je peux vous aider?** May I help you? (5)
aïe ouch
aigu(ë) acute (P), shrill
ail *(m)* garlic
aile *(f)* wing
ailleurs elsewhere; **par ailleurs** furthermore
aimable kind, amiable
aimer to like, to love (2); **Aimeriez-vous... ?** Would you like . . . ? (8); **aimer mieux** to like better, to prefer (2); **Est-ce que tu aimes/ vous aimez... ?** Do you like . . . ? (1); **J'aime/ Je n'aime pas...** I like/I don't like . . . (1); **J'aimerais...** I would like . . . (8); **J'aimerais autant...** I would just as soon . . . (10); **s'aimer** to love each other (7)
aîné(e) oldest *(child)*
ainsi thus; **ainsi que** as well as
air *(m)* air, look, appearance; **avoir l'air** *(+ adjective)* to look / to seem *(+ adjective)* (4); **Ça a l'air bien.** It/That seems nice. (3); **de plein air** outdoor (4)
aise *(f)* ease; **mal à l'aise** ill at ease
aisé(e): classe aisée *(f)* upper class
ajouter to add
alcool *(m)* alcohol (8)
alcoolisé(e) alcoholic
Algérie *(f)* Algeria (9)
algérien(ne) Algerian

alignements *(mpl)* aligned standing stones
aliment *(m)* food
alimentaire food
Allemagne *(f)* Germany (9)
allemand *(m)* German
allemand(e) German
aller (à) to go (to) (2); **aller à la chasse** to go hunting; **aller à la pêche** to go fishing; **aller à pied** to walk, to go on foot (4); **aller simple** *(m)* one-way ticket (9); **aller très bien à quelqu'un** to look very good on someone; **aller voir** to go see, to visit *(a person)* (4); **billet aller-retour** *(m)* round-trip ticket (9); **Ça va?** Is it going okay? *(familiar)* (P); **Ça va.** It's going fine. (P); **Comment allez-vous?** How are you? *(formal)* (P); **Comment ça va?,** How's it going? *(familiar)* (P); **Comment vas-tu?** How are you? *(informal)*; **je vais** I go, I am going (2); **Je vais très bien** I'm doing very well. (P); **On va... ?** Shall we go . . . ? (4); **Qu'est-ce que vous allez prendre?** What are you going to have? (2); **Qu'est-ce qui ne va pas?** What's wrong? (10); **s'en aller** to go away
allergie *(f)* allergy (10)
allier unite, bring together; **allié(e)** allied
allô hello *(on the telephone)* (6)
allumer to light
alors so, then, therefore (1); **alors que** whereas
alphabet *(m)* alphabet (P)
alpinisme *(m)* mountain climbing; **faire de l'alpinisme** to go mountain climbing
amande *(f)* almond
amant(e) *(mf)* lover
améliorer to improve
amener to take, to bring
américain(e) American (P); **à l'américaine** American-style (8)
Amérindien(ne) *(mf)* Native American
Amérique *(f)* America (9); **Amérique centrale** *(f)* Central America (9); **Amérique** *(f)* **du Nord** North America (9); **Amérique** *(f)* **du Sud** South America (9)
ami(e) *(mf)* friend (P)
amitié *(f)* friendship
amour *(m)* love (6); **film** *(m)* **d'amour** romantic movie (6); **le grand amour** *(m)* true love (7)
amoureux(-euse) (de) in love (with) (6); **tomber amoureux(-euse) de** to fall in love with (6); **vie amoureuse** *(f)* love life
amphithéâtre *(m)* lecture hall
ampleur *(f)* scale, scope
ampoule *(f)* light bulb
amusant(e) fun (1)
amuser to amuse; **s'amuser** to have fun (7)
an *(m)* year (5); **avoir... ans** to be . . . years old (4); **jour** *(m)* **de l'An** *(m)* New Year's Day

ananas *(m)* pineapple
anchois *(m)* anchovy
ancien(ne) former, old, ancient
anciennement formerly
ange *(m)* angel
anglais *(m)* English (P)
anglais(e) English
Angleterre *(f)* England; **Nouvelle-Angleterre**
  (f) New England
anglophone English-speaking
angoisse *(f)* anguish
animal *(m)* *(pl* **animaux)** animal (3)
animé(e) animated; **dessin animé** *(m)* cartoon
année *(f)* year (4); **les années** *(fpl)* **soixante**
  the sixties
annexion *(f)* annexation
anniversaire *(m)* birthday (4); **anniversaire** *(m)*
  de mariage wedding anniversary
annonce *(f)* advertisement, announcement
anorak *(m)* ski jacket, anorak (5)
antillais(e) West Indian
Antilles *(fpl)* West Indies (9)
antimicrobien(ne) antimicrobial
antipathique disagreeable, unpleasant (1)
antique ancient
août *(m)* August (4)
apéritif (apéro) *(m)* (before-dinner) drink (8)
appareil *(m)* device, apparatus, appliance
apparence *(f)* appearance
apparenté(e) related
appartement *(m)* apartment (3)
appartenir (à) to belong (to)
appeler to call; **appelé(e)** called; **Comment**
  s'appelle... ? What is . . . 's name? (4);
  Comment t'appelles-tu? What's your
  name? *(informal);* **Comment vous appelez-**
  vous? What's your name? *(formal)* (P); **Il/**
  Elle s'appelle... His/Her name is . . . (4); **Je**
  m'appelle... My name is . . . (P); **s'appeler**
  to be named (7), to be called; **Tu t'appelles**
  comment? What's your name? *(informal)*
  (P)
appétit *(m)* appetite
apporter to bring
apprécier to appreciate (6), to like
apprendre to learn (4)
apprentissage *(m)* apprenticeship
approcher: s'approcher (de) to approach
approprié(e) appropriate
approximatif(-ive) approximate
après after, afterwards (P); **après les cours** after
  class (2); **d'après** according to
après-demain the day after tomorrow (4)
après-midi *(m)* afternoon (P); **cet**
  après-midi this afternoon (4); **Il est une**
  heure de l'après-midi. It's one o'clock in
  the afternoon. (P); **l'après-midi** in the
  afternoon, afternoons (P)
arabe *(m)* Arabic
araignée *(f)* spider; **araignée** *(f)* **de mer** spider
  crab
arbre *(m)* tree (1)
arc *(m)* arch, bow
archéologique archeological
archipel *(m)* archipelago
argent *(m)* money, silver (2)
Argentine *(f)* Argentina (9)
armée *(f)* army
arracher: s'arracher les cheveux to pull out
  your hair
arrêt *(m)* stop; **arrêt** *(m)* **de bus** bus stop (3)
arrêter to arrest, to stop; **s'arrêter** to stop (7)
arrivage *(m)* delivery
arrivée *(f)* arrival (9)

arriver to arrive (2), to happen
arrogance *(f)* arrogance (7)
art *(m)* art (1); **les arts** the arts (1); **les beaux-**
  arts the fine arts
article *(m)* article (9)
artisanal(e) *(mpl* **artisanaux)** handcrafted
artiste *(mf)* artist, performer
ascenseur *(m)* elevator (3)
Asie *(f)* Asia (9)
aspect physique *(m)* physical appearance (7)
asperge *(f)* asparagus
aspirine *(f)* aspirin (10)
assassiner to murder, to assassinate
asseoir: Asseyez-vous. Sit down.; **s'asseoir** to
  sit (down)
assez fairly, rather (P); **assez (de)** enough (of) (1)
assiette *(f)* plate
assis(e) seated (9)
assister à to attend
association caritative *(f)* charitable
  organization
associer to associate; **associé(e)** associated
assurance *(f)* insurance
atelier *(m)* workshop
Atlantique *(m)* Atlantic
atroce atrocious, dreadful
attaque *(f)* attack; **attaque** *(f)* **d'apoplexie**
  stroke; **être d'attaque** to feel fit
attendre to wait (for) (7); **s'attendre à** to
  expect to
attente *(f)* waiting
attention: faire attention (à) to pay attention
  (to), to watch out (for) (8)
attirant(e) attractive
attirer to attract
attraper to catch, to get hold of
aube *(f)* dawn
auberge *(f)* inn; **auberge** *(f)* **de jeunesse** youth
  hostel (10)
aubergine *(f)* eggplant
auburn *(inv)* auburn (4)
aucun(e): ne... aucun(e) no, none, not one
audacieux(-euse) audacious, bold
au-dessus above
auditif(-ive) auditory
augmenter to augment, to raise
aujourd'hui today (P)
auparavant beforehand
auprès de among
auquel (à laquelle, auxquels, auxquelles) to
  which
aussi too, also (P); **aussi... que** as . . . as (1)
austral(e) *(mpl* **austraux)** southern
Australie *(f)* Australia (9)
autant (de)... (que) as much . . . (as), as many
  . . . (as); **J'aimerais autant...** I would just as
  soon . . . (10)
autobus *(m)* bus (4); **en autobus** by bus (4)
autocar *(m)* bus (4); **en autocar** by bus (4)
automne *(m)* autumn, fall (5); **en automne** in
  autumn (5)
autoportrait *(m)* self-portrait
autour de around
autre other (P); **autre part** somewhere else;
  dans un autre cours in another class (P);
  quelquefois... d'autres fois sometimes .
  . . other times (7); **Qu'est-ce que je peux**
  vous proposer d'autre? What else can I get
  you? (8)
autrefois formerly, in the past
Autriche *(f)* Austria
auxiliaire *(m)* auxiliary
avance *(f)* advance; **à l'avance** in advance (9);
  en avance early

avancer to advance
avant before (P); **avant de (faire)** before
  (doing) (7); **avant tout** above all
avantage *(m)* advantage
avec with (P); **avec moi / toi / lui / elle / nous /**
  vous / eux / elles with me / you / him /
  her / us / you / them *(m)* / them *(f)* (2);
  avec ma famille with my family (P); **Avec**
  plaisir! With pleasure! (6)
avenir *(m)* future
aventure *(f)* adventure; **film** *(m)* **d'aventure**
  adventure movie
avenue *(f)* avenue (10)
avion *(m)* airplane (4); **en avion** by airplane (4)
avis *(m)* opinion; **à votre avis** in your opinion
  (8)
avoir to have (3); **avoir... ans** to be . . . years
  old (4); **avoir besoin de** to need (4); **avoir**
  chaud to be hot (4); **avoir cours** to have
  class (6); **avoir de la fièvre** to have fever;
  avoir du mal à... to have difficulty . . . ,
  to have a hard time . . . ; **avoir envie de**
  to feel like, to want (4); **avoir faim** to be
  hungry (4); **avoir froid** to be cold (4); **avoir**
  l'air (+ *adjective)* to look / to seem
  (+ *adjective)* (4); **avoir le nez bouché**
  to have a stopped-up nose; **avoir le nez**
  qui coule to have a runny nose; **avoir**
  les cheveux/les yeux... to have . . . hair/
  eyes (4); **avoir lieu** to take place; **avoir**
  l'intention de to plan on, to intend to (4);
  avoir mal (à) one's . . . hurts (10), to ache;
  avoir peur (de) to be afraid of, to fear
  (4); **avoir pitié (de)** to have pity (on / for)
  (10); **avoir raison** to be right (4); **avoir soif**
  to be thirsty (4); **avoir sommeil** to be sleepy
  (4); **avoir tort** to be wrong (4); **il y a...**
  there is/there are . . . (1), ago (5); **Quel âge**
  a... ? How old is . . . ? (4)
avril *(m)* April (4)
ayant having

B

baccalauréat (bac) *(m) a comprehensive*
  examination at the end of secondary school
bacon *(m)* bacon (8)
bagages *(mpl)* baggage
baguette *(f)* loaf of French bread (8)
baie *(f)* bay
bain *(m)* bath (7); **maillot** *(m)* **de bain**
  swimsuit (5); **prendre un bain** *(m)* **de soleil**
  to sunbathe (4); **salle** *(f)* **de bains** bathroom
  (3)
baiser *(m)* kiss
baisser to lower
bal *(m)* ball, dance (6)
balcon *(m)* balcony (10)
baleine *(f)* whale
ballet *(m)* ballet (9)
ballon *(m)* ball
banal(e) *(mpl* **banaux)** commonplace, banal
banane *(f)* banana (8)
bancaire banking; **carte** *(f)* **bancaire** bank card,
  debit card (9)
bande-annonce *(f)* movie trailer
bande déssinée *(f)* comic strip, comic book
banlieue *(f)* suburbs (3); **en banlieue** in the
  suburbs (3)
banque *(f)* bank (10)
banquier *(m)* banker
barbe *(f)* beard (4)
barrer to cross out
bas *(m)* bottom
bas(se) low; **table basse** *(f)* coffee table

basant: en vous basant sur based on
base: à base de made from
basé(e) sur based on (6)
baseball *(m)* baseball (2)
basilique *(f)* basilica
basket *(m)* basketball (1)
baskets *(fpl)* sneakers, tennis shoes (5)
bataille *(f)* battle
bateau *(m)* boat (4); en bateau by boat (4); faire du bateau to go boating (5)
bâtiment *(m)* building
batterie *(f)* drums (2)
battre to beat; se battre to fight
BD (bande déssinée) *(f)* comic strip, comic book
beau (bel, belle, *pl* beaux, belles) beautiful, handsome (1); beau-frère *(m)* brother-in-law; beau-père *(m)* father-in-law (4); beaux-arts *(mpl)* fine arts; beaux-parents *(mpl)* stepparents, in-laws (4); belle-mère *(f)* mother-in-law (4); belle-sœur *(f)* sister-in-law; Il fait beau. The weather's nice. (5)
beaucoup a lot (P); beaucoup (de) a lot (of) (1)
beauté *(f)* beauty (7)
bébé *(m)* baby
beige beige (3)
beignet *(m)* fritter
belge Belgian
Belgique *(f)* Belgium (9)
bénéficier to benefit
bénéfique beneficial
bénévole benevolent, volunteer
berbère Berber
berceuse *(f)* lullaby
besoin *(m)* need; avoir besoin de to need (4)
bête *(f)* beast (6), animal
bête stupid, dumb (1)
bêtise *(f)* foolish thing, stupidity
beurre *(m)* butter (8); beurre *(m)* de cacahuète peanut butter
beurré(e) buttered
bibliothèque *(f)* library (1), bookcase
bien *(m)* good; biens *(mpl)* goods
bien well (P), very; à bien des égards in many regards; bien d'autres many others; bien que although; Bien sûr! Of course! (5); Ça a l'air bien. It/That seems nice. (3); c'est bien de... it's good to . . . (10)
bien-être *(m)* well-being
bienfait *(m)* benefit
bienfaiteur *(m)*, bienfaitrice *(f)* benefactor
bientôt soon; À bientôt. See you soon.
bienvenu(e) welcome
bière *(f)* beer (2)
bifteck *(m)* steak (8); bifteck hâché *(m)* ground meat
bikini *(m)* bikini (5)
bilan *(m)* assessment
bilingue bilingual
billet *(m)* ticket (9), bill; billet *(m)* d'avion plane ticket (9); distributeur *(m)* de billets ATM machine (10)
bio organic; produits bio *(mpl)* organic products (8)
biologie *(f)* biology (1)
biscotte *(f)* melba toast
bise *(f)* kiss
bistro(t) *(m)* restaurant, pub (6)
blanc(he) white (3); vin blanc *(m)* white wine (2)
blanquette *(f)* stew *(usually veal)*
blessure *(f)* injury
bleu(e) blue (3); carte *(f)* bleue credit card (9)
blog *(m)* blog (9)

bloguer to blog
blond(e) blond (4)
blouson *(m)* windbreaker, jacket
Blu-ray: lecteur *(m)* Blu-ray Blu-ray player (3)
bœuf *(m)* beef (8); bœuf bourguignon *(m)* beef burgundy
bohème bohemian
boire to drink (4)
boisson *(f)* drink (2)
boîte *(f)* box, can (8); boîte *(f)* de nuit nightclub (1)
bol *(m)* bowl
bon(ne) good (1); Bon anniversaire! Happy birthday!; Bonne année! Happy New Year!; Bonne idée! Good idea! (4); Bonne journée! Have a good day!; Bon séjour! Enjoy your stay! (10); Bon week-end! Have a good weekend!
bonbon *(m)* candy
bonheur *(m)* happiness (7)
bonhomme *(m)* man, guy, fellow
Bonjour. Hello., Good morning. (P)
bonne *(f)* maid, nanny
Bonsoir. Good evening. (P)
bord *(m)* edge; à bord on board; au bord de at the edge of; bord *(m)* de la mer seaside
border to border
botanique botanical
botte *(f)* boot (5)
bouche *(f)* mouth (10)
bouché(e) stopped-up; cidre bouché *(m)* bottled cider
boucherie *(f)* butcher's shop (8)
boudin *(m)* blood sausage
bouger to move
bouillabaisse *(f)* fish soup
bouillir to boil
bouillon *(m)* broth
boulangerie *(f)* bakery (8); boulangerie-pâtisserie bakery-pastry shop (8)
boule *(f)* ball, scoop
boulevard *(m)* boulevard (10)
bouleversant(e) overwhelming, very touching
boulot *(m) (familiar)* work
bouquiniste *(mf)* secondhand bookseller
bourg *(m)* town
bout *(m)* end (3); au bout (de) at the end (of) (3)
bouteille (de) *(f)* bottle (of) (8)
boutique *(f)* shop (10); boutique *(f)* de cadeaux gift shop (10)
bras *(m)* arm (10)
bref (brève) short, brief; Bref,... In short, . . ., To be brief, . . .
Brésil *(m)* Brazil (9)
Bretagne *(f)* Brittany
breton *(m)* Breton *(language)*
breton(ne) Breton, from Brittany
brevet *(m)* certificate, diploma
bricoler to do handiwork
brioche *(f)* brioche *(a type of soft bread)*
brique *(f)* brick
britannique British
brochette *(f)* skewer
brocoli *(m)* broccoli
bronzer to tan (9)
brosser to brush; se brosser (les cheveux / les dents) to brush (one's hair / one's teeth) (7)
brouillard *(m)* fog, mist, haze
bruit *(m)* noise (10)
brûler to burn; se brûler la main to burn your hand

brun(e) *(with hair)* medium/dark brown (4), brunette, darkhaired
Bruxelles Brussels
bruyant(e) noisy
bulletin *(m)* d'abonnement subscription form
bureau *(m)* desk (3), office (1); bureau *(m)* de change currency exchange (10); bureau *(m)* de poste post office (10); bureau *(m)* de tabac tobacco shop
bus *(m)* bus (3); arrêt *(m)* de bus bus stop (3); en bus by bus (4)
but *(m)* goal

C

ça that (P); Ça fait combien? How much is it? (2); Ça fait... euros. That's . . . euros. (2); Ça lui plaît? Does he/she like it? (9); Ça s'écrit comment? How is that written? (P); Ça s'écrit... That's written . . . (P); Ça te/vous dit? How does that sound to you? (2); Ça te plaît. You like it. (3); Ça va? Is it going okay? *(familiar)* (P); Ça va. It's going fine. (P); C'est ça! That's right! (1); comme ci comme ça so-so (P); Comment ça va? How's it going? *(familiar)* (P)
cabine *(f)* d'essayage fitting room (5); cabine *(f)* téléphonique telephone booth
cacahuète *(f)* peanut; beurre *(m)* de cacahuète peanut butter
cacher to hide; se cacher to hide oneself, to be hidden
cadeau *(m)* gift, present (10); boutique *(f)* de cadeaux gift shop (10)
cadien(ne) Cajun (4)
cadre *(m)* frame, surroundings
café *(m)* café (1), coffee (2); café *(m)* au lait coffee with milk (2)
cahier *(m)* workbook, notebook (P)
calcul *(m)* calculation, calculus
calculer to calculate
Californie *(f)* California (9)
calme calm (10)
calmement calmly
calmer: se calmer to calm down
calorie *(f)* calorie (8)
calorique high in calories
camarade *(mf)* pal; camarade *(mf)* de chambre roommate (P); camarade *(mf)* de classe classmate
camerounais(e) Cameroonian
campagne *(f)* country (3), campaign; à la campagne in the country (3)
camping *(m)* camping, campground (5); faire du camping to go camping (5)
campus *(m)* campus (1)
Canada *(m)* Canada (9)
canadien(ne) Canadian (P)
canapé *(m)* couch (3), open-faced sandwich
canard *(m)* duck (8)
candidat(e) *(mf)* candidate, applicant
canne à sucre *(f)* sugar cane
canoë *(m)* canoeing
caprice *(m)* whim
car *(m)* bus (4); en car by bus (4)
car because
caractère *(m)* character; en caractères gras boldfaced; trait *(m)* de caractère character trait (7)
carafe (de) *(f)* carafe (of) *(a decanter)* (8)
caraïbe Caribbean; mer *(f)* des Caraïbes Caribbean Sea
caramélisé(e) caramelized
caritatif(-ive) charitable
carotte *(f)* carrot (8)

carré (m) square; **Vieux Carré** (m) French Quarter (4)

carrière (f) career

carte (f) menu (8), card (9), map; **carte** (f) **bancaire** bank card, debit card (9); **carte** (f) **bleue** credit card (9); **carte** (f) **de crédit** credit card (9); **carte** (f) **d'identité** identity card; **carte** (f) **postale** postcard (9); **carte** (f) **téléphonique** telephone card (10)

cas (m) case; **dans tous les cas** in any case

cascade (f) waterfall

casquette (f) cap

casser to break; **se casser la jambe** to break one's leg

casserole (f) pan

catégorie (f) category

cathédrale (f) cathedral

catholique (mf) Catholic (1)

cauchemar (m) nightmare

cause (f) cause; **à cause de** because of

cave (f) cellar

CD (m) CD (3); **lecteur** (m) **CD** CD player (3)

ce (cet, cette) this, that (3); **ce (cet, cette)... ci** this . . . over here (5); **ce (cet, cette)... là** that . . . over there (5); **ce que** what, that which (7); **ce qui** what, that which (7); **ces** these, those (3); **ce semestre** this semester (P); **ce soir** tonight, this evening (2); **Ce sont...** They are . . ., These are . . ., Those are . . . (1); **C'est...** It's . . . (P), He / She / This / That is . . . (1); **c'est-à-dire** in other words, that is to say; **Qu'est-ce que c'est?** What is it? (2); **Qui est-ce?** Who is it? (2)

céder to give up

ceinture (f) belt

cela that; **depuis cela** since then

célèbre famous (4)

célébrer to celebrate

céleri (m) celery

célibataire single, unmarried (1)

cellule (f) cell

celtique Celtic

celui (celle) the one

cendre (f) ash

cendrier (m) ashtray

censé(e) supposed

censure (f) censorship

cent (m) one hundred (3)

centime (m) centime (one hundredth part of a euro) (2)

central(e) (mpl centraux) central; **Amérique** (f) **centrale** Central America (9)

centre (m) center; **centre administratif** (m) administration building; **centre commercial** (m) shopping center, mall (4); **centre** (m) **d'étudiants** student center

centre-ville (m) downtown (3)

cependant however

céréales (fpl) cereal (8)

cerise (f) cherry (8)

certain(e) certain; **certains** some, certain people (3)

certainement certainly

cesser to cease

ceux (celles) those (ones) (8)

chacun(e) each one

chagrin (m) sorrow

chaîne (f) chain; **chaîne de télévision** television channel; **chaîne hi-fi** (f) stereo (3)

chaise (f) chair (3)

chalet (m) **à la montagne** ski lodge (10)

chaleur (f) warmth

chaleureux(-euse) warm

chambre (f) bedroom (3); **camarade** (mf) **de chambre** roommate (P); **chambre** (f) **d'hôte** bed and breakfast; **chambre double** (f) double room (9); **chambre simple** single room (f) (10)

champ (m) field; **champ** (m) **de bataille** battlefield

champignon (m) mushroom

chance (f) luck (5); **Quelle chance!** What luck! (5)

change: **bureau** (m) **de change** currency exchange (10)

changement (m) change

changer to change (6); **changer de l'argent** to exchange money (9)

chanson (f) song

chanter to sing (2)

chanteur(-euse) (mf) singer

chapeau (m) hat

chapelle (f) chapel

chapitre (m) chapter

chaque each, every (3)

charcuterie (f) delicatessen, deli meats, cold cuts (8)

charger to charge, to load; **chargé(e) (de)** busy (schedule), in charge (of); **se charger de** to take charge of

charmant(e) charming

chasse (f) hunt, hunting; **aller à la chasse** to go hunting

chasser to hunt, to make go away

chasseur (m) hunter

chat (m) cat (3)

châtain light/medium brown (with hair) (4)

château (m) castle

chaud(e) hot (2); **avoir chaud** to be hot (4); **chocolat chaud** (m) hot chocolate (2); **Il fait chaud.** It's hot. (5)

chauffeur (m) driver

chaussette (f) sock

chausson (m) **aux pommes** apple turnover

chaussure (f) shoe (5)

chef (m) head, boss, chief

chef-d'œuvre (m) masterpiece

chef-lieu (m) administrative center

chemin (m) road; **chemin** (m) **de fer** railroad; **indiquer le chemin** to give directions, to show the way (10)

chemise (f) shirt (5); **chemise** (f) **de nuit** nightgown

chemisier (m) blouse (5)

chèque (m) check (9); **chèque** (m) **de voyage** traveler's check

cher(-ère) expensive (3), dear

chercher to look for (3), to seek; **aller / venir chercher quelqu'un** to go / come pick up someone (10)

chéri(e) (mf) honey, darling

cheval (m) (pl chevaux) horse; **faire du cheval** to go horseback riding

cheveux (mpl) hair (4)

cheville (f) ankle; **se fouler la cheville** to sprain one's ankle

chèvre (m) goat cheese

chez... at / in / to / by . . . 's house/place (2); in (a person) (7)

chien (m) dog (3)

chiffre (m) number, numeral

Chili (m) Chile (9)

chimie (f) chemistry (1)

Chine (f) China (9)

chinois (m) Chinese

chirurgie (f) surgery

chocolat (m) chocolate (2); **gâteau** (m) **au chocolat** chocolate cake (8); **pain au chocolat** (m) chocolate-filled croissant (8)

choisir (de faire) to choose (to do) (8)

choix (m) choice (8)

chose (f) thing (3); **quelque chose** something (2)

chou (m) cabbage; **choux** (mpl) **de Bruxelles** Brussels sprouts

choucroute (f) sauerkraut

chou-fleur (m) cauliflower

chrysanthème (m) chrysanthemum

chute (f) waterfall

ci: **ce (cet, cette)...-ci** this . . . (5); **ce mois-ci** this month (4); **ces...-ci** these . . . (5); **ci-dessous** below; **ci-dessus** above; **comme ci comme ça** so-so (P)

ciao bye (informal)

ciel (m) sky

cimetière (m) cemetery

cinéaste (mf) filmmaker

ciné-club (m) cinema club (2)

cinéma (m) movie theater (1); **aller au cinéma** to go to the movies (2)

cinématographique film

cinq five (P)

cinquante fifty (P); **cinquante et un** fifty-one (P)

cinquième fifth (3)

circonstance (f) circumstance

circuler to circulate

cithare (f) zither

citoyen(ne) (mf) citizen

citron (m) lemon (2); **citron vert** (m) lime; **thé** (m) **au citron** tea with lemon (2)

civilisé(e) civilized

clair(e) light, clear; **bleu clair** light blue

claire (f) oyster bed

clairement clearly

classe (f) class (1); **classe** (f) **économique** economy class, coach (9); **première classe** (f) first class (9)

classé(e) ranked

classement (m) ranking

classique classical (1), classic (2)

clavier (m) keyboard

clé (f) key (10)

client(e) (mf) customer

climat (m) climate (9)

climatisation (f) air conditioning

climatisé(e) air-conditioned

coca (m) cola (2); **coca** (m) **light** diet cola (2)

coco (m) coconut

cocotier (m) coconut tree, palm tree

code (m) code; **code postal** (m) zip code (3)

cœur (m) heart; **au cœur de** in the heart of

coin (m) corner (3); **au coin de** on the corner of (10); **café** (m) **du coin** neighborhood café; **dans le coin (de)** in the corner (of) (3)

collation (f) snack

colle (f) glue, detention

collectionner to collect

collectivité (f) community

collège (m) middle school

collègue (mf) colleague

colline (f) hill

colocataire (mf) housemate (3)

Colombie (f) Colombia (9)

colon (mf) colonist

colonne (f) column

combien (de) how much, how many (3); **Ça fait combien? / C'est combien?** How much is it? (2); **Combien font... et / moins... ?** How much is . . . plus / minus . . . ? (P);

Pendant combien de temps? For how long? (5); **Vous êtes combien dans votre (ta) famille?** How many are there in your family? (4)

combinaison *(f)* slip, combination

comédie *(f)* comedy (6); **comédie musicale** *(f)* musical

comique comical

commander to order (2), to command

comme like, as, for (1), since (7); **comme ci comme ça** so-so (P); **comme tu vois** as you see (3); **tout comme** just as

commencement *(m)* beginning

commencer (à) to begin (to), to start (2); **Le cours de français commence à...** French class starts at . . . (P)

comment how (P); **Ça s'écrit comment?** How is that written? (P); **Comment allez-vous?** How are you? *(formal)* (P); **Comment ça va?** How's it going? *(familiar)* (P); **Comment dit-on... en français/en anglais?** How does one say . . . in French/in English? (P); **Comment est-il/elle (sont-ils/elles)?** What is he/she (are they) like? (1); **Comment? Répétez, s'il vous plaît.** What? Please repeat. (P); **Comment s'appelle... ?** What is . . . 's name? (4); **Comment vas-tu?** How are you? *(informal)*; **Comment vous appelez-vous?** What's your name? *(formal)* (P); **Tu t'appelles comment?** What's your name? *(informal)* (P)

commentaire *(m)* commentary

commerçant(e) *(mf)* shopkeeper (8), merchant

commerce *(m)* business (1)

commercial: centre commercial *(m)* shopping center, mall (4)

commettre to commit

commode *(f)* dresser, chest of drawers (3)

commode convenient

commodité *(f)* convenience, comfort

commun(e) common

communauté *(f)* community

communiquer to communicate (10)

compagnie *(f)* company; **en compagnie de** accompanied by

comparaison *(f)* comparison

comparer to compare (6); **comparé(e)** compared

compatibilité *(f)* compatibility (7)

compétence *(f)* skill, competency

complément d'objet direct / indirect *(m)* direct / indirect object

complet(-ète) complete (8); **avec une phrase complète** *(f)* with a complete sentence (P); **pain complet** *(m)* (loaf of) whole-grain bread (8)

complètement completely

complicité *(f)* bonding

comporter: se comporter to behave

composer to compose; **composé(e) de** composed of; **se composer de** to be made up of

compréhension *(f)* understanding

comprenant including

comprendre to understand (4), to include (8); **compris(e)** included (10); **Oui, je comprends. / Non, je ne comprends pas.** Yes, I understand. / No, I don't understand. (P); **Vous comprenez?** Do you understand? (P)

comptabilité *(f)* accounting

comptable *(mf)* accountant

compte *(m)* **en banque** bank account

compter to count, to plan on (9); **Comptez de... à...** Count from . . . to . . . (P)

concentrer: se concentrer sur to concentrate on

concerner to concern; **concernant** concerning

concert *(m)* concert (4); **de concert avec** along with

concombre *(m)* cucumber

concours *(m)* competition, competitive entrance examination

confiance *(f)* confidence; **avoir confiance** to have confidence (4); **faire confiance à** to trust

confirmer to confirm (10)

confit *(m)* **de canard** conserve of duck

confiture *(f)* jam, jelly (8)

confort *(m)* comfort

confortable comfortable (3)

conforter to comfort

confus(e) confused

congé *(m)* day off

conjuguer to conjugate

connaissance *(f)* acquaintance, knowledge; **faire la connaissance de** to meet *(for the first time)* (7)

connaître to know, to get to know, to be familiar / acquainted with (4); **Connaissez-vous...?** Do you know . . . ? (6); **faire connaître** to inform

connecter to connect; **se connecter à Internet** to log on to Internet

connu(e) known

conquérant(e) *(mf)* conqueror

conquête *(f)* conquest

consacrer to devote; **consacré(e) à** devoted to

conseil *(m)* piece of advice (8), council, committee

conseiller(-ère) *(mf)* counselor, adviser

conséquent: par conséquent consequently

conserver to keep

conserves *(fpl)* canned goods (8)

considérer to consider; **se considérer** to consider oneself

console *(f)* **de jeux** game console (3)

consommation *(f)* consumption, drink

consommer to consume

consonne *(f)* consonant

constamment constantly

construire to construct, to build; **construit(e)** built

consulat *(m)* consulate

contact *(m)* contact; **en contact** in contact (9)

conte *(m)* story (6); **conte** *(m)* **de fées** fairy tale (6)

contempler to contemplate

contemporain(e) contemporary

contenir to contain

content(e) happy, glad (8)

contenter: se contenter de to be happy to / with

continent *(m)* continent (9)

continu(e) continuous

continuer (tout droit) to continue (straight ahead) (10)

contraire *(m)* contrary; **au contraire** on the contrary

contrat *(m)* contract, agreement

contre against; **par contre** on the other hand

contrôle *(m)* control

contrôler to control (8); **contrôlé(e)** controlled, supervised

convenable appropriate, suitable

convenir to be suitable; **Ça te/vous convient?** Does that work for you? (9)

cool: assez cool pretty cool (P)

copain *(m)* boyfriend, *(male)* friend, buddy (2)

copier sur to copy from

copieux(-euse) copious, large (8)

copine *(f)* girlfriend, *(female)* friend, buddy (2)

coq *(m)* rooster

coquilles St-Jacques *(fpl)* scallops

corde *(f)* rope, cord

corporel(le) of the body

corps *(m)* body (7)

correctement correctly

correspondant(e) corresponding

correspondre (à) to correspond (to)

Corse *(f)* Corsica

corse *(m)* Corsican *(language)*

costume *(m)* suit *(for a man)* (5)

côte *(f)* coast; **Côte d'Azur** *(f)* Riviera; **côte** *(f)* **de porc** pork chop (8); **Côte d'Ivoire** *(f)* Ivory Coast (9)

côté *(m)* side (3); **à côté (de)** next to (3); **côté cour** on the courtyard side (10); **d'à côté** next-door

cou *(m)* neck

couchant setting

coucher: se coucher to go to bed (7); **chambre à coucher** *(f)* bedroom

couler to run *(liquids)*

couleur *(f)* color (3); **De quelle couleur est/sont... ?** What color is/are . . . ? (3)

coulis *(m)* purée

couloir *(m)* hall, corridor (3)

coup *(m)* stroke, blow; **coup** *(m)* **de foudre** love at first sight (7); **coup** *(m)* **de téléphone** telephone call; **tout à coup** all of a sudden (6); **tout d'un coup** all at once (6)

coupe *(f)* dessert dish

couper to cut; **se couper le doigt** to cut one's finger

cour *(f)* court, courtyard; **côté cour** on the courtyard side (10)

couramment fluently

courant(e) present, current, common; **au courant de** aware of

courgette *(f)* zucchini

courir to run (2)

courrier *(m)* mail; **courrier électronique** *(m)* e-mail

cours *(m)* class, course (P); **au cours de** in the course of, during, while on (10); **avoir cours** to have class (6); **cours** *(m)* **de français** French class (P); **cours** *(m)* **en ligne** online course (1); **dans un autre cours** in another class (P); **en cours** in class (P); **salle** *(f)* **de cours** classroom (1); **suivre un cours** to take a course

course *(f)* errand (5), race; **faire des courses** to run errands (5); **faire les courses** to go grocery shopping (5)

court(e) short (4)

cousin(e) *(mf)* cousin (4)

coûter to cost (5)

coutume *(f)* custom

couvert(e) de covered with

couverture *(f)* blanket, cover (3)

covoiturage *(m)* carpooling

cravate *(f)* tie (5)

crayon *(m)* pencil (P)

créancier(-ière) *(mf)* creditor

créatif(-ive) creative

crèche *(f)* *(government-sponsored)* day care

crédit: carte *(f)* **de crédit** credit card (9)

créer to create

crème *(f)* cream (8)

créole Creole

creuser to dig

crevette *(f)* shrimp (8)
crier to shout
crise *(f)* crisis
critique *(f)* criticism
Croatie *(f)* Croatia (9)
croire (à) (que) to believe (in) (that); **je crois** I think
croiser to run across, to bump into
croisière *(f)* cruise
croissant *(m)* croissant (8)
croissant(e) growing
croix *(f)* cross; **en croix** crossed
croque-madame *(m)* toasted ham-and-cheese sandwich with an egg on top
croque-monsieur *(m)* toasted ham-and-cheese sandwich
cru(e) raw
crudités *(fpl)* raw vegetables (8)
cruel(le) cruel (6)
crustacé *(m)* shellfish
cuiller (cuillère) *(f)* spoon
cuir *(m)* leather
cuisine *(f)* kitchen (3), cuisine, cooking (4); **faire la cuisine** to cook (5)
cuisinier(-ère) *(mf)* cook
cuisinière *(f)* stove
cuivre *(m)* copper
cultiver to cultivate (7); **cultivé(e)** cultivated
culture *(f)* culture (9), cultivation
culturel(le) cultural (4)
curieux(-euse) curious, odd
cyclisme *(m)* cycling

D

dame *(f)* lady
Danemark *(m)* Denmark
dans in (P); **dans la rue...** on . . . Street (10); **dans le centre-ville** downtown (3)
dansant(e) dancing
danse *(f)* dance
danser to dance (2)
danseur(-euse) *(mf)* dancer
date *(f)* date (4); **C'est quelle date?** What is the date? (4); **Quelle est la date?** What is the date? (4)
dater de to date from
de of, from, about (P); **de la, de l', du** some, any (8); **de luxe** deluxe (10); **De rien.** You're welcome. (P); **du lundi au vendredi** from Monday to Friday *(every week)* (P); **parler de** to talk about
débarquement *(m)* landing
déboussolé(e) disoriented
debout standing
début *(m)* beginning (6); **au début (de)** at the beginning (of) (6)
décédé(e) dead; deceased (4)
décembre *(m)* December (4)
décidément decidedly, for sure
décider to decide (6); **se décider** to make up one's mind
décision *(f)* decision (7); **prendre une décision** to make a decision (7)
décorer to decorate
découper to cut out
découverte *(f)* discovery
découvrir to discover; **découvrant** discovering
décret *(m)* decree
décrire to describe (9); **décrit(e)** described
dedans inside
défaut *(m)* fault (7)
défini(e) definite
définir to define
degré *(m)* degree

dégustation *(f)* tasting, sampling
déguster to sample
dehors outside; **en dehors de** outside of
déjà already (5)
déjeuner *(m)* lunch; **petit déjeuner** *(m)* breakfast (5)
déjeuner to have/eat lunch (2)
délicieux(-euse) delicious (6)
délirer: faire délirer to crack up
demain tomorrow (P); **À demain!** See you tomorrow! (P)
demande *(f)* request
demander to ask (for) (2); **se demander** to wonder
demi *(m)* draft beer (2)
demi(e) half (P); **demi-heure** *(f)* half hour (7); **Il est deux heures et demie.** It's half past two. (P); **un kilo et demi de** a kilo and a half of (8)
dénoncer to denounce, to turn in
dent *(f)* tooth (7)
dentaire dental
départ *(m)* departure (9)
département *(m)* department *(a French administrative region)*
dépassement *(m)* **de soi** surpassing oneself
dépendre (de) to depend (on) (5); **Ça dépend.** That depends.
dépense *(f)* expense
dépenser to spend
déplaisant(e) unpleasant
depuis since, for (7), from; **depuis cela** since then; **depuis que** since
dérivé(e) derived
dernier(-ère) last (5)
derrière behind (3)
des some (1)
dès since, right after; **dès que** as soon as
désaccord *(m)* disagreement
désagréable unpleasant (1)
désastreux(-euse) disastrous
descendre (de) to go down, to get off (5); **descendre dans / à** to stay at *(a hotel)* (5)
déshabiller to undress; **se déshabiller** to get undressed (7)
désigner to designate, to indicate
désirer to desire; **Vous désirez?** What would you like?, May I help you? (2)
désolé(e) sorry (8); **être désolé(e) que...** to be sorry that . . . (10)
désordre: en désordre in disorder (3)
dessert *(m)* dessert (8)
dessin *(m)* drawing; **dessin animé** *(m)* cartoon
dessiner to draw
dessous: ci-dessous below
dessus: au dessus de above; **par dessus** over
destin *(m)* destiny
détaillé(e) detailed
détendre: se détendre to relax
détenir to hold, to possess
détester to hate; **se détester** to hate each other (7)
détruit(e) destroyed
dette *(f)* debt
deux two (P); **deux-tiers** two-thirds
deuxième second (3)
devant in front of (3)
développement *(m)* development
développer to develop; **se développer** to be developed; **développé(e)** developed
devenir to become (4)
deviner to guess
devinette *(f)* riddle
devoir must, to have to, to owe (6); **il/elle doit** he/she must (3)

devoirs *(mpl)* homework (P); **Faites les devoirs en ligne** Do the homework online. (P)
diabète *(m)* diabetes
diable *(m)* devil
diamant *(m)* diamond
dictée *(f)* dictation
dictionnaire *(m)* dictionary
dieu *(m)* god
différemment differently
différer to differ
difficile difficult (P)
dimanche *(m)* Sunday (P)
diminuer to diminish
dinde *(f)* turkey
dîner *(m)* dinner (8)
dîner to have dinner (2), to dine
diplôme *(m)* diploma, degree
dire to say, to tell (6); **Ça te/vous dit?** How does that sound to you? (2); **Ça veut dire...** That means . . . (P); **Comment dit-on... en français/en anglais?** How do you say . . . in French/in English? (P); **On dit...** One says . . . (P); **On dit que...** They say that . . . (4); **Que veut dire... ?** What does . . . mean? (P)
directement directly
directeur(-trice) *(mf)* director
direction *(f)* direction, management
disciplinaire disciplinary
discothèque *(f)* dance club
discrètement discreetly
discuter to discuss
disparaître to disappear; **disparu(e)** having disappeared
disponible available
disposer de to have available
disputer to dispute; **se disputer (avec)** to argue (with) (7)
disque *(m)* record; **disque compact** *(m)* compact disc
dissiper to dissipate
distraction *(f)* entertainment (5)
distributeur *(m)* **de billets** ATM machine (10)
divers(e) diverse, different
divisé(e) divided
divorcer to divorce; **divorcé(e)** divorced (1)
dix ten (P); **dix-huit** eighteen (P); **dix-huitième** eighteenth (3); **dix-neuf** nineteen (P); **dix-sept** seventeen (P)
dixième tenth (3)
doctorat *(m)* doctorate
dodo: faire dodo *(m)* to go beddy-bye *(familiar)*
doigt *(m)* finger (10); **doigt** *(m)* **de pied** toe (10)
dollar *(m)* dollar (3)
domaine *(m)* estate, domain
domestique *(mf)* servant
domestique domestic, household
domicile *(m)* place of residence
dominer to dominate
dommage: C'est dommage! It's a shame!, It's a pity!, That's too bad! (7)
donc so, therefore, thus, then (7)
données *(fpl)* information, data
donner to give (2); **donner à manger à** to feed (9); **donner lieu à** to give rise to; **Donnez-moi...** Give me . . . (2)
dont of which, (among) which, whose (7)
dormir to sleep (2)
dos *(m)* back (10); **sac** *(m)* **à dos** backpack
dossier *(m)* file
doté(e) endowed
douane *(f)* customs (9)

double double; **chambre double** *(f)* double room (10)

douche *(f)* shower (7)

doute *(m)* doubt; **sans doute** without doubt, doubtless, probably (8)

douter to doubt (10)

douteux(-euse) doubtful

doux (douce) sweet, soft, gentle (6)

douzaine (de) *(f)* dozen (8)

douze twelve (P)

drame *(m)* drama

drap *(m)* sheet

droit *(m)* law *(field of study)*, right *(legal)*; **droits** *(mpl)* **de l'homme** human rights; **tout droit** straight (ahead) (10)

droite *(f)* right *(direction)*; **à droite (de)** to the right (of) (3); **de droite** conservative (7)

drôle funny, odd

du (de la, de l', des) some, any (8)

dû (due, dus, dues) à due to

duc *(m)* duke

duché *(m)* dukedom, duchy

dur(e) hard; **œuf dur** *(m)* hard-boiled egg (8)

durant during

durer to last

DVD *(m)* DVD (3); **lecteur** *(m)* **DVD** DVD player (3)

dynamique active (1)

E

eau *(f)* water (2)

échange *(m)* exchange

échanger to exchange

échapper to escape; **s'échapper** to escape

échouer to fail

école *(f)* school (6); **école** *(f)* **secondaire** secondary school

économie *(f)* economy; **faire des économies** to save money

économique economic; **classe** *(f)* **économique** economy class, coach (9); **sciences économiques** *(fpl)* economics

écossais(e) plaid

écossé(e) shelled

écouter to listen (to) (2); **Écoutez la question.** Listen to the question. (P)

écran *(m)* screen

écrevisse *(f)* crawfish

écrire to write (9); **Ça s'écrit...** That's written . . . (P); **Ça s'écrit avec un accent ou sans accent?** That's written with or without an accent? (P); **Ça s'écrit comment?** How is that written? (P); **écrit(e)** written; **Écrivez la réponse avec une phrase complète.** Write the answer with a complete sentence. (P)

écrivain *(m)* writer

éducateur *(m)*, **éducatrice** *(f)* educator

éduquer to educate

effectuer to carry out

effet *(m)* effect; **effets personnels** personal belongings; **effets spéciaux** special effects (6); **en effet** in fact

égal(e) *(mpl* **égaux)** equal; **Ça m'est égal.** It's all the same to me.; **sans égal** unequaled

également also, as well, equally, likewise

égalité *(f)* equality

égard *(m)* respect

église *(f)* church (4)

égoïste selfish

Égypte *(f)* Egypt (9)

électrique electrical

électronique electronic; **billet** *(m)* **électronique** e-ticket; **courrier** *(m)* **électronique** e-mail

élève *(mf)* pupil, student

élevé(e) high, elevated, raised

elle she, it (1); **avec elle** with her (2); **elles** they (1); **avec elles** with them (2); **elle-même** herself

embarquement *(m)* boarding; **porte** *(f)* **d'embarquement** departure gate

embarquer to embark, to set sail

embêtant(e) annoying (3)

embrasser to kiss; **s'embrasser** to kiss each other, to embrace each other (7)

émincé *(m)* thin slice, strip

émission *(f)* broadcast, show

emmener to take

empêcher (quelqu'un de faire quelque chose) to prevent (somebody from doing something)

emplacement *(m)* location

emploi *(m)* employment, use; **emploi** *(m)* **du temps** schedule

employé(e) *(mf)* employee (10)

employer to use; **s'employer** to be used

emporter to take (along), to carry (away) (5)

emprisonner to imprison

emprunter (à) to borrow (from)

en some, any, of it/them (8), about it/them; **Je vous/t'en prie.** You're welcome. (2); **s'en aller** to go away

en in (P); **de temps en temps** from time to time (4); **en avance** early; **en avion** by plane (4); **en désordre** in disorder (3); **en espèces** in cash (10); **en face (de)** across from, facing (3); **en ligne** online (P); **en même temps** at the same time; **en ordre** in order (3); **en outre** in addition; **en retard** late (10); **en solde** on sale (5); **en vacances** on vacation (4); **être en train de...** to be in the process of . . . ; **partir en voyage** to leave on a trip (5); **partir en week-end** to go away for the weekend (5)

enceinte pregnant (10)

enchanter to enchant; **enchanté(e)** enchanted

encore still (4), again, more (8); **ne... pas encore** not . . . yet (5)

endormir: s'endormir to fall asleep (7)

endroit *(m)* place (9)

énergique energetic

énerver to irritate

enfance *(f)* childhood

enfant *(mf)* child (4)

enfin finally (7)

enflé(e) swollen

enfouir to bury

engagé(e) involved

enlever to take off, to remove

ennui *(m)* trouble

ennuyer to bore; **s'ennuyer (de)** to get bored (with), to be bored (with) (7)

ennuyeux(-euse) boring (1)

énorme enormous

enquête *(f)* investigation, survey

enregistrer to record

enseignement *(m)* teaching, education; **enseignement supérieur** higher education

enseigner to teach

ensemble *(m)* whole group

ensemble together (2)

ensuite then, next, afterwards (4)

entendre to hear (7); **Entendu!** Understood!; **s'entendre bien/mal (avec)** to get along well/badly (with) (7)

enthousiaste enthusiastic

entier(-ère) entire, whole; **à part entière** complete

entièrement entirely, completely

entre between (3), among

entrée *(f)* appetizer, first course (8), entry ticket, entrance, entry; **entrée** *(f)* **au cinéma** cinema attendance

entreprise *(f)* firm, enterprise

entrer (dans) to enter (5), to go in

entretien *(m)* conversation, interview, maintenance

envahir to invade

envers towards

envie: avoir envie de to feel like, to want (4)

environ around, about (4)

envisager to consider, to imagine

envoyer to send (2); **envoyer un texto** to send a text message (2)

épaule *(f)* shoulder

épice *(f)* spice

épicerie *(f)* grocer's shop (8)

épinards *(mpl)* spinach

époque *(f)* time period (6); **à cette époque-là** at that time, in those days

épouser to marry; **s'épouser** to get married

épouvante: film *(m)* **d'épouvante** horror movie

équilibre *(m)* equilibrium, balance

équipe *(f)* team

équipé(e) equipped

ère *(f)* era

escalade *(f)* (rock) climbing

escalier *(m)* stairs, staircase (3)

escargot *(m)* snail (8)

escarpé(e) steep

esclavage *(m)* slavery

esclave *(mf)* slave

espace *(m)* space

Espagne *(f)* Spain (9)

espagnol *(m)* Spanish (P)

espagnol(e) Spanish

espèce *(f)* species; **en espèces** in cash (10)

espérer to hope (3)

espion(ne) *(mf)* spy

espoir *(m)* hope

esprit *(m)* mind, spirit (7)

essayage: cabine *(f)* **d'essayage** fitting room (5)

essayer to try on (5); **essayer (de faire)** to try (to do)

essentiel(le) essential; **Il est essentiel de...** It's essential to . . . (10)

est *(m)* east; **la partie est** the eastern part

est-ce que *(particle used in questions)* (1)

estomac *(m)* stomach

et and (P); **et quart/et demi(e)** a quarter past/ half past (P); **Combien font... et... ?** How much is . . . plus . . . ? (P)

établir to establish; **s'établir** to establish oneself, to settle

établissement *(m)* establishment

étage *(m)* floor (3); **à l'étage** on the same floor, down the hall; **À quel étage?** On what floor? (3); **au premier étage** on the first (second) floor (3)

étagère *(f)* shelf, bookcase (3)

étape *(f)* stopping place, step

état *(m)* condition; **État** *(m)* state (3), government; **États-Unis** *(mpl)* United States (3)

été *(m)* summer (5); **en été** in summer (5)

étendre: s'étendre to extend; **étendu(e)** stretched out

éternuer to sneeze (10)

étoile *(f)* star

étonner to amaze, to astonish; **être étonné(e) que...** to be astonished that . . . (10)

étouffant(e) stifling

étrange strange

étranger(-ère) foreign (5); **à l'étranger** abroad (9)

être to be (1); **c'est** it's (P), he is, she is, it is, this is, that is (1); **C'est ça!** That's right! (1); **C'est quel jour aujourd'hui?** What day is today? (P); **Comment est / sont... ?** What is / are . . . like? (1); **être à** to belong to; **Je suis...** I'm . . . (P); **Je ne suis pas...** I'm not . . . (P); **le français est...** French is . . . (P); **Nous sommes...** There are . . . of us. (4); **Quelle est la date?** What is the date? (4); **tu es/vous êtes** you are (P)

étroit(e) tight, narrow

études *(fpl)* studies, going to school (1)

étudiant(e) *(mf)* student (P)

étudier to study (1); **J'étudie/Je n'étudie pas...** I study/I don't study . . . (1); **Qu'est-ce que vous étudiez/tu étudies?** What are you studying?, What do you study? (1)

euro *(m)* euro (2)

Europe *(f)* Europe (9)

européen(ne) European

eux them; **avec eux** with them (2); **eux-mêmes** themselves

évader: s'évader to escape

événement *(m)* event

éviter to avoid (8)

exact(e) accurate, exact

exactement exactly (10)

examen *(m)* test, exam (P)

excessivement excessively

exclamer: s'exclamer to exclaim, to cry out

excuser to excuse, to forgive; **Excusez-moi.** Excuse me. (P)

exemple *(m)* example; **par exemple** for example

exercice *(m)* exercise (P); **faire de l'exercice** to exercise (2); **Faites l'exercice avec un(e) autre étudiant(e).** Do the exercise with another student. (P)

exiger to require

exotique exotic (9)

expérience *(f)* experience, experiment

explication *(f)* explanation

expliquer to explain (10)

explorateur(-trice) *(mf)* explorer

exploser to explode

exposition *(f)* exhibit (4)

expression *(f)* expression (P)

expresso *(m)* espresso (2)

exprimer to express

expulser to throw out

exquis(e) exquisite

extérieur *(m)* outside, exterior

extra(ordinaire) great, terrific (4)

extrascolaire extracurricular

extraterrestre *(mf)* extraterrestrial

extraverti(e) outgoing, extroverted (1)

F

fabrication *(f)* production

fac *(f)* university, campus (2)

face *(f)* face; **en face (de)** across from, facing (3); **face à** across from, confronted with; **faire face à** to face

facile easy (P)

facilement easily (7)

faciliter to facilitate, to make easy

façon *(f)* way

faculté *(f)* university, campus, school, faculty; **la fac** the university, the campus (2)

fade tasteless

faim *(f)* hunger; **avoir faim** to be hungry (4)

faire to do, to make (2); **Ça fait... euros.** That's . . . euros. (2); **Ça ne se fait pas!** That is not done!; **Combien font... et / moins...?** How much is . . . plus / minus . . . ? (P); **faire attention (à)** to pay attention (to), to watch out (for) (8); **faire connaître** to inform; **faire de l'aérobic** to do aerobics; **faire de l'alpinisme** to go mountain climbing; **faire de la méditation** to meditate (8); **faire de la musculation** to do weight training, to do bodybuilding (8); **faire de la planche à voile** to go windsurfing; **faire de la plongée sous-marine** to go scuba diving; **faire de la varappe** to go rock climbing; **faire de l'exercice** to exercise (2); **faire des courses** to run errands (5); **faire des économies** to save up (money); **faire des projets** to make plans (4); **faire des randonnées** to go hiking (5); **faire du bateau** to go boating (5); **faire du camping** to go camping (5); **faire du cheval** to go horseback riding; **faire du jardinage** to garden (5); **faire du jogging** to jog (5); **faire du patin (à glace)** to go (ice-)skating; **faire du roller** to go in-line skating (6); **faire du shopping** to go shopping (2); **faire du skateboard(ing)** to skateboard (6); **faire du ski** to go skiing (5); **faire du sport** to play sports (2); **faire du vélo** to go bike-riding (2); **faire du VTT** to go all-terrain biking (5); **faire du yoga** to do yoga (8); **faire face à** to face; **faire la connaissance de** to meet *(for the first time)* (7); **faire la cuisine** to cook (5); **faire la fête** to party; **faire la lessive** to do laundry (5); **faire la vaisselle** to do the dishes (5); **faire le ménage** to do housework (5); **faire les courses** to go grocery shopping (5); **faire mal** to hurt; **faire mieux (de)** to do better (to) (8); **faire noir** to be dark; **faire partie de** to be a part of; **faire quelque chose** to do something (2); **faire sa toilette** to wash up (7); **faire sa valise** to pack your bag (9); **faire une promenade** to go for a walk (5); **faire une réservation** to make a reservation (9); **faire un tour** to take a tour, to go for a ride (4); **faire un voyage** to take a trip (5); **Faites les devoirs en ligne.** Do the homework online. (P); **Faites l'exercice avec un(e) autre étudiant(e).** Do the exercise with another student. (P); **Il fait beau / chaud / (du) soleil / du vent / frais / froid / mauvais.** It's nice / hot / sunny / windy / cool / cold / bad. (5); **Il fait bon / du brouillard.** It's nice / foggy.; **Il va faire...** It's going to be . . . (5); **Je fais du...** I wear size. . . . (5); **Quelle taille faites-vous?** What size do you wear? (5); **Quel temps fait-il?** What's the weather like? (5); **Quel temps va-t-il faire?** What's the weather going to be like? (5); **Qu'est-ce que vous aimez faire?** What do you like to do? (2); **Qu'est-ce que vous faites/tu fais?** What are you doing? What do you do? (2); **se faire passer pour** to pass as

fait: en fait in fact

falaise *(f)* cliff

falloir: il faut... it is necessary . . . , one must . . . , one needs . . . (8); **il me/te/nous/vous/lui/leur faut** I/you/we/you/he (she)/they need(s) (9); **il ne faut pas** one shouldn't, one must not . . . (10); **Qu'est-ce qu'il vous faut?** What do you need? (8)

fameux(-euse) famous

familial(e) *(mpl* **familiaux)** family

familier(-ère) familiar, informal; **salutation** *(f)* **familière** familiar greeting (P)

famille *(f)* family (P); **nom** *(m)* **de famille** family name, surname, last name (3)

fantastique fantastic; **film fantastique** *(m)* fantasy movie

far Breton *(m)* far Breton *(a type of cake)*

farci(e) stuffed

farine *(f)* flour

fascinant(e) fascinating

fast-food *(m)* fast-food restaurant (1)

fatigué(e) tired (2)

faut *See* **falloir.**

fauteuil *(m)* armchair (3)

faux (fausse) false

favoriser to favor, to further

fée *(f)* fairy; **conte** *(m)* **de fées** fairy tale (6)

femme *(f)* woman (1), wife (2); **ex-femme** *(f)* ex-wife; **femme** *(f)* **d'affaires** business woman (5)

fenêtre *(f)* window (3)

fer *(m)* iron; **chemin** *(m)* **de fer** railroad

férié(e): jour férié *(m)* holiday

ferme *(f)* farm

fermer to close (2); **Fermez votre livre.** Close your book. (P)

féroce ferocious (6)

festival *(m)* festival (4)

fête *(f)* holiday, celebration (4), party (1); **faire la fête** to party; **fête** *(f)* **des Mères** Mother's Day; **fête** *(f)* **des Pères** Father's Day; **fête** *(f)* **du travail** Labor Day; **fête nationale** *(f)* national holiday

fêter to celebrate

feu *(m)* fire, traffic light

feuille *(f)* **de papier** sheet of paper

feuilleté(e) flaky (pastry)

février *(m)* February (4)

fiancé(e) engaged (1)

fiancer: se fiancer to get engaged (7)

fidélité *(f)* faithfulness

fier(-ère) proud

fièvre *(f)* fever; **avoir de la fièvre** to have fever

figure *(f)* face (7)

fille *(f)* girl; daughter (4); **fille unique** *(f)* only child

film *(m)* movie, film (1); **film** *(m)* **à grand spectacle** epic film

fils *(m)* son (4); **fils unique** *(m)* only child

fin *(f)* end

fin(e) fine

finalement finally (6)

financier(-ère) financial

finir (de faire) to finish (doing) (8); **finir par faire** to end up doing; **Le cours de français finit à...** French class finishes at . . . (P)

fissure *(f)* crack, fissure

fixe fixed; **menu à prix fixe** set-price menu (8)

fixer to set, to fix

flamand *(m)* Flemish *(language)*

fleur *(f)* flower

fleuri(e) with a floral pattern

fleuve *(m)* river

flic *(m)* cop

Floride *(f)* Florida (9)

foie *(m)* liver

fois *(f)* time (5), occasion; **à la fois** at the same time; **d'autres fois** other times (7); **Il était une fois…** Once upon a time there was . . . (6)
folique: acide *(m)* **folique** folic acid
folklore *(m)* folklore (4)
foncé(e) dark; **bleu foncé** dark blue
fonction *(f)* function; **en fonction de** according to
fonctionnement *(m)* functioning, operation, running
fond *(m)* bottom, back, background; **au fond de** at the end of; **dans le fond** really, basically
fondateur(-trice) *(mf)* founder; **père** *(m)* **fondateur** founding father
fonder to found; **fondé(e)** founded
fontaine *(f)* fountain
football *(m)* soccer (1); **football américain** *(m)* football (1); **match** *(m)* **de football américain** football game (1)
force *(f)* force, strength; **à force de** as a result of
forcément necessarily, inevitably
forêt *(f)* forest
forme *(f)* shape; **en forme** in shape (8); **en forme de** in the shape of
formel(le) formal; **salutation** *(f)* **formelle** formal greeting (P)
former to form, to educate
formidable great (7)
formulaire *(m)* form
formule *(f)* formula, expression
fort(e) strong (8)
fort very
fou (folle) crazy
foudre *(f)* lightning, thunderbolt; **coup** *(m)* **de foudre** love at first sight (7)
foulard *(m)* dress scarf
fouler: se fouler la cheville to sprain one's ankle
four *(m)* **(à micro-ondes)** (microwave) oven
fourchette *(f)* fork
frais (fraîche) fresh (8); **Il fait frais.** It's cool. (5)
fraise *(f)* strawberry (8)
framboise *(f)* raspberry
franc (franche) frank, honest
français *(m)* French (P); **cours** *(m)* **de français** French class (P)
français(e) French (1); **à la française** French style
France *(f)* France (1)
franciscain(e) Franciscan
francophone French-speaking
francophonie *(f)* French-speaking world
frapper to strike; **frapper à la porte** to knock on the door
fréquenté(e) visited, frequented
frère *(m)* brother (1); **beau-frère** *(m)* brother-in-law; **demi-frère** *(m)* stepbrother, half-brother
frigo *(m)* refrigerator
frire to fry
frisson *(m)* shiver (10); **avoir des frissons** to have the shivers (10)
frit(e) fried
frites *(fpl)* French fries (2); **steak-frites** *(m)* steak and fries (8)
frivole frivolous
froid(e) cold (4); **avoir froid** to be cold (4); **Il fait froid.** It's cold. (5)
fromage *(m)* cheese (2)
frontière *(f)* border
frottoir *(m)* rubboard

fruit *(m)* fruit (8); **fruits** *(mpl)* **de mer** shellfish (8); **jus** *(m)* **de fruit** fruit juice (2)
fuir to flee, to run away
fumé(e) smoked (8)
fumée *(f)* smoke
fumer to smoke (3)
fumeur(-euse) *(mf)* smoker; **fumeur/ non-fumeur** smoking/non-smoking
furieux(-euse) furious (10)
fusée *(f)* rocket
fusiller to shoot down
futur *(m)* future (tense)

G

gagner to win (2), to gain; **gagner de l'argent** to earn money, to make money
gai(e) gay, lively
galette complète *(f)* ham, egg, and cheese crêpe
gamin(e) *(mf)* kid
garçon *(m)* boy (4)
garder to keep
garde-robe *(f)* wardrobe
gare *(f)* train station; **gare routière** bus station
gaspiller to waste
gastronomie *(f)* gastronomy, cooking
gâté(e) spoiled (6)
gâteau *(m)* cake (8)
gauche *(f)* left; **à gauche (de)** to the left (of) (3); **de gauche** liberal (7)
général(e) *(mpl* **généraux)** general; **en général** in general (2)
généralement generally (8)
génial(e) *(mpl* **géniaux)** great (4)
génie *(m)* genius, engineering
genou *(m)* knee; **sur ses genoux** on one's lap
genre *(m)* gender, kind, type, genre
gens *(mpl)* people (1)
gentil(le) nice (1)
géographie *(f)* geography (9)
géographique geographical
germanique Germanic
geste *(m)* gesture
gilet *(m)* vest
glace *(f)* ice cream (8), ice; **glace à la vanille** vanilla ice cream (8)
glace *(f)* mirror
glacier *(m)* ice cream shop
golf *(m)* golf (2)
golfe *(m)* gulf
gorge *(f)* throat (10); **soutien-gorge** *(m)* bra
gosse *(mf)* kid
goût *(m)* taste
goûter to taste (9)
gouvernement *(m)* government
grâce *(f)* grace; **grâce à** thanks to, due to; **jour** *(m)* **d'Action de Grâce** Thanksgiving
gracieux(-euse) gracious (6)
graisse *(f)* fat, grease
grammaire *(f)* grammar
gramme *(m)* gram (8)
grand(e) big, tall (1); **grande surface** *(f)* superstore (8); **le grand amour** *(m)* true love (7)
grand-chose: ne… pas grand-chose not much, not a lot
grandir to grow, to grow up, to get taller (8)
grand-mère *(f)* grandmother (4)
grand-père *(m)* grandfather (4)
grands-parents *(mpl)* grandparents (4)
gras(se) fatty; **en caractères gras** boldfaced; **matière grasse** *(f)* fat (8)
gratuit(e) free (of charge) (10)
grave serious, grave

Grèce *(f)* Greece (9)
grillé(e) grilled, toasted (8); **pain grillé(e)** toast (8)
grippe *(f)* flu (10)
gris(e) gray (3)
grog *(m)* **au rhum** rum toddy
gros(se) fat (1)
grossesse *(f)* pregnancy
grossir to get fatter (8)
groupe *(m)* group (6); **en groupe** in a group
gruyère *(m)* Swiss cheese
guerre *(f)* war
guichet *(m)* ticket window
guide *(m)* guide, guidebook (9)
guitare *(f)* guitar (2)
Guyane *(f)* French Guiana (9)
gym: aller à la gym to go to the gym (2); **salle** *(f)* **de gym** gym, fitness club (1)
gymnase *(m)* gym

H

habiller to dress; **s'habiller** to get dressed (7)
habitant(e) *(mf)* inhabitant
habiter to live ; **j'habite à** *(+ city)* I live in *(+ city)* (P); **Tu habites… ?** Do you live . . . ? (P)
habitude *(f)* habit; **comme d'habitude** as usual; **d'habitude** usually (2)
habitué(e) à used to, accustomed to
*****haché(e)** chopped (up)
*****hamburger** *(m)* hamburger (8)
*****haricots verts** *(mpl)* green beans (8)
harmonieux(-euse) harmonious
*****hasard: par hasard** by chance
*****haut(e)** high; **en haut** on top; **là-haut** up there
*****hein?** huh?
héritage *(m)* inheritance, heritage
hériter to inherit
hésiter to hesitate
heure *(f)* hour, time (P); **à l'heure** on time (4); **À tout à l'heure.** See you in a little while. (6); **heure locale** local time (9); **heure officielle** official time (6), 24-hour clock; **heures d'ouverture** business hours (6); **Il est… heure(s).** It's . . . o'clock. (P); **Quelle heure est-il?** What time is it? (P); **tout à l'heure** a little while ago
heureusement luckily
heureux(-euse) happy (7)
hideux(-euse) hideous
hier yesterday (5); **hier soir** last night, yesterday evening (5)
hi-fi: chaîne *(f)* **hi-fi** stereo (3)
histoire *(f)* history (1); story (9)
historique historic (9)
hiver *(m)* winter (5); **en hiver** in winter (5)
*****hockey** *(m)* hockey (2)
*****homard** *(m)* lobster (8)
homme *(m)* man (1); **homme** *(m)* **d'affaires** businessman (5)
honnête honest
honnêteté *(f)* honesty
*****honteux (-euse)** shameful
hôpital *(m)* *(pl* **hôpitaux)** hospital
horaire *(m)* schedule (6)
horreur *(f)* horror
horrible horrible (6)
*****hors de** outside of
*****hors-d'œuvre** *(m)* *(inv)* hors d'œuvre, appetizer (8)
hôte *(m)* host; **chambre** *(f)* **d'hôte** bed and breakfast

hôtel *(m)* hotel (5)
hôtelier(-ère) *(mf)* hotel manager (10)
hôtesse *(f)* hostess
huile *(f)* oil
*__huit__ eight (P); **huit jours** one week
*__huitième__ eighth (3)
huître *(f)* oyster (8)
humain(e) human; **sciences humaines** *(fpl)* social sciences (1)
humeur *(f)* mood; **de bonne humeur** in a good mood
humour *(m)* humor; **sens** *(m)* **de l'humour** sense of humor (7)
hurlement *(m)* howl
hypermarché *(m)* superstore

I

ici here (P); **d'ici** from here (P); **par ici** this way (5)
idéaliste idealistic
idée *(f)* idea (4)
identité *(f)* identity; **carte** *(f)* / **pièce** *(f)* **d'identité** identity card
ignorer to ignore; **en ignorant** while ignoring
il he (1), it (P); **il faut...** it is necessary . . . , one must . . . (8); **il ne faut pas...** one shouldn't . . . , one must not . . . (10); **ils** they (1); **il y a...** there is . . . , there are . . . (1), ago (5); **Quelle heure est-il?** What time is it? (P); **Qu'est-ce qu'il y a?** What is there? (1), What's the matter?; **s'il vous plaît** please (P)
île *(f)* island (9)
illustré(e) illustrated
image *(f)* picture
imaginaire imaginary
imaginer to imagine
immédiatement immediately
immeuble *(m)* apartment building (3)
immigré(e) *(mf)* immigrant
imparfait *(m)* imperfect
impatient(e) impatient (4)
impératif *(m)* imperative
imperméable *(m)* raincoat (5)
impoli(e) impolite
importance *(f)* importance (7)
important(e) important (10)
importer to be important; **n'importe où** (just) anywhere; **n'importe quoi** (just) anything
impressionnant(e) impressive
impressionner to impress
imprimé(e) printed
inattendu(e) unexpected
inciter à to encourage
inclure to include; **inclus(e)** included
inconnu(e) *(mf)* stranger
inconvénient *(m)* disadvantage, inconvenience
incroyable incredible
Inde *(f)* India
indécision *(f)* indecision (7)
indéfini(e) indefinite
indicatif *(m)* indicative
indications *(fpl)* directions (10)
indifférence *(f)* indifference (7)
indigène native
indigestion *(f)* indigestion (10)
indiquer to show, to indicate (3); **indiqué(e)** indicated; **indiquer le chemin** to give directions, to show the way (10)
indiscret(-ète) indiscreet
industrialisé(e) industrialized
industrie *(f)* industry
inégalé(e) unequaled
infidélité *(f)* unfaithfulness (7)

infinitif *(m)* infinitive
infirmerie *(f)* health center
inflexibilité *(f)* inflexibility
influencer to influence; **s'influencer** to influence each other
informatique *(f)* computer science (1); **salle** *(f)* **d'informatique** computer lab (1)
informer to inform; **s'informer** to find out information (9)
infos *(fpl)* info (9)
infusion *(f)* herbal tea
ingénieur *(m)* engineer
inhospitalier(-ière) inhospitable
inoubliable unforgettable
insaturé(e) unsaturated
inscrire to register; **s'inscrire** to register (3)
inscrit(e) registered
insensibilité *(f)* insensitivity (7)
insipide tasteless, insipid
insister to insist (10)
inspecteur *(m)* inspector
inspirer to inspire; **s'inspirer de** to draw inspiration from
installations *(fpl)* facilities
installer: s'installer (à / dans) to settle (in), to move (into) (7), to set up business
instant *(m)* instant; **Un instant!** Just a moment!
institut *(m)* institute
instrument *(m)* **de musique** musical instrument
insuffisant insufficient
intellectuel(le) intellectual (1)
intelligent(e) intelligent (1)
intention: avoir l'intention de to plan on, to intend to (4)
intéressant(e) interesting (P)
intéresser to interest; **s'intéresser à** to be interested in (7)
intérêt *(m)* interest
intérieur *(m)* inside
international(e) *(mpl* **internationaux)** international (1)
internaute *(mf)* Internet surfer
Internet *(m)* Internet (2); **surfer sur Internet** to surf the Internet (2); **sur Internet** on the Internet (2)
interrogatif(-ive) interrogative, question
interroger to question
interrompre to interrupt
intime intimate; **ami(e) intime** *(mf)* close friend
intrigue *(f)* plot
inventaire *(m)* inventory, list
investir to invest
invitation *(f)* invitation (6)
invité(e) *(mf)* guest
inviter (à) to invite (to) (2)
Irlande *(f)* Ireland (9)
irréel(le) unreal
irresponsable irresponsible
irriter to irritate
isolé(e) isolated
Israël *(m)* Israel (9)
Italie *(f)* Italy (9)
italien(ne) Italian
italique: en italique in italics
itinéraire *(m)* itinerary
ivoirien(ne) from Côte d'Ivoire

J

jalousie *(f)* jealousy (7)
jaloux(-ouse) jealous (7)
jamais: ne... jamais never (2)

jambe *(f)* leg (10); **se casser la jambe** to break your leg
jambon *(m)* ham (2); **sandwich** *(m)* **au jambon** ham sandwich (2)
janvier *(m)* January (4)
Japon *(m)* Japan (9)
japonais *(m)* Japanese
jardin *(m)* garden (5), yard
jardinage *(m)* gardening; **faire du jardinage** to garden (5)
jaune yellow (3)
je (j') I (P)
jean *(m)* jeans (5)
jet *(m)* stream
jeter to throw
jeu *(m)* game; **jeu** *(m)* **vidéo** video game (2)
jeudi *(m)* Thursday (P)
jeune young (1); **jeunes** *(pl)* young people
jeunesse *(f)* youth (7); **auberge** *(f)* **de jeunesse** youth hostel (10)
jogging: faire du jogging to jog (5)
joie *(f)* joy
joindre: se joindre à to join
joli(e) pretty (1)
jouer to play (2), to act *(in movies and theater)* (6); **jouer à** to play *(a sport or game)* (2); **jouer de** to play *(an instrument)* (2)
jour *(m)* day (P); **C'est quel jour aujourd'hui?** What day is today? (P); **jour** *(m)* **de l'An** New Year's Day; **jour J** *(m)* D-day; **tous les jours** every day (P)
journal *(m)* *(pl* **journaux)** newspaper (5), journal; **journal** *(m)* **télévisé** news broadcast
journalier(-ère) daily
journée *(f)* day (2), daytime; **Bonne journée!** Have a good day!; **journée continue** nine-to-five schedule; **toute la journée** the whole day (2)
joyeux(-euse) happy, joyful; **Joyeux Noël!** Merry Christmas!
juger to judge
juif(-ive) *(mf)* Jew
juillet *(m)* July (4)
juin *(m)* June (4)
jumeau (jumelle) twin (1)
jupe *(f)* skirt (5)
jus *(m)* **(de fruit)** (fruit) juice (2)
jusqu'à until, up to (2)
juste just (10), fair; **juste là** right there
justement precisely, exactly, as a matter of fact (3)

K

kilo (de) *(m)* kilo(gram) (of) *(2.2 pounds)* (8)
kilomètre *(m)* kilometer *(.6 mile)*
kiosque *(m)* kiosk (10)

L

la the (1), her, it (5)
là there (8); **à ce moment-là** at that time; **ce (cet, cette, ces) ...-là** that/those . . . over there (5); **là-bas** over there (9); **là-haut** up there
laboratoire *(m)* **de langues** language laboratory (1)
lac *(m)* lake
laid(e) ugly (1)
laïque lay, secular, civil
laisser to leave (behind) (3), to let; **laisser tomber** to drop
lait *(m)* milk (2); **café** *(m)* **au lait** coffee with milk (2)
laitue *(f)* lettuce (8)
lampe *(f)* lamp (3)
lancer to throw, to fire

langouste (f) spiny lobster
langue (f) language (1); tongue
lapin (m) rabbit
laqué(e) lacquered, with a gloss finish
large wide
largement widely
lavabo (m) washbasin, sink (10)
lave (f) lava
laver to wash; **se laver la figure/les mains** to wash one's face/one's hands (7)
lave-vaisselle (m) dishwasher
le the (1), him, it (5); **le lundi** on Mondays (P); **le matin** in the morning, mornings (P); **le week-end** on the weekend, weekends (P)
leçon (f) lesson
lecteur (lectrice) (mf) reader; **lecteur** (m) **CD / DVD / Blu-ray** CD / DVD / Blu-ray player (3); **lecteur** (m) **MP3** MP3 player
lecture (f) reading
léger(-ère) light (8)
légume (m) vegetable (8)
lendemain (m) the next day (5)
lent(e) slow
lentement slowly (8)
lequel (laquelle, lesquels, lesquelles) which, which one(s) (6)
les the (1); them (5)
lessive (f) laundry (5)
lettre (f) letter (9); **lettres** (fpl) study of literature
leur (to, for) them (9)
leur their (1)
lever: se lever to get up (7)
liaison (f) linking, link
liberté (f) freedom
librairie (f) bookstore (1)
libre free (2); **temps libre** (m) free time (2); **Tu es libre ce soir?** Are you free this evening? (2)
licence (f) *three-year university degree*
lien (m) link, tie
lier to connect, to link; **lié(e)** linked
lieu (m) place; **au lieu de** instead of; **avoir lieu** to take place
light: coca (m) **light** diet cola (2)
ligne (f) figure; line; **en ligne** online (P)
limiter to limit, to border; **limité(e)** limited; **se limiter à** to limit oneself to
linguistique linguistic
liquide (m) liquid (10)
lire to read (2); **Lisez la page 17.** Read page 17. (P)
liste (f) list
lit (m) bed (3); **rester au lit** to stay in bed (2)
litre (m) liter *(approximately one quart)* (8)
littéraire literary
littérature (f) literature (1)
livre (m) book (P); **Fermez votre livre.** Close your book. (P); **Ouvrez votre livre à la page 23.** Open your book to page 23. (P)
livre (de) (f) pound (of), half-kilo (of) (8)
livrer: se livrer à to participate in
local(e) (mpl **locaux**) local (9)
locataire (mf) renter
location (f) rental; **voiture** (f) **de location** rental car (5)
logement (m) lodging (3)
logique logical
logiquement logically
loi (f) law
loin (de) far (from) (3); **au loin** in the distance; **de loin** by far
loisir (m) leisure activity, pastime (2)

Londres London
long: le long de along; **de long** in length
long(ue) long (4)
longer to go alongside
longtemps a long time (5)
longueur (f) length
lors de at the time of
lorsque when
louer to rent (4)
Louisiane (f) Louisiana (3)
loyer (m) rent (5)
lui him (2), (to, for) him/her (9); **avec lui** with him (2); **lui-même** himself
lumière (f) light
lumineux(-euse) luminous (*not in image, omit*)
lundi (m) Monday (P)
lune (f) moon; **lune** (f) **de miel** honeymoon
lunettes (fpl) glasses (4); **lunettes** (fpl) **de soleil** sunglasses (5)
luth (m) lute
lutter to struggle, to fight
luxe (m) luxury; **de luxe** deluxe (10)
luxembourgeois (m) Luxembourgish (*native language of Luxembourg*)
lycée (m) high school (6)
lycéen(ne) (mf) high school student (6)

M

madame (Mme) (f) Mrs., madam (P)
mademoiselle (Mlle) (f) Miss (P)
magasin (m) store (4), shop
magazine (m) magazine (9)
magnifique magnificent
mai (m) May (4)
maigre skinny
maigrir to get thinner, to slim down (8)
mail (m) e-mail (9)
maillon (m) link
maillot (m) **de bain** swimsuit (5)
main (f) hand (7)
maintenant now (P)
maintenir to maintain
mais but (P)
maïs (m) corn
maison (f) house (1); **à la maison** (at) home (P)
maître (m) master
majorité (f) majority
mal (m) bad, evil; **avoir mal à...** one's . . . hurt(s) (10); **faire mal (à...)** to hurt (one's . . .)
mal badly (P); **mal à l'aise** ill at ease; **pas mal** not bad(ly) (P)
malade (mf) sick person
malade ill, sick; **tomber malade** to get sick (10)
maladie (f) illness
malaise (f) discomfort
Malgache (mf) Madagascan
malgré in spite of
malheureux(-euse) unhappy
malhonnête dishonest
maman (f) mama, mom
mamie (f) granny, grandma (7)
Manche (f) English Channel
mandarine (f) tangerine
mandat (m) money order, mandate
manger to eat (2); **donner à manger à** to feed (9); **salle** (f) **à manger** dining room (3)
manière (f) manner, way
manifestation (f) demonstration; **manifestation sportive** (f) sports event
manquer to miss, to lack, to be in shortage
manteau (m) overcoat (5)
maquiller: se maquiller to put on make-up (7)

marais (m) swamp
marbre (m) marble
marchand(e) (mf) merchant, shopkeeper (6)
marchandise (f) merchandise
marché (m) market (8)
marcher to walk (8), to work
mardi (m) Tuesday (P); **Mardi gras** (m) Fat Tuesday
marge (f) margin
mari (m) husband (2); **ex-mari** (m) ex-husband
mariage (m) marriage (7)
marié(e) married (1)
marier: se marier (avec) to get married (to) (7)
marionnettiste (mf) puppeteer
marketing (m) marketing (1)
Maroc (m) Morocco (9)
marocain(e) Moroccan
marquer to mark
marrant(e) funny (1)
marron (inv) brown (3)
mars (m) March (4)
martiniquais(e) from Martinique
masque (m) mask, face pack
massif (m) group of mountains, clump
match (m) match, game (1)
matelas (m) mattress
matérialiste materialistic
maternel(le) maternal; **école maternelle** (f) kindergarten
mathématiques (maths) (fpl) mathematics (math) (1)
matière (f) matter; **matières grasses** (fpl) fats (8)
matin (m) morning (P); **À huit heures du matin.** At eight o'clock in the morning. (P); **le matin** mornings, in the morning (P)
matinée (f) morning (2)
mauvais(e) bad (1); **Il est mauvais de...** It's bad to . . . (10); **Il fait mauvais.** The weather's bad. (5)
maxidiscompte (m) discount supercenter
me (to, for) me (9), myself (7); **il me faut...** I need . . . (9)
mec (m) (familiar) guy
méchant(e) mean (1)
mécontent(e) displeased
médecin (m) doctor (10), physician
médicament (m) medication, medicine (10), drugs
Méditerranée: (mer) Méditerranée (f) Mediterranean (Sea)
méditerranéen(ne) Mediterranean
méfiance (f) mistrust
mégalithe (m) megalith (*a large stone*)
meilleur(e) best, better (1)
mélange (m) mixture
membre (m) member
même same (1), even; **moi-même** myself; **quand même** all the same
mémoire (f) memory
menacer to threaten
ménage (m) housework (5), household; **femme** (f) **de ménage** cleaning lady
menthe (f) mint
mentir to lie
menu (m) menu (8); **menu à prix fixe** set-price menu (8)
mer (f) sea (9); **bord** (m) **de la mer** seaside; **fruits** (mpl) **de mer** shellfish (8)
merci thank you, thanks (P)
mercredi (m) Wednesday (P)
mère (f) mother (4)
mérité(e) deserved, earned
messager(-ère) (mf) messenger (6)

messieurs (MM.) gentlemen, sirs

mètre *(m)* meter

métrique metric

métro *(m)* subway (4); **en métro** by subway (4)

mettre to wear, to put (on) (5), to place; **mettre en place** to put in place; **mettre en scène** to stage, to present; **mettre la table** to set the table; **se mettre à** to start, to set out; **se mettre d'accord** to come to an agreement

meubles *(mpl)* furniture, furnishings (3)

meurtre *(m)* murder

Mexico Mexico City

Mexique *(m)* Mexico (9)

mi- mid-, half-; **cheveux mi-longs** *(mpl)* shoulder-length hair (4)

micronutriment *(m)* micronutrient

micro-ondes *(m)* microwave oven

midi *(m)* noon (P)

mie: pain *(m)* **de mie** soft sandwich bread

mien(ne): le/la mien(ne) mine

mieux (que) better (than); **aimer mieux** to prefer (2); **il vaut mieux…** it's better . . . (10); **le mieux** the best (7)

milieu *(m)* middle, milieu, environment; **au milieu (de)** in the middle (of)

mille one thousand (3)

mille-feuille *(m)* mille-feuille *(a layered pastry)*

million: un million (de) *(m)* one million (3)

mince thin (1)

minéral(e) *(mpl* **minéraux): eau minérale** *(f)* mineral water (2)

mini-bar *(m)* mini-bar (10)

minuit *(m)* midnight (P)

minute *(f)* minute (5)

miroir *(m)* mirror

misère *(f)* misery

mobile *(m)* motive

mobilier *(m)* furnishings

mode *(f)* fashion; **mode** *(m)* **de vie** lifestyle

modèle *(m)* model

moderne modern (3)

moi me (P); **avec moi** with me (2); **Donnez-moi…** Give me . . . (2) **Excusez-moi.** Excuse me. (P); **moi-même** myself; **Pour moi… s'il vous plaît.** For me . . . please. (2)

moindre: le moindre the least

moins minus (P), less (1); **au moins** at least; **Combien font… moins… ?** How much is . . . minus . . . ? (P); **de moins en moins** fewer and fewer, less and less; **le moins** the least; **moins de** fewer, less (8); **moins le quart** a quarter until (P); **moins… que** less . . . than (1)

mois *(m)* month (3); **ce mois-ci** this month (4); **par mois** per month (3)

moitié *(f)* half

moment *(m)* moment; **à ce moment-là** at that time; **au dernier moment** at the last minute

mon (ma, mes) my (3); **ma famille** my family (P); **mes amis** my friends (1)

monarchie *(f)* monarchy

monastère *(m)* monastery

monde *(m)* world, crowd; **faire le tour du monde** to take a trip around the world; **tout le monde** everybody, everyone (6)

mondial(e) *(mpl* **mondiaux)** world(-wide)

monétaire monetary

monnaie *(f)* change (2), currency

monotonie *(f)* monotony

monsieur (M.) *(m)* Mr., sir (P)

monstre *(m)* monster (6)

mont *(m)* mount

montagne *(f)* mountain (5); **aller à la montagne** to go to the mountains (5); **chalet** *(m)* **à la montagne** ski lodge (10)

montagneux(-euse) mountainous

monter (dans) to go up; to get on/in (5), to set up, to climb, to raise

montre *(f)* watch (5)

montrer to show (3)

morceau de *(m)* piece of (8)

mort *(f)* death

mort(e) dead (5)

morue *(f)* cod

mosquée *(f)* mosque

mot *(m)* word (P); **Étudiez les mots de vocabulaire.** Study the vocabulary words. (P)

motif *(m)* reason, motive

mouchoir *(m)* handkerchief

moule *(f)* mussel (8)

moulin *(m)* mill

mourir to die (5)

moustache *(f)* mustache (4)

moutarde *(f)* mustard

mouton *(m)* sheep

moyen *(m)* means; **moyen** *(m)* **de transport** means of transportation (4)

moyen(ne) medium, average; **de taille moyenne** medium-sized (4); **Moyen-Orient** *(m)* Middle East (9)

moyenne *(f)* average; **en moyenne** on average

muet(te) silent

mur *(m)* wall (3)

musculation: faire de la musculation to do weight training, to do bodybuilding (8)

musée *(m)* museum (4)

musical(e) *(mpl* **musicaux): comédie musicale** *(f)* musical

musicien(ne) *(mf)* musician

musicien(ne) musical

musique *(f)* music (1); **musique zydeco** zydeco music (4)

mutation *(f)* transfer

muter to transfer

myrtille *(f)* blueberry

mystère *(m)* mystery

mystérieusement mysteriously

mythique mythical

N

nager to swim (2)

naissance *(f)* birth

naître to be born (5); **être né(e)** to be born (5)

natation *(f)* swimming

national(e) *(mpl* **nationaux)** national (4)

nationalité *(f)* nationality (3)

nature *(f)* nature (7); **omelette nature** *(f)* plain omelet

naturel(le) natural

naturellement naturally

nautique: faire du ski nautique *(m)* to go water-skiing (5)

navette *(f)* shuttle (10)

ne: je ne travaille pas I don't work (P); **ne… aucun(e)** none, not one; **ne… jamais** never (2); **ne… ni… ni…** neither . . . nor . . .; **ne… nulle part** nowhere; **ne… pas (du tout)** not (at all) (1); **ne… pas encore** not yet (5); **ne… personne** nobody, no one; **ne… plus** no more, no longer (8); **ne… que** only; **ne… rien** nothing (5); **ne… rien que** nothing but; **n'est-ce pas?** right? (1); **n'importe où** (just) anywhere

né(e) born (5); **être né(e)** to be born (5)

nécessaire necessary (10)

néerlandais(e) Dutch

négliger to neglect

négocier to negotiate

neige *(f)* snow (5)

neiger to snow (5)

nerveux(-euse) nervous

n'est-ce pas? right? (1)

neuf nine (P)

neuf (neuve) brand-new

neutre neutral

neuvième ninth (3)

neveu *(m)* *(pl* **neveux)** nephew (4)

nez *(m)* nose (10); **avoir le nez bouché** to have a stopped-up nose

ni: ne… ni… ni… neither . . . nor . . .

niçois(e) from Nice

nièce *(f)* niece (4)

niveau *(m)* level

Noël *(m)* Christmas

noir(e) black (3); **Il faisait noir.** It was dark.

noisette *(inv)* hazel *(with eyes)* (4)

nom *(m)* name, noun (3); **au nom de** in the name of; **nom de famille** family name, last name (3)

nombre *(m)* number (P)

nombreux(-euse) numerous

nommer to name; **nommé(e)** named

non no (P); **non?** right? (1); **non plus** neither (3)

nord *(m)* north; **Amérique** *(f)* **du Nord** North America (9)

normalement normally

normand(e) from Normandy

Normandie *(f)* Normandy

Norvège *(f)* Norway

notamment such as, in particular

note *(f)* note (4), grade; **régler la note** to pay the bill (10)

noter to note, to notice

notre *(pl* **nos)** our (3)

nourrir to feed, to nourish, to nurture (8); **se nourrir** to feed oneself, to nourish oneself, to nurture oneself (8)

nourrissant(e) nourishing

nourriture *(f)* food, nourishment

nous we (1), (to, for) us (9), ourselves (7); **avec nous** with us (2); **Nous sommes…** There are . . . of us. (4)

nouveau (nouvel, nouvelle) new (1); **de nouveau** again, anew; **Nouvelle-Angleterre** *(f)* New England; **Nouvelle-Calédonie** *(f)* New Caledonia (9); **La Nouvelle-Orléans** *(f)* New Orleans (4)

novembre *(m)* November (4)

nu(e) naked; **pieds nus** barefoot

nuage *(m)* cloud

nuit *(f)* night (5); **boîte** *(f)* **de nuit** nightclub (1)

nuitée *(f)* overnight stay

nul(le) (en) no good (at), really bad (at); **ne… nulle part** nowhere

numérique digital

numéro *(m)* number (3), issue

nutritif(-ive) nutritional

O

obéir (à) to obey (8)

objectif *(m)* objective

objet *(m)* object

obligatoire required, obligatory

obliger to force, to make; **obligé(e)** obliged, forced

observer to observe

obtenir to get, to obtain (9)

occasion *(f)* occasion; **vêtements** *(mpl)* **d'occasion** second-hand clothes

occasionnellement occasionally

occidental(e) *(mpl* **occidentaux)** western

occupé(e) busy (6)

occuper to occupy; **s'occuper de** to take care of

Océanie *(f)* Oceania (9)

octobre *(m)* October (4)

odeur *(f)* odor, smell

œil *(pl* **yeux)** *(m)* eye (10); **avoir les yeux...** to have . . . eyes (4)

œuf *(m)* egg (8); **œuf dur** *(m)* hard-boiled egg (8)

œuvre *(f)* work

office *(m)* **de tourisme** tourist office (10)

offrir to offer; **offert(e)** offered; **offrant** offering

oignon *(m)* onion (8); **soupe** *(f)* **à l'oignon** onion soup (8)

oiseau *(m)* bird

omelette *(f)* omelet (8)

omniprésent(e) ever-present

on one, they, we, people, you (2); **Comment dit-on... en français/en anglais?** How does one say . . . in French/in English? (P); **On...?** Shall we . . . ?, How about we . . . ? (4); **On dit...** One says . . . (P); **On dit que...** They say that . . . (4)

oncle *(m)* uncle (4)

Ontario *(m)* Ontario (9)

onze eleven (P)

opéra *(m)* opera (9)

optimiste optimistic

or *(m)* gold

orage *(m)* storm

orange *(f)* orange (8); **jus** *(m)* **d'orange** orange juice (2)

orange *(inv)* orange (3)

Orangina *(m)* Orangina *(an orange drink)* (2)

orchestre *(m)* orchestra, band (4)

orchidée *(f)* orchid

ordinateur *(m)* computer (2)

ordonnance *(f)* prescription (10)

ordre *(m)* order; **en ordre** in order (3)

oreille *(f)* ear (10)

organiser to organize; **s'organiser** to be organized

originaire de originally from

origine *(f)* origin; **d'origine...** of . . . origin (7)

orné(e) (de) decorated with, adorned with

orphelin(e) orphan

orthographique spelling

os *(m)* bone

OTAN (Organisation du Traité de l'Atlantique Nord) NATO

ou or (P)

où where (P); **d'où** from where (P); **n'importe où** (just) anywhere

oublier to forget (8)

ouest *(m)* west

oui yes (P)

outre-mer overseas

ouvert(e) open

ouverture *(f)* opening; **heures** *(fpl)* **d'ouverture** business hours (6)

ouvrable: jour ouvrable *(m)* workday

ouvrage *(m)* work

ouvrir to open; **Ouvrez votre livre à la page 23.** Open your book to page 23. (P)

P

pacifique pacific, peaceful

page *(f)* page (P)

paiement *(m)* payment

paillasson *(m)* doormat

pain *(m)* bread (8); **pain au chocolat** *(m)* chocolate-filled croissant (8); **pain complet** *(m)* loaf of whole-grain bread (8); **pain grillé** *(m)* toast (8)

palais *(m)* palace (6)

pâle pale

palier *(m)* (floor) landing

pamplemousse *(m)* grapefruit

panique *(f)* panic

paniqué(e) panicked

panoramique panoramic

pantalon *(m)* pants (5)

pantoufles *(fpl)* slippers

papa *(m)* dad, papa

pape *(m)* pope

papier *(m)* paper (P)

papillon *(m)* butterfly

pâque juive *(f)* Passover

Pâques *(fpl)* Easter

paquet *(m)* package, bag (8)

par per (3), by (5); **par ailleurs** furthermore; **par conséquent** consequently; **par contre** on the other hand; **par exemple** for example; **par *hasard** by chance; **par ici** this way (5); **par la fenêtre** through the window; **par mois** per month (3); **par terre** on the ground / floor (3)

paradis *(m)* paradise, heaven

paraître to appear

parapluie *(m)* umbrella (5)

parc *(m)* park (1); **parc naturel** *(m)* natural park, nature reserve

parce que because (P)

parcourir to scan

Pardon. Excuse me. (P)

pardonner to forgive, to pardon

pareil(le) (à) similar (to)

parent *(m)* parent (4), relative (5); **chez mes parents** at my parents' house (3)

paresseux(-euse) lazy (1)

parfait(e) perfect (7)

parfaitement perfectly (7)

parfois sometimes (5)

parfum *(m)* perfume

Parisien(ne) *(mf)* Parisian (9)

parking *(m)* parking lot (1), parking garage

parler to talk, to speak (2); **Je parle/Je ne parle pas...** I speak/I don't speak . . . (P); **parler au téléphone** to talk on the phone (2); **se parler** to talk to each other (7); **Tu parles... ?** Do you speak . . . ? (P)

parmi among

paroisse *(f)* parish

parole *(f)* word, lyric

part: à part... besides . . . ; **mettre à part** to set aside; **ne... nulle part** not . . . anywhere; **quelque part** somewhere

part *(f)* share

partager to share (3), to divide up; **partagé(e)** shared, divided (3)

partenaire *(mf)* partner (7)

participer (à) to participate (in)

particulier(-ère) particular, private; **en particulier** especially

partie *(f)* part; **en grande partie** mostly, in large part; **en partie** partially; **faire partie de** to be a part of

partir (de... pour...) to leave (from . . . for . . .), to go away (4); **à partir de** starting from; **partir en voyage** to leave on a trip (5)

partout everywhere (3)

pas not (P); **je ne comprends pas** I don't understand (P); **ne... pas (du tout)** not (at all) (1); **ne... pas encore** not . . . yet (5); **Pas de problème!** No problem! (3); **Pas mal.** Not badly. (P); **pas plus** no more (4); **pas tellement** not so much; **Pas très bien.** Not very well. (P)

passant(e) *(mf)* passer-by

passé *(m)* past (6); **dans le passé** in the past (6)

passé(e) past (5)

passeport *(m)* passport (9)

passer to spend, to pass (2); **passer chez** to go by . . .'s house (2); **passer le week-end / la matinée** to spend the weekend / the morning (2); **passer un film** to show a movie (6); **s'en passer** to do without; **se faire passer pour** to pass as; **se passer** to happen (7)

passion *(f)* passion (7)

passionnant(e) fascinating

passionné(e) (de) passionate about, fascinated by

pastèque *(f)* watermelon

patate *(f)* *(familiar)* idiot

pâte *(f)* paste, dough; **pâtes** *(fpl)* pasta

pâté *(m)* pâté, meat spread (8); **pâté de cochon** pork pâté

patience *(f)* patience; **avoir de la patience** to have patience (4)

patient(e) patient (6)

patin *(m)* skate; **patin** *(m)* **à glace** ice-skate, ice-skating

pâtisserie *(f)* pastry shop, pastry (8)

patrimoine *(m)* patrimony, heritage

patron(ne) *(mf)* owner, boss

pauvre poor

pauvreté *(f)* poverty

pavé (de) *(m)* thick slice (of) (8)

payer to pay (2)

pays *(m)* country (3)

paysage *(m)* landscape (9)

Pays-Bas *(mpl)* Netherlands

Pays-de-la-Loire *(mpl)* Loire Valley

pêche *(f)* peach (8), fishing; **aller à la pêche** to go fishing

peigner: se peigner to comb one's hair (7)

peine: à peine barely

peintre *(m)* painter

peinture *(f)* painting (1)

pendant during for (5); **pendant que** while

penser to think (3) **penser à** to think about; **Qu'en pensez-vous?** What do you think about it? (5)

penseur (penseuse) *(mf)* thinker

perçu(e) perceived

perdre to lose (7); **perdre du temps** to waste time (7); **perdu(e)** lost; **se perdre** to get lost (7)

père *(m)* father (4)

période *(f)* period; **à cette période** at that time

permettre (de) to permit, to allow; **permis(e)** permitted, allowed

Pérou *(m)* Peru (9)

Perse *(f)* Persia

personnage *(m)* character

personnalisé(e) personalized; **service personnalisé** personal service (8)

personnalité *(f)* personality

personne *(f)* person (6); **ne... personne** nobody, no one, not . . . anyone

personnel(le) personal

pessimiste pessimistic

pétanque *(f)* lawn bowling, petanque

petit(e) small, short (1); **petit à petit** little by little (6); **petit déjeuner** *(m)* breakfast (5); **petite annonce** *(f)* classified ad; **petits pois** *(mpl)* peas (8)

petite-fille *(f)* granddaughter (7)

petit-fils *(m)* grandson (7)

petits-enfants *(mpl)* grandchildren

peu little (P); **à peu près** approximately, about; **un peu difficile** a little difficult/ hard (P)

peuple *(m)* people

peuplé(e) populated

peur *(f)* fear; **avoir peur (de)** to be afraid (of) (4), to fear; **faire peur à** to frighten

peut-être perhaps, maybe (3)

pharmacie *(f)* pharmacy (10)

pharmacien(ne) *(mf)* pharmacist

philosophie *(f)* philosophy (1)

phrase *(f)* sentence (P); **Écrivez la réponse en phrases complètes.** Write the answer in complete sentences. (P)

physiologique physiological

physique *(f)* physics

physique physical; **aspect physique** *(m)* physical appearance (7)

piano *(m)* piano (2)

pièce *(f)* room (3); **pièce** *(f)* **de monnaie** coin; **pièce** *(f)* **de théâtre** play (4); **pièce** *(f)* **d'identité** identity card

pied *(m)* foot (10); **aller à pied** to walk, to go on foot (4); **doigt** *(m)* **de pied** toe (10); **pieds nus** barefoot

pin *(m)* pine

pique-nique *(m)* picnic

pire worse (1)

piscine *(f)* swimming pool (4)

pistache *(f)* pistachio

pitié *(f)* pity; **avoir pitié (de)** to have pity (on / for) (10)

pittoresque picturesque

pizza *(f)* pizza (8)

placard *(m)* closet (3)

place *(f)* place (3), square, plaza (10); **à sa place** in its place (3)

plage *(f)* beach (4)

plaindre: se plaindre to complain

plaine *(f)* plain

plaire to please; **Ça m'a plu!** I liked it! (6); **Ça t'a plu?** Did you like it? (6); **Ça te plaira!** You'll like it! (9); **Ça te plaît!** You like it! (3); **Il/Elle me plaît.** I like it. (5); **s'il vous plaît** please (P)

plaisant(e) pleasant

plaisir *(m)* pleasure; **Avec plaisir!** With pleasure! (6); **faire plaisir à** to please

plan *(m)* map (10), level; **plan** *(m)* **d'eau** stretch of water

planche *(f)* **à voile** windsurfing; **faire de la planche à voile** to windsurf

plante *(f)* plant (3)

plastique *(m)* plastic

plat *(m)* dish (8); **plat préparé** *(m)* ready-to-serve dish (8); **plat principal** main dish (8)

plat(e) flat; **œuf** *(m)* **au plat** fried egg

plateau *(m)* tray

plein(e) full; **de plein air** outdoor (4); **plein de** full of, a lot of

pleurer to cry

pleuvoir to rain (5)

plongée sous-marine *(f)* scuba diving

pluie *(f)* rain (5)

plupart: la plupart de *(f)* the majority of; **la plupart du temps** most of the time (7)

plus more (1), plus; **À plus (tard)!** See you later! (P); **de plus** in addition; **de plus en plus de** more and more of (8); **en plus** besides, furthermore; **ne... plus** no more, no longer (8); **non plus** neither (3); **pas plus** no more (8); **plus de** more (8); **plus... que** more . . . than (1); **plus tard** later (4)

plusieurs several (8)

plutôt rather (1); instead (4); **plutôt que** rather than

poche *(f)* pocket

poché(e) poached

poème *(m)* poem (9)

poésie *(f)* poetry

poing *(m)* fist

point *(m)* point; **au point de** to be about to; **point** *(m)* **de vue** viewpoint

poire *(f)* pear (8)

pois: petits pois *(mpl)* peas (8); **pois chiche** *(m)* chickpea

poisson *(m)* fish (8); **poisson fumé** smoked fish (8); **poissons** *(mpl)* **d'avril** April Fool's Day

poissonnerie *(f)* fish market (8)

poivre *(m)* pepper (8)

poivron vert *(m)* green bell pepper

poli(e) polite

police *(f)* police

policier(-ère) detective, police

politesse *(f)* politeness

politique *(f)* politics (7), policy

politique political; **homme politique** *(m)* politician; **sciences** *(fpl)* **politiques** political science (1)

politiquement politically

polo *(m)* knit shirt (5)

Pologne *(f)* Poland

Polynésie française *(f)* French Polynesia (9)

pomme *(f)* apple (8); **pomme** *(f)* **de terre** potato (8)

pont *(m)* bridge

populaire popular, pop

porc *(m)* pork (8); **côte** *(f)* **de porc** pork chop (8)

portable: (ordinateur) portable *(m)* laptop (3); **(téléphone) portable** *(m)* cell phone (3)

porte *(f)* door (3); **porte** *(f)* **d'arrivée** arrival gate; **porte** *(f)* **d'embarquement** departure gate

portefeuille *(m)* wallet (5)

porter to wear, to carry (4)

portugais *(m)* Portuguese

poser to place; **poser une question** to ask a question (3)

posséder to possess, to own

possibilité *(f)* possibility (4)

possible possible (10); **il est possible que** it is possible that (10); **Pas possible!** I don't believe it!

postal(e) *(mpl* **postaux): carte postale** *(f)* postcard (9); **code postal** *(m)* zip code (3)

poste *(f)* post office; **bureau** *(m)* **de poste** post office (10)

poster *(m)* poster (3)

pot (de) *(m)* jar (of) (8)

pote *(mf) (familiar)* buddy, pal

poubelle *(f)* trash can

poudre *(f)* powder

poulet *(m)* chicken (8)

poumon *(m)* lung

pour for (P), in order to (1); **pour cent** percent; **pour que** so that

pourboire *(m)* tip

pourcentage *(m)* percentage

pourquoi why (2); **Pourquoi pas?** Why not? (2)

pourtant however, yet (8)

pouvoir *(m)* power

pouvoir to be able, can, may (6); **Je peux vous aider?** May I help you? (5); **on peut** one can (4)

pratique *(f)* practice

pratique practical, convenient (3)

pratiquer to practice, to play *(a sport)*, to do

précédent(e) preceding

préciser to specify

préférable preferable (10); **il est préférable que** it's preferable that (10)

préféré(e) favorite (3)

préférence *(f)* preference

préférer to prefer (2); **je préfère** I prefer (1)

premier(-ère) first (3)

prendre to take (4); **Ça prend combien de temps?** How long does it take? (4); **Je vais prendre...** I'm going to have . . . (2); **prendre possession de** to take possession of; **prendre son petit déjeuner** to have one's breakfast (5); **prendre un bain** to take a bath (7); **prendre un bain de soleil** to sunbathe (4); **prendre une décision** to make a decision (7); **prendre un verre** to have a drink (2); **Prenez votre cahier, du papier et un crayon ou un stylo.** Take (out) your notebook / workbook, paper, and a pencil or a pen. (P); **Qu'est-ce que vous allez prendre?** What are you going to have? (2)

prénom *(m)* first name (3)

préoccuper to worry; **se préoccuper (de)** to worry (about)

préparatifs *(mpl)* preparations (9)

préparer to prepare (2); **plat préparé** ready-to-serve dish (8)

près (de) near (1), nearly; **à peu près** approximately, about

présentation *(f)* introduction, presentation

présenter to introduce, to present; **Je vous/ te présente...** I would like to introduce . . . to you.; **se présenter** to arise, to introduce oneself

presque almost, nearly (2)

prêt(e) ready (4)

prêter to loan, to lend

prier to beg, to request, to pray; **Je vous/t'en prie.** You're welcome (2).

prière *(f)* prayer

primaire: école primaire *(f)* elementary school

principal(e) *(mpl* **principaux)** main (8)

principalement mainly

principauté *(f)* principality

printemps *(m)* spring (5); **au printemps** in spring (5)

prioritaire having priority

priorité *(f)* priority

prisonnier(-ère) *(mf)* prisoner

privatif(-ive) private

privé(e) private (10)

privilégié(e) privileged, favored

prix *(m)* price; **menu** *(m)* **à prix fixe** set-price menu (8)

probablement probably

problème *(m)* problem (3); **pas de problème** no problem (3)

procédé *(m)* process, method

prochain(e) next (4); **le prochain cours** the next class (P)

producteur(-trice) producer

produit *(m)* product (8); **produits bio** *(mpl)* organic products (8)

professeur *(m)* professor (P); **Le professeur dit aux étudiants…** The professor says to the students . . . (P)

profession *(f)* profession (7)

professionnel(le) professional (7)

profil *(m)* profile

profiter de to take advantage of (9)

profond(e) deep

programme *(m)* program

projet *(m)* plan (4); **faire des projets** to make plans (4)

promenade *(f)* walk (5); **faire une promenade** to take a walk (5)

promener: se promener to go walking (7)

promettre (de...) to promise (to . . .) (6)

promouvoir to promote

pronom *(m)* pronoun

prononcer to pronounce

prononciation *(f)* pronunciation

propos: à propos de about

proposer to offer, to suggest, to propose; **Qu'est-ce que je peux vous proposer d'autre?** What else can I get you? (8)

propre clean (3), own

propreté *(f)* cleanliness

protéger to protect; **protégé(e) par** protected by

provençal *(m)* Provençal

Provence *(f)* Provence

provenir de to come from

province *(f)* province (3)

proviseur *(m)* principal

provoquer to cause

prune *(f)* plum

pruneau *(m)* prune

psychologie *(f)* psychology (1)

public: le grand public the public at large

publicité *(f)* advertising, advertisement

puis then (4)

puisque since

puissant(e) powerful

pull *(m)* pullover sweater (5)

pureté *(f)* purity

pyjama *(m)* pajamas

Q

quai *(m)* quay, wharf

quand when (2); **quand même** all the same

quantité *(f)* quantity

quarante forty (P); **quarante et un** forty-one (P)

quart *(m)* quarter; **Il est deux heures et quart.** It's a quarter past two. (P)

quartier *(m)* neighborhood (1)

quatorze fourteen (P)

quatre four (P)

quatre-vingts eighty (2); **quatre-vingt-un** eighty-one (2); **quatre-vingt-dix** ninety (2); **quatre-vingt-onze** ninety-one (2)

quatrième fourth (3)

que that (P), than, as (1), what (2), which, whom (7); **ce que** what, that which (7); **ne... que** only; **ne... rien que** nothing but; **que ce soit** whether it be; **qu'est-ce que** what (1);

Qu'est-ce que c'est? What is it? (2) **Que veut dire...?** What does . . . mean? (P); **quel(le)** which, what (3); **À quelle heure?** At what time? (P); **C'est quel jour aujourd'hui?** What day is today? (P); **n'importe quel(le)...** (just) any . . . ; **Quel âge a... ?** How old is . . . ? (4)

quelque some; **quelque chose** something (2); **quelque part** somewhere; **quelques** a few (5); **quelques-un(e)s** *(mf)* a few; **quelqu'un** someone, somebody (6)

quelquefois sometimes (2)

quelques-un(e)s *(mf)* a few

question *(f)* question (P); **Écoutez la question.** Listen to the question. (P); **Répondez à la question.** Answer the question. (P)

quête *(f)* quest

qui who (2), that, which, who (7); **ce qui** what (7); **Qu'est-ce qui ne va pas?** What's wrong? (10); **Qu'est-ce qui s'est passé?** What happened? (6); **Qui est-ce** Who is it? (2)

quinze fifteen (P)

quinzième fifteenth (3)

quitter to leave (4); **se quitter** to leave each other (7)

quoi what; **n'importe quoi** (just) anything; **à quoi bon** what's the point

quotidien(ne) daily (7)

R

rabbin *(m)* rabbi

raccompagner to (re)accompany

racine *(f)* root

raconter to tell (7), to recount

radio *(f)* radio, X-ray

raffiné(e) refined

raie *(f)* skate (fish), rayfish (8)

raisin *(m)* grape(s) (8); **raisins secs** *(mpl)* raisins

raison *(f)* reason; **avoir raison** to be right (4); **en raison de** because of

raisonnable reasonable

rajouter to add

ralentir to slow down

randonnée *(f)* hike (5); **faire une randonnée** to go for a hike (5)

rangé(e) orderly, put away, in its place (3)

ranger to arrange, to order (7)

rapide rapid (8)

rapport *(m)* relationship, report

rapporter to bring back; **se rapporter à** to be related to

rarement rarely (2)

raser: se raser to shave (7)

rassembler: se rassembler to gather

rater to miss

rayé(e) striped

réagir (à) to react (to)

réaliste realistic

récemment recently (5)

réception *(f)* front desk (10), receiving

recette *(f)* recipe

recevoir to receive (9)

recherche *(f)* research, search

rechercher to seek; **recherché(e)** sought

réciproque reciprocal

recoins *(mpl)* the nooks and corners

recommander to recommend (10); **recommandé(e)** recommended

réconcilier: se réconcilier to make up with each other (7)

reconnaître to recognize (9); **se reconnaître** to recognize each other (7)

recoucher: se recoucher to go back to bed (7)

recours: avoir recours à to resort to

recouvert(e) covered

recréer to recreate

récrire to rewrite

récupéré(e) recuperated, salvaged

rédaction *(f)* composition (9)

redéfinir to redefine

réduire to reduce

réel(le) real

réfléchi(e) reflexive

réfléchir (à) to think (about) (8), to reflect (on)

refléter to reflect

réflexion *(f)* reflection, thought

réfrigérateur *(m)* refrigerator

réfugié(e) *(mf)* refugee

regard *(m)* look

regarder to look at, to watch (2); **se regarder** to look at each other (7)

régime *(m)* diet; regime; **être au régime** to be on a diet

région *(f)* region (4); area (9)

régional(e) *(mpl* **régionaux)** regional (4)

réglable adjustable

règlement *(m)* payment

réglementé(e) regulated

régler to adjust; **régler la note** to pay the bill (10)

regretter to regret (6)

régulier(-ière) regular

régulièrement regularly (8)

rejoindre to join

relation *(f)* relationship (7)

relativement relatively

relaxant(e) relaxing

religieux(-euse) religious

religion *(f)* religion (7)

relire to reread

remarquable remarkable

remarquer to notice

rembourser to reimburse

remercier (de) to thank (for) (10)

remettre to put back

remonter to go back (up)

remplacer to replace

remplir to fill up / out

remporter to win

renaissance *(f)* revival, renaissance

rencontre *(f)* meeting, encounter (7)

rencontrer to meet for the first time or by chance, to run into (1); **se rencontrer** to run into each other (7)

rendez-vous *(m)* date, appointment; **Rendez-vous à...** Let's meet at . . .

rendre (quelque chose à quelqu'un), to return (something to someone) (7); **rendre (+ *adjective*)** to make (+ *adjective*); **rendre visite à quelqu'un** to visit someone (7); **se rendre (à / chez)** to go (to)

renommé(e) renowned

renommée *(f)* fame

renoncer renounce, give up

renouvelable renewable

rénover to renovate

renseignement *(m)* piece of information (3)

renseigner: se renseigner to inquire, to get information (10)

rentrer to return, to come / go back (home) (2); **rentré(e)** having returned

réparti(e) distributed

repartir to start again, to leave again

répartition *(f)* distribution

repas *(m)* meal (6)

répéter to repeat (2); **Répétez, s'il vous plaît.** Repeat, please. (P); **se répéter** to be repeated

répondre (à) to answer (6); **Répondez à la question.** Answer the question. (P)

réponse *(f)* answer (P); **Écrivez la réponse avec une phrase complète.** Write the answer with a complete sentence. (P)

reposer to set down; **se reposer** to rest (7)

reprendre to catch again

représenter to represent

république *(f)* republic

réputé(e) known, renowned

réseau *(m)* network (9)

réservation *(f)* reservation (9); **faire une réservation** to make a reservation (9)

réserver to reserve (9); **réservé(e)** reserved

résidence universitaire *(f)* dormitory (1), residence hall

résoudre to solve

respecter to respect; **se respecter** to respect one another

respiration *(f)* breathing

respirer to breathe

responsable responsible

ressemblance *(f)* similarity

ressembler à to look like, to resemble

ressortir: faire ressortir to make stand out

restaurant *(m)* restaurant (1); **dîner au restaurant** to have dinner in a restaurant (2)

reste *(m)* rest (7); **le reste (de)** the rest (of) (7)

rester to stay (2); **rester au lit** to stay in bed (2)

resto-U *(m)* university cafeteria (6)

résultat *(m)* result

résumé *(m)* summary

resvératrol *(m)* resveratrol

retard *(m)* delay; **en retard** late (10)

retirer (de l'argent) to take out, to withdraw (money) (10); **se retirer** to retire

retour *(m)* return (9); **billet aller-retour** *(m)* round-trip ticket (9)

retourner to return (5); **se retourner** to turn around

retrouver to meet (4), to find (again); **se retrouver** to meet each other *(by design)* (7)

réunion *(f)* meeting

réunir: se réunir to meet

réussir (à) to succeed (at/in), to pass *(a test)* (8)

revanche: en revanche on the other hand

rêve *(m)* dream

réveil *(m)* alarm clock (7), awakening

réveiller to wake up; **se réveiller** to wake up (7)

réveillon *(m)* **du jour de l'An** New Year's Eve

révélateur(-trice) revealing

révéler to reveal; **se révéler** to be revealed

revendre to resell, to sell back (7)

revenir to come back (4)

revenu *(m)* income

rêver (de) to dream (about, of) (7)

réviser to review (5)

révision *(f)* review, revision

revoir to see again; **Au revoir.** Good-bye. (P)

revue *(f)* magazine

rez-de-chaussée *(m)* ground floor (3)

rhum *(m)* rum

rhume *(m)* cold (10)

riche rich (2)

richesse *(f)* wealth

rideau *(m)* curtain (3)

ridicule ridiculous

rien nothing; **de rien** you're welcome (P); **ne... rien** nothing, not . . . anything (5); **ne... rien de spécial** nothing special (5); **ne... rien que** nothing but; **rien à voir avec** nothing to do with; **rien du tout** nothing at all (6)

rillettes *(fpl)* potted meat or fish

ringard(e) old-fashioned

rire to laugh

ris *(m)* sweetbread

rive *(f)* bank

rivière *(f)* river

riz *(m)* rice (8)

robe *(f)* dress (5); **robe** *(f)* **de chambre** robe

rocheux(-euse) rocky

rock *(m)* rock music

rockeur(-euse) *(mf)* rock singer

roi *(m)* king

rôle *(m)* role; **à tour de rôle** taking turns

roller: faire du roller to go in-line skating (6)

romain(e) Roman

roman *(m)* novel (9)

romanche *(m)* Romansh

romantique romantic

rompre to break (up)

rond *(m)* circle

rosbif *(m)* roast beef (8)

rose pink (3)

rosier *(m)* rosebush

rôti(e) roasted; **rôti** *(m)* **de porc** pork roast

rouge red (3); **vin rouge** *(m)* red wine (2)

route *(f)* route, way

routine *(f)* routine (7)

roux (rousse) red *(with hair)* (4)

royaume *(m)* kingdom; **Royaume-Uni** *(m)* United Kingdom (9)

rue *(f)* street (3); **dans la rue...** on . . . Street (10)

ruine *(f)* ruin

rural(e) *(mpl* **ruraux)** rural

ruse *(f)* trick

russe *(m)* Russian

Russie *(f)* Russia (9)

rythme *(m)* rhythm

S

sable *(m)* sand

sac *(m)* purse (5); **sac** *(m)* **à dos** backpack

sage good, well-behaved (4)

sain(e) healthy (8)

saint(e) holy

Saint-Jacques *(f)* scallop

Saint-Valentin *(f)* Valentine's Day

saison *(f)* season (5)

salade *(f)* salad (8); **salade** *(f)* **de tomates** tomato salad (8)

salarié(e) *(mf)* wage earner

sale dirty (3)

salé(e) salted

salle *(f)* room; **salle** *(f)* **à manger** dining room (3); **salle** *(f)* **de bains** bathroom (3); **salle** *(f)* **de cours** classroom (1); **salle** *(f)* **de gym** gym, fitness club (1); **salle** *(f)* **d'informatique** computer lab (1)

salon *(m)* living room (3)

saluer to greet

Salut! Hi! (P)

salutation *(f)* greeting (P)

samedi *(m)* Saturday (P)

sandale *(f)* sandal (5)

sandwich *(m)* sandwich (2)

sang *(m)* blood

sans without (P); **Ça s'écrit avec ou sans accent?** That's written with or without an accent? (P); **sans égal** unequaled

santé *(f)* health (8)

satisfaisant(e) satisfying

satisfait(e) satisfied

saucisse *(f)* sausage (8)

saucisson *(m)* salami (8)

sauf except (2)

saumon *(m)* salmon (8)

sauter to jump; **faire sauter** to blow up

sauver to save; **sauvé(e)** saved

savane *(f)* savanna

saveur *(f)* flavor, taste

savoir to know (how) (9); **Je ne sais pas.** I don't know. (P)

savon *(m)* soap

savoureux(-euse) tasty

science *(f)* science (1); **sciences humaines** *(fpl)* social sciences (1); **sciences politiques** *(fpl)* political science, government (1)

scientifique scientific

scolaire school; **extra-scolaire** extracurricular

scolarité *(f)* education

se herself, himself, itself, oneself, themselves (7); **Il/Elle s'appelle...** His/Her name is . . . (4); **Il/Elle se trouve...** It is located . . .

séance *(f)* showing (6)

sec (sèche) dry

sécher to dry, to skip (class)

secondaire secondary

seconde *(f)* second (5)

sécurité *(f)* security, safety

séducteur(-trice) seductive

séduire to seduce

séduisant(e) attractive

sein *(m)* breast; **au sein de** within

seize sixteen (P)

seizième sixteenth (3)

séjour *(m)* stay (7)

sel *(m)* salt (8)

self-service *(m)* self-service restaurant (8)

selon according to

semaine *(f)* week (P); **en semaine** weekdays; **les jours de la semaine** the days of the week (P)

semblable similar

sembler to seem

semestre *(m)* semester (P)

Sénégal *(m)* Senegal (9)

sénégalais(e) Senegalese

sens *(m)* meaning, sense; **sens** *(m)* **de l'humour** sense of humor (7)

sensible sensitive

sentiment *(m)* feeling (7)

sentimental(e) *(mpl* **sentimentaux)** sentimental, emotional (7)

sentir: se sentir to feel (8)

séparément separately

séparer to separate; **séparé(e)** separated

sept seven (P)

septembre *(m)* September (4)

septième seventh (3)

sérieux(-euse) serious

serrer to squeeze

serveur *(m)* waiter, server (2)

serveuse *(f)* waitress, server (2)

serviable helpful, obliging

service *(m)* service (2)

serviette *(f)* napkin, towel

servir to serve (4); **servi(e)** served (10); **se servir de** to use

seul(e) alone (P), only (3), single, lonely; **le/la seul(e)** the only one

seulement only (8)

shopping: faire du shopping to go shopping (2)

short (m) shorts (5)

si if (5), yes (in response to a question in the negative) (8); **s'il vous plaît** please (P)

siècle (m) century

siège (m) seat

sieste (f) nap

signaler to point out, to draw attention to

similaire (à) similar (to)

simple simple; **aller simple** (m) one-way ticket (9); **chambre simple** (f) single room (10)

simplement simply (10); **tout simplement** quite simply (10)

sinon if not, otherwise

site (m) site (9)

situé(e) situated

six six (P)

sixième sixth (3)

skateboard(ing): faire du skateboard(ing) to skateboard (6)

ski (m) skiing (5); **faire du ski** to go skiing (5); **faire du ski nautique** to go water-skiing (5)

smartphone (m) smartphone (3)

social(e) (mpl **sociaux**) social

société (f) company, society

sœur (f) sister (1); **belle-sœur** (f) sister-in-law; **demi-sœur** (f) stepsister (6), half-sister

soi oneself

soif (f) thirst; **avoir soif** to be thirsty (4)

soigner to treat, to cure

soin (m) care

soir (m) evening (P); **à huit heures du soir** at eight in the evening (P); **ce soir** tonight, this evening (2); **le soir** in the evening, evenings (P)

soirée (f) evening (4), party (6)

soixante sixty (2); **les années soixante** the sixties; **soixante-dix** seventy (2); **soixante et onze** seventy-one (2); **soixante et un** sixty-one (2)

sol (m) ground

solaire solar

soldat (m) soldier

solde: en solde on sale (5)

sole (f) sole (fish)

soleil (m) sun; **Il fait (du) soleil.** It's sunny. (5); **lunettes** (fpl) **de soleil** sunglasses (5); **prendre un bain de soleil** to sunbathe (4)

sombre dark, gloomy

sommeil (m) sleep; **avoir sommeil** to be sleepy (4)

sommet (m) summit

son (m) sound

son (**sa, ses**) her, his, its (3)

sondage (m) poll

sonder to poll

sonner to ring (7)

sorte (f) kind, sort; **en sorte que** so that

sortie (f) outing (6), exit

sortir to go out (2); to take out

soudain suddenly (6)

soudain(e) sudden

soudainement suddenly

souhaiter to wish (10)

soupçonner to suspect

soupe (f) soup (8); **soupe** (f) **à l'oignon** onion soup (8)

sourire to smile

sous under (3); **sous réserve de** subject to

sous-marin(e) underwater; **plongée sous-marine** (f) scuba diving

sous-sol (m) basement (3)

sous-vêtements (mpl) underwear

souterrain(e) underground

soutien (m) support

souvenir (m) memory

souvenir: se souvenir (de) to remember (7)

souvent often (2)

spatial(e) (mpl **spatiaux**): **industrie** (f) **spatiale** space industry

spécial(e) (mpl **spéciaux**) special (5); **effets spéciaux** (mpl) special effects (6); **ne... rien de spécial** nothing special (5)

spécialisé(e) specialized

spécialité (f) specialty (4)

spectacle (m) show

spectateur(-trice) (mf) spectator, viewer

spiritualité (f) spirituality (7)

spontané(e) spontaneous

sport (m) sports (1); **faire du sport** to play sports (2)

sportif (m) athlete

sportif(-ive) athletic (1)

stade (m) stadium (1)

stage (m) internship

stagiaire (mf) intern

station (f) station; **station-service** (f) service station

statistique (f) statistics

statut (m) statute, status

steak-frites (m) steak and fries (8)

stimuler to stimulate

stratégie (f) strategy

stress (m) stress (8)

stressé(e) stressed (out)

stylo (m) pen (P)

subventions (fpl) subsidies

sucre (m) sugar (8)

sucré(e) sweet, sugary

sud (m) south; **Amérique** (f) **du Sud** South America (9)

Suède (f) Sweden

suffire to suffice; **Suffit!** That's enough!

suffisant(e) sufficient

suggérer to suggest (6)

Suisse (f) Switzerland (9)

suisse Swiss

suite: tout de suite right away (6)

suivant(e) following (3)

suivre to follow (7); **à suivre** to be continued (6); **suivi(e) de** followed by; **suivre un cours** to take a course

sujet (m) subject; **au sujet de** about

sulfureux(-euse) sulferous

super great (P)

superficie (f) area

supérieur(e) superior, higher

supermarché (m) supermarket (8)

supplément (m) extra charge (10)

supporter to bear, to tolerate, to put up with (7)

sur on (1); **sept jours sur sept** seven days out of seven

sûr(e) sure; **Bien sûr!** Of course! (5)

suranné(e) old-fashioned

surface: grande surface (f) superstore (8)

surfer sur Internet to surf the Net (2)

surgelé(e) frozen (8)

surgir to arise, to come up, to appear suddenly

surnom (m) nickname

surprenant(e) surprising

surprendre to surprise; **surpris(e)** surprised (10)

sursauter to jump

surtout especially (8), above all

survêtement (m) jogging suit (5)

survivre to survive

sympathique (sympa) nice (1)

symptôme (m) symptom (10)

synonyme synonymous

T

tabac (m) tobacco (8); **bureau** (m) **de tabac** tobacco shop

table (f) table (3); **à table** at the table; **table basse** (f) coffee table

tableau (m) board (P), painting, picture (3), scene, chart; **au tableau** on the board (P); **tableau** (m) **d'affichage** bulletin board

tache (f) spot

tactile: écran (m) **tactile** touch screen

taille (f) size (4); **de taille moyenne** medium-sized, of medium height (4); **Quelle taille faites-vous?** What size do you wear? (5)

tailleur (m) woman's suit

talon (m) heel; *****haut talon** (m) high heel

tambour (m) drum

tandis que whereas, while

tant (de) so much, so many; **tant que** as long as

tante (f) aunt (4)

tapis (m) rug (3)

tapisserie (f) tapestry

tard late (4); **À plus tard!** See you later! (P); **plus tard** later (4)

tarif (m) rate, fare

tarte (f) pie (8); **tarte** (f) **aux pommes** apple pie (8);

tarte tatin (f) tarte tatin (an upside-down fruit pastry)

tartelette (f) **(aux fraises/aux cerises)** (strawberry/cherry) tart (8)

tartine (f) bread with butter and jelly (8)

tas (m) pile; **un tas de** a bunch of

tasse (f) cup

taxi (m) taxi (4); **en taxi** by taxi (4)

te (to, for) you (9), yourself (7); **Ça te dit?** How does that sound to you? (2); **Ça te plaît?** Do you like it? (3); **Je te présente...** I would like to introduce . . . to you.; **s'il te plaît** please; **Te voilà!** There you are!

technologie (f) technology (1); **technologies** (fpl) technical courses (1)

technologique technological

tee-shirt (m) T-shirt (5)

tel(le): tel(le) que such as; **un(e) tel(le)** such a (7)

télé (f) TV (2)

téléchargement (m) downloading

téléphone (m) telephone (2); **au téléphone** on the telephone (2); **numéro** (m) **de téléphone** telephone number (3)

téléphoner (à) to phone (3); **se téléphoner** to phone each other (7)

téléphonique: carte (f) **téléphonique** telephone card (10)

télévisé(e) televised

télévision (télé) (f) television (2)

tellement so much (1), so (6); **pas tellement** not so much (5)

temple (m) temple, Protestant church

temporaire temporary

temps (m) time (2), weather (5); **Ça prend combien de temps?** How long does it take? (4); **de temps en temps** from time to time (4); **emploi** (m) **du temps** schedule; **en même temps** at the same time; **en tout temps** at all times, at any time; **passer du temps** to spend time; **Pendant combien de temps?** For how long? (5); **Quel temps fait-il?** What's the weather like? (5); **temps libre** (m) free time (2); **temps verbal** (m) tense

tendance *(f)* tendency

tendre tender

tendresse *(f)* tenderness, affection (7)

tenir to hold, to keep; **Ah tiens!** Hey!; **tenir à** to value, to be keen on

tennis *(m)* tennis (1); **court** *(m)* **de tennis** tennis court

terme *(m)* term; **mettre terme à** to put an end to

terminaison *(f)* ending

terminer to finish

terrasse *(f)* terrace (9)

terre *(f)* earth; **par terre** on the ground / floor (3); **pomme** *(f)* **de terre** potato (8)

terrine *(f)* earthenware bowl, terrine

territoire *(m)* territory

test *(m)* test (7)

tête *(f)* head (10); **prendre la tête** to take charge

Texas *(m)* Texas (9)

texto *(m)* text message (2)

thé *(m)* tea (2)

théâtre *(m)* theater, drama (1)

thon *(m)* tuna (8)

tiers *(m)* third

timbre *(m)* stamp (10)

timide shy, timid (1)

tiroir *(m)* drawer

toi you (P); **avec toi** with you (2); **Et toi?** And you? *(familiar)* (P)

toilette: toilettes *(fpl)* toilet, restroom (3); **faire sa toilette** to wash up (7)

tomate *(f)* tomato (8)

tomber to fall (5); **tomber amoureux(-euse) (de)** to fall in love (with) (6); **tomber malade** to get sick (10)

ton *(m)* tone

ton (ta, tes) your (3); **tes amis** your friends (1)

tongs *(fpl)* flip-flops (5)

tort: avoir tort to be wrong (4)

tôt early (4)

touche *(f)* key

toucher to touch

toujours always (2), still

tour *(m)* tour, ride (4); **à tour de rôle** taking turns; **faire un tour** to take a tour, to go for a ride (4)

tour *(f)* tower

tourisme *(m)* tourism; **office** *(m)* **de tourisme** tourist office (10)

touriste *(mf)* tourist

touristique touristic (9)

tournedos *(m)* **de bœuf** rounds of beef

tourner (à droite/à gauche) to turn (right/left) (10), to stir, to film; **se tourner (vers)** to turn (toward); **tourné(e)** filmed

tousser to cough (10)

tout (toute, tous, toutes) everything, all, every, whole (2); **À tout à l'heure!** See you in a little while. (6); **C'est tout.** That's all. (8); **ne... pas du tout** not at all (1); **rien du tout** nothing at all (6); **tous (toutes) les deux** both; **tous les jours** every day (P); **tous les soirs** every evening; **tout à coup** all of a sudden (6); **tout à fait** completely; **tout à l'heure** a while ago; **tout de suite** right away (6); **tout droit** straight (10); **tout d'un coup** all at once (6); **tout en** while; **toute la journée** the whole day (2); **tout le monde** everybody, everyone (6); **tout près (de)** right by, very near (3); **tout simplement** quite simply (10)

toutefois however

toux *(f)* cough

traditionnel(le) traditional (8)

traduire to translate

train *(m)* train (4); **en train** by train (4); **être en train de...** to be in the process of . . .

trait *(m)* trait (7); **trait** *(m)* **de caractère** character trait (7)

tranche *(f)* slice (8)

tranquille tranquil, calm

transformer: se transformer en to change into

transmettre to transmit; to pass on

transport *(m)* transportation (4); **moyen** *(m)* **de transport** means of transportation (4); **réseau** *(m)* **de transports en commun** public transportation system (9)

travail *(m)* *(pl* **travaux)** work (6); **fête** *(f)* **du travail** Labor Day

travailler to work (2); **Je travaille...** I work . . . (P); **Je ne travaille pas...** I do not work . . . (P); **Tu travailles?** Do you work? (P)

travers: à travers across

traverser to cross, to go across (10)

treize thirteen (P)

trekking *(m)* backpacking

tremblant(e) trembling, shaky

trente thirty (P)

très very (P); **Je vais très bien.** I'm doing very well. (P)

tribu *(f)* tribe

trinité *(f)* trinity

triomphe *(m)* triumph

triste sad (10)

trois three (P)

troisième third (3)

trompe *(f)* horn

trompette *(f)* trumpet

trop too, too much (3); **trop de** too much, too many (6)

tropical(e) *(mpl* **tropicaux)** tropical (9)

trou *(m)* hole

trouver to find (4); **Il/Elle se trouve...** It is located . . ., He/She/It finds himself/herself/itself

truc *(m)* thing (1); **Ce n'est pas mon truc.** That's not my thing. (1)

truite *(f)* trout

tu you (P)

tuer to kill

Tunisie *(f)* Tunisia

Turquie *(f)* Turkey

typique typical (2)

typiquement typically

tyran *(m)* tyrant

U

un(e) one, a (P)

uni(e) (à) close (to), united, solid-colored; **Royaume-Uni** *(m)* United Kingdom (9)

union: Union *(f)* **européenne** European Union

unique only, single, unique

uniquement only (6)

unité *(f)* unity, unit

universel(le) universal

universitaire university (1); **résidence** *(f)* **universitaire** university dorm (1)

université *(f)* university (P); **à l'université** at the university (P)

urbain(e) urban

urgence *(f)* emergency

usage *(m)* use

usine *(f)* factory

utile useful (P)

utiliser to use, to utilize

V

vacances *(fpl)* vacation (4); **partir en vacances** to leave on vacation (4)

vacancier(-ière) *(mf)* vacationer

vachement really *(slang)*

vadrouille *(f)* stroll

vague *(f)* wave

vaisselle *(f)* dishes; **faire la vaisselle** to wash dishes (5); **lave-vaisselle** *(m)* dishwasher

valeur *(f)* value

valise *(f)* suitcase (9); **faire sa valise** to pack your bag (9)

vallée *(f)* valley; **la Vallée de la Loire** the Loire Valley

valoir to be worth; **il vaut mieux (que)...** it's better (that) . . . (10)

valse *(f)* waltz

vanille *(f)* vanilla (8)

vanité *(f)* vanity (7)

vaniteux(-euse) vain

varié(e) varied

varier to vary

vaut See **valoir**

veau *(m)* veal

végétal(e) *(mpl* **végétaux)** **huile végétale** *(f)* vegetable oil

végétarien(ne) vegetarian

vélo *(m)* bicycle (2); **à vélo** by bike (4); **faire du vélo** to go bike-riding (2)

velouté *(m)* cream soup

vendeur(-euse) *(mf)* salesperson (5)

vendre to sell (7)

vendredi *(m)* Friday (P)

venir to come (4); **venir de** (+ *infinitive*) to have just (+ *past participle*); **Viens voir!** Come see! (3)

vent *(m)* wind; **Il fait du vent.** It's windy. (5); **Il y a du vent.** It's windy. (5)

vente *(f)* sale

ventre *(m)* stomach (10), belly

verbe *(m)* verb

verdoyant(e) green, verdant

verdure *(f)* greenery

verglas: Il y a du verglas. It's icy.

vérifier to check, to verify (10)

vérité *(f)* truth

verre *(m)* glass (2); **prendre un verre** to have a drink (2)

vers *(m)* verse

vers toward(s), about, around (2)

verser to pour, to pay

vert(e) green (3)

vêtements *(mpl)* clothes (3); **sous-vêtements** *(mpl)* underwear

veuf *(m)* widower (7)

veuve *(f)* widow (7)

vexé(e) offended

viande *(f)* meat (8)

victime *(f)* victim

vidéo *(f)* video; **jeu** *(m)* **vidéo** video game (2)

vie *(f)* life (6)

vieillir to age, to get old

vieillot(te) outdated, old-fashioned

viennois(e) Viennese

viennoiserie *(f)* *baked goods sold at a bakery*

vierge *(f)* virgin

Viêt Nam *(m)* Vietnam (9)

vieux (vieil, vieille) old (1); **Vieux Carré** *(m)* French Quarter (4)

vif(-ive) lively, bright; **bleu vif** bright blue

vignoble *(m)* vineyard

village *(m)* village, town

villageois(e) *(mf)* villager
ville *(f)* city (3); **en ville** in town (3)
vin *(m)* wine (2)
vingt twenty (P)
vingtième twentieth (3)
violence *(f)* violence (6)
violet(te) violet (3)
virus *(m)* virus (10)
visage *(m)* face
visite *(f)* visit; **rendre visite à quelqu'un** to visit someone (7)
visiter to visit *(a place)* (1)
visiteur(-euse) *(mf)* visitor
vitamine *(f)* vitamin (8)
vite quick(ly), fast (7)
vitesse *(f)* speed
vivre to live; **Vive…! Long live…!, Hurray for…!**
vocabulaire *(m)* vocabulary (P); **Étudiez les mots de vocabulaire.** Study the vocabulary words. (P)
vœu *(m)* wish
voici here is, here are (2)
voilà there is, there are (2); **Te/Vous voilà! There you are!**
voile *(f)* sailing; **faire de la planche à voile** to go windsurfing
voir to see (1); **aller voir** to go see, to visit (4); **comme tu vois** as you see (3); **rien à voir avec** nothing to do with; **se voir** to see each other (7); **Voyons!** Let's see! (5)
voisin(e) *(mf)* neighbor (9)

voiture *(f)* car (3); **en voiture** by car (4); **voiture** *(f)* **de location** rental car (5)
voix *(f)* voice
vol *(m)* flight (9)
volaille *(f)* poultry (8)
volcan *(m)* volcano
voleur *(m)* thief
volley *(m)* volleyball (2)
volonté *(f)* will, wish
volontiers gladly, willingly
vomir to vomit (10)
voter to vote
votre *(pl* **vos)** your (2); **Ouvrez votre livre à la page 23.** Open your book to page 23. (P)
vouloir to want (6); **Ça veut dire…** That means . . . (P); **Je voudrais (bien)…** I would like . . . (2); **Que veut dire…?** What does . . . mean? (P); **Qu'est-ce que vous voudriez faire?** What would you like to do? (2); **Tu voudrais…?** Would you like . . . ? (2)
vous you (P), (to, for) you (9), yourself(-selves) (7); **avec vous** with you (2); **Ça vous dit?** How does that sound to you? (2); **Et vous?** And you? *(formal)* (P); **Je vous présente…** I would like to introduce . . . to you.; **s'il vous plaît** please (P); **vous-même** yourself; **Vous voilà!** There you are!
voyage *(m)* trip (4); **agence** *(f)* **de voyages** travel agency (9); **agent** *(m)* **de voyages** travel agent (9); **chèque** *(m)* **de voyage**

traveler's check; **faire un voyage** to take a trip (5); **partir en voyage** to leave on a trip (5); **voyage** *(m)* **de noces** honeymoon
voyager to travel (2)
voyageur(-euse) *(mf)* traveler
voyelle *(f)* vowel
vrai(e) true (8)
vraiment really, truly (2)
VTT **(vélo** *[m]* **tout-terrain): faire du VTT** to go all-terrain biking (5)
vue *(f)* view (3); **point** *(m)* **de vue** viewpoint

W

wallon(ne) Walloon
W.-C. *(m)* toilet, restroom (10)
week-end *(m)* weekend (P); **Bon week-end!** Have a good weekend!; **le week-end** on the weekend, weekends (P)
Wi-Fi *(m)* Wi-Fi (1); **accès** *(m)* **Wi-Fi** Wi-Fi access (10)

Y

y there (4); **il y a** there is, there are (1), ago (5)
yaourt *(m)* yogurt (8)
yeux *(mpl)* *(sing* **œil)** eyes (4)

Z

zéro *(m)* zero (P)
zydeco: **musique** *(f)* **zydeco** zydeco music (4)

INDEX

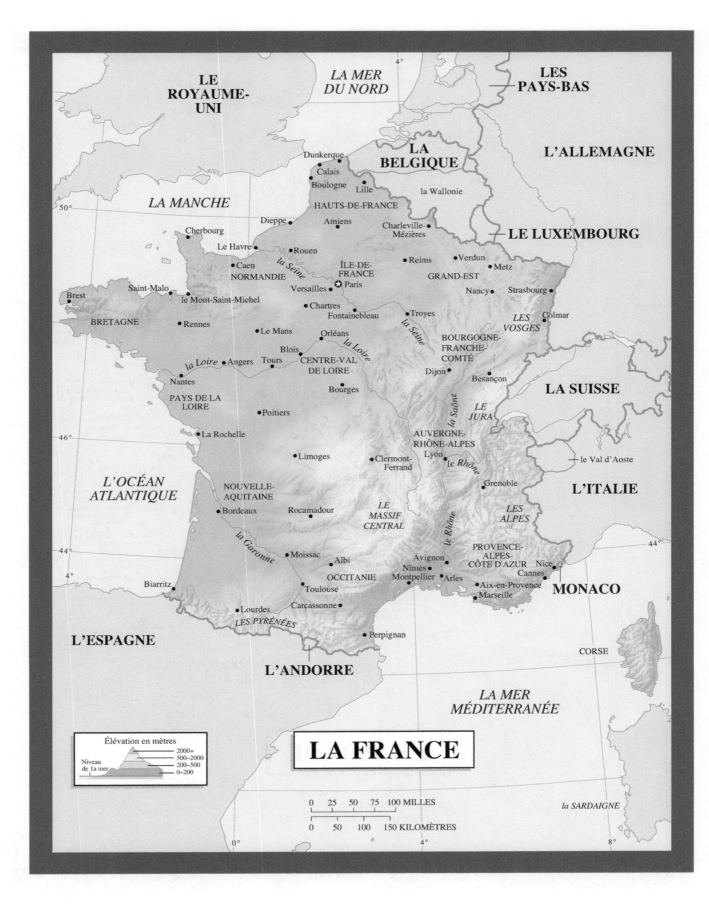

LA FRANCE

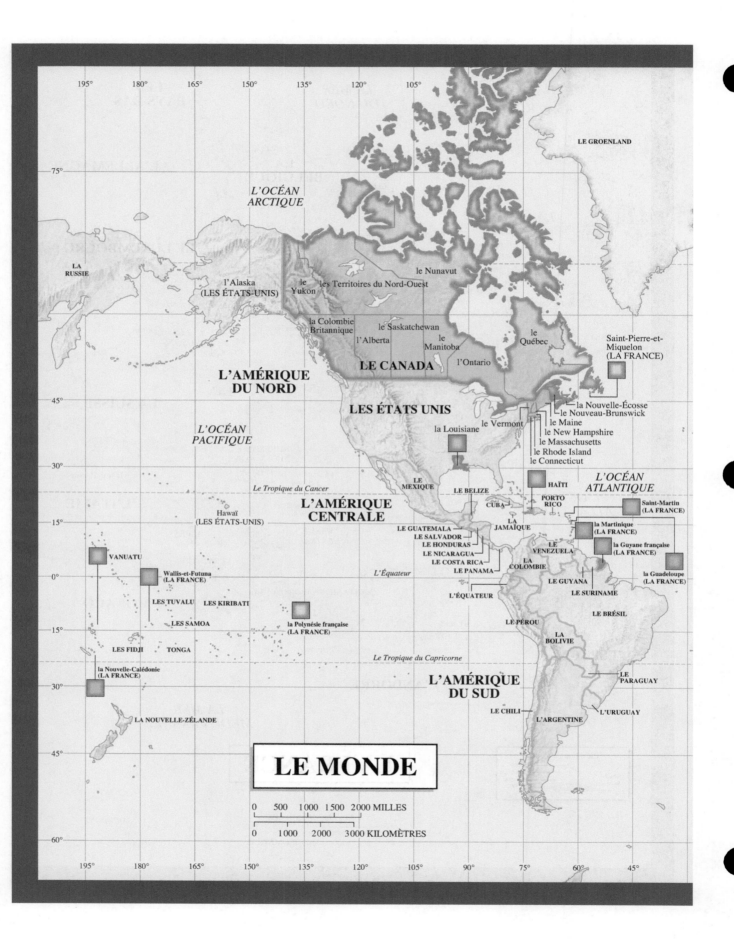

LE MONDE

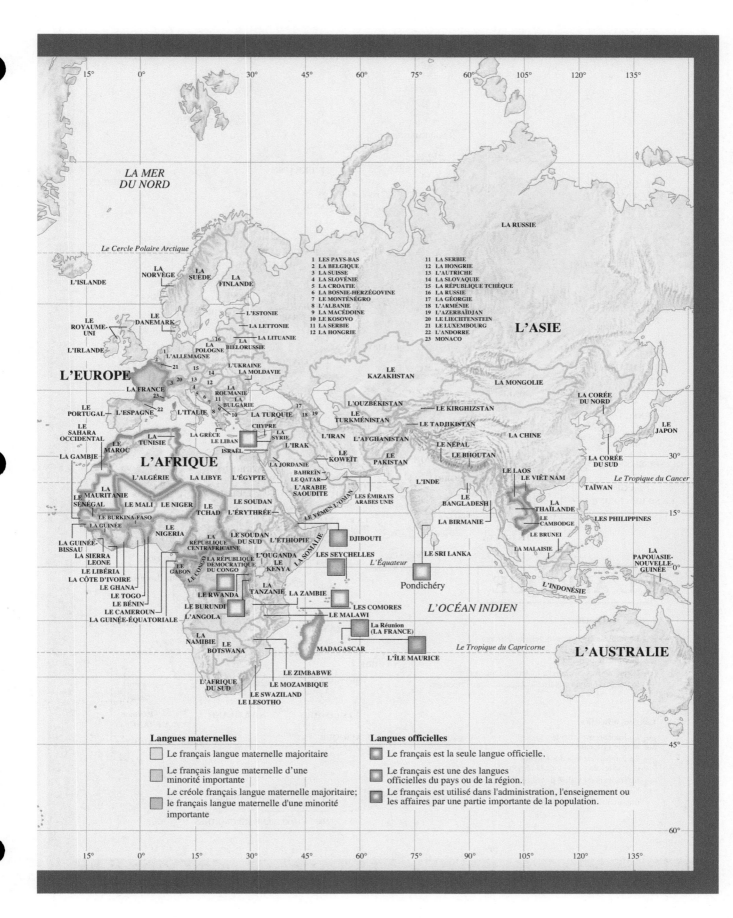

LA MER
DU NORD

Le Cercle Polaire Arctique

LA RUSSIE

1 LES PAYS-BAS
2 LA BELGIQUE
3 LA SUISSE
4 LA SLOVÉNIE
5 LA CROATIE
6 LA BOSNIE-HERZÉGOVINE
7 LE MONTÉNÉGRO
8 L'ALBANIE
9 LA MACÉDOINE
10 LE KOSOVO
11 LA SERBIE
12 LA HONGRIE

11 LA SERBIE
12 LA HONGRIE
13 L'AUTRICHE
14 LA SLOVAQUIE
15 LA RÉPUBLIQUE TCHÈQUE
16 LA RUSSIE
17 LA GÉORGIE
18 L'ARMÉNIE
19 L'AZERBAÏDJAN
20 LE LIECHTENSTEIN
21 LE LUXEMBOURG
22 L'ANDORRE
23 MONACO

L'ASIE

L'ISLANDE

LA NORVÈGE LA SUÈDE LA FINLANDE

LE ROYAUME-UNI
LE DANEMARK
L'IRLANDE

L'ESTONIE
LA LETTONIE
LA POLOGNE LA LITUANIE
LA BIÉLORUSSIE
L'ALLEMAGNE
L'UKRAINE
LA MOLDAVIE

LE KAZAKHSTAN

LA MONGOLIE

LA CORÉE DU NORD

L'EUROPE

LA FRANCE
LE PORTUGAL L'ESPAGNE
LE SAHARA OCCIDENTAL

LA ROUMANIE
LA BULGARIE
L'ITALIE
LA TURQUIE
CHYPRE
LA GRÈCE
LE LIBAN
ISRAËL

L'OUZBÉKISTAN
LE TURKMÉNISTAN
LE KIRGHIZSTAN
LE TADJIKISTAN
L'IRAN
LA SYRIE
L'IRAK
L'AFGHANISTAN
LA JORDANIE
LE KOWEÏT

LA CHINE
LE NÉPAL
LE BHOUTAN

LE JAPON

LA CORÉE DU SUD

Le Tropique du Cancer

LE MAROC
LA TUNISIE

LA GAMBIE
L'AFRIQUE
L'ALGÉRIE LA LIBYE L'ÉGYPTE

BAHREÏN
LE QATAR
L'ARABIE SAOUDITE
LES ÉMIRATS ARABES UNIS
L'INDE
LE BANGLADESH
LE LAOS
LE VIÊT NAM
TAÏWAN

LA MAURITANIE
LE SÉNÉGAL LE MALI LE NIGER
LE TCHAD
LE SOUDAN
L'ÉRYTHRÉE
LE YÉMEN L'OMAN

LA BIRMANIE
LA THAÏLANDE
LE CAMBODGE
LES PHILIPPINES

LE BURKINA-FASO
LA GUINÉE
LA GUINÉE-BISSAU
LA SIERRA LEONE
LE LIBÉRIA
LA CÔTE D'IVOIRE
LE GHANA
LE TOGO
LE BÉNIN
LE CAMEROUN
LA GUINÉE-ÉQUATORIALE

LE NIGERIA
LA RÉPUBLIQUE CENTRAFRICAINE
LE SOUDAN DU SUD
L'ÉTHIOPIE
LA SOMALIE
DJIBOUTI
LES SEYCHELLES

LE SRI LANKA

LE BRUNEI
LA MALAISIE
LA PAPOUASIE-NOUVELLE-GUINÉE

LE CONGO
LE GABON
LA RÉPUBLIQUE DÉMOCRATIQUE DU CONGO
LE RWANDA
LE BURUNDI
L'ANGOLA

L'OUGANDA
LE KENYA
LA TANZANIE LA ZAMBIE

Pondichéry

L'Équateur

L'INDONÉSIE

LES COMORES
LE MALAWI

L'OCÉAN INDIEN

LA NAMIBIE LE BOTSWANA

La Réunion (LA FRANCE)
MADAGASCAR
L'ÎLE MAURICE

Le Tropique du Capricorne

L'AUSTRALIE

L'AFRIQUE DU SUD
LE ZIMBABWE
LE MOZAMBIQUE
LE SWAZILAND
LE LESOTHO

Langues maternelles

- Le français langue maternelle majoritaire
- Le français langue maternelle d'une minorité importante
- Le créole français langue maternelle majoritaire; le français langue maternelle d'une minorité importante

Langues officielles

- Le français est la seule langue officielle.
- Le français est une des langues officielles du pays ou de la région.
- Le français est utilisé dans l'administration, l'enseignement ou les affaires par une partie importante de la population.

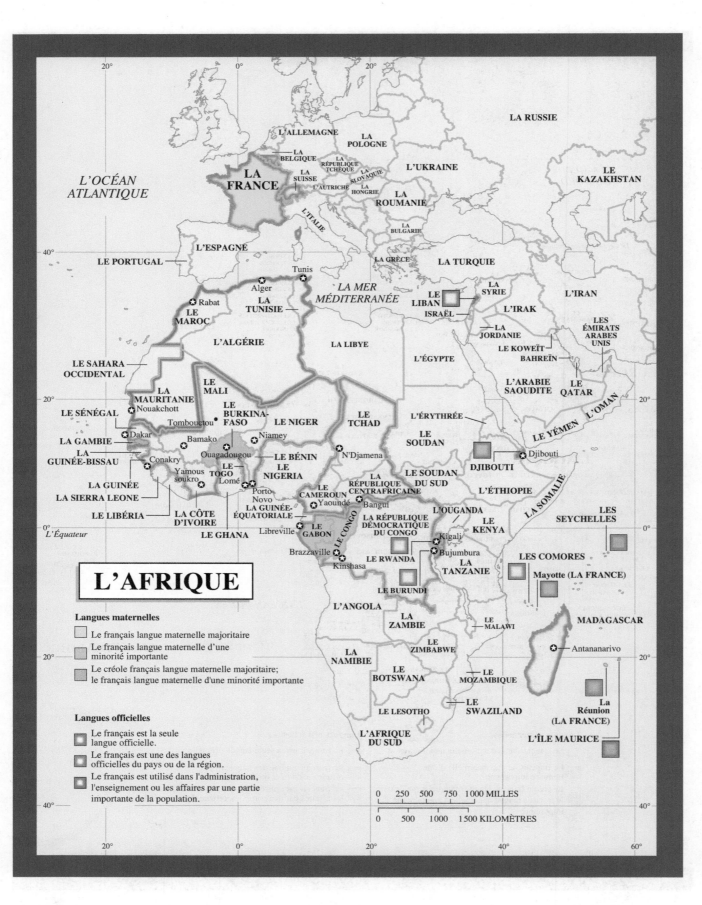

L'AFRIQUE

L'OCÉAN ATLANTIQUE

LA RUSSIE

L'ALLEMAGNE
LA POLOGNE
LA BELGIQUE
LA RÉPUBLIQUE TCHÈQUE
LA SUISSE
LA SLOVAQUIE
L'AUTRICHE
LA HONGRIE
LA FRANCE
L'UKRAINE
LE KAZAKHSTAN
LA ROUMANIE
L'ITALIE
LA BULGARIE

L'ESPAGNE
LE PORTUGAL
LA GRÈCE
LA TURQUIE

Tunis
Alger
★ Rabat
LA MER MÉDITERRANÉE
LE LIBAN
LA SYRIE
L'IRAN
ISRAËL
LE MAROC
LA TUNISIE
LA JORDANIE
L'IRAK
LES ÉMIRATS ARABES UNIS
LE KOWEÏT
BAHREÏN

L'ALGÉRIE
LA LIBYE
L'ÉGYPTE
L'ARABIE SAOUDITE
LE QATAR

LE SAHARA OCCIDENTAL
LA MAURITANIE
LE MALI
L'ÉRYTHRÉE
L'OMAN
LE YÉMEN

LE SÉNÉGAL
★ Nouakchott
Tombouctou●
LE BURKINA-FASO
LE NIGER
LE TCHAD
LE SOUDAN
LA GAMBIE
★ Dakar
Bamako
★ Niamey
N'Djamena
Djibouti
LA GUINÉE-BISSAU
Conakry
Ouagadougou
LE BÉNIN
LE SOUDAN DU SUD
DJIBOUTI
LA GUINÉE
Yamous- soukro
LE TOGO
Lomé
LE NIGERIA
LA RÉPUBLIQUE CENTRAFRICAINE
L'ÉTHIOPIE
LA SIERRA LEONE
Porto Novo
LE CAMEROUN
LE SOUDAN DU SUD
LE LIBÉRIA
LA CÔTE D'IVOIRE
LA GUINÉE-ÉQUATORIALE
★ Yaoundé
Bangui
L'OUGANDA
LES SEYCHELLES
L'Équateur
LE GHANA
Libreville
LE GABON
LE CONGO
LA RÉPUBLIQUE DÉMOCRATIQUE DU CONGO
Kigali
LE KENYA
LA SOMALIE
Brazzaville
LE RWANDA
★ Bujumbura
LES COMORES
Kinshasa
LA TANZANIE
Mayotte (LA FRANCE)
LE BURUNDI
L'ANGOLA
LA ZAMBIE
LE MALAWI
MADAGASCAR
LA NAMIBIE
LE ZIMBABWE
★ Antananarivo
LE BOTSWANA
LE MOZAMBIQUE
La Réunion (LA FRANCE)
LE LESOTHO
LE SWAZILAND
L'ÎLE MAURICE
L'AFRIQUE DU SUD

Langues maternelles

☐ Le français langue maternelle majoritaire

☐ Le français langue maternelle d'une minorité importante

☐ Le créole français langue maternelle majoritaire; le français langue maternelle d'une minorité importante

Langues officielles

☐ Le français est la seule langue officielle.

☐ Le français est une des langues officielles du pays ou de la région.

☐ Le français est utilisé dans l'administration, l'enseignement ou les affaires par une partie importante de la population.

```
0   250  500  750  1000 MILLES
0    500   1000   1500 KILOMÈTRES
```

Seventh Edition

HoRIZONS

Joan H. Manley
University of Texas—El Paso,
Emeritus

Stuart Smith
Austin Community College

John T. McMinn-Reyna
Austin Community College

Marc A. Prévost
Austin Community College

✦ CENGAGE

Australia • Brazil • Mexico • Singapore • United Kingdom • United States

Horizons, **Seventh Edition**
Manley | Smith | McMinn-Reyna | Prévost

Product Director: Marta Lee-Perriard

Senior Product Team Manager: Heather
Bradley-Cole

Senior Product Manager: Lara Semones Ramsey

Content Development Manager: Anika
Bachhuber

Senior Content Developer: Isabelle Alouane

Senior Content Project Manager: Esther Marshall

Senior Marketing Manager: Sean Ketchem

Market Development Specialist: Patricia
Velazquez

Digital Content Designer: Andrew Tabor

VP, Technical Product Manager: Matthew D.
Nespoli

Manufacturing Planner: Fola Orekoya

Senior Designer: Lisa D. Trager

Art Director: Brenda Ciaramella

Text Designer: Brenda Ciaramella

Cover Designer: Lisa D. Trager

Cover image: aixpin/Getty Images

Library of Congress Control Number: 2017951375

ISBN: 978-1-337-56826-5 [Student Edition]
ISBN: 978-1-337-56825-8 [IAC MindTap]
ISBN: 978-1-337-56834-0 [Loose Leaf Edition]

Cengage Learning
20 Channel Center Street
Boston, MA 02210
USA

Cengage Learning is a leading provider of customized learning solutions
with employees residing in nearly 40 different countries and sales in more than
125 countries around the world. Find your local representative at:
www.cengage.com.

Cengage Learning products are represented in Canada
by Nelson Education, Ltd.

For your course and learning solutions, visit **www.cengage.com**

Purchase any of our products at your local college store or at our
preferred online store **www.cengagebrain.com**

Printed at CLDPC, USA, 04-21